Auckland
The Twentieth-Century Story

Paul Moon

Published by Oratia Books, Oratia Media Ltd, 783 West Coast Road, Oratia, Auckland 0604, New Zealand (www.oratia.co.nz).

Copyright © 2023 Paul Moon
Copyright © 2023 Oratia Books (published work)

The copyright holders assert their moral rights in the work.

This book is copyright. Except for the purposes of fair reviewing, no part of this publication may be reproduced or transmitted in any form or by any means, whether electronic, digital or mechanical, including photocopying, recording, any digital or computerised format, or any information storage and retrieval system, including by any means via the Internet, without permission in writing from the publisher. Infringers of copyright render themselves liable to prosecution.

ISBN 978-1-99-004235-5

Editor: Mike Wagg
Designer: Sarah Elworthy

First published 2023

Printed in China

Contents

Preface 5

1 | **Auckland before 1900** 11
2 | **The 1900s** 33
3 | **The 1910s** 66
4 | **The 1920s** 94
5 | **The 1930s** 121
6 | **The 1940s** 149
7 | **The 1950s** 174
8 | **The 1960s** 204
9 | **The 1970s** 231
10 | **The 1980s** 263
11 | **The 1990s** 289
    Epilogue 317

Bibliography 320
Endnotes 337
Index 357

Preface

At the time of writing this book, twentieth-century Auckland is still a lived memory for many of us, although how far those recollections extend back into the period depends on our age. But beyond what we may be able to recall directly is a sort of prosthetic memory[1] of an earlier Auckland — one not experienced personally, but of which traces are still all around us, and which help to prop up our perceptions of the city's past.

This book is, in part, an immersion into those perceptions of the history and character of Auckland — a mosaic of its cultures and lifestyles, anxieties and hopes, disasters and triumphs, virtues and vices — over the course of the twentieth century. As the title hints at, this work is not a formal history of the labyrinthine world of Auckland's local body politics and its deadening bureaucracy. Instead, it delves more into the city's changing personality, exploring where memory and materiality mingle. And instead of providing a scrupulously detailed inventory of happenings in Auckland over the century, the approach here is more impressionistic. At certain points, events are chosen not necessarily because of their importance, but because they serve like daubs of paint, adding to the overall perception and experience of the era. The result is a journey through Auckland's houses and gardens, its offices and factories, harbours and farms, and above all, its cultures and communities. It charts the struggles of tangata whenua to retain and regain land, and of immigrants to adapt to the place. It contends with the city's transport arteries becoming increasingly clogged, the steady ascent of a shopping culture, and the paradoxical sense that Auckland is simultaneously at the edge of the world yet at the centre of it.

Perceptions of Auckland's past are built partly on collections of memories which accumulate on top of each other, leaving a variety of layers of impressions of how the city was seen, both by its inhabitants and visitors to it. This work delves into some of these memories, and the changing way the city's history has been prioritised over the century by various groups of its inhabitants. These differences in perception can be considerable. As one example, in the 1960s, small clutches of refugees from Eastern Europe landed in Auckland and saw the city as a stable, idyllic sanctuary from the tribulations of communism, and eagerly embraced its social norms. Yet, at the same time, a handful of Aucklanders were trying to wriggle free from what they saw as the city's stifling cultural conservatism, and started experimenting with communes and 'alternative' lifestyles. The significant point about such diversity is not so much that it existed, but that conformism and subversion managed to live side by side, usually with relatively little chafing between the two.

For the whole of the twentieth century, there was no single governing body that presided over the needs and interests of the entire city. Auckland knew how to put on a unified face when it had to, but such displays often tended to mask administrative, regulatory, economic, social, and cultural divisions. From different specifications for roads and footpaths in certain parts of the city, to the virulent divisions aroused by the Springbok tour in 1981, the notion of Auckland as a single, indivisible community in this era is easily dispelled.

The case of the Springbok tour is instructive also because it illustrates how Auckland has never really been fully sealed off from the rest of the country. At various points in this book, the intersections between city and nation inevitably surface. Auckland is ambiguously a part of New Zealand yet apart from it — a relationship that has generated both vibrancy and, on occasion, tension. As much as the city acted increasingly as the country's cultural and economic entrepôt during the twentieth century, there was an opposing gravitational force exercised

PREFACE

on it by the rest of New Zealand. The political heart of the country pulsed in Wellington, Auckland's electricity came from outside its perimeter, and various cultural and social trends that exercised an influence on the city were generated elsewhere in the country, as was some of the source of Auckland's wealth. The result was a symbiotic relationship between Auckland and the rest of New Zealand — as though it was a civic ecosystem contained within a larger, national ecosystem.

Such biological comparisons are well established, and have their roots in the Chicago School of sociologists, who in the early twentieth century turned their minds to the nature of cities and the causes and effects of urbanisation on communities. Among much else, they identified how there is an evolutionary force at play in cities that shapes and reshapes their physical, economic, social and cultural forms.[2] While such organic models are not beyond criticism, they are useful for explaining the dynamics of cities at particular junctures in their history, and certainly provide insights into Auckland's evolution over the century. More recently, other explanations of the nature of cities have emerged, and these are drawn on as well to illuminate characteristics of the way the city functioned at various times.[3] However, these theories are applied sparingly. The preference here is to allow the recollections of events and periods to speak largely for themselves, without imposing extraneous meaning on them.

Geographical scope

Although there are various definitions of what constitutes Auckland's boundaries, for the purpose of this work, the region extends from Waiuku in the south to Te Hana in the north, and encompasses the islands of Rangitoto, Waiheke, Pōnui and Motutapu — a combined land area of around 4900 square kilometres. In a straight line, the distance from Auckland's northern- to southern-most point is around 115 kilometres — a latitude greater than London, New York, Berlin or Beijing.

Particularly in the early decades of the twentieth century, much of the Auckland region was sparsely inhabited, but by the 1990s, many of the former towns and smaller, isolated, rural settlements had been engulfed by the city's relentless urban sprawl. In terms of built area, the city grew over this period from under 2500 hectares to almost 50,000 hectares, with its population density increasing from 13 people per hectare in 1900, to 23 people per hectare by 1999.⁴ And very little of this expansion has occurred in an orderly and planned manner. Unlike some cities around the world, with their streets and suburbs neatly set out in preordained grids, Auckland has grown more like an abandoned garden, with a tangle of roads and a chaotic mix of buildings encroaching into any unoccupied space they can find. Stand on any of the city's volcanic peaks, and the view beneath is one of a mesh of urbanisation, hugging the region's contours as it spreads seemingly inexhaustibly.

Population

One of the most prominent characteristics of the city in this era is that of growth. Within this one hundred-year period, Auckland's population expanded rapidly, transforming the region from a colonial settlement to a large metropolitan city. In 1899, there were 66,500 people living in the greater Auckland area, which represented around 8.6 per cent of the colony's population. A century on, the city's seams were stretching as the population had expanded to 1,184,800, making Auckland home to almost a third of the nation's residents.⁵ (It should be noted, though, that calculations of population become slightly problematic at various periods during the twentieth century because of the use of different boundaries by authorities to define the city.)

The roots of Auckland's population may have spread outwards from the old centre over this period, but they did not necessarily deepen for everyone. At the close of the twentieth century, almost a third of the city's residents had been born overseas.⁶ One consequence of this was that settlement patterns were being constantly modified, and some suburbs were increasingly being categorised by the ethnic groups who were perceived to be dominant in those areas. The idiom of an 'Aucklander' was in many ways more chimeric and certainly more diverse in 1999 than it had been in 1900. What did this mean for the identity of those living in the city towards the end of the century — was there even such a thing as an Aucklander? The answer is a resolute 'yes', and although the definition continued to evolve over this period, it was always based in a sense of belonging to the place. Even when the old ideas of what it meant to be an Aucklander fell out of favour and withered, the genus of that notion of belonging to the city proved to be remarkably tenacious, and continued to propagate itself across the region, albeit in new and different forms.

Structure of the book

This work is organised into chapters, each one corresponding to a decade in the century. This compartmentalisation is largely arbitrary, and done chiefly to give some sense of the progression of the century, but also to help rein in some material that otherwise might begin to ramble. The delineations between each chapter are sufficiently porous, though, to allow topics and themes to be dealt with over the period in which they naturally occurred. As readers will discover, the result is a history that in some ways represents a scrapbook of historical memories, assembled and curated in order to give, as mentioned above, an impressionistic view of Auckland in this era.

No history is ever complete, though, and this work is no exception. So much of the period has already vanished — gone with the memories of those who have since died. In addition, the archival record is patchy, and what does exist is unavoidably fragmentary. However, this reconstruction of Auckland's past hopefully goes a small way towards giving some form to Auckland in the twentieth century in ways that illuminate, and maybe even surprise.

Paul Moon
Auckland, 2023

1
Auckland before 1900

Eighty-five million years ago, the land that is now known as New Zealand began to separate from the supercontinent of Gondwanaland. However, it was not until just five million years ago that gargantuan tectonic shifts and convulsive volcanic eruptions thrust the area that is now Auckland from the sea. Geologically, the oldest parts of Auckland are some of the islands in the Hauraki Gulf, along with portions of the hilly terrain on the mainland to the southeast, which date back to the Jurassic and Triassic periods. These were followed by the emergence of South Kaipara and land to the south of Manukau, including the Manukau Heads. The region then continued to be shaped by changes in sea levels, erosion and further volcanic activity until roughly a thousand years ago, when its terrain settled into what is roughly its current form, with around 50 small volcanic cones and craters punctuating the landscape as a reminder of its turbulent past (the most recent eruption being the island of Rangitoto, which emerged from a single explosive episode around AD 1400).[7] Settled might be too optimistic a term, though. The likelihood of future volcanic or earthquake activity in the city is high — the only unknown factor being when either will occur.[8]

Even as the land was cooling in the aftermath of volcanic eruptions, vegetation was already starting to spread across the region. In the shallow, swampy, sediment-laden estuaries, mangroves took root and began their slow process of land reclamation along portions of the coast. The rest of the landscape become dominated by forests of tōtara, pūriri, kahikatea, pukatea, kānuka, tawa, pōhutukawa, rimu, tōwai and kauri, rising from a thick, entangled bed of fern and other subcanopy trees.[9] With a climate in that middling area between subtropical and temperate, and with moderate rainfall experienced for most of the year, the conditions were ripe for these forests to flourish.[10] By the time the first humans tentatively began to explore the area, this primeval terrain was barricaded with dense vegetation.

It was probably one summer sometime in the early fourteenth century that the earliest Polynesian arrivals to what is now known as Auckland hauled their large ocean-going canoe onto shore (summer because oral traditions recount how the pōhutukawa was in bloom at the time).[11] Confronted with a land mass greater than anything they were accustomed to, these migrants conjured up supernatural explanations for the forms of the region's topography. Conflicts between tohunga (traditional healers and spiritual leaders) living in Hūnua and Waitākere, for example, accounted for subterranean volcanic forces bursting through to the surface. At the same time, one tohunga was said to have brought about torrential rains which lashed the Waitākere Ranges, preventing its forests from burning. This was part of a process of explaining the form of the region's geology, and imbuing it with a religious dimension. In addition, genealogies (whakapapa) connected the occupants of the region with the deities responsible for its creation,[12] and in a symbolic amalgamation of the people and place, following someone's birth, their placenta would be interred in the ground.[13] In every way, the first Polynesians who settled in the region were becoming connected to the land, with each successive generation being more strongly linked to the location than the preceding one.

Of the various canoes that visited the region — *Te Arawa*, *Tainui*, *Māhuhu-ki-te Rangi*, *Moekaraka* and *Tākitimu* — none of their crews initially decided to establish themselves there, although at least some may have dropped off a few of their number in the area.[14] One legend relates how Tama Te Kapua (captain of the *Te Arawa* canoe) continued on a journey north after first arriving at Maketū in the Bay of Plenty. He had brought with him a piece of rock from Hawaiki — the location in the South Pacific where the voyagers originally departed from. Tama Te Kapua placed this rock on the small island of Te Matā (now known as Boat Rock, to the west of the Harbour Bridge). The name was a contraction of Kahumatamomoe — Tama Te Kapua's son. This rock gave the area its mauri (in this context, a distinct, living personality) and was regarded as so important that the waters that lapped around it were named Wai Te Matā (the waters of Matā, from which the harbour derives its name: Waitematā).[15] Kahumatamomoe encamped at Ōrākei, from where he sailed to Waiheke Island and established a pā (a fortified village) at Pūtiki Bay, which he called Motu nui nō Kahu (the large island of Kahu).

Another site named by Te Arawa was the 260-metre-tall island of Rangitoto. Its full name was Te (or Ngā) Rangi i Totongia a Tama Te Kapua (which translates roughly as the day the blood of Tama Te Kapua flowed). According to one account (which is disputed by other iwi), Tama Te Kapua cut his feet on some scoria when he landed at what later became known as Islington Bay, to explore the island. From a distance, this forest-clad peak looked to him like a possible future settlement, defended as it was by being located over three kilometres from the mainland. However, its lush appearance belied the fact that there was no fresh water on the island, and the plants that blanketed its surface survived by their roots seeking out thin seams of soil in the crevices of the volcanic rock. Tama Te Kapua abandoned the idea of founding a settlement there, and eventually left the region.[16]

These early arrivals established small, huddled settlements on the coast of the Waitematā Harbour, which proved a more suitable site to survive on. One of these settlers, Ihenga (Tama Te Kapua's grandson) was a founding ancestor of Ngāti Whātua, while another grandson, Taramainuku, settled in Kaipara (the traditional name for the bar at the entrance of the Manukau Harbour was Te Kupenga o Taramainuku — the fishing net of Taramainuku).[17] Over several succeeding generations, these communities expanded into hapū (subtribes) and iwi (tribes), and were responsible for many parts of the region being extensively named, with each name acting as a capsule, containing histories, whakapapa, geological descriptions, navigational prompts and sometimes even warnings about the location.

In the following centuries, one of the region's most distinct geological features — the fact that it was an isthmus with a small, pinched piece of land separating two coasts of the North Island — led to it being the most used portage site in the country. It was, therefore, even at this very early stage, a distinctly cosmopolitan settlement, with numerous other iwi, particularly from the North Island, visiting the region to haul their canoes across Te Tō Waka (the canoe portage), where around 250 metres of land separated the Tāmaki River and Manukau Harbour.[18] The name given to this site, Tāmaki Herenga Waka (the place where canoes are moored), reflected its importance as a location for canoe portage, and as the population grew, and the geographical desirability of the region became more pronounced, the area took on the name Tāmaki Makaurau, which was a personification of Tāmaki as a maiden sought after by a hundred lovers.[19]

In the century or more that followed, the interlacing accounts of canoe arrivals, settlement legends and histories of people moving around the region reached a degree of byzantine complexity that became even more intricate as the population on the isthmus increased. Only a handful of these early Māori settlements in the region have been located and examined, though. One such excavation took place in the 1980s in the suburb of East Tamaki Heights, on the fringe of the commercial and industrial zones at the Harris Road end of Te Rakau Drive. The streets, with affected English names such as Heathridge Place, Elderberry Road and Dulwich Place, suggested an enthusiasm by its developers for a neighbourhood with genteel, northern hemisphere, 'old-world' allusions. Just prior to the site succumbing to urban sprawl, though, archaeologists explored the remnants of its occupation by Māori in the sixteenth century. What they unearthed was evidence of extensive horticultural enterprises, with terraced gardens taking full advantage of the volcanic and sedimentary soils to enable intense crop production. There were also traces of a wāhi tapu (a sacred site) indicating that this was more than a temporary garden hastily organised by a transient community. And as the archaeologists fossicked through the location, they also discovered the remnants of an earth oven, along with deposits of cockle shells, fish bones, charcoal and other detritus of communities.

Yet, even though these settlements may have had housing, food-growing and storage areas, manufacturing locations and even urupā (cemeteries), and tended to be situated close to supplies of fresh water and sources of seafood, after some years or even decades, the residents of these sites would move on,[20] for reasons that can only be speculated on. However, by the seventeenth century, the tendency was for more permanent communities, dependent on vast gardens, and protected by fortifications from potential enemies. Far from this trend leading to isolation, though, trade seems to have flourished in the region. On Pōnui Island, for example, tools were excavated that were found to have been manufactured from greywacke sourced from a quarry in the Coromandel area,[21] and more generally, there is evidence of trade funnelling through the area in the pre-European era.[22]

The largest traditional settlement in the region prior to European arrival was centred at Maungakiekie (One Tree Hill). The name might mean the mountain of the kiekie plant, or the mountain culminating in a pinnacle. Either way, though, by the eighteenth century, it had grown to become home to the most substantial population in Tāmaki Makaurau. It was originally settled in the 1400s by Te Waiohua, but a century later was selected as a site for a community by the Ngāti Awa chief Tītahi, and was given the name Ngā Whakairo a Tītahi. At some point, Te Waiohua reoccupied the peak, possibly with some members of Ngāti Awa remaining (the son of a Ngāti Awa chief, who was given the name Korokī — sometimes referred to as Korokino — was born there, and his placenta buried on the summit, on top of which was planted a tōtara tree, giving the summit another name, Te Tōtara i Ahua).[23]

By the eighteenth century, Maungakiekie had become a tribal crossroad. It was centrally positioned on the isthmus, being around two and a half kilometres from the Manukau Harbour, and roughly four and a half kilometres from the Waitematā Harbour. It was also under ten kilometres from the main portage route across the area, and so was ideally positioned strategically. Maungakiekie was occupied at this time by several groups affiliated with Tainui, and clustered under the umbrella of Te Waiohua, including Ngā Iwi, Ngāti Te Awa, Ngā Oho, Ngā Riki and others. In the 1730s, the area came under the leadership of the chief Kiwi Tāmaki. During his rule, the mountain and the land in its vicinity reached their apex in the scale of their horticultural productivity. Through burning and chopping, the wildness of the forest-clad surrounds succumbed to the tameness of ordered gardens. Acre after acre of fertile land was cultivated, feeding hundreds of occupants who lived on this site.[24] From a distance, it was possible to see how the slopes of Maungakiekie had undergone massive earthworks, and were substantially terraced. Closer up, it was possible to see the storage pits, cooking areas, scarps, shellfish middens, living areas and a complex web of defences — in the form of trenches, banks and palisades — built into the slopes, behind which its residents could defend this prize location.[25] In its totality, it was 'the most magnificent structure of all the Auckland pa, daunting in its extent and complexity'.[26]

The tenure of this seemingly idyllic existence could only ever be limited, however. It was precisely the productivity of Maungakiekie that made it coveted by other iwi. Furthermore, the strategic position of the settlement for trade and access to two harbours was ironically also a point of potential military vulnerability. Geographically, Te Waiohua was effectively clamped between Ngāti Whātua on the north-west, and Ngāti Pāoa on the Thames Estuary. Eventually, it was Te Taoū — a branch of Ngāti Whātua from South Kaipara — which raised a force to challenge Te Waiohua's supremacy on the isthmus, and to quell its leader's increasingly aggressive acts against Ngāti Whātua. Under the leadership of the Te Taoū rangatira (chief) Wahaakiaki, a small war party (perhaps just one hundred) was assembled, and made its way east in the general direction of Maungakiekie (anticipating that Kiwi Tāmaki was likely to leave the confines of his pā to meet this war party before it even got close to his settlement). The clash of these two forces, probably in 1741, took place at Paruroa, on the Manukau Harbour. There, Kiwi Tāmaki was killed in the fighting, and Ngāti Whātua accomplished a victory that was so complete that Te Waiohua was banished from the isthmus and shunted to the southern perimeters of the region.[27] The Te Taoū rangatira Tuperiri now occupied Maungakiekie, and renamed it Hikurangi. This occupation was a clear signal to other hapū and iwi in the vicinity that Ngāti Whātua's period of dominion over the region had commenced.

With such a commanding victory on a scale that even some in Ngāti Whātua may have been shocked by, what was next? More conquest? More battlefield glory? No. The iwi's pragmatic leaders appreciated that further fighting would be futile. There was just one exception, though. Possibly around 1742, Ngāti Whātua decided to press its advantage that bit more, and attacked one of the surviving outcrops of Te Waiohua at Māngere. It was a battle too far, and with the support of other members of Tainui, Te Waiohua mounted a spirited defence which quickly turned into an offence. The vanquished suddenly looked like becoming victors, and in a series of surprise raids Te Waiohua managed to recapture Kohimaramara (now Kohimarama), Ōrākei and Taurarua (Judges Bay). However, within a year, Ngāti Whātua had managed to reverse these triumphs. But instead of annihilating their enemy, the Ngāti Whātua leaders expelled some, and intermarried with others, thus stitching together a new set of alliances where previously there had been just animosities.[28]

On the surface, the prospects of peace may have appeared good, but there were subterranean pressures that had yet to be resolved. Relations among the principal iwi in the region were fragile, and at times nervous, with various groups eyeing up opportunities to make political and territorial gains for themselves. One of these pretenders was Ngāti Pāoa. The iwi was numerically small, which had led it to implementing a strategy of making selective and comparatively slight territorial acquisitions. Key to this strategy, though, was ensuring that each new acquisition was connected to the previous one, leading to the emergence of what could be called the Ngāti Pāoa corridor. And to ensure that this thin, exposed strand of territory was not left vulnerable to attack, the iwi adopted a policy of allowing other hapū to use it. Co-existence rather than exclusivity was the means by which Ngāti Pāoa's foothold in the region was secured. However, Ngāti Whātua's victory in 1741 put it on an eventual collision course with Ngāti Pāoa. In a series of short, sharp battles, Ngāti Pāoa was shunted off the mainland and was forced to seek refuge and then re-establish itself in some of the islands in the Hauraki Gulf.[29] The impetus for Ngāti Whātua's attacks was that its adversary had been building closer relations with Te Waiohua, and so the threat of a combined assault on Ngāti Whātua's still tentative claim over the centre of the region meant that some pre-emptive measure was called for.

The remainder of the eighteenth century was characterised by political jostling and military skirmishing in the region. Old alliances were either renewed or weakened, and the fickle fortunes of war variously invigorated some and demoralised others. What fundamentally changed the political and military calculus of the region was an act of colonisation — not initially in the form of European settlers, but of a piece of European technology: the musket. The acquisition of large quantities of the weapon by the Ngāpuhi rangatira Hongi Hika had given him a tremendous advantage over those hapū and iwi which were not similarly armed.[30] By 1820, Hongi had become a leviathan whose ability to vanquish his enemies seemed unstoppable. The following year, he cited utu (a need for revenge or a desire to restore balance) as the basis for his plan to launch an attack on Ngāti Pāoa at Mauinaina pā in Mokoia (now known as Panmure), which was then under the control of the Ngāti Pāoa chief Te Hīnaki.[31] A year before this assault, one of the first written accounts of the region was produced by Richard Cruise, a traveller on the storeship HMS *Dromedary*, which briefly visited the Waitematā Harbour in late 1820. Cruise described the site that would soon fall to Hongi's forces:

> *This village was about a mile long and half a mile broad, and the houses were larger, and more ornamented with carving, than those we had generally observed. Each family occupied an allotment .... These allotments contained many houses; and the intermediate passages or streets were as clean as the season would permit. The adjacent country was flat, with the exception of a high round hill, which formed the pah .... The ground was good and under cultivation ... and, a profusion of potatoes lay in different parts of the village. An immense number of people received us upon landing, and ... showed us every civility.*[32]

In September 1821, Hongi assembled a taua (war party) of up to 2000 soldiers of whom perhaps 1000 were armed with muskets. They sailed in a flotilla of waka from Northland to the Waitematā Harbour in November, and following Ngāti Pāoa's unsuccessful panicked attempts to avert the impending attack through diplomacy, the Ngāpuhi forces launched a heavy assault on the Mauinaina pā at Mokoia the same month. After some setbacks, Hongi stormed the defences 'and a fearful slaughter took place, men, women and children all shared the same fate'.[33] The Ngāti Pāoa death toll in this battle (and its aftermath) was immense. In 1844, a visitor to the site recorded that 'the bones of 2,000 men still lay whitening on the plain, and the ovens remain in which the flesh of the slaughtered was cooked for the horrible repasts of the victorious party'.[34]

The effects of the Musket Wars on the region's population were calamitous. It is possible that the number of Māori killed in the area in the early 1820s was up to 5000[35] — an astonishingly high figure, given that the entire Māori population in the country at this time was approximately 80,000.[36] The result was that the isthmus gave the appearance of being almost deserted in the period immediately following the fighting. When exploring the area on 24 February 1827, the French naval officer

Jules Dumont D'Urville recorded that '[w]e did not notice any trace of inhabitants, nothing but one or two fires a very long way off in the interior. There can be no doubt that this extreme depopulation is due to the ravages of war.'[37]

European arrivals

The early history of European involvement in Tāmaki Makaurau has only left the faintest of traces. In the case of Ngāpuhi's 1821 raid on Mauinaina pā, one narrative reveals that there were three European sailors 'who were living with the people in the pa' at the time of the attack.[38] Who these sailors were, and how they came to be residing with Ngāti Pāoa is unknown. Captain James Cook sailed past the Waitematā Harbour in November 1769, but saw no need to explore the land in its vicinity.[39] For the remainder of the eighteenth century, the record of European visitors to the region is very scant.

In the early nineteenth century, there were occasional excursions to the region by Europeans (such as that of D'Urville), but a rash of battles between various hapū and iwi factions, both within the area and from outside, deterred most visitors.[40] In 1831, Tāmaki Makaurau was 'a dangerous place to visit, let alone one in which to live'[41] — an assessment confirmed as late as 1837 when the missionary William Fairburn gauged that peace in the region remained a scarce commodity.[42] However, despite the risks, in January 1835 the trader Thomas Mitchell paid several local chiefs a total of £500 (roughly $300,000 in present-day currency) to acquire 256,000 acres on the isthmus. It was a risky speculative venture. New Zealand was not a British colony at this time, and British notions of property tenure barely applied in the country. There was no title, no precise survey was carried out in this case, no means of registering a purchase, and practically no way of enforcing one's ownership of a territory, other than by consent or force. However, Mitchell was convinced that the region was 'the most eligible situation in the island in expectation of the country being colonised by England',[43] and it was this vision that motivated his purchase.

The attraction of the area may initially have been geographical, but its sparse Māori population may have suggested to some potential buyers that there was less likely to be any resistance from indigenous communities in the area once a transaction had been completed and the land began to be developed by the purchaser. A low number of residents and a desirable location was a combination that the missionary Henry Williams observed in February 1835. He wrote in his journal one morning in February that '[a]fter breakfast, went on shore to see if we could discover any signs of natives. All was quietness around; no appearance of smoke, though the fern had been recently burned off in the neighbourhood.' However, despite its deserted appearance, Williams had enough foresight to see the value of this location. 'At sunset,' he noted, 'weighed and made sail through the northern passage by Waiheke, and was much struck with the beauty of the harbour, which is accessible at all times; it will some day make a valuable place, being by far the best anchorage, and deep water.'[44]

Exactly a year after Mitchell's massive purchase, Fairburn acquired 83,000 acres of land on the isthmus, some of which overlapped with other European purchases.[45] Fairburn's payment for this vast span of territory comprised 90 blankets, 24 axes, 24 adzes, 26 hoes, 14 spades, 80 dollars, 900 pounds of tobacco, 24 combs and 12 plane irons. He soon increased the payment amount, perhaps sensing that the initial price in no way fairly reflected the scale of the acquisition, and in 1837 formally returned a third of the purchase to the original vendors.[46] Russell Stone has pointed out that such transactions did not necessarily constitute a sale in the sense that Europeans understood the term: 'Apihai Te Kawau was too intelligent a chief, and too experienced and adroit a politician, to let slip for a paltry sum those lands which were the birthright of his tribe.'[47] As in other parts of the country at the time, having Europeans settle in an area was often an effective means of boosting trade, and the Ngāti Whātua chief appreciated the opportunities that such arrangements offered. The notion that land could somehow be given in perpetuity to someone else, with the giver prohibited from that point onwards from living on it or using it, was an alien notion to most Māori at this time.[48]

In April 1840 the trader John Logan Campbell and his business partner, William Brown, sailed to Tāmaki Makaurau, where they similarly became convinced that the location would make an ideal European settlement.[49] One of the sights that particularly grabbed his attention was 'a volcanic mount, some five hundred feet high, rising suddenly from the plain'. This was Maungakiekie, which had been abandoned for decades by this time. He wrote prematurely that 'it had one solitary large tree on its crater summit .... we christened it "One-Tree Hill," which for ever obliterated the Maori name from Pakeha vocabulary'.[50]

A capital idea

The designation of the region as Tāmaki Makaurau — the place sought after by a hundred lovers — was on the verge of becoming a dramatic understatement. In January 1840, William Hobson arrived in the Bay of Islands. He had been despatched to New Zealand to conclude a treaty with Māori and become governor of the colony. He established the country's first capital in Russell, but it did not take too much foresight to realise that this small town, on a small finger of land protruding into the Bay of Islands, would be unsuitable in the future for the administrative centre of a growing colony.[51]

Hobson's mind turned to possible alternative locations, including Whangārei, Mahurangi, Thames and Tāmaki Makaurau, and in June 1840 he sailed from Russell to the Waitematā Harbour to see for himself what the area offered as a potential seat of government. Having dismissed sites towards what is now Whenuapai and Greenhithe, because the channel there was too shallow, he sailed to what would soon be renamed Freemans Bay. There, he went on shore, and cautiously came to the view that this could be a suitable general location for the capital. However, he held off from selecting a specific site in the area.[52] Three months later, Hobson sent a small group of officials to Tāmaki Makaurau to acquire some land in anticipation of establishing a settlement there.[53] In correspondence with his superior in London at this time, he listed several positive attributes of the location, including its central position (it was not central in the North Island, but was approximately 200 kilometres from the Bay of Islands and 500 kilometres from Wellington — the other major European settlement in the colony), the fact that it had two harbours, and its agricultural potential as reasons for his decision to plant his capital there.[54]

As soon as news spread of Hobson's intention to shift his administration, speculators were aroused by the possibility of profits in the planned capital (including even some of Hobson's own officials).[55] However, the governor was either oblivious to this, or turned a blind eye to it, as he proceeded to establish what he decided to name Auckland, after George Eden, the first Earl of Auckland (who had become First Lord of the Admiralty in 1834, shortly before Hobson had been given command of HMS *Rattlesnake* and posted to the East Indies).[56] Hobson instructed his surveyor, Felton Mathew, to carry out initial planning for the layout of the proposed capital, and on 1 September 1840 a postmaster was appointed to Auckland, with the union flag hoisted on the town's shore 17 days later, symbolising the official commencement of the colonial settlement.[57] The first sale of land to the government took place on 20 October, with Ngāti Whātua being paid £341, along with blankets, clothing, tobacco and tools, for 3000 acres, which would form the basis of the new town.[58]

By December 1840, allotments in the capital were already being advertised for sale — most of which were the unusual size of half an acre.[59] However, it was not until 1841 that Mathew completed his plan for the layout of the town.[60] He envisaged a settlement made up partly of a gridded street network interspersed with quadrants, squares, crescents and a circus[61] (inspired by Georgian urban planning of the sort that had been undertaken in Bath,[62] and parts of London).[63] It proved to be a challenge keeping up appearances, though, with ambition racing away from actuality.[64]

Shortland Crescent (now Shortland Street), which hugged Commercial Bay, was the main business area in the town, behind which was empty land where Mathew's grand design was supposed to have unfurled. The only other artery that showed some slight signs of life was Queen Street, which was lined with a smattering of shops and houses.[65] One of the challenges for businesses and householders in this area was adjusting to the town's topography. This was made frustratingly evident in what became mockingly known as the Queen Street River. Officially, it was designated the Ligar Canal (named after the second surveyor general), and was designed to direct the flow of the Waihorotiu Stream that ran along the street. At its lower reaches, it was affected by tidal surges, and could also rise dramatically depending on the run-off waters entering it from Wyndham Street. It was also often contaminated with raw sewage and other waste emanating from the buildings lining its banks,[66] making it resemble more of an open drain. In the early years of the town, the best that officials could manage to deal with this problem was to fence off parts of this fetid stream, which in turn bisected this part of town, and led to makeshift footbridges being constructed over the canal.[67] Such problems reflected more broadly the underdeveloped nature of the settlement.[68]

Despite having fewer than 600 residents in 1841, and being surrounded by enormous tracts of land, only some of which was needed for cultivation, Auckland was already succumbing to pressure relating to land use. As a small example, some of the side roads and lanes in the town were unusually narrow, even by the standards of the time, because the owners of buildings that lined them had to supply the land, and so offered the bare minimum.[69] As a result, congestion was becoming a problem along some of these routes. Added to this was a far more complex and deeply rooted problem: the seemingly intractable issue of who rightfully owned what land. One official noted that '[t]he good people of Auckland are divided into two parties[:] the supporters of the Government and a clique of Land Sharks styling themselves "The Old Settlers". These [are] noxious vermin.'[70] Such a disparaging view of those who had purchased land in the area prior to 1840 masked the issue of competing settler claims to land previously in Māori ownership — a matter that would still not be fully resolved in the twenty-first century, and that was the source of much ill-will in the nineteenth.

Colonial Auckland

Being the capital of the colony, Auckland inevitably attracted settlers, but even a decade after its establishment it retained the trappings of a frontier town, and had yet to expand significantly. Remuera, for example, was still regarded as a small settlement outside of Auckland, and even within a kilometre of the central business district there were farms and gardens large enough to supply the bulk of the town's food. However, practically all the native forest in the central area of the isthmus had been removed.[71] A visitor in the 1850s observed that 'the only drawback of the country round Auckland, is the almost total absence of trees, except such as are planted by the settlers; yet within eight miles of Auckland the vast forests begin'.[72] Demand for land in Auckland was driven to a significant extent by speculators, forcing land prices to surge. Indeed, so dramatic was the increase in the value of land that Sir James Stephen, the permanent head of the Colonial Office in London, issued a veiled caution to the New Zealand Government about the situation. 'I confess,' he wrote in January 1842, 'that I cannot partake of the pleasure which the Governor feels in the high prices obtained for these Town Allotments. It is surely quite preposterous that Land should fetch as high a price at Auckland as in the immediate vicinity of London or Liverpool. This must be one of the bubbles which burst as surely as they are blown.'[73]

Throughout the 1840s and 1850s, immigrants were pouring into Auckland (the population reached almost 23,000 by the end of this period), which had the effect of swamping numerically the existing

Māori residents of the region (for whom immigration was not an option to bolster their numbers). However, in the 1850s, Māori were still playing an important part in the Auckland economy. In addition to their heavy involvement in the region's agriculture sector,[74] they contributed significantly to the volume of trade in the town.[75] Without the industrial scale of food production that many surrounding Māori communities were engaged in, Aucklanders would have been unable to feed themselves. In one three-month period alone, an Auckland resident recorded that Māori 'brought to market ... upwards of 1100 kits of onions (about twenty tons), upwards of 4000 kits of potatoes (more than one hundred tons), besides corn, cabbages, and kumeras; peaches grown by the natives, and sufficiently good for culinary purposes, are very abundant and cheap'.[76] The relationship between tangata whenua (the indigenous people of the region) and settlers was continually evolving during this period. The trend towards integration or assimilation (depending on your perspective) was encapsulated in the case of a Māori girls' boarding school run in Remuera. It was described by one visitor to Auckland as 'a most excellent institution which promises to be of infinite value to the rising generation of natives', and where 'the native girls are well educated and *trained*, and after many years of patient labour are formed into useful and respectable members of a civilized community: many of them have married the native young men educated at St John's College'.[77] For the settler population as a whole, this is how the future of Māori in Auckland was perceived — as a group that would eventually acquire the traits of their European neighbours.

By the 1850s, satellite settlements were popping up in seemingly remote locations around the Auckland region, but all within the gravitational force of the central town. Vicesimus Lush, the Anglican minister at Howick in 1850, jotted down some of his impressions of 'greater Auckland' at this time when travelling on horseback to his parish: 'I passed through Panmure, a Pensioner Settlement, numbering about a 100 neat wooden cottages, each in its own acre of land — the acres being well cultivated, and each Cottage surrounded by a garden resplendent with beautiful flowers, the whole village looked the picture of health, peace and contentment .... Onehunga and Panmure, though like Howick, pensioner villages, [are] far smaller and far less picturesquely situated.'[78]

A decade later, central Auckland, a least, had a more substantial appearance. Immigrants arriving in the Waitematā Harbour witnessed an expansive settlement stretched along the coast, together with many more substantial buildings that had recently been erected.[79]

By this time, statistics were beginning to be assembled in the settlement, which offer some quantifiable perspectives on Auckland as it entered the 1860s. At the opening of the decade, for example, the town had a European population approaching 5000 (of whom a fifth were illiterate), with all but 20 of them having been born overseas. There were approximately a thousand houses in the town, and churches reflecting a broad range of religious denominations.[80] The figures on the indigenous population were less accurate, but according to one assessment the total number of Māori living in the town in 1859 was a mere 157, suggesting that as settlers flowed into Auckland, the existing residents were being squeezed out.[81]

The commercial epicentre of Auckland for the remainder of the nineteenth century was its port. It was the source of most goods consumed by the town's residents, it was where produce from the region was exported, and importantly, it was the single biggest employer of Aucklanders. Around the port, infrastructure soon grew, with warehouses, shops, offices, banks and factories required to meet the growing scale of trade.[82] Auckland's prospects threatened to sour, though, when in 1863 relations between the government of Sir George Grey and the Kīngitanga (the King movement, based in the Waikato) deteriorated sharply. There were genuine popular fears at the time for the town's safety and survival in the face of a possible Māori invasion from the south.[83] Grey's invasion of the Waikato, and the subsequent confiscation of 1.2 million acres of land in the region,[84] assuaged these fears, even though the cost included destroying the entire Māori economy in the Waikato, forcibly displacing much of its population, and misappropriating vast swathes of iwi land.[85]

Without enduring an invasion, Auckland Māori had suffered a land loss of similarly dramatic proportions. Through a variety of dubious and often quasi-legal manoeuvres, Grey succeeded in alienating territories that had been unethically or illegally acquired from iwi in the region by vesting it in Crown ownership. According to one estimate, by 1855, just under 700 acres of land on the isthmus — known as the Ōrākei Block — remained in Māori possession.[86] And within 15 years the Crown alienated most of that paltry remnant as well, followed by its decision to use the Public Works Act in 1886 to appropriate land at Kohimaramara (popularly known by its slightly shorter name of Kohimarama) and Bastion Point (formerly

Takaparawhā) for defence purposes.[87] Thereafter, the presence of Ngāti Whātua increasingly came to be seen in a derogatory way by some of the city's residents as an impediment to Auckland's development.[88]

The colonial troops despatched to New Zealand to wage the governor's war in 1863 did not all regard Auckland to be as desirable as some of its residents believed it to be. One soldier wrote how the town 'appeared a poor dirty sludgy place'.[89] And in Drury, 34 kilometres south of Auckland's centre, soldiers found the roads 'unmetalled and unfascined', and generally 'in a fearful state'.[90] Most of those living in Auckland, though, tended to 'quietly submit to the rate being levied, quietly pay it, and quietly grumble at seeing it wilfully squandered', with the result that they continued to endure 'darkness, bad streets, muddy roads, starving carters, and hungry stone-breakers and road-menders'.[91]

By the close of the 1860s, the Waikato War was over, and Auckland had steadied itself from any nervous wobbles it may have experienced during the conflict. Signs of progress now seemed to be sprouting up in every direction.[92]

Settlements further away from the town were also beginning to take root in this decade. By 1866, for example, Onehunga had a population of around a thousand, and a railway line connecting it with Auckland was on the verge of completion. Ōtāhuhu at this time, while slightly smaller, was regarded as a 'beautiful township' that was accessible for small coasting cutters, and which was connected to Auckland by the Great South Road.[93] Between these villages and the town of Auckland were large expanses of farmland, dotted with occasional clumps of primordial forest and scrub that had survived earlier Māori and more recent European efforts at clearing.

Auckland's comfortable growth momentarily looked at risk, though, when it lost its position as the colony's capital. The arguments about the need for a capital to be centrally located had been mounting during the 1850s, and won out in 1854 when the seat of government was shifted to Wellington. However, losing the apparatus of the state's bureaucracy was more than compensated for by Auckland's growing commercial activity. Its population continued to increase, and in 1871 went from being regarded as a town to a city, housing 21,000 residents. Cargo vessels were entering the port at an average of one every two days, and the city's industries were both expanding and diversifying. Among the principal areas of industrial activity were timber, kauri gum, flax, rope manufacture, soap-boiling, foundries, distilleries and breweries, furniture-making and coal mining. And when it came to accommodation costs, a tenant renting a four-roomed house close to the city would be charged the current equivalent of as little as $60 a week. The cost of building 'a substantial four-roomed weatherboard cottage, lined and papered' was around $20,000 in current values. A much less expensive option was building a raupō (bulrush) house, which tended to be used for accommodation while more permanent dwellings were being erected. Arrivals to the city in the 1870s were advised that 'these raupo whares [houses] may be made tolerably comfortable, and, if kept in repair, will last for years. The Maoris will put one up for from £3 to £5.'[94]

In keeping with a theme that would echo repeatedly in the twentieth century, in the 1870s infrastructure in the city was struggling to meet the demands of Auckland's population. One case illustrating this occurred in January 1872, when much of the country was enduring a drought.[95] The supply of fresh water in Auckland — drawn mainly from wells fed by springs — was insufficient to meet demand. In order to avert a crisis, authorities resorted to pumping around 130,000 litres of water daily from the well at Seccombe's Brewery in Khyber Pass to a reservoir at the Domain.[96] Three years later, the City Council spent £20,000 to acquire Western Springs as a more reliable source of water for the city, but eventually that too would prove to be insufficient as authorities played an endless game of catch-up with the demands of a rapidly increasing population.

At first glance, Auckland was growing and, despite the ebbs and flows of the economy in general, was prosperous. Yet, even in the final decades of the nineteenth century, there was still a strong tinge of colonial outpost about the place.[97] The great English novelist Anthony Trollope felt that the city was lacking slightly in the relative refinement of Wellington, Christchurch, or Dunedin, and snidely claimed in 1873 that its streets 'are still traversed by Maoris and half-castes, and the Pakeha Maori still wanders into town from his distant settlement in quest of tea, sugar, and brandy'.[98] It was hardly the image of a vibrant, urbane 'Britain of the South', which Auckland (and, indeed, New Zealand) had increasingly been depicting itself as.[99]

Gradually, though, Auckland was acquiring the fixtures and fittings of a modern city: in May 1883 Auckland University College (a part of the University of New Zealand) was opened, albeit in a disused courthouse and gaol, which was the only available building at the time that could accommodate the 95 students who had enrolled;[100] plans were also under way at this time to build a canal between the Waitematā and Manukau harbours that was expected to make the city a crucial transit point for international shipping;[101] the Auckland Public Library's collection exceeded 5000 books; and in 1881 the population of the central city had reached 16,664 — an increase of roughly 20 per cent on what it had been just three years earlier.[102] The ascent of Auckland was far from smooth during this period, though. In the field of education, 'numerous schools were proposed and some were started, only to sink without trace',[103] while there were intermittent spikes in unemployment, for which there was little in the way of state relief.[104] Worse still, that original sin of societies — racism — was festering in Auckland. Onto the well-established anti-Māori sentiment held by some settlers in Auckland was grafted a new form in the 1880s: anti-Chinese protests, which were comprised of 'wild yahoos, breathing forth threatenings and slaughter' and who exhibited 'a most determined resolution to maintain one insular dominion in these seas sacred to the Anglo-Saxon race'.[105]

Auckland's relentless growth also brought into focus its transition from a ramshackle colonial settlement to a fully-fledged city. Its identity was being transformed, and some fractures were appearing in the process. A new phrase had begun to enter the parlance of Aucklanders: the 'old settlers', which was used to distinguish those who had been in the region from the early years of Auckland's inception from more recent arrivals. 'Newcomers' were said to be 'not a little confused and bewildered' by the ways of the old settlers. Meanwhile, the latter could get frustrated at these recent arrivals. 'They hardly know the difference between the *volcanic*, the *semi-volcanic*, and the *clay* soils', one long-term Auckland resident grumbled. 'They do not know the relative merits of the *red*, *black*, *brown*, or *grey* soils. Nor can they understand the advantages peculiar to each. Again, they are puzzled by what is said about *fern-lands* and *bush-lands*.' The newcomers typically made their way 'by dint of many questions and much groping about for stray scraps of information', but still, for those looking to settle in Auckland's rural areas, the challenges ahead of them were substantial and even bewildering at times: '[h]e wonders what he shall do for a house. He is advised to take a tent, or a framed house from town — if the latter, at a cost of £12 or £14 exclusive of carriage, to nobody knows where, at an expense of nobody knows what.'

An old settler, however, could 'run up a "settler's first home" at a tithe of the expense. *He* knows that either raupo, ti-tree, tree-ferns, nikau-palms, bark, or slabs, are to be found everywhere, and in double-quick time.'[106] Out of the social morass of early settler society, gradually (and sometimes not so gradually) distinct classes were emerging.

The establishment of men's clubs in the city reflected some of this emerging social stratification. The Northern Club, on Princes Street, was in the upper echelon of such institutions. 'Many distinguished visitors to the colony have been the guests of the club …. The Duke of Edinburgh was … the club's guest on the occasion of his visit to New Zealand', one writer boasted at the end of the nineteenth century. Descending the scale, next on the pecking order was the Auckland Club in Shortland Street. Although it had a larger membership than the Northern Club, its facilities were fewer, and its location slightly less desirable. Further down, still, was the Auckland Working Men's Club, which met the social needs of a different sector of Auckland society.[107] Numerous other clubs and organisations were formed in Auckland in the latter nineteenth century. Many reflected the overseas origins of their members (such as the Yorkshire Society) and tended to have a lifespan of little more than a generation or two. Others, like the Auckland and Suburban Poultry, Pigeon and Canary Association, were self-explanatory in their purpose, and focused on narrow aspects of life in the city. Amid the din of these various groups, though, a few emerged that hinted at Aucklanders taking a more far-sighted view of their city. One such example was the Auckland Scenery Conservation Society. The city's mayor was its president, and among its vice-presidents were such notables as John Logan Campbell, Laurence Nathan and James Russell, with its committee consisting of 'twenty of the leading citizens of Auckland'. The society was formed in July 1899, with its chief objectives being 'the conservation of the natural beauties of the district of Auckland, to prevent the destruction of native trees and shrubs, to encourage tree planting, the general beautification of public places, and generally, to make travelling to all places of interest easier and pleasanter'.[108] In a way, the very existence of the society showed that at least some Aucklanders believed their city had aesthetic values that deserved to be preserved (even though the society's success was modest, despite its august membership). Auckland was not just the sum total of various commercial enterprises, or a colonial settlement that had succeeded (unlike many others) in becoming more established and surviving the century. It was emerging as an amalgam of people, cultures, and interests who were connected by geography, and who were bound by the city's economy, but who still exhibited a strong diversity of interests, views, beliefs, and aspirations.

After Auckland's economy had enjoyed a boom in the 1880s, in the following decade the pendulum swung in the opposite direction, with the city's residents enduring a slump from which they only crawled out at the tail end of the century. The city's financial fluctuations were mirrored to some extent in its population shifts. In 1891 the population fell by a staggering 18 per cent compared with what it had been five years earlier. Yet, in the remaining nine years of the century, that loss had been fully reversed, with the number of people in urban Auckland reaching 36,000 by 1899.[109] This sort of demographic volatility was a tell-tale trait that the settlement had yet to sink its foundations sufficiently deep in the location. Too many people who lived in the city had sufficiently few attachments to it that they could pack up and leave if better opportunities appeared elsewhere.

Yet, the city had acquired many of the accretions of a modern city by the end of the century, with outbreaks of institution-building suggesting that despite economic and other setbacks, Auckland was here to stay. One of the major steps in this direction was the founding of the Auckland Public Library (which had emerged from the nearly defunct Auckland Mechanics' Institute) in 1870.[110] Its collection soon grew to around 15,000 volumes, a large portion of which came from books amassed by Sir George Grey.[111] Grey was also responsible for a substantial contribution of works to the city's Art Gallery, whose collection was augmented by the gift of an eclectic set of works that had been built up by the businessman James Tannock Mackelvie.[112]

Demographically, at the close of the nineteenth century Auckland was still largely a city of immigrants. Residents might have identified as Aucklanders by virtue of their location, but sentimentally and nostalgically, for many in its population, Britain was still regarded as 'home'.[113] This attachment to Britannia manifested itself when waves of patriotism and passion washed over Auckland in June 1897 for the celebrations of Queen Victoria's Diamond Jubilee. There was a large public procession to the Domain, a military tournament, and night-time street illuminations, which attracted thousands of people.[114] But as a hint that the ties that bound Aucklanders to Albion were beginning to loosen, one journalist noticed that the crowds 'strangely' were having trouble remembering the lyrics of 'Rule, Britannia!': 'No one seemed to know more than two lines of the chorus ... it is somewhat of a wonder that no loyal son of John Bull thought of enlightening the general public as to the precise words'.[115] The fondness for Britain was undiminished among most of the city's population, but politically and economically New Zealand was establishing its own niche in the world, and the drift away from 'home', while slow and uneven, was nonetheless inexorable.[116]

This drift was still very much at its embryonic stages as the nineteenth century came to a close. At the end of 1899, Aucklanders were among those from other parts of the country fighting alongside the British in South Africa in the Boer War. As one newspaper editor put it, while the final 'sands remain in the glass in ... the year 1899', South Africa was 'bathed in blood', and New Zealand was 'sending forth its martial manhood to do and die for Queen and Empire'.[117]

Walking around Auckland in 1899, the city was already wearing a patina of age, despite its comparatively recent inception. Albert Park (constructed in 1881 on the site of the former military barracks) was laid out with starchy Victorian formality — a throwback to an earlier sort of peculiarly English landscape design.[118] Similarly, the Auckland Baptist Tabernacle in Queen Street, completed in 1885, had references to the London Metropolitan Tabernacle, both of which were classically inspired. The Customshouse, on Customs Street West, which opened in 1889, strongly resembled the Marshall and Snelgrove building in Oxford Street, London,[119] and so the list went on. Many of the buildings that lined the city's principal streets were a conscious evocation of older architectural styles, as though antiquity somehow bestowed respectability, or at least pedigree. Yet, there were already signs of Auckland struggling to writhe free from this cult of the old. Not only in architecture, but in technology, values, belief, culture, and identity (among much else), the city was on the cusp of rapid, often radical, and sometimes incendiary change. And as much as the arrival of 1900 was a mere arbitrary punctuation point in the calendar, in some ways it also gave confidence to those who felt it was not too late to seek a newer world. Living standards in Auckland were higher than in most parts of Europe,[120] wars — while raging —

raged elsewhere, and technology would be the panacea for most of society's existing ills. As the twentieth century dawned, at least one New Zealander was in full prophet mode, informing readers of what could be expected in the ensuing hundred years:

> *The number of ocean-going vessels will increase beyond the limits of imagination. Ships will be propelled solely by electricity .... Slum life ... will be a thing of the past, as also will that curious paradox of modern life — involuntary poverty .... In the twentieth century men will always be assured of abundance of all they need, and hence they will "take no thought for the morrow" .... The span of human life will be much longer .... Marriage will be early, and unmarried people, except in the cases of people of scientific pursuits or of religious orders, will be so rare as to excite remark .... Atheism, scepticism, pessimism, and many allied vagaries will be unknown, and historians will regard them as the eccentricities of unnational and unjust social conditions .... The microbe of cancer will be known, as also will that of baldness, and both will be mastered by the men of the twentieth century .... Railways, telegraph lines, telephones, and postal services will be free .... One grand result of all this will necessarily be to do away with the congestion of people in towns; indeed, in the twentieth century it will be very difficult to tell where the town ends and the country begins.*[121]

Top marks for audacity, but as with all human prophecies, this was little more than a concoction of mildly informed guesses and wishful thinking. However, its importance lies in the degree of unbridled optimism it conveys about the twentieth century. Auckland's future was about to be shaped, not by this sort of hyperventilating optimism, but by the relentless flux of history, with its oscillation of torpor and regeneration sculpting the history of the city and its people.

2
The 1900s

For a few hours that Monday morning, Auckland was still. The sky was almost cloudless, with just a faint breeze occasionally wafting across the isthmus.[122] On the previous night — New Year's Eve — people from across the city had thronged to Queens Wharf to see the old year out, and at midnight the ships and boats anchored in the harbour set off their horns and rang their bells, to the sound of cheers from those standing on shore. Shortly afterwards, though, with no other entertainment on offer,[123] the crowds began to thin as people dawdled back to their homes in an atmosphere of slight anticlimax: 1900 had arrived.

The peace of that glittering morning of 1 January was eventually interrupted, however, by the arrival of hordes of children and attendant guardians descending on the tree-rimmed Domain for the annual festival of the Auckland Sunday School Union. Led by a Salvation Army band, this procession of young Aucklanders made its way to the large field. It was comprised of Methodists from Pitt Street Church, Baptists from the tabernacle in Queen Street, Congregationalists from Beresford Street Church, and members of St Andrew's and Knox Presbyterian churches. Races and games were organised, interspersed with refreshments, with the event finally finishing around six that evening. The Devonport Wesleyan Sunday school arguably had an even more exciting day, with the children being taken by steam paddle ferry to Motutapu Island, where they swam and explored until dusk.[124] Not to be outdone by its denominational rivals, a thousand children (along with their parents) from the Central Mission held a 'railway picnic' in Spencer's Paddock in Swanson — a popular location for picnics in this period — owned by the 68-year-old farmer Stephen Spencer (who was to die in his cottage next to the paddock just six weeks later).[125]

While the mass Sunday school activities occupied much of the city's youth, Auckland's adults were left with very few entertainment options on the first day of the twentieth century. The main social event was the Ellerslie Races. Up to 14,000 people attended[126] — roughly half the city's entire population — to parade in their fashionable finery, and to watch the horses. Colonial opulence may not quite have met the standards of an Ascot or Cheltenham, but it was an indication of a city that was reasonably confident in itself, relatively prosperous, and that aspired to the measures of status found in Britain.

For those not drawn to horse racing, 'water excursions' were the main pastime on this holiday. Ferries were crammed with people exploring Auckland's outer reaches. Trips to Waiheke and Kawau islands were heavily patronised, and around 45 kilometres north of the city was the 'delightful health resort' of Waiwera (originally Waiwerawera, meaning very hot water), which was becoming an increasingly popular destination, with visitors drawn to its hot springs that allegedly had various curative properties.[127] There was a 'fine swimming bath and private hot mineral baths for both sexes', and there were opportunities for 'boating, sea and hot spring bathing, fishing, lawn tennis, etc.', along with the promise that 'pleasant walking and driving can be had in the neighbourhood'.[128] Even Riverhead drew visitors on this day, despite the fact that it was little more than the site of a paper mill that lay along the banks of this shallow, muddy tributary of the Waitematā.[129] (Probably the nearby tavern was the sole point of interest for many of these travellers.)

With Auckland's residents at the races, the Domain, or messing around in the harbour, the city itself looked 'practically deserted'.[130] But there is more to these activities than Aucklanders simply occupying their day off from work or school. Beneath all these frolicsome comings and goings lie clues about the character of the city. For example, the fact that several thousand children participated in church-organised events in a city with a population approaching just 34,000[131] attests to the substantial influence that Protestant Christianity exercised in Auckland. And the fact of half of the people in the city attended a race meeting hints that Auckland's society was not tightly wedged into a rigidly hierarchical class system, but rather was more socially relaxed and mobile. Indeed, many people in this era used deliberately vague labels for their occupational roles as a means of sidestepping the risk of class categorisation. Distinctions did exist, of course, but were often more informal, and more likely to be flexible than was the case in in Britain.[132] Certainly, in Auckland, professionals and labourers could meet and mingle more easily than in the countries that they or their parents originated from, and in general, they seemed to prefer things this way.[133]

The nature of these New Year activities in Auckland also point to a city that, while still largely wedded to the idea of Britain as 'home', was flirting with new ways of living and of seeing itself. This was particularly evident in how Christmas and the New Year was celebrated. The *New Zealand Herald* reminded its readers that unlike in northern hemisphere countries, Aucklanders did not gather around fires for New Year's celebrations, or gorge on large feasts. Instead, the newspaper observed that

> *picnics are rapidly becoming an institution ... [as they] fit well with all our surroundings and our circumstances .... Auckland itself is said to be the most inveterate and uncompromising picnic town in all the provinces. We have all heard that Queen-street, at holiday-time, is often like the main thoroughfare of an extinct civilisation .... By boat, by train, by tram, by bus, by vehicles of all descriptions ... Auckland has lately poured itself into the surrounding country .... Hardly a nook for a radius of 20 miles but has been seized upon for bivouac by the tented scouts of the invading army of picnickers.*[134]

So, while in 1900 Auckland was still very much a product of its recent heritage, which was predominantly British and colonial, it did not wallow exclusively in this inheritance. Instead of constantly looking backwards, captivated by the imperial glow of previous generations, the city's residents seemed more self-assured that their future would be defined by where they lived as much as by where they came from. Much of this budding confidence in Auckland grew from the presence of institutions in the city. These were the firm symbols on which residents could moor their identities to some extent.[135] Not all were grand in scale, and few could claim any deep tradition, let alone antiquity in the region. Nonetheless, they were one of the means by which Aucklanders became attached to the area, just as various iwi had to their wāhi tapu (sacred sites), and the whakapapa (family and genealogical) connections that anchored them to the place both historically and metaphysically.[136]

In Princes Street there were two museums, which among much else served to provide a slightly romanticised impression of aspects of the city's past, and which cast this history in distinctly nostalgic hues.[137] Auckland Museum was 'principally remarkable for its Maori carvings, weapons, and implements, and South Sea Island curios',[138] that were housed in 'the charming Maori room'.[139] However, by 1900 the museum had run out of space for its collections, and had a slightly cramped and cluttered appearance in parts of the building. What Māori culture was on display appeared moribund and displayed partly for its decorative attributes. In one example of this, curators positioned the maihi (diagonal bargeboards) and koruru (the point of the gable) of a small pātaka (storehouse) in the Main Hall, flanked by classical statues, including one of the Venus de Milo.[140] One no doubt well-meaning visitor, in an effort to achieve a sense of cultural miscegenation, depicted a carving of Māui (the mythological Polynesian discoverer of the country) as 'the Maori Hercules, hauling up New Zealand from the bottom of the sea'.[141] Another jarring juxtaposition of artefacts could be seen in the Statue Hall, where various reclining figures and busts from the classical world were presided over by the upright skeleton of a giraffe.[142] Elsewhere, rooms were teeming with multitudes of curios, including numerous stuffed animals, which constituted the bulk of the natural history display. This was history reduced to artefacts — stripped of context, and assembled together as much for visual effect as for any sense of educative purpose. But it was a museum nevertheless, and evidence, in a way, of Auckland's maturation. Here was a building housing traces of the past, which gave Aucklanders a feeling of historical pedigree, even if that pedigree came from locations often unconnected with the city.

Nearby, on a much more modest scale, was Craig's Museum, which had a floor space of perhaps 50 square metres at most. It was an institution housed on the first floor of a small building, and was accessible by entering Eric Craig's Fern & Curiosity Shop, which was on the ground floor. In addition to having exhibits on display, visitors to this museum had the added advantage of being able to purchase 'Polynesian curios'[143] from 'every part of the Southern Hemisphere',[144] including carvings from wharenui (meeting houses),[145] although the provenance of these items was seldom provided.

One of the other signs of the city having become an established settlement by 1900 was the presence of a range of churches. The skyline of Auckland's urban topography was pierced by steeples and towers belonging to various places of worship, and in addition to the spiritual function they fulfilled for their members, the construction of churches in the region signalled that they were very much intended to be a permanent fixture of the city. In this period, churches tended to be one of the first buildings constructed in fledgling suburbs, which in turn gave the impression to potential residents that those settlements would be enduring ones. As there was no state church in the country, and no financial assistance was allocated by the government to any religion, these churches were built by their respective denominations on the basis of a great deal of faith that there would eventually be congregations to fill them.[146] By the turn of the century, in the central city area alone, there were seven Anglican churches, four Presbyterian, three Catholic, three Wesleyan, and two each for the Primitive Methodists, the Congregationalists and the Baptists. The Church of Christ also had its own building by this time, the Salvation Army had two places of worship, and Auckland's Jewish community had a synagogue. In total, there were 27 houses of worship excluding all the suburban churches that had been established more recently.[147]

Churches also played a significant role in the city's welfare. Two of the four orphanages in Auckland in this period, for example, were wholly run by churches,[148] and a host of other charitable activities were financed by religious organisations, which committed churches to a seemingly endless cycle of fundraising. One of the most popular means by which churches raised money for themselves and their community work was through holding community events such as charity bazaars. Usually, months of preparations would go into such occasions, with women undertaking most of the organising and work for them.[149] A typical example of what Aucklanders could expect at one of the larger church bazaars was that run by Knox Presbyterian Church, in Parnell. The church was less than a year old in 1900, and in the first week of May held its fundraising bazaar in the Choral Hall to assist with the church's finances. One attendee recorded that there was 'a very large attendance ... and the stall-holders did exceedingly good business'. It was the particular combination of (largely secular) entertainment that brought the crowds out to attend these events, and which made them such a success:

> *The numerous attractive side-shows were all well patronised. An excellent entertainment was provided for visitors in the evening. The beautiful tableaux shown on the previous evening were repeated, and the Victoria Rifles detachment gave an exhibition of bayonet drill and other exercises. Miss Mabel Maxwell sang "Soldiers of the Queen," Miss Gilmour "The King's Own," and Mr Horace Stebbing "The Deathless Army" and "When the Empire Calls." ... The ladies' khaki march, arranged by Professor Carrollo, which was so successful at the Benevolent Society's Easter fair, will be given during the evening, with limelight effects.*[150]

To modern audiences, such diversions from the daily grind might seem quaint and even whimsical, but at this time, options for entertainment in Auckland were limited. There were concerts (ranging from classical music to minstrel shows), visiting shows (such as waxworks), 'interesting' lectures (such as one offered in July 1900 on 'Village Life in the North of England forty years ago') and comic artists,[151] in addition to the normal run of sporting events. And even though the content or style may have changed, many of these forms of entertainment were generally the same as when Auckland had been founded, 60 years earlier.

However, flickering its way into Auckland at the beginning of the twentieth century was something new to occupy the city's residents in their leisure time: the kinematograph, and its variant, the kinetoscope. These were rudimentary forms of film, but to a populace to which anything represented by moving pictures was entirely unknown, they were a technological and visual revolution. A journalist captured this new age of entertainment at the very moment it dawned in the city:

> *What is justly described as the "crowning triumph" of photographic art, the kinetoscope, Edison's latest and greatest*

invention, is now on exhibition in Auckland. Several of these ingenious contrivances are now on view at Bartlett's studio, Queen-street .... The kinetoscope reproduces motions of any kind with remarkable reality. The pictures are marvels of art, are magnified in the machine, and are illuminated by electric light. The first series of scenes include remarkably life-like pictures on work in the barber's shop, the fire rescue, a Chinese laundry and a skirt dance. The skirt dance is a living picture of a new order, the graceful danseuse goes through her figures just as one sees her on the stage. The kinetoscope is a most remarkable invention, and all Aucklanders should see it.[152]

These early 'movies' were sometimes screened in tents, and due to the scarcity of the projection machinery (along with the sparsity of material available), they initially were toured around the country, rather than becoming a fixture in any one location They were regarded by many, however, to be a bit tawdry and down-market — a sort of sideshow attraction dependent on a technological novelty, and not much more.[153] Admittedly, they attracted good audiences, but as yet, no one was certain if this form of entertainment would be a passing gimmick, or become something more permanent. The kinematograph was a harbinger of impending change, though. The slow strides of advancing technology, which had gathered a bit of pace in the nineteenth century, were about to take a series of giant leaps, with developments ranging from powered flight, to electric street lighting, cars, vacuum cleaners, fridges, radio broadcasts, public telephones and electric stoves approaching on the horizon for Auckland — and all within just a couple of decades. The arrival of the twentieth century was becoming a convenient marker for the advent of the modern world.

City life

Throughout the 1900s, the majority of Aucklanders lived in some form of villa. There were still clutches of workers' cottages in pockets of the inner city, and cruder huts in the surrounding countryside, but increasingly the villa had come to dominate the urban landscape. Most villas in this period were built of timber (although examples constructed from masonry were favoured by some of the city's wealthier homeowners), and were influenced by the Gothic Revival style that had spread across the English-speaking world in previous decades. The English architect Charles Eastlake thought it 'strange that a style of design which is intimately associated with the romance of the world's history should now-a-days find favour in a country distinguished ... for the plain business-like tenour [sic] of its daily life'.[154] Yet its appeal was widespread, with the Victorians' fetish for frill being satiated in Auckland by the increasingly intricate and ornate decorative finishes on villas. They ranged from earlier incarnations, that were comparatively subtle, 'to the almost unnervingly riotous', as one architectural historian described it:

> *Rooflines now sported complicated folds and from the air they must have looked like an orderly geology of valleys, ridges, and intersections. Bargeboards delineating the lines of dormer windows and gables became brave with decoration which at its most delicate looked like architectural lace .... Symmetry as well as syncopation of appearance were employed unabashedly, as was the use of complex floor plans which resulted in bays, angles, courtyards and wings spouting in diverse directions.*[155]

Auckland's residential architecture was not to everyone's taste, however. A visitor from England commented at the time, while holding his nose, that the city's villas were 'extremely ugly and mean, painted wood and galvanised iron, making up into hideous streets'. The insides fared no better, being condemned for 'thick common carpets, [and] hideous chromos, typical of the ordinary lower-middle-class English household'.[156] Generally, though, villas were regarded more with appreciation than approbation, and reached the peak of their popularity in this decade.[157]

The grandest room in these villas was the parlour. It was the most lavishly decorated of the spaces in the house, and was where guests were entertained (and hopefully impressed).[158] Parlours also served as a sort of sanctuary the family could occupy that was separate from the more utilitarian parts of the home.[159] They nearly always faced the street, with their bay windows serving as a sunlit backdrop to their ornately arranged interior. And nearly always, villas had verandas — a feature which at the time had an exotic association with the Indian subcontinent (where they had been the preserve of the elite),[160] and which served both as somewhere to enjoy refreshments, or to slowly stroll along.[161]

The price of these houses ranged depending on their location in the city. In 1900, a villa in Prospect Terrace, Mt Eden, cost £315 (equivalent to a present value of around $55,100) while a similar house in Khyber Pass sold for £525 (roughly equivalent now to $91,800).[162] The accelerated growth in villa production was attributed in large part to Auckland's increasing economic prosperity in this period, and the ability of residents to afford these houses. At a meeting of the Auckland branch of the New Zealand Institute of Architects, held in 1906, Edward Bartley (who had designed the city's synagogue and the Mercury Theatre) pointed out to his audience that there had been an 'unmistakable [increase in] spending power of the people', and that as a consequence,

> *it was only necessary to drive through the miles of newly-formed streets and roads, to witness the vast number of villas which had been erected, more especially during the last 15 years, villas of considerable size and variety of design and colour. It could not now be said, as it used to be, that the Auckland villa designs were of the same type and monotonous in colour .... [T]he designing and colouring in Auckland would compare favourably with those of any district in New Zealand.*[163]

The principal challenge the city was facing by the end of the decade, as the villa-filled suburbs enlarged in scale and increased in number, was one of supply. In 1909, a land agent put the situation bluntly: 'People can't get houses ... [and] the position is becoming more and more acute. Dozens of people come into my office every day on the look-out for houses.' The proposed solution was expansion, and in this, there seemed to be some hope for the housing shortage to abate: 'a tremendous amount of suburban land is being thrown on the market shortly .... I find a general feeling of confidence in the future of Auckland, especially when the native lands are opened up.'[164] So that was the solution: make more land available (including Māori land, apparently regardless of how it was acquired) and a happy equilibrium would be reached between demand and supply. But mass supply required mass production, which had led in this decade to the growth in factories with steam-powered machines that were churning out identical parts for villas in mass quantities.[165] And when it came to raw materials, there were timber-felling and milling operations throughout rural Auckland. The heavily forested Waitākere

Ranges was the principal source of wood for the city's houses, with kauri being the favoured timber. (This was before any large-scale exotic forests had been planted in the country.)[166] Such was the voracious appetite for kauri that, by 1906, the Kauri Timber Company — a Melbourne-based syndicate — had secured harvesting rights for almost 450,000 acres of forest, and at its height had a staff of 3500, producing almost half a million cubic metres of timber annually.[167] This degree of industrial-scale production was undertaken with little if any state direction, let alone financial support,[168] and was successful, to a large extent, because of the potent mix of a growing population and the large supply of relatively inexpensive land on the outskirts of the city.

However, Auckland was not the urban utopia that some residents liked to depict it as. Just out of sight of the spacious streets lined with 'pretty villas and well-trimmed lawns'[169] were the squalid and fetid crevices of the city — places where the houses were dilapidated and the occupants destitute. The conditions were sometimes so wretched that they seemed inhumane, even by the standards of the time. Struggling sewerage systems led to some streets wallowing in a constant stench. Houses were rotting, leaking, fungal-filled and occasionally beset by infestations of mice and rats. Diseases soon found a ready home in these seedy slums, thus exacerbating the hardship of those who had resorted to such areas out of sheer desperation.

Outraged by accounts of impoverished housing in Auckland, in 1903 the chief health officer of the Department of Public Health decided to investigate the situation. Although he was initially obstructed by the Auckland Council, he eventually succeeded in uncovering the state of the city's slums. His report was critical of several areas of hygiene, including the habit of some Aucklanders dumping their rubbish on vacant sections, where it was 'left to breed rats and evil odours'. In Mt Roskill he witnessed (and smelt) fish remains, which were used for fertiliser, left stagnating on fields by farmers who did not wish to go to the effort of ploughing it into to the soil. The situation was even worse in the inner-city suburbs. Twenty-five 'ruinous and insanitary houses' had been condemned by the Health Department, but these represented just a fraction of the scale of depths of dilapidation, 'since the city is liberally supplied with hovels which would disgrace a Whitechapel slum', as the chief health officer bluntly assessed the situation. Part of the Council's reticence when it came to tackling this blight on the city seem to have stemmed from the fact that certain slum blocks were owned 'by more influential persons'. Only when pushed did officials take some remedial steps, but these were often little more than window-dressing: '[i]n one case a few bits of tin and wood and a coat of paint on the wall next the street was accepted as sufficient to place the house in good sanitary condition'.[170]

In addition to human excrement and urine sometimes being placed in shallow pits on people's sections and then covered over with soil, there was the 'filthy custom' of keeping chickens in back yards, with little effort made in most cases by residents to remove the refuse produced by these animals. In general, many sections were 'dirty and ill-kept'.[171] And predictably in such conditions, diseases took hold. Tuberculosis, typhoid, polio, smallpox and diphtheria ripped through these slum areas of Auckland, and astonishingly, even a few cases of the plague broke out in the early years of the twentieth century.[172]

Yet housing continued to be constructed in blatant breach of recent regulations. Legislation passed in 1900 had prescribed some basic standards,[173] but the Council appeared to honour such rules more in the breach than the observance. However, as the problems with Auckland's slums became more serious and more widely known, the Council eventually took the initiative to overcome some of the worst excesses on its doorstep. A board was established to acquire land, and tenders were put out for the construction of suitable dwellings for workers. The Department of Labour, which oversaw this scheme, hoped that it would present opportunities for 'bringing up families in decency and comfort', providing them 'the strongest contrast to the conditions which are fast obtaining a hold on the towns — conditions which have the germs of the evil slum in them, and of rabbit-warren dwellings housing many families, such as are to be found in London and New York'.[174]

As with most housing markets, there were leads and lags when it came to affordability. At some points, demand outstripped supply, while at other times there was a small glut of housing, and too few buyers. In an effort to offset some of the homelessness and overcrowding that resulted during those long periods of sharp demand, in 1906 the Government Advances to Workers Act was passed, which entitled workers (manual or clerical) earning under £200 a year, and owning no land, to be eligible for a low-interest loan to enable them to build a house on an urban lot.[175] The effect of such measures was considerable, and contributed to Auckland's steady urban growth in this period by enabling thousands of workers to erect their own homes,[176] where otherwise they might have been forced to move out of Auckland to wherever living was more affordable.

Arrivals and departures

The announcement that there would be a royal tour in June 1901 saw many Aucklanders scurrying to prepare the city for this rare and prestigious event. For the staff and owners of Auckland's Grand Hotel, in Princes Street, the impending arrival of the Duke and Duchess of Cornwall and York had an added urgency as it was there that the royals would be staying during their brief visit to the city. The hotel's exuberant interior was fully refurbished, at a cost of £3000, which included a 100-square-metre dining room ('handsomely furnished and decorated, with a ceiling of asbestos'), balconies, a billiard room and fittings throughout 'of chaste design'.[177]

All the effort and expense that went into the hotel's refurbishment produced only short-lived satisfaction, though. Shortly after midnight on 31 May, in circumstances that were never fully explained, a fire started in the hotel. At first, there was nothing to alert passers-by that anything was wrong, although at the subsequent inquest one pedestrian recalled a burning smell, but saw no sign of a fire and so kept walking. However, the flames raced quickly across the corridors and up the walls, devouring the timber structure with growing ferocity, while smoke billowed into every corner of the building. At about quarter to one that morning, the first cries of help had come from some of the guests. A passing cab-driver noticed the flames and raised the alarm.

Fifteen minutes later, the fire bell at the Albert Street Fire Station rang, and Auckland's fire brigade stumbled into action. The sight was a pathetic one. A handcart containing hose and fittings was hauled uphill towards Princes Street by two men, with another two rushing to help them pull this heavy apparatus towards the direction of the hotel. More equipment, including ladders, was brought to the site of the fire in handcarts — a journey of less than a kilometre, but which took more than ten minutes on foot with the heavy load. By the time the firemen had reached the Grand Hotel, it was engulfed in flames. Above the roar of the conflagration was the sound of crashing of walls and collapsing ceilings as the fire strengthened its hold on the hotel. Attempts were made by firemen to enter the building but the flames easily beat them back.[178]

THE 1900s

A rough count provided by management as the hotel blazed was that there had been 22 occupants inside the building. Some had leapt from windows, others had fled from ground-floor doors, but not everyone was accounted for. Meanwhile, doctors in the vicinity had raced to the location to tend to the injured, and crowds began to build around the perimeter of the carnage — curious and horrified at the inferno in front of them. An eyewitness reported that

> [f]or some time the suspense was awful. The cries of those who had friends or relatives in the building, and who were not sure whether they had escaped or not, were heartrending. The proprietor of the hotel, Mr Johnston, was in terrible agony, believing that three of his children were in the burning building. It was at first hoped that they had escaped unnoticed and [been] taken into the house of some neighbours.[179]

It was not until morning that the fire was finally brought under control, although control was an ambitious claim. In fact, it had nearly burnt itself out, and practically destroyed the building, with the cost of the damage estimated at £12,000. It was only when the charred skeleton of the hotel had cooled that the grim task of recovering bodies could begin. Five people had died as a result of the fire. Three of them were the daughters of the hotel's manager, Alexander Johnston. They were Leonore, aged 14, Eva, aged 12, and Nina, just six. Their badly burned bodies were located in the basement beneath their bedroom. A housemaid, Dora Wallace, attempted to escape the flames by jumping from her bedroom window, but was fatally injured in the fall. Five days later, the final victim was located amid the rubble: Fred Ayres, a 41-year-old bank employee.[180]

The three girls killed in the fire had been boarders at St Mary's High School, Ponsonby, and were due to return to school in the next week or so. The Catholic bishop of Auckland knew all of them, and had coincidentally been one of the first people present to console witnesses of the fire that morning. Consolation soon began to curdle with anger, though. The Auckland Fire Brigade bore the initial brunt of public outrage over their obvious inadequacies in both equipment and response times. 'Imagine,' one commentator wrote, 'a body of men tugging behind them to a fire in our hilly city appliances weighing 30 tons, and expecting them, after such exertion, upon reaching the scene of the fire to cope successfully with it.' Public opprobrium then turned in the direction of the Council, which had been warned of the risk of fires in the city, and the near-complete absence of safety measures (such as external fire escapes and water supplies close by) in Auckland's buildings. 'The majority of them are veritable death-traps .... The whole thing is a disgrace to the people of the largest city in the Colony.'[181]

Wellington's Chief Fire Superintendent, Thomas Hugo, was called to investigate what could be done to improve Auckland's readiness for such fires in the future. Among the recommendations were the installation of 60 telegraph alarm boxes throughout the city, the use of horse-drawn vehicles to transport equipment to fires, the provision of accommodation for at least 16 men at fire stations (including beds and mess facilities), and the supply of steam pumps, longer hoses and taller ladders.[182]

'Inclement'[183] is how the press euphemistically described the bitingly cold, windy, rain-drenched weather that tormented Auckland the day that the Duke and Duchess of Cornwall and York arrived in the city, at the start of their brief royal tour of the country. Whipping in the wind was the 'Welcome Arch' that had been mounted on the wharf where the royals would be disembarking. This 12-metre-tall edifice was decorated with arum lilies and pampas grass, with the main towers lined with punga and nīkau fronds. And across the arch in large white lettering was the word 'Welcome'.[184] It was a construction that paid deference to the royals, but that was also wreathed, literally, with an idiosyncratically indigenous[185] aesthetic — signs, perhaps, of the 'glimmerings of a new national consciousness'.[186] One British writer frothed over the success of the tour, claiming that it was 'unique', 'triumphal', and 'a progress such as Roman conqueror never enjoyed'.[187] This not only wildly overstated the case, but missed a crucial aspect of this visit: the opportunity it gave for the colony to assert its distinct role in the Empire. It was as much about local patriotism as imperial obeisance.

To the loud thuds of saluting cannon fire, the royal couple set foot in Auckland at two o'clock in the afternoon of 11 June 1901. Church bells rang out in unison across the city, and hundreds of flags — sagging in the rain — lined streets in the central business district to celebrate this event. The duke and duchess were welcomed officially by the mayor — Sir John Logan Campbell — who was a surviving relic from the earliest days of Auckland. Thousands of children were present to cheer on the royals, and various deputations of the good and great of the city met these august visitors. In response, the duke's speech reaffirmed the importance of peace, prosperity, racial harmony, loyalty[188] — the sort of platitude repeated around the Empire in this period and for decades to come.

The following morning, there was a military parade at Potter's Paddock[189] (later named Alexandra Park) where the duke presented medals to some of the Auckland soldiers who had fought in South Africa. There was then a chance to return indoors, with a luncheon held at the Choral Hall for 400 veterans of 'all the wars of the Great Queen'. In the afternoon, the duchess was driven to Parnell, along with her husband, where she laid the foundation for the future Queen Victoria High School for Maori Girls.[190] The day concluded with yet another reception — this one hosted by the mayor at the Art Gallery — with the royals departing for Rotorua the following day. It had been a celebration partly of Auckland as it wished to be seen at the time as much as of the visiting royals.[191] The governor, the Earl of Ranfurly, pronounced that the expressions of support and affection that the duke and duchess had received had come 'spontaneously from a free and devoted people, and breathed loyalty to His Majesty'.[192] This was a popular and, no doubt, sincere sentiment. However, there had been a minor fly in the ointment relating to the role that Māori would play in the ceremonies. Planners of the tour had presumed that the indigenous population was a single, amorphous people, and so organised for the royal couple to travel from Auckland directly to Rotorua, where they would receive a Māori welcome. However, Waikato Māori took offence at their exclusion, with the leader of the Waikato-based King movement — Mahuta — suggesting that he personally present the duke with the great war canoe used by his predecessor in the 1863 war against the Crown. Symbolically, this would serve 'as an indication that the Waikato Natives had no further use for it, and were now, and would be in the future, loyal subjects of the King'.[193] Mahuta hoped to lead a procession of waka along the Waitematā Harbour to meet the royal couple, but organisers quashed the idea, and the main 'Māori' component of the tour remained scheduled for Rotorua.

Perhaps it was an act of gratitude to the city he had lived in for most of his life and that had enriched him, or a sudden rush of euphoria, or maybe a craving to be remembered after his death, but whatever the reason, John Logan Campbell used the occasion of the royal visit to Auckland to present the city with a 230-acre park descending from the slopes of

One Tree Hill. Campbell invited the duke to accept this gift on behalf of the people of New Zealand, and that it be named Cornwall Park to commemorate the visit.[194] However, rather than simply hand over the land to the people of Auckland in its existing condition, Campbell assembled a committee to devise a plan on how the proposed public park might be improved. Among the recommendations of the committee's report was that any of the remnants of Māori life on the site be left 'sacredly intact'. Other suggestions, such as a children's playground, proved too costly, and were abandoned. Just the roading and planting elements of the plan ended up as an expensive undertaking, with Campbell donating £2000 of his own money to subsidise it. The gift of the park was proclaimed in Parliament as 'an example of beneficence and kindness, the benefits of which will be felt by rich and poor alike for all time'.[195]

The ceremonial opening of Cornwall Park took place on 26 August 1903, with the 85-year-old Campbell leading an almost two-kilometre-long procession from the Market Road entrance to the park. As they proceeded through the grounds, the newly laid road took the crowd through a tunnel of trees that Campbell had planted 27 years earlier.[196] Finally, he reached the spot where a platform had been especially erected for the occasion, and from which he delivered a speech to the assembled mass of the city's residents beneath him. He commenced by quoting a passage from Socrates that he felt applied to his fellow Aucklanders: 'Our citizens must not be allowed to grow up among images of evil lest their souls assimilate the ugliness of their surroundings.' The crowd were absorbing every word of the city's great patriarch, and with his voice 'broken with emotion', he concluded his speech by announcing that 'this ovation now accorded to me ... constitutes the crowning happiness of my life .... Once more, I bid you all welcome to ... Cornwall Park. Its gates are open to you. May God bless you all.' Cheering instantly erupted from the crowd as he then proceeded to climb to the summit.[197]

Campbell had one remaining wish for 'his' park: that a monument be erected on the summit of One Tree Hill, 'dedicated to the great Maori race'. He made this proposal in 1906, when the Māori presence in Auckland was economically, socially, demographically and politically peripheral.[198] Campbell foresaw his proposed obelisk one day acting as a commemorative marker to the time just prior to Māori disappearing from the country for ever. The belief of Māori as a 'dying race' had been gathering pace since the 1830s,[199] and by the early twentieth century was pervasive in New Zealand. The indigenous population was tentatively on the road to recovery from the late 1890s, but at that time the signs of this were still too faint to be detected, and it would still be a few decades until this revival was plainly evident to the general public.[200] However, by the time Campbell's obelisk was erected, in November 1940, his wish for 'a towering obelisk uprearing heavenward from the summit of One Tree Hill in memoriam to the great Maori race' was already outdated, and although it was a gesture of affection for Māori in Campbell's mind, in subsequent decades different and often erroneous meanings and interpretations were projected onto it.

The sentimentality directed towards Māori at the beginning of the century arose largely from the commonly held view that the country's indigenous people would soon be gone for ever. However, when it came to another minority group — the Chinese — the attitude was far more abrasive. Chinese had come to New Zealand principally to work in the gold-mining industry in the middle of the nineteenth century.[201] When the mining went into decline, though, many left the country — a trend that continued for the remainder of the century. Just how substantial this pattern of departure was can be gauged by the fact that between 1896 and 1901 the nation's Chinese population fell by 23 per cent.[202] In Auckland, however, the trend was a reversal of this. In the entire Auckland province, there were just 206 Chinese in 1901 (of whom only two were women),[203] and all of whom had arrived relatively recently (in 1874, there were no Chinese at all recorded living in the city).[204] The minute presence of Chinese in the city, though, was preceded by major prejudices about them. These 'outsiders' were associated by some white New Zealanders with opium-smoking, prostitution and even white slavery and piracy.[205] The government had responded punitively to their presence, most notoriously by introducing a poll tax on Chinese immigrants. This was initially set at £10 per immigrant in 1881, but 15 years later was raised to £100 for each Chinese person wishing to settle in New Zealand.[206] As discriminatory as such regulations were, they proved insufficient to quell the racism that propped them up. In June 1904 the *Auckland Star* — the city's principal evening newspaper — reported on how the 'hatred of the Asiatic' was gathering momentum in various 'white' nations. Anti-Chinese leagues were being formed 'with the object of ... the rooting out of Chinese and other Asiatics in the Commonwealth',[207] and New Zealand was not immune to the contagion.

This hostility has been explained in part as being an offshoot of New Zealand's growing colonial nationalism in this era. In which forming 'a cohesive, egalitarian community of like-minded citizens required excluding all those ... who stood apart from or threatened to undermine' that society.[208] The 'yellow peril' may have been seen by a minority as a 'hollow' threat,[209] but the popular lure of a scapegoat for any misfortune, or a caricature of an impending Asian invasion, provided sufficient nourishment for racism in the region. Auckland was a latecomer to adopting the fears over the yellow peril, chiefly due to the fact that the Chinese presence in the city was still small and slowly growing in this period. However, enthusiasm for restrictions on Chinese immigration were gathering momentum,[210] and the undercurrent of anti-Asian racism was beginning to spill over more frequently in public. It was fear, primarily, that fuelled this prejudice, as one Auckland newspaper editor inadvertently revealed in 1904: 'In every bazaar in India from end to end of China, in tent and tea-house throughout Central Asia, in Afghanistan, in Siam, in the Philipines [sic], in Arabia, in Egypt, in Turkey, the leaven of unrest, of hope, of the always smouldering enmity to the Western man ... seethe[s] and swell[s].'[211] And with the local press portraying Asian immigration in other parts of the Empire as 'one of the gravest dangers'[212] to those countries, the message to Aucklanders could not have been clearer.

Getting around

Until 1902, Aucklanders had been accustomed to decades of horse-drawn trams. They were slow, smelly and increasingly unsuited to the demands of a growing population that needed more effective forms of moving people around the city.[213] The solution arrived on 24 November, when the city's first electric tram service began operation (running from the city to Ponsonby via Karangahape Road). Better transport drew even more patronage, and by the middle of the following decade a network of trams criss-crossed the metropolis, transporting Aucklanders along Great North Road, New North Road, Sandringham Road, Dominion Road, Mt Eden Road, Manukau Road and Remuera Road.[214] (Some of these routes had been recently renamed, however. Prior to 1907, Dominion Road was known as Mt Roskill Road, and Sandringham Road was initially Cabbage Tree Swamp Road, then Kingsland Road, then New Edendale Road, then Edendale Road, until finally acquiring its present name in 1929.)[215] In what was to become a perpetual cycle, the extension of transport routes hastened the growth of existing suburbs and the formation of new ones, and this, in turn, heightened the demand for the development of additional transport routes. One of the most far-sighted initiatives in suburban planning at this time was a scheme to create a suburb along the railway line between Avondale and Henderson 'with a view to selecting a suitable place for the homes of workmen whose occupations are in the City of Auckland, and who would travel to and from the city daily between their work and their homes'. The planners acknowledged that the land in question was not 'first class', but regardless, they assessed that with some cultivation, the sections 'would carry a cow, and give room for a homestead and garden'. When asked about the viability of such a plan, the assistant general manager of railways was confident that there were at least 'a hundred steady, reliable married men, in constant employment in Auckland ... who would gladly leave their town dwellings ... to go and live in the country'. However, because these men most likely had no savings, it was recommended that the government advance them £100 each towards the construction of a cottage for themselves, and subsidise their rail travel.[216]

Although the scheme did not eventuate in precisely the form that planners had anticipated, there was a rapid rise regardless in rail travel from West Auckland in this era. The purchase of commuter tickets from the Henderson railway station illustrates the enormous increase in train patronage, with ticket sales going from 187 in 1905 to 23,237 in 1929. And between 1900 and 1930, commuter tickets sold in Avondale rose from 313 to 56,700.[217] The opportunities that increased road and rail routes created were quickly capitalised on: 'Large areas of open fields were bought by speculators who ... cut the land up into building sections; as a consequence suburbs came into being, which had never been thought of.' And in keeping with the American aphorism — 'put in your railways and population will follow' — Auckland's suburbs flourished with the extension of tram and train lines.[218]

The other form of transport making its presence felt in this decade was the car. For £485 — roughly the price of the average house in the city — Aucklanders could purchase a 15-horsepower car, capable of travelling at an impressive 24 kilometres an hour.[219] To meet the needs of the growing number of car enthusiasts in the city, in May 1902 the

Auckland Automobile Association (the first of its kind established in the southern hemisphere) was formed. Its membership was made up of car and motorbike owners, importers, and anyone else with an interest in this comparatively new mode of transport, and who was happy to pay the £1 annual subscription. The main requirement for membership eligibility was passing the Association examination, which comprised 'the theory and practice of motor driving (steam, electric or petroleum)'. The Association had its club rooms at 52 Queen Street, where members met on the second Tuesday of every month to swap car stories, and to prepare for the monthly automobile run, which was held the following Saturday afternoon.[220]

And as an indication of the appetite for automobiles at this time, although it was probably as late as 1898 that the country's first car was imported, within 25 years New Zealand had one of the highest levels of car ownership in the world. By 1907, there were already 3000 vehicles in the country, representing one for every 316 people.[221] Any future transport planning for Auckland could not avoid anticipating the impact of this increasingly popular means of transport, although for decades afterwards the effect of increasing rates of car ownership tended to be underestimated by those responsible for the city's roading.

The humble cyclist was not forgotten in the expansion of Auckland's transport networks, though, thanks to the lobbying of the Auckland Cyclists' Road League. Formed in 1900, the League aimed to 'remedy the disgraceful state of the roads in and around Auckland', and to consider 'ways and means for the laying down of cycle paths or improved roads'.[222] In April the following year, it appealed to Parliament for the need for dedicated cycle lanes, and made its case by first tackling the main objection cyclists faced:

> *It may be claimed that the subsidising of a small portion of the public streets and roads would be detrimental to vehicular traffic, or that cyclists ... would seek to conserve the sole rights of the section laid by them. Our ... position is that the League only seek sufficient legislation to allow them to lay the proposed tracks ... and that no interference by them would be offered to any other kind of traffic.*[223]

At the other end of the scale of planned transport routes was the ambitious suggestion of a canal linking the Manukau and Waitematā harbours. The idea of connecting the two harbours had been floating around since the 1840s,[224] but was revived in the early twentieth century principally through the work of the Waitemata-Manukau Canal Promotion Company. The prospect of levying shipping traffic through this proposed passage was enough to enthuse promoters to the point where they tended to diminish the colossal engineering undertaking it would involve. In 1903 the Company sent a letter to the Auckland Harbour Board seeking support for an engineering report on the scheme. The Harbour Board had been toying with a similar idea for a canal, and committed itself to investigating the matter further.[225] The Company's fortunes had faded by 1907 (due to its questionable business practices),[226] but by that stage enthusiasm for the planned canal had spread much more broadly. Subsequent lobbying by various groups led, in 1908, to the passage of the Auckland and Manukau Canal Act. This statute authorised the Auckland Harbour Board to acquire land for the canal's construction, but did not commit the Crown to financing the project.[227] Nonetheless, planning got under way for the canal,[228] but rising estimates of its eventual costs, coupled with the extension of terrestrial transport routes, made the project unviable, and it was eventually abandoned.

As roads, railway tracks and tramlines increasingly straddled the city's terrain, and ferries criss-crossed the harbour, enabling new suburbs to germinate along these routes, the impression of Auckland at this time was of a technologically advanced metropolis, where the clamour of commerce and the clank of industry was heard everywhere.[229] However, the survival of the city was still very much dependent on the activities of the surrounding rural sector. Meat and dairy were thriving on Auckland's periphery,[230] with large processing factories having recently been established at Penrose and Ōtāhuhu to prepare the produce for export. Smaller-scale factories were also a feature of rural Auckland at this time. One such example was the Ambury, English and Co. Creamery at Māngere, which by 1901 was producing 150 tons of butter annually for the British market.[231] Over 868,000 sheep were being farmed in the vicinity of the city at this time,[232] while local forestry earned Auckland almost £23,000 annually.[233]

Further to the west of the city, another pocket of commercial activity was also intensifying. In New Lynn, brick-making had been the dominant industry since being established there in the 1850s. The area experienced a production boom in the 1860s and 1870s, but towards the end of the nineteenth century the number of brickworks declined sharply as timber became more popular as a building material.[234] New Lynn's brick industry then burst back into activity in the 1900s, as demand once again swung in its favour. Firms such as J. J. Craig set up a factory there with the capacity to produce 200,000 bricks per day.[235] Albert Crum, who had previously manufactured bricks in Ashburton, established a ceramics plant in New Lynn in 1905, and by the end of the decade there were around 26 brick, tile and pottery factories operating in the area.[236] And even further west, at Limeburners Bay in Hobsonville, a firm run by Rice Owen Clark was producing a range of ceramic fittings, employing a staff of 200 men.[237] These brick and pipe works were located on sloping land leading to a channel into which barges could enter and be loaded with products to be transported just ten kilometres across the harbour to the central-city wharves.

Elsewhere in the west, areas such as Henderson and Oratia were being cleared for orchards and vineyards. In 1902 a Lebanese immigrant, Assid Abraham Corban, purchased a block of marginal land bordering the Henderson railway line, and planted grapevines in the clay soils, which soon were supplying the winery he built on the site.[238] At the same time, several Croatian families had also moved to Henderson to establish their own vineyards and orchards, and in December 1901 the first meeting of the Henderson Fruitgrowers' and Farmers' Association was held. It was an opportunity to share ideas about growing, marketing and distributing produce from the area, and encouraged innovations such as ventilated train wagons to ensure the fruit sent to Auckland remained as fresh as possible.[239]

The commercial success of Henderson's viticulturalists and orchardists cultivated interest in the settlement's annual horticultural show, which in November 1902 was the biggest yet held. There were flower-arranging events, competitions for the largest vegetables and the best bottled fruit, as well as contests for jams, cream and baking.[240] By the close of the decade, Henderson had come to be regarded as possibly the best fruit-producing area in the North Island[241] — a claim to fame that rested much more with the skills and enterprise of Henderson's horticulturalists than the mediocre quality of the soils and growing conditions in the area.

The city's rural outskirts were also a place of leisure — somewhere urban-bound Aucklanders could escape to, even if only for a day. Among the more popular destinations were the Waitākere Ranges (then known as the Titirangi Ranges) and the Nihotupu Falls. The chance to see a few of the surviving ancient kauri trees towering above 'majestic tree ferns' in picturesque settings was a major attraction.[242] And for the slightly more adventurous, Aucklanders could take a steamer to Great Barrier Island in the Hauraki Gulf — a distance of around a hundred kilometres. A 1902 tourist guide described how on approaching the Great Barrier, the vessel

> *threads its way through a beautiful series of outlying islands, crags, and rocks which girt the coast for about ten miles. Then passing through an extremely narrow opening, the harbour of Port Fitzroy is gained. Here, a series of wild, romantic hills rise peak behind peak till the highest, Mount Hobson, towers like a lofty pyramid to a height of 2,000 feet. This ... harbour is indented by numerous bays and long arms, the steep hills rising on either side compose a charming picture, while the homesteads of the thriving settlers dotted here and there give life and animation to the scene.*[243]

The notion of a spacious, arboreal paradise within easy reach of home was a welcome antidote to the often stifling urban living conditions to which so many Aucklanders were accustomed. These stretches of wilderness were also an opportunity for the city's residents to exercise their imaginations as much as their bodies, and some were inspired to write of their experiences, producing highly romanticised accounts of their excursions into these largely unspoilt areas. Yet, for all the brooding beauty and great antiquity of these forests, the more pragmatic visitor acknowledged that such wilderness areas would eventually have to succumb to the trenchant advances of civilisation that bordered them:

> *Anyone who knows our native bush, if he have any imagination or poetry in his nature, cannot help entering in some degree into the feeling of reverence with which the ancients regarded the forest primeval. Primitive people looked with something like awe on the great green kings of the woods, those solemn pillars which had seen so many generations of men live their little lives and pass away .... the grand growths of the deep woodlands were, in many cases, objects to be approached with ceremonial care*

and reverential feeling. The vast and gloomy woods exercise an overpowering awe .... I can almost share the cries of regret of the shy wood-birds for the vanished trees when I visit some locality where the well-remembered dense bush, affording shelter to all sorts of pretty feathered creatures, has given place to blackened stumps and charred logs. Yet it is not reasonable to object to the wiping-out of the forest by the settler, for the heroic work of colonization must go on; the tangled wilds must disappear to make way for homesteads and tilled fields and flocks and herds.[244]

It was not that the city was all stone, concrete and tar. Most houses had some land around them, which was used for growing fruit trees and vegetables, and sometimes keeping chickens (and in a few cases, rabbits). There were also small parks scattered seemingly at random in some suburbs, and areas of land that remained undeveloped. One of these was what was commonly known as Cabbage Tree Swamp, in eastern Kingsland.[245] As a young child, at the turn of the century, Percy Cross would take his dinghy to the swamp after a period of heavy rain, and with his friends would paddle around in the shallow muddy waters.[246] A section of this swamp was drained and filled in to become a sports field, with its name changing from the Kingsland Cricket Ground to Eden Park in November 1907.[247] Through developments such as this, small pockets of nature across Auckland were being converted into spaces suited for an increasingly urbanised community.

Signs of war

If the extent of newspaper coverage is any indication, at the start of the twentieth century, Aucklanders were captivated by the progress of the Boer War. It was the first time New Zealand troops had fought overseas, and was popularly depicted as a chance for the Empire to reassert its superiority in one of its troublesome corners. Auckland's reaction, as with that of the rest of the country, was swift and impressive when the premier, Richard Seddon (who was also defence minister), put out the call for troops to volunteer. The response was portrayed as 'evidence of the dash and decisiveness of our national character'. Finally, there was an opportunity for the country to bang the patriotic drum, but in a manner that emphasised its own emerging identity[248] as much as its commitment to Britannia: 'New Zealand has grown into Nationhood, and is paying the penalty, but our boys have already justified the step, and added lustre to the name of our bright young colony. "Be brave!" was the monition of the Maori warriors of old; to-day it is the pennant of the New Zealand boy',[249] was how one Auckland writer conflated nationalism, ethnicity, history and international allegiances into a patriotic amalgam in April 1902.

However, on the morning of Monday 2 June 1902, a cable reached Auckland from South Africa, containing just two words: 'Peace declared'.[250] Britain had secured an exhausting victory in the Boer War, even if it was far from a comprehensive or enduring one. As soon as news was announced of the end of hostilities, Auckland's fire bells were rung, accompanied shortly by church bells throughout the city, along with the bell of the Town Hall clock. To this cacophony was added the blaring of steam sirens from ships docked at the city's ports, and the blasts of guns from the Devonport naval base. The combined sounds lasted for half an hour. Ships in the harbour immediately decked themselves with flags to celebrate the victory, and the streets of the city were soon teeming with people wearing red, white and blue, waving union flags, and parading in a 'festive mood'. In Auckland's outer suburbs and the surrounding rural areas, jubilation over the end of the war was no less pronounced. Bonfires were lit that night, bands played patriotic songs, and there were rifle salutes. The following day, after the initial rush of euphoria had settled slightly, Auckland's schools were closed for a special holiday, most government offices were likewise shut for the day, and various businesses celebrated with toasts of champagne.[251]

On the following Sunday, Auckland's churches held special thanksgiving services for the end of the war to packed congregations. Most of the denominations recognised the human cost of the fighting and the importance of peace. However, at St Matthew's Anglican Church the tone of the sermon was noticeably more jingoistic. Blame for the war was placed exclusively with the Boers, with the British victory having been secured through 'the spontaneous loyalty and patriotism of all the sons of our Empire'. The renewed sense of unity in the Empire was pronounced to be a divine blessing, and was achieved because 'our cause was just'.[252] In contrast to this triumphalism, the Women's Christian Temperance Union's publication — *The White Ribbon* — was significantly more magnanimous. It criticised the boasts of victory as being 'not in the best taste', but noted with consolation that, on the whole, 'the feeling shown has been one of heartfelt thankfulness, mingled with respect for our brave foes'.[253]

While the British Empire was already by this stage slowly drifting towards dissolution, a new power was appearing on the horizon — literally. On 9 August 1908, 16 American battleships steamed into the Waitematā Harbour, at the beginning of what would be a six-day stopover.[254] It was one of those goodwill visits that also served as a muscle-flexing exercise, signalling growing American influence in the region. This was militarism of a different stripe, with the Great White Fleet (as the ships were popularly known) evoking popular celebrations even larger than those at the end of the Boer War, yet without a shot having been fired in conflict. A description of the fleet's arrival gave the ships an almost spectral character as they emerged into sight:

> *At first there was a feeling of disappointment, because all over the great Hauraki Gulf lay a dense fog. It hid the sea approaches northward, and enveloped Rangitoto, so that only the crater cones on its summit were visible .... It seemed as if a whole navy might sail through those vaporous clouds unseen. But ... [a]s the sun rose higher it melted gaps in the mist bank, and a light breeze drove it aside in places. Still the fog lay dense to the northward, and the people watched it anxiously. Suddenly the guns boomed out from the forts, and then, as if by magic, an opening appeared in the white mist, widening to a broad sea lane along the Rangitoto Channel. And down this lane glided the white fleet, ship after ship in stately procession. It was an impressive sight. Few more perfect seaways exist anywhere than this approach to the Auckland Harbour, but it seemed as if nature in a gracious mood had specially beautified it for the occasion.*[255]

The visit by these vessels 'was one of the gayest and most spectacular events in the history of Auckland', according to one spectator. An astonishingly large crowd, estimated to be up to 100,000, squeezed into every vantage point along the harbour edge to see the great ships dock.[256] Given that the total Auckland population just two years earlier was 82,100,[257] the number of people swarming to the occasion must have included a large portion from well outside the city. Auckland was 'decorated in a most extensive manner' for the event, with 'the illuminations, in which electricity was used for the first time, being particularly elaborate'. What followed was nearly a week of celebrations in the city on a scale 'never previously indulged in', and which included 'banquets, receptions on land and aboard the ships of the fleet, reviews, race meetings and sports, both general and aquatic'.[258] Most Aucklanders would have flinched at even a hint at this time that this American naval visitation in any way diminished their loyalty to King or Empire. However, the presence of the American fleet in Auckland nonetheless served as an indication that the country's foreign policy was being directed more for regional than necessarily imperial purposes, and that, increasingly, the South Pacific was becoming a sphere of American interests.[259]

The trend towards New Zealand assuming a more independent stance internationally had accelerated in 1907 when the country was granted Dominion status. Although 'constitutionally meaningless', it was symbolically significant.[260] New Zealand was no longer identified as a 'colony', and the declaration of Dominion status became a shorthand for the nation having achieved greater autonomy.[261] Perhaps titular adjustments to the country's status were a hard sell when it came to exciting the public's imagination, because although a half-day holiday was declared in Auckland on 26 September to celebrate Dominion Day, it was not taken up 'with much enthusiasm'.[262] The previous night, there had been steady rain, causing the ground at Victoria Park — where the festivities were to be held — to become soggy. The weather remained threatening on Dominion Day, which probably accounts for why the numbers in attendance were so small. Various dignitaries delivered speeches (although the Minister of Education arrived too late for his address) and there was a military parade preceded by a 21-gun salute. And that was it.[263] In the afternoon, Aucklanders returned to their homes, shops and offices, with little sense that anything monumental in the country's history had been commemorated. In years to come, achieving Dominion status was looked on as one of those totemic rites of passage leading to New Zealand becoming an independent nation, but at the time, this accomplishment barely kindled the interest of most Aucklanders. Still, though, it was an advance of sorts (even if few understood precisely what practical benefits being a dominion would entail), and cause at least for satisfaction if not celebration.

However, there was a handful of Auckland residents who did not see history simply as patriotic pageantry, and who were uncomfortable with the shows of imperial swagger that were regularly on display in the city. And it was from this group that the Auckland Peace Association came into being. Formed in May 1899, its objects included combatting 'the spirit of selfishness, militarism, and rapacity', fostering a 'heathy public opinion in favour of peace', reducing armaments, resolving international conflicts through arbitration, and the promotion of a 'high standard of national righteousness'. Above all, the Association held the view that 'boastfulness, revenge, and disregard for the rights and feelings of others were inconsistent with national honour'.[264] The Association's subsequent lobbying for an end to hostilities in South Africa, though, put it off-side with the majority of Aucklanders who were rallying for the Empire's victory in the Boer War. Given the generally warm affection which the city's residents felt for the imperial cause, it was predictable that there would be some opposition to the Association's mission. A newspaper editorial from the winter of 1900 was representative of the disparaging attitude held by the many towards the few on this issue:

> *Relative to the growing population and intelligence of the city and province ... we are glad to inform the public that faddists[,] cranks, and people with a craze, in church and State, do not really appear to be on the increase. Their tendency, however, is to spring up suddenly as pseudo mushrooms, and not being troubled, as other men with "the slightest remains of the modesty of youth," they keep themselves, for a time, well to the front in the public press. They make a good deal of din, our hobby-horse men — like their prototypes in the nursery — but little progress. The small battalion of mounted heroes we specially refer to now would not bring much honour to the city as troopers in the Transvaal. Their tongues would be longer and sharper in complaints against their friends than their swords and spears against the enemy. One of these valiants for the truth in the Auckland Peace Association — so-called — has become truly alarming .... all Christians can sympathise with [t]he reign of peace they all pray for. But to conceal under this the most violent pro-Boer affection and hatred of the Empire that gives us life, and law, and liberty; to act in such a way that oppression and ignorance and lawlessness [sic] would have been established in*

> Africa, and our Empire broken in the dust, this cannot be a kind of conduct to be commended in the community, under any show of superior morality and religion.[265]

Perhaps stung, but certainly undaunted by such public opprobrium, the Association continued through the 1900s with its dogged pursuit of world peace. Occasionally, its outbursts seemed almost consciously provocative, such as a statement a spokesperson for the Association issued when the American fleet arrived in 1908. He welcomed 'our American cousins', but then went on to say, 'I would rather see them come as civilians, not as butchers'.[266] This rhetoric was almost engineered to offend, but tended to be an exception. More typical of the Association's work was a resolution its committee passed in July 1907, urging the government to negotiate with the world's powers to declare the Pacific Ocean region 'neutral'.[267] There was plainly no interest at all in government circles for such an outlandish proposal, and so like all the preceding motions of the Association, it ended up falling on stony ground, and withered. Still, though, the Association battled on, and by 1909 had around a hundred members, and was attracting up to 500 people to some of its rallies.[268]

'Destined to increase'

Auckland's growth in this decade was uneven demographically, and sporadic geographically. However, a snapshot of the city gives an impression of how far it was stretching out, and how, at just 60 years old (making it one of the youngest cities on earth at this time), distinct traits were already revealing themselves in certain suburbs. The more 'established' areas of the region were, naturally, in the close orbit of the commercial centre, but proximity did not always equate with prosperity. Suburbs such as Ponsonby and Freemans Bay, for example, were a short walk from Queen Street, but were run-down, sometimes disease-ridden, and had deserved reputations as places of prostitution, crime and drunkenness.[269]

In contrast, Parnell, an equally old Auckland suburb, was 'a favourite place of residence' in the city, and was heavily provisioned with schools, churches, libraries, halls and other facilities,[270] in addition to being well endowed with more lavish homes. Neighbouring Newmarket was the province's smallest borough, but one of the busiest due to its heavy road and rail traffic.[271] The adjoining suburb of Remuera was also 'very popular', and although slightly further from the city centre, was regarded as one Auckland's more prestigious locations.[272]

One of the faster-growing areas of Auckland at this time was Mt Eden, principally because of its proximity to the city centre, combined with it being well serviced by trains and buses.[273] It was distinguished from the rest of Auckland, however, by being the location of the city's prison. Auckland Gaol, as it was then known, was a grim edifice, with a dark outer wall of stone — almost six metres in height — behind which prisoners were incarcerated in its 167 cells. (It was also one of the first places in the country where the fingerprints of criminals were taken.)[274]

These suburbs constituted the more densely settled satellites of the city. Beyond them, Auckland's character altered. In Mt Albert, for example, instead of a heavily housed suburb, visitors to the area in the 1900s would have encountered a 'wide stretch of pleasant undulating country', which still retained its rural appearance, but was 'being rapidly acquired by business men seeking suburban homes'.[275]

Nearby Grey Lynn was slightly more developed, but during most of this decade still consisted primarily of 'undulating land ... dotted with large clumps of trees'.[276] Mt Roskill was also in the category of those suburbs that were predominantly rural, but had begun to grow partly as a result of the establishment of the Ranfurly Veterans' Home in the area in 1903.[277] However, it was sparsely populated, and was sometimes used by hunting clubs, who would set their hounds on the trail of hares and pursue them through the fields of Mt Roskill and neighbouring Three Kings.[278] Optimism in the area's growth was sufficient at this time, though, for local Congregationalists to build a church in Three Kings in the faith that a congregation would soon fill it.[279]

One of Auckland's more substantial suburban settlements in the 1900s was Onehunga. It had immediate access to the Manukau Harbour (which until 1908 offered Aucklanders the fastest means of transport to Wellington, by steamer) and was also a favoured port for taking passengers from Auckland to Australia. At the beginning of the century, it had a population of 3000, but unlike many other parts of the city, Onehunga did not expand at the same rapid rate in the early twentieth century. When the main trunk railway line was opened in 1908, trade began to bypass the settlement and this, coupled with the increasing suitability of the Waitematā Harbour as a port, diminished Onehunga's commercial importance.[280]

THE 1900s

Around 15 kilometres southeast of the centre of Auckland was the smaller settlement of Ōtāhuhu. Like Onehunga, it had a rail connection and access to the Manukau Harbour. However, in the 1900s it was still very much a rural location, with just a sprinkling of buildings lining a short length of Great South Road, which was the principal arterial route running through the area.[281] Being relatively remote from central Auckland could have been an impediment to Ōtāhuhu's growth (on occasion, the train journey from Ōtāhuhu to central Auckland could take up to two hours),[282] but the settlement did not languish at this time. While it retained the appearance of a diminutive rural town encircled by paddocks and patches of bush, it was expanding and had ambition. A group of residents had formed the 'Otahuhu Progressive League' in this decade, and sought an increase in train services, lobbied for a canal scheme in the area, submitted a proposal for a tram link to Onehunga and Māngere, and helped establish a technical school. And in the five years leading up to 1908, property prices in the area had trebled,[283] suggesting that there was optimism among buyers in the town's future.

Auckland's North Shore was connected to the main part of the city in the 1900s by a ferry service. This acted as a bottleneck to its growth, preventing the rate of settlement that was occurring in other parts of the city. It was possible to get to the North Shore over land, but that entailed an 80-kilometre trek along dirt roads and rutted paths carved through marginal farmland, scrub and forest.[284] This contributed to the North Shore's comparative isolation from the rest of Auckland, and led to a slightly different pattern of suburban evolution at this time. In the case of Devonport, its proximity to the ferry service, along with its separation from 'mainland' Auckland, made it a favoured location for some of the city's 'leading residents' who favoured a slightly more isolated setting to live in. Devonport was also alluring to some Aucklanders because of its 'sandy beaches and rocky inlets',[285] which together with its slightly grander houses made it 'one of the most salubrious and attractive spots in the environs of Auckland'.[286]

Directly north across the Waitematā Harbour from Herne Bay was the North Shore suburb of Birkenhead. In the 1900s this was 'a large tract of undulating country, well wooded, and dotted with pretty patches of native bush', and was 'unsurpassed for fruit growing'. Around two hundred people lived in Birkenhead, most involved in horticulture. A canning factory had been established near the Birkenhead wharf,[287] but the area was most well known as the location of the Colonial Sugar Refining Company, which had been operating there since 1884.[288] The commercial scale of the sugar refinery's operation was so great that by the end of the 1900s it had begun to finance one out of every three new houses built in Birkenhead.[289]

Of all the North Shore suburbs, at the beginning of the twentieth century Takapuna was regarded as being by far the most prestigious. The area consisted of 'first-class land', and was 'dotted with thriving homesteads, gardens, villas and picturesque heights'. And this elegant built environment was set against 'a crescent-shaped shelly beach, washed by the waters of a sheltered channel, and pohutukawas with their crimson bloom overhang[ing] the roads'.[290] Takapuna was also renowned by the end of the decade for the Mon Desir Hotel. Initially a spacious private home, its owner acquired a licence (following the Lake Hotel in Killarney Street burning down in 1909), and expanded the house to accommodate the demand for guests in the suburb (it subsequently underwent a succession of modifications and expansions) at a cost of £3000 (a current value of approximately half a million dollars).[291] It was billed as a 'magnificent', 'beautifully furnished' and 'picturesque resort', and offered guests an opportunity to indulge in the latest in Edwardian elegance.[292]

Thirty-five kilometres north of Takapuna was the modest settlement of Pūhoi, which straddled the Pūhoi River. It had been formed in 1863 by a group of German-speaking Bohemians, and in the early twentieth century retained much its distinctly central European heritage.[293] The road leading to Pūhoi was not sealed, and so travelling there was not advised if any rain was forecast.[294] One of the more popular attractions of this part of north Auckland was the small village of Waiwera — optimistically described by one entrepreneur as the 'Brighton of New Zealand'.[295] It was an uncomfortable four-hour coach trip from Devonport, but most people arrived there by steamer directly from central Auckland. A sanatorium had been developed around the supposedly curative properties of its thermal spas.[296]

A further 20 kilometres north was where Auckland began to taper off into Northland. Warkworth was one of Auckland's final settlements. By the 1900s it had developed into a fully-fledged town, which included 'a post and telegraph office, a courthouse, public school ... three churches ... a hotel, two temperance boarding houses, three large general stores, a blacksmith's shop and carriage factory, a livery stable, and a newspaper office which prints the "Rodney Times"'.[297] Its expansion to this point had been due to the success of its cement works, which by 1903 had an annual output of 20,220 tons.[298] It was from Warkworth that cement for most of Auckland's construction products was shipped at this time.

This, then, was Auckland at the opening of the twentieth century. A city brimming with commercial opportunities for some, but an inescapable sink of squalor for others. Its class structure was already settling into place, and there was a gathering trend to identify one's prestige with the particular part of Auckland one lived in. And geographically, it had the makings of a strongly urbanised city, but with its outer limits still overwhelmingly rural and remote. Towards the end of the decade, Sir John Gorst, who had spent time in the country in the early 1860s, returned to Auckland, and recorded his sense of how the city had developed by the 1900s:

> *all the country is parcelled out into gardens and houses and orchards which exhibit signs of wealth and prosperity, far in excess of the appearances of former days. The authorities of the city are quite alive to the danger of allowing the population to become too concentrated .... The industrial population is spread over a large area of ground, served by electric trams, and ... the population is no doubt destined to increase enormously.*[299]

If what's past is prologue, then Gorst was more than justified in pronouncing this prophecy.

3
The 1910s

Contrary to all previous predictions (and for some, expectations), the 'dying race' was stubbornly refusing to die.[300] The 1911 Census revealed that the number of Māori in the country (which included 'full-blooded Maoris' and 'half-castes living as members of Native tribes') had reached 49,884 — an increase of 16 per cent in a decade.[301] Still, though, in the 1910s, the Auckland artist Charles Goldie continued to paint portraits of mainly elderly Māori, with mournful titles such as 'A Noble Relic of a Noble Race' (1910), 'One of the Old School' (1912), 'The Last of Her Tribe' (1913) and 'The Whitening Snows of Venerable Elder' (1914).[302] Goldie knew that there was popular interest in this sort of maudlin depiction of a race on the cusp of extinction,[303] and offered viewers a final nostalgic glimpse of what was then referred to as the 'old-time Maori'.[304] He was thus painting both for posterity and for profit, with his favoured subject — elderly Māori — posed in ways that accentuated their 'antiquity', and which, in the process, rendered them as mildewy anthropological specimens. A once vibrant culture was now being depicted in paint as docile, moribund and exhausted,[305] with individuals being reduced to archetypes.

Goldie was also skilled at self-promotion, and carefully curated his public image. He had established his studio on the top floor of Hobson's Buildings, which at the time was next to the *Auckland Star* office in Shortland Street. In a series of highly staged photographs, Goldie portrayed his workplace as it might have been popularly imagined. It was a cornucopia of clichés — palms, plaster busts, exotic drapery, paints, palettes, props, easels, small piles of books, works in progress, and all the other bric-a-brac which cumulatively aimed to convey the image of a slightly bohemian but unmistakably great artist.[306] Even the way Goldie's walls were lined — with the portraits he had painted — made his studio appear like a miniature version of the Royal Academy of Arts' Exhibition Room at Somerset House as it had been famously caricatured by Thomas Rowlandson a century earlier.[307] All that was missing in these images was the permanent stench of cigarette smoke that choked his studio.[308] Yet, by 1912, for all his output and self-promotion, Goldie's fortunes appeared to be ebbing. It reached the point where he ended up visiting various Auckland law offices in an effort to sell them his works.[309] At one stage, he had been the brightest star in the firmament of Auckland's art scene,[310] but time was dimming his reputation. It started, as is so often the case, with murmurs. His works were repetitious in their subject matter, some viewers felt. Others thought they were too photographic. And in an age that saw the introduction of abstract art, cubism and expressionism, Goldie's staid hyperrealism was not even considered to be art at all by some.[311]

The enthusiasm for artistic 'progress' was not merely a topic for idle pondering, though. In 1911 it had led to a serious schism in the Auckland Society of Arts. The Society had championed artists (including Goldie), and saw itself as the bastion and promoter of the city's aesthetic tastes. However, a fundamental divergence in people's artistic penchants at this time was driving a wedge between its members. In September there was a 'hot discussion' within the Society over a number of issues, leading to one faction becoming 'galvanised into activity along sound lines of progress'. This group was at odds with the Society's more traditionalist members, with the result that the 'progressives' (which included several Auckland artists) announced plans to form an alternative arts organisation for the city.[312] Disputes of this nature persisted throughout the decade. Three years after this burst of acrimony, Auckland artists were complaining that the Society (which still held sway in the city) lacked any artistic discretion. It was variously accused of being 'indiscriminate' when it came to how paintings were hung in the Art Gallery, incapable of seeing art as anything more than an 'array of canvas and paint', and an outmoded organisation that favoured the popular over the progressive.[313] For most Aucklanders, reading about the artistic elites at war with each other was probably a source of mild amusement, but at another level it signified a cultural growing pain that the city (along with most other Western cities at this time) was experiencing. Changes in technology, values, beliefs and tastes were accelerating at a rate that threatened to trip up some, and leave others behind. The modern world was displacing much of what had been taken for granted before, and disruption was an inevitable by-product.

A particular moment that symbolically signified the end of the 'old world' for Auckland occurred on 22 June 1912, when John Logan Campbell died, at the age of 94. Physically, he was described as someone who ought to serve as an inspiration to Auckland's younger generation (who were belittled as 'the leg-tired and the luxury-loving'),[314] and for his contribution to the development of the city he was widely lauded. Three days later, his funeral was held, on a brilliantly fine, cold afternoon. Most businesses in the city closed for the day, and a crowd of thousands turned out for the funeral — the largest yet held in Auckland. As the cortège made its way towards One Tree Hill, the crowds grew in number, and eerily for such a large gathering, assembled in total silence. One observer recorded how 'a certain stillness and reverence seemed to possess the crowds' as the procession of one of the city's founding fathers wound on. Finally, the coffin reached its destination, and Campbell was interred on the peak of One Tree Hill. '[F]acing the glorious east,' one journalist reported, 'was Auckland's great benefactor laid peacefully to rest.' And then, captured by the moment, he continued in an even more elegiac fashion, 'his tomb on the crest of the hill beneath the broad arch of the sky shall stand like a beacon to the race — a memorial to titanic energies, an inspiration to those who would serve New Zealand'.[315] The city had grown now to a population of 88,000 (of whom around 840 were Māori)[316] and had a built environment that matched this scale — a dramatic difference to Auckland in 1840, which Campbell later recalled as then being 'a few boats and canoes on the beach, a few tents and break-wind huts along the margin of the bay, and then — a sea of fern stretching away as far as the eye could reach'.[317]

Building Auckland

Inseminated with capital, capability and confidence, and grappling with the demands of demographic and commercial growth, Auckland experienced a burst of construction in the 1910s. And it was not just a case of producing a greater volume of what was already there. This was a period of imagination and experimentation in large-scale building projects, giving Aucklanders something outside of the art galleries and museums to gaze at in wonder. But it was not an unhindered stampede to embrace the new. Just like the conservative/progressive split that had fractured the Auckland Society of Arts, architecture and design in the city in this decade was torn between the radical and the reactionary. Either way, though, Auckland was shedding its rural and colonial skins more rapidly now than at any other previous time.

Grafton Bridge was one such example, not only of a large-scale building project, but also an innovative one. It was conceived of as a replacement for the ageing and increasingly unsafe footbridge that linked Symonds Street, bordering the central part of the city, with Grafton Road, where Auckland's main hospital stood. Separating these two points was Cemetery Gully (later known as Grafton Gully). Part of this crevasse was occupied by the city's oldest European graveyard, beyond which, clumps of workers' cottages (some of which were now almost 60 years old) clung to the scrub-covered slopes.

As the city's population increased, the footbridge leading to Auckland Hospital had become inadequate for purpose, and Auckland Council responded by committing itself to construct a more substantial bridge linking these two important parts of the city — a decision that immediately met with much popular support.[318] The Council raised a loan of £20,000, and sought tenders for a bridge that would be able to cope with the traffic demands expected of one of the busiest parts of the city. By June 1907, when the tendering process was closed, two bids were before the Council for consideration. One was for a trussed girder design on latticed piers, and the other, more experimental, proposal was for a reinforced concrete design by the Ferro-concrete Company of Australasia, costing £31,890. The Council chose the latter option, largely because in the longer term it would incur fewer maintenance costs, and within a month of the decision being reached, construction was already under way.[319]

This was Auckland flaunting its industrial muscle, with a colossus that straddled a span in a way that no other bridge in the world had yet done. At

97.5 metres, it had the widest arch of any reinforced concrete bridge in the world at the time, and demonstrated to doubters that this comparatively new construction method was viable for engineering works on this scale.[320] When it came to construction, iron belonged to the nineteenth century, and wood to the preceding ones. The material for the modern age, however, was concrete strengthened by steel, and in this Auckland momentarily was a world-leader.[321] Understandably, though, there was some apprehension among the public over whether this new bridge was as strong as it was purported to be. To reassure doubters, at the opening on 10 April 1910, two lumbering steamrollers were driven across it, and engineers announced that 'exhaustive tests' had confirmed the structure's soundness.[322] The other measure designed to make Aucklanders feel more secure about the bridge was the construction of the fake piers at each end of the arch, which were made 'to create the visual impression of strength associated with traditional masonry construction', even though the actual load-bearing support came from much slimmer reinforced concrete structures based within the piers.[323] The progressive design had to be concealed by a traditionalist skin in order to satisfy everyone.

For Auckland, this was an age of potential, with technology fuelling hopes of endless progress and improvement. The completion of Grafton Bridge was linked with other feats of the period around the world. By the end of 1910, aeroplanes were crossing the English Channel, cars were being mass-produced and becoming more affordable in the process, ships were larger and more powerful, the Panama Canal was nearing completion, and ships were starting to communicate by wireless.[324] And yet, just two generations earlier, these sorts of developments languished in the realm of fantasy — the provenance of fiction writers rather than the domain of engineers. Aesthetics were rushing to keep pace with this change, and inevitably in such a race, there were relapses. In the midst of modernism, expressionism, avant-garde and the work of the Chicago School of architects, Auckland lurched backwards when designing a town hall for the city, choosing a Baroque Revival style for this centrepiece of the city. It was a patchwork quilt of influences, with the exterior closely modelled on London's Lambeth Town Hall,[325] and the interior of the Great Hall designed as a pastiche of the Gewandhaus Concert Hall in Leipzig, making it a 'dignified venue'[326] housing one of the largest pipe organs in the country[327] (donated by the Auckland philanthropist Sir Henry Brett). However, in 1909, one cynic suggested that the building would end up looking 'like a distorted flat-iron', due to its shape and position on Queen Street.[328]

Another of these 'landmark[s] of civic pride'[329] was the Ferry Building on Quay Street, completed in 1912,[330] and designed to be the central building from where city passengers could depart by ferries to Bayswater, Birkenhead, Chelsea, Devonport, Kohimarama, Northcote, Ōrākei, St Heliers and Stanley Bay.[331] It soon became one of the busiest pedestrian spots in the country as travel across the Waitematā Harbour continued to increase.[332] Like the Town Hall, Auckland's Ferry Building was conceived in the Imperial Baroque style, and also like the Town Hall, was reminiscent of an overseas design — in this case, San Francisco's ferry building.[333]

The third civic edifice constructed in Auckland in this style, and which similarly was meant to impress on viewers the importance and gravitas of the city's institutions, was the Chief Post Office, which, like the Ferry Building, was completed in 1912. And as with the Town Hall and Ferry Building, the architects of the Chief Post Office did not hesitate in looking overseas for inspiration, on this occasion finding it in Sir Henry Tanner's General Post Office, in King Edward Street, London[334] — a resemblance that was consciously seen as a reason for Aucklanders to be proud of their post office.[335] And Aucklanders were indeed proud, with 10,000 of the city's residents turning up for its opening.[336]

Yes, these buildings were products of the fleeting fashion for the Edwardian Baroque/Imperial Baroque/Baroque Revival style; and, yes, they were increasingly out of step with international architectural trends in the United States and Europe at the time, but their faux antiquity did serve a purpose: it lent these edifices an established presence and an aura of permanence. In an age when the physical appearance of buildings contributed to the credibility of institutions, the design of these structures[337] — with their vestiges of imperial authority, and their ambiguous European cosmopolitanism — reinforced the intention (if not the accomplishment) of Auckland's planners to have their city taken seriously by locals and visitors alike. And it was precisely the juxtaposition of different architectural styles that gave the city its particular charm. 'Auckland's buildings', one resident wrote,

> *are a quaint mixture of past and present. In the main streets large buildings of modern design stand side by side with one, two, or three storey structures which have passed their prime in terms*

of years. This contrast is not to be deplored from an artistic point of view, for what it lacks in symmetry is more than compensated by the effect of a broken sky-line. The sky-scraper happily does not exist — an eight-storey building being the tallest in the City.[338]

There was a further plunge into the past with the opening of the Old Colonists' Museum in March 1916 (located in two rooms on the top floor of the same building as the Auckland Art Gallery and Auckland Public Library). Founded by the city's chief librarian, John Barr, it remained operational for the next 41 years, serving as a depository for colonial-era ephemera.[339] Within two years of opening, though, it was already in a 'very congested state', according to one researcher who was trawling through its archival collection,[340] and it soon became a cluttered cornucopia of nineteenth-century objects, ranging from coins to chairs, pianos to ploughs, and nearly anything else that could be squeezed through its doors.[341]

On 6 November 1911 a building of much more modest proportions, but more entertaining pretensions, opened at 160–162 Symonds Street. The Lyric Theatre (renamed the New Lyric Theatre from 1926, then the State Theatre from 1935, before becoming the Oriental Ballroom and then the Rainbow Roller Skating Rink until it was demolished at the end of the century) became the first building in the city with an electric flashing sign (pronouncing 'Hayward's Pictures', named after the theatre's operator, Henry Hayward), and had a luxuriantly carpeted interior, with armchairs as well as the more conventional seats.[342] Audiences were treated to silent movies (the only sort of film shown at the time) accompanied by an all-female orchestra,[343] with up to 1400 patrons capable of being seated inside (although an extra 100 managed to squeeze in for the opening night). Arthur Myers, a local MP who spoke at the opening, declared that '[o]ne of the greatest things of the century was the rise of the moving picture', which 'provided pleasure and instruction to countless thousands'. The crowd applauded enthusiastically as this major advance entertaining Aucklanders got under way.[344] One indication of the remarkable ascent of movies in this era is that, just five years later, more people in the country were attending movies each week than were going to church.[345] The Lyric was also the venue for the premier screening in 1914 of possibly the earliest New Zealand-produced feature film (sometimes known at the time as a 'photo play').[346] The publicists for this film — *Hinemoa* — boasted that it was 'the first picture on record which has been acted entirely by natives', and was '[f]ilmed in Rotorua! On the original spots which have been handed down by generations of Maoris as authentic landmarks in the lives of their ancestors.'[347] Beyond its immediate entertainment and novelty value (a New Zealand-made film was reason in itself for some to attend), *Hinemoa* introduced Aucklanders to a new kind of Māori — one who was not a neighbour, a colleague, or an associate of any kind, but an artefact.[348] The film itself has long been lost, but its hypersentimentalised depiction to Auckland audiences of the country's indigenous population is apparent in accounts of its early screenings. 'The sweet and romantic Maori story of "Hinemoa"', one reviewer wrote,

> *is being done in beautiful pictures at the Lyric Theatre. The gratifying feature to New Zealanders is the excellence of the pantomime, and it is seen that the Rotorua Maoris are born actors and actresses. Characteristic country is used for the development of the typical Maori love story, and there is a real savour of romance about it that charms the audience. It is one of the few pictures seen of late that the audience applauds .... "Hinemoa," ... should not be missed.*[349]

From one of the newest forms of technology to one of the oldest, in 1910 the Waitākere Dam was completed, offering Auckland's growing population a new and secure source of water. The concrete foundations, which were sunk 11 metres into the ground, had been put in place two years earlier, and a wooden auxiliary dam had been constructed as an interim measure. However, in May 1910 a storm crashed into Auckland, with torrents of rain causing landslides in the reservoir, and washing trees and debris downstream until they began to build up against the makeshift dam's wooden wall. Eventually, the immutable laws of physics did their work, and the dam was punctured. Water surged through the ruptured wall and down the valley, sweeping away just about everything in its path. However, as soon as the storm had abated, workers returned to the site, and by December the Waitākere Dam was finally operational,[350] with the certainty of its concrete construction (one of the first of this scale in the country) washing away any concerns about the security of the city's water supply in the foreseeable future. The completed structure was 25 metres tall, and had a capacity of 1,761,000 cubic metres of water.[351] This provided Auckland with three million litres of water daily, which were transported 26 kilometres through a cast-iron pipe with a 68-centimetre diameter.[352] In addition to the dam itself was a plethora of assorted infrastructure. Tramways were carved into hillsides to assist transporting materials and equipment to the site, tunnels and filter stations were built, water-treatment equipment was installed, and when work began on connecting the Upper Nihotupu Dam, a track — eventually known as Exhibition Drive — was constructed (and converted into a road in January 1914).[353]

The opening of Exhibition Drive was an important event on the city's calendar for 1914. Auckland's mayor, Christopher Parr, presided over the occasion, along with members of the Auckland Automobile Association, which had contributed £250 towards the cost of the new road. However, the highlight was 'an imposing procession ... [of] between 50 and 60 motor cars making the run from the Town Hall' to Titirangi. That trip took half an hour to complete, but the drive along the five-and-a-half kilometre length of Exhibition Drive took a further 25 minutes as the convoy snaked its way along the tree-lined road. There may have been no direct economic benefit obtained from the construction of this remote route, but as the mayor emphasised in his speech, this was part of 'an effort to open up this magnificent bush scenery of the ranges to the public of Auckland'.[354] Evidently, the forested side of the city was one few residents were exposed to at this time. One newspaper editor wrote hopefully in January 1914 that

> *the opening of this drive for three miles along the ridge of the Titirangis [sic] will help to make the people of Auckland more familiar with the beauties of their hill-country, and will prepare the way for the opening up of the forest reserve on the Waitakeres, which though one of the loveliest and most impressive of all our public possessions, is still practically unknown to the vast majority of Aucklanders.*[355]

Over the course of the twentieth century, the desire to construct roads around Auckland purely for the scenic benefits they offered diminished. Gradually, roads came to be perceived as a means to get to a destination, and if there happened to be a view to enjoy along the way, that was an incidental advantage.

Exhibiting Auckland

Exhibition Drive's naming was no accident. A month before its opening, the 'Auckland Industrial, Agricultural and Mining Exhibition' (popularly known as the Auckland Exhibition) had commenced at the Auckland Domain, and ran until April 1914. It was, according to one contemporary observer, 'a striking proof of the commercial and industrial advancement of the city and province', and given its scale, this was a fair assessment. The Exhibition occupied a space of 48 acres, and cost £30,000 for the layout and erection of temporary buildings on the site. Despite the substantial cost, it managed to make an overall profit of £21,758, due largely to the extraordinary interest it generated. In the five months it was open, an estimated 870,000 people visited the Exhibition, at a time when the entire nation's population was around one million. Of course, the visitor numbers included those who attended more than once, but nonetheless, the interest overall was extraordinary. The profit the Exhibition generated was set aside for 'beautifying the Domain', which included 'the laying-out of paths, flower beds, playing areas, and the erection of the winter-garden, which stands on the site of one of the exhibition buildings'. Other features of the Domain, such as the tea kiosk and the bandstand, became 'permanent survivals of the exhibition'.[356]

Among the 'amusements' at the Exhibition was Wonderland Park — an Edwardian architectural extravagance (bordering on a fantasy), which was made all the more novel for nocturnal visitors owing to its 'illumination by electricity'.[357] It was by far the most popular attraction at the Exhibition, and was comprised of a rollercoaster, toboggans, a water chute and various stalls and rides, such as 'Dreamland', 'the House of Trouble', 'Jim's Fun Factory' and 'the Laughing Gallery'.[358] Elsewhere, there were hot-air balloon ascents, concerts, a chrysanthemum show, movies and predictably, souvenirs. However, beneath the fun and frivolity was a more serious side to the Exhibition. This was Auckland's opportunity to show itself to the rest of the country and the rest of the world (although distance meant that the rest of the world gave it, at best, a quick glance and nothing more). The city's industry, arts, technological and social advancements were all on show here, like some extended civic trophy cabinet.

More than 28,000 people attended the final day of the Exhibition, on 18 April 1914. No formal closing ceremony had been organised, but towards ten o'clock on the evening when the Exhibition was due to finish, 'the vast crowd, with one accord, made their way to the terraces and steps in front of the Palace of Industries'. George Elliot, the Exhibition's president, accompanied by his officials, walked through the throng of people, during which 'an expectant hush fell upon the sea of upturned faces'. Elliot then spoke to the crowd, followed by the prime minister, William Massey, who reflected on the changes the city had gone through in recent years. 'If I remember correctly,' he commenced,

> *it was 15 years ago that the last Exhibition was held in Auckland. Since that event the population has more than doubled. When another great Exhibition is held in Auckland 15 years hence, I venture to predict — and it hardly requires a prophet to do so — that the population of the city of Auckland and its suburbs will then be a quarter of a million. The city will then stretch from sea to sea, from the Waitemata to the Manukau, and it will be like the city written of in ancient times, beautiful in situation, and a joy of the whole earth.*[359]

After the sun had set, the stalls closed, and the lights went out, the crowd accompanied by a massed band sang "Auld Lang Syne"[360] as a spontaneous tribute to the event before departing the Domain.

Sifting through the paraphernalia of the Exhibition, an overall impression emerges of an Auckland that was not only proud of its accomplishments and progress, but that also had a growing sense of civic solidarity. And to be fair, there was also a seam of loyalty to the city that ran through most of its residents. However, such an impression should not mask the tensions and strains that also existed below the surface. There was confidence and optimism in Auckland at this time, but so too was there plenty of anger and disgust, particularly over the working conditions so many were forced to endure.

Out of this swamp of discontent came a period of sharp anger, as dissatisfaction among workers from a range of occupations spilled over into open revolt against their employers and the system by which wages were set. Auckland, as one of the biggest economic centres of the country, had little chance of shielding itself from this spreading discontent. Strikes in Wellington, Huntly, Westport and Dunedin revealed to the non-union public how intense the feelings were among workers in certain industries. Since the beginning of the decade, industrial disputes had been growing in frequency, and also in terms of the number of people involved. In 1910, for example, just 15 disputes were registered, involving a total of 255 workers. In 1912, the figures stood at 24 industrial disputes involving 5756 workers, and the following year — when the Great Strike (or General Strike, as it was sometimes referred to in Auckland) took place — there were 73 separate disputes, dragging in 13,400 workers.[361] Over the same period, the number of union members in the country rose from 57,091 to 60,622.[362]

It was ostensibly out of a sense of solidarity with the Huntly strikers that a group of Auckland waterside workers downed tools on 28 October 1913, and were joined by the rest of the city's watersiders the following day — a strike that lasted until 23 November. The background to this industrial unrest has been attributed variously to the birthing pains of the country's labour movement, the failure of wages to meet the basic expectations of many workers, the emergence of a modern class system, a general rise in union militancy, the particular evolution in the country's industrial relations, and changes in the fundamental nature of work in some industries.[363]

But if the strike reflected various splits in society, it also accentuated others. The fact that up to 5916 Auckland workers in various trades stopped working in support of the watersiders had a severe impact on the city's economy: 'there was a complete stoppage of cargo traffic for some days, the coastal steamer services were almost entirely suspended owing to the action of seamen in leaving their ships after giving twenty-four hours' notice, and great inconvenience was thereby caused to residents of outlying districts'.[364] Even the city's trams ceased running,[365] and quickly the 'strike fever' caught on, with other trades — from plumbers, drivers and timber workers, to bakers, carpenters and bricklayers — joining this action by similarly refusing to work.

By the time the strike was over, it had cost the city an estimated £60,000 (equivalent now to around $16,800,000) in lost wages and business.[366] The strikers took complete control of the waterfront, and marched in squads — each comprising a few hundred men — along the wharves to prevent any movement of cargo.[367] One Auckland employer, expressing the sentiments of many of his counterparts, responded to the strike by insisting that '[t]he only thing to do now is to make a fight of it to the bitter end, no matter how long it lasts — three, or even six months .... This is the only way to get peace for a year or two. We must fight the strikers with their own weapons.'[368] Then, like some Newtonian principle of physics, a deficit in one area caused a reaction to compensate for it elsewhere. Two weeks into the strike, special police intervened. They were made up of 1700 mounted and 1200 'specials'[369] (some of whom were farmers drawn from Auckland's outlying rural areas), and prevented the strikers from getting within a kilometre of the wharves. The response was instantaneous:

> *Howling mobs of strikers congregated in the lower part of the city and jeered, hooted and stoned the "specials." The patience of the mounted men really was remarkable. They were submitted to the greatest provocation, but stood it without attempting to retaliate. Now, their turn has come. First they extended lines well up into the city, allowing no one to penetrate beyond a certain limit. Now, they patrol the whole city at will, and there is never as much as a "boo" at them.*[370]

It must be remembered, though, that the press was largely unsympathetic to the strikers, and so such swashbuckling accounts of Auckland's rescue represent a fairly narrow view of the conflict. However, it was not just the newspapers that were opposed to the strike. A new waterside union was formed at this time to keep the wharves operating, thus displacing those watersiders who were on strike. These 'scab' workers required police protection while working, but at last from the point of view of Auckland's business and civic leaders, this vital trade artery was again functioning. This move had the added consequence of disillusioning many of the strikers, and instilling in them a fear that their jobs might be permanently lost. With livelihoods at risk, the resolve of the striking workers soon crumbled.[371]

It would be mistaken, though, to see the collapse of the strike as the end of the divisions in Auckland that had fuelled it. On the contrary, in some ways, the rhetoric of worker against employer, the perceived militant socialism of the union movement, and the social turbulence and economic disruption that the strike had inflicted on Auckland served to harden stances on both sides of the dispute. On the day that the strike officially ended in Auckland, rather than any shows of regional reconciliation, a special meeting was held in the Domain of those who had volunteered to serve as 'specials'. They resolved to form a Farmers'

Union Constabulary Corps, so that whenever additional policing was required in the future against groups such as the unionists, they could be 'called together at a moment's notice'.[372]

Crime in the city

While the Great Strike represented one of those periodic ruptures in civic order, which after spiking tend to collapse just as quickly, crime in Auckland was rising more steadily in this era, roughly in keeping with the city's increase in population. In contrast to later in the century, however, the rate at which crimes were solved by the police was especially high. In 1913, for example, in the Auckland district, 5611 crimes were reported, of which 5396 resulted in arrests or summonses being issued. In police parlance, this represents a 'clearance rate' of 96 per cent. By far the most common form of crime was burglary, followed by forgery, then receiving stolen property, assaults and arson. Drunkenness was a frequent source of public disorder, with 2432 Aucklanders charged for alcohol-related offences in 1913, although over this decade there was a slight downward trend in this category of offence. When it came to sexual offending, indecent exposure made up the majority of offences (62 per cent), followed by indecent assaults (19 per cent) and '[c]arnally knowing girls' (9 per cent). Rape, and attempted rape, were only four and a half per cent,[373] although as with many categories of sexual offence, reported offences did not necessarily line up with the actual number of offences, particularly when women were the victims.[374]

However, violence against women — often stemming from drunkenness — was an ongoing concern for some organisations, particularly the Women's Christian Temperance Union, which had been founded in 1885, and had sought to promote Christian values and to reform society through aiming to prohibit alcohol and drugs. Its most famous victory was in 1893, when its relentless campaigning led to women in New Zealand gaining the right to vote. However, the movement was far from a spent force afterwards, and in the 1910s it was becoming a public voice in sexual matters.[375] In 1915 the Union's publication, *The White Ribbon*, issued an opinion piece critical of the sentencing of male sex offenders. It examined the case of a middle-aged Auckland man who was convicted of 'the dastardly crime of assaulting little girls'. He was sentenced to six months' imprisonment, but was released after just a few weeks, when he was then 'brought up again for another little girl ruined'. This time, he received only a 12-month custodial sentence. At the same time as New Zealanders were condemning sexual offences being committed by German troops in Europe, the editor pointed out that 'we express no indignation when little girls in our own Dominion are treated in the same awful manner'. Reform was needed:

> *Six months for a girl's life ruined and life-long torture; 12 months for a second offence. How light the value placed on a little child's purity and innocence. But imprisonment for life for manslaughter when the victim is a man. Is it not time that we had laws to adequately punish these "Huns" in our midst? Also women police and women Magistrates to see them properly administered .... We women, who have the vote, are responsible for every little sufferer until we rise, unite, agitate, and demand protection for our children.*[376]

This sort of published sentiment dispels any stereotypes about Auckland's female population existing as little more than demure chattels of their male counterparts. Although women continued to be depicted (principally, although not exclusively, by men) as 'invariably chaste, innocent, passive, perhaps naïve and easily led astray', and likely to fall 'victim to designing men at the drop of a hat, sometimes quite literally',[377] the fact was that women in this decade were mobilising in various ways. The Women's Christian Temperance Union, for example, sought 'to give political expression to uniquely female values',[378] and did so in a way that was well organised, and from an overtly women's perspective.[379] And it looked to some people in this decade that women's rights were finally reaching parity with those of men. In 1919, Kate Sheppard, who had spearheaded the campaign to secure the right of New Zealand women to vote in the early 1890s, announced with perhaps premature confidence that the 'fossilized prejudices' of patriarchal society had 'crashed in all directions', and 'that opposition to the right of women to full citizenship is breaking down'.[380] Auckland became a sort of incubator for a nationwide campaign for greater women's rights in the country at this time. In 1917, Ellen Melville (who was later one of the first women to stand for Parliament) convened a group of women from the city to contribute to the formation of the National Council of Women. Several women's groups in Auckland participated in this campaign, including the Civic League, the Young

Women's Christian Association (YWCA), the Society for the Protection of Women and Children, the Auckland Women Teachers' Association, the Auckland Women's National Reserve, the Business Girls' Club, the Girls' Friendly Society, the Women's Mutual Aid, the Women's International League, the Auckland Mothers' Union and the Women's Political League.[381] Their object was simple but also urgent: to influence the laws affecting women, and to improve social conditions generally.[382]

As the intricate extent of this political organisation shows, women were already well along the bumpy path leading to equality with men. A snapshot of the general situation of the city's female population was produced in February 1915, which revealed some evidence of this growing parity. Auckland had an 'army of women workers', and purportedly, there was 'no country on earth where women work under better conditions, and are better safeguarded from the evils of "sweating," overcrowding, lack of sanitation and ventilation'. And although precise figures had not been collected, it was estimated that factories were the single biggest employer of women in the 1910s. Roughly 4000 were employed in various types of factory work, followed by the clothing trade (mainly manufacturing), which had close to 3000 female employees across the city. Shops and hotels employed roughly 1500 women, with possibly just as many working each in printing, bookbinding, shoemaking, laundry work, and the biscuit and confectionery trade. Teaching was also a popular profession for women to pursue in this era, with approximately 700 working in schools, 'despite the demand it makes on vital forces'. Nursing was rapidly attracting an increasing number of women, which almost completes this sketch of women's employment at this time. Almost, because when it came to domestic work, the (presumably) male author of this overview had something of a complaint to make. Annoyingly, there was apparently 'no enthusiasm whatever on the part of Auckland girls, and year by year the problem of domestic service grows more acute'.[383]

Auckland was one of the first locations in the country where a designated women's branch of the Government Labour Bureaux was established. Increasingly, this office was becoming

a centre for women — friendless, often destitute — who desire information and advice as regards chances of employment. All the female immigrants from overseas are under the direction of

> *the officer in charge. Girls belonging to all branches of women's work, women physically unfit for active employment, yet forced to earn a living, have received encouragement and practical assistance; strangers have been directed to safe and suitable accommodation, while countless harassed housewives have had their need supplied through this agency.*[384]

Accommodation in Auckland was usually harder for women to secure in this period than for men, but one way in which many women managed to acquire shelter was by boarding with a family, or what was known as 'baching', in which 'a couple of girls will pay five shillings a week and share a room "with use of kitchen," but this is at best a poor makeshift, resulting as a rule in lack of proper nourishment and corresponding detriment to physical well-being'. The result of such challenging circumstances was that many resorted to marriage, even though it was not always the panacea that they hoped it would be. Many had to return to work even when married, 'certainly sadder, possibly wiser, but thankful indeed to have a business to turn to in their need'.[385]

One route out of destitution and squalor (or so some women believed) was to engage in an older profession — prostitution — which in many cases sunk them into the very circumstances they were desperate to avoid, with degradation, disease, social ostracism and criminal convictions the only long-term dividends. Prostitution aroused various responses among Aucklanders, ranging from moral outrage to resigned sympathy, and anxiety over the health implications of the practice. The intensity of reactions waxed and waned, but at their peaks led to the righteous calling for the city to be 'purged and cleaned'.[386] The particular focus of opprobrium for various upholders of social morality in Auckland this decade was the so-called 'one-woman brothels'. It was not that other forms of brothels were regarded as being any more acceptable, but that the growth of this relatively new service was seen as an added threat to the city's virtues. One cleric had written to Auckland Council in 1912, complaining that 'prostitutes now rent shops, ostensibly for the sale of soft drinks and confectionery — a mere pretence of carrying on a legitimate business — and then pursue their calling as prostitutes', resulting in a 'notorious and growing evil' gnawing at the city's morals.[387] What also made these small enterprises troublesome to authorities was that they seemed to slip through a loophole in the city's bylaws relating to brothels, which dealt with 'disorderly house[s]', or 'houses of ill-fame'.[388] However, a conviction was eventually entered against a woman charged for operating one of these establishments, with an accompanying £10 fine. The police, for their part, promised 'to leave no stone unturned to clean up the city of these houses of ill-fame', which included prosecuting the owners of any house 'used for immoral purposes'.[389] Yet, without exaggerating the point, there were small traces of tacit tolerance for prostitution at this time. 'So long as one-woman brothel keepers were not too flagrant about their business, not too noisy or too public in their activities,' one historian has noted, 'neighbours and the police were often prepared to ignore the nature of their livelihood. Even when the police and local residents were ... aware of the number of men seen entering and leaving the premises — quiet, modest establishments could remain free from overt disapproval.'[390] The puffing outrage of those offended by prostitution was one side of the moral coin. On the other were those Aucklanders who were prepared to turn a blind eye to what was going on in their neighbourhood, even if they disapproved of it, for the sake of keeping the peace. And as salacious as the issue of prostitution was to Auckland society generally, it brought to the fore issues that the city nonetheless had to contend with, including changing gender roles in society, female poverty, and the (for some) uncomfortable fact that these women of 'corrupt morals' relied on a clientele drawn from the city's male population to make a living. The moral blame was clearly not being shared evenly. The Women's Christian Temperance Union was explicit on this point, suggesting that there was a 'double standard' being applied by the police: 'If prostitution is a crime for a woman, it is equally so for a man .... Women must fight for perfect equality for treatment for both sexes.'[391]

As the moral to-ing and fro-ing over prostitution in Auckland dragged on, the health issue associated with brothels held up the issue to a different light. In 1915, one newspaper editor made a forceful plea for regulation rather than prohibition to be the means of dealing with this age-old feature of society. 'Experience has shown,' he claimed,

> *that there is but one successful measure in dealing with the prostitute and venereal disease, and that is in a system of licensed prostitution, and the medical examination of prostitutes. True, wowserism would urge that, it would be merely licensing and not restricting vice .... Whatever way it is looked at, one thing*

> *is certain — wherever prostitution is carried on, venereal disease will spread. As it is impossible to abolish the worst evils of prostitution, except by licensing it, so therefore will it be impossible to prevent the spreading of disease, and death.*[392]

Overall, at this time, prostitution continued to be popularly regarded as a malignant presence in Auckland's social fabric, but no one was seriously convinced that it could be eliminated altogether. Instead, moral, legal and health imperatives continued to collide (and occasionally collude) during this decade, with no clear sense in sight of a resolution to the issue.

The war

New Zealand had entered the twentieth century at war, but a comparatively small war involving a handful of combatant nations. In 1914 the country was about to become involved in another war, but this time it would be a conflict without precedent — so vast, so prolonged, so macabre that it defied comprehension for those who lived through it. All the recent trumpeting of technological advances was silenced because of the nature of this war. Modernity, it turned out, was a two-edged sword, equally capable of mass killing as mass progress. Most New Zealanders experienced the war by proxy, with the fighting taking place in locations about as remote from the country as it was possible to get, and with censorship obscuring much of the brutality of the conflict. Thus, on the home front, the sense of the war was largely one of horror viewed through a veil.

The ledger of New Zealand's involvement seems to defy the country's diminutive size at the war's outbreak in 1914. From a population of just over a million people, 120,000 New Zealanders enlisted, of whom 103,000 served overseas, with another 3370 men serving in forces in other parts of the Empire, mainly Australia, and with a further 2600 Māori and 346 Pacific Islands troops contributing to the New Zealand forces. There were also 550 nurses who accompanied the New Zealand Expeditionary Force, plus more who enlisted with other Allied countries, mainly Britain. Of this combined contribution, 18,500 died either in the fighting or directly because of it, with a further 50,000 wounded.[393]

Unaware of the carnage to come, there was a spontaneous, and in some ways superficial, surge of public support in Auckland when King George's declaration of war against Germany was announced on 5 August 1914.[394] (The fact that conscription had to be introduced in New Zealand just over a year later shows how cosmetic these shows of support were.) The *Auckland Star* reported on the scenes in the hours following the declaration:

> [T]he pent-up feeling of the crowds which thronged the city streets gave way in frequent outbursts of enthusiasm. As the evening wore on feeling became more intensified, and groups of young men, waving Union Jacks, marched up and down Queen Street, cheering and singing national airs. Sometimes the crowd forming these processions swelled to a couple of thousand, and traffic in the main thoroughfares was frequently blocked. Interest mainly centred outside the newspaper offices. The "Star" has made arrangements for posting the latest information outside the office each evening, and last night each time a fresh message was posted a surging crowd blocked Shortland Street. In fact, at 9 o'clock, when an announcement was posted that the New Zealand Government had decided to call for volunteers for active service, there was a remarkable scene. A crowd of at least 1500 men, marching up Queen Street, reached Shortland Street corner, just as a cheer from those waiting outside the "Star" Office greeted this last message. Immediately the crowd in Queen Street stampeded up Shortland Street, and the scene was one of wild enthusiasm when those in a position to see called out the news to the surging hundreds who blocked the full width of the street. Flags were wildly waved, and the cheering was tremendous. In the theatres, restaurants, and other places where the public gathered, there were scenes of great enthusiasm. In one of the leading restaurants dinner had not been completed when those present were moved to send up ringing cheers for the British flag.[395]

At the same time, notices of the mobilisation of the Garrison Companies were posted around the city, ordering local Territorials to muster on Queens Wharf, in preparation of being sent to various military bases around the country. In August 1914 about 400 men gathered, with a small crowd at the wharf cheering them off.[396] However, this patriotic passion for the war was not shared by all the city's residents. The Anglican Bishop of Auckland took a more cautionary stance on the impending conflict. 'War,' he preached to his congregation, 'can only be a blight and a curse under such circumstances as exist in Europe at the present time, and it seems monstrous that thousands of valuable lives should be lost and untold misery created because two nations have a personal disagreement. We are driven to the conclusion that much of our civilisation and so-called Christianity is a delusion.'[397] This was very much a minority view at this moment, and was drowned out by the popular roar of support for the war. Such support derived partly from the long-standing sense of loyalty that so many in the city had to what they still regarded as their 'mother-country' — Britain.[398] And to mix the metaphor a bit, since fighting alongside Britain in the Boer War, and subsequently acquiring Dominion status, New Zealand was now as much a sibling as a son of Britain.

Then there was the grandeur of war that occupied the minds of the public (despite some of the atrocities committed by both sides during the Boer War that had managed to slip through the censor's net). There was a manly nobility in fighting in a war, particularly one where King and country were seen to be at stake. And there was also the prospect of returning as a hero (one of the paramount virtues in the British Empire at this time) making participation in the fighting even more enticing,[399] even if volunteers were blissfully unaware of the conflict's intricate causes and meaning.[400]

The euphoria of the announcement that there would be a war soon gave way to more practical aspects, including the need to finance the troops beyond the meagre pay the government gave them. Within two weeks of the declaration of hostilities, Prime Minister William Massey had established the Patriotic Fund, enabling various groups in society to contribute to the war effort. The response from communities was swift and energetic:

> *Every lawful means of raising money that ingenuity could devise, was called into play. Side by side with the mite of the poorest was placed the handsome but not more philanthropic donation of the wealthy. Giving for war purposes was generally regarded as a national duty, and to such a degree was the process of collection systematized, that it is safe now to assert that had twice the sum provided been required, the public of New Zealand would willingly have met the demand.*[401]

Raising money by holding carnivals and competitions was also a means of coping with the 'dull days of war'. One of the more extravagant of these events was the Auckland Queen Carnival, organised by the Auckland Patriotic and War Relief Association, which took place in October and November 1915. Competitions, tugs-of-war, wrestling, boxing and jiu-jitsu were held, but the real interest was in the pageant, in which 12 'queens' (one representing each district in Auckland) campaigned for votes (at a cost of 3d per vote, with multiple voting allowed) to be 'crowned'. The winner — based on a popular vote — was a Mrs Bollard. The 'coronation' ceremony was held at the Town Hall — a lavish event, with red velvet hangings, a throne, regal-looking carpets and various attendants in satin regalia.[402] More important than the gaudy opulence of the event was the fact that it had encouraged Aucklanders to donate £264,547 for the war effort.[403]

A more enduring gesture of generosity prompted by the war came from Auckland businessman Henry Partridge. In March 1915 he offered to donate to the Auckland Art Gallery a collection of Lindauer paintings, provided that the city's residents donated £10,000 to the Auckland Belgium Relief Fund. Details of donors and their contributions were published in the newspapers, and by May the target had been reached.[404]

One feature of fighting in foreign fields is that formerly unknown places become familiar. Two of these far-off locations — which most Aucklanders had probably never heard of in 1914 — were to become scorched into the national psyche: Gallipoli (1915) and Passchendaele (1917). Naturally, everyone expected there to be fatalities in the war, but no one was really prepared for the river of death to brim its banks (as Henry Newbolt put it)[405] in such an abominable way. Aucklanders reading their newspapers were sold these battles as Armageddon-type encounters of good versus evil.[406] Phrases such as 'great gallantry', 'sacrifice', 'struggle', 'splendid conduct and bravery', and 'a great crusade of Right against Wrong'[407] not only elevated and even sanctified these battles, but also buried the truth of what soldiers were experiencing, and even what the war was about. The fact is that the battles at Gallipoli and Passchendaele were not fought as part of any great contest of ideas or ideological struggle, and nor was New Zealand's security threatened by their outcome. And with the resting place of roughly a third of

New Zealanders killed in the conflict remaining unknown at the war's conclusion,[408] it was hardly surprising, then, that the mood respecting the war was soon clouded with bitterness.[409]

It was not until 19 July 1919, eight months after the war had ended, that official peace celebrations were held (it took this long for most of the remaining troops to return from Europe). A public holiday was declared, and Auckland 'wore a gala appearance, bunting and decorations being everywhere in evidence'. There was an official procession from Queen Street to the Domain, where troops who had returned from the conflict paraded. There were around 5500 soldiers present, and the march-by concluded with a message from the king being read out, followed by a 21-gun salute being fired from Mt Eden. That night, 'the city was transformed into a carnival. Bonfires were lit, and the spirit of revelry was abroad, but owing to the coal shortage only limited illuminations were permitted'.[410] Relief at the return of the troops pulsed through Auckland. An account of this day gives some impression of the feeling of release from four years of war that the population felt:

> *The multitudes that filled the streets this morning made up what is without doubt the greatest crowd that has ever gathered along the road between Quay Street and Grafton Bridge, and they watched the greatest procession that has ever marched through this ... City ... From the suburbs they came by tram and motor, crowded ferry boats brought them from the marine environs across the Waitemata, and from the inland districts they were carried in train loads. They changed Queen Street into a great mile of life and movement .... Before half-past nine all the special transport services brought these tens of thousands of cheering people in, and long before the great Memorial March began the throng with its holiday raiment, its fluttering flags and all the other insignia of festival began packing the line of [the] route, craning necks to see the aeroplanes droning overhead .... As the boys who have seen Gallipoli marched along they were cheered greatly all along the line, and these were repeated wave upon wave as the diggers came swinging along .... Some of them, unable to walk, were in motor cars, others walked with sticks, most were in uniform, some were without, some wore decorations, some did not, some, alas, had an empty sleeve, and all were cheered ....*

> [W]hen the noon hour struck. Immediately the movement ceased .... and the parade stood while a bugle band rolled out the "Last Post" in honour of the dead .... It was an inspiring moment in a great day.[411]

Not all the troops who returned to Auckland participated in this bittersweet occasion. Throughout the war, the bodies (or remnants of bodies) of those killed had been shipped back home, and as the death toll climbed, the northwestern portion of Waikumete Cemetery, in Glen Eden, was set aside as a war grave. At its entrance, the Returned Soldiers' Association 'erected a fine obelisk of Nelson marble, with Sicilian marble panels, in memory of those who lost their lives in the Great War',[412] and eventually the land became lined with rigid rows of tombstones. Was there any way of giving meaning to all this meaninglessness? Escapism through commemoration seems to have been the principal response to the physical and psychological trauma that had been inflicted. As a result, a spate of memorial-building followed, with these shrines to grief promising to remember the fallen — the Anzacs.[413]

Throughout the war, a few Auckland civilians battled not to fight. Exemptions to military service on religious grounds were possible,[414] but around the country just 73 objectors had been granted a formal exemption.[415] Many of Auckland's churches showed an unusual degree of ecumenical co-operation when it came to the war, with delegates from the Anglicans, Presbyterians, Catholics, Methodists, Baptists, Congregationalists, Salvation Army, Church of Christ and the Society of Friends forming a 'Peace Committee', which was founded on the principle that war 'as a means of settling disputes between nations is utterly opposed to the mind of Christ'.[416] Percy Gill, from Mt Eden — 'a respectable-looking young man' — was one such religious objector. A Quaker, Gill was opposed to all forms of war, and was brought before the Military Service Board for questioning in January 1918. He refused even to sign the form to be excluded from military service, such was his opposition to have any part in it at all. As a consequence, he was duly placed under arrest — an episode that illustrated not only the strong feelings the war evoked in some, but also the clash of convictions that so many individuals had to contend with at the time.[417] However, in general, most churches cautiously supported sending troops overseas on the basis that the conflict was a 'righteous war'.[418] Some in the union movement, and a handful of socialists, Irish nationalists and secular pacifists, were also among those who refused to be conscripted, but more commonly, in an apparent effort to be moved further down the list of those being called up for service, some men chose to get married, with one observer quipping, 'a fellow's got to do something to avoid being pushed off to the front'.[419]

'Bordering on panic'

On 11 October 1918 — the day before arriving at Auckland — the captain of the ship *Niagara* wired the following anxious message to the Union Steam Ship Company's Auckland office: 'Please advise Health Department, *Niagara* arriving with Spanish 'flu cases on board: increasing daily. Present time over 100 crew down, urgently requiring hospital assistance and accommodation for 25 serious cases.'[420] However, knowledge about how diseases spread was still in its relative infancy at this time, and authorities in Auckland saw no reason for the ship to be quarantined.[421] The *Niagara*'s arrival was soon blamed for the introduction of the influenza epidemic to the country, even though six people had already died of the highly contagious virus three days before the ship had even docked.[422]

Regardless of its source, though, by the end of October, Auckland Hospital was filled with people dying of the disease, with almost 30 of the medical staff also contracting the virus because of their close proximity to the patients. The symptoms included headaches, rapid heartbeats, high fevers, profuse sweating, exhaustion, depression, chest and limb pains, mottled skin, vomiting, diarrhoea, bloody saliva and mucus, delirium and occasionally even some haemorrhaging.[423] Given such suffering, death lost its sting for many of those in the terminal stages of the disease. However, in an instance of absurd legalism in the face of this horror, in December 1918 an elderly Auckland woman who was succumbing to the symptoms of the virus cut her wrist with a razor blade in an effort to end her life. The attempt was unsuccessful, though, and she was subsequently charged with attempted suicide. And even though the delirium had erased her memory of the episode, she was convicted nonetheless.[424]

The unscrupulous in Auckland saw profit to be made from people's pain at this time. One example that illustrates this sordid view of their fellow citizens was the owner of the appropriately named Fear's Pharmacy, in Pukekohe. Under the misleading heading of 'Public Notice', the chemist was selling 'Aggresso' tablets, which promised to 'guard against the serious consequences' of the epidemic.[425] And with a journey of almost 50 kilometres to Auckland Hospital, the residents of this small Auckland settlement may well have been tempted to part with their money for this 'medicine'. Like the other 'miracle' cures on offer at the time, it was ineffective. And meanwhile, hospitals could no longer cope with the upsurge in influenza patients. At nearby Papakura, the Parish Hall was transformed into a makeshift hospital with ten beds to accommodate 'the most urgent cases' in the area, and when that soon reached capacity, the Methodist Sunday school building was also converted into a hospital.[426] In the face of an invisible but highly contagious threat, Auckland authorities clamped down on places where the public could congregate. Schools,[427] theatres, pubs, social clubs, followed by shops, hotels, tearooms and courts, were all forced to close their doors. Even the remote sawmills at Piha, 40 kilometres west of the city centre, had to shut down as workers fell to the virus. By the first week of November, many Aucklanders were said to be 'in a state of mind bordering on panic'.[428]

In Auckland's central suburbs there was a rush to set up temporary hospitals. Seddon Memorial Technical College, 'Kilbryde' (John Logan Campbell's former home in Gladstone Road, Parnell), the three-storey Sailors' Home at the corner of Albert and Quay streets, the Avondale Racecourse building, Myers Kindergarten, the YWCA hostel, Vermont Street School and St Joseph's School in Grey Lynn all became makeshift hospitals, while the Auckland Racing Club's buildings at Ellerslie were converted into a convalescent home.[429]

Focus on the scale of the epidemic, though, risks overlooking the impact it had on individuals. One of the most poignant and tragic episodes recorded in Auckland during the influenza outbreak involved a Salvation Army volunteer who was going door to door in late November to check on the condition of residents. After no response to his knocks on the front door of one inner-city house, the volunteer let himself inside. There was one room that was locked, and so he called a colleague to assist in breaking it open. When they did, they saw that they were too late: '[a] mother lay dead in the one bed, and clinging to her was a little child, also dead. This was not all, for there were also two young children, both lying on the floor. Evidently all four in the little family were suddenly attacked by the sickness, and had died in neglect unable to help themselves.'[430] And there were similarly despondent stories from across the city. One account from the same month involved a motorist who saw two small children on the footpath, standing hand in hand and 'crying bitterly'. The motorist stopped his car and tried to ask the children what the matter was, but they were too young to speak and simply looked back at a house. He then went inside the house and found both the children's parents dead.[431]

Within the next few weeks, though, there were signs that the virus was in retreat, and by the end of the year Auckland was tentatively emerging from its enforced hibernation. Shops began to open, people wandered onto the streets with less anxiety than before, and factories returned to operation, while hospitals and halls across the city slowly emptied of their patients. But given the sudden and serious nature of the onslaught of the epidemic, officials and politicians felt something needed to be done to avert a similar catastrophe. The Influenza Epidemic Commission was formed to investigate, among other things, what could be improved on. When it came to Auckland and other main centres, the personal habits of the population were held up as being deficient:

> *evidence was given ... that there exists very widespread ignorance of the simplest rules of personal hygiene and ordinary housekeeping .... It would appear that a large proportion of girls are not receiving in their houses that teaching which would enable them to maintain a well-directed healthy home life .... Whilst nothing can fully take the place of good home teaching, we counsel that both in the primary and secondary schools much more attention should be given to domestic science, hygiene, first aid, and home nursing as subjects for girls.*[432]

As 1919 hobbled to a close, with Auckland grappling with victims of war and virus, the reaction to death diverged. For the soldiers who had fallen in battle, communities across Auckland erected memorials, and annual commemorations were held in remembrance. Yet, for the approximately 1200 Aucklanders killed by the flu, the response of the public and officials was to avert their gaze, almost as though if the epidemic was out of sight, it would soon be out of mind.[433]

Yet for all the tragedy of the decade that Aucklanders had endured, they finished 1919 surprisingly optimistic. There was a surge in weddings in the city (up by 70 per cent on the previous year), the annual number of deaths had halved in the previous 12 months to under 1500, the economy was performing well,[434] the population of the city and its suburbs was approaching 158,000 (triggering another building boom), the city was exporting nearly ten million pounds' worth of goods annually,[435] and rail traffic was up by 30 per cent.[436] The city's residents looked to be climbing out of the pit of war and sickness that they had occupied since 1914, and were anticipating 'with enthusiasm'[437] the new year and the new decade.

4
The 1920s

Into temptation

Wood was slabbed everywhere — pews, panels, pulpits, floors, altars, window arches — so much timber that the grandeur of the church's interior, with its high, vaulted ceiling and wide transept, was almost subverted by this visual wasteland of exhaustively panelled, drably varnished wood. Almost, because the kaleidoscopic imagery of the sunlit stained-glass windows punctured the monotony, giving the space a sense of sanctity. Knox Presbyterian Church, in Birdwood Crescent, Parnell, was being readied for its Sunday-morning service. Volunteers (apart from the minister, the entire operation was run by volunteers) had prepared the floral arrangements, cleaned the inside of the building, and were now handing out hymn books as members of the congregation filed in and took their seats. The organ hummed quietly in the background as the parishioners greeted each other and thumbed through their hymn books to find the first piece to be sung (the numbers were displayed — similar to the way cricket scores were — on the hymn board). The organ then thundered the opening chords of the first chorus, the congregation rose to its feet, and the singing commenced. Church had started.

The idiom of the church service, repeated throughout the city every

Sunday morning, was part of the weekly ritual for most Aucklanders. However, although measuring the faith of churchgoers is notoriously challenging,[438] the crude calculus of attendance offers a hint of the devotion that congregants may have had — at least to their denomination if not all its tenets. Census figures show a gentle decline in churchgoing between 1921 and 1926, with Auckland having one of the lowest rates of overall attendance in the country. The change from the nineteenth century, however, was more abrupt. In 1896, a quarter of Aucklanders were regular churchgoers, but 30 years later this had fallen to 16 per cent. And of all the major denominations, the biggest discrepancy between affiliation and attendance was with the Anglicans, with only 11 per cent of them regularly occupying a church pew (followed by Presbyterians, with an attendance rate of 20 per cent). At the other end of the scale, 50 per cent of Congregationalists regularly went to church, while 78 per cent of members of the Salvation Army attended services.[439]

As urban Auckland continued its geographic expansion during this decade, the fate of some churches was beginning to be dictated by the accompanying changes in their neighbourhoods. One of the challenges for many inner-city churches was that their construction methods bequeathed expensive maintenance costs to later generations of congregants. St Matthew-in-the-City, for example, faced thousands of pounds of repair costs in the interwar period, as well as the costs of contributing to measures to alleviate acute poverty in the parish.[440] St David's Presbyterian Church, in Khyber Pass, was in debt for several thousand pounds for most of the decade, even though its congregation grew throughout the 1920s.[441]

Further away from the central city, the situation was quite different. There were growing local populations, and churches built in these areas were free from some of the social and demographic difficulties facing some of the older inner-city churches. In addition, these new suburban churches were more likely to be constructed from timber rather than masonry (making them less expensive to build and maintain). In St Heliers (which many Aucklanders in the city still accessed by ferry at this time, and which was still regarded as a seaside resort),[442] when the local Presbyterian church needed to be relocated to 100 St Heliers Bay Road, rather than build a new edifice, the existing structure (built in 1916 on leasehold land near St Heliers beach) was simply shifted to the new, permanent site by a traction engine.[443] The same sort of flexibility in church positioning was exhibited in Mt Albert, when in the summer of 1921–22, the Presbyterian church in that suburb was hauled by a steam roller from its location on the corner of New North Road and Mt Albert Road to its current location at 14 Mt Albert Road. The reason for this shift was that church leaders feared that if the building remained at its former address, it could end up 'in the heart of a future shopping centre' — a concern that proved to be prophetic.[444] Throughout Auckland in this decade, there was a flurry of new churches appearing. In August 1921 the foundation stone was laid for the Anglican church in Waimauku, which was planned as a memorial to the area's fallen in the Great War. Two years later, a Presbyterian church, built in late Gothic Revival style, was opened in Papatoetoe, and in 1926 a church was opened at Pākiri, with a Māori choir from Port Albert leading the event. The following year, there were Anglican churches opened in New Lynn and Helensville, and in 1929 a more substantial Presbyterian church was erected in Northcote.[445]

However, planting places of worship in emerging suburbs or rural parts of Auckland that did not yet have the populations to sustain them was seen as risky by some church leaders. For all the doctrinal differences between denominations, the real villain was secularism, and the threat it posed to these new churches having viable congregations. In the outskirts of Auckland, this fear was well established in the mind of the chair of the Wesleyan Home Missions. He regarded it as 'a sad thing ... to see in the thinly populated country districts so many churches', because he felt that this 'played into the hands of the free-thinkers and those opposed to Christianity' as it gave an impression that the faith was characterised by sectarian divisions. More ecumenical co-operation was the prescription he believed was necessary to overcome some of the fundamental challenges to belief that the churches in Auckland collectively faced.[446] By the 1920s, there were already signs that even among churchgoers there was an 'indefiniteness' about religious ideas and certain points of doctrine that defined their denomination.[447] For such people, their churches were effectively becoming halfway houses between religious commitment and unbelief.

Other faiths were also present in the city, and although their numerical size tended to be slight, their contribution could be significant. Auckland's Jewish community was a case in point. In the mid-1920s the number of Jews in the city was around 600, at a time when Auckland's population was 236,000.[448] Yet, despite this diminutive presence, groups like the Auckland Jewish Women's Benevolent Society proved to be energetic fundraisers for the city's poor.[449] The cultural epicentre of the city's Jews was the Princes Street synagogue, which served variously as a place of prayer, worship, study and assembly.[450] In addition, it was where local efforts were made to rally support for the restoration of the Jewish state, in what was then called Palestine, and where talks were given by visiting Zionists to encourage local Jews to back this cause. However, this group of Aucklanders was singled out by the press, with some journalists resorting to prejudicial Jewish tropes in a way that was designed to set them apart from others in the city. In 1927, one Auckland newspaper went as far as to refer to a guest speaker at the synagogue as a 'tall pale-faced Jew, black of eye, and long in nose'.[451] Old ethnic and religious stereotypes evidently died hard.

For those Aucklanders whose religious curiosity drove them to the esoteric fringes, a home for their inquisitive urges was opened in March 1928, in the form of the Higher Thought Temple. Drawing on an eclectic mix of eastern mysticism, Christianity, theosophy (which itself was a hybrid belief), philosophy and the prevailing fad in spiritualism,[452] the doctrines of the Higher Thought Temple were sufficiently vague so as not to curdle when brought together, provided that no one probed them too deeply or took them too seriously. It proclaimed that it was a 'Universal Church, without fixed creed, dogma or ritual', where people could study 'the principles of Higher Thought as a religion, a science and a philosophy'.[453] The building where devotees gathered was designed by Henry Robinson (who was a theosophist and had designed his sect's building in Queen Street in 1923),[454] and seated around 180 people (although there are no records suggesting that the temple regularly reached capacity in attendances). The Higher Thought Temple's leaders regularly advertised in newspapers about their forthcoming meetings, but seem to have struggled to develop much of a following.

Among the established Christian denominations in the city, struggles of a different sort were emerging. As the creep of secularism was gathering pace in this decade, some churches in Auckland were still more sensitive to sectarianism than to declining membership.[455] Old denominational prejudices and rivalries were still a feature of Auckland society in the interwar period, and although generally dormant, they did occasionally erupt. One of the most incendiary of such occasions took place at the Auckland Town Hall on 17 March 1922. The event was the Grand Irish

Concert, at which the memorably dour-faced Bishop James Liston was scheduled to address the audience (between a performance of 'The Mistral Boy' and 'Erin, The Tear and the Smile').[456] Liston had donned priestly vestments for the first time in 1904, and in 1920 was promoted to Bishop of Auckland.[457] As with many Catholics of Irish descent in this period, his aversion to English Protestantism was congenital and close to the surface. However, for the most part, he had managed to exercise sufficient discretion so as not to draw the attention of Auckland's Protestant majority to his views.

Maybe it was the nostalgic music that tugged at his Irish nationalism that day, or maybe it was a growing resentment with the political situation in his parents' homeland, but whatever the reason, on St Patrick's Day 1922, in front of 3000 concertgoers in the Town Hall, Liston made a highly charged political speech that was to bring to the surface so many animosities that had lain relatively undisturbed in the city for years. The press was almost incredulous over the content of the bishop's speech as he told the audience that his parents had been 'driven from the country in which they were born' by 'their foreign masters [who] did not want Irish men and women peopling their own land, but wished to use it as a cattle ranch for the snobs of the Empire', and that he hoped that his parents' compatriots could achieve a 'complete deliverance from the house of bondage'. He promised that 'there would be many to fight, and even die' for an independent Ireland, and went on to praise those who had fought in the Easter Rising in 1916. But perhaps the aspect of this event that would have enraged some Aucklanders more than Liston's severe pro-Irish rhetoric was the fact that '[n]either at the beginning nor at the close of the concert was the National Anthem played or sung. Instead, at the end of the programme, the whole audience rose and sang "God Save Ireland."'[458]

The newspapers pounced on the bishop's speech in a manner that bordered on hysteria.[459] In a week, the matter had become one of national significance, with Cabinet voting in favour of the bishop's prosecution for sedition[460] under the Crimes Act.[461] Liston's clumsy attempts to extricate himself from this mess of his own making only worsened things, with the editor of the Catholic publication *The Tablet* accusing the bishop of 'being a snob pure and simple', lacking in 'dignity', and exemplifying in the wrong way 'the difference between being pig-headed and courageous'.[462] Following an acrimonious trial, Liston was acquitted (ironically by a Protestant jury), but the effect of this episode was vividly evident in Auckland (as well as elsewhere in the country). The timing of the bishop's comments — just three and a half years from the end of the Great War, in which thousands of Aucklanders had fought for the imperial cause — was bound to inflame feelings around the city, and the reaction was quick in coming. The *New Zealand Herald* accused Liston of 'insulting disloyalty',[463] the mayor of Auckland rebuked the bishop,[464] the Manurewa Town Board held a meeting and voted to support any protest action organised against Liston, the Pukekohe Chamber of Commerce voted in favour of a recommendation that all local body representatives henceforth take an oath of loyalty to the Crown,[465] and at an Auckland Rotary Club luncheon there was 'long and loud applause' at the mayor's criticism of the bishop's controversial comments.[466] Unexpectedly, though, Auckland's Catholic Māori also made public their disapproval of Liston's speech, specifically for the 'pain' he had caused by attacking Britain. They also pointedly reflected that it was Irish soldiers (led by the Home Rule advocate George Grey) who had dispossessed Māori of their land in the Waikato region.[467]

For all the sparks that flew in the aftermath of Liston's comments at the Town Hall, they failed to generate any sustained heat. Auckland's Protestant churches had not risen to the bait, and offered no collective rebuke, and for the remainder of the decade denominational division remained largely what it had been prior to Liston's outburst. Of more immediate concern to most churches was their engagement in the community, brought on by a growing awareness that some of their flocks were beginning to wander off. The need to reach those not attending church encouraged a group of Anglican priests meeting in Auckland in 1927 to propose religious addresses be broadcast on the 'wireless'. Of particular interest was the possibility that radio broadcasts could reach the city's children, who were slowly drifting away from Sunday school attendance. Harnessing the new technology of radio was seen as 'a possible solution to the church school problem, and also to the vexed Bible-in-schools question'. The committee of clerics charged with investigating the use of radio proposed that '[a] half-hour Bible bedtime story three times a week would be listened to by thousands of children. Country Sunday schools, even in very small centres, could be taught by an expert teacher speaking from Auckland.' And more generally, those people in the more remote parts of Auckland, 'cut off from the ministrations of their Church', could hear a weekly church message. Of course, the priests insisted, 'the wireless can [n]ever take the place of church attendance, which will always be necessary for the maintenance of public worship and the reception of the sacraments', but they hoped that those who had 'drifted out of touch with the Church, may be reclaimed by the message received by wireless'.[468]

Outreach of a more traditional Christian variety took a step forward in the 1920s in Auckland when an Anglican priest, Jasper Calder, proposed to his diocese on 13 April 1920 that a mission be established to help the city's poor.[469] Just 16 days later, the plan had been approved by the Church, a basic structure had been established, and Calder was appointed as the leader of what they named the Auckland City Mission.[470] The Mission combined evangelical work with material assistance, and by the end of the decade had a medical clinic, a hospital, library and a night shelter, and was even involved in working with prisoners.[471] Women volunteers also played a role in the Mission, administering to the needs of mothers, single women and girls of a 'difficult age', whose requirements were similarly not only material, but also emotional and spiritual.[472] In 1929 a dedicated shelter, accommodating up to 50 men, was opened by the Mission in Federal Street, and immediately was filled by the 'down and outs' as these people in need were disparagingly referred to in the press.[473] In the 1930s, Calder looked back on the formation of the Mission and recalled that 'when we began our ministrations we had no set programme, other than that we were out to help the underdog in his grim battles against life's difficulties .... We started with no money, no rules, but with an excellent committee, a lot of enthusiasm and a mighty big faith.'[474]

Aucklanders' relationship with faith and churches was complex, though, and at times ambivalent in this era. Even though nominal affiliation with Christianity was strong, and churches were still popularly regarded as the source of moral authority in the community, there was nonetheless an appetite for salacious stories involving clerics.[475] It was as though a portion of the population delighted in the formal, pompous, puritan image of (mainly Protestant) Christianity being subverted in this way. One newspaper in particular — the *New Zealand Truth* — seemed to relish in heaping ridicule on the killjoy attitudes of some church leaders, and their apparent hypocrisy in the area of sexual morality. When reporting, for example, on the 1922 Presbyterian General Assembly, held in Auckland, it referred to the condemnation some ministers had made of the 'awful pictures and the more awful advertising posters' that were eroding society's morality. The journalist then snidely commented, as an aside, that '[t]hese parsons always seem to know about the lurid films'.[476] Three years later, the *Truth* went further. It addressed the 'shivering fit' some Auckland churchgoers were suffering 'over the alleged epidemic of infantile immorality and impurity which has been unearthed by a mixed assortment of parsons'. In August 1925 Anglican canon Percival James addressed a Mothers' Meeting in Auckland, drawing attention to the advancing depravity among the city's youth. When questioned about the evidence to support his claim, the canon replied 'with a long-winded wail about the beastliness observable' on beaches, and complaining with perhaps a bit too much detail that his concern lay with '[b]oys and girls, young men and young women, as near to complete nudity as they can be ... sporting about and lying together'.[477] William Parry, the Labour MP for Auckland Central, was dismissive of James' apparently blanket condemnation of the city's youth,[478] but it was the media's focus on what they depicted as the double standards of some clergy that engaged readers.

These sorts of barrages garnered such great interest partly because Christianity in Auckland at this time was not merely some bland backdrop to people's lives, or something of interest to small huddles of moral purists.[479] The numbers of Aucklanders attending church each Sunday in this decade was still very high, and although it is difficult avoiding the sense that, for some, it was more a perfunctory undertaking, or maybe a means of putting their moral credentials on display, for most, the spiritual and social functions of churches remained important. Churches were still overwhelmingly the places where christenings, weddings and funerals were held, and were where social events took place.[480] In the case of Knox Presbyterian Church in Parnell, for example, there was a series of winter socials, a typical one of which took place in an evening in late May 1929, with a 'good programme of varied items, competitions and games', all conducted by the church's minister, Rev. MacDonald Aspland. By modern standards, the entertainment on offer may seem tedious: 'Elocutionary items were supplied ... a pianoforte solo was given .... Maori choruses by the pupils of Miss Ebba Gunman were much appreciated ... and ... [s]upper was served at the close of the evening by the committee members ...'.[481] But, in an era when the radio was at its infancy, television was yet to appear, and the movies operated at limited times, these sorts of church-organised diversions proved a popular alternative to staying at home.

However, competition for people's interests (and perhaps their souls) was coming in new forms in this decade. The rapid growth in the popularity of radios, and access to music through gramophone records,[482] enabled people across the city to indulge in the new music craze of the era: jazz. The Cakewalk, Bunny Hug, Turkey Trot, Foxtrot, Tickle Toe, Black Bottom, Charleston and Texas Tommy became part of the lexicon of dancing — bound to entice the youth as much as bewilder and perturb their parents. The origins of jazz were African-American rather than European, which added to its exoticness for some, and its moral danger to others. Its powerfully pulsing syncopated rhythms, daring harmonies and free melodies led to wild speculation about its threat to society. The *Auckland Star* alleged in 1921 that jazz could not really be classified as music, and that it had the effect of making its listeners 'more savage'.[483] The Women's Christian Temperance Union warned three years later that the elegant, stately dances of the previous generation had given way 'to the wild revels of the jazz, with its utter absence of dignity, with its wild license, its abandonment of self-control, its mad romp and unseemly contact'.[484] Not to be outdone by its fellow moralists, the Catholic Church argued that when it came to the city's youth,

> *jazz seems to have gone to their heads; and indeed, those who have watched a roomful of young people squirming through the modern dances, must have given up all the knowledge of mankind's weak and passionate nature if they could say that such performances held no danger for those who seemed to be suffering from a rush of jazz to the head .... Can young people twist and squirm and wriggle in a close embrace for hours at a time and evening after evening, without having their sense of modesty impaired, at the very least?*[485]

This slightly more secular post-war Auckland seemed to be dipping its toes in a more hedonistic way of living.[486] Yet, there was no objection raised by the upholders of Auckland's social standards when venues such as Fuller's Opera House, on Wellesley Street, performed pieces with names like 'Mammy's Coal Black Coon', or hosted performances such as 'Ye Old Nigger Minstrels Fun Show'.[487] The suggestive hint of sexual impropriety clearly outstripped any anxiety over the thickly daubed racism that also characterised so much entertainment in the jazz age.

Much of this antipathy to emerging forms of entertainment was a case of the shock of the new. There was an almost instinctive moral aversion held by some people towards anything that was veering away from the traditional. Calder experienced this first-hand in 1923, when he began screening films at some of his mission services. The Bishop of Auckland frowned at this innovation, claiming it was more an obstacle than an opportunity, and by the close of the decade the use of 'moving pictures' by the Church, although not openly declared as sinful, was nonetheless banned.[488]

Meanwhile, Auckland was fast becoming an arena for pursuers of pleasure. It was as though the city was finally shaking off some of its Edwardian dowdiness and entering into the vitalising cultural experiment of the 'modern' age.[489] Clubs, cabarets and dance halls (the distinctions overlapped) led the charge — not only in unleashing new forms of music and entertainment on Auckland, but also in dissolving some of the barriers that had existed between public and private life. These venues were places where the conventional expectations of younger, single people could briefly be set aside, and where notions of 'respectability' were more relaxed.[490] And there was no shortage of such spaces for Aucklanders eager to be transported into this modern milieu in the 1920s. From late 1922, residents of the quiet suburb of Milford were able to attend the Picturedrome, which screened movies,[491] but then afterwards, on certain evenings, would be converted into a dance hall where jazz music took over.[492] At the Dixieland Cabaret in Queen Street, the clientele included (according to one newspaper report from 1926) 'young jazz weeds, dashing sheiks, effeminate nincompoops and frivolous flappers', and there were '[m]any young ladies … [who] could hardly carry themselves. They were holding their partners round the necks and were gone at the knees.' Alcohol saturation seemed to be a common theme in these venues. Some of the patrons were reported to 'mix their ideas of the conventions with as much abandon as they mix their drinks', and then take advantage of 'the cabaret "cuddle cubicles"', which requires little imagination to picture.[493]

Despite the inevitable condemnation that such places attracted, particularly from prohibitionists, demand for dance venues ballooned.

Aucklanders could choose from the Dixieland Cabaret, the Click-Clack Cabaret in Newmarket (which ran exotic carnival nights),[494] Nixon's Cabaret in Mission Bay (which had a Māori dance band from nearby Ōrākei), the Orange Hall in Newton Road,[495] the Manchester Hall at the corner of Hobson and Victoria streets, and the Burlington Dance Club in Parnell, among others.[496] One of the clubs that took on a more eccentric form from the outset was Ye Olde Pirate Shippe, in Milford. With music provided by Ye Versatile Pirates' Band, this ship-shaped venue, with two 'decks' for dancing, attracted up to 600 patrons on its busier evenings, and completed its nautical-themed entertainment by arranging for these patrons to be ferried back to central Auckland when the club closed, usually around midnight.[497]

This new dance culture did not meet with universal appeal, though. Away from the central city, the more 'traditional' forms of dance and socialising maintained a toehold, with courting couples shuffling around country halls (observed by 'admiring matrons') to staid musical accompaniments. '"Jazz" did not enter into it at all.'[498] However, even getting to such events (and returning) could be an effort, as one visitor recalled: 'The young folk ... even the girls, often ride a considerable distance to attend a dance. In the winter, when the roads are bad, horses form the only means of conveyance. Their homeward journey over somewhat narrow and dangerous roads is sometimes a risky business.'[499] This was hardly the way to finish a fun night out, and the venues themselves were barely able to compete with the glamour of their city counterparts. One rural dance-goer in this era described how their local hall 'would be decorated with nikau palms, pampas heads or streamers .... Floors were buffed up by either grating candle wax over the floor or otherwise sprinkled with boric acid and then getting children to sit on sacks, while a male or two dragged them round the floor.'[500] Given such outmoded and dreary scenes, it was little wonder that the rural dances at this time were beginning their descent to a dull, slow death.

At home

One of the incidental spin-offs from the growing craze for movies in the 1920s was the rise in the influence of American tastes on the New Zealand public, and nowhere was this more evident in Auckland at this time than in the ascendance of the bungalow. These were adaptations of the 'Californian bungalow' (which in turn drew on Indian and Sri Lankan architecture).[501] A description of this new style of house published during the early period of bungalow construction in New Zealand gave readers a tempting hint of what to expect:

> *The house is surrounded by a deep verandah, a real substantial verandah, eight feet wide, but the spacious windows give beautiful soft light on the most glaring days. In the drawing room there are two of these windows, each six feet wide, to light up an area of 17 feet by 16. A central vestibule gives access to both the drawing and dining rooms by means of sliding doors, and the dining room is lighted by a flat arch seven feet wide, opening on to the verandah. The sliding doors of the drawing and dining rooms are both seven feet wide, and being situated directly opposite to each other practically make one room of both apartments in case of festivity. The dining room is 23 feet by 20 feet, so that the length of the combined rooms for entertainment is 16 x 8 x 20 — 44 feet — a charming apartment for such purposes. The two subsidiary bedrooms open on to the side verandah, and are fitted with the American oscillating portal wall beds placed in such a position that the occupant can sleep on the verandah or inside at will. It will be noted that provision has been made for guests by the installation of one of these useful devices in the drawing room beside the fireplace. On the other side is a beautiful china cabinet, which gives the whole apartment perfect balance and makes the line of wall and fireplace symmetrical. Throughout this lovely modern home the architect has carried out the idea of built-in furniture, in addition to the wall beds, and home makers will do well to follow the lead. Built-in furniture is a leading feature in all the homes of the latest design in the garden cities of England.*[502]

In keeping with the spirit of the age, bungalows represented a conscious break with the conventions of the past. Unlike their principal predecessor — the villa — they had lower ceilings, which made them easier to heat. And instead of overwrought Gothic references, they were inspired more by the Arts and Crafts movement, making them an 'artistic' house that the 'average' person could afford to own. They were also cheaper to build than villas, and more practical for their inhabitants.[503] In 1928 a demonstration of the speed at which a bungalow could be constructed was held inside the Town Hall. A team of carpenters, bricklayers and other tradesmen, working around the clock, finished the house in just 36 hours, to the amazement of onlookers.[504] By the early 1920s, bungalows were sprouting in some of the city's newer suburbs, dominating places like Epsom, Mt Eden, Mt Albert, Mt Roskill and Pt Chevalier. They were also appearing in smaller numbers throughout Auckland's rural hinterland. However, despite their relatively inexpensive construction costs, the fact that they were mass-produced, and their rapid spread across Auckland, in the following decade bungalows were being displaced by other forms of housing, as they began to fall out of fashion.

From the perspective of the twenty-first century, bungalows did not offer the cute, cosy, charming living that they were sometimes later credited with. Yes, they were an improvement in various practical ways on villas, but they were still without many of the conveniences of subsequent generations of housing. One resident of an Aberfoyle Street bungalow in Epsom later recalled what these 1920s homes were like.[505] The exterior walls were prone to borer,[506] and the weatherboards smelt of tar after being painted with creosote. There was a concrete path leading to the front door, but around the sides of the house, paths were made of seashells that the occupants would collect at a beach, then simply lay on top of the ground as a cheaper alternative to concrete. Typically, the salt from the shells would soak into the soil and kill most of the weeds, and when the mud eventually began to make its way through to the surface, a few more sackloads of shells would be collected and distributed along the path. Like many houses in this era, boundaries were delineated with hedges rather than fences or walls. In this case the hedges were Cape honeysuckle (*Tecomaria capensis*). As for the house's interior, when it was windy, draughts often found their way through the floorboards, although this was usually insufficient to get rid of the condensation that built up on the windows during winter. The bungalow's interior walls were made of scrim and sarking, over which wallpaper was pasted in some rooms. In the kitchen was a safe — in this case a cavity in the wall with a cupboard door on the inside and wire mesh on the outside. Butter and sometimes small cuts of meat were stored there as the coolest place in the house, but it was plainly unsatisfactory, as one Aucklander advised in 1928: 'No part of the house offers a bigger problem in hot weather, than the kitchen and larder. These are the departments which it is most essential to keep cool, and at the same time the very nature of the work carried on therein makes it exceedingly difficult to keep the temperature down.'[507] For most of this decade, very few Auckland households were prosperous enough to afford a refrigerator, and so devices like safes were common. When it came to washing clothes, most bungalows had a dedicated laundry. In this Aberfoyle Street house, the laundry room was dominated by the 'copper'. This was a metal container that was filled with water and soap powder, and which was heated beneath by a fire. Clothes were then placed in the hot water and agitated with a dolly — a sort of wooden paddle. Gas-heated coppers were making an appearance by this time, but like refrigerators, few households could afford them.

However, these homes were more than just houses. In certain ways, they reflected Auckland's accelerating transition to being a predominantly suburban region. Yet, while bungalows epitomised the city's new suburbs in the 1920s, they also referenced its recent rural past. Next to the front doors of many of these houses in this period was a native tree fern (ponga), reminiscent of a similar planting pattern in farmhouses a generation earlier. And free from the land constraints of the inner-city areas, sections in Auckland's new suburbs could be more spacious. Lots of around 300 square metres had been common in pre-war Auckland, but in the 1920s new sections averaged from 800 to 1000 square metres.[508] These effectively brought a memory of the farm to town, symbolically serving as urban meadows.[509] There were also trees planted on these sections (which were largely absent from houses in the centre of the city) and expansive vegetable gardens were established in many cases. The bungalow suburbs were practical, new, built along spacious roads (which unlike older parts of the city, were designed to accommodate motorised traffic), and were aesthetically pleasing. But in addition to these more obvious features, they were also in some ways a 'remnant of an old pastoral dream'[510] — an echo of Auckland's farming past reverberating in an urban setting. And for all their newness, Auckland's suburban expansion in this decade still had to contend with old local body administrative structures. For the most part, the differences were merely bureaucratic, but sometimes they could spill over into aspects of day-to-day life, as one Aucklander noted in 1927:

> I went for a trip out Edendale way on Sunday. Alighting from the tram in Dominion Road, I walked down Paice Avenue accompanied by a local resident. A few hundred yards along,

the well-kept road and wide, tidy footpath ended, and there began a broken road, the sides of which raised profuse growths of grass, fennel and blackberry, which encroached on a narrow track misnamed a "footpath." "What's this?" I inquired in astonishment. "Oh," said my friend, "this is where the Mount Albert borough begins — you can always tell when you leave Mount Eden and pass on to the Mount Albert Borough by the same signs; you see it all along the boundary." I went to the corner and there ten feet from my friend's front gate I stood in the centre of a veritable thicket of fennel, with the tops seeding two feet over my head.[511]

Auckland was still overwhelmingly rural in the 1920s, though, which is partly why countryside motifs featured so strongly in urban landscaping in this period. At the beginning of the decade, heading east from the centre of the city, Greenlane was roughly where Auckland transitioned from predominantly urban to mainly farmland. Onehunga was part of suburban Auckland by this time, but to the southeast, Ōtāhuhu was the only sizeable residential area left, and it was surrounded by agricultural land. To the west, urban Auckland dissolved around Avondale and New Lynn, and on the North Shore, the stretch of land from Devonport to Milford, along with Northcote, were the only areas that were reasonably populated. And even in areas that were nominally urban at this time, such as Mt Roskill, there could be large expanses of horticultural land being worked, with just a few small areas with housing on their boundaries.[512] Likewise, when Mount Albert Grammar School was built in 1922, it was not only positioned on a large field, but in 1933 acquired an adjacent 27-acre block, which was then used as a farm for students (who initially had the task of 'reclaiming neglected land from the mastery of gorse, blackberry and hawthorn').[513] For anyone flying over the city in the 1920s, they would have seen that approximately 90 per cent of the greater Auckland area was still scrub, forest or field.[514]

How the city's emerging suburbs would be designed was still only a loosely conceived notion in this era. Throughout the early decades of the twentieth century, pockets of rural Auckland were sometimes earmarked (usually by local landowners) for urban development, only for the plans to fall through, and the dream left to languish. Names like 'Waari', 'Plumer', 'Selwyn Abbey Estate', 'Waimarie' and 'Winstone Park' were attached to plans that either never eventuated, or were subsumed by the organic growth of suburbia from surrounding areas.[515] As far as any co-ordinated plan for Auckland's expansion was concerned, neither local nor central government had managed to assemble a coherent scheme for the city. A local body official acknowledged at this time that the 'importance of town-planning and its effect on the health, comfort, and convenience of the people have not yet been realised. Public opinion in New Zealand has yet to be educated. Our Parliament ... is lamentably ignorant of the question ...'. The intention among Auckland civic leaders was that the city would 'grow and extend according to a well-concerted plan, rather than by present haphazard methods', but acknowledgement and intention were generally as far as things went. Among the regrets one planner had was that '[t]he whole of the magnificent waterfront should never have been alienated to private individuals'. Instead, a 'wide sweeping esplanade, say, 150 yds wide along the foreshore, should have been reserved to the people, from Ponsonby to Tamaki'. And likewise, 'Auckland's most characteristic feature ... its glorious hills ... were desecrated and destroyed', because of a lack of town planning. The convenient villain in Auckland's unregulated expansion was 'the building speculator', who was responsible for roads that were too narrow, suburbs with too few trees or footpaths, and the 'almost wicked neglect of provision for open spaces'. Meanwhile, the Council 'looked helplessly on, unable to do anything, while new suburb after new suburb was added to the city'.[516] There was occasionally a utopian tinge to some of these pleas for better town planning in this era, as one report made explicit:

> *The country whose towns are systematically planned with a view to health and beauty, whose roads, railways and every means of transit are thoroughly organised and whose traffic and whole business operations run through most smoothly and efficiently is in a fair way to realise the highest ideals of progress and advancement, material and moral. Sickness, premature death and industrial unrest are the price of want of organised control of land and town-building ....*[517]

This sentiment was drained of its idealism during the 1920s as a consequence of a series of practical changes that affected the way that many Aucklanders lived. The passage of the 1922 State Advances

Amendment Act enabled workers to obtain generous loans to build their own houses,[518] and in the case of Auckland, this meant people choosing — in their thousands — to live in new suburbs that were distanced from the perceived decrepitude of the central city.[519] But unlike urban planning in parts of England, where collective green spaces dominated some of the new 'garden suburbs' being carved out at this time,[520] in Auckland in the 1920s (and beyond), having one's own plot of land for exclusive use mattered much more. Affordable houses built on cheap land became the standard formula for Auckland's urban expansion in this period.

Beautiful Auckland

'Beautification' became one of the catchwords of 1920s Auckland.[521] There was a growing awareness among some residents that while the city was expanding, it was not necessarily getting any more visually appealing. Apart from a few of the more substantial churches denting the skyline, suburban Auckland in this era was increasingly uniform and bland. The central city was the most architecturally diverse part of Auckland, but radiating out from there was a sprawl of generally unplanned suburban expansion. House, section and road seemed to be the only three elements in the equation for growth, and as long as this formula was followed, little else appeared to matter (a tourist visiting in 1922 expressed 'surprise ... that Auckland was not a city of beautiful private gardens').[522] There were, admittedly, parks in most suburbs, but often these had the appearance of being a perfunctory afterthought. They were not great recreational spaces as much as zoning anomalies — pockets of land that were designated as parks with the faint hope (but little care) that they might serve some leisure purpose. In 1924 the editor of the *Ladies' Mirror* acerbically wrote that '[i]t has, aforetime, been alleged against Auckland that amongst the cities of New Zealand she is the Arch Philistine. She is, or so her detractors assert, like the fair, but frail, ladies of History, who sat enthroned in beauty, yet considered that the loveliness so lavishly bestowed upon them by Nature exonerated them from the trouble of cultivating beauty of soul ...'.[523] It may have come across as a mean-spirited assessment, but with such scant interest apparently shown by city planners to Auckland's appearance, it rang true for some in the city. In response to this official lethargy, throughout this decade groups of Auckland residents began to take it on themselves to challenge the way their city looked, with the hope of bringing about what they regarded as visual improvements.

One of the features of these movements was that they were grass-roots groups, sprouting from communities rather than being ordained by some centrally planned body. In July 1921, one such organisation was formed in Pukekohe. A president and secretary were chosen, a committee established, and discussions held on how the area could be made to look more appealing.[524] With similar intent, beautifying societies were set up in other parts of the city to rein in, usually in a very modest way, some of the worst excesses of what was generously described as urban design.[525] However, there were often several challenges strewn in front of these would-be improvers. In 1929, for example, the Auckland Beautifying Society sought to tackle an unloved patch of land at the junction of Great South Road and Panmure Road, but was overwhelmed with regulatory obstacles and a jungle of bureaucratic processes to the point where they eventually had to abandon their plans altogether.[526]

One of the perennial targets of the beautifiers was the old dock site in Quay Street. In 1929 a group of 'prominent citizens' petitioned the Council to develop the area 'along aesthetic lines such as was the case in other large cities of the world'. The petitioners sought the formation of 'a place in the dignified architectural manner and befitting the principal entrance to the city'. The principal argument used by proponents of the plan was that beautifying this space would increase the capital value of the surrounding buildings, and that it would draw people to the area through converting the decaying dockland into 'lawns and ornamental gardens'.[527] Once again, though, there was resistance among officials to such initiatives, and hopes for revitalising this part of the city similarly withered.

One of the common pleas in calls for Auckland's beautification at this time was for the planting of more native flora. Gladys Sandford, an 'intrepid lady motorist', raised this matter in an address at the Town Hall in the spring of 1927, when she supported the idea of the roadside of Great South Road being planted with native shrubs and trees, which she suggested would have the additional function of serving as a living memorial to the fallen in the Great War.[528] The dearth of indigenous planting was becoming one of the more frequent criticisms of some of Auckland's parks in this period. 'The Albert, Western and other parks', one resident wrote in 1929, 'are glaring examples of lost opportunities', and then warming to this theme, argued that 'the Auckland Domain outer park wants prompt attention to ensure the preservation of the native flora against its gradual but sure displacement by aggressive exotics such as oak, privet, pine, etc., which should be ruthlessly extirpated'.[529] However, while reinstating indigenous plants and establishing flower beds in the city's commercial precincts preoccupied many beautifiers, one of the grandest efforts to adorn Auckland with something deemed aesthetically and culturally worthy of the city was under way, with the Domain as its focal point.

At the beginning of the 1920s the highest point of the Auckland Domain was a volcanic mound (originally known as Pukekawa) — the remnant of one of Auckland's oldest volcanoes[530] (part of which had been quarried for the 1913–14 Auckland Exhibition).[531] It was carpeted in grass, with its northern slopes falling away to an area of stream-riven gullies, shielded by dense scrub. Where the undergrowth had been cleared in certain sections, Aucklanders were able to meander through the 'sunlit glades',[532] with mature trees offering dappled shade for those keen on an afternoon stroll, while for some of the city's homeless it afforded a degree of shelter and concealment at night.[533] It was on this elevated portion of the Domain that the decision was made in 1920 to build a museum that would serve both as an institution where exhibits would be collected and curated, and as a war memorial (the site had been secured two years earlier for this latter purpose). It needed to be a building that was not just big in scale (when it was finished, it was one of the largest buildings in the country), but one whose grandeur imposed itself on Auckland. The resulting neoclassical design produced by the architects (who themselves had fought in the First World War)[534] had the appearance of a vast Greek temple at its entrance, and the atmosphere of a sepulchre in its war memorial section. A massive nationwide fundraising campaign was launched in 1920 to pay for this colossus, and on 28 November 1929 the governor-general, General Sir Charles Fergusson, officially opened the Auckland War Memorial Museum.[535]

Designing a museum of national significance was always bound to excite public opinion, but combining that undertaking with a memorial for the war dead compounded the controversy. Inevitably, there were public exchanges and private disagreements about almost every aspect of the building's design and function, but the end result seemed to assuage all the disputes leading up to its completion. In its finished form, the museum became a secular temple to the cult of the Anzacs — one deserving 'of public worship and national solicitude'.[536] In addition, it was a manifestation of the pride Aucklanders had for their city — one which trumpeted Auckland's accomplishments to the rest of New Zealand and even to other nations in the Empire.[537] But most importantly, the museum commemorated the fallen in the Great War. At its opening in 1929 the Archbishop of New Zealand addressed the crowds assembled at the cenotaph (modelled on the one at Whitehall in London, designed by Sir Edwin Lutyens),[538] which was situated in the Court of Honour in front of the museum. He then announced that he would pray, and 'silence fell over the multitude' gathered. 'May it be a constant reminder to present and future generations', he began,

> *of those who heard the call to service and sacrifice in defence of ... the fundamental principles of justice and righteousness in the world! May this 'stone of witness' ever stand as a monument, eloquent in its silence and sanctity, of our deep-rooted gratitude to those who died that others might live in peace and security, and of our duty to complete the great work for which they laid down their lives, so that lasting peace may be established upon the earth! May this Cenotaph be a link between the dead and the living and a solemn appeal to present and future to remember the past and give honour to whom honour is due!*[539]

The archbishop then consecrated the site, and the brief stillness that followed was pierced by the playing of "The Last Post". At its conclusion, Kipling's "Recessional" was recited, with the injunction 'lest we forget',[540] spoken by the many thousands present who had lost a loved one.

From the solemnity of the cenotaph, it was just a 300-metre walk to the winter gardens — a 'plant palace'[541] that opened in May 1928, and which in some ways served as a counterpoint to the severity of the museum. The winter gardens comprised two barrel-vaulted iron and glass houses — one temperate and one tropical — separated by a courtyard and pond, and at the southern end joined to a fernery. The style of the glass houses was derived from the similar buildings that had gained enormous popularity in Britain,[542] and the Auckland incarnation of these proved just as attractive to the public. It was a chance for Aucklanders to see plants that existed nowhere else in the country. Exotic specimens, including palms, creepers and flowering plants, were put on display in a manner that was carefully curated and designed to impress. The aim of the gardens was 'to provide a symmetrical setting that is entirely new in the architectural features of the city, and give an impression of orderliness in the arrangement and growing of delicate plants. From whatever point the new palace is viewed the effect will be to give delightful vistas, with bright colours and tasteful form in the general lay-out.'[543]

For seekers of exotic delight, there was something even more startling to be found in Queen Street at this time: the newly opened Civic Theatre. The exterior of the building was modern but unremarkable for the period. However, on stepping inside, patrons were confronted with hyper-stylised oriental exoticism,[544] on a scale and to an extent unequalled anywhere in the country. The entrance had the surreal appearance of how the English-speaking world might have seen the Far East in this era, with excessively ornate mouldings, faux-Hindu reliefs, subdued lighting and exaggerated 'Eastern' architectural features. It was a scrambled aesthetic that owed more to Western cultural stereotypes of 'the other' than to any efforts at faithful reproduction. But after all, as its purpose was fantasy and escapism, nobody in Auckland seemed to mind that it was not architecturally accurate. In the theatre area, before the movie started, patrons were overawed in every direction. Above them, the ceiling was rendered as a dark blue evening sky, with painted clouds and even small lights to mimic stars. And on either side of the screen were minarets stretching from floor to ceiling, elaborately latticed and coloured with Islamic motifs, and each guarded at their base by a gilded lion, with the walls completely made up of facades of stylised Indian and Byzantine palaces and temples. It was as close as any building could come to offering 'Eastern enchantment'. A guest on the opening night later wrote how everyone present was 'taken almost completely by surprise', and that

> [a]ll the glamour of the Orient is spread before the audience and vice-like holds its attention .... It is astonishing to what great lengths the atmospheric style of architecture has been earned .... the audience might have been forgiven for thinking that it was not in a theatre at all. There is a wonderful atmosphere about the palatial building and not all of it is due to novelty.[545]

Ugly Auckland

In a way, this oriental opulence represented a problem in Auckland. Yes, its deployment at the Civic was an outlandishly extravagant caricature that nobody seriously saw as a genuine depiction of any Asian culture. Yet, it was also suggestive of a pervasive view of Asians as something different — a people apart from 'normal' Aucklanders. Sometimes it was the slightest slither of a comment that slipped into the newspapers that revealed this view. 'Dirty as they are in some of their ways'[546] was an observation made about the city's small Indian population in 1926. One Auckland resident wrote to the Minister of Internal Affairs at this time urging the government 'to stop India's teeming millions from swamping out the labour market here', or else 'we will soon have a colour problem here, as they will come here direct from India by the shipload and then things will be similar to Natal'.[547] Meanwhile, Chinese, who were a more sizeable minority in the city,[548] were officially known as 'race aliens',[549] and were frequently subject to bitter stereotyping and racism. In 1923, one such example appeared in the *New Zealand Truth*, with its editor appearing to bundle together all his bigotry when addressing the presence of this minority ethnic group in Auckland:

> *Chinese carry the atmosphere of China into every country they penetrate. A row of dirty, dingy shops, with shuttered windows and a display of fantastic lettering, where bent Asiatics squat in the gutters, or file in and out of stealthily-opened doors in Indian fashion ... grimy by day and gaudy by night with dope and sin .... to pass within any of these filthy dens is to have revealed a lamentable state of affairs. Behind the shuttered windows is the sound of clinking money, the coarse laugh of the harlot, the huddled form of the opium slave ... behind the dilapidated walls are piled mounds of tins, bottles, bones and vile-smelling refuse.*[550]

This was no off-the-cuff comment, but a sustained and aggressive strike at a group of Aucklanders whose lives in no way reflected the vicious depictions in this editorial. Moreover, it emerged from a culture in which notions of a white-only New Zealand had become insinuated among portions of the population. Some of the concerns were economic, with claims that Asians 'sell their wares at a much cheaper rate than white men do', and that instead of spending their earnings, they kept them 'within their own little colonies .... All the evidence that can be gathered points to the fact that they conspire to drain the country.'⁵⁵¹ Other bases for this racism were faux-patriotic. The Returned Soldiers' Association, for example, was adamant that the government needed to take action on the 'Chinese issue'. In 1920 it cautioned that 'the man who fought for his country did not do so with the idea of making it a happy hunting ground for Asiatic labour, and it is the business of Parliament to preserve the country for the men who have made its prosperity'.⁵⁵²

The government's response, in the form of the Immigration Restriction Amendment Act 1920, certainly aided and abetted such views,⁵⁵³ serving almost as a parliamentary ordination for anti-Asian sentiment in the country, with its underlying goal being 'to prevent a single Chinese from landing in New Zealand'.⁵⁵⁴ The Act specified 'that no person other than a person of British birth and parentage shall ... enter into New Zealand unless he is in possession of a permit to enter', and that when it came to defining what constituted British birth or parentage, even those who were naturalised British subjects, or born in another part of the Empire, but of 'aboriginal Native' descent were excluded.⁵⁵⁵ Yet even such restrictions, as abhorrent as they were, were insufficient to appease those intent on pursuing a white-only policy, especially for Auckland. The reason why Auckland was one of the sources of this mounting anti-Asian feeling was that in areas such as Pukekohe there were comparatively high concentrations of Indians and Chinese involved in market gardening, and this proved to be a fertile ground for prejudices to be played out.⁵⁵⁶ However, legislative changes and restrictions on immigration were at best delaying tactics as far as some of the more vociferous racists in the area were concerned. In 1926 the *Franklin Times* (which covered the Pukekohe area) warned its readers that

> [t]he serious danger with which civilisation is threatened does not come from actual savages .... The peril is from those dark-skinned races which have long ago put on a thin veneer of semi-civilisation, but have remained for centuries without rising any higher .... No better example of this class of people can be found than the Hindus [who are] ... mentally and morally incapable of real civilisation ....⁵⁵⁷

The notion of Auckland facing an existential threat from its Asian population was one which relied on a wilful avoidance of the city's demographic composition. In 1926 the combined number of Chinese and Indians in the Auckland area was roughly 1900,[558] out of a total provincial population of around 334,000.[559] Yet the fears and the racist fantasies persisted, leading in December 1925 to the formation in Pukekohe of the White New Zealand League. Its creation was represented by its founders as a moderate defensive measure against an alien group that was expanding aggressively into an area:

> *If someone well acquainted with the Auckland Province were asked to name the choicest districts, he would probably mention Pukekohe and Mangere first. And it is toward these districts that the discriminating Oriental has gravitated. Pukekohe has suddenly awakened to the fact that white settlers are being squeezed out as Orientals can ... sell the produce at lower rates, and still have a margin that will more than supply their lower standard of living. The white residents of that district are now thoroughly alarmed at the increasing numbers of Asiatic landholders and have formed a White New Zealand League in an endeavour to check the movement.*[560]

Anti-Asian feeling in South Auckland was intensified in the era by the addition of moral concerns that agitators tacked on to commercial anxieties. Indians and Chinese, for example, were seen as posing a risk to 'public morality', and were represented at times more explicitly as a sexual threat to women in this part of Auckland.[561] And in a perverse twist, one of the new sources of anti-Asian racism came from a handful of Māori in the area. The Akarana Maori Association, formed in mid-1927, claimed to represent 'educated Maoris', with its membership made up of Māori and Europeans (all of whom were men).[562] The Association did not object to 'the presence of Asiatic professional men', but did lobby to restrict the entry of the 'Chinese and Indians of the market gardening class'. Their prime aim, though, was 'the regulating of the employment of Maori women with Asiatics'.[563] However, racism begat more racism, and by the end of the decade perspectives of the relationship between Māori and Asians in South Auckland were frequently a subject for jaundiced analyses. '[T]he Maori has failed in his first encounter with the despised Asiatic', one Panmure resident assessed the situation in 1929.

> *His women-folk perform menial tasks for Chinese and Hindu masters, while the men lounge in hotel bars between rare and spasmodic bursts of work .... The racial superiority of the Chinese over the Maori is demonstrated by the fact that the Chinese becomes the employer and the Maori the employee. The inferiority of the Maori is shown by his treatment of his women folk in sending them out to work for alien men. It is simply a modern instance of a superior race dominating an inferior one .... The Maori girls are not to blame if, seeing their elder sisters with lazy Maori husbands living in abject poverty, they choose to marry Chinese.*[564]

Sexism and racism made especially pernicious bedfellows, but it was also a coupling that was generating increased anxiety and animosity throughout Auckland, and led ultimately to the Minister of Native Affairs — Apirana Ngata — requesting a report on the situation in the city's market gardens. The committee established to investigate this were charged with determining '[w]hether it is in the interests of public morality that the employment of Maori girls and women by Chinese and Hindus should be permitted to take place'.[565] It reported back to Parliament in September 1929, and based on the evidence it had gathered found that 'as a general principle it is not in the interests of public morality that the employment of Maori girls and women by Chinese and Hindus should be permitted to take place'. This pronouncement was followed by the committee elaborating on what it saw as the consequences of interracial relationships in areas like Pukekohe particularly:

> *The indiscriminate intermingling of the lower types of the races — i.e., Maoris, Chinese, and Hindus — will ... have an effect that must eventually cause deterioration not only in the family and national life of the Maori race, but also in the national life of this country .... The mode of living amongst the Chinese and Hindus, and their ideas of comfort and cleanliness, were crude and insanitary in the extreme compared with European standards, and inferior to the suburban standard now set by the Maoris themselves under the influence of health and educational authorities .... Cases have been brought before the Committee where Maori women who have had children by Chinese fathers have been abandoned and left destitute.*[566]

This is about as close as the government got to recommending a eugenics-inspired programme in this decade. Ironically, though, as Chinese and Indians continued to settle in South Auckland, their economic activity helped to elevate living standards in the area,[567] and in the longer term the racist rump was whittled away, although, as events later in the century would show, it was never completely uprooted.

Crash

Throughout 1929, investors in the United States had continued to stoke an already overheated stock market, despite the Federal Reserve cautioning that the nine-year period of growth in the value of many leading shares was unsustainable. In the final days of October these warnings mercilessly materialised. Investors (many of whom had borrowed heavily to buy shares) stampeded to sell their stocks as values plummeted.[568] The panic of this crash made headlines in the United States, but for most Aucklanders this was a story of something happening overseas, with little premonition of how, or even if, there would be any local consequences. Indeed, the initial reaction was subdued. Bank shares were weak, but '[p]opular local stocks … retain their value, and a number of these changed hands this morning without any concessions being made by the vendors'. And on the final day of October the *Auckland Star* reported that the New York stock market had made 'a powerful recovery', with 'prices jumping', and the 'tension relieved'.[569] Even more reassurance came from the United States, where it was reported that 'it is agreed in practically all quarters that the basic causes [of the crash] were purely technical and psychological'.[570] There looked to be no reason at this moment for Aucklanders to fear for the future, and as the year drew to a close, the biggest shock residents had to contend with was the cyclone that tore through the west of the city in November. Large trees were torn out from the ground in Kumeū, and houses were shaken to the point where pictures on the wall fell to the floor. The violent winds then swung to the southeast, crashing into New Lynn with such force that chimneys were toppled and roofs were blown off buildings.[571] Then, as quickly as the cyclone had arrived, it had gone — in much the same way as the New York stock market crash appeared to have a few days earlier. As Aucklanders counted down the final weeks of the decade, it looked as if most things in the city had settled back to their usual ways. There was 'renewed confidence' in Auckland's businesses, the central railway station was reaching its busiest week of the year with holidaymakers coming and going,[572] the first round of matches organised by the Auckland Cricket Association were being held in several suburbs, the Auckland Trotting Carnival was under way,[573] Christmas trees were being put up in houses, there was an end-of-year school concert in the Matakana Hall, an evening social in the Methodist schoolroom in Port Albert run by the local Ladies' Guild, a Boy Scout gathering in Warkworth, a working bee at the Devonport Yacht Club, a horticultural lecture in Howick,[574] and carol concerts in halls and churches throughout the city. Auckland seemed to be experiencing a glut of normality.

5
The 1930s

Stench

Walking west along Alford Street from Great North Road, in the recently established suburb of Waterview, the road was flat until the final 150 metres, when it lowered slightly before reaching a dead end. From there, the terrain fell away into a small bush-clad bank, and then to a mangrove swamp, beyond which languished a shallow, silted estuary, where the difference between mud and water was often indistinguishable. During the day, even the slightest breeze would waft the marshy aroma of the sea through the area. On still nights, though — especially those muggy, warm summer evenings — a more pungent smell hung in the street, even if only briefly. In 1930, Alford Street was one of those areas where the 'night-cart men' were still in operation. With no reticulated drainage system in Waterview, human sewage (known only slightly euphemistically as 'night soil') was collected (usually weekly) from each house in carts and transported by horse and cart to a dumping ground away from human settlement (in the 1880s, for example, Mt Albert was one of the favoured sites for depositing the city's waste, but by this time locations further afield were used).[575] As the carts trundled their way along streets, they were 'very capable of distributing filth',[576] and despite this means of waste collection being known for decades to be 'very insanitary',[577] it still remained the only option for many Auckland neighbourhoods at this time.[578] And, as the city continued to expand, the night-soil method of managing sewage was creating more problems. In Tūākau in 1936, for example, authorities discovered that some of this extremely odorous and insanitary waste was being dumped on empty sections along the main road, representing 'a danger to the township'.[579] However, although deplored, there was simply no alternative to such an odious practice until the costly option of sewage pipes was extended to those areas still without them.

Of course, there have been challenges with sewage disposal since there have been cities, but in Auckland's case it was not until 1908 that the Auckland and Suburban Drainage Board was established to deal with the city's mounting waste problem. The Board soon commenced work on a sewerage system for the city, with waste flowing to subterranean storage tanks at Ōkahu Point, from where the screened but otherwise untreated household sewage was discharged 300 metres off the coast into the sea each high tide. Predictably, flushing the raw sewage of tens of thousands of households into this one point caused chronic pollution around Ōrākei.[580] The Director-General of Health acknowledged that complaints had been received regarding sewage disposal into the harbour at this location, but the Health Department confidently assured politicians and the public that the matter had been examined, and improvements were being made, in the form of the use of 'extra-fine screens for further screening sewage before its discharge'.[581]

For the Māori community at Ōrākei, which relied on seafood from the area where Auckland's sewage was being emptied, this represented no improvement whatsoever. Surveying their shellfish beds and fishing areas from the coast, the dwindling members of the local Ngāti Whātua settlement could smell the stench of human excrement as it curdled with the surrounding waters. And if they could stomach looking closer at the sea lapping against the shore, occasionally they could see flakes of sewage, some of it coagulating into a paste that broke up again as the small waves carrying it reached the beach. Not that it was much of a beach by this stage anyway. A special Act of Parliament had previously enabled Auckland's drainage authority to construct a sewer pipe running above ground, along the length of Ōkahu Bay. Not only did this obstruct Ngāti Whātua's access to one of its principal food supplies, but it also caused the iwi's adjacent settlement to become waterlogged at certain times. And to top it all off, the Crown had compulsorily acquired the necessary land from local Māori for these works.[582] It was the worst possible set of consequences stemming from the city's drainage planning, and its conscious disregard for its oldest community.

In 1935 the Native Land Court judge, Justice Frank Acheson, visited the surviving Māori settlement at Ōrākei, which had been diminished by avaricious Crown land acquisitions, and viewed the defiling of the coast that made up the community's northern boundary. He rejected suggestions that the location was a slum, and conceded that while the housing was in poor condition, nonetheless,

> *these Maori homes are comfortable. Inside they are remarkably clean. In these homes the Orakei people reared their children .... The people are close to their customary fishing grounds. By netting fish and gathering pipis they keep down the cost of living, a most important consideration for Maoris with big families. They are close to the City where many of the people work. The houses certainly look poor, but at any rate they are free from debt, unlike the palatial residences frowning down upon them from the hill.*[583]

Two years later, the poet and journalist Robin Hyde visited Ōrākei, and having met with some of the residents and toured the settlement, identified certain issues that were central to the area. She conceded that the standard of housing was poor, but also informed her readers that 'they are the dwelling places of very decent people, who, given a chance, would probably keep their premises as creditably as anyone could expect, and who have hung on to their long threatened shacks at Orakei with the courage of despair'. And as one of the community members pointed out, 'one could not expect the Maori people to put much heart into their homes until they knew that those shacks were their homes .... it is impossible for them (their titles to land or dwellings having been under dispute for years) to obtain facilities for proper sanitation, drainage or lighting'. As an example of the drainage problems affecting the site, when it rained, a poorly built road along part of its perimeter suffered from erosion, which blocked up the drains around the houses to the point where they no longer functioned.[584]

The appearance of 'squalor' at Ōrākei in this decade, with houses at the settlement exaggeratedly described as 'grotesque shanties',[585] drew public attention to the site, generating a tediously protracted debate among letter writers to the city's newspapers on what was best for the area. In 1932, one of the suggestions that appeared to be gaining support was more housing to be built on some of the vacant Ngāti Whātua land at Ōrākei, 'combining the best features of Maori and European'. The reason that such a discussion was occurring in the first place was the emerging prospect of the area's Māori owners being evicted altogether from the site by the Crown.[586] The process of removing the iwi from the land had commenced in the nineteenth century, and had accelerated in the early decades of the following century. By the 1930s, after arbitrary law changes, forced sales and other means used by the Crown to secure this site, Ngāti Whātua at Ōrākei were left with a depleted population, and nearly completely landless.[587]

Just as nature abhors a vacuum, so too, it seems, do urban planners loathe vacant land. So, in the 1930s, when a group of Auckland city planners turned their sights towards the quickly emptying land at Ōrākei, they saw it as an obvious target for development. These planners were fixated with the latest trend in urban design — the Garden City[588] — and concocted a scheme for the transformation of Ōrākei with almost utopian zeal. The idea of the Garden City, which manifested itself more commonly as the Garden Suburb, was one that had taken hold in several countries from the late nineteenth century, and was being applied in more refined forms by the 1920s and 1930s.[589] The overwhelming trend in Auckland's urban development to that time was one in which suburbs evolved almost organically — usually clinging to an arterial route, but otherwise largely free to take on the form that was the culmination of the choices of hundreds or thousands of homeowners. House colour, design, positioning and gardens, were all the product of individual choice, leading in some suburbs to the appearance either of character or chaos (the line between the two was not always clear). The passage of time affected suburban forms too. As some areas in Auckland aged, older, frailer buildings were either replaced or repaired, leading to in some instances jarring juxtapositions between the decrepit and the renovated, as well as between the outdated and the contemporary. Services sometimes struggled to cope with the extra demand placed on them, and what were once remote rural roads on the outskirts of the city were often becoming cramped and congested as urbanisation greatly increased the volume of traffic on them.

Now, though, instead of simply allowing the organism of suburban growth and renewal to proceed as it had in the past — with few restrictions, little co-ordination and even less foresight — it was possible to give form to suburbs in ways that reflected the social and aesthetic ideals of the time. And in order for the model Garden Suburb to be successful, it required good planning, sufficient funding, an appropriate site and popular enthusiasm for the project, which would make the suburb be perceived as a desirable place to live.[590] However, in looking forward, these planners were also looking back, to an idealised vision of a village. It was an irony of the modern age that the most advanced state of urban planning drew on nostalgic motifs of pre-industrial English village life, with its close-knit communities, cosy houses, park-like green spaces for shared community events and sympathetic landscaping, free of squalor, overcrowding and 'ugliness'. Yet, at the same time, these retrospective references would be coupled with modern roading (to accommodate the city's growing car cult), gas, electricity, phones and all the other amenities looked for in the modern home — the best of the past and the present would be consummated in the Garden Suburb. Such developments also had the potential to function as a civic centrepiece — one that could attract an audience of hundreds of thousands, and that could demonstrate Auckland's credentials as a 'beautiful' city. In its ideal form, the Garden Suburb would serve as a horizonal monument to the city and its leaders.

However, before Ōrākei could be transformed into a patch of urban utopia, there was the issue of its existing inhabitants to contend with, and at this point some of the arguments for suburban improvement at this location were shown to be little more than a fig leaf concealing deeply rooted racism. In 1937 the *Auckland Star* published a letter from an anonymous reader, which spoke of the perceived need to 'sweep away the eyesore' of the remaining Māori on the site. The Ōrākei settlement was depicted as an 'insanitary jumble of huts ... a blot on the landscape', and those Māori living there were 'selfish' for wanting to 'squat on Auckland's front door'. The writer then pushed the point further: 'The good of the very considerable majority must take precedence. What must overseas visitors think of this blemish on the seascape? .... By all means provide the Maoris with another settlement, and a good one at that. The tide of progress cannot be stemmed. The Maoris have been bought out and must go.'[591]

Plans to establish a Garden Suburb at Ōrākei had commenced in 1925, when a competition was launched to find a suitable urban design for the site (even though the land on which the suburb was to be built had yet to be acquired fully from Ngāti Whātua). The winner, Reginald Hammond, was an architect and surveyor, with town-planning experience in Britain.[592] His design was dominated by two straight roads emanating from a central point at the southern end of the proposed subdivision, with one thoroughfare penetrating north, and the other northeast. The streets radiating from these two prongs were curved, and designed to follow the contours of the land.[593] Provision was included in the plans for parks, a university campus, shops, gardens, playing fields, churches, playgrounds, carparks, a civic centre and a school (but no marae).[594] Section sizes would vary from 800 to 1300 square metres, and the wide roads would have the appearance of being wider still through the use of broad berms and extensive tree-planting.[595] It all looked so promising, and so enticing. Here was a suburb produced not by chance and the collision of a multitude of often ill-conceived individual decisions over decades, but from the intellectual laboratory of experts. Instead of small, old and increasingly impractical dwellings, crowded together cheek by jowl, what was being offered was spacious, luxurious and stylish modern living. By the beginning of 1930, over 60 sections had already been purchased,[596] and the Garden Suburb at Ōrākei looked to be on course to blossom in the near future.[597]

However, just as this utopian vision for a slice of Auckland suburbia was about to materialise, the sunny economic mood that had prevailed for much of the 1920s began to be overshadowed by the deteriorating global economy. Within three years, half of all the sites that had been purchased in the planned suburb (under the deferred payment system) had been returned to the Department of Lands as purchasers were no longer able to meet their payments.[598] This was not quite the end of the suburban project for Ōrākei, though. From 1937, the government used some of the land for its newly instituted state housing scheme,[599] although the sights were now set at a practical rather than utopian level.

Depression

What later became known as the Depression (or the Great Depression) was making its effects more widely felt in New Zealand from 1930, as the collapse of the world's economy gathered pace. No one was prepared for its severity or longevity, and few could even account for its occurrence.[600] There was a certain irony in the fact that technology, which had delivered mass production and modern communications at the beginning of the century to serve economies and connect nations, was now instrumental in cannibalising those very same economies. Businesses buckled, and the banking system broke down, leading to plummeting production and mass unemployment in most of the world's developed economies.[601]

New Zealand was hit hardest by a crash in export prices, which swiftly flowed on to a fall in farm incomes,[602] which in turn rippled out to other sectors. By the middle of 1930, cracks in the Auckland economy were beginning to show. Teachers graduating from training college were finding it significantly harder to get jobs — a problem the Ministry attempted to resolve by creating more teacher-assistant positions in schools, even though these were only temporary roles.[603] As job losses accelerated, fewer people were building houses, and brickmakers in the city had to cut production and staff. Builders were beginning to struggle to find work, furniture sales dropped as spending reduced, and people had to 'make do' with what they had.[604] Everywhere, the economy looked to be spiralling downwards. Auckland's unemployment rate was higher than the rest of the country, in part because many of those without jobs in the rural areas migrated to the city in the hope of finding some work there.[605] The cost of providing relief for the unemployed surged as a consequence. In 1927 the sum spent on unemployment in the Auckland Hospital District was £25,038. By 1930, when the Depression was still in its early stages, this amount had risen to £42,900.[606] The existing benefit regime and the system for delivering welfare were ill-equipped and underfunded for an economic crisis of this magnitude. At the peak of the Depression, around 1933, the unemployment rate nationally approached 30 per cent[607] (although official figures were lower, because they excluded Māori and women).[608]

The human cost in Auckland was becoming apparent to all — there was practically nobody in the city who was unaffected by the Depression in some way, and the hardest-hit in Auckland were in a desperate state by 1932. For much of that year, the Auckland City Mission was providing 5200 beds and 14,600 meals a month, while thousands of others in the city simply went without food at times, to the extent that signs of malnutrition among part of the population were beginning to present themselves. Marriage rates and birth rates fell, while the number of abortions increased — all attributable to the social pressures that the Depression was bringing to bear on society.[609]

In May 1930 the Member of Parliament for the Auckland West electorate, Michael Joseph Savage, sent a telegram to the acting prime minister, alerting him to the worsening situation in the country's largest city. Savage claimed that unemployment had reached a 'desperate stage' in Auckland, with thousands either partially or fully without work:

> *Their families are not getting sufficient to eat and winter is upon them. Local benevolent organisations, both public and private, are doing good work, which is totally inadequate to meet the position. Men, and women, too, want work and are willing to face anything. They are human and must be fed and housed. What will the Government do to give relief? It is no use talking about next year. People are starving now.*[610]

How, though, do you grapple with an unprecedented economic and social calamity? If you are in charge, you apply common sense, which is precisely what the New Zealand Government did, with disastrous consequences. As wages, production and employment rates were in free fall, the government decided that frugality would lead the country out of the crisis. When times got tough, so the conventional logic went, penny-pinching was the best way of preventing things from getting worse. Only it was not. Reduced government expenditure almost guaranteed that there would be no stimulus for spending in the economy, while pensions, state-sector salaries, hospital expenditure and public works were slashed in an increasingly vain and ideologically driven yet futile effort by the government to balance its books.[611]

But as politicians and officials laboured, largely unsuccessfully, to save the economy, the rest of the country bore the brunt of the crisis. Among much else, there was a feeling of overwhelming powerlessness among many people. The Depression was a beast that no amount of effort appeared to be able to contain, and the effects on communities were severe. As one worker described it at the time, there was a feeling of 'greyness' in society: 'It's the only way I can describe a sort of hopelessness that seemed to spread around among people who, in the earlier parts of their lives, had been accustomed to security. It was the result of a discovery, a shock really ... that life was no longer secure. People ... tended to draw in upon themselves, to be rather cagey about other people, to keep to themselves, to not become involved if possible.'[612]

The writer John Mulgan, who lived in Auckland during the early years of the Depression, conjured up something of the atmosphere of the city at this time, and the experience of its residents. In his 1939 novel *Man Alone*, he observed how '[i]t was strange to see how things changed now that the luck had turned, how people grew uneasy and careful with each other, and kept to themselves, watching and saving what they had'.[613] By the winter of 1931, the Depression's hold on the country was tightening. In a gloomy, abandoned warehouse in Fort Street, in the centre of the city, a journalist captured 'one of the many tragic sights' of Auckland: a long, slow-moving line of former soldiers waiting stoically for food:

> [O]n this Monday morning they stand in a queue, waiting for a little sustenance, which is the present "bread line." Whatever feelings of despair may haunt them, they are not blaming any Government …. Their philosophy is to endure. All they ask is a little "tucker." Some of these men are hungry …. Yesterday one man who had received a meal ticket on Saturday said he had not had any food on Sunday, and there was every reason for believing him. It is a significant fact that these ex-soldiers never ask for more than one meal ticket at a time and Sunday intervenes between issues.[614]

By 1931, most Aucklanders had witnessed or were experiencing unemployment, hunger, homelessness and hopelessness. This was the debris of the Depression, piling up throughout the city. People had reached 'a state of desperation',[615] with no apparent respite in sight. For all its efforts (misdirected or otherwise), the government had been unable to bring about any material improvement, resulting in this desperation transmuting into discontent. With a growing number of Aucklanders angry, frightened and feeling that there was little left to lose, it was only a short step from discontent to disorder, and in the autumn of 1932 that disorder was unleashed. Since Monday 11 April, the temperament of Auckland had abruptly darkened, with increasing numbers of people gathering in and around Queen Street, agitated by unionists — in particular Jim Edwards, who had been one of the founders of the Unemployed Workers' Movement the previous year (and who had a string of convictions and arrests for various forms of disorder). On Wednesday afternoon, Edwards had addressed a crowd consisting mainly of unemployed men, delivering a rabble-rousing speech that was enough to incite a clash between protesters and police outside the Bycroft's biscuit factory in Shortland Street. As soon as he saw what was happening, Edwards jumped into the fray and managed, after a while, to help rein in some of the more belligerent protesters. As journalist Robin Hyde laconically put it, '[a] small detachment of police was mobbed there, and it is very generally admitted that had not Edwards made an attempt to control the crowds (who were slowly jamming "the defence" against a lorry), some of the police might have fared worse and gone a very long way farther, in a direction not likely to be popular with them'.[616]

Another gathering was planned for the following day, this one involving employees facing government-proposed salary cuts. On that Thursday, the union members involved entered the Town Hall for this meeting, while outside a large, unruly crowd assembled. Relief workers, the unemployed and onlookers loitered — fidgeting and chatting. They had no plan of action. They were simply exasperated with their circumstances, and saw this gathering as an opportunity to demonstrate their feelings to what seemed like an uncaring government. Over the course of that afternoon, the unwieldy crowd swelled to several thousand, and as the sun lowered, the mood became more sullen.

Edwards then prepared to address this throng of disaffected Aucklanders, but precisely what happened next later became a subject of bitter dispute. The police version of events (possibly skewed by their experiences in Shortland Street the previous day) was straightforward: Edwards was intending to provoke the crowd, and they feared that his actions might lead to a riot. Thus, as he rose to his feet in an effort (so Edwards and his supporters claimed) to calm the crowd,[617] a policeman dissuaded him from speaking. However, it was the nature of this dissuasion that had such an incendiary effect. Hyde, who was reporting on the event, later noted that Edwards 'was bludgeoned by a police official from behind .... but whether he first provided considerably more provocation than he admits is, as I have said before, a matter on which one forms one's own opinion'.[618] She retreated from lumping the blame entirely on the police, however, and conceded that the immediate responsibility for the riot that followed could be spread over all parties involved to some degree:

> *At its very best, the bludgeoning must have looked uglier than it really was .... It's an unpleasant enough spectacle to cause a good deal of righteous indignation. The truncheons (wooden, and not lead-loaded, as was incorrectly and unofficially stated later), cause a scalp wound and much gore. If the police wanted to provide a tame dragon with a taste for blood, they must confess to having supplied the wherewithal.*[619]

Edwards' own account of this moment reveals that he felt powerless to restrain the mob, and that whatever he might have said was practically impossible to hear anyway:

> *Now the mob was infuriated .... I staggered to the balustrade to try and address the crowd. By this time the police had arrived in force and were wielding their batons against the demonstrators and driving them back from the town hall doors, and within seconds the crowd in their thousands had become a frenzied leaderless mob. Whatever I said was drowned in the tumult and uproar and all I could see through the blood that was blinding me, from the wound on my head, was the dark bodies of my fellow men in violent conflict as police and demonstrator encountered one another.*[620]

What followed on from the assault on Edwards was the sort of descent into chaos that no reporter had really anticipated was possible on this scale in the city. 'Riotous scenes without precedent in Auckland were witnessed in Queen Street last evening', was how the *Auckland Star* began its coverage.

> *Trouble commenced with stone-throwing by processionists in Queen Street. It developed into severe rioting in the vicinity of the Town Hall, where, amid pandemonium, batons and sticks were used, and it spread over the greater length of Queen Street, where shop windows were shattered and stock looted. It was a startling instance of mob impulse and the lawlessness and abandon that is bred of contagion. For over two hours sporadic raiding went on over a big section of Auckland's main shopping area amid the cries of excited people and the tinkle and crash of breaking glass.*

> *The police were hopelessly outnumbered. A naval detachment was sent over to the city from the naval base, special constables were hurriedly sworn in and at the height of the trouble the Fire Brigade turned out. The members of the St. John Ambulance worked at peak pressure to rush casualties to the Auckland Hospital, and over 200 cases — several of a serious nature — were dealt with. For nearly three hours Queen Street was more or less in the hands of a lawless crowd bent on destruction, while thousands of citizens helplessly and amazedly looked on.*[621]

Slowly, but with mounting success, authorities took control of the melee, with the crowds of rioters and onlookers encouraged to disperse when confronted with sailors with fixed bayonets advancing through Queen Street and surrounding areas towards them. Two hundred people were injured in the riot, and the shattered glass from hundreds of shop windows carpeted the footpaths where the riot had occurred. The next morning, curious Aucklanders converged in the city centre to survey the carnage, and were deeply shocked by the sights that confronted them. 'Incredulity and dismay were written on every face', according to one report, which concluded that 'the orgy of destruction and thieving that suddenly developed in the heart of the city strikes the average citizen as all the more horrible because he has never seen anything like it before in his own country …. [T]hough the actual damage done is serious, it is not nearly as grave as the exhibition of savagery that produced it.'[622] Ordered Auckland, with its prim public standards, had succumbed to the ugly forces of the mob. The recently elected mayor, George Hutchison, helped with the return of some sense of normality to the streets, but in the immediate aftermath of the riot, that was achieved largely by the deployment of 300 special constables and two squadrons of the Waikato Mounted Rifles, the imposition of a blanket ban on public meetings, and the passage of legislation in Parliament that enabled draconian states of emergency to be imposed.[623] Superficially, Auckland returned to normal within days of the riots, but there was a residue of horror for many at the gravity of the event. In summing up at a trial of some of the rioters, the presiding judge reminded jurors that 'New Zealand has always been regarded as a happy and peaceful country', and that he could not recall 'any incident [that] … has so shocked the public mind' as this riot. 'It was never realised before,' he concluded, 'that there was in this community a number of men who would not hesitate for the purpose of having their wrongs redressed to resort to violence.'[624]

'Ground floor: perfumery'

The damage done to central Auckland's perception of itself as a result of the riots in April 1932 was significant. However, the effects on shops in the area was relatively short-lived. Retail's relentless advance in the city was to be stopped neither by the Depression nor the rioters that it spawned, even though both had their effects on business. Shops in the central business district continued to exercise a gravitational pull on people throughout the greater Auckland region, and, in an odd way, the more distant Aucklanders were from the city's principal shopping precinct, the more attractive — even glamorous — a visit to this retail area became. Most of Auckland's larger suburbs had their own rows of tightly packed shops lined along the main road, including dairies, which made their appearance in this decade. Dairies — with their allusion to milk products — were the stores where locals could buy eggs, milk and other food products.[625] Suburban shops also tended to include ice-cream stores, butchers, fish shops, bakers, drapers, pharmacists, confectioners[626] and, depending on the size of the surrounding population, a cinema. However, there was a certain banality to these smaller shops at this time — they fulfilled more a functional activity than a leisure one. Central Auckland, by contrast, offered retail activity almost as a form of recreation. The biggest drawcard for shoppers were the department stores, which had existed for decades in Auckland, but which by the 1930s were experiencing if not exactly a golden age, then at least a gilded one. The range of goods on sale in these stores vastly exceeded anything available in suburban shops, and they had an atmosphere that was modern, airy and sophisticated.[627] Particular floors were devoted to specific categories of goods, and instead of the product-clotted displays of the city's modest, often cavernous, shops, there was space and some care and subtlety in the arrangement of items for sale. The names of these grand department stores were familiar to all Aucklanders in this era, and they were synonymous at this time with an all-day excursion to 'town', as the central business district was known. Just the mention of plans to visit Milne & Choyce, George Court's, Rendells or Smith & Caughey's would be enough to signal what the shopper was about to enjoy (or endure). And there was no shortage of features and services in these palaces of consumption and modernity that aimed to appeal to customers.[628] Staff were neatly dressed, and most had received some training in 'salesmanship',[629] there were tearooms with an emphasis on elegance, the buildings themselves had large windows, high ceilings, decorative displays and lavish furnishings, and there were services such as barbers and tailors available.

Some of the experiments in enticing customers to these retail monoliths achieved only temporary success. At Smith & Caughey's, for example, the fourth floor of its Roy Lippincott-designed building on Queen Street[630] was home to the Lyceum Club. Formerly the Auckland Women's Club, and committed to social and political issues (one of its founding members, Ellen Melville, was the first woman elected to the Auckland City Council, in 1913),[631] by the 1930s it had transformed into more of a social group, run along similar lines to the sort of gentlemen's clubs that were popular in this era, and reached a membership of one thousand in this period.[632] There was an effort at forging an element of old-world, upper-middle-class character in the Lyceum, with its library, auditorium, dining, meeting and cards rooms, and the occasional musical programme and plays put on for members.[633] However, although the club persisted, its membership declined in later years, and it eventually shifted out of Smith & Caughey's,[634] partly because it was no longer seen as fitting with the store's commercial aims.

On an even bigger scale, but with noticeably less prestige than some of Auckland's other department stores, was the Farmers' Trading Company. In 1910 a group of farmers from the Auckland region had formed the Farmers' Union Trading and Indenting Association — a co-operative which six years later became the Farmers' Union Trading Company, and which in 1920 opened several shops in the province. The purpose of these stores was to allow 'country folk' to supply 'themselves direct with all their requirements without having to pay middlemen's profits'. Those who had shares in this co-operative received discounts on saddlery, sugar, kerosene, lime, cement, galvanised piping, flour and other essentials.[635] The company grew partly because of its distinct organisational structure, but also thanks to sustained advertising, and for providing for mail-order purchases. Among the popular products Aucklanders ordered from the firm in the 1930s were tea, toys and especially bicycle accessories, including tyres, oil and acetylene lamps.[636]

THE 1930s

Farmers was based in a large building in Hobson Street, which initially served as its offices and warehouse. Its central location, though, made it an obvious candidate to join the other department stores in the city, and in 1921 it opened some of its space as a shopping area. Like some of the other central Auckland department stores, Farmers had tearooms, a broad range of stock and comfortable surrounds. It also had one attraction that for generations to come would have children pressing their parents to take them there: the rooftop playground. Billed as 'one of the sights of Auckland',[637] the playground was the bait the firm needed to entice people to their shop, particularly as it was a 650-metre walk for shopping-laden customers from Smith & Caughey's. Going to Farmers was an alluring prospect for many children in this period, and the management ensured that the attractions it offered them would draw them in. Advertisements in the 1930s told parents that their children could go

> to our Pets' Department to see "Hector," the Farmers' Parrot, who, though 90 years old, is still going strong. After that you will, of course, go up to our Roof Playground, where motor-cars, tricycles, swings and roundabouts are provided for the amusement of our wee visitors. The Kiddies will certainly enjoy themselves while you are shopping in our Warehouse or having refreshments in our beautiful Tearoom.[638]

There was even a bus service provided from Queen Street and a tram connection to Karangahape Road to make it easier for shoppers to get to the Hobson Street site. The Farmers building was extended in this decade (with the design — like Smith & Caughey's — produced by Lippincott), and boasted the first free carpark for shoppers in Australasia.[639] And despite the Depression diminishing much of the firm's profitability, in the 1930s new Farmers stores were opened in Avondale, Devonport, Grey Lynn, Mt Albert, Mt Eden, Mt Roskill, New Lynn, Onehunga, Papakura, Parnell, Ponsonby, Pt Chevalier, Pukekohe, Sandringham and Westmere, as well as a Queen Street branch in 1932.[640] It became the largest shopping company in the city, and by 1931 was already employing over a thousand Aucklanders.[641]

Farmers also had one other trick up its marketing sleeve: its annual Santa Parade. There had been Santa parades in Auckland since 1912, although these tended to be modest affairs. The first one was made up of '[t]hree Motor Cars filled with Happy Children', which was ambitiously described as forming 'a Grand Procession' leading to Morris's department store in Karangahape Road.[642] However, the Farmers parade was a much grander spectacle. Santa was 'drawn by gaily-decked horses up Pitt Street, along Karangahape Road, and down Queen Street', before arriving back at Hobson Street, where he took up residency in the toy department. He was accompanied on the parade by 'six lovely fairies, and a lot of funny folk', including 'Waggles and Goggles', 'The Fat Boy', 'the Man That Walks On His Hands', 'The Giant' and 'The Big Fiddle'.[643] It was hardly a great cultural triumph, but that was not its function. Children were enthralled by it, and the Farmers brand was imprinted on the memories of generations of Auckland shoppers as a consequence.

Hike, drink, dance, sing

But if it all got a bit too much — the crowds and the commercialism — respite was not far away. In August 1930, plans were finalised for a sealed road leading from New Lynn (which was on the city's rural fringe at the time) into the wilderness of Titirangi, a further six kilometres southwest.[644] Titirangi was close enough to urban Auckland to be accessible in the 1930s, but remote enough to retain its unspoilt appearance. A guide for motorists at the time offered a truncated assessment of Titirangi's appeal, while noting the fairly challenging route to get there: 'Glorious Views. Native Bush and Park. Tea Kiosk. Road metalled, steep from New Lynn, very rough. Leave Auckland G.P.O. via Anzac Avenue, Symonds St., New North Rd., passing through Eden Terrace, Kingsland, Mt. Albert, Avondale. Beware railway crossing, New Lynn.'[645] At the other end of the literary spectrum, Miss Louie Harrison, of Northcote, resorted to overwrought verse in a paean to the area:

> *Far away from the city's turmoil*
> *In the midst of wooded hills,*
> *Lies a spot of wondrous beauty*
> *Where forgotten are life's ills —*
> *A place of delight and enchantment,*
> *Green fern and soft murmuring rills.*
> *They have named it Titirangi,*
> *The place where skies are blue,*

And mayhap some day an artist
Will paint it in picture for you[.][646]

In this decade, tramping in the Waitākere Ranges was an activity that was gaining ground among those looking for an inexpensive weekend leisure activity. Maybe for some Aucklanders, it was a means of nostalgically recovering their city's recent frontier past. Certainly, for many, a day spent wandering through parts of the 29,100 hectares of native rainforest[647] close to where they lived was an appealing prospect (and for those affected by the Depression — which was practically everyone — an inexpensive one too). One of the options for an adventure into the unspoilt Waitākeres was the mystery train, which was 'intended to facilitate healthful outings for large numbers of people under the most comfortable conditions'.[648] For the price of a few shillings, you could join a group of other booted and backpacked trampers who would be taken by train to an unknown venue from where they would be given a map with their route for the day.[649] Many of these excursions occurred on Sundays, which was a dilemma for some of the city's churchgoers, but one that others managed to resolve, as one participant explained:

> *As one of the hikers in last Sunday's "Mystery Train," I think it is due to them to state that a more orderly and, indeed, reverent Sabbath crowd could not be desired. Arrived at Waitakere we commenced the tramp and soon found ourselves taking lunch at a convenient spot, amidst charming surroundings. Continuing the walk, I feel sure every one of us was at times lost in admiration of the beautiful scenery we passed through. I reached home about 5.30, in good time for the evening church service; this is as it should be. My whole life, a fairly long one, has been such that I might well be looked upon as a professing Christian, and I have yet to learn that an occasional Sunday morning's country walk, enjoying and contemplating the wonderful works of God, can be regarded as a desecration of the Sabbath.*[650]

It was not just the change of scenery that lured hundreds of Aucklanders to these walking expeditions They also served an important social function, and even as a de facto 'matrimonial agenc[y]'.[651] Whether enamoured or just inquisitive, by 1930 the number of Aucklanders being drawn to this wilderness on the outskirts of their city represented an opportunity to some to capitalise on the area's growing popularity. The most prominent and enduring of these undertakings was the Titirangi Hotel (later known as Lopdell House), which was opened on 30 November 1930 by Prime Minister (and MP for Kaipara) Gordon Coates. Every effort was invested in ensuring that this would be a luxurious and modern establishment, despite its distance from the city's urban centres. Rooms had their own bathrooms, with hot and cold running water, there was a tearoom and cabaret, which accommodated two hundred people, and which opened 'out on to a spacious balcony, commanding a wonderful view of the bush and Manukau Harbour', and the hotel's dining room was 'the acme of comfort, carpeted from wall to wall, and furnished in dark oak'. An added feature was the building's roof garden, which offered guests 'a wonderful panorama of Auckland's Blue Mountain scenery and the ever-changing glories of the Manukau Harbour Heads'. The Titirangi Hotel was the latest word in Auckland accommodation:

> *An innovation, as far as hotels in New Zealand are concerned, will be the installation of a Wireless and Talking Machine, which will operate in the Cabaret, on the Roof Garden, and all landings, permitting dance music to be rendered on one floor, while broadcasting may be indulged in on the others .... Included in the equipment of the Hotel are bowsers and oil supplies, for the ever-present motorist. Central heating and electric elevator .... In the summer days the wants of the tourist are well catered for in the matter of ice cream, cooling drinks, and general picnic requirements.*[652]

This 'mountain guest house'[653] could accommodate around 60 guests, and was designed in the Spanish mission style. One of the architects involved was William Bloomfield, the first Māori to practise as an architect in the country.[654] However, for all its opulence, modernity and its slightly exotic setting,[655] the timing proved unfortunate. The hotel struggled to attract guests as the Depression sunk its teeth deeper into the economy in the 1930s. Its principal source of revenue was the restaurant and tearoom, and the hotel limped along until 1942, when the Education Department acquired it as a school for the deaf.[656] However, while the Depression took with one hand, it gave with the other. As one of the government's work schemes, 200 'unemployed married men of Auckland City and suburbs' were employed at this time in the construction of what was originally named the Waitakere Ridgeway Drive, but which soon became known as the Scenic Drive.[657] This eventually provided a 16-kilometre route from Titirangi to Swanson. Unlike other arterial routes of this length built in Auckland, though, carving a road through forest on the edge of the urban area did not lead to the development of the surrounding lands. There was some pressure for this to happen, but local authorities pushed the government into taking measures to protect the forest in the vicinity of Titirangi, and in 1941 the Auckland Centennial Memorial Park Act was passed, which created 'a Scenic Park, to be known as the Auckland Centennial Memorial Park'.[658]

While some Aucklanders relished venturing into their local Arcadia to exercise their imaginations as well as their bodies in the bucolic serenity of the Waitākere Ranges, others were being drawn to the engine-whining, fume-belching, dust-churning spectacle of speedway. From 1923 to 1934, these modified cars were raced in Māngere on land leased from the Auckland Harbour Board by George Henning.[659] The racing then moved to a new circuit in Onehunga, and from there to Western Springs in 1937, where it remained for the remainder of the century. The first races there, involving 'miniature racing cars', or midget cars, took place in December 1937,[660] and it was soon attracting crowds of up to 21,000,[661] at a time when Auckland's urban population was just over 210,000.[662] The spectacle of cars racing in circles was said to be 'keen and exciting', and at one meeting in January 1938, 'a couple of thrills were provided when two of the miniature cars caught fire, although in both instances a very promising blaze was quickly got under control'.[663]

Less inflammatory entertainment was on offer in some of Auckland's dance halls and nightclubs, which were offering a more sophisticated and varied range of entertainment than had been the case even just a decade earlier. And it was spreading from the city centre out into the suburbs. In Mt Eden's Crystal Palace Theatre (where among the first movies in Auckland had been screened) there were regular Saturday-night dances, with hundreds of people shuffling and jumping on the dance floor to one of the city's most popular jazz bands: Epi Shalfoon and his 'Melody Boys'. Shalfoon took up residence at the theatre in 1934, and remained a regular performer there for the next 19 years. Part of his popularity was due to his band's appearance on the radio station 1ZB, in the 'Musicians' Ball' segment, but Shalfoon also took care of the business side as well, including the establishment of what he termed the 'dance band bureau', in which eight jazz bands (of various sizes) were available for just about any function that required them. It was, in effect, a band franchise, and the service remained popular throughout the 1930s.[664]

Licensing laws dogged the operation of some clubs, though, and on occasion Auckland police showed a thirst for enforcing liquor regulations, partly in response to the fears of moral decay that certain clubs allegedly cultivated. Writing from her own experience, Robin Hyde was sceptical about such claims. 'As a matter of fact,' she recalled, 'having trailed wearily from one cabaret to another during a period of years which I hate to think about, I can't honestly say that I've seen a single youth or maiden in a condition which, were I a police sergeant, I would unhesitatingly docket as "Soused".'[665] Her assessment extended to the Peter Pan Cabaret (on the corner of Rutland and Lorne streets), which was targeted by police late in the evening of 23 July 1931. There were rumours that patrons smuggled in alcohol under their coats, or leaned out of windows to hoist up bottles by string.[666] Undercover police constables, dressed in evening attire, witnessed whisky being poured from bottles by patrons, and at one cubicle 'two couples went out to dance and left an empty whisky bottle exposed to the gaze of the dancers'.[667] Hyde, who was at the Peter Pan Cabaret during the raid, jotted down the farcical nature of the police action:

> *That occasion was rather fun. The humour was made all the more pointed by the fact that Auckland's Mayor, Mr. Geo W. Hutchison ... a man of most temperate habits, was among those present. He bore it manfully, but didn't look happy. Everyone, at first, had two theories: one was that the police squad was part of a rag: the other was that the police squad felt thirsty. There was much tasting of glass contents, anyhow.*[668]

For those Aucklanders who sought less raucous surrounds, and had what they believed to be more refined musical tastes, the formation of the Dorian Singers of Auckland in 1936 (by Albert Bryant, who remained as the choir's conductor until 1941)[669] catered to some of their cultural needs. The choir was comprised of trained singers (including many of the city's singing teachers) and had as one of its aims 'to introduce to the public, works which are of the highest cultural value, but which are seldom heard in New Zealand'.[670] On 14 May 1936 the Dorian Choir (as it was popularly known almost from its inception) gave its inaugural performance in the Concert Chamber in the Town Hall where, probably for the first time in the country, Rossini's *Stabat Mater* was performed. The concert was regarded as a success, although one critic remarked how there was 'room for improvement'.[671] The performance might have been more earnest than expert, but for those of the city's residents eager to appear (and be seen) at more cultivated events, such concerts were a welcome addition to Auckland's cultural calendar.

The social expanse between various cliques and classes in Auckland was continuing to widen during this decade, but not just for the usual disparities in income and education that accompanies any growing society. For the city's British-rooted majority, the growing ethnic diversity of Auckland was becoming harder to overlook. One of the signs of this diversity during this era was the emergence of clubs and societies based around particular immigrant communities. For many of the members of these clubs, English was a second language, and New Zealand society remained largely a foreign culture, and so, naturally, the desire to meet and socialise with people from the same country of origin drew some Aucklanders to found groups to enable this interaction. One of these was the Yugoslav Society, which was established in 1930 with the merging of the Yugoslav Club and the Yugoslav Benevolent Society. On arrival in Auckland, many Yugoslav immigrants — most of whom were from what is now Croatia — found accommodation in boarding houses in the vicinity of Hobson and Victoria streets. And as with any concentration of immigrants, their presence aroused adverse reactions among a few of the city's residents, as the *New Zealand Herald* reported in 1931: 'This really is a natural development. Foreign communities anywhere tend to "hive" and it is not surprising that Slavs have .... There is also the influence of race, and no doubt another factor is that the prejudice exhibited the world over by those in possession to a foreign element tends to create a "quarter."' There were accusations made that Yugoslavs in Auckland were manufacturing alcohol illegally at this time, to which the newspaper responded that 'while, perhaps, these foreigners may be inclined to regard our licensing laws as absurd, it remains to be proved whether the proportion of them who flout the laws is greater than in the British community'.⁶⁷² The Yugoslav Society occupied a building in New North Road, in Eden Terrace (which was renamed the Dalmatian Cultural Society following the dissolution of Yugoslavia in the 1990s), and in addition to weekly functions at 'the club', as it was referred to by members, there were annual events, such as balls and picnics. The Dalmatian author Amelia Batistich wrote a vignette of one of these picnics, which captures in a certain way how this specific group of Aucklanders saw themselves, and how their immigrant experience set them apart from their non-Dalmatian neighbours.

> *And the matchmakers, whose daughters are already married, or are not yet old enough, or who have no daughters. They sit together and watch and nod — this boy and that girl — that boy and this girl. It is the eternal business they are on, the securing of generations, the carrying on of names. Each village has its ... representation here, excluding the pretensions of others .... Names caught in the cobwebs of history, all that richness given to new ground, its children given to a new race. In these far antipodes, who will remember Dalmatia in a thousand years? Yet something must survive. In the high cheekbone, in the black eyes, the gesture of a hand, it will be there unsung.*⁶⁷³

There was an unmistakable melancholia in such transitions from immigrant to local, as Batistich rendered it. The process might take a few years or a few generations, but it was precisely out of such amalgamations that Auckland's identity was becoming more intricately marbled.

Help

In the nineteenth century, Patumāhoe was 'a small native village'⁶⁷⁴ around 18 kilometres west of Papakura, bordering the upper course of the Taihiki River, and by the early decades of the twentieth century it was known mainly for its success as a potato-growing district.⁶⁷⁵ It was on these stretches of flat land that the government made the decision in 1927 to build a new 'mental hospital' to service Auckland,⁶⁷⁶ replacing the small, relatively makeshift facility that was already on the site. By 1928 the government reported that '[g]ood progress has been made in the development of this new institution for the Auckland Province', and that '[t]he population of this institution has increased far beyond the limit which is recognized to make for the highest efficiency, and 110 additions to patients' accommodation are contemplated'.[677] Kingseat was the location in Patumāhoe where this facility would be built, with the intention that it would be the most advanced of its type in the country.[678] There had been a surge in the number of people needing institutional care following the First World War, with ex-servicemen suffering from conditions that were regarded as incurable.[679] At the same time, concerns were being expressed from a number of quarters that the country's 'public asylums' were defective, leaving patients prone to abuse.[680]

Kingseat opened in 1931 (after two years of construction), and in one of those anomalies that plague small, new cities, a shortage of local architects forced the government to employ British-trained ones. Consequently, when the director of the hospital insisted that the patients' room face the sun (for their therapeutic benefit),[681] the architects accordingly designed these rooms to be south-facing, perhaps as a reflex response stemming from their northern hemisphere training.[682] Within six years, though, the hospital was already overcrowded, with over a hundred patients squeezed into its facilities. Not only did Kingseat's accommodation need to be expanded, but 'ample provision' had to be made 'for all the most modern forms of treatment, including massage, continuous baths, light, electricity ... X-rays ... a laboratory, dispensary, and operating-theatre'.[683]

All this was understandable from a medical viewpoint, but surprisingly, public perception about mental health issues in this decade was far removed from that of the Victorian era, when a patient would be 'submitted to depressing treatment that alone would have sufficed to drive the healthiest to madness'.[684] Instead, the *Auckland Star* advised its readers in 1937 that '[i]t is particularly necessary to have the type of hospital where the patient can live in an environment most nearly approaching the normal, because in this way lies most hope for the patients' ultimate cure'.[685]

Another advance in what was seen as an enlightened approach to health came from the Auckland Community Sunshine Association. It was formed in the late 1920s with the aim of offering health camps for children who were underprivileged. The Association took up residence in a former school building in Nelson Street and, with the support of the Health Department,[686] engaged in a vigorous programme of fundraising in order to pay for its first camps.[687] Auckland's Jewish Girls' Club held a dance to raise money for the camps, jumble sales were organised, Auckland businessman Louis Arnoldson provided a venue on Waiheke Island for the first camp, and the Union Steam Ship Company offered free transport to take the children to the venue.[688] From 1931, the camps took place on the 179-hectare Motuihe Island.[689] Located in the channel between Waiheke and Rangitoto islands, Motuihe had served as an internment camp for German prisoners in the First World War,[690] and immediately afterwards as a quarantine station during the influenza epidemic.[691] The buildings on the island could accommodate around 80 children, and the Association provided a cohort of staff that included specialists in physical education, nurses and teachers. At its height, up to 1500 children spent time at the health camp on the island every year.

In 1930 the Health Department reported on the work of the Association, emphasising that its object was 'to improve the health of the children, especially those of school age who are undernourished or who suffer from frequent illness which interferes with their education and with their development into healthy men and women'.[692] Among those attending the camps were children 'suffering from debility or malnutrition and tuberculosis', or who came from difficult 'home circumstances'.[693] In 1937 six-year-old Marjorie Hennum, along with her sister, attended one of these camps on Motuihe Island, and later recalled aspects of her experience:

> *We were sent there because we were too thin and skinny. They came through our school and picked us out so we were sent to the Camp to get some fresh air and exercise and to fatten up .... My sister and I were put in different dormitories which didn't help our homesickness .... We were woken by a bell every day and we all had tasks to do before school. Mine was to polish the brass doorknobs, which seemed to be a waste of time to me. We also had PT — physical exercises — on the courtyards between the dormitories before school started as well .... I don't remember exactly what we ate but there was all the food you could eat! We hadn't seen so much food in all our lives. I remember being allowed to eat pudding before the main course if you wanted. Food was available all day .... My family was poor .... We had a vegetable garden but there wasn't ever food to spare. We had very few clothes — mainly just one set of everyday wear. We*

couldn't afford sheets on the beds either. We slept on the bare mattresses with a blanket over us. On cold nights we would put the coats we could find over us, and there was always a race to grab the tablecloth as well.[694]

This degree of poverty was portrayed by one Auckland church minister as a 'creeping paralysis' moving through the city, while another likened it to 'a canker which is eating right down into our social life', and a 'vicious system', warning that 'it is not fair to the rising generation, and if we don't try to improve it they will rise up and curse us'.[695] However, for all the hand-wringing over the descent into seemingly ever-deeper pits of poverty, there was only so much that individuals could do. Churches offered assistance where they could, but often many in their own congregations were facing similar circumstances to those of the recipients of their aid. And likewise with the children's health camps — the support they depended on came from a very narrow range of benefactors, meaning that they could only offer temporary respite[696] from the corrosive poverty that was evident throughout the city. Although the arc of the Depression was drawing to a close by the second half of the 1930s,[697] for those in the grip of often ruinous poverty there was no certainty when, or even if, things would improve. Hard times might not last for ever, but if a family lost their assets, their house, their business, their employment or their health, the struggle to crawl back to their pre-Depression levels of relative prosperity would be gruelling.

Help was on its way, though. The election of the country's first Labour Government in 1935 heralded a new approach to welfare and housing, with the state playing a significant role in both of these areas. There had been earlier attempts by the state in providing housing for the poor,[698] but these were comparatively small-scale, and certainly not designed to deal with the crisis delivered by the Depression. In an effort to understand the extent of the housing problem that the country faced, the United–Reform coalition government organised a survey of the situation.[699] The government's view was that the cost of new houses 'must be in keeping with the income of the lowest-paid class of the community'.[700] And the requirement for this became painfully evident when the housing review was completed. Around 13 per cent of Auckland's houses were overcrowded (defined as more than two people having to occupy a bedroom) and 12 per cent were below the minimum standards for a dwelling set by the government.[701] Across the country, there were nearly 7000 houses in urban areas that were so dilapidated that they needed to be demolished, with the situation being so serious in some areas that towards the end of the decade the government contemplated special slum-clearance legislation.[702] There was some debate, though, about what constituted a slum (the New Zealand Town-Planning Institute, for example, claimed in 1934 that there were no slums at all in Auckland), but the fact that in the first half of the 1930s around 2000 houses had been demolished in the city suggests that there was a problem in the quality of residential buildings.[703] However, in replacing residences with new, social housing, there was a fear that one problem might simply be displaced by another. When Auckland Council resolved in November 1935 to raise a loan to pay for the construction of workers' dwellings in Greys Avenue,[704] there was some opposition, on the basis that concentrated residential living in the city centre would turn the proposed new development into some sort of ghetto.[705] Meanwhile, the trickle of Māori entering the city in search of employment were finding it especially hard to secure accommodation. A combination of discrimination by landlords and low incomes forced many of these arrivals to exist in some of the city's worst inner-city hovels.[706] In the rural outskirts of Auckland, though, the situation was, if anything, even worse:

> *The conditions under which Maoris are living in Pukekohe have been described as deplorable by those who have taken the trouble to investigate the position for themselves .... Today the position is worse than ever, it having reached a state of alarm. At no stage during the depression, when thousands were unemployed, did death take such a heavy toll as it has during the last few months, of Maori children in Pukekohe. .... There may be cases elsewhere where the housing of Maoris is not all that could be desired but they cannot, by any stretching of the imagination, approach anywhere near the deplorable conditions existing in Pukekohe. When upwards of 20 Maori children die, due to the inadequacy of housing, it is time something was done and that quickly, to arrest this appalling death rate.*[707]

Auckland's housing crisis was not just one of crumbling standards. The scarcity of housing was becoming more acute due to changes in occupancy rates. Over the whole of the country, the average number of people per dwelling fell from 4.28 persons per household in 1921 to 3.9 by 1936.[708] Claims were even made that housing conditions were responsible for the country's falling birth rate, with women obtaining abortions because of the inadequate housing conditions they were enduring.[709] In response to the desperation of so many in the face of the worsening accommodation shortage, towards the end of 1936 the plans for a major state housing scheme for the nation were firming up. One of the guiding principles the government insisted on was that the houses would be built from the best materials and to the highest standards, so that they would end up being 'better than ... houses inhabited by ordinary typical citizens'.[710] The designs of these state houses would be modern, but also, varied. This was so that they would be unidentifiable as state houses, and their occupants would therefore not feel any stigma about living in them.[711] One anonymous state house tenant (who had previously worked at the Ōtāhuhu railway workshops) wrote to the Minister of Finance, Walter Nash, in 1938, about the standard of his house, concluding with the observation that 'I can safely say that from a practical point of view that the materials, workmanship and design are the best I have ever seen put into houses. I have, therefore, always replied to any adverse criticism by those who know nothing about building but condemn the houses on hearsay.'[712] Another principle on which the state house model was based was that the prevailing nature of New Zealand domestic life be retained. This meant that the roles men and women fulfilled at home would not be altered, with men — as breadwinners — travelling to and from work each day — while women remained at home, tending to the children, doing the housework and supporting their husbands when they returned home from work.[713]

On 3 May 1937, construction commenced on Auckland's first state house, in Coates Avenue, Ōrākei,[714] and on the morning of 10 December the first tenants moved in. The occupants were the Bonham family. The father, Jack Bonham, was a physical director at the YMCA (from 1932 until 1961),[715] and lived in the house with his wife and two young children.[716] By the end of the year, demand for state houses had grown beyond the ability of the state to keep up,[717] and in the following decade, '[t]he homes of the town workers ate wide into the country, red-roofed, with their small gardens, concrete paths, and modern sanitation. The red-and-yellow "trams de luxe" carried them clanging to their work, some of them in this period a little less regularly to work',[718] as Mulgan slightly disparagingly put it. In December

1939 the Minister of Housing visited Auckland, and announced that the city now had 1842 state houses, with a further 784 under construction. The bulk of these homes had been built in Ōrākei, Pt Chevalier, Mt Albert, One Tree Hill and Grey Lynn, while Takapuna, Mission Bay, Onehunga and Ellerslie had few if any state houses.[719] The buildings were modelled on English cottage designs (with many having central corridors reminiscent of villa layout), and were small, functional, street-facing, with many components (such as doors and window frames) being mass-produced.[720] Garages were also included in an increasing number of state houses in Auckland at this time, and it was a condition of tenancies that cars could not be parked on the property of a state house unless they were in a garage. If there was no garage, though, a car could be parked on the section, but only if there was a kerb crossing (and if there was not, the tenant would have to install one at their own expense in order to be permitted to park their car on their property).[721]

State housing was introduced not to replace private property, but to complement it. Born out of the desperation of the Depression, these dwellings not only alleviated the risk of homelessness for hundreds (and later thousands) of Auckland families, but enabled the city's workforce to grow, and in that sense were a productive addition to Auckland's economic as well as built landscape. And crucially for the character of Auckland's social make-up, this early, experimental stage in state housing did not produce an identifiable underclass in the city. There were no 'state house people' confined to conclaves of visible destitution. However, there were segments of Auckland society that, according to one newspaper editor in 1938, were falling through the cracks of this state-sponsored utopia. These were people 'who have enjoyed little or no increase in their incomes — retired people living on the yield from fixed-interest securities, widows, superannuitants and so on. They represent a forgotten class and find their means shrinking as prices rise. Many are being severely pinched by Labour's regime but are too independent to cry their need.'[722] The fissures of class, wealth, ethnicity and, increasingly, location were becoming more conspicuous as Auckland was maturing and enlarging. The chimerical hope of an egalitarian civic society still clung to Auckland's collective consciousness[723] but the reality of a classless city had long since been exiled.

6
The 1940s

Behind enemy lines

Not since John Logan Campbell's death in 1912 had there been a funeral like it. Michael Joseph Savage — affably referred to as 'Mickey' Savage by his many acolytes in the country — succumbed to cancer on 27 March 1940 (a few days short of his sixty-eighth birthday). The prime minister's death had been anticipated, but when news of it broke, the shock was no less severe. The 1940 Labour Party conference was being held at the time, and when attendees were told that Savage had passed away, a 'deep silence, broken only by the sound of subdued sobbing, filled the conference hall'.[724] That silence and sobbing soon echoed across the country. This secular saint, who in the popular imagination had wrested New Zealand from the clench of the Depression, was now dead. Just how much of a presence Savage had been in people's lives can be gauged by the fact that thousands of Auckland homes had, above their mantlepiece, a framed picture of the avuncular saviour of the nation.[725]

Savage died in Wellington, and after lying in state for two days, his body was brought to Auckland, where it would be interred in Bastion Point (Takaparawhā). Formerly Fort Bastion, the site had been a harbour-defence gun emplacement in the 1880s, and before that, part of a pre-

European Māori settlement.[726] As the train carrying the casket arrived at the Ōtāhuhu railyard, workers held a spontaneous ceremony — their way of expressing their sorrow and gratitude. Meanwhile, the gorse and rubbish that had accumulated on Bastion Point for years was quickly being cleared, and the old military road rebuilt by a team of 60 Public Works Department staff — a job that was completed in just one day.[727]

The train reached Auckland Railway Station shortly after two o'clock in the afternoon on 31 March.[728] Already by that time, mourners were gathering in huge numbers along the five-kilometre route that the cortège would take to Bastion Point. As one of those present recorded, the procession took place 'in the golden sunshine of a late summer afternoon', with extra train and bus services being put on to accommodate those who wished to pay their respects to the former prime minister. This went beyond partisan political loyalties. It was as though history and grief were converging at this location. Certainly, it was a 'never-to-be-forgotten spectacle'[729] for the city:

The flashing bayonets and service uniforms of the armed escort, the interludes of native ceremonial and the burial service, carried out in accordance with the ancient rites of the Roman Catholic Church, all combined to make an occasion of impressive solemnity. The humble spirit of the man whose memory was being honoured found its true reflection in the hushed and reverent crowd of at least 200,000 people who lined the route of the funeral procession and thronged the green slopes around the burial ground .... the casket was placed on a gun carriage. Preceded by an armed escort, the funeral procession commenced its ... journey to the heights of Orakei. On the green headland that is Fort Bastion, the cortege made its way through a hushed crowd, and then the casket was borne to the catafalque, where the burial service was conducted by Bishop Liston. The casket was then raised for the last time to be carried through an avenue of wreaths into the dim quiet of the burial chamber.[730]

At no other time in Auckland's history had such a proportion of people attended a single event. More than 200,000 people were present to witness the procession of Savage's casket in Auckland at a time when the city's urban population was just over 221,500. But after the mass of crowds had dispersed, the casket containing Savage was removed and placed in a small chapel attached to St Patrick's Cathedral in Wyndham Street, so that it would 'not be disturbed by rock-blasting operations' at Bastion Point while the permanent tomb was being constructed.[731] It was not until 1942 that the works at Bastion Point were complete. Auckland architects Tibor Donner and Anthony Bartlett had designed a memorial that was expansive and unlike any other commemorative edifice in the city (and was the last major example of Art Deco architecture in Auckland). On top of the mausoleum was an obelisk, which towered over the forecourt, that was comprised of a sunken memorial garden and reflective pool, all symmetrically laid out and dissected by paths, low hedges and flower beds.[732] It remains the largest memorial to any New Zealand prime minister. Yet, apart from the small relief of Savage on the base of the obelisk, there is an almost startling lack of iconography anywhere. The design was tactful and discreet, with the spaciousness of the memorial making it a place where absence becomes mournful substance.

Savage's funeral took place while New Zealand (along with the rest of the Empire) was at war with Germany. At the outbreak of the Second World War, six months earlier, the prime minister had committed the nation to the conflict in one of his most memorable lines: '[W]e range ourselves without fear beside Britain. Where she goes, we go, where she stands, we stand.'[733] It was stirringly patriotic without being bellicose. In a way, this reflected how far the mood of the country had shifted in the last two and a half decades. The *Boy's Own* thrill evident at the start of the First World War had matured into adult apprehension by this time.

By the beginning of 1940, Auckland was already shuffling to a war footing. Things were a bit different now, though, from how they had been at the outbreak of the First World War. Then, the fighting was taking place on another continent. Local communities provided men, money and materials, and then waited for news on the progress of the conflict. Now, though, advances in military technology, coupled with the greater geographical scope of the war, meant that New Zealand could be a target in the fighting, rather than a faraway contributor and observer. Thus, the surge of enthusiasm to support the war effort was strong from the outset. Since October 1939, Auckland volunteers had been training in Papakura and Ngāruawāhia, and on holidays their khaki-clad presence in the city was one of the more visible signs that the country was at war. Now, they were ready for battle, or so they felt. On 3 January 1940, troops comprising the first echelon of the Second Expeditionary Force paraded at a civic farewell organised at the Domain, just prior to their departure. These troops (some veterans of the Great War, but most new volunteers) were '[s]plendid in their bearing [as] they marched with conscious pride'[734] in sight of the cenotaph honouring the city's dead from the previous world war. There was also, it has to be said, a certain cachet in enlisting — that 'aura of here-today-and-gone-tomorrow about them, a hint of force and danger …. In the streets the sound of heavy black boots, moving in rapid groups, made heads turn with a tinge of awe, a self-conscious awareness of their protectors.'[735] Various means were deployed in Auckland to maintain recruitment levels throughout 1940. Vans drove around beaches and sports grounds, blaring out recruitment messages on loudspeakers; concert parties were held where recruiting sergeants would be present; on a few occasions, planes took off from Hobsonville airbase and flew over the city dropping leaflets known as 'bomphlets', which urged men to sign up; and recruitment 'barometers' were prominently positioned to illustrate the growing enlistment numbers.[736]

By the end of the year, though, this burst of martial fervour was in retreat. A ballot system had been introduced to conscript men, but by December more than 28 per cent of those drawn from the ballot had lodged appeals with the Auckland Area Manpower Committee. Employers, arguing that they could not afford to lose their staff, were the main category of appellant, followed by those men who argued that they had family members who were dependent on them, and who would suffer hardship in their absence. Of the 2886 appeals lodged in Auckland in 1940, around 300 were on the basis of conscientious objections to war.[737] Typically, these objectors opposed their conscription not on the basis that the war did not have a moral cause, but that the act of fighting was contrary to their beliefs. Support came from some quarters of the churches. The Congregationalists went further than most denominations, supporting 'the right of a sincere objector to a sympathetic hearing by an appeal board, on which should be one person competent to understand such scruples; [and] that ministers and church leaders should assist sincere objectors by advice and testimony'.[738] There were also secular bodies offering to aid those who were morally opposed to fighting, but they were forced to operate more in the shadows. The Auckland Conscientious Objectors' Advisory Committee was one such body. It distributed circulars in 1940 asking those who were called up on the ballot to write to a post-box address where they would get further details on how to oppose their conscription. However, the group advised respondents that 'if you do not receive a prompt reply, you will know your letter has been retained or delayed by the censor'.[739] The government was not completely unsympathetic to some of the arguments, but Bob Semple, the Minister of National Service, cautioned churches in particular that '[w]e do not want wholesale exemptions .... If we are too liberal and too sympathetic with the fellow who wants to dodge we will have trouble.'[740]

As part of the campaign to prop up solidarity for the war effort, from 1940, Aucklanders, like the rest of the country, were faced with wide restrictions on expressing their views on the war. Society's unanimity had to be preserved against the common foe, and although it was hard to conceive of a foe more likely to galvanise the nation against it than Nazi Germany, censorship was imposed by the Labour Government nonetheless, perhaps from the memory of conscientious objectors among its own ranks in the First World War, and the potentially demoralising effect this could have on the war effort. On 11 February 1940 the ailing prime minister made one of his final broadcasts to the country, warning precisely of the risks to a united front that unfettered expressions of opinions could have. 'Freedom, such as we enjoy[,] breeds the truest patriots; but', and here was the argument against such freedoms, 'its genial climate permits also the growth of cranks, and ingrates; of dreamers of fantastic dreams; of ideological freaks, oddities and ne'er-do-wells; a diversity of creatures having ... in common, the urge to propagate error'.[741] Within days, regulations to this effect were introduced. Peter Fraser, the Minister of Police, but in many ways the de facto prime minister as Savage's health deteriorated, explained the wide scope of these restrictions: 'freedom to incite damage, and do injury to New Zealand and New Zealand's war effort is not freedom of speech; freedom to sabotage this country by deliberately disseminating false statements is not freedom of thought; endeavouring to prevent men enlisting is not political freedom ... but a gross abuse of freedom'.[742] Society was now caught in a web of censorship, where any reckless comment could have serious repercussions for those involved. Given enough time, it is possible that people would have grown restless with these impositions on their freedoms, but Aucklanders were soon to get a taste of how real and direct the threat of the war was to them.

On 13 June 1940 the German raider *Orion*, disguised as a merchant ship,[743] slipped into New Zealand waters with a cargo of 228 mines. German Naval Command had ordered the ship to lay moored contact mines across the east coast approaches to Auckland. Shortly after sunset, with the weather fine and calm, the ship's crew began laying the first row of mines, stretching from Great Mercury Island (Ahuahu) to Cuvier Island (Rēpanga). Once this was accomplished, the *Orion* sailed north to lay an additional cluster of mines in parts of Colville Channel and around Great Barrier Island (Aotea). The biggest barrage of mines was the set from Great Barrier Island extending around the Mokohinau and Hen and Chickens Islands (Taranga and Marotere). Over the seven hours that this task took, the crew on the *Orion* spotted four vessels passing by, but none detected anything suspicious about this enemy ship. As soon as the final set of mines was laid, the *Orion* steamed northeast at full speed, away from New Zealand.[744]

The string of mines that the Germans had laid around the Hauraki Gulf now acted as a noose on Auckland's shipping, and it was only a matter of time before a vessel fell victim to these explosive devices. Shortly before four o'clock on the morning of 19 June, the 13,500-ton Royal Mail steamer *Niagara*, which had just departed Auckland for Suva, struck one of the mines and sank within two hours. First reports mentioned an explosion, but its cause was initially uncertain. However, by that evening it had been established that the vessel had struck a mine.[745] Although no lives were lost (apart from the ship's cat), the shock of the event reverberated throughout the entire country, but especially Auckland. When more mines were discovered a week later, the city's port was closed until a minesweeping operation could be undertaken. Among the city's population, there was palpable apprehension born of the realisation that the tentacles of Nazi Germany had now stretched into the Waitematā Harbour.

In the wake of the *Niagara*'s sinking, there was the predictable bout of finger-pointing among officials and politicians as they attempted to direct blame for the seemingly effortless way in which the enemy had so successfully avoided detection when laying its mines,[746] but recriminations did little to settle the anxiety of many Aucklanders. In the days that followed, there was so much fear and panic among some of the city's residents that Auckland's telephone system became completely congested. An urgent radio appeal had to be broadcast, requesting that calls be limited to essential business only.[747] Aucklanders could almost inhale the scent of war by this time. It was no longer something that happened 'over there', but very much a threat that now loomed 'right here'. This fear of the country's vulnerability intensified after the bombing of Pearl Harbor (1941) and the fall of Singapore (1942).[748] After all, who would there be to protect the nation if the enemy continued its advance in the region?

This foreboding undoubtedly energised undertakings at home to support the war. Across Auckland, the 'war effort quickened, giving shape and life to all departments for home defence',[749] with one of the first lines of this defence being the Home Guard. Initially established under the provisions of the Emergency Precautions Scheme,[750] the Home Guard was formally constituted in August 1940,[751] just two months after the *Niagara* sinking. The head of the Auckland Home Guard revealed, however, that the resistance it could offer to an enemy invasion would be more symbolic than substantial:

> *We had been issued with a few thousand rifles, some old machine guns and, of course, our armbands. We made up with impressed pea rifles and shot-guns and also had large numbers of Jam Tin Grenades and Molotov Cocktails stored up ready for use .... In January ... I was given the job of forming a highly secret force ... In case of invasion this portion of the Home Guard, after acting as guides to any of our troops in their area, was to go into prepared hideouts as the Japs passed through and then generally play the devil behind the enemy lines.*[752]

As the war progressed, Aucklanders began to experience various privations. There were ration books with coupons that were needed to purchase essential items and foods. Shortages affected butter, sugar, meat, vegetables and tea supplies — the staples of most households[753] — ironically in part because the country was exporting so much of the food it produced to its allies.

Some of the efforts to prepare for the perpetually imminent invasion were perhaps aimed partly at consoling Aucklanders that they were at least doing something worthwhile. Boys at King's College, in Ōtāhuhu, dug trenches in the sports field, but when a siren was sounded for a drill, one student observed the manner in which everyone rushed to these shallow pits: 'It wasn't very well organised because a whole crowd would go to one trench and there would be another trench nobody had gone to

.... I don't think anybody was taking it as seriously as they should. Before I left school in 1942, I think we filled them [the trenches] in.'[754] Defences at home were just as rudimentary, and just as futile. One Aucklander created an air-raid shelter at home from an old septic tank: '[f]ive or six of us could get in there .... [It was a h]uge concrete tank, very big too in those days. We just broke into the side of it, and we only played in it. Nobody ever thought of going into it really.'[755]

On the work front, in January 1942 the government introduced what became popularly known as 'manpower'.[756] This enabled the state to direct labour to areas where it was most needed, and ironically — given its name — led to a surge in women entering the workforce.[757] (This required adjustments in some cases, such as the Auckland Power Board reversing its previous policy of not employing married women.)[758] By the end of 1942 it was a common sight in the city to see women driving delivery vans, labouring in factories, doing clerical work that was formerly the preserve of men, driving taxis and working on trams (where Auckland authorities calculated that although it would take 12 women to do the job of ten, they would be 30 per cent cheaper to employ).[759]

Prior to the war, it was common for women in paid employment to leave their jobs once they were married. The reasons for this ranged from the opinion that to do so constituted being a 'good wife', to the belief that by remaining at home, men would not have to compete with women for work.[760] It was a view of the construct of work and families that the government supported,[761] and it was only the extreme labour demands imposed by the war that accelerated the shift of women out of the home and into paid employment. This shift of women into areas of work previously dominated by men was not seen universally as a progressive move. There was 'an almost masculine plainness' among women, according to one female writer, which had 'ousted the fulness and the fripperies' of the past. 'Women dress the part as they face up to war-time tasks. Clothes consciousness is apparent only in the cut of a garment, and in unobtrusive accessory touches.'[762] Form was following function in fashion, but there were bigger concerns surrounding women's participation in the workforce. Some saw a social cost attached to this relatively sudden exodus of women from their 'rightful' place at home. For a start, there was little in the way of professional childcare services available in Auckland, leaving many mothers constantly making arrangements with friends and relatives for the care of their children while they were at work. There was an additional anxiety that some social workers expressed over women — or more accurately, girls — entering the workforce. 'The problem of young girls in Auckland is grave,' one social worker wrote, 'and it all goes back to lack of parental control. If we are fighting for the future of our race, we must look after our race. There is something wrong in our planning if we have to ride to victory on the backs of our 12-year-olds.'[763]

The other, more widespread, contribution that Auckland women made to the war effort was in the form of what was called 'patriotic fundraising'. Although some men were involved in this drive, many of the activities were organised and led by women. One of the more popular forms of fundraising were the Paddy's markets, where the public were offered a cornucopia of homemade specialities to purchase, with proceeds going to support the troops. Jams, preserved fruit, pickles, fruit, cakes (especially sponges), scones, pikelets and sandwiches were stacked on stalls along with children's clothing, knitted tea cosies, flowers, aprons and the odd outgrown toy or doll thrown in.[764] Such events served as a way of demonstrating community solidarity, and of enabling people to feel that they were doing something practical to assist with the war effort.

Spurred on by the growing demand for money and other forms of support, there were also spontaneous gestures of assistance throughout Auckland at this time. The staff of Flamingo Frocks, in Queens Arcade in lower Queen Street, for example, decided to raise funds for the military hospital at Narrow Neck on the North Shore. They managed to collect a sufficient amount to purchase various items for the hospital, and also donated their own time to make bedding and pyjamas for the patients.[765] This initiative was 'entirely the girls' effort', and came about through staff discussing how best they could assist with the war. Such was their commitment that they contributed a total of £35 from their miserable earnings in order to purchase materials.[766] And throughout the city, there were similar ad hoc efforts by groups keen to play their part,[767] and perhaps also motivated by the fear that if not enough was done, then the country would be that bit more vulnerable to attack.

An invasion of Auckland commenced in 1942, but by a friendly force. On 12 June the first shipment of American troops from the 145th Regiment of the 37th Division, US Army, arrived in the city.[768] However, this military migration was carried out in secrecy (as much as the movement of thousands of men could be kept secret), and it was only in later months that the details began to be made public. The initial stages of this cultural encounter were cordial, no doubt motivated by the fact that Auckland's residents and their American guests shared a common enemy. The editor of the *Auckland Star* offered an assessment of the situation at the beginning of September, which was cordial, but also with a subtle measure of restraint. As much as these American saviours were welcomed, it was still a case of 'their ways are not our ways'. Both sides would clearly need to adjust to some degree to accommodate each other:

> *Actual experience, supporting first impressions, enables all New Zealanders who have had contact with the Americans to endorse wholeheartedly the tribute which Mr. Fraser in the United States has paid them. "They have impressed us by their physique and soldierly bearing, and particularly by their courtesy and discipline." They have also impressed us by a quality of open-mindedness which is refreshing and exemplary. Their presence in our midst should be regarded as a unique opportunity — an opportunity for all of us to meet them in the spirit of goodwill which in them is evident, and to create a relationship between New Zealanders and Americans that will remain sweet and strong long after they depart, and endure in the days of peace.*[769]

The government attempted to smooth the temporary integration of American troops by issuing a book — *Meet New Zealand* — which was an effort to explain some of the idiosyncrasies of the local culture. Linguistic differences were prominent in the work, with words that remained familiar for the remainder of the century, such as 'Aussie', 'biscuit', 'sheep station', 'scone', 'petrol', being explained for these arrivals. Other terms were also included, like 'cobber' (friend), 'jakealoo' (good), 'sheila' (woman), 'up the pole' (ruined) and 'the dinkum oil' (the real truth),[770] even though, ironically, they would become foreign to future generations of Aucklanders.

The reactions in Auckland to this influx of American soldiers varied. One woman recalled how the United States soldiers 'seemed so different from the New Zealand men that I'd known, they were more courteous, they had more social graces. Or so it seemed at first. But when you got to know them, you found it was all a veneer. They were really very … callow underneath.'[771] Navigating the sexual politics of this occupation was always going to be challenging. The phrase 'getting in trouble' — sometimes spoken in an anxious or condemnatory whisper — was code for the unplanned pregnancies that resulted from some of these liaisons. As one woman remembered from this period, temptation, risks and opportunity were now more overtly present:

> *a lot of girls got into trouble. A lot of girls went to America to live, and a lot of them came back again. They [the American soldiers] weren't so good back home as they were as servicemen .... The Americans were charming of course, all of them. You got the odd one that you had to keep in his place .... I think the first time that I went to Auckland it would have been around 1943/44 .... It was a long journey. I had this young American sit beside me uninvited. And he got a little bit amorous through the night hours. And I was very innocent. I was a virgin when I was married .... so I didn't take too kindly to being attended to like that.*[772]

Even without the presence of foreign temptation, though, sexual dynamics were evolving. Statistics reported by one Auckland newspaper in 1942 revealed that a quarter of all first births were conceived out of wedlock (for which rushed weddings when the evidence emerged prevented the illegitimacy rate from being higher than around the stated 4 per cent).[773] In addition, contraceptive use was widespread, abortions were common, and 'venereal disease, the usual aftermath of war [was] ... spreading like a plague'. The morally troubling conclusion was that 'pre-marital intercourse must be common, and, in spite of claims to the contrary, the results are anything but beneficial to the community'.[774] The reaction of some religious groups to this situation was not always what might be expected. The Women's Christian Temperance Union insisted that the country needed 'to adjust our outlook' on the matter of births occurring outside of marriage: 'the cruel stigma imposed on an unmarried mother by society has played into the hands of the most vicious of social evils — the abortionist'. The organisation stressed that it did not wish to minimise the sanctity of marriage, but 'when a girl falls we should pity her and not brand her child with that filthy name of bastard'.[775] In Auckland, there was a category of homes, 'in the nature of clearing houses', where the children 'are not as a rule detained there for lengthy periods'. Instead, these homes were where young children born out of marriage were admitted on a temporary basis before being adopted.[776] For those not adopted, they remained in one of Auckland's 14 orphanages, which relied largely on donations from the Auckland Rotary Club, along with street collections and bequests in people's wills.[777] Institutions such as the Leslie Presbyterian Orphanage, the Manurewa Children's Homes, the Henry Brett Memorial Home, the Methodist Children's Home and Orphanage in Mt Albert, and the Salvation Army Girls' Home at Ponsonby were all regularly engaged in public appeals to cover the costs of those hundreds of Auckland children who for various reasons were without parents.

Paint, victory and beyond

The glorification of 'our boys' doing battle with 'Jerry', the 'Eyeties', or the 'Japs'[778] persisted for the duration of the war, although it was more measured than the chest-thumping passion that was evident at the beginning of the First World War. By the 1940s, such global conflagrations were no longer seen as adventurous military jaunts, wrapped up in the chivalry of war. Instead, they were something to be endured rather than exalted. The Second World War certainly roused issues of moral ambivalence in a more pronounced way. The sober business of killing had to be set against the evil that the enemy embodied. Auckland artist Lois White grappled with the moral entanglements of the war and its aftermath in the 1940s in a distinct way. While artists in other parts of the country in this era were drawn to regionalist landscape or modernist abstraction, White was more interested in figurative and allegorical themes.[779] Her works from this period convey something of the way the war was seen from home, by a woman, and in an aesthetically moralised manner. White was a graduate of the Elam School of Art, and during the 1940s worked from her family home in Richardson Road, Mt Albert (in the following decade, she moved to Taunton Terrace, Blockhouse Bay, where she painted in a small fibrolite studio at the rear of the house). White avoided sentimentalising the war, but she also shunned emphasising its literal brutality.[780] In her 1941 oil *Victims of Invasion*,[781] the focus was on grieving women who are variously wailing and praying as smoke billows through destroyed buildings around them. Their stylised poses amid the curls of smoke gave the work a rhythmic quality, achieving a sort of choreography of the pangs of lament. Her 1944 work *Collapse*[782] tilted towards a more symbolic rendition of the consequences of war, with the buildings (including a church) and a group of people caught in a vertiginous fall. Society itself was collapsing, literally and figuratively, not from the physical destruction of the war (there are no bombed buildings), but through the malign forces responsible for the conflict. But as soon as the fighting ended, the pessimism dissipated. White's 1948 painting *Jubilation*[783] was inspired by an excited crowd celebrating the announcement of victory. The figures' arms sway and writhe as they dance, in a symbol of liberation from the terror of war. The unrestrained elation on their faces captured the burst of relief that accompanied the end of the conflict.

On 8 May 1945, Aucklanders' spontaneous urge to celebrate the end of the war collided with officials' attempts to delay any public activities relating to the Allies' victory. International time differences meant that Aucklanders woke up to the news of the Victory in Europe (VE) before Londoners were aware of it. Anxious about how premature celebrations might appear to other nations, the government urged people to hold their fire until the official announcement of VE Day had been made, after which there would be various planned events to mark the occasion. Thus, on the day that Nazi Germany was defeated and Europe was liberated, Aucklanders were obliged to go about their normal business, leaving some with the impression that what would eventuate was 'celebration by regulation'.[784] When the festivities were finally allowed, from the following day, they were slightly lacklustre, although still generally joyful. People gathering in Queen Street initially seemed more curious than celebratory.[785] One Auckland newspaper editor was left underwhelmed by the events of that day:

> *It cannot be said that the celebrations on VE Day added to the reputation of the city. The brief service of thanksgiving over, the Auckland crowds were left to their own devices. After their habit, they flowed down the city's main street, a trifle bewildered and with little aim or purpose. The attempts of more sanguine spirits to rouse community singing broke on Auckland's traditional self-consciousness. Processions, begun by youthful enthusiasts, lost cohesion in passive crowds. A little ashamed of the carpet of brown glass, Auckland drifted home, and the celebration was over.*[786]

The most the city was capable of mustering by way of entertainment was the Papakura Camp Band, which after performing at an official event at the Town Hall, marched and played its way down Queen Street. However, the band members then caught a bus and departed, leaving the Salvation Army Band to regale the crowds with a succession of hymn tunes. That afternoon, there were a few sparks of spontaneity among those Aucklanders who had gathered in the city centre, but it was slightly clumsy, with the cheering becoming increasingly more raucous as the day wore on. With nothing planned to occupy the crowds, many saw little other choice than to 'get a skin full of booze'.[787]

Victory over Nazi Germany did not quite denote the end of the war, however. It was not until Japan's surrender on 15 August that the six years of fighting across much of the world was officially over. A public holiday was announced for the country, but yet again, Aucklanders were sluggish rather than passionate in their response. Maybe it was the drizzly winter day that dampened moods, and despite the fact that crowds once again gathered, any sense of excitement seemed absent, and as time went on, and more alcohol was consumed, the atmosphere became even less jovial, and efforts at spontaneous fun more forced. A few people began pushing and shoving, and soon bottles were being hurled through the air. The aftermath was predictable, and represented a deeply disappointing way of the city 'celebrating' the end of the Second World War:

> *Numbers of shop windows were cracked or broken and here and there rough wooden shutters had been nailed into position to avoid further damage to fittings and stock .... Sodden and tattered flags and bunting hung limply from poles or clung wetly to shop and office facades, while the roadway the entire length of Queen Street was coated with a sticky brown slime. Much broken glass had been removed by cleaners overnight, but their efforts were confined principally to the main street .... the side streets were still thickly littered with remnants of bottles and glasses.*

Those most responsible for this mayhem were said to be males aged between 15 and 20:

> *youths who have earned high wages in the past few years and have escaped the discipline of service life .... In semi-drunken*

condition they roved the city in bands of ten, twenty or thirty, completely out of control, hurling bottles, shouting obscenities, and brazenly molesting young girls unfortunate enough to cross their paths. Schoolgirls aged 12 and 14 were pursued screaming down the centre of the street, to have beer forced down their unwilling throats when caught, or handed struggling round a throng of shouting youths to have their faces smothered with alcoholic kisses.[788]

'Fill the land'

Would life be any different, though, or more particularly, any better, after the war? In one way, the conflict that had just ended served as a psychological punctuation point.

'Now that the war is over'[789] was the refrain being heard everywhere. Surely, this was a new, post-war world that would shed most of its pre-war shortcomings? Alluding to the biblical books of Joel and Acts, John Mulgan foresaw with guarded optimism an improved future for the country (albeit one which could appear undermined to a degree by his suicide on 26 April 1945). 'If the old world ends now with this war', he wrote,

I have had visions and dreamed dreams of another New Zealand that might grow into the future on the foundations of the old. This country would have more people to share it. They would be hard-working peasants from Europe that know good land, craftsmen that love making things with their own hands, and all men who want the freedom that comes from an ordered, just community .... few would be rich, none would be poor. They would fill the land and make it a nation.[790]

In the remaining years of this decade, Mulgan's prescription for a modest utopia would play out (to some extent) in Auckland more than anywhere else in the country. Part of the reason for this is that the city was becoming the destination for an influx of arrivals from Europe in the wake of the war.

In 1947 the government introduced the assisted-passage scheme for Britons wanting to immigrate to New Zealand. Already, the source of the country's immigrants was narrow, with around 74 per cent of the overseas-born population coming from England or Ireland, and a further 15 per cent from Australia.[791] British immigrants were chosen on the basis of their occupation, age, marital status and health, and were often directed to particular jobs by the Department of Labour.[792] The purpose of the scheme was to ensure that the workforce was sufficiently skilled to cater for the growing economy,[793] as one British academic noted on the eve of the introduction of the scheme: '[i]n New Zealand there is a feeling that any delay in initiating an immigration policy will mean losing ... potential British settlers ... The New Zealand Government's programme of industrialisation cannot go very far unless the supply of certain grades of labour can be increased.'[794]

New Zealand officials were aware that resettlement could be challenging, so when the first batch of immigrants under the assisted-passage scheme arrived in Auckland on 23 August 1947, they were welcomed on the ship by the mayor, Labour Department personnel, and even the president of the Returned Services' Association. And in a further effort to encourage these arrivals, a truck with loudspeakers was parked next to the ship, and blared out what organisers hoped would be welcoming music, in order to create 'a suitable atmosphere for disembarkation'.[795] One of the officials who had been involved in selecting migrants for the assisted-passage scheme stressed to a New Zealand audience in 1948 the need to make these newcomers feel welcomed, and inadvertently revealed some of the issues Britons encountered on arrival:

> *After ... what the British people went through ... the effects of bombing and the inevitable war tiredness, we promised them that their stay in the Dominion would be made as happy as possible. These youngsters have been through the mill, and they will prove fine citizens, so give them every assistance. It is a big change for them, and many of them are very homesick, even after many months. Letters received from girls sent out showed that they were generally satisfied except regarding the difficulty of securing board with private people. The men are satisfied with quarters except in Public Works camps and such places — and then there is only criticism by those who did not serve in the forces.*[796]

Britons' keenness to relocate to New Zealand was so great by the end of the decade that the government had to build immigration hostels to accommodate them. In Auckland, a men's hostel was established at North Head, with a women's one built at Narrow Neck.[797] The motives for Britons wanting to leave for New Zealand were often a combination of domestic circumstances pushing them, and ideas of what New Zealand might offer them, as one migrant explained:

> *We lived in that grey area of the ... 'poverty stricken' .... It was a time when people were, in many cases, too hard up to pay the rent, so the only recourse was to wheel the furniture on a handcart in the dead of the night to a new address .... With the end of the war the future didn't hold great prospects .... I was corresponding with a friend in New Zealand. I was out of work for the second time and so picked up his challenge to come to New Zealand. I had everything to gain as far as I could see.*[798]

Most immigrants arrived in New Zealand in the 1940s by ship. But also, 15 kilometres in a straight line northwest of central Auckland, on low-lying land bordering the upper Waitematā Harbour, an airfield had been constructed in the 1930s, and from 1945 to 1965 served both as a base for the Royal New Zealand Air Force and as the city's civil international airport. Despite the name of the area (Whenuapai, which translates as 'good earth'), the surrounding land was regarded as marginal for farmers and orchardists. The airport occupied 311 hectares, but the facilities for passengers were limited and rudimentary.[799] Being located in what was still rural Auckland, arrangements for travel had to be made in the city, as one domestic flyer later described: 'in those days most passengers checked in at the NAC Air centre in the city and then took the Johnstones bus to the airport. This bus trip was included in the fare that you had paid, so your trip was literally from town centre to town centre rather than airport to airport as it is now. There was a separate bus dedicated for each scheduled flight.'[800]

By the end of the decade, there were four commercial airlines flying internationally to Whenuapai: Tasman Empire Airlines; New Zealand National Airways Corporation; Pan American World Airways; and British Commonwealth Pacific Airlines. Between them, they carried close to 39,000 passengers overseas annually.[801] For some immigrants from

Europe, their first impression of New Zealand was when they got off the plane at Whenuapai, and it was not always what they anticipated: 'We thought Auckland was a city, and when we arrived, all I could see was fields and cows. I thought "was all of New Zealand like this?" I wanted to get back on the plane and go back home. This wasn't what I expected.'[802]

In addition to immigration, Auckland was just starting to experience the internal population pressures brought about by what became known as the baby boom. The country's pre-war Pākehā birth rate was 2.3 births per woman. In the second half of the 1940s this had risen to over 3.5 births per woman (and continued to grow until reaching its high point in 1961).[803] The causes of this boom lay in a combination of circumstances. The affordability of having a family — that had become such a pronounced consideration for many during the Depression — was now less of a concern. Likewise, the war was now over, and so the social and economic uncertainties of that period were also diminished. There was also the trend of women having children at a younger age, and the emergence of economic circumstances that gave the impression that New Zealand was a good place to bring up children. Those children needed schools, though, and in 1947 the Ministry of Education reported that school enrolments over the previous few years had increased by 10,000[804] (an increase attributable to the school leaving age being raised to 15 in 1944),[805] which led to a further spurt in school establishment and expansion in the suburbs.

Auckland's growth was uneven in the post-war years, however. The inner-city suburbs of Arch Hill, Eden Terrace, Freemans Bay, Grafton, Grey Lynn, Herne Bay, Newmarket, Newton, Parnell and Ponsonby experienced a decline in residents, brought about by the growth of new suburbs, a drop in the perceived status of living in inner-city areas, changes in tastes for houses, the improvement of transport routes connecting the inner city with the suburbs, the spread of state housing in new subdivisions, and the decline in the quality of housing in the inner city.[806] The central suburbs were generally places to avoid having to live in if you possibly could. Meanwhile, Auckland was undergoing a surge of suburban expansion to the east of the central-city area. Point England, Glen Innes and northern Panmure became part of the single largest state housing project in Auckland to that time, and aimed eventually to house 30,000 people.[807] The Viennese architect Ernst Plischke[808] (who had arrived in the country as a refugee from the Nazis in 1939) played a central role in the design of some stages of this vast development. His ambitious intention was *to combine the archetypes of European public space with a rigorous modernist functionality and aesthetic, and a sensible response to the burgeoning technical demands of mid-twentieth-century traffic management. The result was an uneasy truce between the traditional city of enclosed and intimate spaces and the freedom and rawness of the low-density suburb.*[809]

However, his plans were compromised by the government suddenly becoming anxious about the risks of unrestrained urban sprawl. Thus, instead of just going out, officials began to explore something that was still barely present in Auckland residential building: going up. Plischke, along with others involved in the planning and design of these new suburbs, therefore began experimenting with small apartments, duplexes and other variants aimed at higher-density living, while at the same time ensuring that there was just enough variety in the forms of these buildings to prevent the oppressive blandness that typified some of the urban developments in parts of Europe at this time.[810]

Still, though, the population density of urban Auckland was historically low at this time. In 1871, there were 22 people per hectare in the city. By 1915, this had risen to 27 people per hectare as Auckland's population increased. However, by 1945, although the population had nearly doubled over the preceding 30 years, the density level had dropped to just 18 people per hectare.[811] (As a measure of comparison, London at this time had a population density of around 54 people per hectare.)[812]

Compared with the options that existed before the war, this state house development occurring in Auckland's eastern suburbs represented an improvement in the standard of living for tens of thousands of the city's residents. Living rooms would (where practicable) be north-facing to capture as much light and warmth as possible, and each home would have a fireplace, which would serve as a focal point for family life. To minimise a monotony of form, there were several different floor plans used, and houses were constructed at different elevations to assist further in making each dwelling feel distinct from its neighbours.[813]

Monotony could not be avoided altogether, though. The terrain was too non-descript, the sections were unvarying in size and use (garage, clothesline, shed, grapefruit tree), and despite the best of intentions, the handful of designs that promised variation were subsumed by the uniformity imposed by having so many thousands of houses built using mainly standardised parts and materials. This enormous experiment in mass state housing solved what would have otherwise been an accommodation crisis for Auckland, but it also stored up other sorts of problems and pressures for the future.

One of the ways in which Auckland managed to supply labour for this building boom was through the various rehabilitation schemes[814] offered to returning servicemen after the war. The main focus of these schemes was to ease these men back into employment, and where necessary provide them training (mainly in trades such as carpentry) where the demand for such skills was greatest.[815] The *Auckland Star* reported that '[m]en who are going through the comprehensive trade training courses of four and five months in carpentry, bricklaying, plumbing, timber working, sawmilling, and so on, are trained under union instructors, and it is held that these intensive courses are producing better results than did the apprenticeship system'.[816] However, a trade and a job could not magically dissolve the trauma that many soldiers suffered from as a consequence of what they had witnessed and what they had done during the war. 'They'd all seen too much in the war,' the novelist Janet Frame observed. As a result, 'the younger men, transformed into imposter soldiers, came home full of anger and hate not at the declared enemy but at their own country and themselves'.[817] Veterans were often reticent in discussing their experiences,[818] and endured nightmares, irritability and sometimes impairment of functioning as a result of the trauma they experienced.[819] The easiest remedy for a lot of these men was alcohol, along with the camaraderie of other former soldiers. Auckland's Returned Services' Assoc-iation clubs peaked in membership at the close of this decade,[820] offering a sanctuary of sorts for these men in a way that no other institution seemed to manage to anywhere near the same extent. And as for the wives of these returned servicemen, they were expected to be dutifully stoic and tolerant:

> *Women must accept and wait; accept in head and heart that their men were changed by the war. If they could not do so, if they blamed and were impatient there would be broken hearts, broken homes, ill feeling and bitterness. They must show all the forbearance and fortitude they could muster, putting up with irrational behaviour and irritability.*[821]

After the war

One of the transitions that was evident throughout the city from the end of the Second World War was a shift away from some of the parsimony of the 1930s. As 'normality' returned, Aucklanders were slowly (and sometimes not so slowly) embracing a more consumerist, leisure-oriented culture. Work arrangements contributed to this new leisure obsession. The entrenchment of the 40-hour week in particular had enshrined weekends as a time for individual and family recreation, with gardening, camping, trips to the beach, bush walks, boating, interior decoration and, of course, sports occupying Aucklanders on Saturdays and Sundays.[822] In the late 1930s, when faith in the state's ability to direct the lives of its citizens was still strong, the Labour Government had created the National Council of Physical Welfare and Recreation. The Council's stated purpose was 'to advise the Government on matters relating to the maintenance and improvement of the physical well-being of the people by means of physical training, exercise, sport and recreation, and social activities', but after the war, the limitations of state-directed leisure became more obvious,[823] and it was individual preference rather than government prescription that shaped how people occupied their spare time.

One of the more notable aspects of leisure in this decade was the rapid increase in the number of women's organisations devoted to activities in the evenings and weekends. These ranged from brass bands to dancing, basketball, bowling, athletics, various housewives' groups and marching.[824] 'Girls' marching' was unique to New Zealand and Australia, in that no other nation practised it in the form and to anywhere near the same scale. Its popularity grew in the post-war years, due to a combination of encouragement from government officials, the presence of ex-army drill officers who could assist in training, and the opportunity it gave women (both as participants and administrators) to free themselves from their domestic routines.[825] In addition to the marchers themselves, there was an army of 'instructors, managers, chaperones, judges and others to help with fundraising, catering and transport'.[826] Those marching on the field were just the tip of a great organisational iceberg that drew in a good portion of communities into the competitions.

An example of the enthusiasm for marching in Auckland occurred in February 1945, at the annual Franklin Caledonian Society's sport day. The local marching girls (together with organisers) were surprised (pleasantly, it should be added) with the unexpected arrival of marching teams from other parts of the city to this event being held in Pukekohe.[827] Any excuse for teams to demonstrate their skills was seized at this time, and the event turned out to be a great spectacle of marching routines. With the end of the war imminent, interest in girls' marching only increased, with a larger competition — involving 19 Auckland teams, and an array of prize cups — organised at Carlaw Park on 24 March 1945. There were teams from Auckland and Epsom Girls' Grammar Schools, Takapuna Grammar School, the Health and Beauty Movement, the Red Cross Transport Corps, the Women's Army Auxiliary Corps (WAACS), among others, with music provided by the Papakura Military Band, the 1st Battalion Auckland Regiment Band, the Auckland District Pipe Band and Te Akarana Girls' Band.[828] Here, the militarism of the war was transmuting into a regimental performance of an entirely peaceful kind. Spectators at Carlaw Park got to see a 'colourful and spectacular display' with '[a] high standard in general bearing, marching, turning, precision, steadiness and drill …. Some of the girls showed fine deportment, and …. [c]olour and gaiety were added to the scene by the snappy uniforms, varying from shorts and blouses to short, pleated frocks, crossed by team ribbons.'[829]

Something of the martial spirit of the war carried on for boys too, in the form of the Boys' Brigade. Although founded in the nineteenth century, it became particularly popular after the Second World War — so popular, in fact, that it had among the highest per capita membership of any country where the Brigade was established. According to one British writer, the attraction of the movement had much to do with the appeal of the landscape:

The N.Z. Companies are run on the usual lines, but camping in those delightful islands can surpass anything we know at home. Often sited in the verdant New Zealand bush, or away up in the lofty snowcapped mountain ranges, these N.Z. B.B. Camps are held at Christmas and New Year. They are real "Holidays in the Open" with unrivalled opportunities for sport, recreation, nature craft and adventure abounding. What could be better than playing, tramping, singing and worshipping in a natural wonderland such as the New Zealand B.B. has around it?[830]

The organisation also played a role in influencing the moral complexion of Auckland society. The thousands of boys in the city who were members were committed to a specifically religious and social outlook, as was made explicit in 1944 during a visit to the Pukekohe Company by the Brigade's dominion secretary:

> Each company ... stands in precisely the same relation to its church as the Sunday School or Bible Class. For this reason and because of its distinctly Christian object, the Boys' Brigade has been called "The Church's Own Movement for Boys." The activities of the Brigade make a strong appeal to the masculine instincts and the manly qualities inherent in boy nature. Discipline comes through drill instruction[,] and esprit-de-corps or "pride of company" is developed as the boys meet together week by week — in their smart uniforms — to train themselves for future Christian citizenship.[831]

There were important functions that the Auckland Brigade members occasionally were called in to assist with, such as the unveiling of the Savage Memorial in 1943 by the prime minister, Peter Fraser (who was himself a former Brigade member),[832] but for most of the participants it was more the activities and camps that held their interest. The prospect of spending a week at Long Bay in summer, sleeping in tents,[833] or just of weekly games nights with other boys in the local church hall,[834] was more than enough to sustain popular enthusiasm for the movement.

In contrast, kicking against this incarnation of Auckland as socially conservative and dutifully uniform was the dancer Freda Stark. By day, she was a clerical worker for the Colonial Ammunition Company in Normanby Road, Mt Eden, but after work, Stark metamorphosised into an exotic dancer without equal in the country. She had acquired some notoriety in 1935 for being in the Mt Eden house of the musician Eric Mareo around the time when he had poisoned his actress wife, Thelma (with whom Freda had been having an affair).[835] But with her reputation apparently unblemished among clubgoers by her connection to the victim and the murderer, Stark's stature as an 'acrobatic dancer' continued to grow — reaching its pinnacle during the Second World War, when she became a favourite performer of American troops stationed in Auckland.[836] The venue with which Stark's risqué performances was most closely identified was the Civic Theatre's Wintergarden. Its honey-lit oriental Baroque decor heightened the exotic nature of her dances, but it was still merely a backdrop to her startling appearance — her body gilded in gold paint, and as she appeared wearing nothing apart from a g-string and maybe a headdress of feathers or a shawl. Her exultant dance routine was suggestive and captivating. 'She was a beautiful mover,' her niece later recalled. 'Talk about poetry in motion .... There was just something about the way she moved that people loved.'[837] Stark was accompanied by a troupe of dancers known as 'The Lucky Lovelies', but there was no mistake that she was the singular attraction of the nightly shows that were put on at the Civic. The Wintergarden had become an informal headquarters for American marines in the city, and Stark's headlining act helped greatly to revive the fortunes of the venue, which had fallen into a financial slump since the Depression. Her statuesque poses, reminiscent of the bronze and ivory figures of the era,[838] elevated the dances out of the status of a striptease, with one dancer describing her routine as being 'rather impersonal, untouchable, slow-moving', as though it was some otherworldly study in aesthetics rendered in human form.[839] In a way, the fact that such extremes of entertainment as Stark's erotic dancing and the more rigid choreography of the city's marching teams could be encompassed in the same region without any real discord was a sign both of Auckland's growing diversity and its increasing maturation.

Auckland's writing scene was also buoyant at this time, with authors and poets including Rex Fairburn, R. A. K. Mason and Frank Sargeson becoming prominent among the public as well as in the city's literary cloisters. Sargeson (born Norris Frank Davey) had moved to Takapuna in 1931, occupying his parents' bach in what was then still a location that was on the fringe of urban Auckland. He described his modest accommodation as 'nothing more than a small one-roomed hut in a quiet street ending in a no-man's land of mangrove mud-flats that belonged to the inner harbour. It was very decayed, with weather-boards falling off.'[840] Cocooned in this hut, Sargeson captured in text the sounds and speech of his fellow Aucklanders. Encountering this prose was a novel experience for most readers, but broadly welcomed, as one reviewer explained:

> *Mr. Sargeson has a terse, colloquial and occasionally slangy style which he uses with remarkable effect. His work is clever without being smart, graphic but in no way laboured; and in a country where it is a popular belief that kauri trees, bell birds and*

the Southern Alps form the topics most suited for good writing, it is something of an achievement for an author to write with penetrating and introspective realism about everyday life.[841]

However, while his literary success was building, Sargeson's living arrangements were crumbling. In 1945, council inspectors gave notice that his bach had to be demolished as it was beyond repair. By scraping together money from friends and his writing, he was able to afford a replacement hut, which was put up in 1948.[842]

While Sargeson's vernacular realism caught the attention of readers and critics, his commentary on a community still captured by a deeply ingrained conservatism offers an insight into how one Aucklander saw the atmosphere of the society he lived in during this era. Writing about his mother as an embodiment of this conformist moral outlook, he wrote how 'again and again she insisted that you must do the right thing because of what people would say or think if you didn't'. He regarded her as 'the impure puritan to whom the bargain of social convention was entirely satisfactory … [and] was indeed truly representative of the prevailing general sentiment about what life in New Zealand should be — the sentiment which powerfully shapes and dominates New Zealand life to this day'.[843] Like Stark, Sargeson was trying to wrestle free from the blandness he felt was smothering Auckland. It was a view shared by the British writer Anna Kavan, who lived in the North Shore (and possibly met Sargeson there) in 1941–42.[844] She recorded that the place 'isn't England and it isn't anywhere else. It's null, it's dull, it's tepid, it's mediocre: the downunder of the spirit.'[845] For all the city's scenic splendour, it appeared to some observers and residents that Auckland had yet to awaken from its reticent, conformist and slightly prudish stupor.

7
The 1950s

Exotica

In a sense, the history of Auckland in the twentieth century is that of a city finding itself. In the 1900s, it still had the strong residue of a colonial settlement in both its appearance and the make-up and loyalties of its population. And like other towns and cities in the country, it was built on the remnants of a Māori community that it had largely displaced (which in Auckland's case, was still happening). However, the two world wars had reminded Aucklanders that their city in the South Pacific was still shadowed by decisions made in London, and, in general, much of the population did not seem to mind this arrangement. Popular support for the British royals — roused by the visit to Auckland of the freshly minted Queen and her prince in December 1953 — seemed to confirm to everyone that the filial affection for Britain was as strong as ever. In one over-egged piece of reporting in January 1954, the distinctions between Britain and New Zealand were almost obscured in a patriotic haze:

> *Her Majesty ... stands above parties, and in John Buchan's words forms "the mystical, indivisible centre of National Union. It is the point around which coheres the Nation's sense of a continuing*

personality. In any deep stirring of heart the people turn from the mechanism of Government, which is their handiwork and their servant, to that ancient, abiding thing behind governments, which they feel to be the symbol of their past achievement and their future hope."[846]

The new queen not only embodied this constitutional connection, but also epitomised the role of the 'modern' woman. For New Zealand women, Elizabeth's ascent to the throne was 'something very special'. According to one women's magazine, '[w]e saw her as a Monarch, one of our own sex, a young mother with children, and as such she makes a special appeal to all wives and mothers. Her wifehood and motherhood have given her an understanding of our problems.'[847] It was an idealisation that may have missed the mark for most Auckland women, but still captured a vision that they could aspire to — one in which loyalty to the Empire and the British outlook on the world, and the importance of local female domesticity, were somehow combined into a single, overarching moral virtue.

Perhaps the most frequent example of this 'Britishness'[848] being put on display in homes at this time was afternoon tea. In a way, this ritual was a display of English upper-middle-class values projected into local households, with fine china tea sets, linen tablecloths and silver service[849] (or electroplated nickel silver — the EPNS hallmark which signified 'inferior' silver cutlery), along with foods that were succinctly summed up as 'something buttered, something biscuity, and something cakey'.[850] It was the accompanying cake, rather than the beverage, however, that was the centre of attention at afternoon teas. Scones, pikelets, pavlova, and especially sponges were ways of demonstrating baking prowess: '[y]ou got a name for being good at something … and you kept on cooking that recipe if you knew it was successful and you kept on at it'. The sponge was the benchmark, though, for many women at this time. According to the prevailing wisdom of some in this era, 'you weren't much of a housewife if you couldn't make a sponge'.[851] The other point of pride for those women hosting an afternoon tea was cleanliness, as a resident of Aberfoyle Street in Mt Eden recalled. 'Oh yes, all the linen had to be washed and ironed, you couldn't use anything that had not been washed, and I had to clean the whole house. People would notice or say something if your house wasn't clean and you didn't want that.'[852]

Yet, appearances could be deceptive, and deliberately so. The outward show of faux-Victorian domestic pageantry that was afternoon tea could conceal hardships in some households. There were challenges in the early 1950s, for example, in simply obtaining the ingredients to bake something. Butter was still being rationed in 1950,[853] and eggs and sugar were not always readily available. However, as the decade progressed, the final wartime restrictions were lifted, and the flow of goods returned to normal. And although seldom mentioned, homelessness was a feature of the lives of some Aucklanders in this period, even though it was later typified as an economic golden age. There was a case in Glenfield in 1950, for example, of a young married couple who were forced to live in a cowshed. The roof leaked, and cooking had to be done on a small oil stove, but they were unable to find any other accommodation, and so had no alternative. As they pointed out, '[i]t was impossible to avoid hardship. There were not enough houses to go around.'[854]

The tradition of afternoon tea was not only a comparatively easy indulgence for many Auckland women, but was also a strand of continuity that stretched back to the nineteenth century — a ritual that could not quite be relinquished whatever else was happening. And changes were certainly under way in this period that were challenging other aspects of home life, including the home itself. Auckland's residential landscape was dominated by three main styles of house at this time: the villa; the bungalow; and the state house. There were numerous variants of each, but overall, most houses in the city were in one of these general types. In the 1950s, though, a radically different style of house began to dot the landscape. At first, they were few in number, but their distinctive style represented an audacious (and not always welcome) challenge to conventional notions of what a house ought to look like. These modernist buildings were experimental, daring and deliberately challenged the fairly staid architectural conventions of the time. But they were also a sign of the city willing to change itself and to re-examine some of its material values. So, although these houses may have struggled to gain widespread acceptance ('it's not to my taste at all' was one Aucklander's defensive verdict at the time),[855] they were nonetheless optimistic (and calculated) expressions of what a 'modern' Auckland could look like. Such futuristic architectural forays were literally the shape of things to come, and they were cropping up throughout the region. The typical features of these modernist houses are easily assembled: flat roofs, large windows (sometimes from floor to ceiling), a linear appearance, with clean lines and minimal ornamentation. In addition, there were distinctive local references, including the use of native wood and stone sourced from the area.[856] These were self-dramatising designs, based on the principle that '[a]rchitecture was not to be clothed in forms of the past, but was to give expression to the industries and technology of the day'.[857]

One example of this embrace of modernism was a farmhouse built in Wellsford for the Grant family in 1955, and designed by the Auckland architect Kenneth Albert.[858] Two mono-pitched roofs converged near the entrance to the house, which was sheltered from the prevailing winds by six framed, frosted-glass panels that extended from the floor to the roofline. The lounge appeared particularly spacious because of the cathedral ceiling, the expanse of windows that allowed light to flood in, and the absence of eaves along one side of the outside wall.[859]

Even more audacious was Erickson House, designed by the architect Edward Erickson for himself and his family, and built deep in the forest in Titirangi in 1954. Like the farmhouse in Wellsford, it had a mono-pitched roof, large windows and an innovative interior layout. However, this building was more nuanced. The pitch of the roof fitted in with the contour of the section, and there were cantilevered eaves on the north-facing side of the house, which stretched out by over a metre to provide some shade. The interior was organised in a way that enabled residents to participate in the design, rather than simply adjust to it:

> *Entry is into a hallway, which offers the choice of turning left, to the west, where social spaces are clustered, or right, to the east, where the private spaces are grouped. The living and dining areas are partially open to each other, separated only by a centrally placed fireplace and chimney .... All spaces and rooms then open out onto the northern deck, providing easy connections between inside and out, as well as panoramic views to the city. To allow for maximum space, and the opening up of one space to the next, sliding doors are used throughout.*[860]

Even the most traditional suburbs were not free from the modernist invasion. Goodman House, in Parnell, was a daring example, designed by Hungarian-born and Czech-trained architect Imric Porsolt, and in keeping with that commitment to exploratory forms that were both functional and engaging. For a start, the house had a pentagon footprint, which was a daring departure from the ubiquitous squares and rectangles from which houses traditionally grew. Windows substituted for walls where there were views to be captured, and on the upper level the cathedral ceiling was supported by exposed Oregon beams that stretched from the living room to the roof of the outside balcony.[861]

Auckland's earlier architectural forms were not suddenly invalidated by the arrival of modernism, but at the time of their appearance these houses were unruly, stark and even startling. Architecture had gone from a 'conversation between styles' to almost an argument, ending in something of a standoff. Attitudes softened over time, though, and by the end of the century such houses were almost passé. The juxtaposition of their materials had gone from confronting to cliché, their low-pitched roofs and big blocks of windows were out of date, and by the 1990s they were suffering from a perception that was worse than contempt: boredom. Modernism had become a spent force in the city's architectural history.

In the 1950s, modernist houses were an exception in Auckland, but were a harbinger of the direction that the city's architecture would take. However, while experiments in house design were confined to those few at this time who had the means and the daring to undertake them, when it came to gardening, the city was taking to new approaches seemingly en masse. The post-war building boom, with houses typically occupying sections from 800 to 1000 square metres,[862] led to a growing demand for horticultural products. This, in turn, led to the emergence of the city's first major retail plant store — Palmers — which opened across the road from Waikumete Cemetery in Glen Eden in 1958. Customers were able to buy fruit trees and roses by extracting the plants from beds of sawdust where they were temporarily rooted. The plants then had their roots wrapped up in newspaper before being purchased. What Palmers had not predicted was the extent of customer demand. The owners responded by getting expert advice and researching overseas for a model to manage the crowds that were turning up at the shop. Eventually, multiple checkouts, trundlers and pre-packaged plants were introduced, along with the entrance having the country's first automated electric doors.[863]

It was not just vegetable seedlings and fruit trees that were being purchased. Aucklanders in the 1950s were changing the atmosphere of their surrounds through gardening. Flower beds, roses and vegetable gardens did not suddenly fade from sight, but the inheritance of the English cottage garden influence was now competing with new ways of seeing and shaping Auckland's suburban horticulture. As one contemporary landscaper summed it up:

> *Auckland's tropical climate allows us to grow [luscious] plants which do not necessarily create a riot of colour (there is too much in our gardens anyway) but make us appreciate the beauty of simple forms. The leaves of taro, the leaves of bamboo, paw paw or flax. We have time for a glance, and we comprehend, much easier and better than if our eye is distracted by a vulgar riot of colour in annual or perennial beds.*[864]

Auckland's subtropical climate lent itself to more regional forms of garden[865] than the 'mediocre'[866] forms that had dominated urban areas for most of the century. By introducing plants from hot climates (including the hibiscus, representing tropical regions, and oleander evoking the Mediterranean), the ubiquitous 'back yard' could summon the impression of warmth and exotic locations, even if the temperature was not always obliging. The idea of the 'tropical' world now seemed almost within reach to some Aucklanders. New hi-fi (high fidelity) audio technology popularised the use of LPs (long-playing records), which coincided with recordings that brought an idealised (and heavily contrived) Pacific music into lounges, accompanied by a growing taste for pseudo-Polynesian décor and tropical cocktail drinks.[867] A specifically Hawaiian-style music, popularised by movies romanticising the South Pacific in this era, appealed to this new fetish in Auckland for the imagined exotic tropical world. Musicians such as the Tongan-born Bill Sevesi and Bill Wolfgramm performed regularly at the Orange Coronation Ballroom on Newton Road from 1954, and drew large crowds to their performances as Aucklanders sought out this alluring faux-tropical sound.[868]

It would be easy to attribute this interest in tropical Pacific exotica to a passing fad — some sort of diversion from the austerity and puritanism of a largely Anglo-Saxon Auckland, except that buried within the superficial ideas of a tropical utopia was a more serious and enduring realisation: even though Auckland was demographically predominantly a European city, it was geographically and historically a Pacific one. This ambiguity was something architects and the population at large were slowly coming to terms with. One response was to tilt towards a more casual form of housing, influenced by perceptions of the easy-living 'Californian style', and combine this with the characteristics of the South Pacific. In 1950, a design journal expressed this ambition in broad brushstrokes:

> If one ... considers the type of house which is beginning to be built in various parts of New Zealand ... one may wonder whether there is not at least the possibility of the development of a unifying 'Pacific Style'. It is an intriguing speculation. After making due allowances for differences of climate, nationality and economics, it can still be claimed that the factors attributed to California, especially the lack of formality and favourable climate, exert a similar influence on life in ... New Zealand.[869]

Of course, all this exploration by Aucklanders looking to make their homes fit their evolving temperament and the ideal of life in the city was set against a much more pragmatic consideration — home ownership, as one expert discussed in 1950:

> In these times of much slick talking and shallow thinking, of economic difficulties and frustration, it is wise to re-examine and restate the policy of individual home ownership. Traditionally, one of the main objects in life of the average family was to own their own home. This still is the object of very many people. We believe that it is a worthy object .... [but] there must always be those who, with the best will in the world, cannot purchase their own homes. Possibly they should be catered for by state housing schemes .... However, [for] the great majority of the community ... the old argument still holds that after twenty-five or thirty years one family owns the house, less depreciation and plus probably appreciation, the other owns only a rent book.[870]

By 1956, roughly 66 per cent of Aucklanders owned their own home, with the remainder in either state houses or private rentals. At the close of the century, despite some fluctuations in the intervening 44 years, this figure was around 65 per cent.[871] However, while ownership rates account for how the city housed itself, the sometimes dramatic evolutionary leaps in design preference reveal much about the way many Auckland residents felt about the location. Architecturally, Auckland had gone from Gothic Revival-inspired villas at the turn of the century — which looked back to England and Victoriana for inspiration — to experimental steps in modernism in the 1950s. The city's mid-century residential design experiments were more than just a case of keeping up with international trends, though. The use of local materials in the finish of these houses, the efforts to make them an almost organic part of their surrounds, and the deliberate rejection of so many of the design approaches inherited from the previous generation of architects, all point to a self-consciousness among some Aucklanders to have a much more intimate affinity with their city. In this case, it involved shedding the last layer of its colonial inheritance — its northern hemisphere residential architecture — in favour of something that was more suited to a South Pacific city. Even at the end of the century, this process was far from complete, and new waves of design influence had reached Auckland shores in the intervening decades, but the fact that the process was under way represents an important phase in the city's self-perception. Aucklanders were beginning to understand that to feel more comfortable in the place, they had to develop a relationship with it.

Māori and the city

None of this was new to Māori — the connections to location and memory were deeply engraved in the culture and the conscience of all hapū. However, these ancient bonds were coming under unprecedented strain in the 1950s as a result of a large and sustained migration of many mainly young Māori from rural areas around the country to the cities. The process had begun shortly after the outbreak of the Second World War, driven initially by the demand especially in Auckland for extra labour, but Māori urbanisation maintained its momentum well into the 1950s. Many of these migrants were effectively exiles from a rural world where life was substantially more challenging. Schools were not always within easy reach, hospitals were remote, and in the evenings and weekends opportunities for entertainment were sparse. Shifting to major centres like Auckland seemed like the simplest and most effective remedy, but the transition was not what most expected. The social seclusion of rural life and dependence on the community largely vanished when these migrants arrived in the city. Notions of hapū and whānau (family) as a governing presence in all aspects of life gradually came to be seem as something that existed more 'back home' (that term of spatial separation really only gained widespread use among Māori once urbanisation had got under way). The initial separation between urban and rural Māori eventually opened up into 'a fundamental cleavage',[872] producing challenges that would be grappled with for the remainder of the century.[873]

One of these challenges was in two competing stereotypes about Māori urbanisation.[874] Some Pākehā could not understand why Māori would want to leave their wholesome, bucolic life in the country, where their language and culture were still largely intact, and move to the more competitive, insular life of suburban Auckland. And some Māori could not understand why anyone would want to remain 'at home' when the cities seemed to offer freedom, 'glamour' and opportunities that were inconceivable in their existing rural homes.[875] The subsequent story of Māori migration to Auckland essentially became one of both groups coming to terms with these stereotypes. However, there was also a lingering prejudice among some Pākehā towards Māori, which Māori urbanisation seemed to bring to the surface at this time, as one contemporary observed,

> *the influx of Maoris to the cities was almost universally deplored. It was popularly referred to as a 'problem'. Common use of the phrase 'drift to the cities' implied something undesirable and badly organised. Maori elders in the country scolded emigrants for their defection from the rural way of life which, they preached, was natural and right for Maoris and the cultivation of Maori virtues. Urban and national leaders, Maoris as well as Pakehas, expressed open concern about bad living conditions, 'footlooseness', absenteeism in employment, thriftlessness, marital instability, crime and delinquency among Maoris living in the city.*[876]

Yet, there was a small degree of perhaps premature optimism creeping in towards the end of the 1950s that the situation for those Māori who had migrated to urban areas was progressing:

> *With improved housing and economic conditions, there is an increase in the group of Maoris who find adjustment easy. More*

and more of our unskilled labourers, are securing permanent homes in and around the city and as they grow domestic roots a change also occurs in their attitude towards their work. The "Will-o-the-Wisp" type of existence is replaced by a more stable one, leading to change in behaviour patterns and social habits. One of the beneficial results is the wider and more spontaneous acceptance by the pakeha of his Maori neighbour as an integral part of his community. A fundamental of good social progress is the sense of belonging to a community, and to reach this there must be a free play of inter-action. The participation of Maori mothers in community projects and the exchange of baby-sitting favours, has already been mentioned, there is also now a much stronger tendency than before to visit each other's homes.[877]

And if the rate of increase in Auckland's Māori population in this decade (by approximately 50 per cent every five years)[878] is a measure, the advantages of urbanisation seemed to appeal more to these migrants than its drawbacks. Whether Māori urbanisation was more integration or assimilation became a point of ongoing debate, but for those Māori who had moved to Auckland in this era the reality was that it was a bit of both. As some of the institutions these migrants left behind gradually receded from their day-to-day life, these arrivals began to form new ones, partly as a substitute for what they had left behind, but partly out of the need for organisations that responded to a very different environment than existed 'back home'. Tribal allegiances remained in place for the most part,[879] but a new sentiment of pan-tribalism was gaining traction. One early example of this was the Maori Community Centre, built in 1947 (and demolished in 2002),[880] which was situated on the corner of Fanshawe and Halsey streets, facing Victoria Park. Administered by various Māori organisations, it was a venue for social gatherings, meals, tangi, kapa haka, carving school, indoor basketball and Sunday church services.[881] In the following decades, membership waned as Māori arrivals to Auckland became more established, had families of their own, developed careers, and found a diminishing need for the sort of support and camaraderie that the Centre offered. But in the 1950s, for those struggling with their move to the city, the Centre was a place where they could feel safe, where there were voices and culture that were familiar to them, and where they could share some of the challenges that they faced.[882]

In April 1952 the Centre was the venue for the second annual conference of the Maori Women's Welfare League. In front of 300 delegates, the Minister of Maori Affairs, Ernest Corbett, was introduced by Te Kani Te Ua, who joked that he felt embarrassed to have to welcome the minister 'to so outlandish and barbaric a place as Auckland'.[883] Corbett then congratulated the delegates for working with 'the zeal of the missionary' and for being 'the mothers of a great race, which over the centuries has survived many tribulations: the migration from Hawaiki to New Zealand and then the impact, the terrible impact of an alien way of life'.[884] The women in attendance had an entirely more practical ambition, though. There were resolutions passed tackling drunkenness, immorality, the need for more apprenticeships for young Māori, better health care for Māori mothers, and the requirement for more Māori teachers.[885]

The goals of the League reflected some of the wider challenges that Māori were facing in this decade. Ben Neho, from Panguru in Hokianga, recounted how even the fundamental requirement of decent accommodation in Auckland could be elusive at this time:

> *My Aunty moved to Cook Street and lived in an old shanty hut. There was hardly any room for a revolving [clothes] line. So they had this big wire running round the house and the washing just flapped and hit the rusty fence. And then my Aunty would boil them up again .... would all sit next to little pot-bellies; that was their cooking [facility]. Some [Māori] were going up Wellington Street, picking up wood so as to boil water. Conditions were really hard. So most of our people lived in Cook Street, Freemans Bay, Ponsonby .... It wasn't easy. I can remember one of us [did not even have enough floor space to lie down], it was so crowded in this little three-bedroom house. We had to open out a closet so the head could sleep there ... and the leg stretched out.*[886]

This was not the experience of all Māori arrivals to the city, however. Mahurangi Mutu and his family left Ruāwai in the 1950s for a new life in Auckland, and settled in Hendon Street, Ōwairaka. He paid off the section there while still working for the Railways Department near Dargaville, and then built the house with a low-interest loan under a Maori Affairs financing scheme.[887] The family then shifted into the house, which was in a predominantly Pākehā-populated street. An account of their situation written in 1959, once they had settled into their home, offers an idealised depiction of Māori urbanisation, and how the assimilationist/ integrationist process supposedly functioned:

> *They [the Mutu family] participate in indoor bowls, league football, basketball and horse riding, which are favourite European activities in Owairaka. Mr Mutu regards mixed housing settlement as the right solution for the Maori; so does the rest of this harmonious neighbourhood .... It is apparent that behaviour rather than colour determines the attitude toward the Maori in the matter of housing. The way the Maori has adjusted himself to urban life has helped to reduce many of the barriers which prevent him from competing on equal terms with the pakeha in this matter. But the Maori still has special problems to overcome which entitle him to special consideration. At present the number of new houses available for Maoris in Auckland is not nearly enough to provide for the growing population.*[888]

It may hardly seem like it, but this era of urbanisation was one of the most convulsive changes to affect Māori arguably since the Land Wars in the 1860s. The migration of tens of thousands of Māori to Auckland in the post-war era was to have drastic effects on the culture, the sense of iwi affiliation and particularly the language. But in the eyes of Pākehā society in the 1950s, it was worth it, and was proof of the oft-repeated claim that the country had the best race relations in the world.[889] It took the assessment of visiting American psychologist David Ausubel, though, to dispel this myth for the self-congratulatory delusion that it was. In 1958 he published an article on Māori–Pākehā relations, which identified various categories that contributed to what he labelled as a 'colour bar'. These included 'the almost universal stereotype of the Maori ... [of being] a lazy, shiftless, unreliable, improvident and happy-go-lucky human being', and the fact that in 'such fields as housing, hotel accommodation, employment, credit, and ordinary social interaction', widespread discrimination was present. He identified Pukekohe as a part of Auckland 'where school segregation is practised', and pointedly observed that 'it is not uncommon for pakeha mothers ... to deplore the fact that their children must travel to school on the same bus with Maori youngsters and to instruct their children not to play with Maori school-mates'.[890] Such deep divisions fractured Auckland society, only most residents seemed to avert their gaze from the problem. The editor of *Te Ao Hou* (the first national magazine published for Māori) similarly pinpointed problems in relations between Māori and Pākehā two years before Ausubel had, and concluded that '[o]nce we have made laws that are just and honest, we are still left with a more difficult job, to be done by each of us individually, of inwardly understanding a member of another race and accept[ing] him as one of our own'.[891]

Except that justice for some Māori was a long way off, and for the surviving community of Ngāti Whātua at Ōrākei was about to go up in smoke. In 1952 the Crown confiscated the remaining 12 acres of the iwi's land in order to establish a park on the site. The inhabitants were forced to relocate to nearby state houses, and the village, which was described at the time as 'a dreadful eyesore and potential disease centre', was razed to the ground. The *Herald* published a photo of the destruction that was callously captioned: 'One of the ramshackle homes at Orakei set on fire after demolition yesterday'.[892] One eyewitness to the burning, however, captured its full horror:

> *I remember the smoke drifting across Tamaki Drive. The smoke was billowing and swirling and illuminated from all sides by the flames of collapsing buildings. The burning, smouldering whares and the embers glowed through the night .... Reports of an old man being dragged from the fire are wrong. He actually cast himself into the holocaust of his home. I remember vividly the [wailing] of the wahine and the confused shouts of the young. It could be clearly heard on the harbour.*[893]

This was the inflammatory edge of race relations in the city in this era, but it was also the exception. More generally, the surge of urbanisation after the war caused both Māori and Pākehā in Auckland to confront each other individually, directly, and often daily to a greater extent than at any other time in the preceding half-century. However, for every shrill note of racism that was sounded, there were probably just as many clumsy gestures of encounter and attempts at understanding each other. This tentative fossicking around in the culture and ways of thinking of neighbours and colleagues was to remain a work in progress, and a constant backdrop to the city's evolution for the rest of the century.

Auckland on parade

In August 1948 confirmation arrived from London that Auckland would host the 1950 British Empire Games.[894] Due to the interruption caused by the war, this would be the first Games held since Sydney in 1938, and as soon as the announcement was made the idling machinery of state revved into life in anticipation of what would be the biggest sporting event in the city to date. Among the array of measures put in place included extra police being brought in from Australia to bolster the local force (an initiative that proved to be 'of substantial assistance in locating or identifying Australian criminals' who were in Auckland during the Games),[895] and amendments to the law to exempt the normal tenancy rules applying to houses to allow rooms to be let on a short-term basis to visitors to the Games.[896]

In several locations, sites were being bulldozed, dug up, renovated and refitted for the sportspeople and supporters who were expected to stretch the seams of the city as they converged in Auckland for the week-long series of competitions. Eden Park was where most of the track events took place, and was where the Games were officially opened. The Town Hall hosted boxing and wrestling, Newmarket was where the swimming was held, and Western Springs was used for the cycling competitions.[897] Accommodation for some of the athletes was at the Ardmore Teachers' Training College, which was around 40 kilometres south of Auckland's central business district. Two concrete swimming pools were constructed there, along with four basketball courts and an athletics field.[898] And when the numbers were eventually calculated, the combined attendance of spectators for the Games added up to 246,694, which would turn out to be higher than for the following three Games.[899]

Yet Aucklanders initially showed little outward enthusiasm in the lead-up to the Games, with one observer describing the popular view in the city as 'one of detached interest only'.[900] Part of the reason for this ambivalence was that the idea of an Empire Games was something few were familiar with (even the name 'Empire' seemed anachronistic in the face of the emerging Commonwealth). The previous event had been held 12 years ago, and for most Aucklanders the affiliation with those Games was confined to clips of some of the competition shown at movie theatres, and maybe radio broadcasts. Also, the 1950 Games were coming two years after the Olympics, which made the imperial competition seem like the diminutive younger sibling. But once the teams from other parts of the Commonwealth began to converge on Auckland, the prophecy made about the Games in 1930 — that if 'we could wave the good old flag ... all would gather round'[901] — was once again borne out.

The organising committee of Auckland's Games echoed this rather sentimental perspective at the close of the 1950 Games, claiming that the event 'was a real reunion of families, races and creeds, once again a fitting testimony to the solidarity of the Empire. Auckland, and New Zealand, took the visitors to their hearts and when the home Dominion team joined the visitors at Ardmore the family was complete. And completely happy.'[902] And in case there were defections from this imperial fealty, Auckland's mayor, John Allum, told teams at a reception before the Games' opening how he detested 'this word "Commonwealth". It always seems to me to have been invented for those who might want to get out. I prefer the old-fashioned term "Empire" and it as citizens of Empire that I welcome you.'[903] To many Aucklanders, the event brought home 'the full significance of the bonds of an Empire',[904] and in a way, the city of 372,000 people felt honoured to have been chosen to host such an event. As for other parts of the country, there was a muted feeling of disappointment that only Auckland was being illuminated by the spotlight of international media attention, and that the rest of New Zealand was being left out of the revelry of the Games.[905]

The Games opened on 4 February, with a modest march-past of the 12 participating teams, followed by a speech delivered by the governor-general, the singing of the national anthem, and finally, a military salute. One journalist euphemistically saw the relative lack of spectacle as a sign of 'dignity',[906] but it was the Games themselves that really animated public interest. Never before had there been so many athletes from so many countries compete in so many sports at one time in Auckland, and when the week-long Games finished almost £84,000 had been taken in gate receipts. One indication of Aucklanders' enthusiasm for the event was shown in the cycling race. A sportswriter found it difficult to explain why a crowd of 50,000 people lined the route of the race for over three hours 'for short glimpses of the riders as they rode past'. Even nuns from a Catholic convent near the route came out to watch and cheer the riders.[907]

Although Eden Park had been the centre of the Games, the closing ceremony took place at Western Springs, where the spectacle was substantially different to the more staid opening a week earlier. Taking place at sunset, the scene was 'a mixture of brilliant colour and eerie shadowy crowds of half-seen and unseen people rising tier on tier'. Floodlights illuminated the centre of the stadium when the teams and their trainers and managers began to parade in front of the spectators, and then all attention turned to the dais, where the prime minister, Sid Holland, and the Games' chairman (and future governor-general), Arthur Porritt, spoke to the crowd, thanking everyone involved. The chairman of the Games Federation then declared the event closed, after which "Auld Lang Syne", "Now is the Hour", and the national anthem were sung. A thunderous four-gun salute then sounded, and that was it.[908] The Games were over (literally closing in a puff of smoke), and amid the general euphoria from the spectacle, size and success of the event (New Zealand was ranked third on the medals tally), there were indications that this choreographed exercise in civic accomplishment had worked. One sign came from the Australian press, which bemoaned the fact that cities such as Brisbane and Sydney, which were substantially more populous, lacked the facilities that matched the 'magnificent' ones seen throughout Auckland.[909]

Whatever warm afterglow of civic pride remained in the wake of the Empire Games' conclusion was swept away in a storm of violent industrial protest the following year. The 1951 waterfront strike repudiated in dramatic fashion the idea of Auckland as a socially cohesive city. The ports were one of the city's main commercial conduits, and so the rise in strike activity that had been occurring among various categories of port workers since 1946 was an economic as well as political concern.[910] In February 1951, 'wharfies', as the waterside workers were popularly known, began to reject demands that they work overtime. Government efforts at breaking this impasse failed, and a nationwide strike followed. The strike paralysed the ports and resulted in hundreds of thousands of tons of cargo piling up.[911] The situation was regarded as so dire by the government that it threatened to impose a state of emergency if the wharfies refused to return to work,[912] but even this was insufficient to budge them. A few days later, according to one observer sympathetic to the union position, the country 'came under the iron heel of the police state'.[913] But it was not just the police. The government ordered the armed services to take over some of the duties on the wharves, while also relying on the public's exasperation with port closures as a means of adding pressure on the strikers to return to work. William Goosman, the Minister of Railways, let slip exactly how the government wished to depict the confrontation — as one of extreme social and political polarisation: 'The instigators of the [waterfront] trouble are anti New Zealand and anti British — they are worse than transferrable diseases, and we have to take steps to deal with them .... All I have to say is that if Hitler had to deal with the same thing, Hitler talked right.'[914]

It was an uncharacteristically incendiary comment, but the mood of the public was swinging more in the government's favour. On 1 May the *Auckland Star*'s editor insisted that '[t]he Government must act rather than talk. A final warning should be issued, and it should take the form of a ban, in the meantime, on any gathering in the vicinity of the wharfs.' And if the wharfies did not come to heel, 'the Government should make it known ... that should individuals or groups defy the ban and challenge the authority of the police, The Police Will Shoot'.[915] The newspaper almost got its wish, with violent clashes between strikers and police in the days that followed. Even the Labour opposition, which was the offspring of the union movement, was uncomfortable with the militancy of the strikers, and on 13 May 1951, before a crowd of 10,000 angry and anxious Aucklanders in the Domain, the Opposition leader, Walter Nash, equivocated. 'We are not for the waterside workers, and we are not against them.'[916]

In Auckland, the worst day of violence occurred on 1 June, in what became known as 'Bloody Friday'. The Auckland City Council had given permission for union supporters to march along Queen Street. Just under a thousand participated, with the procession getting under way around eleven o'clock that morning. However, the police decided to block the march by Myers Park. The anger of the marchers was still palpable, leading to an ugly clash, as one of the strikers recorded:

> *These unarmed and peaceful men and women halted and looked at the serried ranks of baton-wielding thugs. Not the slightest move was made to continue .... That women were in the forefront was of no concern to those uniformed bastards. Row after row charged; batons rising and falling on defenceless men and women.*[917]

Lacerated faces, bruised bodies and possibly even a fractured skull had to be nursed in the aftermath of the confrontation, and was too much even for the largely anti-union public to stomach. The next day, around 17,000 Aucklanders converged at the Domain to listen to various union-affiliated speakers voice their outrage at the events of the previous day.[918] However, this proved to be a momentary stand of defiance. The wharfies' strike was already on its last legs, and collapsed completely by mid-July. But such was the depth of division carved out by the strike that even decades later, animosity between the various factions remained close to the surface for some Aucklanders.[919]

Part of the reason this tension was expressed to such a degree in Auckland was that, financially, so much was at stake. The city had experienced a post-war boom in industrial activity, and the ports were a vital link in the commercial chain connecting the city to other parts of the country and the rest of the world. The extent of the commercial and industrial expansion was such that it was altering the shape of the city. Prior to the war, around 85 per cent of industrial workers in the region (amounting to 13,000 people) were employed in factories in inner-city areas (with the exceptions of Westfield and New Lynn). By 1956, though, the numbers employed in this area had risen to 19,000, but that figure now represented only 43 per cent of Auckland's industrial workers. Another 25,000 workers (57 per cent) were employed in commercial and industrial zones further away from the city centre, in areas such as Ellerslie, Penrose, Mt Wellington, Panmure and Onehunga. Some of this expansion was made up of an increase in the number of small businesses (bakers, printers and suchlike) that had grown to meet the needs of a burgeoning population. It was complemented by a rise in service industries, producing machinery, fittings and spare parts for other factories, and the emergence of new industries (such as those based on plastics manufacturing), or those relying on new technology.[920] In turn, suburban growth around these industrial zones intensified as the demand for labour increased. One such case involved the firm of Fisher and Paykel, which manufactured washing machines, vacuum cleaners and refrigerators. In the 1940s the company was operating from a two-storey building in Carlaw Park Lane in Parnell,[921] but rapid growth in demand for its products, coupled with a shortage of space for expansion in the inner city, led to it opening a new, purpose-built factory in Mt Wellington in 1956, with a 4500-square-metre floor space.[922] At this time, much of the area was still in fields,[923] and with plentiful land available the cost of houses was much more affordable for workers. In one way, though, this represented a reversal in the impetus of Auckland's expansion. For most of the century up until this point, suburban growth was a way for the city's residents to live in areas that were comparatively pleasant, and that were far enough away from the ugly and polluted industrial locations where they worked. Improvements in transport over this period — particularly the rise of the car — had made this achievable by this time.[924] Now, however, this pattern was appearing in reverse in places such as Mt Wellington, with low-value housing clustering around factories, and with fewer of the social and leisure facilities that were available in other parts of residential Auckland. It was a case of growth not always being for the better, and an illustration of the possibilities of an egalitarian city slipping ever further from view.

The moral city

For the most part, Auckland church-attendees in the 1950s knew what they were in for every Sunday morning, and were content with what they got. Services in many churches followed a similar format, commencing with the congregation singing a hymn, followed by a prayer, some more hymns, church notices, a children's address, then the sermon and finally a closing hymn.[925] It was a format with no surprises, and one that was endearing partly because of its comfortable predictability. And with over 82 per cent of the population belonging to the top four religious denominations — Anglican, Presbyterian, Catholic and Methodist[926] — churchgoing was very much a social norm, even though attendance levels (around 20 per cent in the 1950s) never matched assertions of affiliation.[927] A series of events in the 1950s, however, jolted Auckland churchgoers out of any pew-bound docility they may have sunk into. The first of these was the publication of the 'Report of the Special Committee on Moral Delinquency in Children and Adolescents', in 1954.[928] Known as the Mazengarb Report, after the chairman of the inquiry on which it was based, its sometimes disturbing contents were paraded as proof of the nation's moral decline, and served as a call to arms for those defenders of Christian virtues. In one incident relayed in the report, an intermediate school headmaster in Auckland had called the police after discovering a student had £22 in his wallet. In the ensuing investigation, details were disclosed of the 'sexual practices of children on their way home from school, at the homes of parents, and elsewhere'. It was no isolated event.

Forty children, most aged between 12 and 15, were found to be involved, including several girls testifying to 'their agreement to sexual intercourse with older men'. Some of the evidence of the 'sordid happenings' in the city was said to be so shocking that 'people who regard themselves as men of the world could scarcely believe [it] possible in this Dominion'.[929] The age at which these transgressions were occurring was alarming too. 'Immorality appears to be more prevalent now among younger groups in the community,' Mazengarb reported. In Auckland, 'most of the cases were of boys and girls whose ages ranged from twelve to fifteen years; but some of the young girls also associated with boys several years older than themselves'. The moral downfall of some girls was set apart for special consideration during the inquiry, expressed in the deadpan finding that 'in many cases girls, by immodest conduct, have become the leaders in sexual misbehaviour and have in many cases corrupted the boys'.[930]

It was not just the fact that such immorality was occurring, its frequency, or even the young age of its participants, but the prevailing attitude of indifference that was most difficult for older generations of Aucklanders to comprehend. What about all the efforts that church, community and sports groups had invested in shaping the city's youth — had it been a colossal waste of time and resources? Maybe that was indeed the case, if some of the findings in Mazengarb's report were anything to go by:

> *Perhaps the most startling feature is the changed mental attitude of many young people towards this evil. Some offend because they crave popularity or want to do what their friends are doing. Some assert a right to do what is regarded by religion, law, and convention as wrongful. It was reported that some of the girls were either unconcerned or unashamed, and even proud, of what they had done .... in one series of cases in Auckland, records were kept, and there was some competition between girls concerning the number of immoral acts in which they were involved .... one girl claimed a total of 148 instances in her favour.*[931]

Mazengarb's proposed solutions were thin on detail, but correspondingly heavily laced with an ideological stance that placed part of the blame for teenage delinquency with the abdication of individual responsibility in society. The encroaching welfare state, with its array of benefits propping up society, was portrayed as an enfeebling force. 'The virtues of thrift and self-denial have been disappearing. Incentive does not have the place in our economy which it used to have', Mazengarb warned. 'The tendency has been to turn to the State for the supply of all material needs. By encouraging parents to rely upon the State their sense of responsibility for the upbringing of their children has been diminished.' To this was added a further conjectural view on the corruption being brought about by excessive materialism:

> *The adolescent of today has been born into a world where things temporal, such as money values and costs, are discussed much more than spiritual things .... The dangers inherent in this materialistic view is that many young people who could profit from further education do not feel a sufficient* inducement to continue study .... In the result, these young people, having too much interest in material things, and not enough in the things of the mind and the spirit, become a potential source of trouble in the community.[932]

Given that Auckland was the country's largest city, it should have been expected that the number of examples of delinquency would be proportionately greater, but it seems that the city's residents were not prepared for the degree of detail contained in the report. The reaction was certainly swift and sharp. Newspapers were showered with letters to their editors from the outraged and the morally upstanding, expressing in often hyperbolic language their anger and dismay at the imminent collapse of society.[933] And soon other targets were selected as the war on immorality escalated. One Auckland Presbyterian minister suggested that '[t]he pressure of sex-laden so-called comics, the cheap escapism of many radio serials, the false glamour of the unreal film world, and many other subtle forces, deliberately catering for the 'teen-ager, present a pseudo-philosophy which has many of our youth in its grip'.[934] Such aftershocks emanating from the Mazengarb Report can be accounted for to some extent by the fact that almost every household in the country where the family benefit was being received was sent a copy. And given some of the lurid details it contained, it is hardly surprising that it induced such hyperventilating bursts of outrage. 'Moral panic' is the term that has come to be associated with the report,[935] although the panic was evidently not so great as to prevent much of the populace picking through the report's often lurid contents — if only to be informed, of course, should any discussion turn to the matter of declining community morality.

The self-appointed arbiters of this morality were determined to leave no stone unturned in their crusade to hunt out the causes of corruption among young people that Mazengarb had exposed. Rock and roll (even the term itself was originally a euphemism for sexual intercourse) was another cultural vice that became an object for condemnation, as did cigarettes, alcohol, along with the perennially concerning illicit sex. In the popular imagination,[936] all these forms of corruption and depravity were epitomised in the 'bodgie', and their female counterpart, the 'widgie' ('the current slang name for youths who avidly follow modern popular music trends and wear extravagant clothes').[937] A popular spot in Auckland for this particular brand of iniquity was Curries' Milkbar, located at 142 Queen Street. There, on Friday nights in particular, 'juvenile delinquents' would loiter, listening to the latest rock and roll songs, with their 'African' rhythms and innuendo-laced lyrics,[938] and then ride motorbikes up and down the road. Much of this activity was designed to attract attention from passers-by, and throw a light on the rebellious nature of this subculture, as one of them recalled:

> *We used to walk up the street with a gallon of gas and spill a bit here and there, say nothing, and then get on the bike and come flying down the road with hobnail boots on, drop your boots and "phwwwh phwwwh", set it on fire with a spark from the boot. It looked good at night. On club nights we used to go mad up there, do all sorts of crazy things .... [but] I never looked for trouble and I don't reckon the rest of the guys ever did either.*[939]

Trouble found some of these youths, though. On 28 March 1955, at Somervell's milk bar (located at 238 Queen Street), Sharon Skiffington, an usherette at the Century Picture Theatre, was having a milkshake around a quarter past two in the afternoon before returning to work. At that moment, her estranged boyfriend, Frederick Foster, walked into Somervell's with a 12-bore shotgun and shot Skiffington in the face at close range, killing her instantly (for which Foster was hanged for the murder on 7 July 1955). Aucklanders were outraged not only over the brutality of the 19-year-old's murder, but because the circumstances seemed to verify all their prejudices about the delinquency of the young. Just about every ingredient in the killing confirmed this view. It had taken place in a milk bar, and involved alleged promiscuity, violence and an absence of adult supervision, all set against a backdrop of rock and roll.[940] But just as the shock and outrage over this murder were beginning to abate, there was another 'milk bar' murder — this one at Ye Olde Barn café, located at 366 Queen Street. This time, another 19-year-old was killed. Alan Jacques was fatally stabbed by Albert Black, apparently in a dispute over a 16-year-old girl they had both met at a party in a boarding house the previous evening.[941] Here was all the proof Aucklanders needed. Encroaching in the midst of their city was 'an American-style teenage wasteland [with] ... warring juveniles, delinquents, teenage sex, no parental supervision, all-night dives, blaring jukeboxes — even a cult built around the banned books of Mickey Spillane'.[942]

What had corrupted the post-war ideal of Auckland, and led to the emergence of such delinquency among a portion of the city's youth? The Epsom-based psychologist Alfred Manning put his professional mind to the question, and in 1958 published *The Bodgie: A Study in Psychological Abnormality*.[943] The book was remarkable in part because he included actual case studies that revealed how some of the city's youths were exposed to a parlous concoction of parties, alcohol, cigarettes, sexual experiences (many non-consensual), violence, parental neglect, prostitution, poverty, truancy and loneliness.[944] In the end, the best that Manning could offer was the hope that the delinquency on show around the city's milk bars almost every weekend could somehow be ameliorated by better upbringing. '[W]here the child has a defective psychological background,' he concluded, 'if he is reared in a good, happy and loving environment ... his chances of avoiding accident in the city streets [are improved].'[945] However, Manning added a note of overall encouragement in what was otherwise a despondent assessment of a small group of Auckland youth: 'Let it be said that the children of today are the best that ... New Zealand [has] ... ever produced. They are freer, they think more, they know more, and they reason more .... These children are the hope of a world that is sick, neurotic and hopeless.'[946]

For many of those Aucklanders still shocked by what they saw as an advancing and seemingly unstoppable mudslide of immorality, in 1959 salvation finally looked to be at hand, though. It came in the form of a tall, attractive, athletic Baptist minister from North Carolina: Billy Graham. With a message that was shaped for the particular moral blights that urban audiences faced,[947] coupled with his use of mass media and marketing, Graham's revivalist-style rallies were believed by some to be the answer to Auckland's imminent moral disintegration. Between 29 March and 4 April 1959, a total of over 160,000 people flocked to the week-long Billy Graham 'crusade' at Carlaw Park. In terms of attendance, it was rivalled in Auckland only by the Empire Games in this decade, and for many attendees and onlookers alike, was something of a corrective to the moral deterioration that appeared to be in evidence all around the city. Of course, one of the ironies in Graham's Auckland crusade was that it was very much his Americanised approach to faith that drew so many Aucklanders for whom much of the rest of American culture was an adulterating force in society.[948]

Graham's arrival was preceded by a great deal of organisation and preparation. Some Auckland churches screened films of Graham's earlier crusades as a foretaste of what to expect,[949] and weeks before the event at Carlaw Park, hundreds of counsellors from Auckland's churches were giving training to support those at the rally who were drawn to make a commitment to Christ. One of the counsellors at the event described in 2018 how the actions of some of the crowd seemed to be governed more by the atmosphere of Graham's crusade: 'I quickly found the decision [by audience members] to come forward was more often a response to the emotion of the moment than any intention to pursue that commitment by joining a local congregation, which was the point of the exercise.'[950] Christian piety required more than a virtuoso performance and the emotional pull of the crowds, but the reach of Graham's message was enormous, and 'boosted the morale' of churches throughout Auckland at this time.[951]

On the road again

In the ancient world, cities were defined by their large, densely accommodated populations, and by possessing some form of fortifications, a government and monumental state or religious buildings.[952] In the latter half of the twentieth century, though, one of the additional markers of a city had become the presence of motorways, and Auckland was eager to develop itself in this direction. By the middle of the 1950s, the city's swelling population was starting to have its movement impeded by a sluggish public transport system and clogged roads, many of which had been built at a time when the number of residents was only a fraction of its present size. Change was clearly required, and one of the first signs of this was the phasing out of trams (the last one trundled from the Central Post Office to Karangahape Road on 29 December 1956).[953] There remained, however, the challenge of Auckland's fleet of buses, trains and trolley-buses struggling to extend their reach into the city's increasingly intricate suburban maze. Attempts were made at boosting the provision of public transport, but the geographical spread of the city, combined with its particular shape (large land masses squeezed by an isthmus in the centre and separated by the harbour to the north), made this an almost impossible mission at the time. As a result, in 1955 the Auckland Regional Planning Authority's 'Master Transportation Plan for Auckland' was devised. This shifted the direction of planning away from public transport, and towards its private alternative in the form of cars. In the words of Auckland's transport policy-makers, '[t]he motor vehicle has been the greatest single factor in forming the pattern of modern urban development. It is probably the greatest mechanical convenience man has yet devised for himself.'[954] A master plan was developed, in which an inner ring road would encircle Auckland's central business district, with vehicles from across the city reaching it through a network of motorways.[955] It would be the transport equivalent of a heart bypass operation. The clogged veins of the existing roading network would be superseded by new arteries that would be wide and swift-moving, allowing a strong flow of cars in and out of the central city. The demand for more roads was definitely growing in the region. By 1951, there were over 72,000 cars registered in Auckland, giving the city one of the highest number of vehicles per capita in the world.[956]

The commitment to motorways had already started in 1952, with the opening of the North-Western Motorway (to Te Atatū), followed by the Southern Motorway a year later (the stretch between the Ellerslie Panmure Highway and the Mt Wellington Highway). And just two years after that, the North-Western Motorway was extended to Lincoln Road.[957] Over the remainder of the century, this growth served as a self-fulfilling prophecy. The decision to build transport infrastructure that favoured private transport for Auckland seemed vindicated as the volume of cars on the city's roads continued to increase. Public transport still dominated (in 1954, almost two-thirds of motorised journeys to the central city were by rail, bus or ferry), but there were now over 25,000 drivers and passengers travelling in and out of the centre every weekday.[958] Ironically, the very argument for an extensive motorway network for Auckland — the scattered character of its urban layout — led to even more dispersal,[959] and greater vehicle usage as a consequence. For the next two decades, car ownership in Auckland increased cumulatively by over ten per cent every year.[960]

And it was not just the suburbs that were growing due to the dominance of cars in Auckland. The central business district was able to draw on a broader geographical base of workers to populate its offices and shops, which at lunchtimes led to congestion of the pedestrian kind. Some subtle changes were made to manage this, including the introduction of the 'Barnes Dance' style of pedestrian crossing.[961] On 21 August 1958, Auckland became the first city in New Zealand to adopt this crossing system, in which all vehicles at certain intersections along Queen Street stopped so that pedestrians could cross in any direction at the same time.[962]

Regaled with motorways and an ambitious road-building, suburb-expanding programme, King Car's advance through the city was now a certainty. At the end of the decade, though, one major rampart remained to be overcome: the connection between central Auckland and the North Shore. Since the nineteenth century, the options for reaching the sleepier side of the city were either by ferry or by road via Taupaki, Whenuapai, Riverhead, Coatesville and Albany.[963] The requirement for a bridge linking the North Shore to the rest of Auckland was plainly evident, as one engineer summarised it in 1958:

> *the number of vacant sections within eight miles from the centre of the city is negligible on the south shore. Across the harbour on the North Shore, however, there are acres of un-subdivided land within five miles from the C.P.O. and the transportation problems of a rapidly expanding population of 50,000 have been apparent for some time. Passenger ferries carrying 11 million per year, vehicular lorries carrying 1½ million vehicles per year, and a 45-mile road route around the head of the harbour are the present inter-area facilities.*[964]

Serious consideration for a harbour crossing (either by bridge or tunnel) had been given in 1946, with a Royal Commission set up to examine the possibility. Over a four-week period, 67 experts were quizzed by the commission on their views of how to connect the North Shore with the city centre. The commissioners eventually recommended a bridge crossing the harbour, which in addition to having two lanes in each direction would also have footpaths and cycle tracks. And as for the enormous cost of the project (around £3,000,000), this would be paid in part by a toll on those crossing the bridge.[965] However, the commission also recommended that a state highway 'from the city boundary at Avondale to Whenuapai and Dairy Flat' would be needed to help expand the development of the area to the northwest of the city, and enable drivers who did not want to pay the bridge toll to have a viable alternative route.

It was plain to all of those involved researching the transport options for the city at this time that the North Shore's projected growth required a major link with the rest of Auckland, and that inaction could lead to the area's underdevelopment:

> *The population at present numbers some 35,000, and the forecast of the population of the North Shore boroughs in 1965, as given in the Metropolitan Planning Report for 1943, is 55,000, to which we have added another 8,000 in the remainder of the North Shore area, making a total of 63,000. This is the largest community in New Zealand not directly served by rail, and the only populous area wholly dependent on a ferry service.*[966]

The necessity for a bridge was accepted by the government, but instead of the recommended six lanes, habitual official frugality pared them back to four, with both the footpath and cycle tracks eliminated from the final plan.[967] After four years of construction, this engineering colossus opened on 30 May 1959 (with each worker receiving a £30 bonus for completing the bridge three weeks ahead of schedule). After crowds had walked along its route in the previous week, the Harbour Bridge was now open to traffic, with more than 20,000 vehicles crossing it on the first day. Just 11 weeks later, that total had reached one million, which more than vindicated the decision to go ahead with the project.

The Harbour Bridge's dimensions were unequalled in the country at the time of construction, and remained so for the rest of the century.

The roadway was 13 metres wide, and 1020 metres in length, with the longest span stretching 243 metres. The bridge had a clearance of 43 metres above the high-water mark, with its reinforced concrete piers supporting the bridge's lattice-work steel trusses extending 31 metres below sea level.[968] In 1969, further lanes were added to each side of the bridge (pejoratively known as 'Nippon Clip-ons' because they were constructed by a Japanese firm),[969] and on 31 March 1984, tolling ceased. The final innovation for the bridge in this century took place in 1990, when a moveable lane barrier was installed to improve traffic flows at peak times during the day.[970] On the day the bridge opened, the *Auckland Star* claimed that Auckland was riding 'the highest wave of elation that has swept our way since the completion of the Main Trunk Railway'.[971] Although this was embellishing the reaction, the opening of the Harbour Bridge was undoubtedly about much more than the placement of a girdered behemoth arching over the Waitematā. Suddenly, the once remote and sparsely populated North Shore was now appended to the central-city suburbs, and its rapid urbanisation from this point onwards was much more certain.

Eventually, the Harbour Bridge, along with Rangitoto, and later, the Sky Tower, became part of that triumvirate of visual symbols that epitomised Auckland in the popular imagination. However, it was not so much the bridge's design — with its awkwardly hunched form, painted in battleship grey — that made it an enduring emblem of the city. Rather, it was its huge scale and its position straddling Auckland's main harbour that lent it this status, along with the fact that no other man-made edifice had the potential to transform the city as this bridge did — triumphing over geography to expand the frontiers of suburbia.

A bigger splash

It was not just the muscular limbs of industry and construction that were flexing at this time. Another sign that Auckland was maturing into a 'proper' city during the 1950s was its small but committed arts scene. The annual Auckland Society of Arts exhibition was one of the main opportunities for the city's creative community to assemble, and to parade their wares to fellow participants and the public. In the 1955 exhibition, modernism featured prominently, leading one critic to speculate about 'whether this is a new direction or possibly only a newly fashionable one', and when addressing the modernist works of one of the artists on display, wondered

> *whether they are not just academic paintings in a new guise or does ... [the artist's] lack of feeling for his subjects show as a new direction in painting, and if it does, should we not question this direction and, questioning this, then look about us to discover where we are heading. It is not enough to be 'modern'. To be modern is to take on a new coat and a new coat does not make us new men. Perhaps the answer is in being neither modern nor unmodern but, with courage, what one is at the time of painting.*[972]

The critic was the Titirangi-based artist Colin McCahon, and while he himself embraced elements of modernism,[973] his questioning of some efforts of those committed to this movement revealed as much about his own developing artistic orientation as it did about the works he was reviewing.

Such a nuanced reflection on the role of modern art was still a relatively rare commodity at this time, though. A more common popular reaction to modern art was consternation or outright denunciation. In September 1956, for example, when the Auckland mayor, John Luxford, walked from his office during his lunch hour to inspect the Henry Moore sculpture exhibition at the Auckland Art Gallery, he returned commenting that he 'had never seen the art gallery so desecrated by such a nauseating sight. There may be technical merit in Moore's work, which is not readily apparent to the ordinary person who goes into the gallery expecting entertainment and enlightenment. These figures, offending against all known anatomy, to me were repulsive.'[974] Yet, once released from its box, there was no way that modern art could somehow be returned to storage. Just two kilometres away from what Luxton berated as Moore's modernist monstrosities were the Parnell Baths — renovated the following year under the supervision of architects Tibor Donner and Ralph Wilkinson in a distinctly modern style. And the star attraction of the pools was a modernist glass-chip mosaic mural with a daily audience of thousands of motorists and train passengers passing along Tamaki Drive. A Matisse-esque work, the mural (principally the creation of the artist James Turkington) depicted swimmers floating and frolicking in an ambiguous mix of air and water, suspended weightlessly above the pools for actual swimmers to look up at as they themselves mimicked this artwork.

By the end of the century, modernism had, in the words of the art critic Robert Hughes, 'turned into a kind of entropic, institutionalized parody of its old self'. It had become less a form of experiment, expression and daring, and instead was reduced to appearing 'like a period room in a museum'.[975] However, for Aucklanders in the 1950s (and for a little while after), something of the spirit of the age was harnessed in works like Turkington's mural. There was a distinct effort to glance into the future, liberated from having to stare at a stuffy, formal past. Architecturally, culturally, socially and technologically, Auckland was transforming at a faster rate than at any previous time in the century. However, these changes were felt unevenly, and were not necessarily embraced happily by all Aucklanders. Instead, tensions rippled across the city's surface. Moral conservatism was juxtaposed with new experiments in social and individual values, traditional housing was slowly being confronted with the appearance of radical alternatives that deviated from so many of the unspoken conventions of what a house 'ought' to look like, Māori were becoming a demographically significant feature of the city (rather than the diminishing cultural remnant they had been treated as in previous decades), and even the shape of the city itself was being swiftly redefined as roads fanned out further into previously sparsely inhabited areas, propagating entirely new suburbs in the process.

8
The 1960s

Upscaled Auckland

Even by 1960, the various brickworks operating in New Lynn still had a Dickensian feel about them. Factory buildings, clad in rusted corrugated iron or soot-coated brick, were connected to each other by a maze of muddy, ill-lit paths, and on still days chimney smoke hung in a thick pall over this industrial area, creeping into every crevice, and draping the nearby swampy fields in a smoggy haze. One stretch of barren, flat, spongy land adjacent to these dilapidated factories covered an area of about three hectares, and it was there that the decision was made to build New Zealand's first shopping mall. This was the era of transformation in how Aucklanders shopped. In 1958 the city's first supermarket — the Foodtown 'all-convenience' store — had opened in Ōtāhuhu (and was closely based on the supermarket model that was proliferating in the United States at this time).[976] The next great stride in this retail revolution took place five years later, on 30 October 1963, when LynnMall (originally named the 'New Lynn Shopping Mall') opened on what had been a bare patch of industrial wasteland just a few years earlier. The contrast could not have been starker. In the midst of an otherwise bland working-class suburb, where residential streets abutted factories, a radically new conception in shopping materialised.

Here, customers could visit 38 shops under one roof covering an area of over 8000 square metres,[977] and there was a large carpark that could accommodate 500 vehicles, making it a convenient shopping destination for people outside the normal retail catchment area.[978] But it was not just the convenience that attracted people to LynnMall. The novelty and newness of its futuristic brutalist form (its 33-metre tower was in keeping with the vogue for space-age aesthetics in this era) drew in customers from across the city, as did the fact that malls functioned as new social spaces — places where the community could mingle and socialise.[979] Here was a place that felt relaxed (its central terrazzo courtyard had seating, and even a fountain), and where people could wander to major stores such as Farmers, Milne & Choyce and Woolworths, as well as smaller shops, like La Gonda Fashion, Kean's, Masco and Curtaincraft.[980] And there was more. Competitions for bed-making were run, as well as a variety of beauty pageants, musical performances, talent quests and other ancillary forms of entertainment designed to lure shoppers. If there was an epicentre of the fantasy of suburban utopia in Auckland at this moment, LynnMall was it, although not everyone was convinced. Some existing retailers in the area thought that building an American-style mall in New Lynn was a doomed experiment from the outset.[981] Surely, they reasoned, the shopping preferences of Aucklanders were more in keeping with their British forebears, who preferred a traditional high street to 'foreign' American tends such as malls? Such Canutes were, of course, completely wrong — the incoming tide of mall-shopping was unstoppable, and would eventually sweep away many of the small, owner-operated shops along the main streets of those suburbs where malls were established.

Not all that was traditional was on its way out, though. One pottery that had been active under various names since its inception in Hobsonville in 1854, and which had shifted to New Lynn in 1925, was Crown Lynn. In the 1940s the firm's mundane designs were aimed at the mass market, which made it an obvious choice for government support during the war, when imported crockery became almost completely unavailable. In the 1950s, sometimes under various subsidiary names, Crown Lynn produced shapes and patterns that were aesthetically the equal of any major producer in the world. However, sales-wise, the success of these innovative works was modest. They suffered from the paradoxical problem of local customers regarding their design as too 'foreign' and their quality too 'local' and therefore inferior.[982] By the 1960s, the patterns of Crown Lynn crockery had become much less adventurous, the shapes more mundane,[983] and sales boomed accordingly. The insertion of more modern production technology went hand in glove with the affordability of their ceramics, and a seemingly insatiable customer demand followed. At the beginning of this decade, the company's factories were churning out over ten million items annually, and employing nearly 500 people.[984] But even though the company's mass-produced products were later perceived as passé, there was great innovation in this era. In 1963, one of the novel designs Crown Lynn introduced was a straight-sided, cylindrical coffee cup. This was a huge departure from the conical forms that had dominated cups for the whole century up until this time, and added some modern chic to the country's kitchens wherever these cups were on display. But there was one aspect of the firm's output that — even beyond the aesthetic appeal of its products — ensured the loyalty of its customers. This was the fact that for the more than 30 dinner-set designs that Crown Lynn was manufacturing by 1965, each piece was replaceable.[985] This meant that owners could ensure they maintained complete sets long after the production runs of imported crockery ended. By 1969, this West Auckland company had become the biggest ceramics producer in the southern hemisphere.[986] And while items like the Crown Lynn white swan vase were a feature of many Auckland mantlepieces in this era, the most popular of the company's items in the 1960s was the dinner and tea set with the 'autumn splendour' pattern. If you were having afternoon tea in Auckland in this decade, this is the most likely set it would have been served in, and it came to epitomise suburban ceramic fashion (even though the transfer pattern had been designed in the United States).[987] Yet, just 20 years later, Crown Lynn closed down, defeated by cheaper imports and changing local tastes. Later, though, a nostalgia-infused affection for the company's ceramics saw popularity for its products surge, with one collector offering a very corporeal reason for his affinity with this locally manufactured crockery: 'The thing I like about Crown Lynn is that it's made out of West Auckland dirt. When you are eating off your Crown Lynn, you're eating off part of this country.'[988]

As the Crown Lynn kilns exhaled their smoke, and the factory workers (mainly women)[989] laboured on its assembly lines, 15 kilometres east of New Lynn, a factory in Fort Richard Road, Ōtāhuhu, was engaged in a much more improbable form of production. Whether it was a calculated entrepreneurial risk, or inflated ambition (or most possibly, a bit of both), in 1963 Phil Andrews and Noel Turner decided to explore the possibility of producing a New Zealand-made car (albeit one assembled from parts from overseas).[990] The catalyst for this inroad into car-manufacturing was the introduction in 1958 of tariffs on almost all private imports to New Zealand, which in turn was the result of a collapse in the prices of cheese, butter and wool in the country in the previous year, which had precipitated a balance-of-payments crisis. One of the aims of the tariffs was to invigorate domestic production,[991] which suited the scheme that Andrews and Turner had devised — involving importing Skoda parts and assembling them to produce a distinctly New Zealand car.

On 2 December 1966, after a great deal of tinkering, experimenting and makeshift solutions to the complex business of car manufacturing, the first Trekka rolled off the production line. The event was modest by the standard of car launches in this era in other countries. A row of chairs was laid out in the back yard of the Ōtāhuhu factory where the vehicles were being assembled, and the Minister of Customs, Norman Shelton, was present to deliver a speech. Then came the climax of the launch. A white curtain had been draped across the factory's doorway, and at the appointed time six dark green Trekkas with brown canvas tops drove through the curtain and into the sunshine (one of the cars had a bumper missing, and was consequently kept away from the photographers present).[992]

At £899, not only was the Trekka among the most affordable cars on sale in New Zealand (the Ford Anglia and Austin Mini were marginally cheaper), but the fact that it bypassed the foreign currency requirements for purchasing an overseas-made car meant that more people in the country could afford one. However, reliability issues with the vehicle, combined with the eventual easing of import restrictions, led to the Trekka's demise, and the few surviving examples ended up as curiosities favoured by collectors. The Trekka was destined to be a very small outcrop of the country's car market — a naively hopeful venture that was doomed by its diminutive scale and technological shortcomings. Despite the car's affordable purchase price, its apparent practicality, and its debatably rustic charm, there was no way an Ōtāhuhu vehicle manufacturer could sustain competition with its major international counterparts in Detroit or Coventry.

Where Auckland was able to muster a more credible and enduring industrial operation was in Glenbrook — one of the more remote parts of Auckland, located 40 kilometres south of the central city, and 15 kilometres west of Pukekohe. In the same dogged spirit of economic self-sufficiency that had spawned the Trekka, the Department of Scientific and Industrial Research had begun to explore possibilities for the ironsands (which contained potentially commercial quantities of iron and titanium)[993] along parts of Auckland's west coast to be smelted for steel production. In 1959 the Crown granted itself the exclusive right to mine these ironsands,[994] and established the New Zealand Steel Investigating Company in the anticipation of converting the sand into steel, and the steel, in turn, into revenue. In 1967 construction of the Glenbrook Steel Mill began in 1400 hectares of flatlands bordering the eastern shore of the sluggish Waiuku River (which is not technically a river at all, but a silt-clogged estuarial branch of the Manukau Harbour),[995] and a year later the mill began operating (soon becoming one of the largest industrial sites in the country). Glenbrook was unique in the world in that it was the only plant to use titanomagnetite sand as its source of iron. It was also one of the biggest single employers in Auckland, even though it lay at the southern extremity of the city's rural limit. However, the industrial processes of the Glenbrook Steel Mill, including its discharge of smoke, and its contamination of local waters, collided with how some local Māori regarded the area ought to be used. These two monolithic views of environmental use — indigenous and industrial — proved to be difficult to reconcile. If Glenbrook was regarded as sufficiently 'out of the way' by most Aucklanders to be of any concern, it was equally seen as central to many local Māori in their campaign to resist this sort of heavy industry.[996]

The ancient and the advanced also squared off in this decade in Māngere. In September 1960 the Māngere Wastewater Treatment Plant (then known less euphemistically as the Manukau Sewage Purification Works) was opened. It was the product of years of deliberation by engineers and politicians on how to treat and dispose of the quantities of sewage that the city's growing number of residents was producing.[997] The works relied on shallow oxidation ponds where sewage would be treated biologically through a combination of algae, sunlight, wind action and the movement of the water in the ponds to break down the contaminants.[998] The ponds at Māngere — then still a largely rural part of Auckland — were the largest of their kind in the world, covering an area of over 500 hectares — sufficient to cater for a population of 500,000, and able to accommodate waste pumped in from a 40-kilometre radius. However, within six years of opening, Auckland's population had reached 535,000,[999] and so extensions to the plant commenced in the following decade.[1000] The science of sewage treatment using natural biological processes may have seemed an elegant solution to a problem that is as old as humanity, but too little forethought had been given to the accompanying stench. As the population in this part of South Auckland grew, the periodic bouts of foul air wafting through the area often went from unpleasant to unbearable. Some residents were forced to close their windows, especially on hot days when the smell seemed to get worse, and its reach occasionally extended as far as Hillsborough, five kilometres to the north of the ponds. Eventually, improved technology eliminated most of these odours, but for decades the ponds were associated with pong.

The ill-effects of the treatment plant were not just olfactory. As with the Glenbrook Steel Mill, there was a sort of cultural contamination involved, with the oxidation ponds not only stretching out next to traditional seafood-gathering areas for local Māori, but also being located adjacent to the Ōtuataua Stonefields, a historic reserve containing the remnants of extensive stoneworks extending back to the earliest period of human occupation of the Auckland region.[1001] This juxtaposition of one of the country's oldest historically significant sites (including the foreshore that borders it) with the country's largest sewage pond is symbolic of how the majority of Aucklanders regarded both this corner of their city, and its Māori heritage at this time. At the beginning of the 1960s, Māngere was a nine-kilometre drive from Great South Road, and was almost stranded on a peninsula that was surrounded by the mudflats of the Manukau Harbour, and was made up of tired and, in some cases, abandoned farms. There was a scattering of houses — some dating back to the colonial era — and Makaurau marae, located at the centre of Ihumātao pā. In 1961 a visitor to this settlement of around two hundred people sketched an account of how it was being modernised:

> *Less than five years ago this village, or as it is commonly called, pa, consisted of several substandard weatherboard houses lying along the banks of an unhealthy tidal creek in a market gardening zone .... Considered a potential slum area by both the Manukau County Council and Maori people of the pa itself, application was made to the Department of Maori Affairs for individual housing*

> loans. On these being granted, section clearing, demolition and building was begun almost immediately with the result that there are at present fourteen new semi-detached houses in the village with others planned for construction in the next twelve months. The building of new houses, of course, is not the only aim of the Ihumatao Maori people; also scheduled for construction is a new meeting house to replace the present wooden building that has served as a picture theatre and dance hall for the past ten years. Impressed by all this constructive activity in the pa, the Manukau County Council also decided to ... lay down new approach roads and make arrangements for the community to be connected with the Auckland Electric Power Supply.[1002]

Such outward signs of progress, however, belied just how culturally insignificant the Māori presence in the area was popularly seen during this period. As an illustration of this, when the Māngere Wastewater Treatment Plant was being constructed, scoria for the ponds' retaining walls was quarried from sites that were regarded as sacred to local Māori. Some of the drystone boundary walls at Ōtuataua were demolished for use in construction of the ponds, and access to the bores and springs used by residents was banned because of the risk that they could be contaminated by sewage seeping from the treatment plant.[1003]

Two years after the sewage treatment plant was opened, work commenced on a major state housing development in Māngere. In an area of 1450 acres, schools, parks, shops, an industrial area and residential zones were mapped out, and over the next two decades this semi-rural outpost was transformed into a modern suburb.[1004] One of the principal reasons for the decision to open up Māngere for urbanisation was its proximity to one of Auckland's emerging industrial zones, and the city's new domestic and international airport. The existing airport, at Whenuapai, had been struggling both with the steady increase in traveller numbers and the fact that its longest runway was not suited to a new generation of passenger jet aircraft, such as the DC-8 and the Boeing 707. In 1955 the government approved plans for a major airport at Māngere, and began acquiring additional land for the project. Construction got under way in 1960 on the site where a grass runway had been in use since the 1930s (Jean Batten had landed there on 16 October 1936 after her solo flight from Britain). The 844-acre site had to be completely levelled, with some of the runway being built on land reclaimed from the Manukau Harbour. A hundred acres of concrete was laid, and the new runway was 2590 metres in length (which was extended to 3292 metres in 1973).[1005]

Auckland Airport officially opened on Auckland Anniversary Weekend (29 to 31 January) 1966 (although the first flight from the new airport had taken place at the end of 1965). Over that weekend, various events with an aeronautical theme were held at this location, attracting more than 100,000 curious Aucklanders to the city's new portal to the rest of the world. In the year it opened, Auckland Airport had almost 700,000 passenger movements, but these travellers were all herded through an interim facility that was regarded by many as an embarrassment because of its cramped and rapidly deteriorating condition. Work soon commenced on a new terminal, that opened in 1977, by which time the airport was dealing with almost two and a half million passenger movements annually.[1006] In 1966, though, despite the shortcomings of the terminal, Auckland Airport was lauded as one of the summits along the city's march of progress; and as one commentator observed, its success was rippling across the city:

> *The city is already the chief point of entry for tourists arriving by air, and this should increase further if the hopes for greater transit traffic materialise. Several airlines are now becoming interested in extending their services from Sydney and thus placing Auckland on a round-the-world route. Large hotel developments are taking place in the city centre in anticipation of the increased tourist traffic, whilst motels are being built in the suburbs along the route to the airport. As with many large scale developments in transport, the full implications of the new airport are probably unforeseen but in any event Mangere will be playing an increasingly significant role in the future economic development of Auckland.*[1007]

New faces

In the 1960s, Auckland became one of the favoured destinations for migrants from Samoa, Tonga, the Cook Islands and Niue. As the demand for factory labour in particular outstripped local supply, New Zealand began to drain the Pacific basin of people at a rate that would result in

Auckland soon becoming the largest Polynesian city in the world.[1008] The lure of employment was strong for many of these immigrants, but often their greater priority was for the educational opportunities New Zealand offered for their children.[1009] But the growth of a large Polynesian diaspora in Auckland was not simply a case of the invisible hand of the city's economy smoothy slotting in labour to where it was needed. Pacific immigrants brought their cultures and languages with them, and for the most part in this decade, maintained the taproots that connected them with their homelands. The ocean border that separated these immigrants from their places of birth may have been vast, but it was also very porous. One of the more visible connections with 'home' was the support that immigrants gave to their families back in the islands in the form of remittances.[1010] This flow of funds became part of the economic infrastructure of Pacific migration in this decade — supporting families left behind, and in some ways serving as a demonstration by some immigrants of the success they had found in Auckland (even if that success was not always what they made it out to be). However, the clock was ticking on this culture of funnelling money back home. While many immigrants adhered dogmatically to the practice — relying on it partly as a means of demonstrating kinship ties that otherwise were severed by geography — their children were generally much less inclined to send some of their earnings to their families in the Pacific.[1011] For this second generation (and even more so the ones that followed) the connections with home were inherited rather than experienced, and more sentimental than tangible.

Pacific immigrants to Auckland in the 1960s faced all manner of obstacles and adjustments as they endeavoured to recommence their lives. The barriers of language, education, appearance and culture were formidable, and exacerbated by the relative poverty many arrivals experienced. One contemporary report revealed how these new Aucklanders were perceived locally, describing Pacific migrants coming from islands that 'are underdeveloped and present limited educational facilities and few opportunities to acquire skills appropriate to an industrial society'. Consequently, on reaching Auckland, 'the vast majority of these people find employment only in labouring and unskilled occupations, insuring [sic] their concentration in the lower socio-economic strata of New Zealand society', including the ghettoisation of these communities in poorer parts of the city.[1012] Around 58 per cent of Pacific immigrants in Auckland in 1964 lived in inner-city suburbs, where typically the housing stock was older, more run-down, but more affordable. The living conditions were made tougher still by the fact that almost a half of Pacific households in Auckland in this decade accommodated extended families, resulting in approximately 40 per cent of inner-city homes housing five or more occupants.[1013]

And to make matters worse, there was a wall of racism that these immigrants faced at almost every turn. One contemporary piece of research noted that by the end of the decade there was a '[p]opular acceptance of a West Samoan reputation for bad behaviour (a reputation shared to some extent by all Pacific Islanders and Maoris), [and] a belief or fear that property values will be depressed by the arrival of West Samoan neighbours'.[1014] In the openly expressed parlance of the time, immigrants from the Pacific Islands were derided as 'over-stayers', 'coconuts', 'bungas' and 'fresh off the boat'.[1015] Yet, for all the waspish comments, contemptuous glares and rampant discrimination (particularly in housing and employment), Pacific immigrants still strived to improve their lot. Of course, there was the relentless struggle to earn enough to put food on the table and a roof over their heads, but beyond this, there were efforts to recreate some of the sense of community that they had left behind when they moved to Auckland. The focal point from the 1960s onwards for the rest of the century was the church. In addition to their obvious spiritual function, Auckland's Pacific churches had sports teams, music groups, choirs and a host of social gatherings. The church was also a place where congregants' native language could be heard and spoken freely[1016] — something perhaps taken for granted by English-speaking Aucklanders. And churches were also where cultural memories were stored and rekindled — not only memories of the islands from where the immigrants originated, but also, over time, of the early experiences of life in Auckland.[1017]

But no church is an island, and the sometimes rigid adherence to traditional structures and boundaries that were evident in many churches came up against a younger generation (many brought up in Auckland rather than in the country their parents were from), who felt that such views were out of place in the city where they lived. One young Samoan church member described how they saw their place in the congregation in a way that captured an emerging tension around Pacific traditionalism in contemporary Auckland:

When you spoke you had to be aware of the reputation of your family and the ways people would see what you did and that tended to be a constraint on what we said and how we said it. There weren't enough of us to make a real difference. We were sort of 'token young people' and sometimes, in the session, you couldn't even be certain that your parents and relations would support you although normally a Samoan family is, as you know, pretty tight.[1018]

When it came to outward shows of solidarity, though, most Pacific communities in Auckland in the 1960s were able to conceal whatever internal fractures they had, and contribute to the common cause. This was especially evident in the formation of Pacific Island churches in this decade. The first specifically Pacific church in the city was in Edinburgh Street, Newton, and opened in 1962. This was a Congregational church (a denomination that had a strong presence in much of the South Pacific), and became the largest Congregational church in New Zealand in this decade, with seating for 700 worshippers.[1019] To outsiders, the most visible sign of the faith of many Aucklanders from the Pacific was in the Sunday-morning procession of churchgoers walking from their homes in suburbs like Ponsonby and Grey Lynn to church, dressed in pristine white (a sign of moral purity). Women wore hats (in accordance with the biblical requirement for women's heads to be covered), with their hair usually pulled back off the face and tied in a bun. Such dress styles were 'associated with Christianity and good pure morals and cleanliness'.[1020] But in inner-city Auckland in the 1960s, sanctity sometimes collided with sin, as one Samoan from this part of the city later recalled:

As a child I remember ... walking home, or often waiting for my bus at the bus-stop at the Pink Pussycat [a striptease club] on Sundays. Oblivious to what the strip clubs represented, I never stopped to think of what I must have looked like — a young Samoan girl in frilly dress and shiny black shoes juxtaposed against a backdrop of a white, seductively beckoning nude temptress. I wondered why the headmistress at the Grammar school forbade us to wait for our bus at that bus stop in our school uniforms![1021]

'246'

Cultural contrasts and clashes were the norm rather than the exception for many immigrants in this era. Knowledge about Auckland as a destination was limited in many instances to whatever little could be gleaned from the newspapers, perhaps a book about the place, but most commonly, word of mouth from friends and relations who had already moved there (thus putting them in the category of what is known as 'chain migrants'). One of the more sizeable groups of such migrants to Auckland in the 1960s came from the present-day Croatian region of Dalmatia. Escaping poor living standards and a communist regime, just under 3000 arrived in the country in this decade,[1022] with the majority settling in Auckland. In addition to having to learn English, and find employment quickly (often to pay off the cost of their airfare to the country), many of these recent migrants had to contend with what they found to be a largely alien culture. For all its territorial scale, the city had a parochial feel to it, with its Anglo-Saxon residents appearing reserved, even withdrawn, and somehow culturally blunted, perhaps as a consequence of their isolation. It was certainly not what some of these freshly arrived Europeans were accustomed to at all:

> I didn't understand anything about it [Auckland]. Here I was, on the other side of the world, and it felt terrible. On our second night here, a few of us — we all came over on the same plane — we went out for the evening. We thought, you know, we'll go to a restaurant, then some cafes, and walk around Queen Street. Everyone had talked about Queen Street. But when we went there, there was nothing. Everything was shut, everyone was at home. All I could think is 'what's wrong with these people? Why aren't they out enjoying themselves?'[1023]

Instead of what these immigrants were used to — the presence of a vibrant nightlife throughout the week — Auckland offered absence. At a quarter to six every evening, bars and pubs announced to their patrons that it was 'supping-up time', and 15 minutes later they were required to close (a hangover from 1917, when the temperance movement convinced the government to introduce this early-closing measure ostensibly to enhance wartime efficiency).[1024] This became known as the 'six o'clock swill' — a term almost as distasteful as the practice it described. Men would rush to the pubs straight after work and often consume as much beer as they could before closing time, sometimes returning home in a fog of intoxication. It was not until 1967 that the law was changed, allowing local authorities to permit closing hours to extend until ten o'clock in the evening. Until then, as one English immigrant remembered it, the country's drinking habits at the pub were squalid and degrading:

> *I arrived ... to be thrown into a culture that was supposedly genteel British, but in fact was marked by the 'six o'clock swill', and the Friday night 'bashes' at which a group of mates each 'shouted' their round, whether they needed it or not. Women were not welcome, and felt very out of place in a public bar. 'Nice' women did not drink beer in public.*[1025]

It was a situation that — to the immigrants arriving in the city, and to the growing number of Aucklanders who were being exposed to different entertainment cultures as they travelled overseas — felt antiquated and lacking in sophistication. One migrant to the city, however, led a campaign to bring a semblance of European normality to Auckland's culturally asphyxiated hospitality sector. For seven years, the Dutch-born Otto Groen had lobbied authorities for the right to allow wine to be served with meals at his Shortland Street restaurant The Gourmet. His customers could select from various cuts of steaks, beef Stroganoff, Vienna schnitzel, Hungarian goulash and roast turkey, but the puritanical prohibition on alcohol was at odds with dining habits overseas. It is probable that alcoholic drinks were surreptitiously consumed at The Gourmet, making the ban one that increasingly was honoured more in the breach than the observance. However, passing bottles in brown paper bags under the table was hardly conducive to elegant dining. Groen persisted, though, and on 13 December 1961 his restaurant became the first in Auckland to obtain a liquor licence.[1026] The genie was now out of the (wine) bottle, and 1960s Auckland experienced a growth in establishments that catered for those who liked the option of drinking alcohol with their meals. Takapuna's response to this more liberated regulatory environment was the new Mon Desir Hotel — a startling, Japanese-influenced modernist building, which boasted the city's first beer garden — an outdoor space where alcohol could be served, and significantly, where women were welcomed.[1027]

THE 1960s

The gastronomic profile of Auckland was altering significantly at this time. In 1960 the city had 94 restaurants (all unlicensed) and two 'ethnic' restaurants. In just over a decade, though, the total figure had nearly trebled.[1028] However, it was not just that the number of eateries was increasing. There was a perceptible shift taking place in the attitudes of Aucklanders to dining out. Rather than settling for somewhere to get food before doing something else, restaurants were becoming talked-about destinations in their own right. They were a way of showing one's sophistication, gentrification or cosmopolitan leanings, and one of the few types of venue where the distinction between public and private space blurred. Restaurant-going in this period was also a subtle act of rebellion against the bland, British-inherited fare Aucklanders had been used to for generations. Now there were exotic ingredients, alchemically combined to produce novel meals, served in venues with ambiences that were radically and glamorously distinctive from the suburban dining room. Even the menus were more like maps of desire, opening up imaginative gustatory possibilities for diners.[1029] But like all bouts of progress, there were reactionaries who resented these changes. Grumbled accusations of 'foreign muck'[1030] were made against the new varieties of food appearing in Auckland restaurants, and the Auckland-based food writer Tui Flower (who became food editor of the *New Zealand Woman's Weekly* in 1965) received letters complaining about recipes she published, on the basis that they included ingredients such as garlic and oil.[1031] Auckland's palate was obviously still acquiring its taste, but eating out was becoming more popular, and at venues throughout the city where choices of food were becoming more varied.

But if you were after lunch or afternoon tea where formality and convention reigned, Auckland offered that too in this decade. In the suburbs, there were cafés (many in malls or shopping arcades) where people could get something to eat, but these places generally lacked much in the way of glamour, and were largely perfunctory. Customers would place a heavy plate on a plastic tray and drag it along a narrow bench as they selected food from plastic cabinets containing mainly sandwiches and a narrow selection of cakes. It was convenient, and a change from making one's own snacks, but not much more than that. In July 1964, though, a new shopping centre opened at 246 Queen Street, and soon became widely known simply as '246'. Advertising for the centre emphasised its refined ambience:

> *Allow yourself a sigh: an old tradition is with us again: the old wonderful idea that shopping is neither route march or bayonet charge ... but an unhurried dallying, a leisurely thing, when the choice of something to wear, or something for the home is as important for the seller as it is for the buyer. Remember when aisles in shops were spacious, the atmosphere unhurried, the people polite, attentive, interested? Refresh your memory at 246.*[1032]

Developed by the cinema owner Robert Kerridge, 246 was intended to be a sophisticated mall that combined high-end shops with places to eat, space for fashion parades, and even beauty salons. Among the more illustrious shops that were housed in 246 were Maitland Knitwear, El Jay, Vance Vivian Menswear, Barker & Pollock and the furniture shop Danske Møbler.[1033] Visiting such a prestigious shopping centre was a highlight for many Aucklanders when going to the city centre, and in this decade they went to some considerable effort to dress for the occasion. 'Whenever you went to 246,' a visitor in the 1960s later recounted, 'it was a big deal. All the ladies wore hats, and when they went for a cup of tea, you would see them with gloves on, all sitting very proudly. And everyone talked about 246 after they had been there.'[1034] This multi-level mall remained popular until at least the late 1970s, but its tilt towards traditionalism and conventionalism was slightly anomalous in the so-called swinging sixties,[1035] where the swing was specifically away from anything staid and conservative, and towards those things that were adventurous and liberated. Youth culture was exalted, and the past was dispensed with like some unfashionable relic from a stuffier, more socially retentive age. Formality was in retreat, and new music, values and styles were taking its place. Mods and hippies, polyesters and acrylics, paisley and psychedelic — these were part of the culturally variegated trends sweeping through Auckland (and much of the rest of the Western world) in this period.

Yet, just as Auckland appeared to be rushing eagerly to experience the shock of the new, at the same time it was also rediscovering some of its past. In the inaugural era of motorways and mass air travel in the city, it occurred to some Aucklanders that it might be a good idea to preserve the remnants of the technology that had helped build the city, and that otherwise might end up in rust and ruin. In 1960, Auckland's mayor, Dove-Myer Robinson, convened a meeting in which members of the augustly named Old Time Transport Preservation League submitted plans for the preservation of a handful of Auckland's trams, which had been put out of service in the previous decade.[1036] Other historical groups — particularly those with a focus on machinery and transport, soon joined the ranks of this project, which culminated in 1964 with the opening of the Museum of Transport and Technology (MOTAT).[1037] The museum was built around the steam-powered Western Springs pumping station — itself a monument of the city's early industrial history.[1038] However, the notion of what constituted a museum exhibit, and the value of certain types of potential exhibits, was not clear to everyone in the city at this time:

> *Old things had not yet acquired intrinsic 'antique' value, and much of what museum members saved would otherwise have been lost forever. Much had already been sacrificed to war-time scrap drives. From barns and attics and wrecker's yards, from phased-out tramways and steam railways, from airline, fire brigades and farms, and even from buried dumps of war-time aircraft, the museum's supporters brought in thousands of items, large and small. And once the project began to become news the public responded with a further flow of relics, heirlooms, and even whole private collections.*[1039]

As MOTAT's collection was being developed, 17 kilometres to the east the Howick and Districts Historical Society (formed in 1962) was engaged in its own plans for a pastiche of the past.[1040] These eventually culminated in the formation of Howick Historical Village — an open-air ménage of cottages and assorted buildings evoking rather than reconstructing a colonial-era Auckland outpost.[1041]

Both MOTAT and the Howick Historical Village were depicting Auckland's history in ways that appealed to the city's view of itself in the 1960s. It was a perception of the past that was largely European, that commenced only a century or so earlier, and that offered a slightly defensive, anaemic rendition of the city's evolution. This particular approach to popularising Auckland's history reached its peak in 1967, with the opening in Auckland Museum of the Centennial Street exhibition (an installation that was dismissively removed in 2015). Centennial Street — which was part cultural archaeology and part kitsch fabrication — was a stylised vision of an Auckland shopping area in 1866.[1042] Visitors wandered around the 'streets' lined with scaled-down stores, they could peer through shop windows to see artefacts from the previous century, and in some cases could enter these buildings — a pub or a drapery, for example. With its dimmed lighting, this conceit of Victorian Auckland was one that everyone bought into. Nobody had any expectation that Centennial Street was a faithful reproduction of part of the city in 1866, but there was just enough authenticity in some of the exhibits to allow this exercise in imagination to draw visitors into a version of Auckland's colonial history. And as with similar efforts to reconstruct the past at MOTAT and in Howick, for the next half-century Centennial Street acted as an indication of the way Aucklanders in the 1960s preferred to remember their city's past.

Elsewhere, though, the city's history was not being treated with nearly as much affection. Symonds Street Cemetery, one of the most significant historical burial sites in Auckland, had lain dormant since it reached full capacity in the beginning of the century. However, whereas when it was opened in 1842 this cemetery was on the outskirts of the embryonic city, it was now (somewhat problematically) a six-hectare site sprawling across what were potentially crucial arterial routes into the city. In 1963 the government took the grave decision to authorise some of the bodies in the cemetery to be disinterred to make way for a new stretch of motorway running under Grafton Bridge.[1043] The following year, work began on digging up around 4100 bodies in the affected area and shifting them to two memorial sites set aside in the remainder of the cemetery (the identity of most of those reburied in this way was not recorded).[1044] It was far from being an entirely fitting solution, but in the calculus of civic progress at that time, road transport took precedence over just about everything else.

Going up

The pressure on land in Auckland was obvious in places like the central business district, where the shape of the isthmus placed additional pressure on an already densely populated and heavily utilised part of the city. However, the formerly happy relationship between population growth and urban sprawl — with each able to satisfy the other — could not last indefinitely. By the end of the decade, the number of people living in metropolitan Auckland was approaching 650,000, and was growing at a rate of nearly 3.4 per cent annually (compared to a growth rate of under

1.8 per cent by the close of the century).[1045] In an effort to manage this expansion, in 1961 the Auckland Regional Planning Authority developed a plan for the region's growth. It laid out the vision of an 'orderly, coherent, decentralised metropolitan region comprising a main or parent area surrounded by a cluster of communities'.[1046] It sounded so simple — defining Auckland's future urban contours with utopian ease — except that reality was marching in a different direction. A pair of academics writing in 1969 diagnosed some of the planning ailments afflicting the city at this time:

> *Auckland ... suffers from the "cult of the quarter acre"; residential densities seldom rise above 16 to the acre so that sprawl on a large scale is evident. Today urban Auckland extends approximately 30 miles from north to south and 20 miles from east to west. Urban motorways, now with a length of 30 miles, and the harbour bridge .... have increased the accessibility of more distant parts and accelerated the outward movement of the city's population. Both the State and group-housing firms have contributed to this by creating large-scale estates and pockets of development on the city's fringe .... Such additions increase the demand for public services while similar facilities in older areas serve fewer people as families move out to the newer suburbs .... Low residential densities make difficult the economic provision of public transport. The motor car is increasingly used for commuter transport, thus aggravating the city's circulation problems.*[1047]

In the course of this inexorable, low-density suburban enlargement, agricultural land was being swallowed up, which caused a few residents at this time to worry that the city's food-production capacity was being diminished.[1048] But in addition to growing out, Auckland was also experimenting with going up, which peaked in this decade with the erection of the Civic Administration Building (credited as being the country's first skyscraper)[1049] at the northern end of Greys Avenue. Design work had got under way in the mid-1950s, led by Auckland City Council's chief architect, the Hungarian-born Tibor Karl Donner, with the resulting modernist structure finally completed in 1966.[1050] The building would be where many of the administrative needs of all the people of Auckland would be co-ordinated — like some bureaucratic

Babel, towering over its citizens. And while the land on which it was built was in the centre of the city, and therefore had a high commercial value, the Civic Administration Building effectively added value to the air above it, leading the way for other multi-storey buildings in Auckland to follow suit. The Civic Administration Building's slim form — 16 storeys high, 40 metres in length, but just under 16 metres wide — was complemented by its stark outward appearance. The long sides were sheeted in glass, with aluminium frames and sunshades, while the north end had a concrete panel running up the entire height of the building on its right side.[1051] This was civic pride confidently thrust heavenward, and changed the city's skyline like few other buildings had to that time. The scale of this building was undoubtedly monumental, but Aucklanders were divided on its aesthetic appeal. Yes, it was very much in keeping with contemporary international trends in skyscraper design (although the 11-year lag from inception to completion meant that it was already dated by the time it opened),[1052] but still some found it unlovable.

Around 300 metres to the south along Greys Avenue from the Civic Administration Building was another of Auckland's architectural innovations of this decade: the city's main synagogue. Similarly designed in a modernist style, its architect (and synagogue congregant) John Goldwater planned the brick-clad building around a central, open courtyard that was surrounded by parts of the building serving differing functions. On one wall was a Holocaust memorial leading to the direction of the octagonal interior of the synagogue — the most spectacular interior space in the complex. Illuminated substantially by natural light from arched windows at ground level, and clerestory windows lining part of the ceiling, this large space was dominated by a modernist holy ark in which the Torah scrolls were housed.[1053] In 1967 the synagogue was opened, making it the newest significant religious building in Auckland in this decade, housing one of the city's oldest religious communities.

One of the potentially most controversial building projects in Auckland in the 1960s (and probably the whole of the twentieth century) never reached fruition, but illustrates how far some were prepared to go to enable the ongoing modernisation of the city at this time. All that population growth, all that urbanisation, and all that industrial expansion could not occur without substantially increasing supply of electricity. The trouble was, though, that such supply was far from certain in this decade. From the end of the Second World War until 1958, there had been periodic restrictions on electricity consumption to cope with a shortfall in generation.[1054] The demand for electricity continued to grow in the 1960s, though, partly as a natural consequence of an increasing population, but also because of the greater dependence on electrical appliances, such as heaters, televisions, fridges, freezers and clothes dryers.[1055] In 1962 the government formed the Electricity Council to provide advice on power supply and distribution,[1056] and in scouring for new sources of electricity, inevitable in this era, the option of generation by nuclear fission came into view.

Nuclear power was seen at the beginning of the decade as the elixir for the country's electricity supply needs. It was inexpensive, inexhaustible and harmless,[1057] and could secure Auckland's growth for decades ahead, particularly as there were questions at this time over how many remaining sites there were that were suitable for hydro-electric generation.[1058] Work soon began on plans for a nuclear power plant, and in 1968 Oyster Point, on the Kaipara Harbour, was selected as the most suitable site — an area of gently undulating farmland about seven kilometres northwest of the small settlement of Kaukapakapa. The plant would comprise four 250-megawatt reactors that planners forecast would meet the electricity needs of the growing city until the end of the twentieth century.[1059] However, just as Auckland was poised to become only the second location in the southern hemisphere to acquire a nuclear power station (the other was in Atucha, Argentina),[1060] other alternative sources of power came into consideration, and eventually resulted in the Oyster Point project being scuttled. The idea was not abandoned altogether, though. In 1976 the Royal Commission on Nuclear Power Generation in New Zealand was established to explore if the possibility was still viable, but a lack of immediate demand for such a facility led the Commission to conclude that a nuclear power programme would not be economically justifiable until 'the early part of the next century', and that 'a firm decision to proceed need not be made until at least about 1992 to 1996'.[1061] By that time, however, popular distaste for anything nuclear had grown considerably,[1062] and any thoughts for reviving the option for nuclear power had been abandoned.

Not so innocent

In 1963, two career criminals — Ronald Jorgensen and John Gillies — put a large-calibre puncture in any faith Aucklanders may have had that they were immune from the sort of gun crime normally associated with mafia-type gangsters in American cities. On Thursday 5 December, both men entered the house at 115 Bassett Road, in Remuera, with Gillies armed with a Reising submachine gun (set to semi-automatic mode).[1063] Inside were Kevin Speight and Frederick 'Knucklehead' George Walker — both of whom had criminal records, and who were involved in various illegal activities around the city. When their bodies were discovered by their landlord (who was visiting to collect their rent), Speight was lying in his underwear, and had been shot in the chest and lip. Walker was in a shirt and underwear, and had been shot in the cheek, arm and back of the head. A future police minister and Auckland mayor, John Banks, recalled an encounter with the victims shortly before they were killed:

> *You know, I never really thought anything of it at the time. I was at home one day when there was a knock at the door. There were these two huge guys asking to speak to Dad. I recognised one of them as George Walker, who had known my parents for years .... [Walker was] absolutely polite and friendly, but couldn't go anywhere without stealing something. Kevin Speight was a big guy too .... They came in and went to speak with Dad. They sat there, heads together talking in whispers, paranoid about the police .... Around the time of my birthday in December, Dad took me to 115 Bassett Road where they had set up a sly-grog. I couldn't believe that just a few days later those jokers would be dead.*[1064]

One of the detectives assigned to the case recalled arriving at the scene:

> *It was a Saturday, and like a lot of other detectives, I was called in from my day off. I went around to 115 Bassett Road and saw the bodies. The stench I just cannot explain. If you could imagine that these men had been lying undiscovered for several days in the height of summer, and the room itself was equally hot as the blinds were drawn. We had two dead bodies here, which was most unusual because in that era, murder was a rarity. But here we had two.*[1065]

The investigation into the shootings was headed by Detective Chief

Inspector Robert Walton, and supported by 32 detectives who spent the next week scouring the area for the weapon used in the killings — exploring local streams, parks, neighbouring gardens, all without success. Aucklanders were shocked by these execution-style murders, and the emerging story of gambling, illegal alcohol trade and the presence of brutal crime syndicates operating in the city.[1066]

Such crimes were indeed rare — something borne out by the fact that the murder of Speight and Walker at Bassett Road accounted for 20 per cent of all the murders in the country for the whole of 1963.[1067]

In the heightened state of vigilance following the discovery of the bodies, all ports and airports in the country were put under surveillance by the authorities, and rewards posted by the police, totalling £1000, were paid to 12 individuals who supplied information on aspects of the crime.[1068] Auckland was awash with rumours about the killings, to the point where the normal flows of intelligence were swelling and bursting their banks. One recipient of information was the National MP for the Tāmaki electorate, Robert Muldoon, who had been in contact with someone whom he believed had useful details about the case. The witness named Gillies as the killer, but when Gillies subsequently refused to co-operate with the police, he was put under covert surveillance while investigations were making headway against his partner, Jorgensen. Both men were arrested on 31 December, and charged with what the entire city was referring to as 'the Bassett Road murders'. It took the jury just four hours to find the killers guilty, after which — predictably — sentences of life imprisonment were pronounced.

Jorgensen completed his sentence in 1984, and in December that year disappeared. His abandoned car was located at the bottom of a cliff in Kaikōura, but there was no body, and despite sightings of him afterwards, he was declared dead in 1998. Gillies was released at the end of the 1960s, but ongoing offending saw him in and out of prison until 1987, when he was given a new identity, after which he disappeared into the anonymity of the general public.[1069]

Reds

Along with the rest of the country, there was disquiet building among some Aucklanders over New Zealand's involvement in the Vietnam War from the mid-1960s. The advance of communism in South-East Asia had been a source of anxiety since the 1950s for many in the West,[1070] and as the Cold War chilled further in the following decade, New Zealand — as a small but loyal member of the Western alliance — contributed to the increasingly futile war to prevent communism taking hold throughout Vietnam. By the time the war was lost, 3890 New Zealand military personnel had served in the conflict (with 35 killed and 187 wounded).[1071]

The 'worry about Asian nations going over to communism'[1072] was widespread and almost innate among many in the country: '[W]ell, at that time, yes, we were worried that the Russians would keep expanding. That's what it looked like then. They were already in control in Eastern Europe and were invading other countries. The feeling was that they would keep going.'[1073] There was a countervailing view at the time, though — probably held by a minority of Aucklanders — which challenged some of the orthodoxy of this Cold War thinking: 'It was always about communist aggression, but when we saw what the Americans were doing in Korea and then Vietnam, we could see that the communists were not the only ones who were aggressive.'[1074]

Auckland became the first location in the country to produce a movement specifically opposed to the country's military entanglement in Vietnam (excluding the five members of the Communist Party of New Zealand, who held an anti-Vietnam War gathering in Pt Chevalier in August 1964).[1075] The 'Peace for Vietnam Committee' was established on 28 March 1965 during the meeting in the Town Hall of a coalition of union, pacifist and religious groups opposed to the war.[1076] The Committee was a left-leaning organisation, and failed to arouse widespread public support. Another body opposed to the war, but comprising principally academics from the University of Auckland, emerged in 1965, and even though its credentials were largely non-communist, it similarly failed to garner much in the way of popular backing.[1077] However, in some of the city's households, the issue of New Zealand's involvement in the conflict was becoming a matter of concern, particularly when the first troops were sent from the country to the war zone. As one Aucklander recalled:

> *At home there was constant talk. Above the table there was a map of the world and that was Dad's sharpening board to get us talking about things that were happening around the world. Politics was always talked about. We argued like hell about it, but Dad always won [Laughter]. The war in Vietnam was going*

> *on and I was part of a group responsible for a big study we did of it at Teachers' College [in Mt Eden] .... Both my parents, of course, were always talking about Vietnam and that the Yanks were bastards and lots of my friends and a lot of their friends were the same. The day that they sent troops to Vietnam we handed out a leaflet in Queen Street — thousands of them .... The leaflet said that we were sending troops to Vietnam, that a decision had been made. That night Holyoake got up and announced that it was just a pack of rubbish and that it hadn't even been considered. About two days later we got the announcement that the troops had already gone.*[1078]

At a time when sources of information were comparatively few, and in some cases more carefully curated than was the case in later decades, it was difficult for opponents of the war to convince others of the value of their cause:

> *in those days you believed everything that was written you know. You didn't question what you were being told. And I didn't have any friends that were as I said that were involved in protesting and that. So, I didn't get any information that way. Because we were so busy doing our stuff at that time. And it was only afterwards when all the other things came out that you really, you know that we talked about it.*[1079]

What did finally mobilise Aucklanders to the streets to protest against the country's collaboration in the conflict was the arrival in New Zealand in January 1967 of South Vietnamese Premier Air Vice-Marshal Nguyen Cao Ky. Opponents to the war gathered in various parts of Auckland, formed committees and subcommittees, and debated and then determined the action they would take. As the country's involvement in Vietnam escalated, and as letter-writing, lectures and pamphlet distribution had proved ineffectual, more drastic and visible forms of protest were resorted to, and Ky's visit was the timely trigger. On 24 and 25 January, around 2400 protesters assembled outside the Star Hotel in Auckland to denounce Ky's visit, with 21 of these protesters arrested in the process.[1080] Further protests occurred in Auckland in May (which even captured the attention of the *New York Times*),[1081] and in October police had a 'pitched battle with Vietnam demonstrators' outside the Paritai Drive home of the American consul.[1082]

Public opinion was slow in turning against the war, but by the close of the decade it was doing so decisively.[1083] In keeping with other nations in the West, popular distaste for the ongoing prosecution of a war that was increasingly looking unwinnable, combined with the monstrous massacres and chemical killings, made claims that it was preventing a greater evil — communism — difficult to digest. Another noticeable sign of this shift in popular attitudes was that, unlike their comrades in the Second World War, those troops returning home from Vietnam were given no parades or laudatory speeches, and their cause was regarded as much one of shame as of glory. One soldier's account of his arrival back in Auckland after serving in Vietnam encapsulates the mood of the time:

After a couple of hours over the Tasman sea we were told to take off our military clothes and put our civies on. We were told once we were on New Zealand soil not to tell people where we had been and that was it. We landed like one in the morning in New Zealand and by 2 am we were on the streets of Auckland. There was no one there to welcome you, but a truck driver.[1084]

In turning their backs on the troops staggering back from Vietnam, Aucklanders were unwittingly displaying a cultural shift that had occurred in the city (where it was probably more pronounced than in some of the country's rural areas). The term that so often surfaces when historians address this decade in the West is that of 'counterculture' — a movement that was contrary to the prevalent culture.[1085] The problem with such a term is that it misses the point that the so-called counterculture was not a defiant aberration, but more a rapid bout of social evolution that altered society's culture and values rather than merely lashing out at them like some fleeting adolescent tantrum.

In some areas, the machinery of the state seemed to be failing to keep pace with the rate of this social change. Once such case of the developing 'youth' culture colliding with government regulation involved the broadcast of music in Auckland. The government's ongoing monopoly of the radio frequencies in this decade gave it little incentive to accommodate all sectors of its potential audience. As long as there was no competition, radio programming could remain stale and even slightly aloof. The thriving popular culture of the city's youth — invigorated in this decade by tours of performers including the Beatles, Tom Jones, the Rolling Stones, the Who, the Yardbirds, the Small Faces and Herman's Hermits[1086] — was confronted continually with a broadcast regime that generally turned up its nose at this raucous, rebellious and even riotous music.[1087] It was routinely rejected as aurally and morally polluting, and nothing more.

The rebelliousness of which rock-and-roll music enthusiasts stood accused was borne out in Auckland on 4 December 1966, when the 30-metre vessel *Tiri* chugged out to a spot in the Colville Channel (between the Coromandel Peninsula and Great Barrier Island). Following a brief introduction, the first song broadcast from this floating (and illegal) radio station was Matt Monro's lethargic ballad "Born Free". It was hardly drug-induced psychedelia or aggressive rock, but it was a poke in the eye to the authorities, and thousands of Aucklanders were soon tuning in to the frequency (1480 AM) to listen to the 'pirate' radio station: Radio Hauraki.[1088] Soon, listeners could hear music by Jimi Hendrix, the Doors and the Kinks — all of which had effectively been banned by the New Zealand Broadcasting Service (although at the other end of the popular music spectrum, it also played songs by the Irish Rovers).[1089] One of the complaints about the station that was of concern to politicians was not its content but the technicalities of its operations. The Auckland opposition MP Hugh Watt questioned (evidently in all sincerity) the postmaster-general in October 1970 over what action he intended to take 'to prevent the interference by Radio Hauraki to the reception of station 2YA in Auckland, as many complaints have been received from listeners that the broadcast of Parliament is affected in the evenings'.[1090] After three years at sea (including a sunken vessel, and numerous challenges from the authorities), Radio Hauraki was eventually granted a land licence. It was a pyrrhic victory for the 'pirates', though, as the basis for the notoriety on which their popularity was built was stripped away as a result of gaining the official authorisation to broadcast they had sought for so long.

Probably more than any other decade in the century, the 1960s has a series of images and motifs attached to it — flower power, hippies, anti-war protests, mini-skirts, psychedelia, sexual liberation, and so forth.

It is true that these elements are part of the iconostasis of the era, but they were neither spontaneous apparitions nor momentary aberrations. Auckland, like much of the rest of the world at this time, experienced many of these social, aesthetic and cultural convulsions, but they should not be allowed to distract from the continuity of life in the city in this time. Shifting social norms in no way diminished the appreciation many Aucklanders were cultivating for their city's past. In the flurry of progress, some residents were increasingly keen to preserve the physical markers — from trams and trucks to cottages and cars, to even a stylised colonial street — that embodied the stages that Auckland had traversed to reach its current state. Such reflection did not bring about stagnation, though. In addition to society readjusting itself to accommodate the different attitudes, fashions, cultures, beliefs, tastes and trends that were arriving at an ever-greater frequency, Aucklanders were also adjusting to the physical appearance of the city evolving more rapidly. Among the most monumental changes in this decade were built ones, in the forms of shopping malls, steel mills, supermarkets, skyscrapers and sprawling subdivisions. If the city had a manifesto in this era, it could be reduced to a single, all-encompassing word: expansion. And as the new decade approached, every indication was that this augmenting Auckland was set to continue.

9 The 1970s

Happening

A grin must have spread across the face of Phil Warren — the Auckland music promoter, agent and manager — when the idea first came to him. Just a few months earlier, almost half a million people had converged at Woodstock, near New York, for a three-day music festival, which also became a parade of American counterculture in this period. Surely, Warren thought, Auckland could host its own music festival, trading on Woodstock's success (and infamy).

In late 1969 he began to assemble a line-up, and selected a venue for this event: Redwood Park, in Swanson. It was 16 kilometres from the centre of the city, in a rural setting that had been a favourite spot for the Avondale Presbyterian Church Sunday-school picnics at the beginning of the century (and was named for the redwood trees planted in the vicinity in 1934).[1091] Warren's timing was out, though. For all its mass appeal, Woodstock signified — as much as anything else — the end of an era.[1092] The generation of peace, love and drugs was growing up, and Woodstock represented more of a final flourish of the period of free-living hippy abandonment than a movement in the first flush of its existence.

'Redwood 70', as it was billed, took place on the weekend of 31 January/1 February 1970. The line-up of musicians was comprised almost entirely of local acts, but the 'special guest star direct from London' was Robin Gibb from the group the Bee Gees,[1093] who was to be backed by a 17-piece orchestra (which was as much of a hint as was needed that this event would be far from the sort of radical countercultural outpouring witnessed at Woodstock).

As an indication of how makeshift the event was, the start of the first performance had to be delayed by half an hour because the food stalls were using up too much electricity, leaving insufficient power for the amplifiers on stage.[1094] Eventually, the festival got under way, and as the relatively disappointing crowd of around 9000 settled in at Swanson, the compère Peter Sinclair (who had until recently presented the popular music television show *C'mon*) introduced the event: 'Hi, welcome to Redwood 70, the first happening of a happening decade .... a love-in, a live-in, a be-in. Thirty-six hours of non-stop top pops.'[1095] So far, so hippy, but there were soon signs that peace and love were not in ample supply at this event. An account of Gibb taking the stage revealed that there was an uncouth element making its presence known in the audience:

> *International pop star Robin Gibb, on asking if the audience is "Having a luvly [sic] time?" gets pelted with a flying tomato. Then a young man dashes for the stage and is intercepted by the under-resourced police and security detail. Breaking away, one arm still held, he dances a fake foxtrot with his captor, drawing laughter from the large crowd and prompting yet more flying cans and missiles .... Soon after, a girl dressed in white makes it onstage and grabs Gibb around the neck, pushing him into the music stands behind. She's quickly followed by a male fan who heads for the microphone before being repelled by a policeman.*[1096]

Sinclair attempted to placate the malcontents in what he thought was the patois of the audience. 'Well guys and gals', he announced with a slightly American inflection in his voice, 'you've been very patient out there .... but I've got to remind you the Police and the security service have promised to remove anybody from the grounds who creates any sort of disturbance at all .... so let's cool it and have a groovy scene'.[1097]

Sinclair's plea, plus the installation of an electric fence near the stage, seemed to deter most from disrupting this event any further.

The low attendance at Redwood 70 resulted in the promoter losing money on the venture, and some of the lacklustre performances failed to rouse anything like the Woodstock spirit. Instead, late on the Sunday afternoon of 1 February 1970, the audience wandered off listlessly once the final song finished. There had been a few arrests during the festival, the usual series of scuffles, and some drug use (although perhaps slightly less than rumours suggested), but nothing more serious. As the daylight faded on that Sunday evening, the food trucks drove away, the stage was taken down, and a gang of cleaners began restoring Redwood Park to its former humdrum state. The city's experimentation with a youth music festival had been a moderate success, but this West Auckland Woodstock concluded with a sense of unfulfilled possibilities.

Massey and its counterpoints

By the 1970s, Auckland had become too big. At the mid-point of the decade, its population had reached just over 707,000, yet its built area covered 37,000 hectares, affording residents a very comfortable density of just 19 people per hectare[1098] (compared to Sydney's 27 people per hectare, and London's 50 residents in each urban hectare).[1099] Spacious it may have been, but in many cases, getting around the city was neither easy nor cheap. This was particularly so after the oil shock of 1973, when over the following nine years petrol prices rose from 10 to 60 cents a litre.[1100] The impact of this increase on some families was significant, as one Swanson resident explained: 'My brother lived in Howick. That was about twenty-five miles away — a fifty-mile round trip — and there were no buses you could catch, so you had to drive there. And that was a lot of petrol at that time, so we'd only go there about once every couple of months.'[1101] Experience and inconvenience were conspiring to mould Auckland into a patchwork quilt of increasingly self-contained suburbs. Even the lure of the centre was being dimmed by the rising popularity of local shopping centres. It was principally the thread of road network that held the pieces of this quilt together. Even administratively, Auckland was a tangle of cities, towns, counties, districts, licensing authorities and boroughs[1102] — each with their own elected bodies and bureaucracies, and all grimly guarding their parochial interests. This manifested itself in numerous ways, from different footpath sizes, berm widths and road design, through to public transport options and even where alcohol could be sold. Paradoxically, however, in a way, part of Auckland's distinctive character was the sum total of all these localised idiosyncrasies (and inconveniences).

This was also the era of peak suburbia, when the city's urban expansion reached its terminal form, epitomised in the West Auckland suburb of Massey. It seemed that all that mattered at this point was to provide housing for people, and little else. At the start of the decade, Massey was characterised by rapid house construction but a dearth of public facilities, such as town halls, shops or parks. And to add indignity to this most functional and dystopian of suburbs, the rich topsoil of the area was removed during the subdivision stage, leaving 'good old Massey clay', as one resident put it, from which gardens later struggled to grow.[1103] Planners had faith that the facilities expected of a suburb at this time would soon appear in Massey, once there were sufficient people living in the area. However, the lag in the provision of many basic services made the suburb seem even less endearing to all except those who could not afford any better. As one example, in the middle of this decade, the residents in Cedar Heights Avenue, Benchmark Drive and Redwood Drive all relied on a solitary phone box if they needed to call anyone.[1104] And until the end of the 1970s, when Woolworths opened at Royal Heights, the nearest supermarket was in Te Atatū South or Henderson — around a seven-kilometre drive away, in an era when not every family had a car. Even planting a church in the suburb was a challenge. The Methodist church built in Waimumu Road in this decade only existed because a local retired farmer decided to donate the land on which it could be constructed.

In the 1970s, areas such as Massey were known as dormitory suburbs — places characterised by affordable mass housing but almost no jobs available locally. Consequently, a tide of mainly male workers drained out of Massey every morning and returned each evening. The combination of few facilities and a sense of isolation was challenging for those left at home, as one housewife explained at the time:

> when I was first left here on my own with just the children I felt as though I had been slammed into somewhere in isolation .... I didn't know any of my neighbours .... Once I got to know them, it was much better. We felt that we needed each other because we were so far away from things.[1105]

This gnawing sense of isolation was compounded by a near absence of any feeling of connection with the location. A Massey school teacher noted in 1978 that none of the students had parents who had attended the school (because it had only recently been built), or who were born in the area, and many had relatives in Auckland who did not even know where Massey was.[1106]

In a pocket of land to the west of the city that until recently had comprised paddocks, scrub and a few small vineyards and orchards, Auckland had now reached its suburban nadir. It took until the end of the century — when plans were finalised to establish a large commercial and industrial zone on Massey's northwestern flank — for the area to begin to move away from its status as a characterless, cultureless, residential outpost. That, at least, was the view from the outside. Some of Massey's residents have a fonder, though possibly nostalgically affected, recollection of their suburb in the 1970s:

Well, it was a struggle for everybody at that time, but we all knew each other in our street, and if someone needed their kids looked after if they had to go to the doctor, or even if your lawnmower was broken and you needed to borrow one, it was never a problem. Not everyone was helpful, but most of them were, and it's stayed that way, really, the whole time I've been there.[1107]

For all its bland, poorly designed and even more poorly resourced form, this was where the nation's egalitarian ideal was played out in its most efficacious manner. It was just that when Massey's incarnation of the egalitarian utopia finally came into view, it was utterly underwhelming. Whereas, earlier in the century, city planners had conceived of 'garden suburbs', or carefully laid-out residential areas with high-quality housing and generous community facilities, Massey instead became the heart of what was then known as 'group housing'. Sections were generally smaller (around 600 square metres on average) and the houses themselves — built by firms including Keith Hay, Universal Homes, Beazley and Neil Housing[1108] — had many of their components (from doors to frames to windows) mass-produced in factories. Buyers could select from a range of standard plans,[1109] but the overall appearance and layout of these houses was very similar. Fibrolite was favoured over weatherboard (brick cladding was a rarity), carports often became a substitute for garages, and the range of exterior house colours was narrow. And instead of being positioned in regimented rows along straight streets, houses in Massey looked more as though they had been scattered on subdivisions, only loosely lining the crescents and cul-de-sacs where they were built. Even on the section, these homes were often positioned at an awkward angle, as if fashionably defying the conventions that buildings should be parallel to their boundaries. One of the most dramatic but relatively rare efforts at injecting the exotic into this mundane housescape was modifying homes to give them the 'hacienda' look. This was a faux-South American aesthetic that materialised variously in the form of arches (rather than doors) connecting one room to another, 'Spanish' style rough plaster (on interior and exterior walls), terracotta tile roofs instead of corrugated iron and maybe even some wrought-iron features over the windows or for gates. Embracing this style was partly a means of escapism from the banality of group housing, although within a decade it had largely fallen from fashion.

Another feature of Massey's freshly housed subdivisions was that they were seldom initially landscaped. Consequently, when it rained, there was often a heavy smell of wet soil, which sometimes resulted in a yellowy sludge of clay washing onto the footpaths and streets. By contrast, in summer, that same clay would bake hard, making planting almost impossible. Eventually, though, some trees struggled into maturity. Bottle brushes, pittosporum and the occasional silver dollar tree took root, softening the look of sections, and as a feature plant, the cactus-like 'Yellow Ribbons' century plant (*Agave americana*) became moderately popular because of its dramatic form and its association with the hot climate of Central America (where hacienda architecture originated). Massey's working-class, low-income-earning residents did what they could to beautify their patch of Auckland. Admittedly, not all the efforts weathered well, but the same could be said for any other part of the city in this period. However, Massey's mass-produced, budget housing, and its emergence in what was almost a case study in the dereliction of planning, left it languishing for the remainder of the century as an example of what Auckland's haste to urbanise looked like when pursued to its ultimate end. The crowing ignominy for this fledgling suburb was the Poultrymen's Co-operative Limited factory — manufacturers of poultry feed — on Don Buck Road.[1110] Although constructed in the previous decade, land in its immediate vicinity was zoned for residential use, and housing appeared around the factory in the 1970s. Visually, it looked prematurely derelict, like some overbearing industrial carcass, with its faded, rust-patched iron cladding, its dreary concrete-block office with dirty frosted-glass windows, and its pipes, vents and vats in all directions. But worse was the smell of the decaying animal matter used to make the poultry feed, which was particularly pungent on still days, without a breeze to disperse it. 'I remember walking home past there every day,' one former student of Massey High School recollected, 'and the whole area stunk. Even when we got to Triangle Road [about 300 metres away], the smell was still really strong.'[1111] This was an example of Auckland planning at its most negligent. And it would be more than a quarter of a century until the factory was finally torn down.

Fifteen kilometres northeast of Massey, on seven hectares of rural land in Albany, lay a promised elixir to suburban neurosis and the grinding gears of Auckland's urban planning system. Opened in 1977, the Centrepoint commune offered its 36 founding members (a group that grew to around 300 at its height)[1112] an 'alternative' lifestyle. Influenced by similar communes that had been established in California in the 1960s, Centrepoint was a response to the decline in traditional communities in Auckland, the increasing breakdown of families, and the fall-off in involvement in organised religion.[1113] The attraction of a promised return to a more intimate form of social connection was understandable for anyone looking at the character of Auckland's newer suburbs — Massey, Glenfield, Wiri, Pakuranga and others — where any sense of community had been hollowed out, and where each household appeared to be socially marooned on its small, barren urban plot. Centrepoint's communalism, in contrast, was infatuating. In a way, Centrepoint was also the logical end point of the unbridled pursuit of sexual liberation in the 1960s — a wilful experiment to see how far the remaining boundaries of propriety and social norms could be pushed. Was it possible for a community to unshackle itself from the rest of the city and, just maybe, become the cradle of a new Auckland? Herbert 'Bert' Potter thought so. As founder, spiritual leader and manager of Centrepoint, Potter, a former vacuum-cleaner salesperson, had already been offering therapy to individuals from his home in Campbells Bay, and in 1975 moved to a house in Gillies

Avenue, in Epsom, where his focus shifted to group therapy (and where a number of like-minded social experimenters moved in with him). Two years later, Potter founded Centrepoint on its Albany site.

With the bare bones of his commune now established, Potter dived head-first into an undertaking that attempted to force together sexual liberation, financial communism and pernicious social control. If the initial enthusiasm of its members was anything to go by, it looked as though Auckland had found its small patch of nirvana. Centrepoint's emphasis on 'encounter group' therapy afforded those in the community the opportunity of catharsis, while its diverse business activities promised the organisation financial longevity. Membership was drawn predominantly from Auckland's Pākehā middle class — those with just enough sense to imagine the utopian possibilities of Centrepoint, but without sufficient sense to anticipate the many pitfalls that lay ahead (and that, if they had bothered to inquire, had hobbled most previous similar attempts at communal living). The commune's loosely articulated aims were also in keeping with the culture of self-exploration and discovery that was gaining ground in the West at this time.[1114] One early member described this progression leading to membership of Centrepoint:

> *It was strange how I got into the spiritual thing. I was in one of those spaces young people sometimes get into where you ask some questions and the next day you meet someone with the answer. I was wide open and having a lot of those kinds of experiences .... I was quite consciously searching. I went around checking out groups like the Hare Krishnas, and I'd been to India and met a lot of people doing the guru circuit .... the next book I picked up was some esoteric Buddhist thing about people who spend all their lives looking for what's right under their nose, so I gave it all away and ... [joined] Centrepoint.*[1115]

Intimacy became one of the governing principles of the commune, with shared showers, toilets and sleeping areas supposedly designed to foster a feeling of closeness and strip away members' inhibitions.[1116] Nudity in the commune became common, as did sexual openness, and eventually, sexual abuse. For the rest of Auckland, speculation and rumour occupied a space created by a dearth of evidence about Centrepoint. In the city's popular culture at this time, the commune became a focal point where moral outrage and sexual titillation existed as confused bedfellows. And there were enough hints that something unusual was taking place at Centrepoint, even if it was in the fact that hundreds of Auckland children were uprooted from their schools and neighbourhoods and effectively were held captive at the commune. When the stories leaked out, they ranged from concerning to chilling:

> when I was really young Dad said to me 'We're going to get an ice cream' and then he drove me up there, so he didn't even tell me the truth from the start. And then the next time we went up there, I tried to run away, because I just didn't like the feel of the place and the look of the place and it was just too different. And the way my father had talked about it, I knew what went on up there. So I just, was scared of going there for that reason too.[1117]
>
> The Centrepoint community just hounded and hounded Mum to get us to go there. Really — just because Bert just wanted to have sex with us. And so, yeah, so basically, yeah, so he got us, got Mum to come and get us, and so, you know. [He] didn't let up until we'd moved in.[1118]
>
> You'd be in group therapy and they would always turn around to sex and how you please people and then the next minute a couple of the group leaders would be doing a demonstration of how you pleasure each other.[1119]

Ultimately, Potter's commune served as little more than a means for him and his coterie to carry out sexual abuse. With their emphasis on nudity, non-monogamous relationships, bogus therapy and the breakdown of conventional inhibitions towards sexuality, some of Centrepoint's leaders were able to perpetrate serious and sustained sexual offences, including against children.[1120] However, it would not be until the following century that the extent of the abuse at the commune was made public. In the 1970s, Centrepoint was still a place of whispered fascination for Aucklanders — a 'free love community'[1121] which was right on the city's doorstep, yet morally out of reach for most people.

Auckland was capable of being just as pious, though, as it was profane. At the same time that Potter's commune was sinking ever deeper into its own iniquity, the solidly working-class suburb of Mt Roskill was developing a reputation as Auckland's Bible belt,[1122] with the highest number of churches (and the lowest number of pubs) per capita in New Zealand (with 26 churches for the 35,000 residents of the area).[1123] The reasons for this religious revival were manifold. There was a rise in the charismatic and Pentecostal movements at this time,[1124] and this combined with the emergence of new denominations in the area (such as the Alliance church) and the success of smaller denominations that were community focused (such as the Church of Christ).[1125] In addition, there was a convergence of young church leaders in the suburb in this decade, shared interdenominational events, and the fact that, at times, success begets success.[1126] If a congregation was large, that in itself could prompt the curious to attend, if only to find out the cause of this church in their neighbourhood being so popular. One couple from the suburb explained how they came to be involved in their local church around 1978:

> *We met the minister one Saturday when a few of the members of the church were having a working bee. We had noticed that in the past year, the building had been cleaned up quite a bit, and we stopped and got talking to him .... we had never really been to church, but he asked us to come next Sunday, and we did. We did and we liked the people there and we liked what they preached, and so we kept going back.*[1127]

This example could just as easily have come from a small village, and in a way, that is the point. Churches in Mt Roskill in this period (but to some degree in other parts of the city too) were inadvertently rediscovering their role as community institutions — a fact borne out by the efforts many churches went to in encouraging groups from the area to use their facilities during the week. However, Mt Roskill was something of an anomaly. Overall, church attendance was in a slow but steady decline in this decade (from around 19 per cent at the start of the decade to 16 per cent at its close),[1128] although it is possible that the reasons were not just religious. Secular groups, from sports teams to clubs devoted to hobbies, experienced a similar contraction of membership in this era.[1129] Secularisation seemed to be going hand in hand with a more general decline in community activity in the city. Churches were hit harder, though. There was a growing perception that they demanded time, were monotonous, irrelevant, old-fashioned, conformist and even authoritarian.[1130] The occupants of late-twentieth-century Western cities, by contrast, were less inclined to long-term commitments to organisations, and favoured involvement with groups that were smaller, more informal and easier to leave.[1131]

This slide away from religion was not the fate of all the city's faiths, though. In 1972 the New Zealand Muslim Association purchased a house in Vermont Street, Ponsonby, with a view to a mosque eventually being erected on the site. This signified a shift in the region's religious make-up. At the beginning of the century, Auckland was a predominantly Anglo-Saxon, Protestant city, with a strong Catholic minority. By the 1970s, advancing secularism among the city's Pākehā population, coupled with a rise in immigration from non-Western European countries, created demand for places of worship that would have been unimaginable in Auckland just eight decades earlier. By 1976, there were 644 Muslims living in Auckland,[1132] and it was a rapidly growing population. Over the next three years, this small community engaged in a concerted fundraising drive to pay for the construction of a mosque in Ponsonby (which would be the country's first purpose-built place of worship for Muslims). On 30 March 1979 its foundation stone was laid, in the presence of representatives from Iran, Indonesia, Jordan, Malaysia and Turkey.[1133]

A much more visible (and audible) religious minority in Auckland at this time was the Hare Krishna movement (an offshoot of Hinduism, founded in New York in 1966).[1134] Distinguished by the shawls, saris and kurtas that they wore, their shaved heads, and the percussive instruments they used to accompany their chanting and dancing, Hare Krishnas were a regular presence on Queen Street in the 1970s, from where they recruited new members to the movement[1135] (and where they were the object of ridicule by some Aucklanders).[1136] They established their first headquarters in Auckland in 1972, at 155 Landscape Road in Mt Eden. Four years later, they shifted to larger premises at 67 Gribblehirst Road, in Mt Albert. In 1978 they finally relocated to what would be their permanent home — a farm they called 'New Varshana', in Coatesville. As with Centrepoint, devotees of this movement favoured a commune in a rural Auckland setting for their base. It was close enough to the centre of the city's population (and source of recruits) but with a sense of remoteness that gave members a feeling of being apart from the world, and which helped to maintain their countercultural image.[1137]

While Auckland's religious profile was becoming much more intricate in this decade, overall, the drift to a more secular population continued, although the Pentecostal/charismatic revival, particularly in places such as Mt Roskill, could have given casual observers the impression that this trend had been reversed. At the same time, there was much greater religious pluralism among those in the city who did profess a faith. Immigration, and the rise of a taste for 'alternative lifestyles', contributed to this more marbled religious landscape, as did a decline in the social strictures that at the beginning of the century had wielded more of an influence, at least in the outward profession of belief by Aucklanders. The social aspect of religion cannot be ignored, though. Earlier in Auckland's history, churches were often the principal or even the sole place of communal activity, particularly in the more remote parts of the region. In a large, urbanised city, however (Auckland's population nudging towards 770,000 by 1979),[1138] there were many more social institutions vying for the community's involvement. This fact, along with greater social and sexual freedoms in society more generally, and greater demands on spare time, militated against the conventional churchgoing routines that had been a much more prominent part of life for Aucklanders in the early part of the century.

'The Colonel'

At the beginning of the 1970s, if Aucklanders wanted a quick meal, the takeaway options were limited to fish and chips, meat pies or perhaps a visit to one of the few Uncle's burgers outlets sparsely sprinkled around the region. By the end of the decade, however, the sharp blade of American fast-food firms had sliced through the city, revolutionising not only Auckland's eating preferences but also the places where food was consumed, and expectations about what constituted 'fast food'. This latter point often gets overlooked. Fish and chips, for example, could involve a wait of more than quarter of an hour at peak time (usually Friday nights), and apart from the various frittered foods that were offered as extras, the essential meal of wilting deep-fried battered fish and deep-fried chips had been unchanged for most people's lifetimes. The monotony of this menu could only be alleviated by people limiting their purchase of fish and chips to just once a week. This cottage industry (the vast majority of Auckland takeaway owners were sole traders) was an easy sector to be pushed aside by the muscular, flashy, industrialised American fast-food chains that so far had refrained from setting foot in the country. By the

1970s, though, they were prepared to stride into markets like Auckland — devouring the local competition and introducing a new food culture to the unsuspecting city.

Aucklanders received their initial entrée of American fast food on 20 August 1971, when Kentucky Fried Chicken opened its first branch on Manukau Road in Royal Oak, on a site facing the large roundabout intersection.[1139] Also referred to as 'KFC' or 'The Colonel's' (the latter a reference to its founder, Colonel Harland Saunders), this takeaway would be open every day of the week, and was the latest incarnation of that lineage of American shopping in Auckland that had started with supermarkets and malls and was now reaching its apogee with the introduction of American fast-food franchises.[1140] In a way, this was one of the inevitable outcomes of the city's intense phase of post-war suburbanisation. Put that trend next to the enduring ardour for most things American (the country that continued to lead the world in consumerism and popular culture), and the success of these takeaway chains looked almost preordained.

KFC's designation as a fast-food outlet applied to more than just the pace at which it could fulfil customer orders. Within 12 months of the first store opening in Royal Oak, others had opened in Panmure, Takapuna and Papatoetoe.[1141] Unsurprisingly, KFC's success encouraged other franchises to test the Auckland market, and in September 1974 the first Pizza Hut in the country opened in New Lynn. Pizza Hut — another American import[1142] — promised a more family-oriented eating environment, and for those who associated fast food with smelly fish-and-chip shops or windswept burger outlets, Pizza Hut's distinctive restaurants (with their trapezoidal windows and red, Dutch-gabled roof) offered an eating environment that was 'spotlessly clean [and] congenial'.[1143] There were menus, tablecloths, ambient lighting and various other trappings of those 'conventional' restaurants that many families could not afford to eat at. Now, restaurant-styled dining (albeit with a menu almost exclusively comprising pizza) was available to a much larger portion of Auckland's population. A nascent culture of dining out was being introduced to the masses.

The triumvirate of American fast-food franchises arriving in Auckland was completed in June 1977, when the burger chain McDonald's opened an outlet in the former Auckland Savings Bank building at 260 Queen Street (it was the second McDonald's in the country — the first having opened in Porirua the previous year). And as with Pizza Hut, McDonald's offered the option of takeaways or 'dining in'. However, with the crowds cramming McDonald's during its first days in operation in Auckland, with customers waiting their turn for a table while those eating were conscious of the throngs of people around them, this was 'dining out' reduced to its lowest common denominator. But they were popular, and as these American franchises spread across the city in a sort of eczema of red roofs, red-and-white-striped walls and red and yellow arches, Auckland's assimilation into the globalised eating industry accelerated rapidly in this decade.[1144]

Given the flush of success of these imported fast-food outlets, local entrepreneurs were keen to cash in on the trend by offering indigenous alternatives. Most of these turned out to be pale imitators of their more ostentatious American rivals, but for this decade at least, they gave Aucklanders a degree of variety in franchise takeaways that was greater than at any other point in the century. Thomas Ah Chee, the Foodtown founder, established the country's first Georgie Pie in Kelston in 1977. This franchise, modelled on McDonald's, but with pies rather than burgers as the principal food, eventually extended to over 32 outlets until it finally succumbed to its competition and closed down in 1998. Its demise prompted a feeling of nostalgia among some Aucklanders that a fast-food brand that was distinctly local was no longer present, as one former customer lamented:

> *I can remember being very upset and confused to [sic] the discontinuation of Georgie Pie. I was at a loss, as a big part of my childhood memories was gone forever. I even used to always look at the building where it used to be situated and feel sad and resent the new restaurant there.*[1145]

Another New Zealand-born fast-food chain, Homestead Golden Fried Chicken, was established in 1973, and mimicked many stylistic and gastronomic aspects of KFC.[1146] However, by 1992 the company had ceased operating, unable to compete with the advertising budgets of its major rivals,[1147] and maybe tasting a little too bland in comparison to its famous competitor.

One of the more intriguing responses to this foreign invasion of franchised food providers was Cobb & Co. It drew on the family restaurant model that Pizza Hut had perfected, but with what it hoped was a distinctive New Zealand strain. Its atmosphere was one dominated in the 1970s by rich red carpets and upholstery, and dark timber panelling, with allusions in the décor to stagecoaches and saloon-style doors, which harked back to nineteenth-century travelling in the colonies (even the name Cobb & Co. came from a Melbourne-based stagecoach service founded in 1854,[1148] although this firm was not connected at all to the 1970s New Zealand restaurant). The first Cobb & Co. restaurant opened in the South Pacific Hotel (on the corner of Queen and Customs streets) in 1974, and by the end of the decade there were 27 around the country, many located in motor inns or hotels, where there was a steady flow of diners to supplement neighbourhood demand (and because it was a division of New Zealand Breweries, it already had an association with these venues). The menu Auckland's famished families could expect if they went to dine at 'The Cobb' (as it was sometimes referred to) was an awkward collision of conventional and curious. Alongside the Cobb schnitzel, oven-roasted half chicken, lamb's fry and bacon, steaks and roasts of the day were shrimp cocktails, a Coach burger and a prawn concoction, together with novelty drinks such as the Traffic Light and Pink Panther.[1149] One thing Cobb & Co. was most certainly not was grandiose. As a manager later explained, '[o]ur food is not pretentious — it's food that people are comfortable and familiar with and we want to put it out to people at a price that is reasonable'.[1150]

Like its other New Zealand counterparts, customer interest in Cobb & Co. declined in subsequent decades, and it can be tempting as a consequence to see such initiatives as failures in the making — an earnest but hopelessly ambitious effort to compete with the 'big boys' from the United States. But such a view would be a case of reading history backwards, and misreading the sentiment of the era. The 1970s was the decade when Aucklanders in their tens of thousands entered the omnivorous realm of the family restaurant often for the first time, and its brasher younger cousin, the fast-food franchise.

These new fast-food outlets and family restaurants — whether local or imported — were not without their detractors, though. 'Mum and dad said it wasn't "proper food" and that it would rot your teeth'[1151] was the household edict on McDonald's for at least one Auckland family in the 1970s, and no doubt others held similar views. However, overall, Aucklanders voted with their stomachs, and by the end of the decade

KFC had become one of the leading fast-food chains in the city, with others following closely in its wake. Family restaurants and takeaways proliferated in number and variety, and became a fixture of life in many parts of suburban Auckland.

At home, culinary variety was also beginning to expand. This was the era when meals diverged into their most social and solitary forms. Potluck dinners — where guests would bring food to contribute to the meal — rose in popularity in the 1970s as an increasing percentage of women entered the workforce, requiring the conventional burden of women doing all the food preparation to be shared for gatherings. It also allowed the cost of a group eating together to be distributed more evenly. An additional attraction of the potluck dinner was the 'luck' element, with no certainty as to who would bring what. The possibilities could tantalise or repulse — that was always the gamble. A recollection by one hostess of some of the options popular in this decade offers a taster of exactly how appetising Auckland gatherings could be:

> *Fondues of all descriptions with choccy and strawberry dip to finish. Beef Wellington. Made those until they came out my ears. Prawn and avo[cado] cocktails with that ghastly orangey sauce that came in a jar. Meatballs in a plum sauce with rice. Curried mince and rice with sides of fresh pineapple, coconut, raisins and bananas .... Puddings had a frothy evaporated milk thing with gelatine on top which you put in the fridge and then beat until frothy, then this went on top of a lime and melon mould or a fresh strawberry and strawberry jelly mould. That was a party piece for me .... Lemon meringue pie always. Still a winner.*[1152]

At the other end of the comestible spectrum were the TV dinners. These frozen meals, with portions of vegetables, potatoes and gravy-coated meat compartmentalised in an aluminium tray, could be heated and ready to serve without the hassle of preparing a cooked meal in the conventional manner. Derived from aeroplane meals, the TV dinner grew in popularity in the United States from the 1950s, and reached their peak in the 1970s, especially in urban areas where there was less time than previously to prepare food.[1153] And as the name suggested, the growing practice of having an evening meal in front of the television, which was still frowned upon by traditionalists, was a habit that was gaining in popularity: '"TV dinners" ... forever changed the family meal. I was unaware of frozen dinners until the early 1970s. TV advertising really promoted "TV dinners" as nutritious, low cost, time saving convenience food and the industry really took off.'[1154]

More acres

In the 1970s, history was once again creeping up on Auckland to remind its residents that there was still unfinished business to be addressed. Just as the city looked to be entering into something of a slumber — induced by the opiates of consumerism and suburban contentment — it was startled back into reality by a succession of shrill reminders if its unresolved past. The first of these abrupt wake-ups occurred in September 1975, when a column of Māori made their way through Auckland as part of a march that had commenced in Te Hāpua, in the far north, and was headed to Wellington.[1155] The group organising the march — Te Ropu o te Matakite — was led by the revered kuia Whina Cooper, and was using this form of protest as a way of drawing the rest of the country's attention to concerns about Māori land alienation,[1156] and about the state of the nation's race relations more generally.[1157] The idea of a land march had been conceived at a hui at Māngere marae at the start of the year, with the axiomatic plea that 'not one more acre' of Māori land be taken by the Crown.[1158]

As the marchers — in excess of 10,000 at times[1159] — threaded their way south, the reaction of some Aucklanders was one of bewilderment. The unspoken presumption that New Zealand was a multi-ethnic paradise started to be challenged as these 'radicals' dispelled this mirage. For some of those on this protest — particularly those urban Māori who had experienced a degree of cultural alienation since moving to the city — this was the right cause at the right time. 'Maoris [sic] have a cultural attitude to land, distinct from that of the Pakeha New Zealander,' the march organisers explained in their manifesto. 'Land is the very soul of a tribal people.'[1160] It was a message that instantly resonated with most Māori, but one that took some time to settle and then register in the minds of some of the city's Pākehā population. Yet, by the time the march reached the North Shore, there were Pākehā walking alongside the Māori marchers in common cause.[1161] But just getting through Auckland would be a challenge, both logistically and legally. The scene of this advancing march was captured at that moment by the poet Graham Lindsay: 'A thousand-eyed eel sweats up the hill / Of the harbour bridge, that chained dinosaur.'[1162] The issue of permission to cross that chained dinosaur had arisen shortly after the marchers had left Whangārei, as Cooper later recounted:

> *When I wanted to go across the Harbour Bridge, it was blasted all over the papers and everything: 'you're not going to come over this Harbour Bridge' .... And the marchers said to me, 'Hey, look Whina, what are we going to do? We can't go over the bridge. What are we going to do?' I said, 'swim across. What's wrong with that?' ... [Then] I said, 'No. you leave that to me.'*[1163]

Cooper sent a telegram to the bridge authorities and the mayor, requesting that the hīkoi be given permission to cross the Harbour Bridge, and to just about everyone's surprise it was granted.[1164] The emblematic crossing was led by Ngāti Whātua's Joe Hawke, which given the iwi's long history of land loss, added poignancy to this stage of the march. One participant later reflected on the emotions that this cause brought to the surface:

> *[W]hen the [protest] flag just started waving in the breeze, my elders wept, because it was almost symbolic of the days of the biblical slaves ... when Moses led the slaves out of bondage .... I was holding on to Mrs Whina Cooper, and she smiled, as if that smile was [saying] 'Here we come, now, the Maori people, to regain what is truly ours — our heritage ... to regain our identity as the tangata whenua o Aotearoa.*[1165]

The route then took the marchers through Queen Street, bringing two New Zealands face to face in the main street of the country's largest city. Onlookers crowded the footpaths and leant out of office windows to witness the spectacle of a determined column of Māori marching for a cause few others fully understood, let alone empathised with. Certainly, some of those watching on were unrepentant in their view that Māori owed the nation gratitude rather than this sort of sullen protest. The mood as the hīkoi slowly advanced through the city centre was uncertain. 'One could sense their [Pākehā] fear of a Maori uprising,' one of the protesters observed. 'I was startled by the realisation that Maori and Pakeha were not familiar with Maori unity of purpose.'[1166]

When it came to the ambivalence of Māori–Pākehā relations in Auckland, the Land March served merely as a dress rehearsal for a far more dramatic confrontation at Bastion Point a few years later. From the perspective of tangata whenua, the issue of land loss had never gone away. It was a scar that did not heal, despite the passage of several generations, and as Ngāti Whātua's landholdings continued to diminish, the need to do something — principally to protect what little remained, and then to address what had previously been appropriated by the Crown — grew more urgent. By late 1976, Ngāti Whātua was almost landless in central Auckland, but remained defiant that some sort of justice would eventually be exacted for the losses that they had endured. The Orakei Maori Committee Action Group decided that protest was the only remaining option to address the pitiless process of land alienation. The issue was made more urgent by the government's announcement of its intention to build a retirement village on some of the 'uncommitted' land that had been taken from the iwi,[1167] by means that were legally opaque as well as ethically dubious.

Ngāti Whātua's protest took the form of an occupation, which got under way on 5 January 1977 — just two days before the subdivision of some of the iwi's land was due to commence. An occupation was a different beast from a march. The latter — however principled — tended to have a short duration, and often served primarily as a means of drawing public attention to an issue. An occupation, on the other hand, implied a more protracted undertaking, with occupiers digging in, literally, in expectation of continuing on to final victory. And in this age of a mass audience for television news, any occupation of this nature was also a visual spectacle, with all the possibilities that went with that for the message being refracted in various ways. Most importantly, though, the occupation was a wero — a challenge to the authorities to do the right thing and return what had been taken.

When the initial group of occupiers — numbering around 150 — moved onto the land, they faced measures of both support and hostility. Whina Cooper, who had become a household name since leading the Land March in 1975, was among the first to visit the protesters. She managed to arrange a large shed to be delivered to the site, which was as good an indication as any that this occupation would not be ending anytime soon. Eventually, other buildings were erected, along with fences and a watchtower. Some of the land was even used to cultivate crops — a form of herbaceous protest in this leafy suburb. Soon, hundreds of supporters converged at the site of the occupation. Māori from other iwi, along with sympathetic Pākehā, either visited or stayed for a while in a show of solidarity.[1168] For one Pākehā visitor, the occupation was a revelation:

> *In that meeting house I saw the flourishing of a vigorous Maori culture that I had never previously experienced. The people in occupation, led by Renee and Joe Hawke, demonstrated to the highest degree, ingenuity, skill, organisation and perseverance under adversity. I saw the development of a sense of pride, discipline and aroha. I saw young Maoris absorbing their language, their culture, their history and their customs. Many admitted to never having had real contact with anything specifically Maori before. Together, on Takaparawha, in the meeting house, which itself was a masterpiece of ingenuity, Maori people discovered a sense of purpose and identity.*[1169]

Confronted with what it saw as a ragged band of intransigent radicals, the government initially adopted a pose of stately nonchalance, in the hope that if the occupation was ignored for long enough (at least until winter), the heat of the protest would dissipate and the planned subdivision would be able to proceed (with any remaining occupants being easily mopped up by the police). In the meantime, there were some meetings between government ministers and protest leaders, but it was apparent from the outset that the gulf separating them was too wide to bridge. The government then turned to a new strategy. Perhaps, it thought, some of the elders might be persuaded to voice their opposition to the occupation, and the ensuing division would bring about an end to the protest. This was a serious misreading of the situation, and ultimately backfired, with one of the protesters noting that the result of the government's surreptitious efforts to fragment the iwi resulted in the opposite to what had been intended: 'The Government strategy was to talk our kaumatua into siding against us .... We discussed our position with the kaumatua and told them the stand we were going to make and in the end we got their full blessing.'[1170]

The greater threat to the protest at this point was a meteorological one. As the weather got colder, there was apprehension among some protesters over how long the occupation would last:

During winter the camp was wet, windy and freezing cold — and the ground became a bog. The physical and emotional demands of staying on the land saw numbers dwindle to just a few people each night. But, whenever the government prepared to pounce, supporters rallied and hundreds returned to the camp.[1171]

But the real low point in the occupation occurred in September 1977, when Joannee Hawke, a niece of the protest leader Joe Hawke, died in a fire on the site.[1172] Hawke rushed to where the accident happened, asking, '"Where is Joannee? Where is Joannee" …. Several of our menfolk ran into the flames covered head and foot with whatever they could find. Her position was too small and the heat too fierce. It was hell on Earth, mind-shattering and spirit-breaking. We lost our little Joannee.'[1173] A poignant memorial was constructed to commemorate this tragedy, but in a further indignity, officials later insisted that it be removed.[1174] One of the protesters described how he 'thought about the emotional burden on the leaders, and wondered how the occupation could continue. It suddenly seemed like a life and death struggle. But they proved that they were deadly serious.'[1175]

By this time, the government was coming around to the view that if attrition and duplicity were not going to get the protesters to budge, a firmer and more direct approach would be needed. After more than a year of the occupation, with no indication that the will of the protesters was in any slackening, senior ministers, including the prime minister (in whose electorate Bastion Point lay), opted for more drastic measures. On the 506th day of the occupation, the government finally abandoned any semblance of moral restraint, opting instead for what amounted to an invasion. Six hundred police (double the number of protesters on the site) formed a human noose around the occupation, and with the assistance of the army and various vehicles, then began tightening it.[1176] From the protesters' perspective, it was a terrifying moment, as one of them explained:

Doc and I were on the daybreak lookout on the meeting house roof the morning the police invasion convoy rolled onto the land. We set off the orange distress flares to summon neighbouring supporters to the Point. With a loud hailer, Doc encouraged the growing numbers of onlookers to join those already assembled

> in Arohanui [the makeshift meeting house erected on the site]. Waiata rang out, tears were shed. Grant [Hawke] led a mighty mass haka in heartfelt defiance and courage. One by one we were dragged off the land. Through grills on the police wagons you could see them rip down our shelters. Heavy machinery tore and shoved Arohanui groaning to the ground.[1177]

A protester later recounted what happened after the mass arrests had been made: 'We were put into busses and carted off to the "pig" [police] … station. We filled the cells, all 222 of us.' Several hours later, most were released from their cells, and some returned to the site of the occupation. There, the scene had changed dramatically:

> I was anxious and tired. I returned to the Point. The gates were locked and the police barricade replaced by army personnel. Every building removed. The clearing of the buildings tore at my heart. I was staring at an empty paddock in disbelief. I felt the loss so deep. My body shook with uncontrollable sobbing. My father held me. He was telling me it would be all right. He comforted me until I could cry no more.[1178]

The police action, even by the standards of the time, had been excessive. Protesters were kicked, had their hair pulled, some were lifted into the air and then slammed to the ground, bones were cracked, with no sparing of such treatment for the elderly.[1179] It was the most militant show of state force against Māori since the Crown's invasion of Maungapōhatu in 1916, and inflicted a serious wound on Auckland's race relations. It took another decade for Bastion Point finally to be returned to Ngāti Whātua, during which time Aucklanders were slowly developing a more nuanced understanding of this aspect of the city's history.

Other people

The general election on 29 November 1975 had delivered a new prime minister to the country — the MP for Tamaki, Robert Muldoon. It had been a brutal and bruising campaign, remembered mostly now for the cartoon advertisement featuring dancing Cossacks in front of a map of New Zealand turning communist red. There was a follow-up advertisement (less well remembered now) aimed mainly at Auckland voters. This cartoon featured a stereotypical Polynesian-looking man being ejected from a pub. As this scene was being played out, the voice-over informed viewers in language that otherwise might be used when addressing only the most dim-witted in society: 'people poured in ... from other countries ... The people became angry and violence broke out, especially among those who had come from other places expecting great things.'[1180] Of course, 'other places' was code for the South Pacific, and 'other people' were unmistakably Polynesians. There was no need to name them specifically — the crude likenesses in these propaganda pieces were all that was required — a nudge and wink to 'proper' Aucklanders about these undesirable immigrants in their midst. With the political party producing these advertisements heading for power, a tacit approval was thus given for quietly held racist views in some sectors of the community to be voiced. Suddenly, headlines began appearing, with vulgar sentiments such as 'Browns out, Whites all right', 'Kiwis must come first', 'Send illegals back home' and 'Fit in or get out'.[1181] Auckland's Polynesian population, already beleaguered by poverty and prejudice, was now facing an onslaught of open racism.

It was just a short distance at this point from rhetoric to deed. In this case, the deed was what came to be known as the 'dawn raids' — a policy every bit as aggressively chilling as the name suggested. It commenced under the Labour Government in 1974, and was pursued with even more determination by the National Government that succeeded it in 1975. Immigration officials tracked down people who had overstayed their work permits (hence the designation 'overstayer'), and in that shadowy period before sunrise, a vanload of police would arrive at the house where a suspected overstayer was sleeping. All the entrances would be covered, and constables would then enter the dwelling and demand to see every occupant's proof of residency. Those whose permits had expired were hauled off, locked in cells at the police station, and usually deported.

The first raid took place on 12 March 1974, commencing just before midnight, and lasting for around four hours. Houses in Onehunga occupied by Tongans were selected, and a total of 15 people were arrested. More raids followed in the ensuing weeks, including later in the month when immigration officers and police with dogs burst in on a church prayer meeting, arresting four in the congregation, including the minister.[1182] The raids continued with even more tenacity in 1976.

Telesia Topping, a Tongan married to a New Zealander, and someone who had been living in the country for decade, was randomly targeted by authorities in February in one of these raids. She was interviewed by the *Auckland Star* shortly afterwards, which enabled her experienced to be preserved. It was a harrowing and legally questionable ordeal:

> At six o'clock we were all asleep except for one, who had to be at work at seven. He was making breakfast when he saw a policeman trying to push up the window. He was pointing towards the door. As the door opened, they burst inside. Four were inside, four more outside the house. A young policeman, about twenty-two years old, came to my room. I'd just opened my eyes because of the noise. I asked him what he was doing in my bedroom. He did not answer. I was really frightened. He went to the bathroom, inspected it, came back and pulled the covers off my bed, looked under the bed. I called out to him again what he was doing in my bedroom. He ignored me. He pulled open the wardrobe, fiddled with the clothing, checked everything. The same policeman went into the adjoining room where my two nephews, aged 19 and 20 were asleep. The policeman shone the light into their eyes, saying "get up and get out." Another policeman was also there. My nephews were very frightened. The police then started dragging them out to their van. One of them said they were taking us in because we were illegal immigrants.[1183]

This was reminiscent more of South Africa than South Auckland. Yet, for all the testosterone-charged bravura of those police involved in these raids, the technique of ambushing households yielded few overstayers. Rather than reappraise the practice, though, the police turned their teeth towards any factories that had a large Polynesian workforce. A Samoan employee caught in the bite of these workplace raids in 1976 later revealed the deplorable nature of what was involved: 'I was at work. I never dreamed that something like this would happen to me that day. I was taken by surprise when these men came and took me from work. They said that I would be questioned and then returned, and that was the last time I saw anyone, including my family.'[1184]

The police evidently needed little encouragement when executing these raids. One senior officer in Auckland went as far as to advise those who did not have a 'Kiwi accent' to carry their passport with them. And further up the chain of command, the police minister responded to protests from Polynesian community leaders over the raids by casually observing that 'in a herd of Jersey cows the odd Friesian cows will stand out'.[1185] This comment was inadvertently instructive, because it revealed that the targets of the raids were singled out because of their ethnicity. Around two-thirds of overstayers were non-Polynesian, yet did not have to experience the state invading their homes, dragging them off and putting them on planes heading out of the country.[1186] And inevitably, the racism that was the operating principle of the raids leached into other areas of police operations. In October 1976 a Māori woman living in Birkenhead recounted an episode that revealed just how far this onslaught on liberty was advancing:

> *I was going to work last Friday morning. We got off the bus at Rawene Road, Highbury about 7:30. There was myself, a Samoan girl, a European and two Fijians. A police car stopped across the road from us. One called 'can we see you?' They asked me and the Samoan girl which island we were from. The Samoan girl said Western Samoa. I realised what it was all about and I said 'I'm a Maori'. The policeman said 'I hope you're a good Maori.' There were two men cops and a lady. They were sniggering through it. They didn't ask me anything else after that. He then questioned the Samoan girl, who luckily had her papers. The Fijians look like Maoris and weren't questioned. They didn't know any of our names and didn't ask questions about anything else.*[1187]

This policy of self-inflicted civic injury reached its most damaging stage at this time. Over Labour Weekend in 1976, police in Auckland stopped 856 people — almost all Polynesian — and demanded to see their passports. At the same time, 200 houses across the city were raided. The result of this vast deployment of manpower and resources was the apprehension of just 23 overstayers. However, the raids, random stops and questioning of people on the street, and roadblocks (on Karangahape Road, for example)[1188] continued in the narrow-minded drive to hunt down those whose immigration status technically breached the law — provided, of course, that they were also Polynesian in appearance.

A bridge too far

It should not have been any surprise that there was a mood of disgruntlement spreading through Auckland during much of the 1970s. The oil shocks, the dawn raids, the Bastion Point occupation, rising unemployment, declining terms of trade,[1189] inner-city poverty (by the mid-1970s, for example, up to 300 families a week were receiving assistance from a local food co-operative in Ponsonby alone),[1190] and industrial action all merged into an amalgam of discontent within the community. Government policies at this time did little to alleviate the challenges many in the city were confronting. In response to a worsening fuel crisis, in March 1979 the sale of petrol was prohibited between seven o'clock on Friday evenings to six o'clock on Monday mornings. The ban was adjusted in November, so that petrol could be purchased on Saturday mornings, and the entire scheme was abandoned in August the following year as it proved utterly ineffective in its aim of reducing fuel consumption.[1191] An accompanying measure to curb petrol use was the reduction of the speed limit on the open road from 100 to 80 kilometres per hour. But by far the most intrusive policy was introduced on 31 July 1979: 'carless days'. Vehicle owners had to nominate a day each week that they would not use their car (and face penalties if they breached this edict). They were then issued with a small sticker (colour-coded for the particular day they had chosen to be carless) which was stuck on the windscreen. It was an 'innovative' attempt to reduce petrol consumption, but faults with this rationing system soon emerged. First, it unduly penalised those families with only one car, and who therefore had no alternative vehicle to use on their nominated carless day. Second, petrol use was not always reduced, as driving that was forbidden on one day could be made up for on a permitted day. Carless days also imposed a burden on businesses and staff, and failed to take into account the extent to which vehicle use had become vital to the economy.[1192]

What little effect carless days had was eroded by the exemptions that began to be granted. It started with those living in rural areas, for whom daily use of a vehicle was vital, especially in the absence of public transport, and was followed by some work vehicles in urban areas being exempted. Exemption stickers were required, and soon an illicit trade in these emerged, which further undermined any remaining effectiveness of the policy. 'It was just a nuisance for us,' as one Aucklander described the carless-days era. 'We only had one car then, so we had to plan around when we could use the car. I ended up not going [to netball on Saturdays] because it was impossible to get to practice from where we lived without a car, and people weren't always able to give you a lift.'[1193] Such disruption was grudgingly accepted by most Aucklanders. After all, there was little alternative than to endure it.

Another facet of life that the city's residents had become accustomed to (though seldom accepting of) was the seemingly perpetual cycle of strikes — which were partly the product of the country's antiquated industrial relations machinery. Towards the end of the decade, Aucklanders endured strikes by marine engineers, brewery boiler attendants, refrigerated truck drivers, Air New Zealand engineers, freight forwarders, domestic pilots, public servants, port workers, secondary school teachers, storemen, motor assembly workers and railway workers, among others,[1194] culminating in a paralysing one-day general strike on 20 September 1979.[1195]

One thing that distinguished Auckland's experience of industrial disruption from that of the rest of the country was that the city had its own, enormous monument to this era of strikes: Mängere Bridge. At least, it would eventually become a bridge. In the late 1970s it was a row of thickset concrete columns rising from the marshy inlet of the Manukau Harbour between Onehunga and Mängere. Planned as part of a new route linking central Auckland to the airport, work on the bridge had halted due to industrial action. The strike lasted longer than any other in New Zealand's history, and it was not until 1983 that construction was finally completed. Until then, Aucklanders travelling along the adjacent route had to cross the harbour along a Bailey bridge (a prefabricated, portable, truss bridge)[1196] that had been constructed over the old Mängere Bridge (the earliest reinforced concrete bridge across a harbour in New Zealand),[1197] which had passed its useful life and was slowly sinking into the mud. The spectacle of the unfinished bridge was the visible reminder of how riven with industrial discord Auckland was at this time. It also left an enduring memory of the era for some residents, as one later recalled: 'I can remember when we drove over that old bridge, Dad would always say to us how the unions were responsible for stopping the new bridge being built. I was too young to know what unions were really, but we sort of knew they were the baddies.'[1198] For some of the workers involved in protesting for better pay, however, their memory was more embittered still. Zac Wallace, a union leader, described the treatment several of the strikers received from their employer during the dispute:

They delayed the payments for as long as possible — some of us had to wait 12 weeks before we got anything. Then when we had to send some of the men out to get jobs, the Labour Department offered them jobs back on the bridge, which they of course refused. So .... their dole was cut for six weeks for refusing to cross a picket line.[1199]

By the end of the decade, Māngere Bridge had become a totem representing the meeting of a broken industrial relations regime with a stalled part of Auckland's roading system. So tangled were the bases of blame that trying to establish cause and effect, let alone responsibility for the situation, proved impossible. However, Auckland's industrial apparatus was not all mess and muddle in this decade. Just 10 kilometres southeast of the half-built Māngere Bridge was the fully functioning Ford factory at Wiri. In 1971, Henry Ford II visited New Zealand to give his blessing to the new Auckland factory that would bear his name in Auckland. He was the son of Edsel Ford, and grandson of Henry Ford, and was as close as the automotive world got to a papal succession. The plant opened in 1972, and the following year the first Ford Falcon rolled off the assembly line. Along with Holden Kingswoods, these were among the most prominent vehicles in the city during this decade, and, to an extent, came to epitomise the popular perception of private transport at this time. 'You were either a Holden man or a Ford man at that time, and you didn't change'[1200] was a common sentiment, even though both makes were facing increased competition from Japanese brands in this period.[1201]

The establishment of the Ford plant at Wiri was part of an industrial growth spurt that South Auckland was experiencing in this decade — and where there were jobs, people were sure to follow. The area's growth was assisted, in part, by the establishment of the Housing Corporation in 1974, which offered mortgage finance to low-income households that otherwise would be unable to secure a loan to buy a house.[1202] State housing was also a prominent feature of South Auckland in this era, but demand continued to outstrip supply, leading to overcrowding and high proportions of people's incomes going to housing costs. In addition, as with West Auckland, the race to provide housing outpaced much thought of urban planning, as one resident bemoaned:

you throw a whole lot of young housewives particularly with young children with bugger all schools and bugger all preschool facilities, shitty parks, all the parks were left over bits of land that the developers found too difficult to deal with so that was their reserves contribution and over it all you had local authorities who ... thought that they had nothing to do with social issues.[1203]

However, the area was not left devoid of facilities for long. South Auckland's spiritual and temporal needs were met in this decade by the construction of churches and shops. Churches in particular became a distinct feature of the area, especially with its high Polynesian population, of whom over 90 per cent claimed a religious affiliation.[1204] They served as places of worship, but also venues for social and cultural expression. However, outside of churches, in the beginning of the decade there were few places for gathering in South Auckland. In no other part of Auckland at this time was there a community that seemed so identifiable geographically (due to its specific ethnic composition) yet that was so scattered socially. This began to change with plans at the start of the decade to build a 'city centre' in Manukau. It would be a combination of an office block for Manukau City Council (Manukau was how the area was known administratively) and a shopping mall. Both projects would be substantial in scale — not only to meet the needs of a growing population in the surrounding suburbs, but as a statement of confidence in South Auckland. There were plans to attract a university, a hospital, a central police station and a court to the area,[1205] and although not all of these materialised in the remaining decades of the century, they were indicative of the ambition some held for the area. The most prominent building to rise up from the abandoned paddocks adjacent to Great South Road was the nine-storey futuristic-looking council office, designed by architect Neville Price. Its stark white walls and elongated curved-cornered windows were unlike any other building in the area, and had an almost space-station-like protrusion leading to an imposing cylindrical council chamber.[1206] Next door was the Manukau City Centre, which when it opened in 1976 was the largest covered mall in the country.[1207] Here, at last, was a place where the residents of South Auckland could congregate in all weather, even if it was just to browse the shops. And reflective of the distinct character of the surrounding society, the third building to appear in this community entrepôt was the Manukau Friendship House, which opened on 17 June 1979. Founded by six church denominations, its purpose was to provide health and social services to the community, and it complemented the commercial and administrative centres nearby.

A significant aspect of this development, aside from the large-scale modern architecture that was suddenly towering over the area, was that as Auckland was expanding geographically, its infrastructure was becoming more decentralised. This was certainly true administratively, with the region divided up into numerous administrative realms, with councils for Auckland City, Birkenhead Borough, Waiheke County, Devonport Borough, East Coast Bays Borough, Ellerslie Borough, Franklin County, Glen Eden Borough, Great Barrier Island County, Grey Lynn Borough, Helensville Borough, Henderson Borough, Howick Borough, Manukau City, Mt Albert Borough, Mt Eden Borough, Mt Roskill Borough, New Lynn Borough, Mt Wellington Borough, Newmarket Borough, Northcote Borough, One Tree Hill Borough, Onehunga Borough, Otahuhu Borough, Papatoetoe Borough, Papakura Borough, Pukekohe Borough, Rodney County, Takapuna City, Waitemata City and Waiuku Borough. The boundaries of these local body entities were more bureaucratic than physical, but the developments such as at Manukau City, along with similar trends in places like Henderson, had implications for the character of the city as a whole. The principal one of these went to the very essence of what constitutes a community. The conventional definition of a community is a place that is geographically defined, where most social and work activity is carried out, where people spend most of their time, and where people have a sense of belonging.[1208] Did someone who lived in, say, Ōtara in the 1970s affiliate more to the broader Auckland community or their specifically South Auckland community? Of course, the two overlapped, but in practice the answer tilted more to the latter, just like a resident in Massey in this era was more a member of the West Auckland community than of the greater Auckland community. It was as though the city was outgrowing itself, and dividing into satellites, each of which were largely geographically and socially self-contained. People worked, shopped, socialised, worshipped and played sports in their specific area of Auckland, and it was to that area that they developed a community affinity.

This was inevitable, especially given the city's dimensions. After all, what reason would there be for Auckland residents in Wellsford to have regular involvement in the Auckland community of Waiuku, which would involve a 300-kilometre round trip by car to visit? Or to put it in another way, the South Auckland suburb of Pukekohe was only 80 kilometres from Hamilton, but 130 kilometres from Wellsford. Distance mattered when it came to a sense of belonging. This evolution was a natural development for a city of Auckland's size. With a population approaching 750,000 people, spread out over a built area in this decade of 37,000 hectares,[1209] it would be unrealistic to expect all the suburbs and areas in the city to function as a single social entity.

But for all the forces detaching Auckland into its increasingly self-contained communities, there were episodes in the 1970s that acted as unifying influences on the city, and that showed that the civic whole was still greater than the sum of its parts. One of these collective undertakings was the Round the Bays 'fun run' — an initiative of the Auckland Joggers Club in 1972, which grew to be the biggest per capita running event in the world. By the end of the decade, thousands of Aucklanders were participating annually, forming a dense column of puffing joggers along Tamaki Drive that extended for several kilometres.[1210] And on the harbour, another annual event reminded residents in the region of their shared past. Every Auckland Anniversary Day (the Monday closest to 29 January)[1211] a regatta was held, which by the 1970s had become the largest single-day event of its kind in the world.[1212] Around one in every ten Aucklanders owned a boat in this era,[1213] and the annual regatta was an opportunity for them to participate in a mass parade of aquatic flamboyance, involving all manner of vessels in the Waitematā Harbour, in what was a distinctly Auckland event.

It is easy, however, to get caught up in a parochial perspective of Auckland in the 1970s — an overly comfortable image that congratulates itself on the city's progress, and too conveniently brushes aside any dissent that was present at this time in the greater cause of civic patriotism. Sometimes, though, it takes a sceptical outsider to bring a different understanding to a place. In 1973 visiting British novelist and social commentator J. B. Priestley delivered just such a service.[1214] With the inquisitiveness of an archaeologist, combined with the acerbic perception of an experienced writer, he left a depiction of Auckland that offers a counterbalance to how some of the residents saw their city. 'I never really took in Auckland, never accepted it, so to speak, as a character, as I had done in the other ... cities,' he wrote while sitting in his room in the White Heron Hotel in Parnell. He seemed unable to connect with the place in the way he had with Christchurch, Dunedin or Wellington. 'We kept going into it or through it but never felt *of it*' was Priestley's sense of the city. Although it had, in his eyes, a 'cheerful and prosperous higgledy-piggledy, yesterday and today all mixed up' appearance, it lacked any distinct personality. In addition, Auckland was 'entirely without glamour'. It was 'too small, looking like so many suburbs, when compared with *real cities*, huge, monstrous and cruel, yet dazzling, fascinating, richly rewarding'. Auckland was not on a par with what he felt a city ought to be. 'Where are the restaurants and night-clubs for the jet set and the Beautiful People? Or the parties, perhaps in fancy dress, that make international news? Or the first nights or the film premieres and the spring or autumn fashion shows?' The wine lists were modest, the cigar selections poor, and 'the mere raw materials of the glamorous life were lacking in such a dead level of bungalows and TV snacks'.[1215] It was slightly unfair of Priestley to lay all these expectations at the feet of a city that had existed for just over 130 years, and that had a comparatively small population, and few of the civic resources that had been pumped into other cities for centuries. Auckland may not yet have acquired the trappings of an 'international' city, but had Priestley stayed in Auckland for longer, he would have seen that it was indisputably heading in that direction.

10
The 1980s

The days the weekend ended

The 1980s were bookended by two legislative developments which in many ways transformed the culture of Auckland. On 12 November 1980, Parliament passed the Shop Trading Hours Amendment Act, allowing for Saturday trading.[1216] Until then, almost all shops (with the exception of dairies and some bakeries) closed on Friday evenings and opened again on Monday mornings — an arrangement that had been in place since the 40-hour week had been legislated for in 1945.[1217] In the intervening 35 years, weekends had grown to serve devotedly non-work activities, and had accordingly become bastions of leisure. But from that Wednesday in 1980, the work/weekend divide was breached, and the Saturdays were no longer sacrosanct. At the time, there were fears that shops opening for an extra day would contribute to inflation, unemployment and the erosion of the 40-hour week, and would have detrimental effects on family life and sporting activities.[1218] Unions were leading the charge against what they saw as this encroachment on workers' entitlements, but their heart was not really in it. A year before the legislation was amended, some retailers in Queen Street were already defying the law, with authorities turning a blind eye to these infringements.[1219] And in January 1980 an opinion poll revealed that 61 per cent of people favoured Saturday trading, with only 21 per cent opposed (the remainder were undecided).[1220] Some of those workers welcomed the opportunity for shopping to be added to the weekend's leisure landscape, while for others it was a chance to earn more money. And once the law was enacted, shopping on Saturday became an appetite that grew with the eating for many Aucklanders. The Saturday-morning suburban slumber was replaced by families driving to their nearest mall or shopping centre, where they could graze without the urgency that accompanied weekday shopping, when purchases had to be squeezed into that hour or so between finishing work and the shops closing.

In the months immediately after Saturday trading was legalised, some Auckland shop owners were more tentative than others about the prospect of extending their working week. A journalist who visited several suburbs seven months after the law change observed that retailers and customers were still adjusting to the transformation:

> *The overall impression we get is that Saturday shopping is still very much in its infancy .... Aucklanders still seem to regard Saturday as sport day .... [N]ew patterns seem to be emerging — city workers are shopping in their suburb in the weekend and relax as they do so. Those working in the suburbs seem to be coming into town ... shopping seems to have taken over from strolling.*[1221]

In July 1981 the idea of Saturday trading was still far from being universally embraced by Auckland retailers. In addition, the trends tended to vary considerably between suburbs, suggesting that shop owners were staring at each other to see who would blink first. In Mt Roskill, fewer than one in ten shops were open on Saturdays, and there were barely any customers in the area. The situation in Avondale was about the same. However, in Henderson, where close to nine out of ten shops were open, there was an abundance of customers and the curious in the shopping precinct.[1222]

Towards the end of the decade, the success of Saturday shopping had helped build up a momentum for an assault on the Sabbath — that final, and as yet unassailed, citadel of the weekend. On the one hand, it made perfect sense. If Saturday trading had been good for business overall, and gave customers greater convenience, why not extend trading to include Sundays? One reason for resistance to the suggestion was that the cultural and religious arguments against Sunday trading were much more entrenched for some Aucklanders than they had been when Saturday trading was introduced. However, also at play was the change that society had undergone in the 1980s.[1223] At the beginning of the decade, there had been a wage-price freeze that represented one of the most severe forms of government intervention in the economy in living memory. There were also carless days (which ended in May 1980), and a society riven by industrial action, and various other pent-up tensions that were soon to burst forth. By the close of this decade, however, the economy had undergone an abrupt and sometimes painful process of deregulation, religious adherence had declined further, alcohol sales had been liberated, homosexuality had been legalised, there was a Ministry of Women's Affairs, and the overall mood of progressivism was on the rise. One of the facets of this evolutionary process was the ascent of secularism in the country. The major influence of the churches on society was reaching its expiry date, and the fight over Sunday trading revealed precisely how far the influence of Christianity in the country had receded. And Auckland was perceived as being at the forefront of this trend. As one representative of the Keep Sunday Free Coalition conceded after Sunday trading was legalised, 'when they did introduce it very little trading was done on Sundays for a long time .... It's really Auckland and places like that, that have the population base to allow it.'[1224]

On 5 December 1989 the Minister of Labour, and MP for Mt Albert, Helen Clark, introduced a Bill aiming to allow for Sunday trading (and which eventually came into force in August 1990).[1225] This put the government on a collision course with both trade unions and churches, who became unlikely allies in opposing the possibility of Sunday trading. There was a flurry of letter-writing at this time from various Christian groups and individuals — both to the Advisory Committee considering the legislation and to newspapers. Bible verses were quoted extensively, and readers of these letters were instructed that New Zealand was 'still a Christian country'.[1226] Union opposition to Sunday trading stemmed from concerns about protecting workers' rights, but was also propelled by a major setback the union movement had suffered in 1987, when the government ended compulsory union membership,[1227] thus depleting many workers' groups of the level of funding that they had previously enjoyed. This was a cause that some unions hoped would help maintain membership. A third group opposed to Sunday trading (partially comprising those in the other two camps) was concerned with the social impacts of this proposed change:

> *Stop and think for a moment about how many national and regional social, sporting and hobby clubs and organizations depend on knowing that most people aren't working across the weekend, so they can get together. Swimming meets and university extramural courses, cricket matches and meeting of the New Zealand Philatelic Federation, table tennis tournaments and tramping and natural history outings: what makes many such activities viable at present is that society is organized so as to take a break at one recognized time. Suppose that regular Sunday trading were legalized and took off just in the Auckland area. That would be enough to cause major disruption of our whole society.*[1228]

On the other side of the fence, an *Auckland Star* editorial in 1988 pointed out that Sunday trading would be beneficial for the city's tourism sector,[1229] and the general economic arguments in favour of the move certainly seemed compelling. When, for example, the Manukau City Centre mall opened on the Sunday before Christmas 1988, over 50,000 people went through the shops in just one day, suggesting that the demand for Sunday trading was substantially stronger than opponents had estimated.[1230] Meanwhile, business leaders were making the case that opening shops on Sunday was better for the workers and shop owners, and was in keeping with the culture of deregulation that had reached into almost all aspects of the economy in this decade.[1231] The government echoed this view, with Clark informing Parliament that the decision to introduce Sunday trading had been made 'simply because the present restrictions are out of date'. She argued that there was 'considerable demand for Sunday shopping, especially during summer. Tourists are leaving ... with money jangling in their pockets because of our outdated laws, and more spending by tourists must mean more jobs and income for New Zealand.'[1232] It would also create a market for casual dining and the so-called 'café lifestyle' that had hardly existed a decade earlier.

Opening up the weekend to shopping brought about a surge of

customers, and made malls in particular places of recreation. Clark's assessment of popular demand seemed to be correct, and the naysayers were either misguided or clinging to ideas that were no longer in tune with where society was heading. However, in the course of this transition to seven-day shopping, the notion of the weekend as a time when barely anybody went to work was permanently lost. These changes were a valediction to a way of life Aucklanders had become used to for decades, and among the casualties were sports clubs, community groups, religious organisations and civic engagement in general.[1233] Commerce may have triumphed, but its victory was at the expense of the city's particular weekend lifestyle. What Aucklanders did with their leisure time from this point onwards would never be the same again.

The types of leisure activity in Auckland were changing in the 1980s in addition to the times they occurred. The traditional activities were still there — sports, movies, bars, clubs and concerts — but there were new options appearing across the city. The first of these in this decade was Leisureland (later Footrot Flats Fun Park) in Te Atatū North, which was established — unusually — in partnership with the Accident Compensation Corporation.[1234] Constructed on a site of bare land previously used as a BMX cycle track, Leisureland offered dodgems, a giant swing, a teahouse, a miniature train, a working farm and a pond with an island in the middle of it. There were also small, motorised cars, which children could drive on a road circuit that had its own intersections and traffic lights. 'When these cars were first run at Leisureland,' a staff member later explained, 'the operators had lessons to become qualified driving instructors. Kids were put through driving lessons with either an instructor or a parent then after so many sessions they were able to sit a test and gain their Driverstown licence.'[1235] One of the main attractions, though, was the Cannonball Express rollercoaster, which was the largest permanent rollercoaster in the country at the time, and which acquired notoriety when it experienced a serious derailment. In 1988 the park emerged in its final iteration as the short-lived Safari Land, where visitors could drive through enclosures amidst lions and other exotic animals.[1236] On a much bigger scale, in December 1982 Rainbow's End opened in Manukau. This proved a more popular venue, with bumper boats, mini golf, Can Am cars and video games drawing strong-enough crowds that the following year the facility was added to with a pirate ship, a maze and an indoor games area. Cafes, dodgems and kiddies' cars were introduced in 1984, along with one of the most popular attractions at the location: the log flume ride, and two years later, a rollercoaster augmented the other attractions. Until the 1980s, and the advent of these amusement parks, Aucklanders generally had to make do with the annual Easter Show, where similar types of activities were on offer, but which were generally on a smaller scale than Rainbow's End, and were both more expensive and slightly more tawdry.

A more novel entertainment initiative that Auckland acquired in this decade was popularly known by its founder's name, the marine archaeologist Kelly Tarlton. Tarlton conceived of an aquarium for Auckland where instead of visitors being confronted with flat plates of glass in front of them displaying fish, they would have a more immersive experience. His plan was to make use of the disused sewage storage tanks on Tamaki Drive to house a subterranean aquarium, and create curved 70-millimetre-thick acrylic tunnels that would arch right over visitors — a world first for an aquarium. There would also be a conveyor belt on the floor to move people through at a regular speed, thus preventing logjams in these aquatic corridors.[1237] Construction began in April 1984, with a budget of just $2.2 million, and was completed in January 1985, literally two hours before the scheduled opening of 'Kelly Tarlton's'.[1238]

Play the game

But just at that point where Auckland looked to be heading towards being a bloated, godless, open-all-hours, consumer mecca, adhering to the decade's creed that greed was good, the city discovered that its moral pulse was still beating after all. Well, at least some of its citizens did. The issue that led to this resuscitation of Auckland's conscience was the planned tour to the country by the South African national rugby team — the Springboks: a team both representing and manifesting its nation's viciously racist apartheid regime. Flouting its international obligations, the government did not intervene to prevent the tour from taking place,[1239] and from the moment that the announcement of the tour was made, groups began to mobilise to oppose it. The result was that a wedge was driven though the country. You were either 'pro-tour' or 'anti-tour', and as the games and protests got under way, the space in between for ambivalence narrowed almost to nothing. Polls showed that the number of supporters and opponents of the tour was evenly split,[1240] and throughout this period there was very little shift in these figures.

The most prominent organisation that was battling against the tour was HART (Halt All Racist Tours). For most of its existence since its formation in 1969, HART was a small activist organisation that was barely known to the public.[1241] However, in the face of a visit by a rugby team representing apartheid South Africa, the number of HART's supporters ballooned, and it soon grew to symbolise the anti-apartheid movement in New Zealand. Its members consisted of a cocktail of groups and individuals opposed to the tour, ranging from Māori anti-racism activists to church leaders, student unions, communists, peace campaigners, civil rights supporters and, it has to be said, some who sought to protest for protest's sake. And there were other anti-apartheid acronyms that soon entered the popular lexicon, such as CARE (Citizens Association for Racial Equality), ACORD (Auckland Committee on Racism and Discrimination), MOST (Mobilisation to Stop the Springbok Tour) and COST (Citizens Opposed to the Springbok Tour).[1242] However, once they were in the streets, banners and adrenalin raised, their ideological distinctions largely fell away. Protesting against the tour, or attending one of the games, became an opportunity for private prejudices to be summoned for public performance.

Moderation was an early casualty during the tour, as the clashes between anti-tour protesters and the police became increasingly violent, and were followed by hundreds of arrests. The police were the physical buttress to the protests, and there was a hardened section of society that supported their approach, either because they were concerned with the nature of the physical unrest they were witnessing, or because they were committed — against all evidence to the contrary — to the self-refuting argument that 'sports and politics shouldn't mix'.

Auckland was the venue for the final and deciding test between the All Blacks and the Springboks, but well before that encounter protests against the tour and what it symbolised had grown in scale and ferocity. The ructions that accompanied matches played in other parts of the country (including a pitch invasion at Hamilton and frequent violent confrontations with the police in other centres) provoked outpourings both of opprobrium and righteous justification, but these shows of resistance proved to be mere curtain-raisers for the real chaos that was about to unfurl in Auckland. By this time, it had become plain that protests and civil disobedience would not shift the government's stance, and so the purpose of some anti-tour leaders swung to garnering international attention for their cause. At that point, even the most hard-headed activists were effectively reduced to actors who were forced to stage ever more riotous protests to ensure that they could continue to gasp the oxygen of international publicity.[1243]

The Auckland test, on the Saturday afternoon of 12 September 1981, was where the city had the most to play for. Even before the sun had risen behind a thinly overcast sky, preparations were under way for a final confrontation, which for many involved had the epic moral dimensions of a deciding fight between good and evil (except that there was no unanimity on which side represented evil). John Minto — the Auckland teacher and established anti-apartheid campaigner — had come to embody the protest movement opposing the tour, and in the days leading up to the Auckland test promised the country demonstrations 'like never before'.[1244] Many of the 7000 protesters[1245] anticipated violence, with some building shields and acquiring helmets in preparation for a clash, while the police erected barricades and prepared to deploy their 'Red' and 'Blue' squads — which were initially formed to protect the rugby teams, but as one former member conceded, 'became the face of police brutality' during the tour.[1246] And in the midst of this anticipated melee would be 50,000 rugby supporters, whose loyalties were firmly pro-tour, and whose response, if circumstances got beyond control, was unknown.

Inside Eden Park, the focus was meant to be on rugby, but even in that tightly secured space the protest movement made its presence felt. At one point, a commentator announced to television audiences around the world that there was 'an unusual feeling of tenseness because there is a light plane circling the ground and dipping in low and dropping things into the crowd .... it seems to be just above the grandstand height'.[1247] The pilot of the Cessna aircraft involved, the appositely named Marx Jones, later unapologetically explained how he undertook his act of protest:

> First, we went round Eden Park three or four times and dropped our leaflets. We tried the soft approach first. Then we had half a dozen parachute flares but I think only two or three landed on the pitch. It's quite difficult getting your speed and your trajectory sorted out. I went quite low and diagonally so I wouldn't tangle with the goalposts.[1248]

Meanwhile, around Eden Park rioters were rampaging through the streets, with police responding in a brutal ebb and flow of attack and retreat. The injured staggered to whatever empty spaces they could find away from the skirmishing, while the combatants continued to lunge chaotically at each other until — after about three hours — the police managed to gain the upper hand. In the aftermath of the final test, Auckland Police District Assistant Commissioner Brian Davies gave a dispassionate account of the clashes around Eden Park:

> *At three locations serious rioting broke out with so called anti-apartheid protestors attacking the police with eggs, paint bombs, incendiary devices, chemicals, fence palings and rocks. These rocks came from residents' walls, as the area contained dozens of boundary walls made up of volcanic rock dug from sections. These provided lethal missiles and after two separate attacks on police lines on the day of the last test in Auckland demonstrators stood back from police lines and rained a barrage of missiles upon the police. At the two main points where rioting broke out, about 1,000 demonstrators were at each of the two confrontation points. Police held back from the fusillade until reinforcements in protective equipment were available and then in a series of charges forced the demonstrators back using their batons where necessary, the philosophy being that protestors cannot effectively throw missiles when retreating. The most vicious riot took place in Marlborough and Onslow Roads and here the battle raged for about one hour with the police driving the protestors ever backwards with at least 10 baton charges. The charges were undertaken by 5 sections of an escort group with other team police sections leap-frogging as the police lines were halted or reformed. During this "battle" 20 police and 30+ demonstrators were injured. All the police injuries came from rocks being thrown or from being hit by shields and fence palings carried by protestors.*[1249]

It was not just a case of order collapsing into anarchy at the Auckland anti-tour protest, but of the will of the individual succumbing to the madness of the mob — on all sides. And in the aftermath, there was the predictable round of autopsies with participants and observers picking over the carcass to see what brought about this unprecedented disorder, and where the blame lay.

One thing was certain, though, to all parties involved, and those watching on from the sidelines: rugby had not been the winner on the day. In fact, even without the disastrous 1981 Springbok tour, the game's hold on the popular affections was loosening, and it was no longer the great unifying social force it had been in previous decades.[1250] Now more than ever, there were competing options for the public's attention. In the sporting field, soccer was on the ascent. The distaste for rugby following the deep acrimony of 1981 contrasted with the success of the country's much more virtuous-looking national soccer team[1251] — the All Whites — in securing a place in the 1982 FIFA World Cup.[1252] This trend of interest in soccer continued to the point where, by the end of the century, there were more people in the country playing soccer for clubs than rugby.[1253] Soccer's expansion was especially evident in the 1980s in Auckland. A sizeable proportion of British immigrants contributed to the growth of the game in the city, to the extent that by 1982 the head of the New Zealand Football Association — Glasgow-born Aucklander Charlie Dempsey — told a journalist that when it came to the New Zealand national team, '[i]n many ways we are more British than the British .... Our manager ... and the coach ... both learned their trade in England, and four of our players are English-born .... We also have three Scots-born lads.'[1254]

Clubs like Papatoetoe, East Coast Bays, Suburbs and Courier went through a golden age of player participation and spectator support at this time. There were also women's teams throughout the city, and a thriving youth competition, with adventurously named teams such as the 'Mangere Town Coyotes' and the 'Papakura Hornets' competing with the likes of the 'Otara Cobras' and the 'Waiuku Spitfires'.[1255] Within a year of the All Whites' entry to the World Cup, the game's popularity in Auckland had risen to the point where Auckland Grammar School, one of the traditional stalwarts of secondary school rugby in the city, had as many soccer teams as rugby teams[1256] — a situation that would have been inconceivable a generation earlier. The attractions of soccer were manifold. It was a professional sport and rugby was still nominally an amateur game. Soccer was the most international of sports, while rugby was played predominantly in the countries of some of the white settler colonies and their former imperial power. As Auckland was increasingly seeing itself as a more urbane city, the need to uphold rugby as the epitome of stoic Kiwi masculinity, where the slightest flicker of emotion was frowned on as a display of weakness, was becoming a harder proposition to sustain. Compared to the ecstatic displays of exuberance when a goal was scored in soccer, rugby's emotional reticence felt suddenly dull rather than heroic. And then there was the element of boredom in rugby. It's stop-start nature, and heavy reliance on brute strength, was struggling against the flowing, fleet-footed nature of soccer.[1257] 'To be honest, I don't think we'd ever watched a full game of soccer before,' one Auckland sports fan reflected on this period, 'but as soon as the All Whites got into the World Cup, we started watching a lot of soccer, and you could sort of understand why so many people everywhere around the world got into it. It's a pretty exciting game really.'[1258]

However, rugby was not about to have the last rites read over it. The vitality of the great sporting beast may have been flagging in recent years, but it was still the national game, and was about to be revived with the sporting equivalent of a blood transfusion. In 1987 rugby acquired what many other sports had — a world cup. For the first time, the world's rugby-playing nations would gather together to compete in a tournament to determine which nation had the greatest team. Auckland was chosen as the venue for the inaugural Rugby World Cup. Sixteen teams participated (although not South Africa, which was still an apartheid state), but unusually for such a major event, there was no opening ceremony — apparently, the budget for the tournament could not extend that far. If this was to be rugby's fightback, the early signs were far from encouraging. In addition to its perfunctory commencement, Aucklanders' initial interest in this World Cup barely registered. Attendances were poor, with the opening game at Eden Park between the All Blacks and Italy failing to fill much more than half the stadium's seats. Holders of season tickets at Eden Park — those who were dedicated to rugby — were not eligible to use their tickets for the World Cup games, and so had to pay like everyone else, which could have affected the crowd size, but there was a pervading sense of wait and see, as Aucklanders looked on to assess how the tournament progressed. Indeed, popular enthusiasm in the city was so sluggish that organisers of the World Cup only managed to secure a sponsorship deal for the event just 30 minutes before the kick-off for the first match.[1259] The schedule of games suited domestic audiences (with matches being played in the afternoons), but this meant that it was difficult to attract northern hemisphere audiences,[1260] and the potential advertising revenue that came with it.

Eventually, though, locals overcame their lethargy and hesitation over the tournament, and by the afternoon of the World Cup final, on 20 June, there was widespread popular interest. Eden Park was packed for the match between New Zealand and France that day, which the All Blacks comfortably won 29 to 9. By the time the William Webb Ellis trophy was handed to the All Blacks' captain, David Kirk, the sun was already just about setting over Eden Park's western stand, and Aucklanders' enthusiasm for rugby had been clearly revived. And then it was over. This time, rugby was the winner on the day, but there was something of an anti-climax in the aftermath. Auckland hooker Sean Fitzpatrick pointed out that

> [t]he celebrations were actually pretty tame, though. For us, it was a case of job done — a job that was expected of us — and now let's move on to the next thing, which was a game against Australia in a few weeks. We went back to the hotel, had one or two drinks in the hotel bar and were in bed by one or two in the morning. You have to remember, we were amateurs, so most of us were back to work on Monday. The final was on a Saturday; being a builder, I was back on site bright and early Monday morning.[1261]

Snap

When an intoxicated and embittered Robert Muldoon slurred to reporters on the evening of 16 June 1984 that there would be a snap election in a month, he had been prime minister for close to nine years, and the MP for Tamaki for nearly a quarter of a century (and at the age of 62, was already eligible for retirement). The mood in Auckland — which had endured much of the brunt of Muldoon's economic interference and social divisiveness — was for change. Muldoon belonged to that generation that remembered the Second World War (and in his case, had served in the New Zealand Army in the South Pacific and Italy). His views of what he wanted the country to be like, and its place in the world, inevitably were framed by the era he grew up in and the formative experiences of that time. In contrast, his main contender in the forthcoming election — the MP for Mangere, David Lange — was two years old when the war ended, and was 41 years old when the snap election was announced.

As these Auckland MPs confronted each other in the month-long campaign, the differences between the two contenders were stark. Muldoon frequently looked like a fatigued behemoth, his growl had become more of a snarl, and his famous cackle was now less audible. Opposite him was Lange the leviathan. Fleshy-faced, and with a wit and intellect that was easily a match for Muldoon's, the Mangere MP was the orator battling against the haranguer. Together with his finance spokesperson, the MP for Manurewa, Roger Douglas, Lange won the election that year in convincing fashion. This was more than just a change of administration, though. It was partly a rebuke of the direction the country had been heading in, and more than most of the elections this century, represented a distinct generational shift in the nation's ruling party. Auckland's verdict on the Muldoon government was especially striking, with National retaining only six of the 22 general seats in the city. Immediately following the election, a survey of voters in three Auckland electorates (Eden, Glenfield and West Auckland) found that perceptions of the leaders played a critical role in the election outcome.[1262] 'We all just felt it was time for a change,' as one Auckland voter explained. 'Muldoon had been there for too long. He'd had his chance and stuffed it up, so we just wanted to get rid of him.'[1263]

The new Labour Government was welcomed by peace campaigners in particular, for its promise to make a stand on nuclear weapons and nuclear-powered ships entering New Zealand waters. In August the previous year, there had been protests in Auckland over the visit of the USS *Texas* — a cruiser that was almost certainly carrying nuclear weapons (although the United States' 'neither confirm nor deny' policy made absolute assertions on the matter impossible).[1264] Also by this time, parts of Auckland, such as Waitākere, had declared themselves nuclear-free, and although it held no legal status, it was still indicative of an anti-nuclear sentiment that was strongly held by some in the city.

Three months after the visit of the USS *Texas*, the nuclear-powered submarine USS *Phoenix*[1265] — another embodiment of American military prowess in the region — entered the Waitematā Harbour. 'Don't we look fabulous steaming into your harbour with flags flying and our missiles and guns ready for action' was the sarcastic message anti-nuclear protesters spread in anticipation of the vessel's arrival.[1266] As the USS *Phoenix* glided into the harbour, it was met with a protest flotilla of around a hundred yachts, speedboats and canoes, supported by several thousand protesters on shore in Devonport. The numerous small aquatic Davids on the water managed to breach the police barrier and forced the lumbering Goliath twice to stop, and even reverse in order to avoid a collision.[1267] And as the submarine moved towards its anchorage point, protesters in two boats succeeded in throwing a fishing net over its bow.[1268] Civil disobedience on this scale against American warships in Auckland was unprecedented, and showed no signs of abating. Polls in 1984 revealed that 49.6 per cent of Aucklanders opposed visits by nuclear-powered or -armed vessels, while 32 per cent favoured them, and the remainder were neutral in their views.[1269] In the months that followed, opposition throughout the country to New Zealand's close military relationship with the United States (principally through the ANZUS alliance) grew, which in turn fortified the government's resolve in this area.[1270] Lange made clear his administration's stance on visiting naval vessels within months of being elected:

> *To ensure that our exclusion of nuclear weapons is complete, the government decided ... that access to New Zealand's ports would be granted only to those vessels which we could satisfy ourselves were neither nuclear-powered nor nuclear-armed .... That policy reflects the fact that there is simply no need for nuclear weapons to be brought into New Zealand. The strategic environment does not call for nuclear weaponry.*[1271]

Auckland would be the test case of this commitment in February 1985, when the guided-missile destroyer USS *Buchanan* (which was conventionally powered and unlikely to be nuclear-armed)[1272] was scheduled to visit the city.[1273] However, Labour stuck to its guns, and refused the vessel entry on the basis that the United States could not offer assurance that it was not carrying any nuclear weapons. The US Government responded by downgrading political and diplomatic relations with New Zealand. Although no one knew at the time how far the relationship would deteriorate, the New Zealand Government, having plotted its course, was now sticking to it.

The murderous irony in this anti-nuclear campaign was that the threat of attack that Auckland faced was neither nuclear, nor from an enemy. Instead, conventional explosives were used by a nominal ally — France — to blast a vessel moored in the Waitematā Harbour on 10 July 1985. And in a further callously ironic twist, the particular vessel that was attacked was selected because it had been involved in anti-nuclear campaigning.

What had piqued the French to the point that they were willing to commit a terrorist act in Auckland was the presence of the Greenpeace ship *Rainbow Warrior* in the Waitematā Harbour. The ship was about to lead a flotilla of vessels to Mururoa Atoll to protest French nuclear testing there,[1274] which would draw global attention to activities that the French Government would have preferred remain clandestine. Somewhere in the bowels of the French security services, the suitably named 'Operation Satanic' was concocted to respond to the Greenpeace 'threat'. The plan — which was even given the blessing of French President (and one-time Vichy collaborator) François Mitterrand[1275] — involved sinking the protest vessel, in the hope that the impending flotilla mission would not go ahead.

The two French foreign intelligence service operatives who organised the attack were Alain Mafart and Dominique Prieur, who arrived in New Zealand under the aliases Sophie and Alain Turenge in the guise of a newlywed couple on their honeymoon. Once in the country, they immediately set to work on their scheme, which involved placing two limpet mines (with different explosive forces) on the hull of the *Rainbow Warrior*, just beneath the waterline. The first, smaller mine, when detonated, would cause panic and result in the crew fleeing the ship. Once the vessel had been abandoned, the second, more powerful mine would be set off, sinking the ship with no casualties. The final stage of the execution of this plan got under way just before midnight on 10 July 1985, but once the first mine was detonated, the terrorists' tactics turned to tragedy. Rather than the crew escaping the vessel as soon as the blast was felt, the opposite happened. Several of those who had been on board went to find out what had happened and what damage had been inflicted on the ship. Among those scurrying through the *Rainbow Warrior*'s compartments was the Greenpeace photographer Fernando Pereira, who was trying retrieve his photographic equipment when the second blast ripped a gaping hole in the hull. Water immediately flooded the vessel, drowning Pereira in the process.

All around the stricken vessel there was confusion and panic. What actually had happened? Would there be further explosions? Was anyone hurt? One of the crew — in a state of shock — told a journalist who had rushed to the scene that '[s]omebody blew up our boat .... They ripped her guts out and killed one of our crew. I feel like someone has ripped some of my guts out in the process.'[1276] Another crew member later recalled how the police initially presumed that the blasts were due to a fault within the vessel, until navy divers found that the tears in the hull were facing inwards, which could only have happened if the explosion had come from outside.[1277] The possibility that this was a terrorist attack in the centre of Auckland was so far-fetched that it was initially rejected by the prime minister as a possible explanation for what had happened.[1278] However, the police quickly began to assemble clues that pointed to the almost unthinkable: that the *Rainbow Warrior* had been bombed. Mafart and Prieur were apprehended and charged just over a day later, but rather than admit its complicity, the French Government initially accused British security services for being responsible for the attack.[1279] However, as the evidence against the French agents began to pile up, this cowardly attempt to deflect blame ground to a halt.

On 4 November, Mafart and Prieur pleaded guilty in the Auckland High Court in Waterloo Quadrant to the reduced charges of manslaughter and wilful damage, after the initial charges of murder and arson against the saboteurs were reduced (their guilty plea ensured that the facts of the police investigation would never be made public). Mafart later recounted the scene in court, in an almost bemused manner:

> *In this auditorium no one suspects the strategy that ... has [been] concocted. The Court is declared open. Judge Ron Gilbert enters, looking extremely formal, wearing a robe and an Elizabethan-style wig. I have an impression of being a mutineer from the Bounty ... but that in this case the gallows would not be erected in the village square. Three courteous phrases are exchanged between [the judge] and our lawyers, the charges are read to us and the Court asks us whether we plead guilty or not guilty, our replies are clear "guilty!". With that one word the trial is at an end.*[1280]

The pair were each sentenced to ten years' imprisonment, but following an intense period of political horse-trading, the New Zealand Government agreed for the two to serve out their sentence under French custody on the French island of Hao, from where they were released after serving fewer than three years, and subsequently re-employed and even promoted by the French Government. For at least one of the crew on board the *Rainbow Warrior* that night, the memory of the attack had no such convenient ending: 'For me, a young ordinary seaman, and for most of the crew, it seemed unreal. When excellent work by the New Zealand Police proved that the French secret service was responsible, we and most of the New Zealand public lost some of our innocence.'[1281]

The *Rainbow Warrior* bombing was one of those very rare occasions where international relations between allies toppled from the lofty realms of political visits and diplomatic functions, and crashed into the lives of everyday people in a murderous manner. In the course of this, Aucklanders received a harsh lesson in geopolitics: the realisation that, for the major nuclear powers, places like Auckland were almost inconsequential in their pursuit of their strategic goals. And as the lifeless carcass of the *Rainbow Warrior* lay slumped at Marsden Wharf after the bombing, it came to serve as a reminder that the Cold War sureties that many in the city had taken for granted up until that point in July 1985 were now anything but certain.

'Looking into Hades'

In November 1986, Auckland residents received another reminder of how the formerly sharp outlines of East and West were becoming blurred as the Cold War began to lose some of its chill. The apparition that embodied this increasingly opaque state of world affairs was a white-frocked Pole. Eight years earlier, Karol Wojtyła had been elected Pope John Paul II, and had lent the moral support of the Catholic Church in his native country to the Solidarity movement — a workers' organisation that was successfully undermining Poland's communist regime. In 1986, John Paul II added another accomplishment to his papacy, by becoming the first pope to visit New Zealand. The flight he arrived on landed on 22 November at Auckland Airport, and after the obligatory tarmac-kissing, he was driven to the Domain, where he received a pōwhiri (ritual welcome) before addressing a crowd of thousands[1282] — both Catholics and the curious — who had gathered for the spectacle. 'I rejoice to be in your midst. Indeed I rejoice that it has been possible for me to come to God's house here, that is, to the People of God, the Church in Auckland, the Church in New Zealand' was his opening comment, and in the brief address that ensued, the pope spoke of the importance of denominations drawing closer together, and stressed a message of peace.[1283] However, despite the homilies delivered at the Domain, the pope was still implacable in his view that homosexuality was a sin,[1284] which placed him at odds with New Zealand's legalisation on homosexuality, that had passed in July the same year.

In the early decades of the twentieth century, homosexuality was a penal offence, and although the penalties were reduced in 1961, the criminality for 'indecency between males', 'sodomy', 'keeping place of resort for homosexual acts' and for 'unnatural ... offences committed with any other male human being', remained in place.[1285] Through the introduction of the Homosexual Law Reform Bill in Parliament, in March 1985, legislators aimed to rectify the situation by decriminalising homosexuality, and prohibiting discrimination on the basis of a person's sexuality. However, research carried out just six years beforehand exposed a general attitude in the community towards gay people that was still heavily steeped in stereotypes:

Overall, male homosexuals were perceived as being effeminate in attitude, posture, and dress and as being more "emotional" and "sensitive" than most New Zealand males.... The perception of lesbians ... [was] uniformly negative. They were seen as being "tough," aggressive, "butch," and "masculine" (in a disparaging sense) in temperament and behaviour.[1286]

It was in such an environment that the legalisation of homosexual acts between consenting adults was being proposed. But it was never going to be a straightforward debate between ardent supporters and strident opponents, even if the media depictions of it sometimes gave this impression. First, there was the matter of morality, which was seldom openly discussed, but which was now being thrust centre stage in public debate. Many Aucklanders may have assumed that their neighbours and friends all shared similar moral views on certain issues, and were surprised to discover that it was not always so. The deepest moral inclinations of different groups in the city were not only now being exposed, but were being torn at from all directions. Allied to this issue was whether the state had any role at all in forbidding consenting adult behaviour that took place in private. For others, there was anxiety (sometimes manifesting as bullishness) that the role of religion was not nearly as influential nor as widespread in the city as they had believed. Then there were overlapping debates about health (particularly with the still poorly understood disease of AIDS), the appropriate age of consent, the discrimination gay people faced, competing ideologies relating to what society should look like, and even the type of sexual intercourse that would be encompassed by the planned law (which some opponents seemed eager to argue in lascivious detail).[1287]

Auckland's responses were varied and nuanced, even if popular representations of the debate at the time only focused on the shrill extremities. Several Auckland church groups, for example, organised a petition opposing the Bill, but were far from hostile in their approach. In their submission on the Bill, they stressed the need for 'compassion, understanding and love from the community', and that, therefore, their approach had been 'to avoid any derogatory publicity against homosexual people'. As they went on to explain:

> *Unlike other protest movements, we have not used any slogans, badges, car stickers, sprayed slogans on buildings, nor organised any protest marches with chanting and placards .... We are therefore deeply disappointed at the way in which the news media have misrepresented our approach in order to discredit out cause.*[1288]

Likewise, the East Coast Bays Methodist Parish submitted its view that homosexuality was a sin, but that 'people should not be jailed for committing the homosexual act with a consenting partner in private'.[1289] Contrary views came predominantly from campaigners for reforming the law, but there was also support from sometimes unexpected quarters. As an indication of how widespread and deeply felt views were in this debate, the Waiheke County Council waded into the issue, and prepared a statement in favour of the Bill, stressing 'the need for the recognition of revoking an antiquated Victorian inspired piece of legislation which discriminates against the sexes'.[1290] In contrast to this approach, in May 1985 the Mt Roskill Church of Christ paid for a full-page advertisement in the *Auckland Star* condemning homosexuality outright.[1291]

As time went on, the debate became more strident, and the more moderate voices were drowned out by the din of demagogues, whose rallies evinced very little in the way of compassion, understanding or love. Most notorious, perhaps, was the speech delivered by the National MP Norman Jones in 1985, when he addressed a vocal minority of gay protesters at one of his speeches. 'Go back into the sewers where you come from,' he told them, 'as far as I'm concerned you can stay in the gutter. We do not want homosexuality legalised. We do not want our children to be contaminated.' And as the partisan crowd began to roar in approval, Jones instructed them derisorily to '[t]urn around and look at them [the gay hecklers] ... gaze upon them ... you're looking into Hades ... don't look too long, you might catch AIDS'.[1292] It felt like just a few steps away from a lynching, but the effect of this type of low-rent rhetoric was probably not what Jones and his ilk expected. While it certainly roused the rabble, it also galvanised supporters of homosexual law reform. James Peters, a member of the Auckland Gay Task Force, which was campaigning for the Bill, explained how such anti-gay tirades motivated him to become more involved in activism at this time:

> *One night on the TV news I saw [gay activist] Peter Wall at a public meeting where the fundamentalists opposing the bill were coming up with rhetoric so inflammatory and unbalanced that Peter couldn't contain himself. I saw a policeman drag him out. There was a meeting at Alfies nightclub the next Wednesday and I went along with some fear and trepidation. I'd never thought of myself as an activist but sometimes you've got to stand up and be counted .... I was 43. I was a businessman. I had been out since I was 18 or 19 and I'd been determined to live an open life, not be a closet gay. I've been one of the lucky ones. But I sometimes helped out Father Felix Donnelly, who ran a home for wayward kids who'd often been thrown out of home because of their sexuality. He told me this bill had to pass, because of the young people who were committing suicide.*[1293]

Sensing that the moral boundaries were shifting into dangerous territory, and desiring to reverse the trend, two Auckland businessmen — Keith Hay and Bill Subritsky — helped form the Coalition of Concerned Citizens. This was a conservative Christian lobby group, modelled on the American Moral Majority movement, which aimed to harness widespread popular support to oppose the Homosexual Law Reform Bill. Their principal weapon in this fight was to be a petition, even though, from the outset, it should have been obvious that such an approach had no chance of bringing about the collapse of parliamentary support for the Bill. In some Auckland suburbs, leaflets were dropped in letterboxes linking the Bill with the increased risk of the spread of AIDS, and petition sheets were widely circulated by church groups in an effort to capture as many signatories as possible.[1294] On 24 September 1985 the petition containing the names of approximately 835,000 New Zealanders was presented to Parliament[1295] (although, subsequently, irregularities with some signatories were detected).[1296]

When it came to the vote on 9 July 1986, Parliament passed the legislation by 49 to 44,[1297] which represented 'a devastating blow for conservative Christians in the political arena'.[1298] In the lead-up to the vote, in an assertion of misplaced optimism, Hay buoyantly suggested that 'Christians are going to take control of this country. The next two years are going to be the most exciting years this country's had',[1299] but even in Auckland's Bible belt of Mt Roskill, where Hay's campaign against the Bill was based, this sort of promise rang hollow. 'The vote didn't go our way, and for a lot of people in the area, they just weren't that worried by it,'[1300] was the frank summation of one local minister. The moral panic over legalising homosexuality soon subsided, and, to a degree, Christianity in Auckland withdrew a few steps further to the periphery of society.

Boom

In the contest between God and Mammon, in the mid-1980s it looked as if Mammon was gaining the upper hand. Auckland was emerging from its stultifying regulatory cocoon into the bright sunlight of the free market. This metamorphosis was possible because of the great economic liberalisation brought about from 1984. In the country's biggest city, the ostentatious displays of wealth that came in the wake of deregulation were at their most vivid, and arguably, at their most vulgar. This blaze of affluence was most luridly embodied in the 'yuppie' — a category made up of young, 'upwardly mobile' urban professionals,[1301] whose sudden auto-gentrification lacked anything particularly refined. Instead, they tended to be more sail and less anchor, to paraphrase Macaulay.[1302] The accoutrements of the yuppie class were most evident in central Auckland. Cars such as BMWs, which had been a rarity in the previous decade, were now seen in comparative abundance, and became a stereotypical status symbol of the era, along with vibrant-hued, shoulder-padded fashion, and any sort of entertainment that cultivated an air of opulence, perhaps veering towards decadence.[1303]

The ideals of this subclass were retooled for the prosperity age. The sexual revolution had been won by the previous generation, and it was now the turn for the elevation of values such as prestige, power, wealth, fame, recognition, status and flamboyance in the cycle of social change.[1304]

There was little distinctly New Zealand about yuppie culture, and in a way, that was the point. Although its members may have lived in Auckland, they strove for a consciously transcultural lifestyle that was affiliated to no particular place. For some of the leaders of this pack, what mattered was the way in which wealth (or the pretence of wealth) could be converted into a form of exhibitionism. Certainly, Ray Smith, the founder of Goldcorp, was not shy in revealing his financial phallus. Having formed his 'investment' company on gold speculation, he was not only determined to enjoy his instantly acquired wealth, but also to flaunt it. 'By the end of September 1987,' he boasted,

> *I owned: a home on Takapuna beach worth $1.5 million; the latest Bentley Turbo R made by Rolls-Royce worth $350,000; a new Ferrari 328 worth $200,000; ... half shares in an Agusta twin turbine helicopter worth $2 million; a 58 foot cruiser — 'Spartacus' worth $500,000; ... 27 million shares in Goldcorp Holdings valued at $36 million; an art collection worth $150,000.*[1305]

And in perhaps the most audacious act of financial hubris, one day, Smith summoned the artist Billy Apple to his Parnell Rise office, where he commissioned him to sculpt an apple from solid gold. Six months later, the item was complete, and Smith was delivered *The Golden Apple*, which was cast from 103.559 ounces of pure gold, and which he sold for $85,000 (making it the most expensive artwork at the time by a living New Zealand artist).[1306]

In 1987, in a case of art imitating artifice, a lavish drama series was produced by Television New Zealand that parodied, yet also captured, Auckland at the peak of its mid-decade hedonism. *Gloss* was the programme's title, and its producer, Janice Finn, consciously set out to depict 'something about the 80s and what was happening in Auckland', and in particular, how 'wealth had changed and become very obvious. People were chucking money around and being very over-the-top in spending their dough.'[1307] One of the actors who starred in the series,

Peter Elliott, reflected on the extent to which Auckland's zeitgeist was reflected in the series:

> *It was the first time Auckland woke up and went, "... it's good to be an Aucklander." It was greedy as hell, it was brash and noisy. Things had changed from a Lion Brown and a doobie; you could go anywhere and be offered a line. We were country bumpkins suddenly moved into this fast-paced new world.*[1308]

It felt that almost everyone was in on the act. While yuppies were leading the way, 'ordinary' Aucklanders were also able to partake in this avaricious culture courtesy of the share market. 'We didn't know all the ins and outs of it, but we thought it was worth a go, especially as everyone else was doing it'[1309] was how one suburban Auckland resident explained what was probably a widespread approach to investing at this time. Buying shares usually involved a visit to a sharebroker (most likely based in a chrome-and-pastel-decorated office in Queen Street), after which the suburban investor could return home and maybe causally mention to a friend or neighbour that they had just visited 'their' sharebroker as they 'dabbled in the market'. And, every morning, these mum-and-dad investors could open the business section of the *Herald* and run their finger down the column of firms until they spotted the company they had invested in. They would then slide that finger along the row of figures to trace whether their shares had gone up or down. And, for a while, the direction was much more often upwards.

All this time, though, there was no prophetic voice in the wilderness warning that speculation comes before a fall. The city could indulge in its *méthode champenoise* tastes while the mysterious machinery of the share market continued to manufacture wealth for everyone in a seemingly perpetual gilded age. Or so it felt. History, though, has a tendency to strike at perceived certainties, and on 19 and 20 October 1987, like some divine judgement, the New Zealand share market crashed, and, along with it, the fortunes and aspirations of all those who had invested in it.[1310] Billions of dollars were wiped off the value of the country's shares, bearing out Marx and Engels' scornful warning about capitalism: that 'all that is solid melts into air', or the earlier biblical injunction not to store treasures on earth. Ilona Rodgers, another star of *Gloss*, recounted the suddenness and unexpectedness of the day the market went bust:

The ultimate scene of the first series is the wedding of Alistair and Gemma. On the day, we're filming in a church somewhere beyond Remuera. My secretary pulls out a gun and shoots somebody, there's blood on the church wall. Gemma rushes down the drive with blood on her wedding dress, and somebody on the street — this is in real life — comes up to us and says, "The stock market's just crashed!" I can't think of a better way to put the relationship between Gloss *and Auckland in context.*[1311]

There was an initial bout of business collapses, and a drastic retreat in public parades of affluence. One Auckland business leader described in straightforward terms the extent of the effects of the crash on the city: '[l]et's assume I had ten friends, I would say two went penniless broke, another five — of which I was one — lost money, and the remainder would have escaped'.[1312] However, unlike in many other economies, New Zealand struggled to get up from the blow of the 1987 share market collapse and brush off its devastating effects. Instead, the economy continued to languish for the remainder of the decade, and well into the following one.

Tuscany?

One of the shifts that the burst affluence in the middle of the decade brought about in Auckland — and that outlasted the share market crash — was a recalibration of how some suburbs were perceived. In the 1970s, a popular T-shirt worn in Auckland bore the names: 'London, Rome, New York, Ponsonby', which played with the irony of the glamour of the first three locations being juxtaposed with the relatively run-down condition of the fourth. Inner-city suburbs like Ponsonby were what could charitably be described as 'tired' by the 1980s. Auckland was continuing with its now long-established pattern of renewal through expansion, with suburbs extending ever further away from the city centre.

By the middle of the decade, Auckland's population had grown to 754,000, occupying a built area of 40,022 hectares, which gave the city an urban density of 19 people per hectare[1313] — roughly what it had been for most of the century. However, the distribution of this density was far from even. In 1986, for example, Mt Eden had a density of 31.2 people per hectare, Ellerslie was at 16.8, Birkenhead at 17.6, Henderson at 12.7, and

Waitakere City (which still had tracts of rural land in its boundaries) had just 2.6 people occupying every hectare on average.[1314]

The availability of comparatively affordable land, supported by slowly improving transport links, encouraged expansion into areas of Auckland that were previously regarded as remote. Suburbs such as Chatswood, Highbury, Meadowbank, St Johns, Rosebank and Albany were either created or enlarged during this period, and for the first time in the century, there was an accompanying trend: inner-city residential rejuvenation. Sometimes referred to as 'gentrification', it boiled down to a process whereby more affordable houses in the inner city, many of which were run-down, were purchased and restored, with improvements. However, the financial viability of this transformation relied on the status of certain suburbs being revolutionised. If young, upwardly mobile, status-conscious people were to spend money, time and effort to overhaul an old villa or bungalow, then there had to be an accompanying expectation that the prestige of the suburb in which they were doing this would rise accordingly. Was it really possible, though, for an area with the slightly decrepit reputation that Ponsonby had to ever really be elevated to fashionable status? It was still an unlikely proposition at the start of the decade, but by its end, against many people's expectations, it was coming to fruition.[1315]

But was this anything more than an act of architectural necrophilia? Moving into Ponsonby, Grey Lynn, Mt Eden or other such suburbs seemed to be little more than an imaginative exercise in immersing oneself into what passed for Auckland's antiquity. It was also partially a repudiation of the present, by bestowing value on a form of house design that was generations old. And maybe the renovation of the villa and bungalow suburbs that gathered pace in Auckland in the 1980s was a way for some of those caught up in the rush of changes affecting the city to seek a sort of refuge and stability. If the present was uncomfortable, perhaps recalling aspects of the past could offer an antidote.[1316]

Not everyone who could afford to, however, was resorting to this embrace of the old. In the greenfield suburbs sprouting on the city's unbuilt edges, radical experimentation in housing was determining the atmosphere of some new suburbs, and changing the expectations of the functions that homes in the city could fulfil. These new houses combined the inflated aesthetic aspirations of their owners with new building materials and unusual approaches to design. The stylistic influences were not confined to any single source. There were elements of modernism, with the scaling-back of some traditional ornamentation, and a tilt towards more abstract and often geometric forms focusing on linear definitions, flat roofs, the use of glass bricks, ubiquitous (sometimes tinted) glazing and a near absence of historical references. Colloquially, these houses had the 'Miami Vice' look, an allusion to a popular television programme of the decade set in Miami, and which sometimes featured houses that accentuated this 1980s take on modernism.

The exception, however, to this conscious break with what had existed before was in the frequent absorption of a generic 'Mediterranean' look. This involved having buildings made from texture-coated fibre-cement sheets (which were a cheap — in every sense — alternative to masonry), accompanied by terracotta tiling or roofing, balconies extending from bedrooms, and outdoor patio areas shaded with thick-beamed open-topped arbour-style covering, waiting for a grapevine to grow through it for the finishing touch. Real estate agents were offering a 'touch of Tuscany' in suburban Auckland. And to accentuate the effect, the landscaping could include citrus trees in terracotta pots, olive trees and cypresses, and, slightly incongruously, palms. Indeed, from this decade until the end of the century, palms proliferated in Auckland gardens. The climate suited them, but more importantly, they brought a sense of the tropics to the isthmus. Yet, to a degree, this was not so much an enhancement of Auckland as it was a denial of it. These styles, particularly those with a Mediterranean tinge, were architectural affectations — in a way, a regurgitation of the 1970s hacienda look writ large. They drew on what was perceived as a type of climate, culture and lifestyle that could be appropriated by homeowners in these aesthetically experimental suburbs, as they shed, like an old skin, what Auckland used to be, and tried to make it something that it was not. And within a decade, the cracks in this approach began to appear — literally — as the gaps in the outer walls allowed moisture to affect the kiln-dried timber framing in some of these buildings. These monolithic-clad houses consequently acquired a new colloquial name that was entirely bereft of any glamour whatsoever: 'leaky homes'.[1317] Auckland's progress was turning back on itself. The caricature of living the lifestyle of another country was short lived, and instead of rustic, Mediterranean chic, thousands of Aucklanders who had bought these houses were instead left with dwellings that were being gradually consumed by mould and rot.

11
The 1990s

This is the moment

Even as the New Year's Day festivities in 1990 were following their predictable route — from celebration to inebriation to recuperation — some Aucklanders were defying tradition, and spent the first day of the decade working. They were putting a myriad of finishing touches on plans for the Commonwealth Games that the city would be hosting a little over three weeks later. The ghosts of the long-dead Empire were now being summoned as blithe spirits, and were scheduled to make their quadrennial apparition at the Games' opening ceremony at Mt Smart Stadium on 24 January. Forty years after Auckland had hosted the event in its earlier incarnation as the Empire Games, the city was once more mustering its enthusiasm for this international event. This time, though, the scale was vastly greater than its predecessor. Teams from 55 nations participated, with a total of 2074 athletes competing in 213 events for one (or more) of 643 medals.[1318] Almost a thousand coaches, trainers and officials accompanied the competitors,[1319] along with thousands of tourists who descended on Auckland for the event. As hotels and motels soon filled with arrivals, residents in the city were encouraged to take people into their homes (costs were up to the hosts and guests to negotiate) to ease the strain. In the age of multi-million-dollar corporate events, which is what the Commonwealth Games were,[1320] the idea of Aucklanders sharing their homes with visitors was a fleeting sign that traces of the city's still quaint character were there to be found, despite its outward pretensions of being just as austere, modern and clinical as any other large international city. However, Auckland was certainly prepared and professional when it came to sporting facilities. The newly built velodrome at the Manukau Sports Bowl hosted track cycling events, a purpose-built pool complex in Henderson held the swimming events, and some of the shooting competitions took place at a new shooting range at Ardmore.[1321] In addition, 305 houses were constructed to accommodate the athletes in a purpose-built village in Glen Innes (that afterwards became the site of the University of Auckland's Tāmaki campus). The players' village included a medical centre, shops, bus lanes, open spaces and the seemingly obligatory accessory for such venues: a fountain.[1322] The closing ceremony at Mt Smart in some ways paraded how Auckland saw itself, and how it wished others to see it. As the ceremony got under way, the audience was treated to a parade of marching girls, whose tight formations and precisely choreographed movements were an echo of an earlier Auckland that seemed slightly whimsical in this setting. The performance of a Scottish pipe band only added to the feeling that Auckland's identity was still a weave of various historical and overseas cultural influences that remained ill at ease in this South Pacific city. Queen Elizabeth II and the Duke of Edinburgh were driven around the stadium's field to the accompanying music of the Games' theme song, "This is the Moment". One of those present at the ceremony described the euphoria of the event: 'It was a mammoth party, the streets around the stadium swarmed with people and athletes dancing, hugging and singing. And what a brilliant anthem "This is the Moment" was. It's a song that will always be part of the national psyche.'[1323] As the international spotlight illuminated Auckland that summer evening (an audience of 83 million watched the closing ceremony), the city looked to be splashing around in a puddle of deserved self-congratulation.

The view of Auckland from the rest of the country, though, was not always so sanguine. The 1990s was the period when the pejorative acronym 'JAFA' came into more widespread use in New Zealand. It stood for 'just another f—king Aucklander', and carried with it a store of stereotypes about what Aucklanders were like.[1324] This particular notion of the archetypal Aucklander was developed in the 1980s, when some of the more extravagant excesses of flaunted wealth in the city came to be seen as symptomatic of a more widespread brashness among its population — something that went against the supposedly parsimonious and self-effacing grain of the rest of the country. 'Auckland-hating'[1325] was nothing new in New Zealand, with examples of it even littering the press in the nineteenth century.[1326] However, in the 1990s, new life was being breathed into the old prejudice. The city was allegedly 'unplanned, polluted, choked with traffic, full of crime, an ethnic volcano, philistine, strident, vulgar, [and] money-grubbing' according to one journalist.[1327] Others saw Auckland as somehow getting more than its fair share of political and economic attention, to the detriment of the rest of the country.[1328] Auckland was also regarded by some outsiders as pretentious — a place of 'cocktails and cool'[1329] that increasingly had severed its cultural connections with the 'real' New Zealand.[1330] However, the attention generally seemed to run in only one direction. While bouts of Auckland-envy occasionally belched to the surface in other parts of the country, for the most part, it was not reciprocated.

Of course, it was not a case of the rest of New Zealand being filled with jealousy or animosity for Auckland. Sometimes, the term JAFA was used jokingly or even as a show of endearment. However, while it would be easy to dismiss this stereotype as just that — an oversimplified depiction of the city — in some ways, it reflected Auckland's migration away from other parts of the country. This was particularly noticeable both in the case of its population growth, and its ethnic and cultural composition. By 1999, Auckland's population was 1,184,000.[1331] How this growth compared with other New Zealand cities is instructive. In 1937, for example, for every 100 people living in Auckland, there were 70 in Wellington and 62 in Christchurch. Auckland was the most populous city in the country, but not by much. However, by 1999, for every 100 people residing in Auckland, there were just 29 in Wellington and 28 in Christchurch.[1332] Or to put it another way, Auckland's population was more than three times greater than the country's next two largest cities. Auckland had become a 'primate city', the traits of which one geographer sketched in the 1930s:

> *The finest wares are always to be found there, the rarest articles, the greatest talents, the most skilled workers in every science and art. Thither flows an unending stream of the young and*

ambitious in search of fame and fortune, and there fame and fortune are found. [It is] ... the market for all that is superlative in intellectual and material productions. Its supereminence as a market runs parallel to its supereminence in size.[1333]

Those drawn to primate cities have been depicted as 'pilgrims who purchase no round-trip tickets'. They come not only from overseas, but also from other parts of the country, and are drawn to these large centres both by what it can offer them and what they can offer it. A primate city 'therefore expresses the national disposition more completely than any other city', and 'contributes much to the unification of the country'.[1334] That was the theory, anyway. The view of Auckland from other parts of the country suggested that, at times, the city was anything but a condensed expression of New Zealand's disposition. As one academic put it: 'seen through South Island or Wellington eyes, Auckland's expansion is a pugnacious aggrandizement; through rural New Zealand eyes, it becomes an extravagant and unnecessary excrescence'.[1335]

Auckland had also always been more diverse than other regions in New Zealand due to it being the first point of arrival for a large portion of the country's immigrants. This diversity became much more pronounced and visible in the 1990s, and led to Auckland becoming increasingly culturally separated from some other parts of New Zealand, even if only to a slight extent. And even within the city itself, there were signs of separation. By the early 1990s, Asian immigration to Auckland was greater than immigration from the rest of the world combined, with these arrivals most likely to settle in Meadowbank, Hillsborough or, especially, Howick.[1336] In fact, the density of Asians in Howick became so noticeable that the suburb was sometimes derogatorily referred to as 'Chowick'.[1337] Such enclaves — known by some as 'ethno-suburbs' — served as places where the recently arrived could live among those from similar backgrounds, and receive the sort of cultural and community support that was not as concentrated in other parts of the city. However, unlike the historic tendency of immigrant groups to cluster in areas that became ghettos because of the relative impoverishment of their occupants, some of the suburbs in East Auckland with comparatively high Asian populations were substantially more affluent than the average for the city.[1338] Still, though, in this decade, the notion of suburbs as sanctuaries persisted for many Asian immigrants to Auckland. But even in the areas of Auckland where Asian populations were at their most concentrated, these groups still remained a minority in those suburbs.[1339]

While it became easy for some longer-standing Auckland residents to sneer at what they saw as these separated ethnic communities apparently mushrooming on their doorstep, the organic processes of integration were already at work, bringing the cultures into contact with each other. Nowhere was this more obvious in this decade than in food. By 1999, over half the restaurants in Auckland were Asian.[1340] 'I remember my mate saying we were going to get some sushi for lunch,' one student in the 1990s recalled. 'I'd never heard the word. I had no idea what he was talking about, but he took me to get some and I loved it.'[1341] In such small ways, not only were the barriers between cultures being dismantled, but the experiences of being an Aucklander were widening. So-called 'ethnic' foods went from being unknown, to exotic, to a normal part of the city's food selection, and to some extent, the perception of who was an Aucklander was undergoing a similar route. Immigration was not undermining Auckland, but rather was bolstering the city. The bigots may have lamented the decline of the 'good old days' of Anglo-Saxon Auckland ('my parents would be turning in their graves if they could see what Sandringham has turned into now. You walk down the street and everyone is speaking Asian [sic]', one octogenarian Pākehā grizzled about the changes in the ethnic composition of the area),[1342] but the fact is that such a location had never existed in the first place. Auckland has always been a cultural amalgam, and perhaps more than anywhere else in the country, has resisted any efforts to be moulded to some preordained form. On the contrary, the 1990s revealed — possibly more than at any other time in the twentieth century — how complex, fluid, ambiguous and unsettled the city's nature was. Yet, at the same time, it was a place where all these diverse groups found their moorings.

It is also significant that whereas in other Western countries — especially the United Kingdom and United States — race riots periodically scarred several cities, Auckland's response to the presence of ethnic minorities (though still far from ideal) largely sidestepped such brutal resentment. Instead, the city voted with its feet for a more integrationist approach. One example of the culture of migrant groups being insinuated into the character of Auckland took place at Western Springs Park in March 1993. This was the inaugural Pasifika Festival, which attracted an audience of 30,000.[1343] On the two stages set up at the park, members of these diaspora groups communicated to the diverse audience through performance the importance of their cultures and their identities to the city.[1344] One of the organisers recounted the circumstances which gave rise to the festival:

> *In 1991, there was something like 30 per cent unemployment, and Pacific peoples were the worst affected by it, especially amongst men. So, I think, within the Island community there was, not shame, but you know, men who worked hard at the freezing works and places that had all gone, there was a lot of frustration, a feeling of uselessness .... there was a need to create something which put some pride into the communities.*[1345]

From the outset, the annual Pasifika Festival had avoided falling into the trap of becoming a culturally frozen depiction of its constituent groups. Instead, its subsequent evolution (which included it becoming the largest Polynesian festival in the world by the end of the decade) revealed how the cultures of these immigrant groups were at once influencing Auckland and being influenced by it. The performances increasingly fused the traditional with the contemporary, and the expected with the innovative, all in an environment of uproarious mayhem, comedy and optimism, nourished with an extravagantly varied cuisine that was available to all festivalgoers. In some ways, this was the inevitable progression brought about as the passage of time shifted the city's Polynesian population from being predominantly immigrant to increasingly Auckland-born and raised:

> *the first generations came in the '70s, and suddenly in the '90s you have first generations born coming-of-age. They were different people; they were educated here and you could see the difference, their outlooks were different. They were striving for different things, wanted to achieve in education and so forth. So I wanted Pasifika to be a forward-looking festival so it would evolve and not be locked in time.*[1346]

And, vitally, the audience was not exclusively comprised of members of the communities represented on stage. Rather, it was a cross-section of the city (albeit a generally younger one) that was drawn to the event — a point not lost on one participant:

I like the fact that there are a lot of other cultures in New Zealand who attend this event which tells me that they are genuinely interested in our cultures, traditions, language but more importantly who we are .... Personally I love the positive light that this sheds on the Pacific peoples.[1347]

The name 'Pasifika' was always a convenient collective term that encompassed several distinct cultures, languages, histories and peoples. With this in mind, the festival organisers ensured that the constituent elements of this Pacific cosmopolitanism remained at the centre of the event, and were not absorbed into some generic South Pacific stereotype. Their specific aim was 'to create little pockets of particular identities, so you could go to Samoa, you could go to Fiji, you could go to Tonga, and the idea was you would start to recognise the diversity within Pasifika'.[1348]

Elsewhere in Auckland, small enclaves bound by their shared heritage were repeating the well-worn routine of asserting their distinct culture in a city where it was otherwise practically absent. In September 1991 the inaugural meeting of the Croatian Cultural Society was held in Auckland, and blushing with the first flush of nascent nationalism as Yugoslavia collapsed into civil war, Croatians in the city (both long-standing immigrants along with recent ones) worked towards establishing a club for themselves. In August 1992 the Society purchased a section in McLeod Road, in Te Atatū South, and through strenuous fundraising built a clubroom on it. That Christmas, around 600 people attended its first major function,[1349] and for the remainder of the decade it became one of the principal locations in the city where selected elements of the members' culture and heritage were conserved and reproduced.[1350] Occasionally, there were differences that reflected the length of time some members had been in the country. The traditional kolo dances, for example, that Auckland Croatians had maintained for generations received an unusual response from some of the more recent arrivals, as one long-time Auckland Croat explained: 'The new immigrants, they do not have that feel for our kolo. And some of them even go as far as to say "it's crap, I hate it"; but it does not matter.'[1351] As with most other cultural groups formed by immigrants, the perpetual rehearsal of cultural activities became acts of dogged preservation as much as anything else. And what of the eventual fate of the Croatian Cultural Society? It is still too early to tell, but if the experience of other such organisations in the past is anything to go by, the succession of generations will leave an ageing and dwindling membership struggling to shore up a culture and values that have reached a dead end in their adopted city. The alternative is to take a lesson from the Pasifika Festival, where evolution as much as preservation is the axiom.

Diverging

The whole matter of the ultimate purpose and persistence of cultural groups in Auckland was complicated by the end of the century due to changes to the complexion of the city itself. At the close of the 1990s, nearly half of the overseas-born population of New Zealand lived in Auckland, with 14 per cent of the city's population identifying as Asian and another 14 per cent as Pacific.[1352] The Asian-born population was approximately 68,000, and, more generally, the traditional sources of immigrants — particularly Britain and Europe — were being displaced by countries in Asia, Africa and the Middle East.[1353] Never in the twentieth century had Auckland been not just as populous, but also as ethnically diverse. In addition, some of the city's former footings in other areas that previously characterised it seemed to be giving way, especially its religious composition. The 1990s saw a continuation of the decline of Christianity, a rise in people who declared they were irreligious and also a growth in faiths that had arrived in the country more recently. This manifested itself in various ways throughout the city, and not all of them tangible. The principal of a Catholic primary school on the North Shore, for example, described how the encounter between faiths could present itself in everyday school life in a way that would have been unfamiliar to Aucklanders a few generations earlier:

> *There's been this ... Islam [sic] family who're quite devout, you know, and that's a lot of learning for us, because it's the first time we've had such a ... a devout family come in to the school, I mean, you know, [Student] goes out on Friday afternoon, for prayer, if he wants to, with Dad. You know, so ... that's been a lot of learning for us, because we didn't know. So there's a bit of ignorance as well.*[1354]

Mosques, along with Buddhist, Hindu and Sikh temples began to appear as part of Auckland's religious architecture, where once Christian places of worship had dominated. Crucially, though, the city avoided the sort of aggressive religious sectarianism that was occurring in other parts of the world in this era. Instead, the pious generally kept their beliefs within the confines of their religious communities, and when in public, instead of collisions between members of different faiths, there was a remarkable degree of civility — a fact perhaps taken for granted by residents, but more fully appreciated by recent migrants from those parts of the world where such religious co-existence was almost inconceivable.

Auckland businesses and bureaucrats contributed to this sense of community solidarity when, in 1994, they collaborated to bring about the inaugural 'Christmas in the Park' concert, which was held in the Domain on 10 December. The event became an annual exercise in slightly contrived civic fellowship, and was also, both in absolute terms and certainly per capita, one of the biggest concerts of its type anywhere in the world. The cricket pavilion was converted into a stage for the event, and a succession of musicians performed from early evening, in front of audiences reclining on picnic rugs strewn across the vast grounds. Attendances reached a pinnacle of around 300,000 by 1998, representing almost a third of the city's population.[1355]

However, by the end of the decade Christmas in the Park was becoming less about Christmas and more about mass entertainment. The crowds were still there every December, but not in their former numbers, and the event was gradually becoming more of an undertaking in predictable self-referential parody.

As the cumbersome weight of Christmas in the Park increasingly leant on tradition to prop it up, another type of festival had been conceived in the early 1990s that superficially represented something very new for the city. The Hero Parade, first held in Queen Street, was organised by some members of the city's gay community Their hope was that it would turn into a local incarnation of Sydney's Gay and Lesbian Mardi Gras — a mass pageant where Auckland's homosexuals could (at least for one evening) escape the moral mausoleum many still felt they were confined to. However, its smaller scale, insufficient funding and lack of the pedigree of its Sydney counterpart (which had been going since 1978) resulted in Auckland's initial efforts resembling more of a sexualised Santa Parade. The early years were undoubtedly the most challenging, as one of those involved explained:

You think it's easy to put on a parade? Get real! The first Hero was small and it didn't almost survive to the second year. At that second parade, hostile rate payers got behind their City Council to try to prevent the parade from taking place on Auckland streets. The third Hero had a bad press to contend with .... During the next parade ... the skies opened up and the rain cometh down.[1356]

The Hero Parade eventually grew in scale and popularity, to the point where by the middle of the 1990s it had become a prominent fixture in Auckland's calendar of public events, even if it came with a trail of controversy. Ostensibly, it was an opportunity for participants to reveal and 'celebrate' their sexual orientation in a hyper-stylised, public and almost ceremonial way. Nonetheless, around three-quarters of the spectators looking on at this revelation were heterosexual, with one participant acknowledging that this was the intended audience:

Well the parade is basically put on for the straight community when it comes down to it. Like a hundred thousand people there, I don't know, 5000 would be gay? Ah, so it's for straights and that's fine. I don't think we should have a problem with that at all. We should encourage it.[1357]

However, the reaction from the onlookers was not always one of unabashed enthusiasm. In 1997 a spectator was heard commenting to a person standing next to her, 'There are some *normal* people in the parade, you know, *straight* people. It's not all gay.'[1358] It was a slightly perplexed response, suggesting that the parade's intended purpose was not always completely clear to audiences. For a portion of Aucklanders, though, the parade was depicted as the last days of Sodom and Gomorrah being played out in the central city. An Auckland talkback radio announcer told his audience, 'I believe that most people in this country still find the sort of behaviour that gays may get up to ... abhorrent, undesirable and a number of other adjectives I could use.'[1359] And at a full council meeting (held in the Town Hall) called in the wake of the first parade, with 1200 people in attendance, one member of the public got up and argued that 'if the whole world became homosexual, within two generations the world would self-destruct'.[1360] Much of this sort of rhetoric was an echo of what had been heard in the mid-1980s during the debate over homosexual law reform, although this time around it was noticeably more subdued, and the arguments often sounded more routine or even defeatist compared to the tenor in the previous decade. Yet, opposition remained strong. The city's mayor, Les Mills, wrote to the New Zealand AIDS Foundation, expressing how he was 'not prepared to personally encourage homosexuality or support the promotion of a homosexual lifestyle as an individual or by the Auckland City Council from city rates'[1361] — a stance endorsed by Deputy Mayor David Hay, who argued that such events were 'not what the silent majority want to see in our city'.[1362]

This was primarily a response to the degree of the parade's sexual explicitness. In addition to outrage emanating from some of the more predictable quarters in Auckland society, a group known as the Gaily Normal also raised concerns about the overt character of the parade: '[The] general public see us as sexual creatures flaunting sex, but really we aren't. We are just average people and what we do behind closed doors is our business.'[1363] By the end of the decade, opponents of the parade had grudgingly become resigned to the fact that it would continue, while its proponents were beginning to diverge on issues relating to the political function of the event, and the groups that ought to be represented in it. In 1996 the parade shifted from Queen Street to Ponsonby Road, enhancing the latter's reputation as the country's gay capital.[1364] For the remainder of the decade, its popularity continued to soar, although whether all attending did so from fascination with the spectacle or some latent voyeurism is impossible to know.

For all its flamboyance and frippery, the Hero Parades at this time had a more serious social purpose. They aimed to challenge the idea that, in public, the only sort of attraction that could be displayed was of the heterosexual variety. It was a boundary that the parades in the 1990s quickly breached, and in the process forced Aucklanders to re-examine their moral positions on homosexuality.[1365] The matter, of course, remained unsettled. The perpetually offended continued to butt heads with the perpetually flagrant, revealing the true nature of Auckland's enduring moral diversity.

It was not just contested moral issues that were more evident in public Auckland in this period. The tangled relationship between culture and landscape in the city — which had played out in a multitude of forms since the first humans hacked their way through the isthmus's undergrowth — took a knotty turn in October 1994, when a Māori activist, Mike Smith

(Ngāpuhi, Ngāti Kahu), decided to attack Auckland's skyline. His particular target was the lone Monterey pine tree on One Tree Hill, which had been one of the city's emblems for most of the century — arching over Cornwall Park and curving into Auckland's horizon. Along with Rangitoto, it was one of the few natural features that was instantly recognisable to residents and visitors as belonging specifically to the city. Smith's stated motive in his assault on the tree was to protest against the government's policy on Treaty of Waitangi settlements, but it soon disassembled into a more generic grievance about colonialism, which this aged pine supposedly embodied.

On that drizzly night in October, Smith took a chainsaw with him to the summit, and cut frantically at the base of the tree, knowing that the noise would soon alert households bordering the park. As the blade sliced deep into the trunk, sawdust sprayed out all around its roots, but, as predicted, the noise carried and the police soon arrived. '[T]hey were in their black overalls,' he recalled. 'They had dogs. They had sidearms, and they didn't look very happy. So I thought, well probably the worst thing to do would be to be standing there with a chainsaw that's revving. So I just turned it off.'[1366] Seriously wounded, the tree received a fatal attack by another protester in 1999, and was removed the following year. And although Smith remained unrepentant for 'interfering' with the tree (as the police worded the charge), he later expressed a small grain of contrition:

> *The only regret I ever felt, was when I read a story in the media, about a woman who talked about how much that tree meant to her. I think her husband, who had died, proposed to her under that tree. She saw it as a touchstone for the love she felt for her partner, to take that away from somebody on a human level, I didn't feel too good about that.*[1367]

The protest passed, the policy it targeted also passed, but One Tree Hill was now deprived of the very thing from which it derived its name, and which had helped make it one of Auckland's most distinctive landscape features.

Play it again

The sharply toned blue skies and alpine-white mountain peaks were reflected perfectly in a tranquil high-country lake — a pristine bucolic scene that slowly shrank as the camera panned away from it, revealing it as a chimera. This was merely a poorly placed tourism billboard. As the scene around it broadened, what was exposed was a scene of 1990s Gothic horror. It was this cruel juxtaposition that was the opening scene of the feature film *Once Were Warriors*. In its first moments, the audiences were transported from the South Island to South Auckland. Although set in a fictional suburb that was supposed to epitomise urban deprivation, there was no shortage of locations in Auckland that fitted the bill, with most of the filming taking place in Onehunga, Glen Innes and Ōtara during 1993. The story revolved around a highly dysfunctional Māori family that eventually found refuge, if not redemption, in its traditional culture. However, judging by the intense response of audiences to the film,[1368] *Once Were Warriors* became the cinematic equivalent of a wrecking ball, demolishing the lazy preconceptions that Aucklanders had built around their city's progress and improvement. Outside the more comfortable suburbs, there was another Auckland — one seething with violence, crippled by poverty and bereft of hope. Yes, it was melodramatic in parts, and visually exaggerated for effect, but it was still recognisable to those familiar with the cavities of dystopia in the city. The film's director, Lee Tamahori, was explicit in his wish for 'a very hard, almost treeless urban experience that not many people in New Zealand would ever have been aware of or even seen',[1369] and he accomplished this by selecting various locations that until this time tended to be bypassed by Aucklanders who lived outside of them. Places like Māngere and Ōtara were not destinations, and neither were they transit points. Instead, they were places where the poor were packed. These were overcrowded, run-down suburbs where substandard health, education and employment, together with a pervading sense of hopelessness, predominated. This, at least, was the stereotype. Many residents, though, hardly felt stranded in an island of suburban despair. John Pule's 1992 novel *The Shark that Ate the Sun* offered a nostalgic rendition of the area, capturing something of the dense matting of relationships that existed in places such as Ōtara — one that would not necessarily be easily detected by outsiders:

> *In this life, in this Otara, there is no such thing as solitude, you become part of a life that is stormy, happy people, languages of ancient migration, mingling in the adopted soil .... Otara is a survivor .... Kid shily staking out the area, and the buses,*

yellow longboats we called them, were the noisiest in the world, and in these machines the many languages of Otara flew like birds down the aisle .... On Sundays the church people, dressed immaculately in white, filled the seats and gave the bus and Otara a sense of pride and harmony.[1370]

Or as it was put more prosaically by one researcher in the 1990s, South Auckland had a 'unique form of suburban communalism which would be the envy of many other hard pressed New Zealand communities'.[1371] In 1993 a member of the portentously titled 'Enterprise Otara' similarly observed that there was 'a wealth of cultural skill and knowledge embedded within the fabric of this community', and that this 'unique multi-ethnic environment could be developed to attract the valuable tourist dollar to boost the local economy'.[1372] Material deprivation clearly did not always equate with deficiencies in other aspects of life. On the contrary, events that achieved city-wide success in this decade, such as the Pasifika Festival or the Ōtara Flea Market (which by the 1990s had become New Zealand's largest street market),[1373] had their genesis in the very types of suburbs that were vilified in *Once Were Warriors*. So which rendition of South Auckland was the more accurate? Was this part of the city really an urban abyss, or was it more a location of unrealised potential? In a sense, the question misses the mark. Auckland was always about the unwieldy cohabitation of 'us' and 'them'. By the end of the twentieth century, it was already far too large to be typecast as anything less. The dull cultural pallor of the city at the beginning of the century had long since been replaced by a more vividly chromatic complexion. Where Auckland's wealth and opportunities fell across the city was uneven, as it always had been, with the inevitability that certain suburbs would fare worse than others. But as had also always been the case in Auckland, there was an element of socio-economic snakes and ladders at play. People dropped in and out of poverty, and the prosperity of some suburbs fluctuated dramatically. Still, though, there was no escaping the fact that parts of the city by the 1990s were showing signs of serious urban decay — both physical and social — in a way than was more than just part of the usual cycle of decline and renewal. Words like 'intergenerational' and 'entrenched'[1374] were starting to preface descriptions of poverty, particularly in suburbs such as Māngere, Ōtāhuhu, Manurewa and Ōtara. It was also becoming more noticeable that with each incoming tide of prosperity that reached Auckland, some areas were still being left high and dry. This was a problem with antecedents extending back for more than a century, and was now at a level of complexity that defeated the best minds in the city to resolve it.

Twenty-five kilometres directly east from Māngere was the setting for another internationally acclaimed movie filmed in Auckland in the 1990s. Jane Campion's *The Piano* — even more so than *Once Were Warriors* — exploited the city's physical attributes, almost to the point of making the location one of the characters in the movie. Karekare, where some of the seminal scenes of *The Piano* were shot, offered the sort of drama and desolation that was crucial for the visual narrative of the film. The forest in this part of Auckland served as a cloistered canopy, concealing activities that were less likely to occur in a wide-open space. It was a forbidding place that characters trudged their way through, with Campion drawing on a palette of greys and darkened greens to convey a sense of perpetual 'nightmarish' moss-laden gloom.[1375] And then there was the shore. The black-sand beach at Karekare, which was encased in a rugged hinterland of bush-clad slopes beneath a vaulted overcast sky, offered a brooding backdrop to the film, and accentuated visually feelings of isolation, abandonment and uncertainty — and all of this just 14 kilometres away from the mundane suburbs of Glen Eden and Henderson. Of course, *The Piano* was set in the Victorian era — a period that was remote from 1990s Auckland, and yet this particular region of wilderness at the edge of the city had remained unspoiled in the intervening time. The same sounds of ocean, birds and wind, and the same scenery, confronted visitors to Karekare in the 1990s as in the 1860s — a claim few other developed cities in the world could make about their natural landscapes.

Metropolis

Auckland's habit of growing outward continued in the 1990s with as much vigour as it had at any other time in the century. Suburbs such as Westgate, Whenuapai and Albany, which until that time were made up mainly of paddocks that were no longer economically viable as farms, and a few strings of old houses lining main roads, were now prized by developers as the next sites of urban intensification. A resident who had lived in the Westgate area for nearly 50 years outlined the sort of changes that were taking place in this decade:

When we moved in here, it was a metal road and only a few houses on it. It was meant to be part of a new subdivision, but that never really took off. It was really just before Westgate [Shopping Centre] opened that you could see things starting to change. All that land behind us, that was all farm-land, and we had gotten used to it. It was nice waking up and seeing those fields every morning. But the next thing you know, it's all being subdivided, and now it's all housing. I suppose that's what they call progress.[1376]

Change the name of the area, and it could easily have been the account of someone living in Massey in the 1960s, Te Atatū in the 1950s or Mt Albert in the 1920s. This was the perpetual cycle of the city's enlargement that had been in operation since the nineteenth century. However, Auckland's surrounding supplies of land were not limitless. By the 1990s, East Auckland was almost completely urbanised, and housing in West Auckland was starting to fill up in areas bordering the city's rural boundaries. Like a balloon being gripped in the middle, pressure for more accommodation was forcing expansion increasingly to the north and south, and perceptions of Auckland were altering as a result. Albany's rapid residential and industrial enlargement was pushing the urban frontiers northward. As a consequence, places like Ōrewa, which were once a 'holiday resort'[1377] where Aucklanders would take a day trip to escape the city, were now not only growing into large suburbs in their own right, but were also becoming tantalisingly close to the rest of the city. By the end of the 1990s, Ōrewa was just 14 kilometres from the northern reaches of Albany, with developing areas such as Silverdale filling in the gap between. Ōrewa and Whangaparāoa, which were formerly sparsely occupied in the winter, but popular with Auckland holidaymakers in the summer, were now evolving into what was described resignedly in the parlance of the time as 'just another suburb'.

However, as the emerging outer suburbs were ever more distant from the city centre, and with transport routes straining to cope with increased demand, the challenges of commuting began to pile pressure on existing suburbs to intensify land usage — something that, on the whole, local authorities were supportive of.[1378] This process had begun in the 1980s but accelerated in the 1990s, leading to another term entering the popular lexicon of Aucklanders: 'infill housing'. Initially, this was financially viable mainly in the city's more desirable suburbs, where there was the available space (that is, where section sizes were generally larger) and where zoning permitted it. Parts of Epsom and Mt Eden became known for infill housing, producing often jarring results, with single-level villas and bungalows at one end of a section now overshadowed at the other end by two-storey houses built in the latest forms, with oversized porticos over the front door supported by imposing pillars, mixtures of brick and monolithic cladding, anaemic pastel tones, and with planting having gone from pōhutukawa to palm.

Like some self-fulfilling prophecy, the more intensification that took place, the more land values rose. While infill housing represented a common approach to achieving greater intensification, there was much more reluctance over another option: apartments. Could Aucklanders, who for generations were accustomed for the most part to living in stand-alone houses on sections, be convinced that an apartment was even a viable let alone desirable alternative? The signs were not optimistic at first. The naysayers, after all, had history on their side:

> *we thought you'd never get New Zealanders living in something like that [an apartment]. It might have suited other countries, but we were more an outdoors place. I couldn't see anyone wanting to be cooped up in little boxes where you couldn't just step outside and have your own private space.*[1379]

To some degree, the emergence of apartments was inevitable as Auckland's density continued to intensify. Between the late 1970s and the late 1990s the city's population grew by around 300,000 without any significant extension of its urban limits.[1380] And despite the doubters, Aucklanders soon went from testing the water with apartment-living to diving into this 'new' form or residential living. In 1991 there were just 356 apartment units in the whole of the Auckland inner city (excluding university accommodation). Within five years, this had risen to over 3000 units in total,[1381] and by July 1999 there had been 3553 apartment units built in the city in the previous 12 months alone,[1382] with the rate of apartment growth only getting faster.[1383] Several factors contributed to this surge towards the inner city. Availability was important. The supply of purpose-built apartment buildings, augmented by lowly tenanted office blocks that were being converted into apartments, made this option relatively affordable. At the same time, improved construction methods and cheaper materials made new buildings a more economically feasible proposition for developers. Residents were not merely moving into a new type of building — there was also increasingly an accompanying lifestyle that tempted some people: commuting was faster and cheaper; there were more recreation and entertainment opportunities; maintenance was much less than on the traditional suburban house (which attracted those whose children had left home and who were looking for an easier lifestyle); the reputation of the inner city had improved thanks to the gentrification of many surrounding suburbs; banks were more willing to lend on apartments; and immigrants from countries where apartment-living was common had been helpful in leading the way,[1384] demonstrating that this form of accommodation was not just for students or people who were unable to afford a conventional house in the suburbs.

Some of the earliest apartments constructed in Auckland in this decade, especially those that were converted office buildings, tended to have more modest finishes, with features that revealed that they had originally been designed for a different purpose. In some cases, the principle that form followed function was no longer a 'spiritual union' between design and purpose, as Frank Lloyd Wright had proposed,[1385] but instead had become a justification for apartments that met the barest expectations at the least possible cost. However, with the notion of apartment-living still in its infancy for most Aucklanders, and with demand still small and volatile, developers could be excused for treading carefully.

Not everyone was convinced though that it was sufficient for people to be boxed into these unappealing buildings. One Auckland property developer, Andrew Krukziener, began tinkering with the possibility of an apartment building that would elevate the quality of inner-city living beyond anything that existed at the time. 'Travelling frequently to New York, I was awed by their romanticism and the inspirational thoughts that these skyscrapers engendered in people,' he explained about his approach to this project. 'Buildings define a city. Together they all form the fabric that makes the city a whole. Each building should increase the quality of the fabric, rather than taking away from it.'[1386] His plan soon took on a clear form, and materialised with the completion, in 1999, of the Metropolis building in Courthouse Lane. At 40 storeys (155 metres), it was by far the tallest residential building in the country, and contained

368 apartments as well as 55 hotel rooms. Its exterior was comparatively austere, with an emphasis on appearing elegant rather than ostentatious. Apart from its obvious height, one of its most visual features were the rows of balconies (rare at that time in Auckland apartment buildings), and the partially stepped copper dome that crowned the building. Inside, Krukziener wanted 'an art deco theme',[1387] which was accomplished by drawing on traits from New York hotel lobbies and apartments from that era, with elements in the foyer such as marble floors, faux skylights, cylinder wall lights and clean-lined neoclassical forms contributing to an ambience of luxurious nostalgia without ever descending to architectural mimicry. However, like its cinematic namesake, Metropolis was an undertaking with a budget that continued to soar, resulting in the final construction cost reaching around $180 million.[1388] More than any other building in the city, though, Metropolis embodied the possibility of no longer owning land, but living in a space above it. And instead of values being determined horizontally, by how far one's section extended, they could now also be defined vertically, by how high one's apartment was. Living in somewhere like the Metropolis apartments was still out of reach for the majority of Aucklanders, and was not yet seen by most people at that time as a desirable alternative to life in the suburbs, but gradually buildings like the one Krukziener conceived were beginning to recalibrate where and how some of the city's residents chose to be housed.

A concern for many people in this era when looking on at Auckland's inner-city regeneration was the loss of the inner-city's heritage as older, smaller buildings were knocked down to make way for new construction. Some developers partially circumvented concerns about the diminution of Auckland's 'historic' appearance by preserving the façades of older buildings, behind which modern skyscrapers were erected. It was usually an incongruous marriage of styles, forced on developers by a growing perception that Auckland had already lost too many of its heritage buildings, and that development needed to be tempered with preservation. The façade option had been employed at 125 Queen Street, where the original Bank of New Zealand building, designed in 1865, had its street frontage preserved when a high-rise office building was constructed on the site in 1986. Another approach was to graft a space with a contemporary design onto a heritage building. The High Court building was once such example, with a large predominantly glass porch appended to its entrance in 1991. Similarly, Holy Trinity Cathedral in Parnell Road, which was constructed between 1958 and 1973, had a wide-span zigzagging nave added to it between 1990 and 1995.[1389] Ultimately, though, such architectural hybrids were bound to remain the exception at a time when population expansion and the demands of a modern city meant that new buildings were the order of the day.

Not all the large-scale buildings constructed in Auckland in this decade were a continuation of the steel-and-glass office blocks that had been appearing since the 1980s. The completion of the Aotea Centre, which opened in 1990, provided Auckland with a 2100-seat theatre (600 more than the capacity of the Town Hall). However, it had been designed in 1974, and so already had a dated appearance by the time it was completed. It was the creation of council architect Ewen Wainscott (also the designer of the Auckland Central Library), who had to grapple with local body bureaucracy, a timeframe that was too short, and the shifting sands of public taste when developing his plans. The result was an edifice that looked out of place in its surrounds, and that suffered from a number of small but irritating design flaws.[1390] The following year, Starship Children's Hospital was completed. The architects were given a brief that required them to design a building that had 'character and personality' and that would appeal to children. The use of a variety of pastel colours, along with a 33-metre-high atrium that flooded the interior with natural light, were some of the ways this brief was fulfilled.[1391] It was also notable for having the first dedicated space of any hospital in the city for whānau to stay when visiting relatives.

Another one of those steps towards acquiring the accoutrements of other modern cities took place in February 1996 with the opening of the city's first casino. Initially, backers of the project considered using the Auckland Railway Station or the Central Post Office, both of which were unoccupied at the time, to house their venture, but eventually a site was acquired 300 metres east of Queen Street, flanked by Federal and Hobson streets, on which the SkyCity Casino was constructed. A year later it was the act of architectural bombast appended to the casino that attracted more attention of Aucklanders. The Sky Tower, which opened in August 1997, was by far the tallest structure in the country. At 328 metres high, it dominated the skyline, and in the central city was one of the few buildings that poked above the brown haze that usually occurred on cold, still, weekday mornings during the peak commuting time[1392] (another trait of most modern cities). It was built using the 'jumpform' method, whereby concrete was pumped into a mould, and once the concrete had set, the mould would be raised to the next stage and the process would repeat. Some 15,000 cubic metres of concrete, 2000 tonnes of reinforcing steel and 660 tonnes of structural steel went into the construction, with a design that included observation decks and a revolving restaurant.[1393]

The Sky Tower became the one structure that was visible in more parts of Auckland than any other. Yet there was nothing especially bold in its design. Its principal boast was its height, with its intrinsic value being measured by the number of metres it extended from the ground. In the calculus of status-by-height, it was taller than the Eiffel Tower (by four metres) and shorter than the Empire State Building (by 115 metres) — respectable but not spectacular. However, the drama of this spire was not so much when looked up at, but rather, when looked down from. Gazing out over Auckland from the observation decks, visitors could get a view of the city that was otherwise reserved for those in aircraft. An added feature on one of the viewing areas was a path with a transparent floor. Here, there was the sensation of stepping above a great void, with just a block of glass separating the visitor from the street 186 metres below. The experience was sublime, and operated on Edmund Burke's theory that '[w]hen danger or pain press too nearly, they are incapable of giving any delight, and [yet] with certain modifications, they may be, and they are delightful'.[1394] The Sky Tower helped add new scenes of Auckland to the popular perception of the city. Like the vistas from the top of Mt Eden or One Tree Hill, this was an omniscient view of Auckland that revealed the vast mosaic of its urban and rural terrain in its horizon-reaching scale.

'Just another day'

Modern cities function like a form of civic ecosystem. Each interrelated part pursues its own ends, and cumulatively this gives the city its character and form. Ironically, it is the complex diversity within cities that ends up reinforcing their solidarity and enabling their adaptability.[1395] Socially and culturally, most modern cities are more diverse now than at any other time in their histories. And economically, the sophistication in the division of labour is more intricate than ever. Yet, like any other ecosystem, there are periods when adjustments to changes in the environment are necessary — times when there are leads and lags, and bottlenecks. A subdivision on the city's periphery, for example, will create a new supply of housing, but there may not yet be sufficient shops in the vicinity, or adequate transport links yet to meet the requirements of those moving into the area. This was the experience of Auckland at many times in the twentieth century. The best intentions of planners and bureaucrats might manage to smooth some of the rougher edges of the process, but the ecosystem is beyond the reach of anyone to control it entirely. Normally, any irregularities eventually get resolved, and a new equilibrium is established — today's uncertainties become tomorrow's sureties. Very occasionally, though, the laissez-faire nature of this civic ecosystem breaks down, exposing its imperfection, and serving as a cautionary reminder that intervention is sometimes necessary to keep everything functioning. And while it might eventually be self-repairing, in the short term the ruptures can be damaging. In early 1998, Auckland experienced one such failure, which had serious consequences for the city.

In this case, the service in question was the central city's electricity supply, which had fallen victim to a tangled process of restructuring during this decade. In 1994 the Auckland Energy Consumer Trust (which had been formed the previous year) brought Mercury Energy Limited (formerly the Auckland Electric Power Board) into being — a company charged with owning and running Auckland's electricity supply.[1396] At this time, around 5000 people lived in the city centre, and more than 70,000 worked or studied there.[1397] Because of this high concentration of people and businesses in one location, the demands on electricity supply were unique in the city. And to make matters worse, those demands were soaring as air-conditioning units throughout Auckland were being relied on more heavily than usual as a result of a heatwave that was languishing over the city. Electricity to central Auckland was supplied by four 110-kilovolt cables from the Penrose Substation. Two of these cables supplied a substation at Liverpool Street, and the other two a substation at Quay Street. The latter pair of cables, dating back to the 1940s, were gas-insulated, and well past their expected life. The other pair dated from the 1970s, and were oil-filled. Increasing heat and hot dry conditions caused movement in the ground, which in turn led to the cables being damaged. The subterranean crisis began on 20 January, when one of the Quay Street cables failed. Although concerning, it was not regarded as warranting undue alarm, as the three remaining cables could manage the load in the meantime until the faulty cable was repaired. But then the second cable at Quay Street failed less than three weeks later. The situation was more worrying now, but hopefully still manageable as far as officials were concerned. However, in a 24-hour period from 19 February, both of the Liverpool Street cables failed.[1398] Above ground, the first Aucklanders knew that something was seriously wrong when Mercury Energy issued a public statement on 19 February, urging those in the city centre to conserve power. This was a forlorn plea, and the next day, at half past five in the afternoon, Mercury Energy made a further announcement, which despite its low-voltage prose was enough to shock residents:

The situation has deteriorated to the point that now the company believes it can no longer supply the central business district with electricity. This raises a civil defence and public safety issue which may lead to a declaration of a civil defence emergency. Mercury Energy is notifying all essential service providers; and asking them to come immediately to an emergency meeting at Mercury Energy headquarters. After the conference, civil defence will decide whether a civil emergency is declared.[1399]

Apart from a few streetlights, the central city was suddenly without electricity. Lifts, alarms and even doors were no longer functioning in many buildings, and in some cases sewage and water that relied on electric pumps were not flowing as intended. Food began to spoil in restaurants as refrigeration units failed,[1400] and Queen Street was almost completely deserted. Gradually, the silence of the abandoned city streets was replaced by the hum of diesel generators brought in to provide emergency electricity to some businesses. This was far from sufficient, but was better than nothing. The situation was occasionally lightened by humour, with one joke drawing out a sardonic grin among some of those affected: '[W]hat did Aucklanders use before candles? Electricity.'[1401] But dark humour did not alleviate the crisis, and the uncertainty over when power would be restored exacerbated the anger and anxiety over Mercury Energy's failure.

The most serious phase of the outage lasted until 27 March. However, it would be several months before the city's electricity supply was reasonably secure, and two years before a new tunnel for the replacement cables was completed.[1402] A Ministerial Inquiry followed, with the finger of blame pointed at the various entities responsible for Auckland's electricity supply for failing to maintain the power-supply infrastructure, and for not having appropriate contingency plans in place, as well as lacking the required expertise to operate the cables.[1403] The suffering caused to businesses and individuals by this prolonged electricity outage varied in severity, but the most serious victim was the Mercury Energy Chief Executive Wayne Gilbert, who died at his desk of a heart attack on the eve of the report of the Ministerial Inquiry being released.

The vulnerability of some of the city's ageing electricity infrastructure was exposed at a time when the city was on the cusp of a revolution in electronic technology. From the middle of the decade, cellular phones were able to transmit SMS (short message service, or text) messages, which increased further the popularity of these devices (although text messages cost around 26 cents each to send depending on the plan users subscribed to). Calls from a mobile to a fixed network in 1999 averaged 70 cents a minute,[1404] but despite such costs, businesses immediately saw the advantages that cell phones brought, and by the end of the decade business users were spending an average of $2070 per phone in user charges annually.[1405] To put these costs into some sort of context, in 1999 the per capita gross domestic product for New Zealand was $22,000 (by 2021, it was around three times this amount). Yet, despite the expense of operating a cell phone, they went from being a convenience to a necessity to many people over this decade. In 1990 there were approximately 18,000 cell-phone users in Auckland. By 1999 this figure had risen to 263,000.[1406] However, surprisingly for such a mass-market product, in the early 1990s purchasing a cell phone in a shop was not possible. There were agents from whom customers would buy these devices. 'It was a different retail environment,' an Auckland cell-phone seller from this time explained:

> *I suppose an analogy would be like buying a car. Those phones cost thousands, and you would go to a dealer just like you would go to a car dealer to get a car. And there was also that mentality of control. Because it was quite a new technology, the government still wanted to control the market.*[1407]

Having purchased the phone, the customer would then sign up to one of the service providers. Companies such as Telecom, Motorola, Ericsson, Cellnet and BellSouth began to occupy billboard space around Auckland in the voracious competition for clients, while a league of salespeople circulated through the city, inseminating the community with a new means of contacting each other.

Auckland was also on the cusp of an even more profound technological change at this time. In larger organisations, as well as a few households to start off with, banks of computers were beginning to connect their users through the internet. It was still very much at its nascent phase, with just 12 per cent of New Zealanders connected to a network by the close of the 1990s, and with roughly a quarter of those using it solely for email.[1408] As one leader of an Auckland organisation during this decade recalled, 'we had Pegasus email. I think we got it around 1994. I remember some staff saying they preferred the old memos that you typed and printed, and then sent in internal mail. But email took off pretty quickly.'[1409] In 1999 the Bank of New Zealand began to provide some banking services online, which was made possible by Telecom introducing the first broadband connections. For nearly all domestic users of the internet, though, connections were still made at this time by a dial-up modem, which relied on a telephone link to an internet service provider. By later standards, the quantity of data that could be transferred this way was small, and the rate at which it flowed was extremely slow. And there was also less reliability in the process, due to the dependence on phone lines, which some found exasperating:

> *I used the internet mainly at night when nobody would call, because if you were downloading something and someone called, the download would be interrupted and you'd have to start all over again. It's probably more frustrating looking at it now, because we're all used to broadband, but it was still frustrating at the time when you had your connection interrupted.*[1410]

In this era of dial-up data, before Instagram, before YouTube, and even before Facebook, the possibilities of the internet were yet to be imagined, let alone understood. Throughout the 1990s, there was a growing yet still hazy inkling about its use as a source of information, and possibly as a means to bring people together, but it was regarded more as something that might complement everyday life, rather than being an undetachable part of it, which was the destiny that it achieved in the following decade.

Lights out

Towards the end of the 1990s, the word 'millennium' was added to the popular lexicon, appearing more frequently in anticipation of the advent of 2000. Not wishing to seem out of step with the zeitgeist, businesses, universities and other organisations latched on to the millennium name, hoping to acquire some of its futuristic lustre by appending it to buildings, products, services, fundraising exercises and academic projects of varying significance. There was even legislation passed defining what constituted a 'millennium event'.[1411] And then, in the final months of the century, technology — which so many had put their faith in as society's redeemer — looked as though it was about to consume its disciples. The numeronym 'Y2K' — an abbreviation of Year 2000 — became a catch-all term for a feared collapse in the world's computer systems that might occur at the stroke of midnight on 31 December 1999. For decades, programmers grappling with small memory space on computers had resorted to shortening year formats from four to two digits. Thus, 1999 would appear as 99 in a computer program. The problem was that 2000 would appear as 00, which could be interpreted as any other date ending with two zeros. How would computers respond to this? The answer at the close of this decade was that nobody knew for certain in all instances. Computers might jump to another time, reset or close down completely. The public reaction to this 'software time bomb',[1412] and the looming possibility that society's infrastructure might collapse, was one of slightly heightened anxiety.[1413] One Aucklander's recollection of this time encapsulated the response of many in the city to the impending mass failure of computers and the associated infrastructure:

> Obviously, no one was going to be flying at that time [midnight on 31 December 1999]. We stayed at home and just kept an eye on things. We had enough tinned food, but we actually thought that things would probably work out okay, which they did. We were probably more curious about what would happen. We definitely weren't worried.[1414]

Some of the apprehension about the Y2K bug was unfounded, even at the time. The MP for Pakuranga, Maurice Williamson, later explained how far popular panic sometimes raced ahead of the evidence:

There were people saying the electrical grid will no longer work, and we'll have no electricity, the aviation system will come undone, because the control towers won't work .... I read stories where there'd be planes just falling out of the sky left[,] right and centre, and of course every briefing we got back said no, that's not the case. We were told some of the cars wouldn't work because they had date depend[e]nt chips. There were things like the traffic lights weren't going to work. I remember someone advocating that at midnight all the traffic lights would all go to red.[1415]

Gavin Ellis, the editor of the Auckland-based *New Zealand Herald*, was one of those who was jittery about the effects of Y2K:

We were the first paper in the world to go through the vortex. I was sweating blood up until the clock ticked over because none of us really knew for sure. We had spent a lot of money and a lot of time ... to upgrade the systems but there was still no absolute guarantee that the power supply, for example, would still be there.[1416]

In the end, there were no failures, and Ellis noted that '[i]t was an extraordinary anti-climax. It was just another day.'[1417]

But in the lead-up to Y2K, modest efforts were made to prepare for the worst. On 23 August 1999, Auckland City Council issued a statement advising residents to 'begin putting together their B Ready Kits', which would help Aucklanders survive a three-day shutdown of the entire city any time in the three months from 31 December. 'All it takes is a little bit of planning, a little bit of thought' was the Council's encouraging advice.[1418] By December 1999, plans were well under way for the end-of-the-year celebrations. The symbolism of entering a new millennium — as meaningless as that was in any practical sense — gave many people an overwrought sense of history to this particular New Year's Eve. The government was quick to wade into this opportunity, allocating Auckland $800,000 for millennium celebrations. The bulk of this money went to fund the ominously titled 'This Is It' celebrations — a 'multi media extravaganza' to be staged in the Domain on New Year's Eve. The Minister of Internal Affairs was exuberant about the show.

> *This is possibly the largest free event ever staged in this country and will have an enormous cast with professional performers featuring alongside cultural and community groups. About 300,000 people are expected to attend and thousands more will be able to see it on television because it is a major focus of TV3's Millennium broadcast.*[1419]

An extra $100,000 was devoted to the event's culmination: 'a cacophony of fireworks, which will then spread out into the harbour and ultimately include the Sky Tower, Harbour Bridge and barges around Rangitoto'.[1420] Like most state-planned pageants, "This Is It" was a triumph of generously budgeted bombast, but who cared when there was a combustible climax of fireworks to be captivated by? For some, however, all the warnings and predictions of impending chaos that had been grinding away for months continued to play on their thoughts. And as the final countdown to the New Year proceeded, watched by hundreds of thousands of Aucklanders on televisions, and shouted out hoarsely by the mass crowds that had gathered in the Domain, and in and around Queen Street in the rain, the point of reckoning finally arrived. Throughout the city, in houses, driveways, garages, parks and streets, the guttural crescendo of the twentieth century's final moments were given unfettered voice: Five! Four! Three! Two! One! ....

Epilogue

A few people closed their eyes. Some watched their television screens attentively. Others squinted skyward. But as the opening seconds of 2000 continued to pulse, the feared catastrophe never eventuated. The minutes clicked on, and as the Sky Tower's peak erupted in euphoric bursts of fireworks, the anxieties soon subsided. By sunrise, the prophetic warnings of a Y2K-instigated doom were quickly receding in people's minds. The mood of bleary-eyed Aucklanders — many of whom had secured positions on beaches or hills to get that much-vaunted glimpse of the 'first day of the new millennium' — was more one of celebration or reflection than of any apprehension, and the hot excitement of the previous night's festivities had simmered down to a more tepid dawn. The century that Aucklanders had lived their lives in was now gone, and they were stepping into a new era. Or so it felt at the time.

Certainly, imaginations remained lit up with hope for Auckland in the 2000s. Its past would now be refashioned as its prologue. A rash of more 'millennium' projects were under way (showing that the currency of the term was still holding its value), the city's barely bridled growth persisted as it had since its inception, more apartment buildings began to clutter central Auckland's skyline, and Auckland continued to bulge outwards as part of its imperishable psyche of suburban enlargement.

AUCKLAND: THE TWENTIETH-CENTURY STORY

Greater Auckland's entire population at the start of the twentieth century had staggeringly increased 35-fold by the century's end. By comparison, London's population over the same period rose by one and a half times, Sydney's grew by eight times, and Wellington's expanded seven-fold. In one way, though, this ferocious growth was a case of catch-up. With a population of around 34,000 in 1900, Auckland's claim to being a city at that time was still a tenuous one. However, by 1999 its demographic and geographical size had seen it slide comfortably into that homogeneous mould of 'modern' Western cities, with its malls, McDonald's, motorways, indistinct suburbs, traffic congestion, perpetually regenerating centres, growing ethnic diversity and a seemingly widening divide between the haves and the have-nots. It was not uncommon, at the end of the twentieth century, for people in the city to comment that Sydney was 'just a bigger Auckland', so similar had the latter grown into the image of the former.

However, for those disillusioned by the city's uncertain character — the inability to pin down precisely what made Auckland distinct from its overseas counterparts — the fact was that its identity was never a straightforward issue. Was the city merely a cluster of disparate suburbs, cultures and communities, corralled into a common civic geography, or was there the kernel of something that made the whole distinctly greater than the sum of its parts? At times, it seemed that the forces binding the city together were losing ground to those inducing its unravelling. Yet, throughout the twentieth century, Auckland's experiences suggest that while it was evolving inexorably to acquire many of the attributes of other cities, it was simultaneously clinging to elements that contributed to its singular character. No other city, after all, shared its iwi history, and by the 1990s, Ngāti Whātua, which had struggled for more than a century to maintain a toehold in the city, was re-establishing itself on a firmer footing. Few cities anywhere could boast that nearly a third of its citizens would assemble annually for a concert, as happened each Christmastime in the Domain. Of immeasurably more importance, despite Auckland's variegated ethnic and cultural composition, it avoided the plague of race riots that afflicted other cities in this century (the United States had 130 in the twentieth century, and Britain experienced over a dozen in the 1980s alone). For all the differences between the peoples that comprised Auckland, internecine violence of the sort that regularly flared up in other countries remained absent. On the whole, Aucklanders preferred to muddle along with each other rather than descend into feuding and fighting.

EPILOGUE

Then there is Auckland's very distinct physical form. This elongated metropolis, with bulbous northern and southern ends joined by a thin central isthmus, built in a field of around 50 volcanic peaks, is flanked by the split personality of its aquatic edges: the desolate, wind-blasted black-sand beaches of the west coast; and the calmer, yellow-sanded shores of the east. Auckland's terrain, and how humans have interacted with it, also inevitably became one of those defining features of the city. In 1959, as the Takapuna-based playwright Bruce Mason was putting the finishing touches to what would be his most famous and enduring work — *The End of the Golden Weather* — he managed to capture some of the interplay between Aucklanders and their surrounds in the nuanced way that would have been familiar to so many of the city's residents at that time, and for decades afterwards. The play was set in the 1930s, and so was already draped in nostalgia by the time it was first performed. However, there was enough of a sense of continuity with the present for it to resonate with Aucklanders in particular. Mason delivered a promised land for his audience where the promise had already been fulfilled:

> *On Sunday nights in the summer, we have tea on the glassed-in verandah facing Rangitoto. My mother prepares a mountain of sandwiches and out they come, mounds of them, on a jingling trolley. There we sit in the summer, while the day ends in gold explosions on the horizon and the lower borders of the sky are suddenly drenched in pink, as though a full brush had been slapped round the rim. Below us on the beach, people are strolling and the thin rarefied tinkle of their voices floats up to us as they approach ....*[1421]

This vignette of a house on an east coast Auckland beach was an archetype that to some degree had probably drifted away from the moorings of memory for those generations born in the twenty-first century. It was an irretrievable time that was a bit quieter, a bit less crowded, and a bit simpler than the incarnation of Auckland in the early decades of the 2000s. Yet, Auckland's landscape continues to insinuate itself into the minds of its residents, as does its history. As the sun set for that final time in 1999, the twentieth century was not simply discarded by Aucklanders. Those who looked back could still bask in the glow of the city's past, and draw on it whenever they turned to face that harsher light of the present.

Bibliography

Abbreviations

AJHR	Appendices to the Journals of the House of Representatives
AL	Auckland Libraries
ALHC	Auckland Libraries Heritage Collection
AM	Auckland Museum
AML	Auckland Museum Library
ANZ	Archives New Zealand
AS	Auckland Star
ATL	Alexander Turnbull Library
AWMM	Auckland War Memorial Museum
AWMML	Auckland War Memorial Museum Library
JNZS	Journal of New Zealand Studies
JPS	Journal of the Polynesian Society
MNZ	Museum of New Zealand
MOTAT	Museum of Transport and Technology
NLNZ	National Library of New Zealand
NZJH	New Zealand Journal of History
NZH	New Zealand Herald
NZPD	New Zealand Parliamentary Debates

Newspapers, magazines

Alexandra Herald and Central Otago Gazette
Ashburton Guardian
Auckland Star
Auckland Weekly News
Colonist
Daily Southern Cross
Eastern Courier
Evening Post
Evening Star
Franklin Times
Gisborne Herald
Grey River Argus
Greymouth Evening Star
Guardian
Hamilton Spectator
Hastings Standard
Hawera Star
Home and Building
Hot Lakes Chronicle
Kai Tiaki: The Journal of the Nurses of New Zealand
Kaipara and Waitemata Echo
Ladies' Mirror
Leisure Hour: An Illustrated Magazine for Home Reading
Listener
Lyttelton Times
Metro
National Business Review
Nelson Evening Mail
New York Times
New Zealand Advertiser and Bay of Islands Gazette
New Zealand Boating
New Zealand Herald
New Zealand Illustrated Magazine
New Zealand Police Gazette
New Zealand Railways Magazine
New Zealand Sportsman
New Zealand Tablet
New Zealand Times
New Zealand Truth
New Zealand Woman's Weekly
New Zealander
North & South
Northern Advocate
Oamaru Mail
Observer
Otago Daily Times
Patea Mail
Press
Progress
Pukekohe and Waiuku Times
Quick March
Rip It Up
Rodney and Otamatea Times, Waitemata and Kaipara Gazette
Salient
Speaker
Stratford Evening Post
Sun
Sunday Mail
Sunday News
Sunday Star-Times
Taranaki Herald
Te Ao Hou
Triad
United Press International
Waiapu Church Gazette
Wairarapa Age
Wanganui Herald
Western Leader
Western Star
White Ribbon

Legislation

Advances to Workers Act 1906
Auckland and Manukau Canal Act 1908
Auckland Centennial Memorial Park Act 1941
Chinese Immigrants Amendment Act 1907
Crimes Act 1908
Crimes Act 1961
Criminal Code 1893
Defence Amendment Act 1912
Electricity Advisory Council Act 1962
Finance Act (No. 2) 1949
Government Advances to Workers Act 1906
Homosexual Law Reform Act 1986
Housing Survey Act 1935
Immigration Restriction Amendment Act 1920
Indictable Offences Summary Jurisdiction Act 1894
Iron and Steel Industry Act 1959
Justices of the Peace Act 1908
Labour Relations Act 1987
Local Government (Millennium Events) Amendment Act 1999
Municipal Corporations Act 1900
Municipal Corporations Act 1954
Physical Welfare and Recreation Act 1937
Public Safety Conservation Act 1932
Rehabilitation Act 1941
Reserves and Other Lands Disposal Act 1963
Servicemen's Settlement and Land Sales Act 1943
Shop Trading Hours Act 1990
Shop Trading Hours Amendment Act 1980
Shops and Offices Amendment Act 1945
State Advances Amendment Act 1922
War Pensions Act 1943
Workers' Dwellings Act 1905

Maps, photographs, art, audiovisual, ephemera, unpublished material

A topographic map of the area in West Auckland, 1940, ALHC, Map 2258, Class. No. 995.

Advertisement and illustration of Maori carvings from Eric Craig Curiosity Dealer, Auckland. British Museum, ref. 2016,2124.5.

Advertisement for 246, 1967, in K. Dix, "24 Shopping Centre," New Zealand Fashion Museum (September 2017).

Advertisement for Hotel Titirangi, 1936, West Auckland Research Centre, Ref: JTD-10A-01675.

Albert Park, ATL, J. N. Taylor Collection, Ref: 1/2-152852.

Andrews, P., interview, 13 April 2004, ATL, ref. OHInt-0899-14.

Anonymous, "Plan of Auckland as it Stood in January, 1842 (traced from the original)," Sir George Grey Special Collections, AL, NZ Map 4601 (1842).

Architects Division, City Engineer's Department plans. Auckland Council Archives Reference: ACC 015-9631-2.

Auckland Art Gallery, Accession nos. 1952/16/1; 1929/4/2; 1911/1/2; MNZ, Registration no. 1973-0007-2.

Auckland City Council, "Listen to Ken! Y2K," media release (Auckland, 23 August 1999).

Auckland Co-ordinator of Petition to Oppose the Homosexual Law Reform Bill, submission to Select Committee, ANZ, ref. R314656.

uckland Industrial, Agricultural and Mining Exhibition (1913–14): Exhibition axemen's carnival. World's & New Zealand 1914 championships, NLNZ, Ref: Eph-A-EXHIBITION-1914-01-cover.

uckland Lyceum Club, Records, 1919–1992, AWMML, MS-1994-52.

uckland Museum, [Craig's Museum, Princes Street], Unknown photographer, ca. 1880, PH-RES-4181.

uckland's Civic Administration Building, 5 October 1970. Sir George Grey Special Collections, AL, Ref: 580-20350.

uckland's Last Tram, AM, ref. PH-CNEG-S1177.

arber, F., *The Christian Science Monitor* (5 December 1983), n.p.; E. Heath "David and Goliath cartoon," ATL, ref. B-144-034.

astion Point Eviction, 25 May 1978, Television New Zealand Archive, Ref: P182678.

ennett, Shani, "Fever of the Fleet," documentary, Auckland University of Technology, (2010).

ourke, C., Blog Post, 11 June 2015.

ritish Empire Games, Auckland, New Zealand, 1950: Closing ceremony [and] Vice-Patrons of the New Zealand Olympic and British Empire Games Association. Official programme. NLNZ, Ref: Eph-A-SPORT-1950-03-20/21.

ommonwealth Games, Mount Albert City Council subject files. Archives Reference: MAC 108 Record C-1-11.

ooper, W., "Māori Land March. Whina Cooper," Radio New Zealand, Sound Archives T7413.

e Tourret, E., photograph of Dominion Road, AL 255A-93; H. Winkelmann, photograph looking north over the harbour to Devonport, AL 995.1101 W33 (1900-09) [33].

iamond, J. T., View across plaza area at the newly opened shopping centre in New Lynn, photograph, AL, record I. D. JTD-11A-02070-2.

oreen McLeod, Items 21–22, AML, ref. Papers MS-99-69.

ast Coast Bays Methodist Parish, 29 September 1985, submission to Select Committee, ANZ, ref. R314656.

lder, J., in Department of Internal Affairs, "Auckland Millennium Celebrations Get Lottery Funding," (Wellington, 16 July 1999).

actory worker, Crown Lynn, Te Papa MNZ, 1964, ref. F.013469; Crown Lynn workers, AWMM, ref. 72204N.

airburn, W., "Journal," ALHC, MJ-0054.

itzpatrick, S., in Talksport Radio (19 November 2010).

lanagan, F. W., *Map of the North Island of New Zealand*, National Library, MapColl-NZGB-5/27/354/ Acc.55040 (Wellington: Lands and Survey Department, 1906).

G. Goodall. Colour postcard of the entrance of the new Mon Desir hotel, Takapuna, 1965. ALHC, ref. T0271.

oldie, C. F. news clippings, MNZ, MS 6.

oldie, C. F., "Studio Interior," Auckland Art Gallery, Accession no. 1990/15/1.

room, C. E. to Russell, G. W., Minister of Internal Affairs, 2 April 1919, AAAC 6015 W4686 13A Misc Affairs, Enemy POWS, ANZ.

ammond, R., "Orakei Garden Suburb General Plan," ATL, ref. MapColl 832.1291gmbd/Re/1925/Acc. 47624.

anly, G., "Crowd below rear of Museum awaiting Pope John Paul II, Auckland Domain," AM, ref. PH-2015-2-GH1596-33.

ay, D., in Auckland Library, "The Hero Parade's Seven Fabulous Outings," (19 February 2019).

enning's Speedway, ALHC, MJ-2436.

eritage New Zealand, "Customhouse (former), Summary," List No. 104.

iggins, N., "Black Monday," Radio New Zealand broadcast, 3:30 pm (7 September 2017).

olland, S., 21 February 1951, in Radio New Zealand Sound Archives Ngā Taonga Kōrero, "Dispute: An Account of the 1951 Waterfront Conflict," 1968, ref no T81.

omestead Chicken, 1973, Dominion Post Collection, ATL (PAColl-7327), Ref: EP/1973/3746/26a.

ouse, yard and Maori children, Nelson Street, Auckland, photographed by H L McNaughton, late 1930s. ATL, ref. PA1-o-914-07-5.

Invitation to the official opening of the Manukau City Centre mall, outer and inner fold. (Ephemera, Commerce, 20/10/76) ALHC, MJ_4935.

Isola Productions, *Dawn Raids*, documentary, Jean, R., producer, Fepuila'e, D., director (Auckland, 2005).

Jackson, H., "Foodlovers," (Auckland, October 2007).

Johnson, J., "The British flag first hoisted on the shore of the Waitemata, September 18th, 1840," Watercolour, Hocken Pictorial Collections, Otago University Research Heritage (1840).

Johnstone, I., "Johnstone's Journey — Settling for Suburbia," (New Zealand National Film Unit, 1978).

Jones, N., addressing a public meeting in 1985, in LAGANZ 0080-B, Peter Nowland Collection.

Journey NZ, "Coca-Cola Christmas in the Park: 25 years of Memories, History and Fun," (Auckland, 31 August 2018).

Keir, J., dir., *Close Up*, "Big Dealers," TVNZ (1987).

Kennedy, D., "Gourmet Restaurant (Auckland): The Gourmet. A la carte menu. Operated by Otto Groen (Amsterdam) and Jim Jennings (New York City) [ca 1960–1961?]," photo, NLNZ, Ref: Eph-C-DINING-1960-02.

Lamb's old mill, Riverhead, about to be converted into a paper mill, ALHC, AWNS-18990728-7-2.

Land March Itinerary, ANZ, ref: AAMK 869 W3074 Box 684/d 19/1/774 Part 1.

LaRoche, A., "From Mt Wellington, 1950," Howick Historical Village, object no. 2017.296.02; Whites Aviation, Mt Wellington and Panmure, Aerial photograph, NLNZ, Ref: WA-45435.

Libreria Editrice Vaticana, "Homily of John Paul II, Auckland (New Zealand), 22 November 1986," (Vatican: 1986).

Livesey, J. v The Dominion, New Zealand Media Council, CN 613 (May 1996), n.p.

Main Hall of Auckland Museum at Princes Street, showing the small pataka, Te Oha, installed about 1885, AML, C4238.

Manukau City Centre shopping mall, Auckland, 20 Oct 1976, NLNZ, Ref: WA-73691-G.

Manukau Sports Bowl, Track marking layout. Archives Reference: MCC Barcode C9424.

Maori Schools — Policy — Closure of native schools owing to influenza epidemic, ANZ, ref. R20390829.

Map of Auckland City to the Waitakere Ranges, and then as far north as the Puhoi River, showing the extent of Auckland City and the surrounding area, and with considerable landscape detail, Sheet South J-60/A-IV, Map 8893 (Wellington: Lands and Survey Dept., 1920).

Map of state and main highways showing load classification under the Heavy Motor Vehicles Regulations 1950, as at 1/4/1959, Auckland, New Zealand. Department of Lands and Survey, NLNZ, NZMS 19A; sheet 2.

Mathew, F., *Original Plan of Auckland, 1841*, Sir George Grey Special Collections, AL, NZ Map 2664.

McGehan, F., Photo of Savage Memorial, Bastion Point, AL, Record ID 255A-35037.

Medical Superintendent, Kingseat Hospital, to the Director-General, MHD, August 8, 1947, ANZ, R20960887.

Michael Joseph Savage. Original photograph, ATL, Box 1, Ref: PAColl-5471-055.

Mumme, M., "Memories of the Motuihe Health Camp," (n.d.).

Newmarket Borough Council photographs. Auckland Council Archives Reference: NMB 020 Item 50.

Oblique aerial photograph of Mt Eden Borough, Whites Aviation photograph. Auckland Council Archives Reference: MEB 029 1j.

Old Time Transport Preservation League, Minutes, correspondence, accounts etc., AML, ref. 88/28, MS-1651.

Opening of the Centennial Street (Auckland 1866) exhibition at the Auckland War Memorial Museum, AM, ref. PH-RES-1699.

Oppose Nuclear Visits, poster, 1983, AML, ref. EPH-2008-1-14.

Overall layout, XIV Commonwealth Games Village Development Company Ltd, 9 December 1988. Plans drawn by KRTA Ltd. Archives Reference: ACC 493 Item 44b.

Ozich, D., "History of the Croatian Cultural Society," (Auckland: Croatian Cultural Society, 2012).

Pan American World Airways DC-4 Clipper "Kathay" at Whenuapai, Museum of Transport and Technology, Accession No. 16-0776.

Papatoetoe A. F. C. Results, 10 & 11 May 1980, unpublished document.

Petersen, O., "Original P. C. L. Massey building fire," AM, ref. H-1988-9-F1-2.

Photograph of Cabbage tree Swamp, Sir George Grey Special Collections, AL, Ref: 4-854.

Presbyterian Church Archives Research Centre, ref. P-A427-1-3.

Programmes for the annual Auckland Regatta, 1970, 1971, 1973, NLNZ, Ref: Eph-A-BOAT-AR-1970/1973.

Quinn, K., interview about 1987 Rugby World Cup, Television New Zealand (11 September 2007).

Radio New Zealand interview, Rainbow Warrior sinking, Radio New Zealand Sound Archives Ngā Taonga Kōrero, ref no COMP 3, 1985, tk6.

Radio New Zealand broadcast, "The night the lights went out in Auckland," 3:30 pm (22 March 2018).

Records of the Young Women's Christian Association (Auckland, N.Z.) (1885–1985), AWMML, ref. MS1131.

Redwood 70 Festival Poster (Auckland, 1970).

Richter, A., "Centrepoint: Neither Free nor Loving," Radio New Zealand broadcast, 7:45 pm (31 May 2021).

Riethmaier, G., photograph of Queen Street, ANZ, Ref. AAQT 6539 W3537 141/B4813.

Riethmaier, Gregory, "Takapuna Beer Garden," ANZ, ref. AAQT 6539, A84942.

Ringer, B., "A History of Manukau City Centre," AL, Ref: LHE-004.

Rowlandson, T. and Pugin, A. C., "Exhibition Room, Somerset House," Royal Academy of Arts, Object no. 03/6170.

Safari Land to move from Massey site to join Footrot Flats Fun Park, in Te Atatu North, AL, Ref: NZCI000128157.

Sheppard, K., 'President's address to the National Council of Women," 1919, NCW Session, ATL, MS-Papers-1371, folder 107.

Showing the main exhibition buildings of the 1914 Auckland Exhibition in the Auckland Domain, ALHC, 4-154.

Sinclair, P., in "Redwood 70," (New Zealand Broadcasting Corporation, 1970).

Smith, M., in "The chainsaw used on One Tree Hill and heard across Aotearoa," in *The Spinoff, The Single Object*, video (13 April 2021).

Statement by Leisureland staff member, June 2019.

Statue Hall of Auckland Museum at Princes Street, AML, C56638.

Stevens, G. (director), *Te Matakite o Aotearoa — The Maori Land March*, television documentary (Auckland: Television Two, 1975).

Stop the Killer Disease Aids, ANZ, ref. R314656.

Television New Zealand commentary (12 September 1981).

The Mon Desir Hotel, Takapuna, postcard, Sir George Grey Special Collections, AL, NZG-19100112-76-1.

"The Wings over New Zealand Aviation Forum," (8 November 2006).

Thorn, C., "Social Services Sunday," St Matthew-in-the-City (5 August 2018).

University of Bradford, "The J. B. Priestley Archive: Interim Catalogue," Archive reference code: (GB 0532) PRI, Special Collections, J. B. Priestley Library (Bradford: University of Bradford, April 2013).

View of the Palace of Industries and towers, Auckland Exhibition, taken at night to show the illuminations, NLNZ, Ref: 1/2-001288-G.

View of Wonderland, Auckland Exhibition, Auckland Domain, looking towards the water chute, NLNZ, Ref: 1/2-001132-G.

Vowles, J., "Social Structure. Political Attitudes and Trade Unionism: An Analysis of Aspects of the Fourth Labour Government's Election Coalition," New Zealand Political Science Association Conference Paper (Auckland: University of Auckland, 1985).

Waiheke County Council, submission to Select Committee, ANZ, ref. R314656.

Wall, M., "National Party election advertisement," (Wellington November 1975).

Ward, P., "Gloss: A Perspective," *NZ On Screen* (22 September 2008).

Welcome to Leisure Land. Theme Park. Te Atatu, Auckland. n.d., AM, ref. GV155 Box 2.

Wells, R. E., "A group of marching girls performing in front of crowd in Dargaville, 1946," ATL, ref. 1/4-091100-F.

West Auckland Swimming and Recreation Centre brochure.

White, A. L., "Jubilation," 1948, Auckland Art Gallery, Accession no. 1990/29.

Williamson, M., in Radio New Zealand broadcast, "Are You Y2 OK?," 7:00 am (13 December 2018).

XIVth Commonwealth Games 1990 — Headquarters Operation Manual (Auckland, 1989), Annex K.

Reports, papers and conference proceedings

Annual Report of Director-General of Health, in *AJHR*, Session I, H-31 (1930); Session I–II, H-31 (1931).

Annual Report of the Department of Internal Affairs, in *AJHR*, Session I–II, H-22 (1923); Session I, H-22 (1940).

Annual Report of the Director-General of Health, Department of Health, in *AJHR*, Session I, H-31 (1930).

Annual Report on Department of Lands and Surveys, in *AJHR*, Session I, C-01a (1926); Session I, C-01 (1930).

Annual Report on the Police Force of the Colony, 20 June 1905, in *AJHR*, Session I, H-16 (Wellington: House of Representatives, 1905).

Annual Report on the Police Force of the Dominion, in *AJHR*, Session I, H-16 (Wellington: House of Representatives, 1914).

Auckland Council, *Albert-Eden Heritage Survey: Historical Context Survey* (Auckland: Auckland Council, 2013).

Auckland Council, "Fact Sheet: Civic Administration Building, (Auckland, 2017).

Auckland Council, *Swanson Heritage Survey — Historical Context* (Auckland: Auckland Council, 2016).

Auckland Hebrew Congregation, "Submission on the proposed amendments to the Auckland Unitary Plan, (Operative in Part) Historic Heritage Overlay Schedule 14.1 as they relate to 108–11 Greys Avenue, Auckland (ID01965)," Appendix 2 (Auckland, 7 March 2018).

Auckland Regional Council, *A Brief History of Auckland's Urban Form* (Auckland: Auckland Regional Council, 2010).

Auckland Regional Planning Authority, "Master Transportation Plan for Metropolitan Auckland," (Auckland: Auckland Regional Planning Authority, 1955).

Auckland Tourism, Events and Economic Development, *Auckland Growth Monitor* (Auckland: ATEED, 2017).

Balance-Sheets and Statements of Accounts of Various Government Departments, in *AJHR*, Session I, B-07 (1929).

Baldwin, T., "History of electricity security in New Zealand," (May 2005).

Best, S. and Furey, L., "Westney Road Denominational Graveyard. Report to the New Zealand Historic Places Trust," (Auckland: GFC Heritage Ltd, 2007).

Bishop, C. D., Landers, T. J. and Goldwater, N. P., "Changes in Indigenous Ecosystems and the Environment within the Boundary of the Waitakere Ranges Heritage Area Act 2008: 2008–2013 Report," (Auckland: Auckland Council, 2013).

Boon, J., "Urban Regeneration in Moderate Size Cities — The Case for Minimal Government Intervention," Asian Planning Schools Association Congress (Bandung, 1997).

Business History Project, University of Auckland, "Fisher and Paykel," (Auckland: University of Auckland 2021).

Child Welfare, State Care of Children, Special Schools and Infant-Life Protection, in *AJHR*, Session I, E-04 (1945).

Clark, S. and Cameron, S., *Oxidation Pond Guidelines 2005* (Wellington: Ministry for the Environment, 2005).

Clough, R., Macready S. and Plowman, M., *R. O. Clark's Pottery (1864–1931), Limeburners Bay, Hobsonville: Archaeological Investigation Report on S18 investigation of site* (Auckland: Clough & Associates Ltd, 2008).

Dave Pearson Architects Limited, *Grey's Avenue Flats Auckland: Conservation Plan* (Auckland, 2006, n.p.).

De Sylva, S., Vale, B. and Holden, G., "The Rise and Fall of the Bungalow," *Proceedings of the 35th Annual Conference of the Society of Architectural Historians of Australia and New Zealand* (Wellington, 2018).

Donovan, E., "State Housing Revival: Sustainable Regeneration Strategies for Post-war Suburban State Housing in New Zealand," *Housing and Welfare Conference: Boundaries, Encounters, Connections. Workshop 1: Polarization, Inequality and Affordable Housing* (Copenhagen, 2014).

Eaves, M. et al., *Onehunga Heritage Survey* (Auckland: Auckland Council, 2013).

Emergency Reserve Corps Regulations 1940, in *New Zealand Police Gazette* LXV, no. 35 (28 August 1940).

Felgate, M., *His Majesty's Theatre Excavations (R11/1624): Final Archaeological Report, Volume 1* (Auckland: Auckland City Council, 1998).

Financial Statement, in *AJHR*, Session I, B-06 (1935); Session I, B-06 (1939).

Foster, R., "NZHPT Authority 2009/171. Michael Joseph Savage Memorial Garden, Bastion Point, Auckland Monitoring Report," (Auckland: Russell Foster and Associates, 2009).

Francis, K., "Learning about Landscape: Odo Strewe and the Group," (Auckland: Unitec, 2010).

Ge, J. and Lai, F. P., "A study into the demand for apartments in central Auckland," *Asian Real Estate Society Annual Meeting and International Conference* (Shanghai: Shanghai University of Finance and Economics, 2008).

Gibson, K., Morgan, M., Woolley, C. and Powis, T., "A different kind of family: Retrospective accounts of growing up at Centrepoint and implications for adulthood," (Palmerston North: Massey University, 2010).

Gilbertson, A. and Meares, C., *Ethnicity and Migration in Auckland. Auckland Council Technical Report, TR2013/012* (Auckland: Auckland Council, 2013).

Greater London Authority, *Population Growth in London, 1939–2015* (London: Greater London Authority, 2015).

Gutman, P., "Auckland's Power Outage, or, Auckland — Your Y2K Beta Test Site," (Auckland, 24 May 1998).

Hart, P., "Alfred Henry Whitehouse; a bootmaker who became a pioneer of New Zealand films," *Te Aroha Mining District Working Papers* 160 (Hamilton: Historical Research Unit, Waikato University, 2016).

Heritage "Consultancy Services, North Shore Heritage — Thematic Review Report," Auckland Council Document TR 2011/010 (Auckland: Auckland Council, 2011).

Hoffman, L., *A Brief History of Auckland's Urban Form* (Auckland: Auckland Council Research and Evaluation Unit, 2019).

Interim Return of Sheep in the colony on the 30th April 1902, in *AJHR*, Session I, H-23a (Wellington: House of Representatives, 1902).

Kawharu, M., *Tamaki Foreshore and Harbour Report: A report prepared for the Orakei Maori Trust Board for the Wai 388 Treaty claim* (Auckland: 2004).

Lawlor, I., *An assessment of heritage resources located within the proposed Otuataua Stonefields Historic Reserve Visitor Centre development 'footprint', and measures to avoid, remedy and mitigate effects* (Auckland: 2009).

Liu, Y., "Visualizing the urban development of Sydney (1971–1996) in GIS," in *Proceedings of the 10th Annual Colloquium of the Spatial Information Research Centre. Dunedin: The University of Otago* (Dunedin, 1998).

Madanovic, M., "Concrete Complexities: Reinforced Concrete in the Architecture of Auckland's Town Hall, Chief Post Office and Ferry Building," *Historiographies of Technology and Architecture: Proceedings of the 35th Annual Conference of the Society of Architectural Historians of Australia and New Zealand*, J. Merwood-Salisbury, M. Dudding and C. McDonald, eds (Wellington: SAHANZ, 2018).

Maré, D. C., Coleman, A. and Pinkerton, R., *Patterns of population location in Auckland*, Motu Working Paper 11-06 (Wellington: Motu Economic and Public Policy Research, 2011).

Mason, J. M., "Report of the Chief Health Officer, Department of Public Health," *AJHR*, Session I, H-31 (Wellington: House of Representatives, 1903).

Matthews and Matthews Architects Ltd, *Mangere Town Centre: Historic Heritage Survey*, Appendix 1 (Auckland: Matthews and Matthews Architects Ltd, 2013).

Mazengarb, O. C. et al., *Report of the Special Committee on Moral Delinquency in Children and Adolescents* (Wellington: Government Printer, 1954).

McCreary, J. R., *Housing and Welfare Needs of Islanders in Auckland: A Report to the Minister of Island Territories* (Wellington: Victoria University, 1965).

McKerrow, J., "Workmen's Homes in the Vicinity of Auckland," *AJHR*, Session I, C-13 (Wellington: House of Representatives, 1900).

Mercury Energy Statement (20 February 1998), in J. Walker, "Auckland lights out from failure to recovery [power system disturbance]," in *21st International Telecommunications Energy Conference. INTELEC' 99*, Cat. No. 99CH37007 (Chester, 1999).

Ministry of Commerce, *Statistics on Information Technology in New Zealand* (Wellington: Ministry of Commerce, 2006).

Ministry of Works Statement, in *AJHR*, Session I, D-01 (1950).

Morrison, P. S., *On the Falling Rate of Home Ownership in New Zealand* (Wellington: Centre for Housing Research Aotearoa New Zealand, 2007).

Muhammad, I., Matthews, L. and Pearce, J., "Political path dependence in public transport in Auckland: an historical analysis," Australasian Urban History Planning History Group, Victoria University of Wellington, 12th Australasian Urban History Planning History Conference (2–5 February 2014, Wellington, New Zealand, 2014).

Murdoch, G., *A Brief History of Muriwai Regional Park and its Environs* (Auckland: Auckland Regional Council, 1994).

Murphy, N., *The Poll-Tax in New Zealand: A Research Paper* (Wellington: The New Zealand Chinese Association, 1994).

New Zealand Government, *Official Volume of the Proceedings of the Town Planning Conference held in Wellington* (Wellington: Government Printer, 1919).

New Zealand Police, "Historic NZ Murder Rate Report 1926–2017," (Wellington, 2017).

O'Connor, K. F. and Simmons, D. G., "The use of islands for recreation and tourism: Changing significance for nature conservation," in *Ecological Restoration of New Zealand Islands*, Towns, D. R., Daugherty, C. H. and Atkinson, I. A. E., eds, Conservation Sciences Publication No. 2 (Wellington: Department of Conservation, 1990).

OECD, *Communications Outlook 1999* (Paris, OECD, 1999).

OECD, *Mobile Phones: Pricing Structures and Trends* (Paris: OECD, 2000).

Paterson, M., "Statement of Evidence of Dr Malcolm Paterson," ENV-2018-AKL-000078 (Environment Court: Auckland, 2018).

Peterson, D., "Petrol Prices and Taxes," (Wellington: Parliamentary Library, 2001).

Polkinghorne, J., "New Zealand and the 1970s oil shocks — more than just 'carless days'," (Auckland, 2014).

Pool, I., Baxendine, S., Cochrane, W. and Lindop, J., "New Zealand Regions, 1986–2001: Population Geography," *Population Studies Centre Discussion Papers* 54 (Hamilton: University of Waikato, 2005).

Primary and Post-Primary Education, in *AJHR*, Session I, E-02 (1947).

Proposed Waitemata-Manukau canal: reports and plans re Whau and Tamaki routes, AM, TC722.6 PRO.

Public Works Statement, Department of Health, in *AJHR*, Session I, D-01 (1936).

Reeves, A. and McNeil, J., "The Design of the New Old Mangere Bridge," *Austroads Bridge Conference, 10th, 2017, Melbourne, Victoria, Australia* (2017).

Rennie, H., *Auckland power supply failure 1998: the report of the Ministerial Inquiry into the Auckland Power Supply Failure* (Wellington: Ministry of Commerce, 1998).

Report by the Chief Health Officer, Department of Health, in *AJHR*, Session I, H-31 (1902).

Report for the Social Security Department, in *AJHR*, Session I, H-09 (1941).

Report of the Auckland Drainage Commission, in *AJHR*, Session I, H-03 (1947).

Report of the Committee on Employment of Maoris in Market Gardens, in *AJHR*, Session I, G-11 (1929).

Report of the Department of Labour and Employment, in *AJHR*, Session I, H-11 (1949).

Report of the Department of Labour, in *AJHR*, Session I, H-11 (Wellington: House of Representatives, 1914).

Report of the Influenza Epidemic Commission, in *AJHR*, Session I, H-31A (1919).

Report of the Minister of Education, in *AJHR*, Session I, E-01 (1944).

Report on Mental Hospitals for the Dominion, in *AJHR*, Session I, H-07 (1928); Session I, H-07 (1937).

Report on Prisons for the year 1924–1925, in *AJHR*, Session I, H-20 (1925).

Report on the Air Department, in *AJHR*, Session I, H-37 (1950).

Royal Commission to Inquire into and Report Upon Transharbour Facilities in the Auckland Metropolitan Area and the Approaches Thereto, in *AJHR*, Session I, D-06 (1946).

Slocombe, A., *Shaw Block Site Survey. Site R11/1525* (Auckland: New Zealand Historic Places Trust, 1986).

Slocombe, A. and Veart, D., *Archaeological Investigation at the Shaw Block (R11/1525), East Tamaki* (Auckland: Department of Conservation, 1989).

State Forests Revenue and Expenditure for the Ten Years Ending 31 March 1903, in *AJHR*, Session I, C-12a (Wellington: House of Representatives, 1903).

Statement, in *AJHR*, Session I, D-02 (1946).

Statistics New Zealand, "Apartments Hit Record High," (Wellington: Statistics New Zealand, 31 August 1999).

Supplementary Estimates of the Expenditure of the Government of New Zealand, in *AJHR*, Session I, B-07, 2 (1943).

Te Roopu o te Matakite, "Why We March," (Auckland, 1975).

The Police Force of the Dominion, in *AJHR*, Session I, H-16 (1949); Session I, H-16 (1950).

Thomsen, S., Tavita, J. and Levi-Teu, Z., *A Pacific Perspective on the Living Standards Framework and Wellbeing*, New Zealand Treasury Discussion Paper (Wellington: New Zealand Treasury, 2018).

Tourist and Health Resorts Report (23 August 1904) by the Minister of Tourist and Health Resorts, Hon. Sir J. G. Ward, KCMG, in *AJHR*, Session I, H-02 (Wellington: House of Representatives, 1904).

Tregear, E., "Report of the Department of Labour," in *AJHR* Session II, H-11 (Wellington: House of Representatives, 1906).

Truttman, L., *Puketapapa — Mt Roskill Heritage Survey 2013* (Auckland: Matthews and Matthews Architects Ltd, 2014).

United Nations Department of Economic and Social Affairs, "2019 Revision of World Population Prospects," (United Nations, 2019).

Vowles, J., "Civic engagement in New Zealand: Decline or demise?," Inaugural Professorial Address (Auckland: University of Auckland, 2004).

Waitakere City Council, *New Lynn Reserves Management Plan 2004* (Auckland: Waitakere City Council, 2004).

Waitākere Ranges Local Board, *The State of the Waitākere Ranges Heritage Area, 2018* (Auckland: Auckland Council, 2018).

Waitangi Tribunal, *Report of The Waitangi Tribunal on The Orakei Claim, Wai-9* (Wellington: Department of Justice, 1987).

Waitangi Tribunal, *The Loss of the Orakei Block* (Wellington: Waitangi Tribunal, 2013).

Walker, D. and Manning, R., "Rationing and Deterrence: General Theory and the Example of New Zealand's 'Carless Days' Scheme," Centre for the Economic Analysis of Property Rights. Economics and Law Workshop Papers, 83-09. London, ON: Department of Economics, University of Western Ontario (1983).

Watercare, "The history of wastewater treatment in Auckland, 1878 to 2005," WWIS1-0918 (Auckland: Auckland City Council, 2010).

Williams, L. et al, *Otahuhu Historic Heritage Survey, Overview Report* (Auckland: Matthews and Matthews Architects Ltd, 2014).

Yoo, S., *Background to Case Study: Sylvia Park and the Mt Wellington Area*, Working Document GUS/SP2.2 (Auckland: University of Auckland, 2019).

Parliamentary Debates (Hansard)

Allen, P. B., in *NZPD* 294 (19 June 1964).

Clark, H., in *NZPD* 503 (5 December 1989).

Earl of Ranfurly, "Governor's Speech," in *NZPD* 116 (2 July 1901).

Goosman, W., in *NZPD* 294 (28 June 1951).

Massey, W., in *NZPD* 116 (5 July 1901).

Parry, W., in *NZPD* 207 (25 August 1925).

Reeves, W. P., in *NZPD* 127 (3 November 1903).

Shrimski, S., in *NZPD* 116 (4 July 1901).

Watt, H., *NZPD* 369 (9 October 1970).

Theses and dissertations

Alleyne, H., "Traversing Memory: the last days of the old Mangere bridge," MA&D thesis (Auckland: Auckland University of Technology, 2014).

Arbury, J. "From Urban Sprawl to Compact City — an analysis of urban growth management in Auckland," MA thesis (Auckland: University of Auckland, 2005).

Arps, J., "Rise, Ruin & Regeneration: An Examination of the Regeneration of Post-War Suburban State Housing in New Zealand," MArch thesis (Wellington: Victoria University, 2012).

Ball, G., "The amazing Jasper Calder, the Auckland City Mission and welfare provision, 1920–1946," MA thesis (Auckland: University of Auckland, 1997).

Bradstock, H., "'Let's Talk about Something Else': Religion and Governmentality in New Zealand's State Primary Schools," PhD thesis (Dunedin: University of Otago, 2016).

Brown, M. N. R., "Packing down the scrum: an historical analysis of the 1981 Springbok tour and the homosexuality issue in the Presbyterian Church of Aotearoa New Zealand," PhD thesis (Dunedin: University of Otago, 1995).

Brown Pulu, T., "Kakai Tonga 'i 'Okalani Nu'u Sila: Tongan Generations in Auckland New Zealand," PhD thesis (Hamilton: University of Waikato, 2007).

Collins, P. R., "The Jewish community in New Zealand: a contribution to the study of assimilation," MA thesis (Palmerston North: Massey University, 1971).

Derbyshire, N. W., "An anatomy of antipodean Anglicanism: the Anglican Church in New Zealand 1945 to 2012," PhD thesis (Auckland: Massey University, 2013).

Dorsey, M., "The Post-War Reconciliation Process of New Zealand Vietnam War Veterans," PhD thesis (Dunedin: University of Otago, 2014).

Hopner, V., "Home from War," PhD thesis (Auckland: Massey University, 2014).

Hucker, G., "'A Time of Sorrow and Misery': Representations of the 1918 Influenza Epidemic in a Rural District of New Zealand," Postgraduate DipArts research essay (Palmerston North: Massey University, 1999).

Ioka, D., "Origin and beginning of the Congregational Christian Church of Samoa (CCCS) in Aotearoa New Zealand," PhD thesis (Dunedin: University of Otago, 1998).

Johnson, L., "Maori activism across borders, 1950–1980s," PhD thesis (Palmerston North: Massey University, 2015).

Johnson, S., "The Home Front: Aspects of Civilian Patriotism in New Zealand During the First World War," MA thesis (Palmerston North: Massey University, 1975).

Katavich, S. M., "Responses in New Zealand to the Vietnam War: a case study of the Palmerston North community," MA thesis (Palmerston North: Massey University, 2020).

Kennedy, A., "Keep Sunday Free: Social Engineering Through Shop Trading Hours in New Zealand," PhD thesis (Auckland: Auckland University of Technology, 2009).

Krivan, M., "The Department of Maori Affairs housing programme, 1935–1967," MA thesis (Palmerston North: Massey University, 1990).

Laurenson, H. B., "Myths and the City: A Social and Cultural History of Auckland, 1890–1990," PhD thesis (Auckland: University of Auckland, 2010).

Lee, B., "Struggling to make the world a better place: Exploring some experiences of activists in the Auckland Progressive Youth Movement (1965–1977)," PhD thesis (Auckland: Auckland University of Technology, 2019).

Lynch, K., "Healthful Housing," MA thesis (Palmerston North: Massey University, 1999).

Lyon, D. K., "The Development and Performance of Airports in New Zealand as Commercial Entities," PhD thesis (Palmerston North: Massey University, 2011).

Mackintosh, L., "Shifting grounds: history, memory and materiality in Auckland landscapes c. 1350–2018," PhD thesis (Auckland: University of Auckland, 2019).

Marsden, L. E., "Hard times?: demographic change and the 1930s depression in New Zealand," MPhil thesis (Palmerston North: Massey University, 1991).

Mason, N. M., "Inspiring and creative public places: what are the crucial ingredients when developing a successful arts precinct? a Waitakere City, New Zealand case-study," PhD thesis (Palmerston North: Massey University, 2007).

Maung, M. T., "Beneficiation of ironsands from Raglan, New Zealand," PhD thesis (Dunedin: University of Otago, 1962).

McColley, S. L., "Historical GIS for Auckland suburbanisation: 1951–1981," MSc thesis (Auckland: University of Auckland, 2017).

McLaughlan, R., "One dose of architecture, taken daily: Building for mental health in New Zealand," PhD thesis (Wellington: Victoria University, 2014).

Metge, R. T., "The House that Jack Built: The Origins of Labour State Housing 1935–8 With Particular Reference to the Role of J. A. Lee," MA thesis (Auckland: University of Auckland, 1972).

Mitchell, J., "Immigration and national identity in 1970s New Zealand," PhD thesis (Dunedin: University of Otago, 2003).

Morrison, M. A., "The Grassroots of the 1981 Springbok Tour: An examination of the actions and perspectives of everyday New Zealanders during the 1981 Springbok Rugby Tour of New Zealand," MA thesis (Christchurch: University of Canterbury, 2017).

Potgieter, S., "'Barbed-Wire Boks': The Long Shadow of the 1981 Springbok Tour of New Zealand and the United States of America," PhD thesis (Stellenbosch: Stellenbosch University, 2017).

Reid, N. E., "Churchman: A Study of James Michael Liston, Bishop of Auckland, 1920–1970," PhD thesis (Auckland: University of Auckland, 2004).

Richardson, P., "An architecture of empire: The government buildings of John Campbell in New Zealand," PhD thesis (Christchurch: University of Canterbury, 1988).

Ross, T., "New Zealand's Overstaying Islander: A Construct of the Ideology of Race and Immigration," MA thesis (Wellington: Victoria University, 1994).

Saunders, C., "The response of grassroots Christians to the introduction of Sunday trading to New Zealand in 1989: by what authority are you doing these things and who gave you this authority?," PhD thesis (Dunedin: University of Otago, 2011).

Snowball, A., "Delineating Nihilism: Colin McCahon's Last Paintings," BFA thesis (Brisbane: Griffith University, 2011).

Sykes, R. C., "The market milk industry in New Zealand," MAgrSc thesis (Palmerston North: Massey University, 1952).

Taule'ale'ausumai, F. J., "The Samoan diaspora church in New Zealand: Patterns of movement and dynamics amongst three generations of Samoan families," PhD thesis (Auckland: Auckland University of Technology, 2019).

Thompson, C., "Confronting design: case studies in the design of ceramics in New Zealand," PhD thesis (Auckland: Auckland University of Technology, 2003).

Tonkin-Covell, J., "The collectors: Naval, Army and Air Intelligence in the New Zealand Armed Forces during the Second World War," PhD thesis (Hamilton: University of Waikato, 2000).

Towers, R. J., "The Mountain, the River, and the Big Blue: The 1951 Waterfront Dispute as it Occurred in the Taranaki and Wanganui Region," BA essay (Palmerston North: Massey University, 2001).

Tulloch, T. C., "State regulation of sexuality in New Zealand 1880–1925," PhD thesis (Christchurch: University of Canterbury, 1997).

Tunufa'i, L. F., "The price of spiritual and social survival: investigating the reasons for the departure of young New Zealand-born Samoans from a South Auckland Samoan Seventh-day Adventist Church," PhD thesis (Auckland: Auckland University of Technology, 2005).

Walling, J., "Is Authenticity Necessary for Heritage? Official and Non-Official Views Through the Lens of the Open-Air Museum Howick Historical Village," PhD thesis (Auckland: University of Auckland: 2016).

Wanninayake, S. P., "Response of a New Zealand tree fern," MPB thesis (Christchurch: University of Canterbury, 2007).

Watson, M., "'Of course you had to keep the cake tins full': Pakeha women and afternoon tea from 1930–50," PhD thesis (Wellington: Massey University, 2011).

Whitcher, G. F., "'More than America': some New Zealand responses to American culture in the mid-twentieth century," PhD thesis (Christchurch: University of Canterbury, 2011).

Wright, H., "Rethinking Facadism: The Contemporary New Zealand Villa," MArch thesis (Wellington: Victoria University of Wellington, 2011).

Journal articles

Abbott, M., "The long-term development of New Zealand's electricity supply industry," *New Zealand Economic Papers* 44, no. 1 (2010).

Aitken, J., "Wives and Mothers First: The New Zealand Teachers' Marriage Bar and the Ideology of Domesticity, 1920–1940," *Women's Studies Journal* 12, no. 1 (1996).

Annabell, A. R., "A Broadwood Square Pianoforte in the Auckland Institute and Museum," *Records of the Auckland Institute and Museum* 25 (1988).

"Auckland Synagogue and Community Centre," *New Zealand Institute of Architects Journal* 37, no. 5 (20 May 1970).

Austin, M., "Round Table Connections: The House in the Auckland Scene," *Interstices: Journal of Architecture and Related Arts* 5 (2000).

Ausubel, D. P., "Race relations in New Zealand: Maori and Pakeha: an American view," *Landfall* 12 (1958).

Ballara, A., "Settlement Patterns in the Early European Maori Phase of Maori Society," *JPS* 88, no. 2 (1979).

Bandyopadhyay, S., "A History of Small Numbers. Indians in New Zealand, c.1890s–1930s," *NZJH* 43, no. 2 (2009).

Barcham, M., "The challenge of urban Maori: reconciling conceptions of indigeneity and social change," *Asia Pacific Viewpoint* 39, no. 3 (1998).

Barrie, A., "Auckland City in the 1970s," *Itinerary No. 39, Block: The Broadsheet of the Auckland Branch of the New Zealand Institute of Architects* 10 (2011).

Barrie, A., "Auckland City in the 1990s," *Itinerary No. 37, Block: The Broadsheet of the Auckland Branch of the New Zealand Institute of Architects* 3 (2011).

Bassett, J., "A Thousand Miles of Loyalty," *NZJH* 21, no. 1 (1987).

Baxendale, J., "'... into Another Kind of Life in Which Anything Might Happen ...' Popular Music and Late Modernity, 1910–1930," *Popular Music* 14, no. 2 (1995).

Beaglehole, R. and Jackson, R., "Coronary heart disease mortality, morbidity, and risk factor trends in New Zealand," *Cardiology* 72, no. 1-2 (1985).

Beattie, J., Heinzen, J. M. and Adam, J. P., "Japanese gardens and plants in New Zealand, 1850–1950: Transculturation and transmission," *Studies in the History of Gardens & Designed Landscapes* 28, no. 2 (2008).

Bedford, R., "Pacific Islanders in New Zealand," *Espace Populations Sociétés* 12, no. 2 (1994).

Bell, A., "Reverberating Historical Privilege of a 'Middling' Sort of Settler Family," *Genealogy* 4, no. 2 (2020).

Bell, C., "'Not really beautiful, but iconic': New Zealand's Crown Lynn Ceramics," *Journal of Design History* 25, no. 4 (2012).

Bell, L. "The Colonial Paintings of Charles Frederick Goldie in the 1990s: The Postcolonial Goldie and the Rewriting of History," *Cultural Studies* 9, no. 1 (1995).

Berry, B. J. L., "The Chicago School in Retrospect and Prospect," *Urban Geography* 22, no. 6 (2001).

Best, E., "Notes on the art of war, as conducted by the Maori of New Zealand, with accounts of various customs, rites, superstitions, &c., pertaining to war, as practised and believed in by the ancient Maori. Part III," *JPS* 11, no. 3 (1902).

Billing, G. C., "The Industrial Pattern and New Zealand's Future," *The Economic Journal* 67, no. 265 (1957).

Bloomfield, G. T., "Geographic Notebook: The Auckland International Airport," *New Zealand Geographer* 22, no. 1 (1966).

Bonwick, R. J. and Morris, P., "Post-traumatic stress disorder in elderly war veterans," *International Journal of Geriatric Psychiatry* 11, no. 12 (1996).

Boon, J., "The interplay of market forces and government action in the achievement of urban intensification: the case of Auckland, New Zealand," *Journal of Urbanism* 3, no. 3 (2010).

Boraman, T., "A middle-class diversion from working-class struggle? The New Zealand new left from the mid-1950s to the mid-1970s," *Labour History* 103 (2012).

Bowman, R., "Public attitudes toward homosexuality in New Zealand," *International Review of Modern Sociology* 9, no. 2 (1979).

Bradshaw, W., "Learning the lessons of the 1918 Spanish influenza epidemic," *Nursing New Zealand (Wellington, NZ: 1995)* 11, no. 10 (2005).

Brailsford, I., "'If there's not one near you now, there soon will be': American Fast-Food Chains Come to New Zealand," *NZJH* 39, no. 1 (2005).

Brailsford, I., "'US Image but NZ Venture': Americana and Fast-Food Advertising in New Zealand, 1971–1990," *Australasian Journal of American Studies* 22, no. 2 (2003).

Brand, D., "Auckland, Slowly Disappearing: Looking for the Felton Mathew Plan," *Journal of Urban Design* 1, no. 3 (1996).

Brand, D., "Ernst Plischke and the Design of Urban New Zealand, 1939–47," *Journal of Urban Design* 19, no. 5 (2014).

Brickell, C., "Heroes and invaders: Gay and lesbian pride parades and the public/private distinction in New Zealand media accounts," *Gender, Place and Culture: A Journal of Feminist Geography* 7, no. 2 (2000).

Brickell, C., "The politics of post-war consumer culture," *NZJH* 40, no. 2 (2006).

Brookes, B., "Gender, work and fears of a 'hybrid race' in 1920s New Zealand," *Gender & History* 19, no. 3 (2007).

Brück, J., "Landscapes of desire: parks, colonialism, and identity in Victorian and Edwardian Ireland," *International Journal of Historical Archaeology* 17, no. 1 (2013).

Brunton, W., "The Scottish Influence on New Zealand Psychiatry before World War II," *Immigrants & Minorities* 29, no. 3 (2011).

Bryder, L., "'Lessons' of the 1918 Influenza Epidemic in Auckland," *NZJH* 16, no. 2 (1982).

Buch, T., Milne, S. and Dickson, G., "Multiple stakeholder perspectives on cultural events: Auckland's Pasifika Festival," *Journal of Hospitality Marketing & Management* 20, nos. 3–4 (2011).

Buckenberger, C., "Meanings of housing qualities in suburbia: empirical evidence from Auckland, New Zealand," *Journal of Housing and the Built Environment* 27, no. 1 (2012).

Butcher, A. P., "Educate, consolidate, immigrate: educational immigration in Auckland, New Zealand," *Asia Pacific Viewpoint* 45, no. 2 (2004).

Callister, S., "*Stabat mater dolorosa*: Death, photography and collective mourning," *NZJH* 41, no. 1 (2007).

Calomiris, C. W., "Financial factors in the Great Depression," *Journal of Economic Perspectives* 7, no. 2 (1993).

Campbell, K. I., "The Beatles at Woodstock," *Popular Music and Society* 43, no. 2 (2020).

Carlyon, R., "Grand Hotel Fire 1901, A Turning Point," *Despatches* (Auckland, 2019), n.p.

Carmichael, G. A., "Non-marital Pregnancies in New Zealand Since the Second World War," *Journal of Biosocial Science* 17, no. 2 (1985).

Chalmers, L. and Hall, B., "Auckland," *Cities* 6, no. 2 (1989).

Clark, P., "Te Mana Whenua O Ngati Whatua O Orakei," *Auckland University Law Review* 9 (2000).

Clarke, A., "Churchgoing in New Zealand, 1874–1926," *NZJH* 47, no. 2 (2013).

Clarke, J., "C.F. Goldie: the old master revisited," *New Zealand Geographic* 38 (April–June 1998).

Clements, K. P., "New Zealand's Role in Promoting a Nuclear-Free Pacific," *Journal of Peace Research* 25, no. 4 (1988).

Cliffe, A. W., "Auckland Harbour Bridge," *New Zealand Engineering* 13, no. 5 (1958).

Coleman, J., "Apprehending possibilities: Tracing the emergence of feminist consciousness in nineteenth-century New Zealand," *Women's Studies International Forum* 31, no. 6 (2008).

Coll, J. A. and Radicella, R., "Nuclear Activities in Argentina. A Short Review. Part 2," *Ciencia e Investigacion* 54, no. 1 (2002).

Colquhoun, D., "Royal Scenes from the Empire City: The Prince of Wales in Wellington, 7–9 May 1920," *Turnbull Library Record* 41 (2009).

Cookson, J. E., "Illiberal New Zealand: The Formation of Government Policy on Conscientious Objection, 1940–1," *NZJH* 17, no. 2 (1983).

Crawford, J., "Overt and Covert Military Involvement in the 1890 Maritime Strike and 1913 Waterfront Strike in New Zealand," *Labour History* 60 (1991).

Culliford, J., "The Commonwealth Games Village — New Solutions to an Accommodation Problem," *New Zealand Engineering* 45, no. 2 (1990).

Currie, E., "Old port town Waiuku," *Heritage Matters: The Magazine for New Zealanders Restoring, Preserving and Enjoying Our Heritage* 29 (2011).

Cusins-Lewer, A. and Gatley, J., "The 'Myers Park Experiment' (1913–1916) and its Legacy in Auckland," *Fabrications* 12, no. 1 (2002).

D'Arcy, P., "Maori and Muskets from a Pan-Polynesian Perspective," *NZJH* 31, no. 1 (2000).

Dahms, F., "Urban Passenger Transport and Population Distribution in Auckland: 1860–1961," *New Zealand Geographer* 36, no. 1 (1980).

Dalley, B., "'Fresh Attractions': White Slavery and Feminism in New Zealand, 1885–1918," *Women's History Review* 9, no. 2 (2000).

Dalley, B., "Lolly Shops 'of the Red-Light Kind' and 'Soldiers of the King': Suppressing One-Women Brothels in New Zealand, 1908–1916," *NZJH* 30, no. 1 (1996).

Dart, W., "Film," in *Rip It Up* 51 (October 1981).

Davies, B. R., "Operation Rugby," *The Police Journal* 55, no. 1 (1982).

de Bruin, A. and Dupuis, A., "The dynamics of New Zealand's largest street market; the Otara flea market," *International Journal of Sociology and Social Policy* 20, nos. 1/2 (2000).

de Bruin, A., "From cultural to economic capital: Community employment creation in Otara," in *Labour, Employment and Work in New Zealand* (1996).

de Lange, P. J. and Crowcroft, G. M., "The Vascular Flora of Motuihe Island Recreation Reserve," *Auckland Botanical Society Journal* 54, no. 2 (1999).

Del Visco, S., "Yellow peril, red scare: race and communism in National Review," *Ethnic and Racial Studies* 42, no. 4 (2019).

Delbruck, F., "Oil prices and the New Zealand economy," *Reserve Bank of New Zealand Bulletin* 68, no. 4 (2005).

Dickens, C., "The Star of Bethlehem," *Household Words: A Weekly Journal* 386 (August 1857).

Douglas, A., "Plan/ditch: Topographic inscription in an early colonial capital," *Interstices* 16 (2015).

Dunstall, G., "Frontier and/or cultural fragment? Interpretations of violence in colonial New Zealand," *Social History* 29, no. 1 (2004).

Edwards, P. N., "Y2K: Millennial reflections on computers as infrastructure," *History and Technology, an International Journal* 15, no. 1–2 (1998).

Elers, S., "A 'White New Zealand': Anti-Chinese Racist Political Discourse from 1880 to 1920," *China Media Research* 14, no. 3 (2018).

Emery, M., Hooks, J. and Stewart, R., "Born at the wrong time? An oral history of women professional accountants in New Zealand," *Accounting History* 7, no. 2 (2002).

Esler, A. E., "Changes in the native plant cover of urban Auckland, New Zealand," *New Zealand Journal of Botany* 29, no. 2 (1991).

Faemani, S. U., "The Impact of Remittances on Rural Development in Tongan Villages," *Asian and Pacific Migration Journal* 4, no. 1 (1995).

Fairburn, M., "Social Mobility and Opportunity in Nineteenth-Century New Zealand," *NZJH* 13, no. 1 (1979).

Fairburn, M., "What Best Explains the Discrimination Against the Chinese in New Zealand, 1860s–1950s?," *JNZS* 2/3 (2003).

Fairfield, F. G., "Maungakiekie. One Tree Hill, Auckland. Description of some Ethnological Discoveries," *JPS* 50, no. 2 (1941).

Fallan, K., "One Must Offer 'Something for Everyone': Designing Crockery for Consumer Consent in 1950s' Norway," *Journal of Design History* 22, no. 2 (2009).

Fox, A., "Pa of the Auckland Isthmus: an archaeological analysis," *Records of the Auckland Institute and Museum* 14 (1977).

Francis, L. J., Lankshear, D. W. and Jones, S. H., "The influence of the charismatic movement on local church life: A comparative study among Anglican rural, urban and suburban churches," *Journal of Contemporary Religion* 15, no. 1 (2000).

Friesen, W., "New Asian migrants in Auckland: issues of employment and status," *Labour, Employment and Work in New Zealand* (1992).

Friesen, W., "The demographic transformation of inner city Auckland," *New Zealand Population Review* 35, no. 1 (2009).

Gaimster, D., "Fitting the colonial museum dashboard? Civic action, curatorial agency and identity building at the Auckland Museum (1852–1929)," *Museum History Journal* 13, no. 1 (2020).

Gatley, J., "The Question of Auckland's Civic Building," *Docomomo Journal* 1 (2015).

Gee, A. and Trapeznik, A., "The Motoring Lobby in New Zealand, 1898–1930," *JNZS* 27 (2018).

Gilling, B. D., "'Back to the Simplicities of Religion': The 1959 Billy Graham Crusade in New Zealand and its Precursors," *Journal of Religious History* 17, no. 2 (1992).

González-Tennant, E., "Using geodatabases to generate 'living documents' for archaeology: A case study from the Otago Goldfields, New Zealand," *Historical Archaeology* 43, no. 3 (2009).

Gottmann, J., "Why the Skyscraper?," *Geographical Review* 56, no. 2 (April 1966).

Goulding, C., "Romancing the past: heritage visiting and the nostalgic consumer," *Psychology & Marketing* 18, no. 6 (2001).

Graham, G., "'Kahu-Mau-Roa and Te Kotuiti.' Two Famous War Canoes of Ngati-Paoa and their History," *JPS* 33, no. 2 (130) (1924).

Graham, G., "Tainui," *JPS* 60, no. 1 (1951).

Greasley, D. and Oxley, L., "The pastoral boom, the rural land market, and long swings in New Zealand economic growth, 1873–1939," *The Economic History Review* 62, no. 2 (2009).

Greenberg, A., "Lutyens's Cenotaph," *The Journal of the Society of Architectural Historians* 48, no. 1 (1989).

Greenwood, J., "The 1908 Visit of the Great White Fleet: Displaying Modern Sydney," *History Australia* 5, no. 3 (2008).

Griffiths, G. M., Talbot, N., Dirks, K. N., Betti, G. and Salmond, J. A., "Forecasting brown haze in Auckland," *Weather and Climate* 39, no. 1 (2019).

Griffiths, P., "Popular culture and modernity: Dancing in New Zealand society 1920–1945," *Journal of Social History* 41, no. 3 (2008).

Grzelewski, D., "Kelly Tarlton," *New Zealand Geographic* 84 (March–April 2007).

Gu, K., "Exploring the fringe belt concept in Auckland: An urban morphological idea and planning practice," *New Zealand Geographer* 66, no. 1 (2010).

Gunder, M., "Auckland's Motorway System: A New Zealand Genealogy of Imposed Automotive Progress 1946–66," *Urban Policy and Research* 20, no. 2 (2002).

Gurley, C. R. and Nicholls, J. S. F., "Earthquake strengthening of old masonry with reference to the Auckland Ferry Building," *Bulletin of the New Zealand Society for Earthquake Engineering* 15, no. 4 (1982).

Guy, L., "Between a Hard Rock and Shifting Sands: Churches and the Issue of Homosexuality in New Zealand, 1960–86," *Journal of Religious History* 30, no. 1 (2006).

Guy, L., "'Moral Panic' or Pejorative Labelling? Rethinking the Mazengarb Inquiry into Underage Sex in the Hutt Valley in 1954," *Journal of Religious History* 33, no. 4 (2009).

Haigh, D. I., "Community development and New Zealand local authorities in the 1970s and 1980s," *New Zealand Sociology* 29, no. 1 (2014).

Hamilton, M., "Sexual politics and African-American music; or, placing Little Richard in history," *History Workshop Journal* 46, no. 1 (1998).

Hamlin, P. K., "The 1981 Springbok Tour of New Zealand," *Auckland University Law Review* 4 (1980).

Hancox, G. G. and Hight, J., "The Labour Movement and the Strike of 1913 in New Zealand," *The Economic Journal* 24, no. 94 (1914).

Hanigan, J. P., "The centrality of marriage: Homosexuality and the Roman Catholic argument," *The Ecumenical Review* 50, no. 1 (1998).

Hannis, G., "From Yellow Peril to Model Minority? A Comparative Analysis of a Newspaper's Depiction of the Chinese in New Zealand at the Start of the 20th and 21st Centuries," *Asia Pacific Media Educator* 1, no. 19 (2009).

Hare, A. and Currie, E., "MOTAT Gems," *Heritage Matters: The Magazine for New Zealanders Restoring, Preserving and Enjoying Our Heritage* 21 (2009).

Hargreaves, R. P., "Maori Flour Mills of the Auckland Province: 1846–1860," *JPS* 70, no. 2 (1961).

Hargreaves, R. P., "The Maori agriculture of the Auckland province in the mid-nineteenth century," *JPS* 68, no. 2 (1959).

Hargreaves, R. P., Hearn, T. J. and Little, S., "The state and housing in New Zealand to 1919," *New Zealand Geographer* 41, no. 2 (1985).

Harper, T., "'Amen, amen!': Christianity, society and visions of the future in 1920s New Zealand," *NZJH* 42, no. 2 (2008).

Harris, C. E., "Slow train coming: the New Zealand state changes its mind about Auckland mass transit, 1949–56," *Urban Policy and Research* 23, no. 1 (2005).

Harris, J., "Definitely maybe: continuity and change in the Rugby World Cup," *Sport in Society* 16, no. 7 (2013).

Hawkins, J., "A Personal Recollection Of Four Years Work In The Crown Lynn Design Studio From 1978 To 1982," *Back Story: Journal of New Zealand Art, Media & Design History* 4 (2018).

Heale, M. J., "The Sixties as History: A Review of the Political Historiography," *Reviews in American History* 33, no. 1 (2005).

Herzog, C., "The archaeology of cinema architecture: The origins of the movie theatre," *Quarterly Review of Film & Video* 9, no. 1 (1984).

Hill, R. S., "Maori urban migration and the assertion of indigeneity in Aotearoa/New Zealand, 1945–1975," *Interventions* 14, no. 2 (2012).

Hillyer, M., "To Dance the Native Dance: Vernacular Modernism in an 'Australian-New Zealand Comedy Romance'," *JNZS* 25 (2017).

Hochstein, G. and Gatley, J., "A Golden Pedigree: Finding Mies in New Zealand Modernism through the Work of Edward Erickson," in *Proceedings of the Society of Architectural Historians, Australia and New Zealand*: 33, Brennan, A. and Goad, P., eds (Melbourne: SAHANZ, 2016).

Hoek, J. A., Gendall, P. J. and West, R. D., "The role of sponsorship in selected New Zealand companies," *New Zealand Journal of Business* 12 (1990).

Höllinger, F., "Does the counter-cultural character of New Age persist? Investigating social and political attitudes of New Age followers," *Journal of Contemporary Religion* 19, no. 3 (2004).

Hook, A., "Macaulay and America," *Journal of American Studies* 9, no. 3 (1975).

Hooks, J. J. and Stewart, R. E., "The geography and ideology of accounting: a case study of domination and accounting in a sugar refinery in Australasia, 1900–1920," *Accounting Historians Journal* 34, no. 2 (2007).

Horton, M., "The Art of Poetry: The (Frank Lloyd) Wright Stuff," *Carolina English Teacher* 31, no. 4 (2005).

Hucker, G., "'The Great Wave of Enthusiasm': New Zealand Reactions to the First World War in August 1914 — a Reassessment," *NZJH* 43, no. 1 (2009).

Hughes, A. and Saxton, P., "Geographic micro-clustering of homosexual men: implications for research and social policy," *Social Policy Journal of New Zealand* 28 (2006).

Hunt, N. and Robbins, I., "The long-term consequences of war: the experience of World War II," *Aging & Mental Health* 5, no. 2 (2001).

Hunter, I. and Wilson, M., "Origins and opportunity: 150 years of New Zealand entrepreneurship," *Journal of Management & Organization* 13, no. 4 (2007).

Husbands, P., "Poverty in Freemans Bay 1886–1913," *NZJH* 28, no. 1 (1994).

Hutchinson, S., "Humanitarian critique and the settler fantasy: the Australian press and settler colonial consciousness during the Waikato War, 1863–1864," *Settler Colonial Studies* 4, no. 1 (2014).

Ignatieva, M., Haase, D., Dushkova, D. and Haase, A., "Lawns in cities: from a globalised urban green space phenomenon to sustainable nature-based solutions," *Land* 9, no. 3 (2020).

Isaacs, N., "House assembly — prefabrication and factory manufacture," *Build Magazine* 108 (2008).

Ishizawa, H. and Arunachalam, D., "Ethnic neighbourhoods in Auckland, New Zealand," *Urban Policy and Research* 32, no. 4 (2014).

James, B., Rehm, M. and Saville-Smith, K., "Impacts of leaky homes and leaky building stigma on older homeowners," *Pacific Rim Property Research Journal* 23, no. 1 (2017).

Jefferson, M., "Why geography? The law of the primate city," *Geographical Review* 79, no. 2 (1989).

Jenks, T. and Wanhalla, A., "Psychological Casualties: War Neurosis, Rehabilitation, and the Family in Post-World War II New Zealand," *Health and History* 22, no. 2 (2020).

Jensen, R. J., "The causes and cures of unemployment in the Great Depression," *The Journal of Interdisciplinary History* 19, no. 4 (1989).

Johnson, M., "'The Land of the Wrong White Crowd': Anti-racist Organizations and Pakeha Identity Politics in the 1970s," *NZJH* 39, no. 2 (2005).

Johnston, R., Poulsen, M. and Forrest, J., "Asians, Pacific Islanders, and ethnoburbs in Auckland, New Zealand," *Geographical Review* 98, no. 2 (2008).

Jones, L., "Frank Sargeson [Norris Frank Davey], 1903–1982," *Kōtare: New Zealand Notes & Queries* 7, no. 2 (2008).

Jones, M. T., "Adam Smith and the ethics of contemporary democratic capitalism in New Zealand," *International Journal of Social Economics* 20, no. 12 (1993).

Jones, N., "Auckland's Māori Community Centre: 1947–1970," *Auckland History Initiative* (7 January 2020).

Jones, S. R. H., "Government policy and industry structure in New Zealand, 1900–1970," *Australian Economic History Review* 39, no. 3 (1999).

Joseph, P., "Maori and the Market: the Waitangi Tribunal," *Race and Class* 41, no. 4 (2000).

Joyce, H., "Out from nowhere: Pakeha anxieties in *Ngati* (Barclay, 1987), *Once Were Warriors* (Tamahori, 1994) and *Whale Rider* (Caro, 2002)," *Studies in Australasian Cinema* 3, no. 3 (2009).

Kattan, L., Acharjee, S. and Tay, R., "Pedestrian Scramble Operations: Pilot Study in Calgary, Alberta, Canada," *Transportation Research Record* 2140, no. 1 (2009).

Kavan, A., "New Zealand: Answer to an Inquiry," *Horizon: A Review of Literature and Art* 8 (1943).

Kawharu, I. H., "Biculturalism and inclusion in New Zealand: The case of Orakei," *Anthropologica* 50, no. 1 (2008).

Keane, W. F., "'Ex-pats' and 'Poofters': The New Zealand All Whites," *Sport in Society* 4, no. 3 (2001).

Kearns, R. A., Coleman, T. M. and Edmeades, J., "New Zealand children's health stamps: Ideological artefacts linking health and place," *Social Science & Medicine* 227 (2019).

Kennedy, A., "The history of New Zealand shop trading hours," *International Journal of Retail & Distribution Management* 38, no. 8 (2010).

Kersey, H. A., "Opening a Discourse on Race Relations in New Zealand: The Fern and the Tiki Revisited," *JNZS* 1 (2002).

Ketola, K., "The Hare Krishna and the counterculture in the light of the theory of divergent modes of religiosity," *Method and Theory in the Study of Religion* 16, no. 3 (2004).

Khouri, P. M., "Conscientious Objection and Compulsory Military Service in New Zealand," *Auckland University Law Review* 1 (1967).

Kim, S. and Law, M. T., "History, institutions, and cities: A view from the Americas," *Journal of Regional Science* 52, no. 1 (2012).

King, A., "The Bungalow," *Architectural Association Quarterly* V (1973): 6.

Krtalić, M. and Grgić, I. H., "Cultural societies and information needs: Croats in New Zealand," *Global Knowledge, Memory and Communication* 68, nos. 8/9 (2019).

Krzanich, A., "Murder, Mazengarb and a Moral Panic: The Intersection of Juvenile Delinquency and the Media in 1950s New Zealand," *Auckland University Law Review* 16 (2010).

Kühn, M. and Stöfen, H., "A reactive flow model of the geothermal reservoir Waiwera, New Zealand," *Hydrogeology Journal* 13, no. 4 (2005).

Kumar, R., "A Comparative Study Between on Pizza Hut and Domino's Pizza," *International Journal of Marketing and Technology* 5, no. 9 (2015).

Kuszewski, K. and Brydak, L., "The epidemiology and history of influenza," *Biomedicine & Pharmacotherapy* 54, no. 4 (2000).

Lange, D., "New Zealand's Security Policy," *Foreign Affairs* 63 (1984).

Lawrence, J. and Kearns, R., "Exploring the 'fit' between people and providers: refugee health needs and health care services in Mt Roskill, Auckland, New Zealand," *Health and Social Care in the Community* 13, no. 5 (2005).

Le Grice, J. S. and Braun, V., "Mātauranga Māori and reproduction: Inscribing connections between the natural environment, kin and the body," *AlterNative: An International Journal of Indigenous Peoples* 12, no. 2 (2016).

Le Rossignol, J. E., "A General Strike in New Zealand," *The American Economic Review* 4, no. 2 (1914).

Leckie, J., "In Defence of Race and Empire: The White New Zealand League at Pukekohe," *NZJH* 19, no. 2 (1985).

Legg, S., "Memory and nostalgia," *Cultural Geographies* 11, no. 1 (2004).

Legg, S. M., "Views from the Antipodes: the 'forest influence' debate in the Australian and New Zealand press, 1827–1956," *Australian Geographer* 49, no. 1 (2018).

Lewis, T., "'A Godlike Presence': The Impact of Radio on the 1920s and 1930s," *OAH Magazine of History* 6, no. 4 (1992).

Lewthwaite, G. R., "Maungawhau and Maungakiekie: Reinterpreting the Cultural Landscape," *Yearbook of the Association of Pacific Coast Geographers* 45, no. 1 (1983).

Leyland, B., "Auckland central business district power failure," *Power Engineering Journal* 12, no. 3 (1998).

Lindsay, J. M., Leonard, G. S., Smid, E. R. and Hayward, B. W., "Age of the Auckland Volcanic Field: a review of existing data," *New Zealand Journal of Geology and Geophysics* 54, no. 4 (2011).

Lindsey, D., "A brief history of conscience voting in New Zealand," *Australian Parliamentary Review* 23, no. 1 (2008).

Lineham, P., "The place of small denominations in the religious landscape of New Zealand," *Stimulus: The New Zealand Journal of Christian Thought and Practice* 21, no. 2 (2014).

Linge, G. J. R., "The diffusion of manufacturing in Auckland, New Zealand," *Economic Geography* 39, no. 1 (1963).

Lipman, P., "Making the Global City, Making Inequality: The Political Economy and Cultural Politics of Chicago School Policy," *American Educational Research Journal* 39, no. 2 (2002).

Little, C., "The forgotten game? A reassessment of the place of soccer within New Zealand society, sport and historiography," *Soccer & Society* 3, no. 2 (2002).

Loto, R., Hodgetts, D., Chamberlain, K., Nikora, L. W., Karapu, R. and Barnett, A., "Pasifika in the news: The portrayal of Pacific peoples in the New Zealand press," *Journal of Community and Applied Social Psychology* 16, no. 2 (2006).

Macdonald, C., "Crime and punishment in New Zealand,1840-1913: a Gendered History," *NZJH* 23, no. 1 (1989).

Mackley-Crump, J., "A 'Pacific renaissance'?: exploring the Pacific diaspora in Aotearoa New Zealand through the evolution of festivals and popular music," *Journal of New Zealand & Pacific Studies* 3, no. 2 (2015).

MacLean, M., "'Almost the same, but not quite ... Almost the same, but not white': Maori and Aotearoa/New Zealand's 1981 Springbok Tour," *Kunapipi: Journal of Postcolonial Writing* 23, no. 1 (2001).

Macpherson, C. and L., "Evangelical Religion among Pacific Island Migrants: New Faiths or Brief Diversions?," *Journal of Ritual Studies* 15, no. 2 (2001).

Macready, S., "A review of urban historical archaeology in Auckland to 1990," *The Australian Journal of Historical Archaeology* 9 (1991).

Maloney, T., "Welfare reform and unemployment in New Zealand," *Economica* 69, no. 274 (2002).

Marker, M., "Geographies of Indigenous leaders: Landscapes and mindscapes in the Pacific Northwest," *Harvard Educational Review* 85, no. 2 (2015).

Martin, J. E., "'Waging War on the Labour Market': The State and Wage Labour in Late Nineteenth-Century New Zealand," *The Turnbull Library Record* 26 (1993).

Matthews, P. J., "Archaeological site survey on Ponui Island, Hauraki Gulf, New Zealand," *Tane* 25 (1979).

Mawer, C. and Kiddle, R., "Suburban shopping malls as spaces for community health and human flourishing: an Aotearoa New Zealand case study," *Journal of Urban Design* 25, no. 2 (2020).

Mazlin, C., "Returned Soldiers in *Owls Do Cry*, *A State of Siege*, and *The Carpathians*: Janet Frame's Subversive Representations," *Antipodes* 28, no. 2 (2014).

McCreanor, T., "'Why Strengthen the City Wall When the Enemy Has Poisoned the Well?' An Assay of Anti-Homosexual Discourse in New Zealand," *Journal of Homosexuality* 31, no. 4 (1996).

McDonald, C., "A Nation Wins its Spurs: Military Performances and National Identity in New Zealand's Royal Visits, 1901-1927," *Royal Studies Journal* 5, no. 1 (2018).

McDougall, H., "'The whole world's watching': New Zealand, international opinion, and the 1981 Springbok Rugby Tour," *Journal of Sport History* 45, no. 2 (2018).

McEwan, B., Campbell, M. and Swain, D., "New Zealand culture of intoxication: Local and global influences," *New Zealand Sociology* 25, no. 2 (2010).

McEwen, J. M., "The Development of Maori Culture Since the Advent of the Pakeha," *JPS* 56, no. 2 (1947).

McKay, A., "Preserving a legacy: an analysis of the role and function of the Mackelvie Trust Board, 1885-2010," *Records of the Auckland Museum* 53 (2018).

Mees P. and Dodson, J., "Backtracking Auckland?: Technical and Communicative Reason in Metropolitan Transport Planning," *International Planning Studies* 12, no.1 (2007).

Metcalf, T. R., "Architecture and the representation of empire: India, 1860-1910," *Representations* 6 (1984).

Millar, G., "'We never recovered': The social cost of the 1951 New Zealand waterfront dispute," *Labour History* 108 (2015).

Miller, B. J., "From 'jungles of terror' to 'God will begin a healing in this city': Billy Graham and evangelicals on cities and suburbs," *Journal of Urban History* (2020).

Miller, C. L., "Theory poorly practised: the garden suburb in New Zealand," *Planning Perspectives* 19, no. 1 (2004).

Mills, E. S. and Tan, J. P., "A comparison of urban population density functions in developed and developing countries," *Urban Studies* 17, no. 3 (1980).

Mitchell, P., "Laurence Binyon," *English Literature in Transition, 1880-1920* 40, no. 4 (1997).

Molloy, C., Shane, P. and Augustinus, P., "Eruption recurrence rates in a basaltic volcanic field based on tephra layers in maar sediments: implications for hazards in the Auckland volcanic field," *Geological Society of America Bulletin* 121, no. 11-12 (2009).

Moloughney, B. and Stenhouse, J., "'Drug-besotten, sin-begotten fiends of filth': New Zealanders and the Oriental Other, 1850-1920," *NZJH* 33, no. 1 (1999).

Monsalve, F., "ASB Theatre," *Architecture Now* 10 (December 2013).

Moon, P., "Prosthetic Nostalgia: History and Memory in 'Art Deco Napier'," *JNZS* 32 (June 2021).

Moore, K., "'The warmth of comradeship': the First British Empire Games and Imperial Solidarity," *The International Journal of the History of Sport* 6, no. 2 (1989).

Moore, P. R., "The Tahanga basalt: an important stone resource in North Island prehistory," *Records of the Auckland Institute and Museum* 13 (1976).

Murphy, L., "Third-wave gentrification in New Zealand: The case of Auckland," *Urban Studies* 45, no. 12 (2008).

Murphy, L., "To the market and back: Housing policy and state housing in New Zealand," *GeoJournal* 59, no. 2 (2004).

Murray-McIntosh, R. P., Scrimshaw, B. J., Hatfield, P. J. and Penny, D., "Testing migration patterns and estimating founding population size in Polynesia by using human mtDNA sequences," *Proceedings of the National Academy of Sciences* 95, no. 15 (1998).

Nash, W., "New Zealand's Total War Effort," *Far Eastern Survey* 11, no. 12 (1942).

Neill, L., Bell, C. and Hemmington, N., "A Pie Cart Story: The longevity of a Vernacular Fast Food Eatery," *Locale: The Australasian-Pacific Journal of Regional Food Studies* 2 (2012).

Newnham, R. M., Lowe, D. J., Giles, T. and Alloway, B. V., "Vegetation and climate of Auckland, New Zealand, since ca. 32 000 cal. yr ago: support for an extended LGM," *Journal of Quaternary Science: Published for the Quaternary Research Association* 22, no. 5 (2007).

Ngoei, W., "The Domino Logic of the Darkest Moment: The Fall of Singapore, the Atlantic Echo Chamber, and 'Chinese Penetration' in US Cold War Policy toward Southeast Asia," *Journal of American-East Asian Relations* 21, no. 3 (2014).

Nichol, R., "The eruption history of Rangitoto: reappraisal of a small New Zealand myth," *Journal of the Royal Society of New Zealand* 2, no. 3 (1992).

Nicholls, K., "Why was there no general strike in 1991? Corporatism, pluralism and neoliberal labour relations in New Zealand," *Commonwealth & Comparative Politics* 40, no. 1 (2002).

Nolan, M., "The reality and myth of New Zealand egalitarianism: Explaining the pattern of a labour historiography at the edge of empires," *Labour History Review* 72 (2007).

Nolan, M., "Unstitching the New Zealand state: Its role in domesticity and its decline," *International Review of Social History* 45, no. 2 (2000).

Nott, J., "Contesting Popular Dancing and Dance Music in Britain during the 1920s," *Cultural and Social History* 10, no. 3 (2013).

November, J., "'The Law as a Profession for Women': A Century of Progress? A Reply to Mary Jane Mossman," *Australian Feminist Law Journal* 33, no. 1 (2010).

O'Connor, P. S., "Keeping New Zealand White, 1908-1920," *NZJH* 2, no. 1 (1968).

O'Malley, V., "A United Front against Capitalism? Unemployed Workers' Organisations in Christchurch, New Zealand, during the Depression," *Labour History Review* 73, no. 1 (2008).

Olssen, M., "In defence of the welfare state and publicly provided education: A New Zealand perspective," *Journal of Education Policy* 11, no. 3 (1996).

Ongley, P. and Pearson, D., "Post-1945 International Migration: New Zealand, Australia and Canada Compared," *International Migration Review* 29, no. 3 (1995).

Osborne, R. J., "Toward Prosperity? Some Aspects of Recent Economic Deregulation in New Zealand," *UCLA Pacific Basin Law Journal* 7 (1990).

Pacheco, G. and Maloney, T., "Are the Determinants of Intergenerational Welfare Dependency Gender-Specific?," *Australian Journal of Labour Economics* 6, no. 3 (2003).

Pearse, A., "Fifty Thousand Miles Under the Union Jack," *The Leisure Hour: An Illustrated Magazine for Home Reading* (1902).

Pepper, D., "Communes and the green vision: counterculture, lifestyle and the New Age," *Utopian Studies* 4, no. 1 (1993).

Petersen, B., "Epi Shalfoon: Loss of a Popular Musician," *Te Ao Hou* 5 (October 1953).

Phillips, J., "Māori and Royal Visits, 1869–2015: From Rotorua to Waitangi," *Royal Studies Journal* 5, no. 1 (2018).

Pool, I., "The baby boom in New Zealand and Other Western Developed Countries," *Journal of Population Research* 24, no. 2 (2007).

Porter, F., "Digging in the Compost Heap," *Turnbull Library Record* 38, no 1 (January 2005).

Pownall, L. L., "Metropolitan Auckland 1740–1945: The historical geography of a New Zealand city," *New Zealand Geographer* 6, no. 2 (1950).

Prescott, E. C., "Some observations on the Great Depression," *Federal Reserve Bank of Minneapolis Quarterly Review* 23, no. 1 (1999).

Press, D. L., "Planned shopping centres: Impacts on retailers," *New Zealand Geographer* 50, no. 2 (1994).

Putnam, R. D., "Bowling Alone: America's Declining Social Capital," *Journal of Democracy* 6, no. 1 (January 1995).

Rabel, R. G., "The Vietnam Antiwar Movement in New Zealand," *Peace and Change* 17, no. 1 (1992).

Ralph, F., "Preserving the Legacy of Crown Lynn: The dedicated excavation efforts of one man have led to a museum that will preserve Crown Lynn's legacy," *Viva* (26 August 2015).

Rankin, E., "Banners, batons and barbed wire: Anti-apartheid images of the Springbok rugby tour protests in New Zealand," *De Arte* 42, no. 76 (2007).

Rankin, K., "How great was the depression in New Zealand? Neglected estimates of inter-war aggregate income," *New Zealand Economic Papers* 28, no. 2 (1994).

Rankin, K., "Unemployment in New Zealand at the peak of the Great Depression," University of Auckland, Working Papers in Economics No. 144 (Auckland: University of Auckland, 1995).

Reynolds, P., "Popular responses to the New Zealand Government's Nuclear Weapons Policy: 1984–1986," *Politics* 22, no. 1 (1987).

Rimmer, P. J., "Planned Shopping Centres in New Zealand," *New Zealand Geographer* 23, no. 1 (1967).

Robb, A., "Bastion Point: A desperate struggle and a dream fulfilled," in *E-Tangata* (3 June 2018).

Roberton, E., "Milk as a Vehicle of Disease," *Transactions and Proceedings of the New Zealand Institute* 23 (1890).

Roberts, E., "'Don't sell things, sell effects': Overseas influences in New Zealand department stores, 1909–1956," *Business History Review* 77, no. 2 (2003).

Roberts, G. and Kerensky, O. A., "Auckland Harbour Bridge: Design (Including Plate)," *Proceedings of the Institution of Civil Engineers* 18, no. 4 (1961).

Robie, D., "The Rainbow Warrior bombers, the media and the judiciary," *Australian Journalism Review* 29, no. 2 (2007).

Robinson, H., "Lest We Forget? The Fading of New Zealand War Commemorations, 1946–1966," *NZJH* 44, no. 1 (2010).

Rochford, E. B., "Recruitment strategies, ideology, and organization in the Hare Krishna movement," *Social Problems* 29, no. 4 (1982).

Ross, A., "Reluctant dominion or dutiful daughter? New Zealand and the Commonwealth in the inter-war years," *Journal of Commonwealth & Comparative Politics* 10, no. 1 (1972).

Ross, D., "Captain William Hobson: the man who would be Governor," *Journal of the C. J. La Trobe Society Inc.* 19, no. 2 (2020).

Ross, K., "'Schooled by Nature' — Pakeha Tramping Between the Wars," *NZJH* 36, no. 1 (2002).

Roth, B., "Chronicle: April–June 1979," *New Zealand Journal of Industrial Relations* 4, no. 2 (1979).

Roth, B., "Chronicle: July–September 1979," *New Zealand Journal of Industrial Relations* 4, no. 3 (1979).

Rowland, D. T., "Maori migration to Auckland," *New Zealand Geographer* 27, no. 1 (1971).

Russell, C. A., Cristel, A., Schau, H. J. and Bliese, P., "Brand afterlife: Transference to alternate brands following corporate failure," *Journal of Business Research* 97 (2019).

Ryan, G., "The Turning Point: The 1950 British Empire Games as an Imperial Spectacle," *Sport in History* 34, no. 3 (2014).

Salmon, E., "The Royal Imperial Tour," *Fortnightly Review* 70, no. 419 (1901).

Salys, R., "Art Deco Aesthetics in Grigorii Aleksandrov's 'The Circus'," *The Russian Review* 66, no. 1 (2007).

Sampson, S., "South Sea Island Magic: Bill Sevesi and the Auckland Music Scene," *Perfect Beat* 4, no. 1 (2015).

Sanders, K., "'The Sensational Scandal which has Worried Wellington': The Kelburn Raid, Sex, and the Law in First World War New Zealand," *NZJH* 48, no. 2 (2014).

Savells, J., "Who are the 'Yuppies'? A Popular View," *International Journal of Comparative Sociology* 27 (1986).

Schmidt, A., "Redwood 70 National Music Convention — West Auckland January 31 to February 1, 1970," in *Audioculture: Iwi Waiata* (12 December 2013).

Schrader, B., "Avoiding the mistakes of the 'mother country': the New Zealand garden city movement 1900–1926," *Planning Perspectives* 14, no. 4 (1999).

Schwass, M., "Invention and reinvention: Greville Texidor meets Frank Sargeson," *Journal of New Zealand Literature* 34, no. 1 (2016).

Sepie, A. J., "Counterculture within a Counter-Culture: New Zealand, Psychedelic Rock, and the Moral Guardians of the 60s and 70s," *Rock Music Studies* 5, no. 3 (2018).

Sharp, I., "The Big Meccano Set," *New Zealand Geographic* 7 (July–September 1990).

Sherburn, S., Scott, B. J., Olsen, J. and Miller, C., "Monitoring seismic precursors to an eruption from the Auckland Volcanic Field, New Zealand," *New Zealand Journal of Geology and Geophysics* 50, no. 1 (2007).

Shonle, R., "The Chicago School of Sociology, 1918–1933," *Urban Life* 11, no. 4 (1983).

Simmons, D. R., "Economic Change in New Zealand Prehistory," *JPS* 78, no. 1 (1969).

Skinner, W. H., "Ancient Maori Canals. Marlborough, N.Z.," *JPS* 21, no. 3 (1912).

Smale, M. C. and Gardner, R. O., "Survival of Mount Eden Bush, an urban forest remnant in Auckland, New Zealand," *Pacific Conservation Biology* 5, no. 2 (1999).

Smart, J., "The Evangelist as Star: The Billy Graham Crusade in Australia, 1959," *The Journal of Popular Culture* 33, no. 1 (1999).

Smith, M. E., "The archaeological study of neighborhoods and districts in ancient cities," *Journal of Anthropological Archaeology* 29, no. 2 (2010).

Smith, P. M., "The 'NZ' in Anzac: different remembrance and meaning," *First World War Studies* 7, no. 2 (2016).

Snyders, H., "Rugby football and the display of New Zealand identity during and beyond the Anglo-Boer war (1899–1907)," *South African Journal of Cultural History* 34, no. 2 (2020).

Sparke, P., "'Covered promenades for wet weather': London's winter gardens and people's palaces, 1870–1900," *The London Journal* 45, no. 2 (2020).

Spoonley, P. and Meares, C, "Laissez-faire multiculturalism and relational embeddedness: Ethnic precincts in Auckland," *Cosmopolitan Civil Societies: An Interdisciplinary Journal* 3, no. 1 (2011).

Stagoll, B., "Coming across: family therapy in Australia and New Zealand," *Australian and New Zealand Journal of Family Therapy* 17, no. 1 (1996).

Star, P., "Great Barrier Island and the Kauri Timber Industry," *Australian Forest History Society Newsletter* 59 (May 2012).

Stocker, M., "'The best thing ever seen in New Zealand': The Henry Moore Exhibition of 1956–57," *The Sculpture Journal* 16, no. 1 (2007).

Storper, M. and Scott, A. J., "Current Debates in Urban Theory: A Critical Assessment," *Urban Studies* 53, vol. 6 (2016).

Strewe, O., "Living in hand with nature," *New Zealand Modern Homes and Gardens* (Winter 1960).

Sturm, J., "Anna Kavan Meets a New Zealand Writer on His Special Day," *Kōtare: New Zealand Notes & Queries* 5, no. 1 (2004).

Summers, A., "Militarism in Britain before the Great War," *History Workshop Journal* 2, no. 1 (1976).

Summers, J. A., Baker, M. and Wilson, N., "New Zealand's experience of the 1918–19 influenza pandemic: A systematic review after 100 years," *New Zealand Medical Journal* 131 (2018).

Sunderland, P. L. and Denny, R. M., "Finding Ourselves in Images: A Semiotic Excursion," *Journal of Research for Consumers* 8 (2005).

Sutton, D. G., "Maori Demographic Change, 1769–1840: The Inner Workings of 'A Picturesque but Illogical Simile'," *JPS* 95, no. 3 (1986).

Tannock, S., "Nostalgia Critique," *Cultural Studies* 9, no. 3 (1995).

Tapsell, P., "Marae and tribal identity in urban Aotearoa/New Zealand," *Pacific Studies* 25, no. 1 (2002).

Taylor, D., "Riots, Strikes, and Radical Politics in Aotearoa New Zealand," *Counterfutures* 7 (2019).

Taylor, G. P., "New Zealand, the Anglo-Japanese Alliance and the 1908 Visit of the American Fleet," *Australian Journal of Politics & History* 15, no. 1 (1969).

Te Rito, J. S., "Whakapapa and whenua: An insider's view," *MAI Review* 1, no. 3 (2007).

Temin, P., "Transmission of the Great Depression," *Journal of Economic Perspectives* 7, no. 2 (1993).

Tennant, M., "Fun and fundraising: the selling of charity in New Zealand's past," *Social History* 38, no. 1 (2013).

Tennant, M., "Sisterly Ministrations: The Social Work of Protestant Deaconesses in New Zealand 1890–1940," *NZJH* 32, no. 1 (1998).

Tewksbury, D., Moy, P. and Weis, D. S., "Preparations for Y2K: Revisiting the behavioral component of the third-person effect," *Journal of Communication* 54, no. 1 (2004).

Thakur, R., "Creation of the Nuclear-Free New Zealand Myth: Brinkmanship Without a Brink," *Asian Survey* 29, no. 10 (1989).

Thijssen, P., "From Mechanical to Organic Solidarity, and back: With Honneth beyond Durkheim," in *European Journal of Social Theory* 15, no. 4 (2012).

Thomas, B., "Does our Migration Policy Make Sense?," *The Political Quarterly* 18, no. 3 (1947).

Thornton, G., "Industrial Archaeology in New Zealand," *Industrial Archaeology Review* 10, no. 1 (1987).

Toomath, W., "From Villa to Bungalow to Jazz Modern: New Zealand Houses between the Two World Wars," *JNZS* 2, no. 4 (1992).

Toynbee, C., "Class and Social Structure in Nineteenth-Century New Zealand," *NZJH* 13, no. 1 (1979).

Trapenznik, A. and Gee, A., "'Each in his narrow cell for ever laid': Dunedin's Southern Cemetery and its New Zealand Counterparts," *Public History Review* 20 (2013).

Traue, J. E., "The public library explosion in colonial New Zealand," *Libraries & the Cultural Record* 42, no. 2 (2007).

Trlin, A. D., "Attitudes Towards West Samoan Immigrants in Auckland, New Zealand," *The Australian Quarterly* 44, no. 3 (1972).

Troughton, G., "Church, Society, and the Challenges of Modernity in the Anglican Diocese of Auckland, 1918–1940," *Anglican and Episcopal History* 84, no. 3 (2015).

Tsimpouki, T., "The Sixties Are Dead: Long Live Their Legacy: The Politics and Poetics of Counterculture," *Gramma: Journal of Theory and Criticism* 16 (2008).

Tuhaere, P. and Tuhaere, P., "An Historical Narrative Concerning the Conquest of Kaipara and Tamaki by Ngati-Whatua. Introductory remarks," *JPS* 32, no. 4 (128) (1923).

Turkington, D. J., "The Trend of Strikes in New Zealand 1946–70: Part II," *Journal of Industrial Relations* 15, no. 2 (1973).

Turner, M., "RAN Sweeping of German Mines in Two World Wars," *Journal of Australian Naval History* 7, no. 2 (2010).

Tyler, L., "Imric Porsolt: The 'Messenger of Modernism' in Exile," *Interstices: Journal of Architecture and Related Arts* (2018).

Van der Wusten, H., "Public authority in European capitals: a map of governance, an album with symbols," *European Review* 12, no. 2 (2004).

Van Ingen, E. and Moor, N., "Explanations of changes in church attendance between 1970 and 2009," *Social Science Research* 52 (2015).

Verran, D., "Mechanics' institutes in New Zealand, and their effect on the development of library services," *Library and Information Association of New Zealand Aotearoa Conference* (8 September 2004).

Walker, R. J., "The genesis of Maori Activism," *JPS* 93, no. 3 (1984).

Wang, Y., "The art of screen passing: Anna May Wong's yellow yellowface performance in the art deco era," *Camera Obscura: Feminism, Culture, and Media Studies* 20, no. 3 (2005).

Wanhalla, A., "Housing Un/healthy Bodies: Native Housing Surveys and Maori Health in New Zealand 1930–45," *Health and History* 8, no. 1 (2006).

Ward, A., "Alienation Rights in Traditional Maori Society: A Comment," *JPS* 95, no. 2 (1986).

Ward, K., "Rugby and Church: Worlds in Conflict," *Reality* 53 (2002).

Ward, K., "Towards 2015: the future of mainline Protestantism in New Zealand," *Journal of Beliefs and Values: Studies in Religion and Education* 27, no. 1 (2006).

Ward, S. V., "The garden city tradition re-examined," *Planning Perspective* 5, no. 3 (1990).

Watson, L. R., "The Perils of Impurity: The New Zealand Purity Crusades of Henry Bligh, 1902–1930," *NZJH* 39, no. 2 (2015).

Weitzel, R. L., "Pacifists and Anti-Militarists in New Zealand, 1909–1914," *NZJH* 7, no. 2 (1973).

Wexler, J., "The Rainbow Warrior Affair: State and Agent Responsibility for Authorized Violations of International Law," *Boston University International Law Journal* 5 (1987).

White, B. R. and Chambefort, I., "Geothermal development history of the Taupo Volcanic Zone," *Geothermics* 59 (2016).

Whitelaw, J. S. and Bloomfield, G. T., "Auckland, New Zealand's Largest Urban Area," *Geography* 54, no. 3 (1969).

Whiteley, N., "Interior Design in the 1960s: Arenas for Performance," *Art History* 10, no. 1 (1987).

Wilcox, M., "Motuihe Island," *Auckland Botanical Society Journal* 54 (1999).

Williams, D. V., "New Zealand Immigration Policies and the Law — A Perspective," *Otago Law Review* 4, no. 1 (1977).

Willis, R., "Ten years of change in New Zealand manufacturing employment," *Labour, Employment and Work in New Zealand* (1994).

Willits, F. K. and Crider, D. M., "Church attendance and traditional religious beliefs in adolescence and young adulthood: A panel study," *Review of Religious Research* 31, no. 1 (1989).

Wilson, G. F., "A Pictorial Survey of Housing in New Zealand, Part Three," *Design Review* 2, no. 5 (February–March).

Wilson, J., "New Zealand Sovereignty: 1857, 1907, 1947, or 1987?," *Political Science* 60, no. 2 (2008).

Wilson-Jackson, P., "Vertigo as Entertainment: Sky Tower Data," *New Zealand Engineering* 52, no. 7 (1997).

Wilton, D. and Soltani, L. Z., "Tram or dam?: A comparison of kauri logging transportation methods in the Kauaeranga valley, New Zealand, 1871-1928," *Australasian Historical Archaeology* 31 (2013).

Wilton, D. E., "A note on the impact of government intervention in the petrol market, 1979-1980," *New Zealand Economic Papers* 17, no. 1 (1983).

Winkelmann, R., "Immigration: The New Zealand Experience," *IZA Discussion Papers*, no. 61 (Bonn: Institute for the Study of Labor, 1999): 4-5.

Witten, K., et al, "New Zealand parents' understandings of the intergenerational decline in children's independent outdoor play and active travel," *Children's Geographies* 11, no. 2 (2013).

Woityra, W., Boda, K. and Davanzo, M., "Lift the Ban on New Zealand Port Visits," *US Naval Institute Proceedings* 145, no. 7 (July 2019).

Wood, G. A., "The Former 'Dominion of New Zealand'," *Political Science* 26, no. 1 (1974).

Wood, V., Brooking, T. and Perry, P., "Pastoralism and politics: reinterpreting contests for territory in Auckland Province, New Zealand, 1853-1864," *Journal of Historical Geography* 34, no. 2 (2008).

Worthy, S., "Communities of Remembrance: Making Auckland's War Memorial Museum," *Journal of Contemporary History* 39, no. 4 (2004).

Wrigglesworth, K., "In retrospect: World-first fish world," *Engineering Insight* 13, no. 2 (2012).

Wright, M., "'Mordacious Years': Socio-Economic Aspects and Outcomes of New Zealand's Experience in the Great Depression," *The Reserve Bank of New Zealand Bulletin* 72, no. 3 (2009).

Wurster, C. B., "The social front of modern architecture in the 1930s," *Journal of the Society of Architectural Historians* 24, no. 1 (1965).

Yoon, H., "Recent East Asian immigrants and their contribution to multi-culturalism in Auckland, New Zealand," *Japanese Journal of Human Geography* 55, no. 3 (2003).

Books

Adam, J., Burgess, V. and Ellis, D., *Rugged Determination: Historical Window on Swanson, 1854-2004* (Auckland: Swanson Residents and Ratepayers Association Incorporated, 2004).

Aldrete, G. S., *Daily Life in the Roman City: Rome, Pompeii and Ostia* (Westport: Greenwood Publishing Group, 2004).

Alison, E. W., *A New Zealander Looks Back* (Auckland: Gordon & Gotch, 1964).

An Old Hand, *Memories of the Past: Auckland from 1847* (Auckland: 1887).

Anae, M., "From Kava to Coffee: The Browning of Auckland," in *Almighty Auckland*, Carter, I., Craig, D. and Matthewman, S., eds (Palmerston North: Dunmore Press, 2004).

Ashford, J., *The Bungalow in New Zealand* (Auckland: Viking, 1994).

Auckland University College, *Calendar for the Year 1898* (Auckland: The University College, 1898).

Bainbridge, S., *The Bassett Road Machine-Gun Murders: New Zealand's Gangster Killings* (Auckland: Allen & Unwin, 2013).

Baker, L., *The Way of the Jafa: A Guide to Surviving Auckland and Aucklanders* (Auckland: Penguin Publishing, 1998).

Banks, J., *The Endeavour Journal of Joseph Banks, 1768-1771*, Vol. I, J. C. Beaglehole, ed. (Sydney: Angus and Robertson, 1962).

Barnes, J., *Never a White Flag: The Memoirs of Jock Barnes*, T. Bramble, ed. (Wellington: Victoria University Press, 1998).

Barr, J., *Municipal and Official Handbook of the City of Auckland* (Auckland: Wilson & Horton, 1922).

Barr, J., *The City of Auckland, New Zealand, 1840-1920, Preceded by a Maori History of the Auckland Isthmus* (Auckland: Whitcombe and Tombs, 1922).

Bartley, B., "Grafton Bridge," in *Evolving Auckland: The City's Engineering Heritage*, La Roche, J., ed. (Christchurch: Wily Publications, 2011).

Bassett, M. and King, M., *Tomorrow Comes the Song. A Life of Peter Fraser* (Auckland: Penguin Publishing, 2000).

Batistich, A. E., *An Olive Tree in Dalmatia* (Auckland: Longman Paul, 1980).

Beaglehole, J. C., *Meet New Zealand* (Wellington: Department of Internal Affairs, 1942).

Beatson, P. and D., *The Arts in Aotearoa New Zealand: Themes and Issues* (Palmerston North: Massey University, 1994).

Belich, J., *Paradise Reforged: A History of the New Zealanders from the 1880s to the Year 2000* (Auckland: Allen Lane/The Penguin Press, 2001).

Bell, L., "Auckland's Centrepiece: Unsettled Identities, Unstable Monuments," in *Settler Colonialism: History and Memory in Australia, Canada, Aotearoa New Zealand and South Africa*, A. Coombes, ed. (Manchester: Manchester University Press, 2006).

Bell, L., *The Maori in European Art: European Representations of the Maori from the Time of Captain Cook to the Present Day* (Wellington: Reed, 1980).

Bertram, G., "The New Zealand Economy, 1900-2000," in *The New Oxford History of New Zealand*, Byrnes, G., ed. (Melbourne: Oxford University Press, 2009).

Best, A. D. W., *The Journal of Ensign Best, 1837-1843*, N. M. Taylor, ed. (Wellington: R. E. Owen, Government Printer, 1966).

Bilborough, M., "The Making of the Piano," in *The Piano*, Campion, J. and Chapman, J., eds (New York: Hyperion, 1993).

Birch, A. E., *The Story of the Boys' Brigade* (London: Frederick Muller, 1965).

Blackburn, A., *Radio Pirates: How Hauraki Rocked the Boat* (Auckland: Shoestring Press, 2014).

Blackley, R., *Goldie* (Auckland: Auckland Art Gallery, 1997).

Boddy, G. and Matthews, J., eds, *Disputed Ground: Robin Hyde, Journalist* (Wellington: Victoria University Press, 1991).

Bodell, J., *A Soldier's View of Empire*, K. Sinclair, ed. (London: The Bodley Head, 1982).

Bonny, M., *Titirangi: Fringe of Heaven*, B. and T. Harvey, eds (Auckland: West Auckland Historical Society, 2011).

Booth, P., *Deadline: My Story* (Auckland: Viking Adult, 1997).

Bourke, C., *Blue Smoke: The Lost Dawn of New Zealand Popular Music* (Auckland: Auckland University Press, 2010).

Bowron, G., "Tamaki State Housing Scheme," in *Long Live the Modern: New Zealand's New Architecture, 1904-1984*, Gatley, J., ed. (Auckland: Auckland University Press, 2008).

Boyd, R. and Baker, A., *Seventy-Five years: A Celebration Record 1915-1990. St Heliers Presbyterian Church, Auckland, New Zealand* (Auckland: St Heliers Presbyterian Church, 1990).

Brookes, B., ed., *At Home in New Zealand: History, Houses, People* (Wellington: Bridget Williams Books, 2000).

Bryson, B., *At Home* (New York: Random House, 2010).

Bunbury, T., *Reminiscences of a Veteran*, vol. 3 (London: Charles J. Skeet, 1861).

Bunkle, P., "The origins of the Women's Movement in New Zealand: The Women's Christian Temperance Union 1885-1895," in *Women in New Zealand Society*, Bunkle, P. and Hughes, B. eds (Auckland: Allen & Unwin, 1980).

Burgess, V., Bishop, G. and Cole, G., *Henderson: Heart of the West* (Auckland: West Auckland Historical Society, 2017).

Burke, E., *Burke's Philosophical Inquiry into the Origin of Our Ideas of the Sublime and Beautiful* (London: J. F. Dove, 1827).

Burton, D., *Two Hundred Years of New Zealand Food and Cookery* (Wellington: Reed, 1982).

Burton, O. E., *The Silent Division: New Zealanders at the Front 1914-1918* (Sydney: Angus and Robertson Ltd, 1935).

Bush, G. W. A., *Decently and in Order: The Centennial History of the Auckland City Council* (Auckland: Collins, 1971).

Butler, J., *Earliest New Zealand: The Journals and Correspondence of the Rev. John Butler*, R. J. Barton, ed. (Masterton: Palamontain & Petherick, 1927).

Campbell, J. L., *Poenamo: Sketches of the Early Days of New Zealand* (London: Williams and Norgate, 1881).

Carlyon, J. and Morrow, D., *Urban Village: The Story of Ponsonby, Freemans Bay and St Mary's Bay* (Auckland: Random House, 2008).

Census of New Zealand 1881 (Wellington: Registrar-General's Office, 1881).

Chapman, V. J., "Mangroves in New Zealand," in *Biology and Ecology of Mangroves*, H. J. Teas, ed. (Dordrecht: Springer, 1983).

Chapple, G., *When the Tour Came to Auckland* (Wellington: Bridget Williams Books, 2014).

Clark, J. and Walker, P., *Looking for the Local: Architecture and the New Zealand Modern* (Wellington: Victoria University Press, 2000).

Clayden, A., *A Popular Handbook to New Zealand: Its Resources and Industries* (London: Wyman and Sons, 1886).

Clements, K., *Back from the Brink: The Creation of a Nuclear-Free New Zealand* (Wellington: Port Nicholson Press, 1988).

Coleman, J. N., *A Memoir of the Rev. Richard Davis* (London: James Nisbet and Co., 1865).

Colgan, W., *The Governor's Gift: The Auckland Public Library: 1880–1980* (Auckland: Auckland City Council, 1980).

Condliffe, J. B., *New Zealand in the Making: A Survey of Economic and Social Development* (London: G. Allen & Unwin Ltd, 1930).

Conley, M. A., *From Jack Tar to Union Jack: Representing Naval Manhood in the British Empire, 1870–1918* (Manchester: Manchester University Press, 2017).

Coutts, B. and Fitness, N., *Protest in New Zealand* (Auckland: Pearson, 2013).

Crawford, J. C., *Recollections of a Travel in New Zealand and Australia* (Edinburgh: Ballantyne Press, 1880).

Cresswell, J., *MOTAT: Museum of Transport and Technology of New Zealand* (Auckland: Paul Hamlyn, 1976).

Crosby, R. D., *The Musket Wars: A History of Inter-iwi Conflict 1806–45* (Auckland: Reed, 1999).

Cross, I., *Such Absolute Beginners: A Memoir* (Auckland: David Ling, 2007).

Cruise, R., *A Journal of Ten Months' Residence in New Zealand* (London: Longman, 1824).

Cryer, M., *The Godzone Dictionary of Favourite New Zealand Words and Phrases* (Christchurch: Exisle Publishing, 2010).

Cumberland, K. B., *Auckland in Ferment: The Present and Future Brew* (Auckland: New Zealand Geographical Society, 1971).

Cyclopedia Company Limited, *The Cyclopedia of New Zealand* (Christchurch: Cyclopedia Company Limited, 1902).

Daley, C., *Leisure & Pleasure: Reshaping & Revealing the New Zealand Body 1900–1960* (Auckland: Auckland University Press, 2003).

Davidson, A. K. and Lineham, P., *Transplanted Christianity: Documents Illustrating Aspects of New Zealand Church History*, 4th edn (Palmerston North: Department of History, 1997).

Davidson, A., *A Home of One's Own: Housing Policy in Sweden and New Zealand from the 1840s to the 1990s* (Stockholm: Almqvist & Wiksell International, 1994).

Davies, G., *Religion in Postwar Britain* (Oxford: Blackwell, 1994).

Dheensaw, C., *The Commonwealth Games: The First 60 Years 1930–1990* (Victoria: Orca Book Publishers, 1994).

Drury, A., *Islam in New Zealand: The First Mosque* (Auckland: Abdullah Drury, 2006).

Dumont D'Urville, J. S. C., *New Zealand 1826–1827 from the French of Dumont d'Urville. An English Translation of the Voyage de L'Astrolabe in New Zealand Waters*, O. Wright, trans. (Wellington: Wingfield Press, 1950).

Dunsford, D., *Mt Albert Then and Now* (Auckland: Mt Albert Historical Society, 2016).

Eastlake, C., *A History of the Gothic Revival* (London: Longmans, 1872).

Edwards, J., *Riot, 1932: An Eyewitness Account of Social Upheaval in New Zealand in 1932* (Christchurch: Whitcombe & Tombs, 1974).

Elder, J. R., *The History of the Presbyterian Church in New Zealand, 1840–1940* (Christchurch: Presbyterian Bookroom, 1940).

Else, A., ed., *Women Together: A History of Women's Organisations in New Zealand: Ngā rōpū wāhine o te motu* (Wellington: Historical Branch, Department of Internal Affairs, 1993).

Everingham, S., *Wild Ride: The Rise & Fall of Cobb & Co.* (Camberwell: Penguin, 2007).

Fairburn, M., "Interpreting 1913: What are the Important Questions?," in *Revolution: The 1913 Great Strike in New Zealand*, Nolan, M., ed. (Christchurch: Canterbury University Press, 2005).

Feinberg, S., *What Makes Shopping Centers Tick* (New York: Fairchild Publications, 1960).

Fenton, F. D., *Observations on the State of the Aboriginal Inhabitants of New Zealand* (Auckland: W. C. Wilson, 1859).

Ferguson, G., *Building the New Zealand Dream* (Palmerston North: Dunmore Press, 1994).

Ferrall, C. and Ellis, R., *The Trials of Eric Mareo* (Wellington: Victoria University Press, 2002).

Firth, C., *State Housing in New Zealand* (Wellington: Ministry of Works, 1949).

Fitton, E., *New Zealand: Its Present Condition, Prospects and Resources* (London: Edward Stanford, 1856).

Frame, J., *The Carpathians* (London: Pandora, 1989).

Fraser, M., *Report on the Results of a Census of the Dominion of New Zealand, Taken for the Night of 2nd April 1911* (Wellington: Government Printer, 1913).

Fraser, M., *The New Zealand Official Year-Book, 1920* (Wellington: Government Printer, 1920).

Fresno-Calleja, P., "Trans/locating Pacific Identities," in *Postcolonial Translocations: Cultural Representation and Critical Spatial Thinking*, Munkelt, M. et al., eds (Amsterdam: Ropoti, 2013).

Gatley, J. and McKay, B., "Beyond Futuna: John Scott, Modern Architecture and Māori in Aotearoa New Zealand," in Grant, E., Greenop, K., Refiti, A. L. and Glenn, D. J., eds, *The Handbook of Contemporary Indigenous Architecture* (Singapore: Springer, 2018).

Gatley, J., "Going Up Rather than Out," in *At Home in New Zealand: History, Houses, People*, Brookes, B., ed. (Wellington: Bridget Williams Books, 2000).

Gatley, J., *Long Live the Modern: New Zealand's New Architecture, 1904–1984* (Auckland: Auckland University Press, 2008).

Gearing, N., *Emerging Tribe: Gay Culture in New Zealand in the 1990s* (Auckland: Penguin, 1997).

Geary, C., *Smith and Caughey's* (Auckland: Smith and Caughey's, 2005).

Gee, S. et al., "Producing and Consuming Masculinity: New Zealand's (Speight's) 'Southern Man'," in *Sport, Beer, and Gender: Promotional Culture and Contemporary Social Life*, Wenner, L. A. and Jackson, S. J. eds (New York: Peter Lang, 2009).

Gopnik, A., "Foreword," in Spang, R. L., *The Invention of the Restaurant: Paris and Modern Gastronomic Culture* (Cambridge, MA: Harvard University Press, 2000).

Gorst, J. E., *New Zealand Revisited* (London: Sir Isaac Pitman and Sons, 1908).

Gorst, J. E., *The Maori King* (London: Macmillan and Co., 1864).

Green, N., *By the Waters of Babylon: The Art of A. Lois White* (Auckland: David Bateman, 1993).

Greig, B. D. A., *Tararua Story: Published in Commemoration of the Silver Jubilee of the Tararua Tramping Club, 1919–1944* (Wellington: Tararua Tramping Club Incorporated, 1946).

Gustafson, B., *From the Cradle to the Grave: A Biography of Michael Joseph Savage* (Auckland: Reed Methuen, 1986).

Hall, P. and Ward, C., *Sociable Cities: The 21st Century: The Reinvention of the Garden City* (Oxford: Routledge, 2014).

Hamer, D., *New Towns in the New World: Images and Perceptions of the Nineteenth-Century Urban Frontier* (New York: Columbia University Press, 1990).

Hamill, I., *The Strategic Illusion: The Singapore Strategy and the Defence of Australia and New Zealand, 1919–1942* (Singapore: Singapore University Press, 1981).

Harper, D., *Food Medicine* 1 (Bloomington: Balboa Press, 2020).

Harris, A., *Hīkoi: Forty Years of Māori Protest* (Wellington: Huia Publishers, 2004).

Hawke, G. R., *The Making of New Zealand: An Economic History* (Cambridge: Cambridge University Press, 1985).

Hawke, S. ed., *Takaparawhau: The People's Story. 1998 Bastion Point 20-Year Commemoration Book* (Auckland: Moko Productions, 1998).

Haworth, D. and Miller, D., *Freda Stark: Her Extraordinary Life* (Auckland: HarperCollins, 2000).

Hayward, B. W. and Diamond, J. T., *Kauri Dam Sites in the Waitakere Ranges* (Auckland: Auckland University Field Club, 1975).

Hayward, B. W. and Diamond, J. T., *Waitakere Kauri: A Pictorial History of the Kauri Timber Industry in the Waitakere Ranges, West Auckland* (Auckland: Lodestar Press, 1980).

Hayward, B. W., Murdoch, G. and Maitland, G., *Volcanoes in Auckland: The Essential Guide* (Auckland: Auckland University Press, 2011).

Hazelgrove, J., *Spiritualism and British Society Between the Wars* (Manchester: Manchester University Press, 2000).

Henry, A., *Old Colonists' Museum Ephemera Collection* (Auckland: Auckland Museum, 2014).

Hitz, A. E., *San Francisco's Ferry Building* (Charleston: Arcadia Publishing, 2017).

Hodgson, T., *Proud Possessions: Architectural Style and the Old New Zealand House* (Wellington: Bookcase, 2003).

Hughes, R., *The Spectacle of Skill* (New York: Alfred A. Knopf, 2015).

Hunter, I., *Farmers: Your Store for 100 Years* (Auckland: HarperCollins, 2009).

Hursthouse, C., *New Zealand, Or, Zealandia, the Britain of the South*, Vol. I (London: Edward Stanford, 1857).

Hutching, M., *Long Journey for Sevenpence: An Oral History of Assisted Immigration to New Zealand from the United Kingdom, 1947–1975* (Wellington: Victoria University Press, 1999).

Hyde, R., *Journalese* (Auckland: National Printing Company, 1934).

Ihimaera, W., *Out There: Portraits of the Hero Parade* (Auckland: Savidan Productions Ltd, 2000).

Institution of Professional Engineers New Zealand, *Engineering to 1990* (Wellington: Engineering Publications Ltd, 1990).

Jackson, H. R., *Churches and People in Australia and New Zealand, 1860–1930* (Wellington: Allen & Unwin, 1987).

Jameson, R. G., *New Zealand, South Australia, and New South Wales* (London: Smith, Elder & Co., 1842).

Jelicich, S. and Trlin, A., "Croatian," in *Book & Print in New Zealand: A Guide to Print Culture in Aotearoa*, Griffith, P., Maslin, K. and Harvey, R., eds (Wellington: Victoria University Press, 1997).

Jenkins, D. L., *At Home: A Century of New Zealand Design* (Auckland: Godwit, 2006).

Jenkins, D. L., *New Dreamland: Writing New Zealand's Architecture* (Auckland: Godwit, 2005).

Johnson, D., *The Auckland Ferry Building* (Auckland: Auckland Maritime Museum, 1988).

Johnston, L., "Borderline Bodies," in *Subjectivities, Knowledges and Feminist Geographies: The Subjects and Ethics of Social Research*, Bondi, L., Avis, H., Bankey, R., Einagel, V., Bingley, A. and Davidson, J., eds (Lanham: Rowman & Littlefield, 2002).

Keith, H., *New Zealand Yesterdays: A Look at Our Recent Past* (Sydney: Readers Digest Services, 1984).

King, M., *New Zealanders at War* (Auckland: Penguin Books, 2003).

La Roche, A., *An Introduction to the Howick Historical Village* (Auckland: Howick and Districts Historical Society, 1997).

Labrum, B., *Real Modern: Everyday New Zealand in the 1950s and 1960s* (Wellington: Te Papa Press, 2015).

Lange, B., *The Stock Market Crash of 1929: The End of Prosperity* (New York: Chelsea House, 2007).

Lange, D., *My Life* (Auckland: Penguin Books, 2005).

Lange, R., *May the People Live: A History of Maori Health Development 1900–1920* (Auckland: Auckland University Press, 1999).

Lange, S. M., *A Rising Tide: Evangelical Christianity in New Zealand, 1939–1965* (Dunedin: Otago University Press, 2013).

Laurenson, H., *Going Up, Going Down: The Rise and Fall of the Department Store* (Auckland: Auckland University Press, 2005).

Law, G. *Auckland, August 1908: A Stop on the Great White Fleet World Cruise* (Auckland: Maruiwi Press, 2008).

Lay, G. and Ross, J., *Golden Weather: North Shore Writers Past and Present* (Auckland: Cape Catley, 2004).

Legget, R., "From Sugar as Industry to Sugar as Heritage: Changing Perceptions of the Chelsea Sugar Works," in *Sugar Heritage and Tourism in Transition*, L. Jolliffe, ed. (Bristol: Channel View Publications, 2012).

Leigh, J., *A Place on the Edge: The Story of St Matthew-in-the-City* (Auckland: Random House, 2005).

Levine, S., *The New Zealand Jewish Community* (Maryland: Lexington Books, 1999).

Leydon, R., "Utopias of the Tropics: The Exotic Music of Les Baxter and Yma Sumac," in *Widening the Horizon: Exoticism in Post-War Popular Music*, Hayward, P., ed. (New Barnet: John Libbey Publishing, 1999).

Lindsay, G., *Thousand-Eyed Eel* (Christchurch: Hawk Press, 1976).

Lineham, P., *Agency of Hope: The Story of the Auckland City Mission, 1920–2020* (Auckland: Massey University Press, 2020).

Lineham, P., *Ventures of Faith and Community: The Development of Churches on the North Shore, Auckland* (Auckland: The Wesley Historical Society and the Anglican Historical Society, 2014).

Logan, M., *Nordy: Arnold Nordmeyer, A Political Biography* (Wellington: Steele Roberts, 2008).

Lomax, M., *The Experiences of an Asylum Doctor* (London: George Allen & Unwin, 1921).

Lush, V., *The Auckland Journals of Vicesimus Lush, 1850–1863*, A. Drummond, ed. (Christchurch: Pegasus Press, 1971).

Macdonald, C., *Strong, Beautiful and Modern: National Fitness in Britain, New Zealand, Australia and Canada, 1935–1960* (Vancouver: University of British Columbia, 2013).

Macdonald, C., *The Vote, the Pill and the Demon Drink: A History of Feminist Writing in New Zealand, 1869–1993*, Charlotte Macdonald, ed. (Wellington: Bridget Williams Books, 1993).

Macdonald, F. and Kerr, R., eds, *West: The History of Waitakere* (Auckland: Random House, 2009).

Mackley-Crump, J., *The Pacific Festivals of Aotearoa New Zealand: Negotiating Place and Identity in a New Homeland* (Honolulu: University of Hawai'i Press, 2015).

Maclean, F. S., *Challenge for Health: A History of Public Health in New Zealand* (Wellington: Government Printer, 1964).

Manning, A. E., *The Bodgie: A Study in Psychological Abnormality* (Wellington: Reed, 1958).

Mason, B., *The End of the Golden Weather: A Voyage into a New Zealand Childhood* (Wellington: Victoria University Press, 1998).

McCan, D., *Whatiwhatihoe: The Waikato Raupatu Claim* (Wellington: Huia Publishers, 2001).

McCarthy, C., *Exhibiting Māori: A History of Colonial Cultures of Display* (Oxford and New York: Berg, 2007).

McCarthy, T. P., *Nuclear Power Generation in New Zealand: Report of the Royal Commission of Inquiry* (Wellington: Government Printer, 1978).

McIntyre, W., *The Significance of the Commonwealth, 1965–90* (London: Springer, 1991).

McLean, G., *Fires and Firefighting* (Wellington: Grantham House, 1992).

McNaughton, T., ed., *Countless Signs: The New Zealand Landscape in Literature* (Auckland: Reed Methuen, 1986).

Metge, J., *A New Maori Migration: Rural and Urban Relations in Northern New Zealand* (Melbourne: Melbourne University Press, 1964).

Mitchell, J., "Has 'foreign' food internationalized New Zealand's cuisine?," in *Culinary Arts and Sciences VII: Global, National and Local Perspectives*, Hartwell, H. H., Lugosi, P. and Edwards, J. S. A., eds (Bournemouth: International Centre for Tourism and Hospitality Research, 2011).

Mogford, J. M., *Onehunga: A Brief History* (Onehunga: Onehunga Borough Council, 1977).

Montgomerie, D., *The Women's War: New Zealand Women 1939–45* (Auckland: Auckland University Press, 2001).

Moon, P., *Hobson: Governor of New Zealand, 1840–1842* (Auckland: David Ling Publishing, 1998).

Moon, P., *New Zealand in the Twentieth Century: The Nation, The People* (Auckland: HarperCollins, 2011).

Moon, P., *The Struggle for Tamaki Makaurau: The Maori Occupation of Auckland to 1820* (Auckland: David Ling Publishing, 2007).

Morgan, W., *The Journal of William Morgan. Pioneer Settler and Maori War Correspondent*, N. Morris, ed. (Auckland: Libraries Department, 1963).

MOTAT, *MOTAT: Moving History* (Auckland: MOTAT, 2006).

Mt Roskill Borough Council, *Roskill: An Illustrated History of New Zealand's Largest Borough* (Auckland: Mt Roskill Borough Council, 1984).

Mulgan, J., *Man Alone* (London: 1939; Hamilton: Paul's Book Arcade, 1960).

Mulgan, J., *Report on Experience* (London: 1947; Barnsley: Frontline Books, 2010).

Murray, R., *Nuclear Energy: An Introduction to the Concepts, Systems, and Applications of Nuclear Processes* (Burlington, MA: Elsevier, 2009).

New Zealand as a Tourist and Health Resort. A Handbook to the Hot Lake District, the West Coast Road, the Southern Lakes, Mt. Cook, Sounds, Etc. (Auckland: Thomas Cook & Son, 1902).

New Zealand: A Handbook for Emigrants (London: F. Algar, 1860).

Niall, T., *The Trekka Dynasty* (Auckland: Iconic Publishing, 2004).

Nicholls, R., "Elite Society in Victorian and Edwardian Wellington," in *The Making of Wellington 1800–1914*, Hamer, D. and Nicholls, R., eds (Wellington: Victoria University Press, 1990).

Nolan, M., "1913 in Retrospect: A Laboratory or a Battleground of Democracy?," in *Revolution: The 1913 Great Strike in New Zealand*, Nolan, M., ed. (Christchurch: Canterbury University Press, 2005).

Oakes, L., *Inside Centrepoint: The Story of a New Zealand Community* (Auckland: Benton Ross, 1986).

Oliver, W. H., *Claims to the Waitangi Tribunal* (Wellington: Department of Justice, 1991).

Orwin, J., *Kauri: Witness to a Nation's History* (Auckland: New Holland Publishers, 2004).

Parr, A., *Home: Civilian New Zealanders Remember the Second World War* (Auckland: Penguin Books, 2010).

Parsons, T., *Essays in Sociological Theory* (New York: The Free Press, 1954).

Petersen, A., *New Zealanders at Home: A Cultural History of Domestic Interiors 1814–1914* (Dunedin: University of Otago Press, 2001).

Phillips, J. and Hearn, T., *Settlers: New Zealand Immigrants from England, Ireland and Scotland 1800–1945* (Auckland: Auckland University Press, 2008).

Platts, U., *The Lively Capital: Auckland 1840–1865* (Christchurch: Avon Fine Prints, 1971).

Pollock, N. J., "Rugby, Racing and Beer in New Zealand: Colonising a Consumer Culture," in *Liquid Bread: Beer and Brewing in Cross-Cultural Perspective*, Schiefenhövel, W. and Macbeth, H., eds (Oxford, Berghahn Books, 2011).

Pomare, M. and Cowan, J., *Legends of the Maori*, vol. 1 (Wellington: Whitcombe & Tombs, 1930).

Powell, A. W. B., Brooker, S. G., Troup, C. O. and Turbott, E. G., *The Centennial History of the Auckland Institute and Museum* (Auckland: Council of the Auckland Institute and Museum, 1967).

Priestley, J. B., *A Visit to New Zealand* (London: Heinemann, 1974).

Pugsley, C., *Gallipoli: The New Zealand Story* (Auckland: Raupo, 2008).

Pule, J., *The Shark that Ate the Sun* (Auckland: Penguin, 1992).

Registrar-General's Office, *Results of a census of the Colony of New Zealand taken for the night of the 29th April, 1906* (Wellington: Government Printer, 1907).

Reidy, J., *Not Just Passing Through: The Making of Mt Roskill* (Auckland: Auckland City Council, 2007).

Rice, G., *Black November: The 1918 Influenza Epidemic in New Zealand* (Wellington: Department of Internal Affairs, 1988).

Richards, T., *Dancing on Our Bones: New Zealand, South Africa, Rugby and Racism* (Wellington: Bridget Williams Books, 1999).

Ridgway, A. and Sons, *Voices from Auckland. New Zealand* (London: Alex F. Ridgway & Sons, 1860).

Robinson, S., *False Flags: Disguised German Raiders of World War II* (Wollombi: Exisle Publishing, 2016).

Rutherford, J., ed., *The Founding of New Zealand: The Journals of Felton Mathew* (Dunedin: A. H. & A. W. Reed, 1940).

Ryan, K., *Justice Without Fear or Favour* (Auckland: Hodder, Moa, Beckett, 1997).

Ryburn, W. M., *The Story of St David's Presbyterian Church, Auckland. 1864–1964* (Auckland: Len Bolton & Co., 1964).

Salmond, J., *Old New Zealand Houses 1800–1940s* (Auckland: Reed Methuen, 1986).

Schama, S., *Landscape and Memory* (New York: Vintage, 1995).

Schrader, B., *We Call it Home: A History of State Housing in New Zealand* (Auckland: Reed Publishing, 2005).

Scott, D., *151 Days: History of the Great Waterfront Lockout and Supporting Strikes* (Auckland: New Zealand Waterside Workers' Union, 1952).

Scott, D., *Fire on the Clay: The Pakeha Comes to West Auckland* (Auckland: Southern Cross Books, 1979).

Shaw, L., "A Woman's Place," in Brookes, B., ed., *At Home in New Zealand: History, Houses, People* (Wellington: Bridget Williams Books, 2000).

Sherrin, R. A. A. and Wallace, J. H., *Early History of New Zealand: From Earliest Times to 1840* (Auckland: H. Brett, 1890).

Shum, L. G., "Remembering Chinatown: Haining Street in Wellington," in M. Ip, ed, *Unfolding History, Evolving Identity: The Chinese in New Zealand* (Auckland: Auckland University Press, 2003).

Simon, D., "Dancing the Kolo Under the Long White Cloud," in *Moving Oceans: Celebrating Dance in the South Pacific*, Buck, R. and Rowe, N., eds (London: Routledge, 2017).

Simpson, T., *The Sugarbag Years: An Oral History of the 1930s Depression in New Zealand* (Wellington: Alister Taylor, 1974).

Sinclair, K., *Walter Nash* (Auckland: Auckland University Press, 1976).

Smith, A. F., *Eating History: 30 Turning Points in the Making of American Cuisine* (New York: Columbia University Press, 2009).

Smith, H., *E Tū Ake: Māori Standing Strong* (Wellington: Te Papa Press, 2011).

Smith, R. W., *Where's The Gold? My Story* (Auckland: R. M. & J. A. Jensen Ltd, 1994).

Smith, S. P., *Maori Wars of the Nineteenth Century* (Christchurch: Whitcombe & Tombs Limited, 1910).

Smythe, M., *New Zealand by Design: A History of New Zealand Product Design* (Auckland: Godwit, 2011).

Stacpoole, J., "James Tannock Mackelvie and his Trust," in Bogle, A. and Muir, B., eds, *The Mackelvie Collection: A Centenary Exhibition, 1885-1985* (Auckland: Auckland City Art Gallery, 1985).

Stevens, G. and Bartholomew, D. H., *Stevens and Bartholomew's New Zealand Directory for 1866-67* (Melbourne: Ferguson and Moore, 1866).

Stewart, D., *The New Zealand Villa: Past and Present* (Auckland: Penguin Books, 1992).

Stone, R. C. J., *From Tamaki-Makau-Rau to Auckland: A History of Auckland* (Auckland: Auckland University Press, 2001).

Stone, R. C. J., *The Father and His Gift: John Logan Campbell's Later Years* (Auckland: Auckland University Press, 1987).

Stringer, T., *The Art of A. Lois White* (Auckland: The Wallace Arts Trust, 2017).

Summerson, J., *The Architecture of the Eighteenth Century* (London: Thames & Hudson, 1986).

Swainson, W., *Auckland, The Capital of New Zealand* (London: Smith, Elder & Co., 1853).

Sweetman, R., *Bishop in the Dock: The Sedition Trial of James Liston* (Auckland: Auckland University Press, 1997).

Swenson, A. and Chang, P., *Architectural Education at I.I.T., 1938-1978* (Illinois: Godwit, 1980).

Taylor, N. M., *The Home Front* (Wellington: Historical Publications Branch, 1986).

Taylor, N., *Early Travellers in New Zealand* (Oxford: Clarendon Press, 1959).

Templeton, M., *Standing Upright Here: New Zealand in the Nuclear Age, 1945-1990* (Wellington: New Zealand Institute of International Affairs/Victoria University Press, 2006).

Tennant, M., *Children's Health, the Nation's Wealth: A History of Children's Health Camps* (Wellington: Bridget Williams Books, 1994).

Terry, C., *New Zealand: Its Advantages and Prospects as a British Colony* (London: T. & W. Boone, 1843).

The New Zealand Official Year-Book, 1986-7 (Wellington: Government Printer, 1987).

Thomas, H., *Dance, Modernity, and Culture: Explorations in the Sociology of Dance* (London: Routledge, 1995).

Thompson, K. M., "Once Were Warriors: New Zealand's First Indigenous Blockbuster," in *Movie Blockbusters*, Stringer, J., ed. (London: Routledge, 2013).

Thompson, M. and Clements, A., *Where New Zealand Touches the World — From Farm Paddock to South Pacific Hub: A History of Auckland International Airport* (Auckland: Auckland International Airport, 2003).

Tripp, L. O. H., "War Relief and Patriotic Societies," in *The War Effort in New Zealand*, Drew, H. T. B., ed. (Auckland: Whitcombe & Tombs Ltd, 1923).

Trollope, A., *Australia and New Zealand* (Melbourne: George Robertson Little, 1873).

Tronson, A., *The Story of the British Empire Games* (Auckland: Organising Committee for the 1950 British Empire Games, 1950).

Truttman, L., *Balmoral and Sandringham Heritage Walks* (Auckland: Auckland City Council, 2009).

Truttman, L. J., *Heart of the Whau: The Story of the Centre of Avondale* (Auckland: Avondale-Waterview Historical Society, 2003).

Turton, H. H., *Maori Deeds of Old Private Land Purchases in New Zealand, From the Year 1815 to 1840, with Pre-Emptive and Other Claims* (Wellington: George Didsbury, 1882).

Tyrrell, H. G., *History of Bridge Building* (Chicago: The author, 1911).

Vaile, E. E., *Some Interesting Occurrences in Early Auckland: City and Provinces* (Christchurch: Whitcombe & Tombs, 1955).

Vaile, P. A., *Peeps at Many Lands: New Zealand* (London: A. & C. Black, 1918).

Verran, D., *The North Shore: An Illustrated History* (Auckland: Random House, 2010).

Vogel, J., ed., *The Official Handbook of New Zealand, 1875* (London: Wyman & Sons, 1875).

Von Dadelszen, E. J., *New Zealand Official Yearbook 1900* (Wellington: John MacKay, 1900).

Von Dadelszen, E. J., *Report on the results of a census of the Colony of New Zealand taken for the night of the 31st March 1901* (Wellington: Government Printer, 1902).

Von Dadelszen, E. J., *The New Zealand Official Yearbook, 1897* (Wellington: John Mackay, 1897).

Walker, R., *Ka Whawhai Tonu Matou: Struggle Without End* (Auckland: Penguin Books, 1990).

Wallace, L., "Queer Chattels and Fixtures: Photography and Materiality in the Homes of Frank Sargeson and Patrick White," in *Domestic Imaginaries: Home in Global Literary and Visual Cultures*, Harper, B. and Price, H., eds (Cham: Palgrave Macmillan, 2017).

Wanhalla, A. and Stevens, K., "'I Don't Like Maori Girls Going Out with Yanks': Māori–American Encounters in New Zealand," in *Mothers' Darlings of the South Pacific: The Children of Indigenous Women and U.S. Servicemen, World War II*, Bennett, J. A. and Wanhalla, A., eds (Honolulu: University of Hawai'i Press, 2016).

Waters, S. D., *German Raiders in the Pacific* (Bennington: Merriam Press, 2005).

Webb, L., *Government in New Zealand* (Wellington: Department of Internal Affairs, 1940).

Webb, S. D., *New Zealand Society: Contemporary Perspectives* (Sydney: John Wiley & Sons Australasia Pty, 1973).

Wendt, R., "The Vavalu Germans," in *Explorations and Entanglements: Germans in Pacific Worlds from the Early Modern Period to World War I*, H. Berghoff et al., eds (New York: Berghahn, 2018).

Wheeler, B. and Nash, M., *An Examination of the Sharemarket Crash and its Aftermath in New Zealand* (Wellington: Economic Development Commission, 1989).

Williams, H., *The Early Journals of Henry Williams*, L. M. Rogers, ed. (Christchurch: Pegasus Press, 1961).

Williams, H., *The Life of Henry Williams, Archdeacon of Waimate*, H. Carleton, ed. (Auckland: Upton and Co., 1874).

Williams, M. M., *Panguru and the City: Kāinga Tahi, Kāinga Rua — An Urban Migration History* (Wellington: Bridget Williams Books, 2015).

Williams, P., *A Passion for Justice* (Christchurch: Shoal Bay Press, 1997).

Wood, F. L. W., *New Zealand in the World* (Wellington: Department of Internal Affairs, 1940).

Wood, F. L. W., *Political and External Affairs* (Wellington: Historical Publications Branch, 1958).

World Nuclear Association, *Nuclear Energy Prospects in New Zealand* (London: World Nuclear Association, 2009).

Wright, M., *Guns and Utu: A Short History of the Musket Wars* (Auckland: Penguin, 2011).

Yska, R., *All Shook Up: The Flash Bodgie and the Rise of the New Zealand Teenager in the Fifties* (Auckland: Penguin Books, 1993).

Zablocki, B. D., "Communes, Encounter Groups and the Search for Community," in *In Search for Community: Encounter Groups and Social Change*, Back, K. W., ed. (New York: Routledge, 2019).

Zedner, L., *Women, Crime, and Custody in Victorian England* (Oxford: Clarendon Press, 1991).

Endnotes

Preface

1. P. Moon, "Prosthetic Nostalgia: History and Memory in 'Art Deco Napier'," *JNZS* 32 (June 2021): 60-80.
2. R. Shonle, "The Chicago School of Sociology, 1918-1933," *Urban Life* 11, no. 4 (1983): 415; P. Lipman, "Making the Global City, Making Inequality: The Political Economy and Cultural Politics of Chicago School Policy," *American Educational Research Journal* 39, no. 2 (2002): 379-419; B. J. L. Berry, "The Chicago School in Retrospect and Prospect," *Urban Geography* 22, no. 6 (2001): 559-561.
3. M. Storper and A. J. Scott, "Current Debates in Urban Theory: A Critical Assessment," *Urban Studies* 53, vol. 6 (2016): 1114-1136.
4. Auckland Regional Council, *A Brief History of Auckland's Urban Form* (Auckland: Auckland Regional Council, 2010), 11, 23, 25.
5. E. J. Von Dadelszen, *New Zealand Official Yearbook 1900* (Wellington: John MacKay, 1900), 91-107; I. Pool, S. Baxendine, W. Cochrane and J. Lindop, "New Zealand Regions, 1986-2001: Population Geography," *Population Studies Centre Discussion Papers* 54 (Hamilton: University of Waikato, 2005), 8-13.
6. A. Gilbertson and C. Meares, *Ethnicity and Migration in Auckland. Auckland Council Technical Report, TR2013/012* (Auckland: Auckland Council, 2013), 6.

Before 1900

7. J. M. Lindsay, G. S. Leonard, E. R. Smid and B. W. Hayward, "Age of the Auckland Volcanic Field: a review of existing data," *New Zealand Journal of Geology and Geophysics* 54, no. 4 (2011): 379-401; R. Nichol, "The eruption history of Rangitoto: reappraisal of a small New Zealand myth," *Journal of the Royal Society of New Zealand* 22, no. 3 (1992): 159.
8. C. Molloy, P. Shane and P. Augustinus, "Eruption recurrence rates in a basaltic volcanic field based on tephra layers in maar sediments: implications for hazards in the Auckland volcanic field," *Geological Society of America Bulletin* 121, no. 11-12 (2009): 1666-1677; S. Sherburn, B. J. Scott, J. Olsen and C. Miller, "Monitoring seismic precursors to an eruption from the Auckland Volcanic Field, New Zealand," *New Zealand Journal of Geology and Geophysics* 50, no. 1 (2007): 1-11.
9. V. J. Chapman, "Mangroves in New Zealand," in *Biology and Ecology of Mangroves*, H. J. Teas, ed. (Dordrecht: Springer, 1983), 81-85; M. C. Smale and R. O. Gardner, "Survival of Mount Eden Bush, an urban forest remnant in Auckland, New Zealand," *Pacific Conservation Biology* 5, no. 2 (1999): 83-93.
10. R. M. Newnham, D. J. Lowe, T. Giles and B. V. Alloway, "Vegetation and climate of Auckland, New Zealand, since ca. 32 000 cal. yr ago: support for an extended LGM," *Journal of Quaternary Science: Published for the Quaternary Research Association* 22, no. 5 (2007): 517-534.
11. R. P. Murray-McIntosh, B. J. Scrimshaw, P. J. Hatfield and D. Penny, "Testing migration patterns and estimating founding population size in Polynesia by using human mtDNA sequences," *Proceedings of the National Academy of Sciences* 95, no. 15 (1998): 9047.
12. A feature common to many cultures. As an example, see M. Marker, "Geographies of Indigenous leaders: Landscapes and mindscapes in the Pacific Northwest," *Harvard Educational Review* 85, no. 2 (2015): 229-253.
13. J. S. Le Grice and V. Braun, "Mātauranga Māori and reproduction: Inscribing connections between the natural environment, kin and the body," *AlterNative: An International Journal of Indigenous Peoples* 12, no. 2 (2016): 151-164.
14. G. Murdoch, *A Brief History of Muriwai Regional Park and its Environs* (Auckland: Auckland Regional Council, 1994), 1.
15. P. Moon, *The Struggle for Tamaki Makaurau: The Maori Occupation of Auckland to 1820* (Auckland: David Ling Publishing, 2007), 17.
16. Nichol, 161.
17. M. Pomare and J. Cowan, *Legends of the Maori*, vol. 1 (Wellington: Whitcombe & Tombs, 1930), 119.
18. G. Graham, "Tainui," *JPS* 60, no. 1 (1951): 80-92.
19. M. Paterson, "Statement of Evidence of Dr Malcolm Paterson," ENV-2018-AKL-000078 (Environment Court: Auckland, 2018), 2269-2271.
20. A. Slocombe and D. Veart, *Archaeological Investigation at the Shaw Block (R11/1525), East Tamaki* (Auckland: Department of Conservation, 1989), 1-42; A. Slocombe, *Shaw Block Site Survey. Site R11/1525* (Auckland: New Zealand Historic Places Trust, 1986), 1-38.
21. P. J. Matthews, "Archaeological site survey on Ponui Island, Hauraki Gulf, New Zealand," *Tane* 25 (1979): 23-33; P. R. Moore, "The Tahanga basalt: an important stone resource in North Island prehistory," *Records of the Auckland Institute and Museum* 13 (1976): 77-93.
22. D. R. Simmons, "Economic Change in New Zealand Prehistory," *JPS* 78, no. 1 (1969): 3-34.
23. F. G. Fairfield, "Maungakiekie. One Tree Hill, Auckland. Description of some Ethnological Discoveries," *JPS* 50, no. 2 (1941): 102-3; A. Fox, "Pa of the Auckland Isthmus: an archaeological analysis," *Records of the Auckland Institute and Museum* 14 (1977): 1-24.
24. L. Mackintosh, "Shifting grounds: history, memory and materiality in Auckland landscapes c. 1350-2018," PhD thesis (Auckland: University of Auckland, 2019), 133.
25. G. R. Lewthwaite, "Maungawhau and Maungakiekie: Reinterpreting the Cultural Landscape," *Yearbook of the Association of Pacific Coast Geographers* 45, no. 1 (1983): 35-39.
26. Fox, 12; R. C. J. Stone, *From Tamaki-Makau-Rau to Auckland: A History of Auckland* (Auckland: Auckland University Press, 2001), 36-37.
27. M. Kawharu, *Tamaki Foreshore and Harbour Report: A report prepared for the Orakei Maori Trust Board for the Wai 388 Treaty claim* (2004), 5-7.
28. P. Tuhaere and P. Tuhaere, "An Historical Narrative Concerning the Conquest of Kaipara and Tamaki by Ngati-Whatua. Introductory remarks," *JPS* 32, no. 4 (128) (1923): 229-237.
29. G. Graham, "'Kahu-Mau-Roa and Te Kotuiti.' Two Famous War Canoes of Ngati-Paoa and their History," *JPS* 33, no. 2 (130) (1924): 130-135.
30. P. D'Arcy, "Maori and Muskets from a Pan-Polynesian Perspective," *NZJH* 31, no. 1 (2000): 123.
31. M. Wright, *Guns and Utu: A Short History of the Musket Wars* (Auckland: Penguin, 2011), 1-2.
32. R. Cruise, *A Journal of Ten Months' Residence in New Zealand* (London: Longman, 1824), 215-16.
33. S. P. Smith, *Maori Wars of the Nineteenth Century* (Christchurch: Whitcombe & Tombs Limited, 1910), 184, 187-88.
34. Ibid., 188; A. Ballara, "Settlement Patterns in the Early European Maori Phase of Maori Society," *JPS* 88, no. 2 (1979): 203; S. Yoo, *Background to Case Study: Sylvia Park and the Mt Wellington Area*, Working Document GUS/SP2.2 (Auckland: University of Auckland, 2019), 2-5.
35. Stone, *From Tamaki-Makau-Rau to Auckland*, 106.
36. D. G. Sutton, "Maori Demographic Change, 1769-1840: The Inner Workings of 'A Picturesque but Illogical Simile'," *JPS* 95, no. 3 (1986): 315, 318.
37. J. S. C. Dumont D'Urville, *New Zealand 1826-1827 from the French of Dumont d'Urville. An English Translation of the Voyage de L'Astrolabe in New Zealand Waters*, O. Wright, trans. (Wellington: Wingfield Press, 1950), 152.
38. Smith, *Maori Wars of the Nineteenth Century*, 188.
39. J. Banks, *The Endeavour Journal of Joseph Banks, 1768-1771*, Vol. I, J. C. Beaglehole, ed. (Sydney: Angus and Robertson, 1962), 434-37.
40. H. Williams, *The Early Journals of Henry Williams*, L. M. Rogers, ed. (Christchurch: Pegasus Press, 1961), 43-44.
41. Stone, *From Tamaki-Makau-Rau to Auckland*, 126.
42. W. Fairburn, "Journal," ALHC MJ-0054.
43. R. A. A. Sherrin and J. H. Wallace, *Early History of New Zealand: From Earliest Times to 1840* (Auckland: H. Brett, 1890), 536-37.
44. H. Williams, *The Life of Henry Williams, Archdeacon of Waimate*, H. Carleton, ed. (Auckland: Upton and Co., 1874), 167.
45. Fairburn Purchase, 22 January 1836, in H. H. Turton, *Maori Deeds of Old Private Land Purchases in New Zealand, From the Year 1815 to 1840, with Pre-Emptive and Other Claims* (Wellington: George Didsbury, 1882), 306-7.

46   Ibid., 306-8.
47   Stone, *From Tamaki-Makau-Rau to Auckland*, 159.
48   A. Ward, "Alienation Rights in Traditional Maori Society: A Comment," *JPS* 95, no. 2 (1986): 259-265.
49   J. L. Campbell, *Poenamo: Sketches of the Early Days of New Zealand* (London: Williams and Norgate, 1881), 104-5.
50   Ibid., 105.
51   P. Moon, *Hobson: Governor of New Zealand, 1840-1842* (Auckland: David Ling Publishing, 1998), 192-93.
52   *NZH*, Supplement, 11 January 1896, 1.
53   N. Taylor, *Early Travellers in New Zealand* (Oxford: Clarendon Press, 1959), 114-15.
54   L. L. Pownall, "Metropolitan Auckland 1740-1945: The historical geography of a New Zealand city," *New Zealand Geographer* 6, no. 2 (1950): 110.
55   T. Bunbury, *Reminiscences of a Veteran*, vol. 3 (London: Charles J. Skeet, 1861), 140-41; J. Rutherford, ed., *The Founding of New Zealand: The Journals of Felton Mathew* (Dunedin: A. H. & A. W. Reed, 1940), 22-23.
56   D. Ross, "Captain William Hobson: the man who would be Governor," *Journal of the C. J. La Trobe Society Inc.* 19, no. 2 (2020): 41.
57   *New Zealand Advertiser and Bay of Islands Gazette*, 3 September 1840, 1; J. Johnston, "The British flag first hoisted on the shore of the Waitemata, September 18th, 1840," Watercolour, Hocken Pictorial Collections, Otago University Research Heritage (1840).
58   A. Bell, "Reverberating Historical Privilege of a 'Middling' Sort of Settler Family," *Genealogy* 4, no. 2 (2020): 8.
59   *New Zealand Advertiser and Bay of Islands Gazette*, 10 December 1840, 1.
60   F. Mathew, *Original Plan of Auckland, 1841*, Sir George Grey Special Collections, AL, NZ Map 2664.
61   A. Douglas, "Plan/ditch: Topographic inscription in an early colonial capital," *Interstices* 16 (2015): 57-71.
62   D. Hamer, *New Towns in the New World: Images and Perceptions of the Nineteenth-Century Urban Frontier* (New York: Columbia University Press, 1990), 26, 195.
63   J. Summerson, *The Architecture of the Eighteenth Century* (London: Thames & Hudson, 1986), 163; Douglas, "Plan/ditch: Topographic inscription in an early colonial capital," 57-71; D. Brand, "Auckland, Slowly Disappearing: Looking for the Felton Mathew Plan," *Journal of Urban Design* 1, no. 3 (1996): 265-279.
64   C. Terry, *New Zealand: Its Advantages and Prospects as a British Colony* (London: T. & W. Boone, 1843), 30-32.
65   Anonymous, "Plan of Auckland as it Stood in January, 1842 (traced from the original)," Sir George Grey Special Collections, AL, NZ Map 4601 (1842).
66   U. Platts, *The Lively Capital: Auckland 1840-1865* (Christchurch: Avon Fine Prints, 1971), 43.
67   Douglas, "Plan/ditch: Topographic inscription in an early colonial capital," 51-71.
68   An Old Hand, *Memories of the Past: Auckland from 1847* (Auckland: 1887), 6.
69   Pownall, 113.
70   A. W. D. Best, *The Journal of Ensign Best, 1837-1843*, N. M. Taylor, ed. (Wellington: R. E. Owen, Government Printer, 1966), 332.
71   A. E. Esler, "Changes in the native plant cover of urban Auckland, New Zealand," *New Zealand Journal of Botany* 29, no. 2 (1991): 177-196.
72   C. Hursthouse, *New Zealand, Or, Zealandia, the Britain of the South*, Vol. I (London: Edward Stanford, 1857), 202.
73   J. Stephen, in Rutherford, ed., *The Founding of New Zealand*, 199.
74   R. P. Hargreaves, "The Maori Agriculture of the Auckland Province in the Mid-Nineteenth Century," *JPS* 68, no. 2 (1959): 61-79; R. P. Hargreaves, "Maori Flour Mills of the Auckland Province: 1846-1860," *JPS* 70, no. 2 (1961): 227-232; V. Wood, T. Brooking and P. Perry, "Pastoralism and politics: reinterpreting contests for territory in Auckland Province, New Zealand, 1853-1864," *Journal of Historical Geography* 34, no. 2 (2008): 220-241.
75   W. Swainson, *Auckland, The Capital of New Zealand* (London: Smith, Elder & Co., 1853), 33-34.
76   E. Fitton, *New Zealand: Its Present Condition, Prospects and Resources* (London: Edward Stanford, 1856), 56.
77   V. Lush, *The Auckland Journals of Vicesimus Lush, 1850-1863*, A. Drummond, ed. (Christchurch: Pegasus Press, 1971), 26 (emphasis in original).
78   Lush, 33.
79   *New Zealand: A Handbook for Emigrants* (London: F. Algar, 1860), 6.
80   *New Zealander*, Supplement, 15 August 1857, 1-2.
81   F. D. Fenton, *Observations on the State of the Aboriginal Inhabitants of New Zealand* (Auckland: W. C. Wilson, 1859) iv.
82   Pownall, 115.
83   J. E. Gorst, *The Maori King* (London: Macmillan and Co., 1864), 375.
84   D. McCan, *Whatiwhatihoe: The Waikato Raupatu Claim* (Wellington: Huia Publishers, 2001), 1.
85   S. Hutchinson, "Humanitarian critique and the settler fantasy: the Australian press and settler colonial consciousness during the Waikato War, 1863-1864," *Settler Colonial Studies* 4, no. 1 (2014): 48-63.
86   L. Hoffman, *A Brief History of Auckland's Urban Form* (Auckland: Auckland Council Research and Evaluation Unit 2019), 14.
87   Waitangi Tribunal, *The Loss of the Orakei Block* (Wellington: Waitangi Tribunal, 2013), 1; P. Clark, "Te Mana Whenua O Ngati Whatua O Orakei," *Auckland University Law Review* 9 (2000): 568-69.
88   P. Tapsell, "Marae and tribal identity in urban Aotearoa/New Zealand," *Pacific Studies* 25, no. 1 (2002): 145.
89   J. Bodell, *A Soldier's View of Empire*, K. Sinclair, ed. (London: The Bodley Head, 1982), 131.
90   W. Morgan, *The Journal of William Morgan. Pioneer Settler and Maori War Correspondent*, N. Morris, ed. (Auckland: Libraries Department, 1963), 53.
91   *Daily Southern Cross*, 27 July 1867, 5.
92   *New Zealander*, 28 December 1864, 5.
93   G. Stevens and D. H. Bartholomew, *Stevens and Bartholomew's New Zealand Directory for 1866-67* (Melbourne: Ferguson and Moore, 1866), 279.
94   J. Vogel, ed., *The Official Handbook of New Zealand, 1875* (London: Wyman & Sons, 1875), 258-62.
95   *Press*, 30 January 1872, 2; S. M. Legg, "Views from the Antipodes: the 'forest influence' debate in the Australian and New Zealand press, 1827-1956," *Australian Geographer* 49, no. 1 (2018): 45.
96   *AS*, 2 February 1872, 2.
97   Hursthouse, 205-6.
98   A. Trollope, *Australia and New Zealand* (Melbourne: George Robertson Little, 1873), 631.
99   *Daily Southern Cross*, 9 March 1860, 2.
100 Auckland University College, *Calendar for the Year 1898* (Auckland: The University College, 1898), 14.
101 A. Clayden, *A Popular Handbook to New Zealand: Its Resources and Industries* (London: Wyman and Sons, 1886), 196-97.
102 *Census of New Zealand 1881* (Wellington: Registrar-General's Office, 1881), table xiv.
103 Lush, 27.
104 *New Zealand Tablet*, 12 July 1889, 13.
105 *New Zealand Times*, 17 May 1888, 6.
106 A. Ridgway and Sons, *Voices from Auckland. New Zealand* (London: Alex F. Ridgway & Sons, 1860), 66-67 (emphasis in original).
107 Cyclopedia Company Limited, *The Cyclopedia of New Zealand* (Christchurch: Cyclopedia Company Limited, 1902) 239-40.
108 Ibid., 253-54.
109 E. J. Von Dadelszen, *The New Zealand Official Yearbook, 1897* (Wellington: John Mackay, 1897), 89; J. Barr, *The City of Auckland, New Zealand, 1840-1920, Preceded by a Maori History of the Auckland Isthmus* (Auckland: Whitcombe & Tombs, 1922), 141.
110 J. E. Traue, "The public library explosion in colonial New Zealand," Libraries & the Cultural Record 42, no. 2 (2007): 151-164; D. Verran, "Mechanics' institutes in New Zealand, and their effect on the development of library services," *Library and Information Association of New Zealand Aotearoa Conference* (8 September 2004), 2.
111 Barr, 147-48.
112 A. McKay, "Preserving a legacy: an analysis of the role and function of the Mackelvie Trust Board, 1885-2010," *Records of the Auckland Museum* 53 (2018): 17-26; J. Stacpoole, "James Tannock Mackelvie and his Trust," in A. Bogle & B. Muir, eds, *The Mackelvie Collection: A Centenary Exhibition, 1885-1985* (Auckland: Auckland City Art Gallery, 1985), 7.
113 *Observer*, 24 January 1891, 12.
114 *AS*, 23 June 1897, 2.

15 *AS*, 26 June 1897, 2.
16 F. L. W. Wood, *New Zealand in the World* (Wellington: Department of Internal Affairs, 1940), 56–77.
17 *NZH*, Supplement, 30 December 1899, 1.
18 J. Brück, "Landscapes of desire: parks, colonialism, and identity in Victorian and Edwardian Ireland," *International Journal of Historical Archaeology* 17, no. 1 (2013): 196–223; S. Macready, "A review of urban historical archaeology in Auckland to 1990," *The Australian Journal of Historical Archaeology* 9 (1991): 14, 18; Albert Park, ATL, J. N. Taylor Collection, Ref: 1/2-152852.
19 Heritage New Zealand, "Customhouse (former), Summary," List No. 104.
20 G. Bertram, "The New Zealand Economy, 1900–2000," in *The New Oxford History of New Zealand*, G. Byrnes, ed. (Melbourne: Oxford University Press, 2009), 538–39.
21 P. J. O'Regan, "One Hundred Years Hence," *New Zealand Illustrated Magazine*, 1 August 1900, 65.

2 The 1900s

22 *Press*, 1 January 1900, 6.
23 *AS*, 2 January 1900, 2.
24 Ibid.
25 J. Adam, V. Burgess and D. Ellis, *Rugged Determination: Historical Window on Swanson, 1854–2004* (Auckland: Swanson Residents and Ratepayers Association Incorporated, 2004), 101; *Lyttelton Times*, 14 February 1900, 2; Auckland Council, *Swanson Heritage Survey — Historical Context* (Auckland: Auckland Council, 2016), 20.
26 *NZH*, 2 January 1900, 6.
27 M. Kühn and H. Stöfen, "A reactive flow model of the geothermal reservoir Waiwera, New Zealand," *Hydrogeology Journal* 13, no. 4 (2005): 606; B. R. White and I. Chambefort, "Geothermal development history of the Taupo Volcanic Zone," *Geothermics* 59 (2016): 150; J. C. Crawford, *Recollections of a Travel in New Zealand and Australia* (Edinburgh: Ballantyne Press, 1880), 209.
28 *New Zealand as a Tourist and Health Resort. A Handbook to the Hot Lake District, the West Coast Road, the Southern Lakes, Mt. Cook, Sounds, Etc.* (Auckland: Thomas Cook & Son, 1902), 20.
29 Lamb's old mill, Riverhead, about to be converted into a paper mill, ALHC, AWNS-18990728-7-2; *NZH*, 2 January 1900, 7.
30 *NZH*, 2 January 1900, 7.
31 J. Barr, *The City of Auckland, New Zealand, 1840–1920, Preceded by a Maori History of the Auckland Isthmus* (Auckland: Whitcombe & Tombs, 1922), 182.
32 M. Fairburn, "Social Mobility and Opportunity in Nineteenth-Century New Zealand," *NZJH* 13, no. 1 (1979): 45; C. Toynbee, "Class and Social Structure in Nineteenth-Century New Zealand," *NZJH* 13, no. 1 (1979): 68–69.
33 R. Nicholls, "Elite Society in Victorian and Edwardian Wellington," in *The Making of Wellington 1800–1914*, D. Hamer and R. Nicholls, eds (Wellington: Victoria University Press, 1990), 195, 218.
34 *NZH*, 3 January 1900, 4.
35 S. Kim and M. T. Law, "History, institutions, and cities: A view from the Americas," *Journal of Regional Science* 52, no. 1 (2012): 10–39.
36 J. S. Te Rito, "Whakapapa and whenua: An insider's view," *MAI Review* 1, no. 3 (2007): 1–8.
37 C. Goulding, "Romancing the past: heritage visiting and the nostalgic consumer," *Psychology & Marketing* 18, no. 6 (2001): 565–592; S. Legg, "Memory and nostalgia," *Cultural Geographies* 11, no. 1 (2004): 99–107.
38 *New Zealand as a Tourist and Health Resort. A Handbook*, 16.
39 Cyclopedia Company Limited, *The Cyclopedia of New Zealand* (Christchurch: Cyclopedia Company Limited, 1902), 57.
40 Main Hall of Auckland Museum at Princes Street, showing the small pataka, Te Oha, installed about 1885, AML, C4238.
41 *New Zealand Illustrated Magazine*, 1 August 1900, 813.
42 Statue Hall of Auckland Museum at Princes Street, AML, C56638.
43 Auckland Museum, [Craig's Museum, Princes Street], Unknown photographer, ca. 1880, PH-RES-4181.
44 *Hot Lakes Chronicle*, 9 October 1895, 2.
45 Advertisement and illustration of Maori carvings from Eric Craig Curiosity Dealer, Auckland. British Museum, ref. 2016,2124.5.

146 E. J. Von Dadelszen, *The New Zealand Official Yearbook, 1900* (Wellington: John Mackay, 1900), 48.
147 *Cyclopedia of New Zealand*, 214.
148 Von Dadelszen (1900), 152.
149 M. Tennant, "Fun and fundraising: the selling of charity in New Zealand's past," *Social History* 38, no. 1 (2013): 49–53.
150 *AS*, 5 May 1900, 3.
151 *AS*, 20 July 1900, 2.
152 Cited in P. Hart, "Alfred Henry Whitehouse; a bootmaker who became a pioneer of New Zealand films," *Te Aroha Mining District Working Papers* 160 (Hamilton: Historical Research Unit, Waikato University, 2016), 20.
153 C. Herzog, "The archaeology of cinema architecture: The origins of the movie theatre," *Quarterly Review of Film & Video* 9, no. 1 (1984): 11–32.
154 C. Eastlake, *A History of the Gothic Revival* (London: Longmans, 1872), 2.
155 T. Hodgson, *Proud Possessions: Architectural Style and the Old New Zealand House* (Wellington: Bookcase, 2003), 10.
156 B. Webb, in T. McNaughton, ed., *Countless Signs: The New Zealand Landscape in Literature* (Auckland: Reed Methuen, 1986), 291–92.
157 D. Stewart, *The New Zealand Villa: Past and Present* (Auckland: Penguin Books, 1992), 7.
158 H. Wright, "Rethinking Facadism: The Contemporary New Zealand Villa," MArch thesis (Wellington: Victoria University of Wellington, 2011), 21.
159 B. Bryson, *At Home* (New York: Random House, 2010), 135; A. Petersen, *New Zealanders at Home: A Cultural History of Domestic Interiors 1814–1914* (Dunedin: University of Otago Press, 2001), 103.
160 T. R. Metcalf, "Architecture and the representation of empire: India, 1860–1910," *Representations* 6 (1984): 37–38; A. King, "The Bungalow," *Architectural Association Quarterly* V (1973): 6.
161 Wright, 21; D. L. Jenkins, *New Dreamland: Writing New Zealand's Architecture* (Auckland: Godwit, 2005), 51.
162 *NZH*, 1 September 1900, 1.
163 *NZH*, 9 February 1906, 5.
164 *NZH*, 13 October 1909, 8.
165 J. Salmond, *Old New Zealand Houses 1800–1940s* (Auckland: Reed Methuen, 1986), 90.
166 B. W. Hayward and J. T. Diamond, *Waitakere Kauri: A Pictorial History of the Kauri Timber Industry in the Waitakere Ranges, West Auckland* (Auckland: Lodestar Press, 1980); B. W. Hayward and J. T. Diamond, *Kauri Dam Sites in the Waitakere Ranges* (Auckland: Auckland University Field Club, 1975), 105–8; D. Wilton and L. Z. Soltani, "Tram or dam?: A comparison of kauri logging transportation methods in the Kauaeranga valley, New Zealand, 1871–1928," *Australasian Historical Archaeology* 31 (2013): 78–87.
167 J. Orwin, *Kauri: Witness to a Nation's History* (Auckland: New Holland Publishers, 2004), 110, 152; P. Star, "Great Barrier Island and the Kauri Timber Industry," *Australian Forest History Society Newsletter* 59 (May 2012): 1.
168 R. P. Hargreaves, T. J. Hearn and S. Little, "The state and housing in New Zealand to 1919," *New Zealand Geographer* 41, no. 2 (1985): 49. The exceptions were *The Workers' Dwellings Act 1905* and *The Government Advances to Workers Act 1906*.
169 *NZH*, 9 September 1903, 6.
170 J. M. Mason, "Report of the Chief Health Officer, Department of Public Health," *AJHR*, Session I, H-31 (Wellington: House of Representatives, 1903), 22–23.
171 Ibid.
172 Ibid., 2–3.
173 s. 352, *The Municipal Corporations Act 1900*.
174 E. Tregear, "Report of the Department of Labour," *AJHR*, Session II, H-11 (Wellington: House of Representatives, 1906), vii.
175 *The Government Advances to Workers Act 1906*.
176 Hargreaves, Hearn and Little, "The state and housing in New Zealand to 1919," 51–52.
177 *AS*, 28 November 1900, 4.
178 G. McLean, *Fires and Firefighting* (Wellington: Grantham House, 1992), 53.
179 *Colonist*, 1 June 1901, 2.
180 R. Carlyon, "Grand Hotel Fire 1901, A Turning Point," *Despatches* (Auckland, 2019), n.p.
181 *New Zealand Tablet*, 13 June 1901, 6.
182 *NZH*, 15 May 1902, 6; S. Shrimski, *NZPD* 116 (4 July 1901), 103.

183 *NZH*, 11 June 1901, 5.
184 *AS*, 11 June 1901, 2.
185 J. Phillips, "Māori and Royal Visits, 1869–2015: From Rotorua to Waitangi," *Royal Studies Journal* 5, no. 1 (2018): 41–42.
186 D. Colquhoun, "Royal Scenes from the Empire City: The Prince of Wales in Wellington, 7–9 May 1920," *Turnbull Library Record* 41 (2009): 30; C. McDonald, "A Nation Wins its Spurs: Military Performances and National Identity in New Zealand's Royal Visits, 1901–1927," *Royal Studies Journal* 5, no. 1 (2018): 82.
187 E. Salmon, "The Royal Imperial Tour," *Fortnightly Review* 70, no. 419 (1901): 780.
188 J. Bassett, "A Thousand Miles of Loyalty," *NZJH* 21, no. 1 (1987): 129.
189 A. Pearse, "Fifty Thousand Miles Under the Union Jack," *The Leisure Hour: An Illustrated Magazine for Home Reading* (1902): 275–293.
190 *Northern Advocate*, 15 June 1901, 5.
191 J. Bassett, 138.
192 Earl of Ranfurly, "Governor's Speech," *NZPD* 116 (2 July 1901), 8.
193 W. Massey, *NZPD* 116 (5 July 1901), 152.
194 Barr, 184.
195 W. P. Reeves, *NZPD* 127 (3 November 1903), 276.
196 R. C. J. Stone, *The Father and His Gift: John Logan Campbell's Later Years* (Auckland: Auckland University Press, 1987), 244.
197 *AS*, 26 August 1903, 2.
198 L. Bell, "Auckland's Centrepiece: Unsettled Identities, Unstable Monuments," in *Settler Colonialism: History and Memory in Australia, Canada, Aotearoa New Zealand and South Africa*, A. Coombes, ed. (Manchester: Manchester University Press, 2006), 117.
199 J. N. Coleman, *A Memoir of the Rev. Richard Davis* (London: James Nisbet and Co., 1865), vii.
200 J. M. McEwen, "The Development of Maori Culture Since the Advent of the Pakeha," *JPS* 56, no. 2 (1947): 173.
201 E. González-Tennant, "Using geodatabases to generate 'living documents' for archaeology: A case study from the Otago Goldfields, New Zealand," *Historical Archaeology* 43, no. 3 (2009): 20–37.
202 E. J. Von Dadelszen, *Report on the results of a census of the Colony of New Zealand taken for the night of the 31st March, 1901* (Wellington: Government Printer, 1902), 40.
203 Ibid., 164.
204 G. Hannis, "From Yellow Peril to Model Minority? A Comparative Analysis of a Newspaper's Depiction of the Chinese in New Zealand at the Start of the 20th and 21st Centuries," *Asia Pacific Media Educator* 1, no. 19 (2009): 87.
205 L. G. Shum, "Remembering Chinatown: Haining Street in Wellington," in M. Ip, ed., *Unfolding History, Evolving Identity: The Chinese in New Zealand* (Auckland: Auckland University Press, 2003), 73–93; *New Zealand Illustrated Magazine*, 1 April 1903, 6.
206 Hannis, 87.
207 *AS*, 28 June 1904, 3.
208 B. Moloughney and J. Stenhouse, "'Drug-besotten, sin-begotten fiends of filth': New Zealanders and the Oriental Other, 1850–1920," *NZJH* 33, no. 1 (1999): 44.
209 *New Zealand Illustrated Magazine*, 1 July 1904, 252.
210 As an example, see *Chinese Immigrants Amendment Act 1907*; P. S. O'Connor, "Keeping New Zealand White, 1908–1920," *NZJH* 2, no. 1 (1968): 44.
211 *Rodney and Otamatea Times, Waitemata and Kaipara Gazette*, 15 October 1904, 2.
212 *AS*, 19 October 1907, 5.
213 K. Gu, "Exploring the fringe belt concept in Auckland: An urban morphological idea and planning practice," *New Zealand Geographer* 66, no. 1 (2010): 50.
214 J. Arbury, "From Urban Sprawl to Compact City — an analysis of urban growth management in Auckland," MA thesis (Auckland: University of Auckland, 2005), 70.
215 Auckland Council, *Albert-Eden Heritage Survey: Historical Context Survey* (Auckland: Auckland Council, 2013), 46.
216 J. McKerrow, "Workmen's Homes in the Vicinity of Auckland," *AJHR*, Session I, C-13 (Wellington: House of Representatives, 1900), 1.
217 F. Dahms, "Urban Passenger Transport and Population Distribution in Auckland: 1860–1961," *New Zealand Geographer* 36, no. 1 (1980): 4.
218 E. W. Alison, *A New Zealander Looks Back* (Auckland: Gordon & Gotch, 1964), 171, in Dahms, 6.
219 *Progress*, 1 February 1909, 143.

220 *Progress*, 1 March 1906, 105.
221 A. Gee and A. Trapeznik, "The Motoring Lobby in New Zealand, 1898–1930," *JNZS* 27 (2018): 131.
222 *Cyclopedia of New Zealand*, 246.
223 *Observer*, 6 April 1901, 2.
224 R. G. Jameson, *New Zealand, South Australia, and New South Wales* (London: Smith, Elder & Co., 1842), 287.
225 *NZH*, 11 November 1903, 5.
226 *AS*, 1 February 1907, 5.
227 *Auckland and Manukau Canal Act 1908*; *NZH*, 22 January 1908, 4.
228 Proposed Waitemata-Manukau canal: reports and plans re Whau and Tamaki routes, Auckland Museum, TC722.6 PRO.
229 E. De Tourret, photograph of Dominion Road, AL 255A-93; H Winkelmann, photograph looking north over the harbour to Devonport, AL 995.1101 W33 (1900–09) [33].
230 Auckland Regional Council, *A Brief History of Auckland's Urban Form* (Auckland: Auckland Regional Council, 2010), 11.
231 *Cyclopedia of New Zealand*, 334; R. C. Sykes, "The market milk industry in New Zealand," MAgrSc thesis (Palmerston North: Massey University, 1952), 7.
232 Interim Return of Sheep in the colony on the 30th April 1902, in *AJHR*, Session I, H-23a (Wellington: House of Representatives, 1902), 1.
233 State Forests Revenue and Expenditure for the Ten Years Ending 31 March 1903, *AJHR*, Session I, C-12a, (Wellington: House of Representatives, 1903), 1.
234 M. Felgate, *His Majesty's Theatre Excavations (R11/1624): Final Archaeological Report, Volume 1* (Auckland: Auckland City Council, 1998), 151.
235 D. Scott, *Fire on the Clay: The Pakeha Comes to West Auckland* (Auckland: Southern Cross Books, 1979), 117–19.
236 R. Clough, S. Macready and M. Plowman, *R. O. Clark's Pottery (1864–1931), Limeburners Bay, Hobsonville: Archaeological Investigation Report on S18 investigation of site* (Auckland: Clough & Associates Ltd, 2008), 20–24.
237 Waitakere City Council, *New Lynn Reserves Management Plan 2004* (Auckland: Waitakere City Council, 2004), 48.
238 N. M. Mason, "Inspiring and creative public places: what are the crucial ingredients when developing a successful arts precinct? a Waitakere City, New Zealand case-study," PhD thesis (Palmerston North: Massey University, 2007), 10.
239 V. Burgess, G. Bishop and G. Cole, *Henderson: Heart of the West* (Auckland: West Auckland Historical Society, 2017), 154.
240 Ibid.; *AS*, 2 December 1902, 2.
241 Burgess, Bishop and Cole, 155.
242 *New Zealand as a Tourist and Health Resort. A Handbook*, 18; S. P. Wanninayake, "Response of a New Zealand tree fern," MPB thesis (Christchurch: University of Canterbury, 2007), 1.
243 *New Zealand as a Tourist and Health Resort. A Handbook*, 19.
244 J. Cowan, "Te Wao-Nui-a-Tane," *New Zealand Illustrated Magazine*, 1 December 1902, 200.
245 Photograph of Cabbage tree Swamp, Sir George Grey Special Collections, 3, Ref: 4-854.
246 Interview with P. C. (January 1980).
247 *NZH*, 7 November 1907, 7.
248 H. Snyders, "Rugby football and the display of New Zealand identity during and beyond the Anglo-Boer war (1899–1907)," *South African Journal of Cultural History* 34, no. 2 (2020): 42–64.
249 *New Zealand Illustrated Magazine*, 1 April 1902, 3.
250 *New Zealand Tablet*, 5 June 1902, 15.
251 *AS*, 6 June 1902, 6.
252 *NZH*, 9 June 1902, 6.
253 *The White Ribbon*, 16 June 1902, 6.
254 J. Greenwood, "The 1908 Visit of the Great White Fleet: Displaying Modern Sydney," *History Australia* 5, no. 3 (2008): 78-9.
255 *NZH*, 10 August 1908, 12.
256 Barr, 189.
257 Registrar-General's Office, *Results of a census of the Colony of New Zealand taken for the night of the 29th April, 1906* (Wellington: Government Printer, 1907), 13.
258 Barr, 189–90.
259 G. P. Taylor, "New Zealand, the Anglo-Japanese Alliance and the 1908 Visit of the American Fleet," *Australian Journal of Politics & History* 15, no. 1 (1969): 59–60; G. Law, *Auckland, August 1908: A Stop on the Great White Fleet World Cruise* (Auckland: Maruiwi Press, 2008), 20–25; G. W. A. Bush, *Decently and in Order: The Centennial History of the Auckland City Council* (Auckland: Collins, 1971), 176.

260 G. A. Wood, "The Former 'Dominion of New Zealand'," *Political Science* 26, no. 1 (1974): 4.
261 J. Wilson, "New Zealand Sovereignty: 1857, 1907, 1947, or 1987?," *Political Science* 60, no. 2 (2008): 45; L. Webb, *Government in New Zealand* (Wellington: Department of Internal Affairs, 1940), 34.
262 *New Zealand Tablet*, 26 September 1907, 23.
263 *Taranaki Herald*, 26 September 1907, 7; *Nelson Evening Mail*, 27 September 1907, 4.
264 *NZH*, 27 May 1899, 3.
265 *AS*, 11 June 1900, 4.
266 *Oamaru Mail*, 7 July 1908, 1.
267 *Wanganui Herald*, 6 July 1907, 5.
268 *NZH*, 3 July 1909, 7; R. L. Weitzel, "Pacifists and Anti-Militarists in New Zealand, 1909-1914," *NZJH* 7, no. 2 (1973): 134.
269 *AS*, 29 January 1901, 2; P. Husbands, "Poverty in Freemans Bay 1886-1913," *NZJH* 28, no. 1 (1994): 3-21.
270 *Cyclopedia of New Zealand*, 509-15; L. Mackintosh, "Shifting grounds: history, memory and materiality in Auckland landscapes c. 1350-2018," PhD thesis (Auckland: University of Auckland, 2019), 124.
271 *Cyclopedia of New Zealand*, 516.
272 *Progress*, 1 September 1909, 386; *Cyclopedia of New Zealand*, 521.
273 *Cyclopedia of New Zealand*, 523.
274 Annual Report on the Police Force of the Colony, 20 June 1905 in *AJHR*, Session I, H-16 (Wellington: House of Representatives, 1905), 6; R. Hyde, *Journalese* (Auckland: National Printing Company, 1934), 202-6.
275 Auckland Regional Council, *A Brief History of Auckland's Urban Form*, 11; *Cyclopedia of New Zealand*, 523.
276 *Cyclopedia of New Zealand*, 524.
277 L. Truttman, *Puketapapa — Mt Roskill Heritage Survey 2013* (Auckland: Matthews and Matthews Architects Ltd, 2014), 15; *New Zealand Illustrated Magazine*, 1 January 1904, 334.
278 *NZH*, 19 August 1901, 6.
279 Truttman, 31.
280 M. Eaves et al., *Onehunga Heritage Survey* (Auckland: Auckland Council, 2013), 4, 20, 30; J. M. Mogford, *Onehunga: A Brief History* (Onehunga: Onehunga Borough Council, 1977), 81-82.
281 L. Williams et al., *Otahuhu Historic Heritage Survey, Overview Report* (Auckland: Matthews and Matthews Architects Ltd, 2014), 15, 43.
282 *NZH*, 15 October 1909, 6.
283 *AS*, 30 September 1908, 5; *AS*, 20 May 1908, 8; *NZH*, 22 May 1907, 8; *NZH*, 6 June 1907, 6; *NZH*, 25 October 1909, 3.
284 F. W. Flanagan, *Map of the North Island of New Zealand*, National Library, MapColl-NZGB-5/27/354/ Acc.55040 (Wellington: Lands and Survey Department, 1906).
285 *Cyclopedia of New Zealand*, 530.
286 *Observer*, 18 May 1907, 2.
287 *Cyclopedia of New Zealand*, 526.
288 J. Legget, "From Sugar as Industry to Sugar as Heritage: Changing Perceptions of the Chelsea Sugar Works," in *Sugar Heritage and Tourism in Transition*, L. Jolliffe, ed. (Bristol: Channel View Publications, 2012), 189.
289 J. J. Hooks and R. E. Stewart, "The geography and ideology of accounting: a case study of domination and accounting in a sugar refinery in Australasia, 1900-1920," *Accounting Historians Journal* 34, no. 2 (2007): 157.
290 *Cyclopedia of New Zealand*, 537.
291 *Progress*, 1 September 1909, 387.
292 The Mon Desir Hotel, Takapuna, postcard, Sir George Grey Special Collections, AL, NZG-19100112-76-1; D. Verran, *The North Shore: An Illustrated History* (Auckland: Random House, 2010), 73, 126.
293 *Cyclopedia of New Zealand*, 539.
294 Ibid., 97.
295 *New Zealand as a Tourist and Health Resort. A Handbook*, 20.
296 M. Kühn and H. Stöfen, "A reactive flow model of the geothermal reservoir Waiwera, New Zealand," *Hydrogeology Journal* 13, no. 4 (2005): 606; B. R. White and I. Chambefort, "Geothermal development history of the Taupo Volcanic Zone," *Geothermics* 59 (2016): 150; Tourist and Health Resorts Report (23 August 1904) by the Minister of Tourist and Health Resorts, Hon. Sir J. G. Ward, KCMG, *AJHR*, Session I, H-02 (Wellington: House of Representatives, 1904), 1-24.
297 *Cyclopedia of New Zealand*, 540.
298 G. Thornton, "Industrial Archaeology in New Zealand," *Industrial Archaeology Review* 10, no. 1 (1987): 23-40.
299 J. E. Gorst, *New Zealand Revisited* (London: Sir Isaac Pitman and Sons, 1908), 321-22.

3 The 1910s

300 J. M. McEwen, "The Development of Maori Culture Since the Advent of the Pakeha," *JPS* 56, no. 2 (1947): 173.
301 M. Fraser, *Report on the Results of a Census of the Dominion of New Zealand, Taken for the Night of 2nd April 1911* (Wellington: Government Printer, 1913), 7, 8, 138-39.
302 Auckland Art Gallery, Accession nos. 1952/16/1; 1929/4/2; 1911/1/2; MNZ, Registration no. 1973-0007-2.
303 R. Lange, *May the People Live: A History of Maori Health Development 1900-1920* (Auckland: Auckland University Press, 1999), 55.
304 W. H. Skinner, "Ancient Maori Canals. Marlborough, N.Z.," *JPS* 21, no. 3 (1912): 105-108; E. Best, "Notes on the art of war, as conducted by the Maori of New Zealand, with accounts of various customs, rites, superstitions, &c., pertaining to war, as practised and believed in by the ancient Maori. Part III," *JPS* 11, no. 3 (1902): 127-162.
305 L. Bell, *The Maori in European Art: European Representations of the Maori from the Time of Captain Cook to the Present Day* (Wellington: Reed, 1980), 70-93; L. Bell, "The Colonial Paintings of Charles Frederick Goldie in the 1990s: The Postcolonial Goldie and the Rewriting of History," *Cultural Studies* 9, no. 1 (1995): 26.
306 C. F. Goldie, "Studio Interior," Auckland Art Gallery, Accession no. 1990/15/1; *New Zealand Illustrated Magazine*, 1 November 1901, 148.
307 T. Rowlandson and A. C. Pugin, "Exhibition Room, Somerset House," Royal Academy of Arts, Object no. 03/6170.
308 C. F. Goldie, news clippings, MNZ, MS 6.
309 J. Clarke, "C.F. Goldie: the old master revisited," *New Zealand Geographic* 38 (April-June 1998).
310 R. Blackley, *Goldie* (Auckland: Auckland Art Gallery, 1997), 15.
311 *AS*, 19 July 1905, 4; *Triad* 16, no. 4, 1 July 1908, 10; *Otago Daily Times*, 24 November 1909, 2; Blackley, 15, 26.
312 *AS*, 29 September 1911, 2.
313 *NZH*, 1 June 1914, 10.
314 J. Cowan, "The Father of Auckland," *New Zealand Railways Magazine* 8, no. 7 (1 November 1933): 17.
315 *NZH*, 26 June 1912, 8.
316 Fraser, *Report on the Results of a Census of the Dominion of New Zealand*, 140.
317 J. L. Campbell, *Poenamo: Sketches of the Early Days of New Zealand* (London: Williams and Norgate, 1881), 316.
318 E. E. Vaile, *Some Interesting Occurrences in Early Auckland: City and Provinces* (Christchurch: Whitcombe & Tombs, 1955), 17.
319 B. Bartley, "Grafton Bridge," in *Evolving Auckland: The City's Engineering Heritage*, J. La Roche, ed. (Christchurch: Wily Publications, 2011), 158-60; *Progress*, 1 May 1908, 239.
320 Institution of Professional Engineers New Zealand, *Engineering to 1990* (Wellington: Engineering Publications Ltd, 1990), 6; H. G. Tyrrell, *History of Bridge Building* (Chicago: The author, 1911), 405.
321 *Progress*, 1 March 1910, 168; J. Gatley, *Long Live the Modern: New Zealand's New Architecture, 1904-1984* (Auckland: Auckland University Press, 2008), 12.
322 *NZH*, 29 April 1910, 6.
323 Institution of Professional Engineers New Zealand, *Engineering to 1990*, 6.
324 *Progress*, 2 January 1911, 497.
325 M. Madanovic, "Concrete Complexities: Reinforced Concrete in the Architecture of Auckland's Town Hall, Chief Post Office and Ferry Building," *Historiographies of Technology and Architecture: Proceedings of the 35th Annual Conference of the Society of Architectural Historians of Australia and New Zealand*, J. Merwood-Salisbury, M. Dudding and C. McDonald, eds (Wellington: SAHANZ, 2018), 329.
326 H. B. Laurenson, "Myths and the City: A Social and Cultural History of Auckland, 1890-1990," PhD thesis (Auckland: University of Auckland, 2010), 57.
327 P. and D. Beatson, *The Arts in Aotearoa New Zealand: Themes and Issues* (Palmerston North: Massey University, 1994), 106.
328 P. A. Vaile, *Peeps at Many Lands: New Zealand* (London: A. & C. Black, 1918), 36.

329 Madanovic, 329.
330 C. R. Gurley and J. S. F. Nicholls, "Earthquake strengthening of old masonry with reference to the Auckland Ferry Building," *Bulletin of the New Zealand Society for Earthquake Engineering* 15, no. 4 (1982): 203–4.
331 D. Johnson, *The Auckland Ferry Building* (Auckland: Auckland Maritime Museum, 1988), 5–6.
332 *NZPD* 195 (11 July 1922), 232.
333 A. E. Hitz, *San Francisco's Ferry Building* (Charleston: Arcadia Publishing, 2017), 18.
334 P. Richardson, "An architecture of empire: The government buildings of John Campbell in New Zealand," PhD thesis (Christchurch: University of Canterbury, 1988), 166.
335 *AS*, 21 November 1912, 9.
336 *Greymouth Evening Star*, 21 November 1912, 3.
337 H. Van der Wusten, "Public authority in European capitals: a map of governance, an album with symbols," *European Review* 12, no. 2 (2004): 143–158.
338 J. Barr, *Municipal and Official Handbook of the City of Auckland* (Auckland: Wilson & Horton, 1922), 17.
339 A. R. Annabell, "A Broadwood Square Pianoforte in the Auckland Institute and Museum," *Records of the Auckland Institute and Museum* 25 (1988): 60.
340 J. Cowan, in W. Colgan, *The Governor's Gift: The Auckland Public Library: 1880–1980* (Auckland: Auckland City Council), 87.
341 *Waiapu Church Gazette*, 1 October 1937, 3; A. Henry, *Old Colonists' Museum Ephemera Collection* (Auckland: Auckland Museum, 2014), n.p.
342 *Observer*, 4 November 1911, 8.
343 C. Bourke, *Blue Smoke: The Lost Dawn of New Zealand Popular Music* (Auckland: Auckland University Press, 2010), 8.
344 A. M. Myers, in *AS*, 7 November 1911, 7.
345 Bourke, *Blue Smoke*, 8.
346 *NZH*, 22 August 1914, 5.
347 Cited in M. Hillyer, "To Dance the Native Dance: Vernacular Modernism in an 'Australian-New Zealand Comedy Romance'," *JNZS* 25 (2017): 46.
348 C. McCarthy, *Exhibiting Māori: A History of Colonial Cultures of Display* (Oxford and New York: Berg, 2007), 2.
349 *Observer*, 22 August 1914, 6.
350 J. Adam, V. Burgess and D. Ellis, *Rugged Determination: Historical Window on Swanson, 1854–2004* (Auckland: Swanson Residents and Ratepayers Association Incorporated, 2004), 67–72, 158.
351 Waitākere Ranges Local Board, *The State of the Waitākere Ranges Heritage Area, 2018* (Auckland: Auckland Council, 2018), 207.
352 Barr, *Municipal and Official Handbook*, 100.
353 Waitākere Ranges Local Board, *The State of the Waitākere Ranges Heritage Area, 2018*, 207–8.
354 *AS*, 24 January 1914, 9.
355 *AS*, 26 January 1914, 4.
356 J. Barr, *The City of Auckland, New Zealand, 1840–1920, Preceded by a Maori History of the Auckland Isthmus* (Auckland: Whitcombe & Tombs, 1922), 211–14.
357 Ibid., 213.
358 View of Wonderland, Auckland Exhibition, Auckland Domain, looking towards the water chute, NLNZ, Ref: 1/2-001132-G; View of the Palace of Industries and towers, Auckland Exhibition, taken at night to show the illuminations, NLNZ, Ref: 1/2-001288-G; Auckland Industrial, Agricultural and Mining Exhibition (1913–14): Exhibition axemen's carnival. World's & New Zealand 1914 championships, NLNZ, Ref: Eph-A-EXHIBITION-1914-01-cover; Showing the main exhibition buildings of the 1914 Auckland Exhibition in the Auckland Domain, ALHC, 4-154.
359 *NZH*, 20 April 1914, 9.
360 *Evening Post*, 20 April 1914, 3.
361 M. Nolan, "1913 in Retrospect: A Laboratory or a Battleground of Democracy?," in *Revolution: The 1913 Great Strike in New Zealand*, M. Nolan, ed. (Christchurch: Canterbury University Press, 2005), 23.
362 J. E. Le Rossignol, "A General Strike in New Zealand," *The American Economic Review* 4, no. 2 (1914): 293.
363 Nolan, "1913 in Retrospect," 27–29.
364 Report of the Department of Labour, in *AJHR*, Session I, H-11 (Wellington: House of Representatives, 1914), 12.
365 Barr, *The City of Auckland*, 216–17.
366 *Press*, 22 December 1913, 8; G. G. Hancox and J. Hight, "The Labour Movement and the Strike of 1913 in New Zealand," *The Economic Journal* 24, no. 94 (1914): 204.
367 *Greymouth Evening Star*, 13 November 1913, 5.
368 Cited in Le Rossignol, 299.
369 J. Crawford, "Overt and Covert Military Involvement in the 1890 Maritime Strike and 1913 Waterfront Strike in New Zealand," *Labour History* 60 (1991): 78.
370 *Greymouth Evening Star*, 13 November 1913, 5.
371 Report of the Department of Labour, in *AJHR*, Session I, H-11 (Wellington: House of Representatives, 1914), 12; Barr, *The City of Auckland*, 216–17.
372 *Wairarapa Age*, 24 November 1913, 5.
373 Annual Report on the Police Force of the Dominion, in *AJHR*, Session I, H-16 (Wellington: House of Representatives, 1914), 2–3.
374 C. Macdonald, "Crime and punishment in New Zealand,1840–1913: a Gendered History," *NZJH* 23, no. 1 (1989): 5–21; G. Dunstall, "Frontier and/or cultural fragment Interpretations of violence in colonial New Zealand," *Social History* 29, no. 1 (2004): 77; T. C. Tulloch, "State regulation of sexuality in New Zealand 1880–1925," PhD thesis (Christchurch: University of Canterbury, 1997), 30–31.
375 L. R. Watson, "The Perils of Impurity: The New Zealand Purity Crusades of Henry Bligh, 1902–1930," *NZJH* 39, no. 2 (2015): 114.
376 *White Ribbon*, 19 July 1915, 9.
377 B. Dalley, "'Fresh Attractions': White Slavery and Feminism in New Zealand, 1885–1918," *Women's History Review* 9, no. 2 (2000): 597.
378 P. Bunkle, "The origins of the Women's Movement in New Zealand: The Women's Christian Temperance Union 1885–1895," in *Women in New Zealand Society*, P. Bunkle and B. Hughes, eds (Auckland: Allen & Unwin, 1980), 59.
379 J. Coleman, "Apprehending possibilities: Tracing the emergence of feminist consciousness in nineteenth-century New Zealand," *Women's Studies International Forum* 31, no. 6 (2008): 465.
380 Kate Sheppard, "President's address to the National Council of Women," 1919, NCW Session, MS-Papers-1371, folder 107 ATL, in *The Vote, the Pill and the Demon Drink: A History of Feminist Writing in New Zealand, 1869–1993*, Charlotte Macdonald, ed. (Wellington: Bridget Williams Books, 1993), 82–83.
381 *AS*, 10 April 1918, 3; 1 March 1919, 20.
382 *NZH*, 19 June 1917, 8.
383 *NZH*, 20 February 1915, 9.
384 Ibid.
385 Ibid.
386 *New Zealand Truth*, 12 February 1916, 5.
387 W. E. Gillam, in B. Dalley, "Lolly Shops 'of the Red-Light Kind' and 'Soldiers of the King': Suppressing One-Women Brothels in New Zealand, 1908–1916," *NZJH* 30, no. 1 (1996): 3.
388 *New Zealand Truth*, 12 February 1916, 5; s. 13, *Indictable Offences Summary Jurisdiction Act 1894*; s. 144, *Criminal Code*, 1893; s. 177, *Justices of the Peace Act 1908*; K. Sanders, "'The Sensational Scandal which has Worried Wellington': The Kelburn Raid, Sex, and the Law in First World War New Zealand," *NZJH* 48, no. 2 (2014): 113–14.
389 *New Zealand Truth*, 12 February 1916, 5.
390 Dalley, "Lolly Shops," 7.
391 *White Ribbon*, 18 June 1918, 9.
392 *New Zealand Truth*, 17 July 1915, 4.
393 C. Pugsley, *Gallipoli: The New Zealand Story* (Auckland: Raupo, 2008), 363–65.
394 Graham Hucker, "'The Great Wave of Enthusiasm': New Zealand Reactions to the First World War in August 1914 — a Reassessment," *NZJH* 43, no. 1 (2009): 59–60.
395 *AS*, 6 August 1914, 6.
396 *New Zealand Truth*, 8 August 1914, 5.
397 A. W. Averill, in *Hastings Standard*, 5 August 1914, 2.
398 A. Ross, "Reluctant dominion or dutiful daughter? New Zealand and the Commonwealth in the inter-war years," *Journal of Commonwealth & Comparative Politics* 10, no. 1 (1972): 28, 37; J. B. Condliffe, *New Zealand in the Making: A Survey of Economic and Social Development* (London: G. Allen & Unwin Ltd, 1930), 431.
399 A. Summers, "Militarism in Britain before the Great War," *History Workshop Journal* 2, no. 1 (1976): 104–23; M. A. Conley, *From Jack Tar to Union Jack: Representing Naval Manhood in the British Empire, 1870–1918* (Manchester: Manchester University Press, 2017), 160–92.
400 O. E. Burton, *The Silent Division: New Zealanders at the Front 1914–1918* (Sydney: Angus and Robertson Ltd, 1935), 121.

401 L. O. H. Tripp, "War Relief and Patriotic Societies," in *The War Effort in New Zealand*, H. T. B. Drew, ed. (Auckland: Whitcombe & Tombs Ltd, 1923), 177.
402 S. Johnson. "The Home Front: Aspects of Civilian Patriotism in New Zealand During the First World War," MA thesis (Palmerston North: Massey University, 1975), 59–60.
403 Barr, *The City of Auckland*, 222-23.
404 *NZH*, 19 May 1915, 6.
405 H. Newbolt, in *The Speaker*, 26 February 1898, 270.
406 R. Hughes, *The Spectacle of Skill* (New York: Alfred A. Knopf, 2015), 18.
407 *Waiapu Church Gazette*, 1 May 1915, 130; *Kaipara and Waitemata Echo*, 6 May 1915, 3; *NZH*, 8 May 1915, 1.
408 S. Callister, "*Stabat mater dolorosa*: Death, photography and collective mourning," *NZJH* 41, no. 1 (2007): 6.
409 Pugsley, 348.
410 Barr, *The City of Auckland*, 224-25.
411 *AS*, 19 July 1919, 7.
412 Barr, *Municipal and Official Handbook*, 118.
413 P. Mitchell, "Laurence Binyon," *English Literature in Transition, 1880–1920* 40, no. 4 (1997): 472–476; P. M. Smith, "The 'NZ' in Anzac: different remembrance and meaning," *First World War Studies* 7, no. 2 (2016): 193–211.
414 s. 65(2), *Defence Amendment Act 1912*.
415 P. M. Khouri, "Conscientious Objection and Compulsory Military Service in New Zealand," *Auckland University Law Review* 1 (1967), 94.
416 A. K. Davidson and P. Lineham, *Transplanted Christianity: Documents Illustrating Aspects of New Zealand Church History*, 4th edn (Palmerston North: Department of History, 1997), chapter 5; R. L. Weitzel, "Pacifists and Anti-Militarists in New Zealand, 1909–1914," *NZJH* 7, no. 2 (1973): 130.
417 *AS*, 15 January 1918, 5.
418 *NZH*, 31 October 1917, 8.
419 *Observer*, 5 February 1916, 7.
420 Cited in W. Bradshaw, "Learning the lessons of the 1918 Spanish influenza epidemic," *Nursing New Zealand (Wellington, NZ: 1995)* 11, no. 10 (2005): 22–23.
421 G. Rice, *Black November: The 1918 Influenza Epidemic in New Zealand* (Wellington: Department of Internal Affairs, 1988), 22.
422 J. A. Summers, M. Baker and N. Wilson, "New Zealand's experience of the 1918-19 influenza pandemic: A systematic review after 100 years," *New Zealand Medical Journal* 131 (2018): 54–69.
423 K. Kuszewski and L. Brydak, "The epidemiology and history of influenza," *Biomedicine & Pharmacotherapy* 54, no. 4 (2000): 188–195.
424 *AS*, 5 December 1918, 4.
425 *Pukekohe and Waiuku Times*, 5 November 1918, 2.
426 Ibid., 12 November 1918, 3.
427 Maori Schools — Policy — Closure of native schools owing to influenza epidemic, ANZ, ref. R20390329.
428 *AS*, 7 Nov 1918, 3.
429 Barr, *The City of Auckland*, 229-30.
430 *Grey River Argus*, 29 November 1918, 3.
431 *AS*, 21 November 1918, 2.
432 Report of the Influenza Epidemic Commission, in *AJHR*, Session I, H-31A (1920), 32.
433 G. Hucker, "'A Time of Sorrow and Misery': Representations of the 1918 Influenza Epidemic in a Rural District of New Zealand," Postgraduate DipArts research essay (Palmerston North: Massey University, 1999), 1.
434 *AS*, 31 December 1919, 7.
435 Barr, *The City of Auckland*, 239, 242.
436 *NZH*, 30 December 1919, 6.
437 *AS*, 31 December 1919, 7.

4   The 1920s

438 F. K. Willits and D. M. Crider, "Church attendance and traditional religious beliefs in adolescence and young adulthood: A panel study," *Review of Religious Research* 31, no. 1 (1989): 68–81.
439 A. Clarke, "Churchgoing in New Zealand, 1874–1926," *NZJH* 47, no. 2 (2013): 109, 127, 129.
440 J. Leigh, *A Place on the Edge: The Story of St Matthew-in-the-City* (Auckland: Random House, 2005), 89–90, 97.
441 W. M. Ryburn, *The Story of St David's Presbyterian Church, Auckland. 1864-1964* (Auckland: Len Bolton & Co., 1964), 60–63.
442 *NZH*, 4 July 1924, 8; 1 February 1929, 4.

443 R. Boyd and A. Baker, *Seventy-Five years: A Celebration Record 1915-1990. St Heliers Presbyterian Church, Auckland, New Zealand* (Auckland: St Heliers Presbyterian Church, 1990), 3.
444 Presbyterian Church Archives Research Centre, ref. P-A427-1-3.
445 *Kaipara and Waitemata Echo*, 18 August 1921, 2; *Sun*, 15 March 1929, 2, 1 November 1927, 16, 14 July 1927, 13; *Rodney and Otamatea Times, Waitemata and Kaipara Gazette*, 21 April 1926, 4; *Franklin Times*, 8 June 1923, 7; J. R. Elder, *The History of the Presbyterian Church in New Zealand, 1840-1940* (Christchurch: Presbyterian Bookroom, 1940), 238–40.
446 P. McArthur, in P. Lineham, *Ventures of Faith and Community: The Development of Churches on the North Shore, Auckland* (Auckland: The Wesley Historical Society and the Anglican Historical Society, 2014), 55.
447 H. R. Jackson, *Churches and People in Australia and New Zealand, 1860–1930* (Wellington: Allen & Unwin, 1987), 125.
448 P. R. Collins, "The Jewish community in New Zealand: a contribution to the study of assimilation," MA thesis (Palmerston North: Massey University, 1971), 23; D. C. Maré, A. Coleman and R. Pinkerton, *Patterns of population location in Auckland. Motu Working Paper 11-06* (Wellington: Motu Economic and Public Policy Research, 2011), 70; S. Levine, *The New Zealand Jewish Community* (Maryland: Lexington Books, 1999), 37.
449 *Sun*, 7 July 1928, 15.
450 Collins, 77.
451 *Sun*, 9 July 1927, 9.
452 J. Hazelgrove, *Spiritualism and British Society Between the Wars* (Manchester: Manchester University Press, 2000), 2–5.
453 *Sun*, 28 December 1929, 4.
454 *NZH*, 8 November 1923, 10.
455 Clarke, "Churchgoing in New Zealand," 115.
456 *AS*, 16 March 1922, 12.
457 N. E. Reid, "Churchman: A Study of James Michael Liston, Bishop of Auckland, 1920–1970," PhD thesis (Auckland: University of Auckland, 2004), 16.
458 *AS*, 18 March 1922, 11.
459 R. Sweetman, *Bishop in the Dock: The Sedition Trial of James Liston* (Auckland: Auckland University Press, 1997), chapter 5; Reid, 143–45.
460 Reid, 146.
461 ss. 118, 119, *Crimes Act 1908*.
462 J. Kelly, in Reid, 148.
463 *NZH*, 23 March 1922, 4.
464 *AS*, 24 March 1922, 4.
465 *Franklin Times*, 31 March 1922, 4, 7.
466 *NZH*, 21 March 1922, 6.
467 *NZH*, 24 March 1922, 4.
468 *Waiapu Church Gazette*, 1 February 1927, 13.
469 P. Lineham, *Agency of Hope: The Story of the Auckland City Mission, 1920–2020* (Auckland: Massey University Press, 2020), 33–36.
470 G. Troughton, "Church, Society, and the Challenges of Modernity in the Anglican Diocese of Auckland, 1918–1940," *Anglican and Episcopal History* 84, no. 3 (2015): 289.
471 Report on Prisons for the year 1924–1925, in *AJHR*, Session I, H-20 (1925), 18.
472 M. Tennant, "Sisterly Ministrations: The Social Work of Protestant Deaconesses in New Zealand 1890-1940," *NZJH* 32, no. 1 (1998): 17.
473 *Stratford Evening Post*, 25 May 1929, 5.
474 J. Calder, in C. Thorn, "Social Services Sunday," St Matthew-in-the-City (5 August 2018), n.p.
475 T. Harper, "'Amen, amen!': Christianity, society and visions of the future in 1920s New Zealand," *NZJH* 42, no. 2 (2008): 138–139.
476 *New Zealand Truth*, 25 November 1922, 6.
477 Ibid., 1 August 1925, 1.
478 W. Parry, in *NZPD* 207 (25 August 1925) 547.
479 Harper, 149.
480 M. Fraser, *The New Zealand Official Year-Book, 1920* (Wellington: Government Printer, 1920), 34.
481 *NZH*, 22 May 1929, 7.
482 T. Lewis, "'A Godlike Presence': The Impact of Radio on the 1920s and 1930s," *OAH Magazine of History* 6, no. 4 (1992): 26–33; J. Nott, "Contesting Popular Dancing and Dance Music in Britain during the 1920s," *Cultural and Social History* 10, no. 3 (2013): 439–456.
483 *AS*, 25 June 1921, 19.

484 *White Ribbon*, 18 November 1924, 1.
485 *New Zealand Tablet*, 3 April 1924, 18.
486 P. Moon, *New Zealand in the Twentieth Century: The Nation, The People* (Auckland: HarperCollins, 2011), 140.
487 *AS*, 19 November 1921, 16; 8 June 1926, 9.
488 G. Ball, "The amazing Jasper Calder, the Auckland City Mission and welfare provision, 1920–1946," MA thesis (Auckland: University of Auckland, 1997), 32–33; Troughton, "Church, Society," 292.
489 H. Thomas, *Dance, Modernity, and Culture: Explorations in the Sociology of Dance* (London: Routledge, 1995), 1–30.
490 J. Baxendale, "'… into Another Kind of Life in Which Anything Might Happen …' Popular Music and Late Modernity, 1910–1930," *Popular Music* 14, no. 2 (1995): 142–43.
491 *AS*, 4 January 1923, 7.
492 Bourke, *Blue Smoke*, 20.
493 *New Zealand Truth*, 5 August 1926, 7.
494 *Sun*, 19 May 1928, 14.
495 Bourke, *Blue Smoke*, 41.
496 *AS*, 23 June 1928, 23; 24 December 1928, 18.
497 *Sun*, 3 May 1929, 15; 2 January 1929, 14.
498 *NZH*, 31 December 1927, 10; J. Griffiths, "Popular culture and modernity: Dancing in New Zealand society 1920–1945," *Journal of Social History* 41, no. 3 (2008): 614.
499 *NZH*, 31 December 1927, 10.
500 Cited in Griffiths, "Popular culture and modernity," 617.
501 S. de Sylva, B. Vale and G. Holden, "The Rise and Fall of the Bungalow," *Proceedings of the 35th Annual Conference of the Society of Architectural Historians of Australia and New Zealand* (Wellington, 2018): 127; J. Ashford, *The Bungalow in New Zealand* (Auckland: Viking, 1994), 59; G. F. Wilson, "A Pictorial Survey of Housing in New Zealand, Part Three," *Design Review* 2, no. 5 (February-March): 97; J. Ashford, *The Bungalow in New Zealand* (Auckland: Penguin Books, 1994), 8.
502 *Progress*, 1 April 1919, 471.
503 W. Toomath, "From Villa to Bungalow to Jazz Modern: New Zealand Houses between the Two World Wars," *JNZS* 2, no. 4 (1992): 3.
504 *Sun*, 21 May 1928, 14.
505 Interview with James 'Jack' Cross (Auckland, August 1992).
506 *Progress*, 1 November 1920, 17.
507 *NZH*, 6 February 1928, 5.
508 Ashford, 27.
509 M. Ignatieva, D. Haase, D. Dushkova and A. Haase, "Lawns in cities: from a globalised urban green space phenomenon to sustainable nature-based solutions," *Land* 9, no. 3 (2020): 3.
510 S. Schama, *Landscape and Memory* (New York: Vintage, 1995), 16.
511 *AS*, 15 January 1927, 8.
512 Mt Roskill Borough Council, *Roskill: An Illustrated History of New Zealand's Largest Borough* (Auckland: Mt Roskill Borough Council, 1984), 24.
513 D. Dunsford, *Mt Albert Then and Now* (Auckland: Mt Albert Historical Society, 2016), 92; *AS*, 16 December 1933, 17.
514 Map of Auckland City to the Waitakere Ranges, and then as far north as the Puhoi River, showing the extent of Auckland City and the surrounding area, and with considerable landscape detail, Sheet South J-60/A-IV, Map 8893 (Wellington: Lands and Survey Dept., 1920).
515 V. Burgess, G. Bishop and G. Cole, *Henderson: Heart of the West* (Auckland: West Auckland Historical Society, 2017), 174; *NZH*, 28 October 1916, 9, 9 November 1912, 3; *Sun*, 22 June 1927, 10.
516 C. J. Parr, in *NZH*, 16 September 1913, 4.
517 New Zealand Government, *Official Volume of the Proceedings of the Town Planning Conference held in Wellington* (Wellington: Government Printer, 1919), 46.
518 *State Advances Amendment Act 1922*.
519 B. Schrader, "Avoiding the mistakes of the 'mother country': the New Zealand garden city movement 1900–1926," *Planning Perspectives* 14, no. 4 (1999): 404.
520 S. V. Ward, "The garden city tradition re-examined," *Planning Perspective* 5, no. 3 (1990): 249–256.
521 A. Cusins-Lewer and J. Gatley, "The 'Myers Park Experiment' (1913–1916) and its Legacy in Auckland," *Fabrications* 12, no. 1 (2002): 61.
522 *NZH*, 27 September 1922, 11.
523 *Ladies' Mirror*, 1 October 1924, 3.
524 *NZH*, 15 July 1921, 4.
525 *Sun*, 20 June 1929, 15.
526 *Sun*, 6 July 1929, 9.
527 *AS*, 26 June 1929, 17.
528 *AS*, 14 October 1927, 5.
529 *AS*, 19 August 1929, 6.
530 B. W. Hayward, G. Murdoch and G. Maitland, *Volcanoes in Auckland: The Essential Guide* (Auckland: Auckland University Press, 2011), 123.
531 L. Mackintosh, "Shifting grounds: history, memory and materiality in Auckland landscapes c. 1350–2018," PhD thesis (Auckland: University of Auckland, 2019), 183.
532 *Ladies' Mirror*, 1 December 1926, 17.
533 *New Zealand Police Gazette*, 24 August 1892, 140.
534 D. Gaimster, "Fitting the colonial museum dashboard? Civic action, curatorial agency and identity building at the Auckland Museum (1852–1929)," *Museum History Journal* 13, no. 1 (2020): 89.
535 A. W. B. Powell, S. G. Brooker, C. O. Troup and E. G. Turbott, *The Centennial History of the Auckland Institute and Museum* (Auckland: Council of the Auckland Institute and Museum, 1967), 29.
536 *AS*, 19 December 1929, 6.
537 S. Worthy, "Communities of Remembrance: Making Auckland's War Memorial Museum," *Journal of Contemporary History* 39, no. 4 (2004): 606.
538 A. Greenberg, "Lutyens's Cenotaph," *The Journal of the Society of Architectural Historians* 48, no. 1 (1989): 5–23.
539 *NZH*, 29 November 1929, 15.
540 Ibid.
541 *AS*, 13 January 1928, 9.
542 P. Sparke, "'Covered promenades for wet weather': London's winter gardens and people's palaces, 1870–1900," *The London Journal* 45, no. 2 (2020): 242.
543 *AS*, 13 January 1928, 9.
544 Y. Wang, "The art of screen passing: Anna May Wong's yellow yellowface performance in the art deco era," *Camera Obscura: Feminism, Culture, and Media Studies* 20, no. 3 (2005): 166.
545 *NZH*, 21 December 1929, 16.
546 *Hawera Star*, 27 May 1926, 7.
547 C. E. Groom to G. W. Russell, Minister of Internal Affairs, 2 April 1919, AAAC 6015 W4686 13A Misc Affairs, Enemy POWS, ANZ, in S. Bandyopadhyay, "A History of Small Numbers. Indians in New Zealand, c.1890s–1930s," *NZJH* 43, no. 2 (2009): 158.
548 Cited in Bandyopadhyay, 162.
549 Annual Report of the Department of Internal Affairs, in *AJHR*, Session I–II, H-22 (1923), 8.
550 *New Zealand Truth*, 6 October 1923, 4.
551 *AS*, 15 April 1920, 4.
552 *Quick March* (10 July 1920), in P. S. O'Connor, "Keeping New Zealand White, 1908–1920," *NZJH* 2, no. 1 (1968): 54.
553 *Immigration Restriction Amendment Act 1920*; S. Elers, "A 'White New Zealand': Anti-Chinese Racist Political Discourse from 1880 to 1920," *China Media Research* 14, no. 3 (2018): 88–98.
554 Cited in N. Murphy, *The Poll-Tax in New Zealand: A Research Paper* (Wellington: The New Zealand Chinese Association, 1994), 51.
555 s. 5(1)(2), *Immigration Restriction Amendment Act 1920*.
556 M. Fairburn, "What Best Explains the Discrimination Against the Chinese in New Zealand, 1860s–1950s?," *JNZS* 2/3 (2003): 65–79.
557 *Franklin Times*, 18 January 1926, 4.
558 Based on Auckland having 45 per cent of the country's Asian population at this time. J. Leckie, "In Defence of Race and Empire: The White New Zealand League at Pukekohe," *NZJH* 19, no. 2 (1985): 104.
559 Fraser, *The New Zealand Official Year-Book, 1920*, 13.
560 *NZH*, 21 December 1925, 12.
561 B. Brookes, "Gender, work and fears of a 'hybrid race' in 1920s New Zealand," *Gender & History* 19, no. 3 (2007): 508.
562 Ibid., 506.
563 *Sun*, 30 August 1929, 8.
564 *AS*, 5 August 1929, 6.
565 Report of the Committee on Employment of Maoris in Market Gardens, in *AJHR*, Session I, G-11 (1929), 1.
566 Ibid., 4–6.
567 Leckie, "In Defence of Race and Empire," 128–29.
568 B. Lange, *The Stock Market Crash of 1929: The End of Prosperity* (New York: Chelsea House, 2007), 22–42.
569 *AS*, 31 October 1929, 7.
570 *AS*, 1 November 1929, 7.

571 Ibid., 8; *NZH*, 2 November 1929, 12.
572 *Sun*, 31 December 1929, 10; 23 December 1929, 1.
573 *Sun*, 24 December 1929, 7; 30 December 1929, 11.
574 *Rodney and Otamatea Times, Waitemata and Kaipara Gazette*, 18 December 1929, 5, 7; *Sun*, 10 December 1929, 14; *NZH*, 12 December 1929, 18.

5 The 1930s

575 *AS*, 13 November 1888, 8; F. S. Maclean, *Challenge for Health: A History of Public Health in New Zealand* (Wellington: Government Printer, 1964), 64; L. Bryder, "'Lessons' of the 1918 Influenza Epidemic in Auckland," *NZJH* 16, no. 2 (1982): 107.
576 E. Roberton, "Milk as a Vehicle of Disease," *Transactions and Proceedings of the New Zealand Institute* 23 (1890): 577.
577 Report by the Chief Health Officer, Department of Health, in *AJHR*, Session I, H-31 (1902), 33.
578 *Sun*, 4 March 1930, 7; *Franklin Times*, 7 November 1930, 4.
579 *AS*, 6 May 1936, 18.
580 Watercare, "The history of wastewater treatment in Auckland, 1878 to 2005," WWIS1-0918 (Auckland: Auckland City Council, 2010), 1.
581 Annual Report of the Director-General of Health, Department of Health, in *AJHR*, Session I, H-31 (1930), 57.
582 Waitangi Tribunal, *Report of The Waitangi Tribunal on The Orakei Claim, Wai-9* (Wellington: Department of Justice, 1987), 4, 79.
583 F. Acheson, in ibid., 112.
584 R. Hyde, in *Disputed Ground: Robin Hyde, Journalist*, G. Boddy and J. Matthews, eds (Wellington: Victoria University Press, 1991), 335.
585 *AS*, 25 August 1939, 14.
586 *AS*, 23 July 1932, 10.
587 I. H. Kawharu, "Biculturalism and inclusion in New Zealand: The case of Orakei," *Anthropologica* 50, no. 1 (2008): 51; P. Clark, "Te Mana Whenua O Ngati Whatua O Orakei," *Auckland University Law Review* 9 (2000): 569.
588 C. B. Wurster, "The social front of modern architecture in the 1930s," *Journal of the Society of Architectural Historians* 24, no. 1 (1965): 49.
589 P. Hall and C. Ward, *Sociable Cities: The 21st Century: The Reinvention of the Garden City* (Oxford: Routledge, 2014), 1–44.
590 C. L. Miller, "Theory poorly practised: the garden suburb in New Zealand," *Planning Perspectives* 19, no. 1 (2004): 38.
591 *AS*, 15 July 1937, 6.
592 Annual Report on Department of Lands and Surveys, in *AJHR*, Session I, C-01a (1926), 6.
593 B. Schrader, "Avoiding the mistakes of the 'mother country': the New Zealand garden city movement 1900–1926," *Planning Perspectives* 14, no. 4 (1999): 407.
594 R. Hammond, "Orakei Garden Suburb General Plan," ATL, ref. MapColl 832.1291gmbd/Re/1925/Acc. 47624.
595 Miller, "Theory poorly practised," 46–47.
596 Ibid., 48.
597 Annual Report on Department of Lands and Surveys, in *AJHR*, Session I, C-01 (1930), 2.
598 Miller, "Theory poorly practised," 48.
599 H. B. Laurenson, "Myths and the City: A Social and Cultural History of Auckland, 1890–1990," PhD thesis (Auckland: University of Auckland, 2010), 153.
600 E. C. Prescott, "Some observations on the Great Depression," *Federal Reserve Bank of Minneapolis Quarterly Review* 23, no. 1 (1999): 26.
601 P. Temin, "Transmission of the Great Depression," *Journal of Economic Perspectives* 7, no. 2 (1993): 87–102; C. W. Calomiris, "Financial factors in the Great Depression," *Journal of Economic Perspectives* 7, no. 2 (1993): 61–85; R. J. Jensen, "The causes and cures of unemployment in the Great Depression," *The Journal of Interdisciplinary History* 19, no. 4 (1989): 553–583.
602 G. R. Hawke, *The Making of New Zealand: An Economic History* (Cambridge: Cambridge University Press, 1985), 137; K. Rankin, "How great was the depression in New Zealand? Neglected estimates of inter-war aggregate income," *New Zealand Economic Papers* 28, no. 2 (1994): 205–209.
603 *AS*, 4 June 1930, 5.
604 Interview with R. T. (February 2021).
605 *NZH*, 6 June 1930, 15.
606 *NZH*, 11 June 1930, 12.
607 K. Rankin, "Unemployment in New Zealand at the peak of the Great Depression," University of Auckland, Working Papers in Economics No. 144 (Auckland: University of Auckland, 1995), 13.
608 Ibid., 5.
609 M. Wright, "'Mordacious Years': Socio-Economic Aspects and Outcomes of New Zealand's Experience in the Great Depression," *The Reserve Bank of New Zealand Bulletin* 72, no. 3 (2009): 50.
610 M. J. Savage, in *Sun*, 8 May 1930, 1.
611 Wright, "'Mordacious Years'," 48.
612 T. Simpson, *The Sugarbag Years: An Oral History of the 1930s Depression in New Zealand* (Wellington: Alister Taylor, 1974), 17.
613 J. Mulgan, *Man Alone* (London: 1939; Hamilton: Paul's Book Arcade, 1960), 42, 67.
614 *NZH*, 23 June 1931, 10.
615 W. Parry, in *AS*, 18 April 1931, 11.
616 R. Hyde, *Journalese* (Auckland: National Printing Company, 1934), 57.
617 D. Taylor, "Riots, Strikes, and Radical Politics in Aotearoa New Zealand," *Counterfutures* 7 (2019): 88.
618 Hyde, *Journalese*, 58.
619 Ibid., 59 (emphasis in original).
620 J. Edwards, *Riot, 1932: An Eyewitness Account of Social Upheaval in New Zealand in 1932* (Christchurch: Whitcombe & Tombs, 1974), 2.
621 *AS*, 15 April 1932, 8.
622 Ibid.
623 s. 3(2), *Public Safety Conservation Act 1932*; V. O'Malley, "A United Front against Capitalism? Unemployed Workers' Organisations in Christchurch, New Zealand, during the Depression," *Labour History Review* 73, no. 1 (2008): 158.
624 *NZH*, 28 May 1932, 12.
625 M. Cryer, *The Godzone Dictionary of Favourite New Zealand Words and Phrases* (Christchurch: Exisle Publishing, 2010), 51.
626 L. Truttman, *Balmoral and Sandringham Heritage Walks* (Auckland: Auckland City Council, 2009), 9.
627 H. Laurenson, *Going Up, Going Down: The Rise and Fall of the Department Store* (Auckland: Auckland University Press, 2005), 7.
628 E. Roberts, "'Don't sell things, sell effects': Overseas influences in New Zealand department stores, 1909–1956," *Business History Review* 77, no. 2 (2003): 266.
629 Ibid., 279.
630 M. Madanovic, "Concrete Complexities: Reinforced Concrete in the Architecture of Auckland's Town Hall, Chief Post Office and Ferry Building," *Historiographies of Technology and Architecture: Proceedings of the 35th Annual Conference of the Society of Architectural Historians of Australia and New Zealand*, J. Merwood-Salisbury, M. Dudding and C. McDonald, eds (Wellington: SAHANZ, 2018), 233–34.
631 J. November, "'The Law as a Profession for Women': A Century of Progress? A Reply to Mary Jane Mossman," *Australian Feminist Law Journal* 33, no. 1 (2010): 167.
632 C. Geary, *Smith and Caughey's* (Auckland: Smith and Caughey's, 2005), 30.
633 *Kai Tiaki: The Journal of the Nurses of New Zealand*, 1 November 1929, 200.
634 Auckland Lyceum Club, Records, 1919–1992, AWMML, MS-1994-52.
635 *Northern Advocate*, 10 September 1920, 3.
636 I. Hunter, *Farmers: Your Store for 100 Years* (Auckland: HarperCollins, 2009), 28–29.
637 *NZH*, 28 December 1933, 13.
638 *AS*, 19 May 1938, 19.
639 Laurenson, *Going Up, Going Down*, 17.
640 Hunter, *Farmers*, 99.
641 Roberts, "'Don't sell things, sell effects'," 267.
642 *AS*, 18 December 1912, 11; Laurenson, *Going Up, Going Down*, 101.
643 *NZH*, 23 November 1934, 17; Hunter, *Farmers*, 115.
644 *Sun*, 1 September 1930, 13.
645 *Ladies' Mirror*, 1 September 1924, 4.
646 L. Harrison, "Titirangi," in *Ladies' Mirror*, 1 January 1926, 11.
647 C. D. Bishop, T. J. Landers and N. P. Goldwater, "Changes in Indigenous Ecosystems and the Environment within the Boundary of the Waitakere Ranges Heritage Area Act 2008: 2008–2013 Report," (Auckland: Auckland Council, 2013), 5.
648 "Mystery Trains," in *New Zealand Railways Magazine* 7, no. 4 (1932): 6.
649 K. Ross, "'Schooled by Nature' — Pakeha Tramping Between the Wars," *NZJH* 36, no. 1 (2002): 58.
650 H. R., in *NZH*, 12 September 1932, 13.

651 B. D. A. Greig, *Tararua Story: Published in Commemoration of the Silver Jubilee of the Tararua Tramping Club, 1919–1944* (Wellington: Tararua Tramping Club Incorporated, 1946), 96, cited in Ross, "'Schooled by Nature'," 58.
652 *NZH*, 20 November 1930, 16.
653 Advertisement for Hotel Titirangi, 1936, West Auckland Research Centre, Ref: JTD-10A-01675.
654 J. Gatley and B. McKay, "Beyond Futuna: John Scott, Modern Architecture and Māori in Aotearoa New Zealand," in E. Grant, K. Greenop, A. L. Refiti and D. J. Glenn, eds, *The Handbook of Contemporary Indigenous Architecture* (Singapore: Springer, 2018), 607.
655 M. Bonny, *Titirangi: Fringe of Heaven*, B. and T. Harvey, eds (Auckland: West Auckland Historical Society, 2011), 179–180.
656 Supplementary Estimates of the Expenditure of the Government of New Zealand, in *AJHR*, Session I, B-07, 2 (1943), 26.
657 Public Works Statement, Department of Health, in *AJHR*, Session I, D-01 (1936), xii; A topographic map of the area in West Auckland, 1940, Auckland Libraries Heritage Collections, Map 2258, Class. No. 995.
658 *Auckland Centennial Memorial Park Act 1941*.
659 "Henning's Speedway," ALHC, MJ-2436.
660 *NZH*, 30 December 1937, 12.
661 *NZH*, 8 January 1938, 20.
662 *Western Star*, 19 July 1938, 2.
663 *AS*, 11 January 1938, 13.
664 B. Petersen, "Epi Shalfoon: Loss of a Popular Musician," *Te Ao Hou* 5 (October 1953): 19.
665 Hyde, *Journalese*, 105.
666 C. Bourke, Blog Post, 11 June 2015.
667 *NZH*, 12 September 1931, 11.
668 Hyde, *Journalese*, 105.
669 Doreen McLeod, Items 21–22, AML, ref. Papers MS-99-69.
670 *NZH*, 14 March 1936, 9.
671 *AS*, 16 May 1936, 13.
672 *NZH*, 9 January 1931, 13.
673 A. E. Batistich, *An Olive Tree in Dalmatia* (Auckland: Longman Paul, 1980), 99.
674 J. E. Gorst, *The Maori King* (London: Macmillan and Co., 1864), 150.
675 *Franklin Times*, 16 September 1921, 5.
676 Balance-Sheets and Statements of Accounts of Various Government Departments, in *AJHR*, Session I, B-07 (1929), 44–45.
677 Report on Mental Hospitals for the Dominion, in *AJHR*, Session I, H-07 (1928), 2–3.
678 W. Brunton, "The Scottish Influence on New Zealand Psychiatry before World War II," *Immigrants & Minorities* 29, no. 3 (2011): 330.
679 R. McLaughlan, "One dose of architecture, taken daily: Building for mental health in New Zealand," PhD thesis (Wellington: Victoria University, 2014), 164–65.
680 M. Lomax, *The Experiences of an Asylum Doctor* (London: George Allen & Unwin, 1921), 13, in McLaughlan, "One dose of architecture," 166.
681 Medical Superintendent, Kingseat Hospital, to the Director-General, MHD, August 8, 1947, ANZ, R20960887, in McLaughlan, "One dose of architecture," 178.
682 McLaughlan, "One dose of architecture," 177–78.
683 Report on Mental Hospitals for the Dominion, in *AJHR*, Session I, H-07 (1937), 5–6.
684 C. Dickens, "The Star of Bethlehem," *Household Words: A Weekly Journal* 386 (August 1857): 146.
685 *AS*, 28 December 1937, 6.
686 M. Tennant, *Children's Health, the Nation's Wealth: A History of Children's Health Camps* (Wellington: Bridget Williams Books, 1994), 97, 99.
687 *NZH*, 4 November 1929, 17.
688 *AS*, 15 November 1929, 11.
689 M. Wilcox, "Motuihe Island," *Auckland Botanical Society Journal* 54 (1999): 42.
690 R. Wendt, "The Vavalu Germans," in *Explorations and Entanglements: Germans in Pacific Worlds from the Early Modern Period to World War I*, H. Berghoff et al., eds (New York: Berghahn, 2018): 306–7.
691 P. J. de Lange and G. M. Crowcroft, "The Vascular Flora of Motuihe Island Recreation Reserve," *Auckland Botanical Society Journal* 54, no. 2 (1999): 20.
692 Annual Report of Director-General of Health, in *AJHR*, Session I, H-31 (1930), 25.
693 Annual Report of Director-General of Health, in *AJHR*, Session I–II, H-31 (1931), 16.
694 M. Mumme, "Memories of the Motuihe Health Camp," (n.d.).
695 *Rodney and Otamatea Times, Waitemata and Kaipara Gazette*, 25 September 1935, 7.
696 R. A. Kearns, T. M. Coleman and J. Edmeades, "New Zealand children's health stamps: Ideological artefacts linking health and place," *Social Science & Medicine* 227 (2019): 40.
697 D. Greasley and L. Oxley, "The pastoral boom, the rural land market, and long swings in New Zealand economic growth, 1873–1939," *The Economic History Review* 62, no. 2 (2009): 346; L. E. Marsden, "Hard times?: demographic change and the 1930s depression in New Zealand," MPhil thesis (Palmerston North: Massey University, 1991), 186–87.
698 *Workers' Dwellings Act 1905*; *Advances to Workers Act 1906*.
699 *Housing Survey Act 1935*; A. Wanhalla, "Housing Un/healthy Bodies: Native Housing Surveys and Maori Health in New Zealand 1930–45," *Health and History* 8, no. 1 (2006): 106.
700 Financial Statement, in *AJHR*, Session I, B-06 (1935), 5.
701 A. Davidson, *A Home of One's Own: Housing Policy in Sweden and New Zealand from the 1840s to the 1990s* (Stockholm: Almqvist & Wiksell International, 1994), 219; G. Ferguson, *Building the New Zealand Dream* (Palmerston North: Dunmore Press, 1994), 130, in K. Lynch, "Healthful Housing," MA thesis (Palmerston North: Massey University, 1999), 36–37.
702 Financial Statement, in *AJHR*, Session I, B-06 (1939), 4–5; *AS*, 8 April 1937, 19.
703 *NZH*, 24 August 1934, 10.
704 Dave Pearson Architects Limited, *Grey's Avenue Flats Auckland: Conservation Plan* (Auckland, 2006, n.p.), 1–29.
705 *AS*, 29 November 1935, 14.
706 House, yard and Maori children, Nelson Street, Auckland, photographed by H L McNaughton, late 1930s. ATL, ref. PA1-o-914-07-5.
707 *Franklin Times*, 15 July 1938, 4.
708 C. Firth, *State Housing in New Zealand* (Wellington: Ministry of Works, 1949), 5.
709 *AS*, 28 July 1937, 3; B. Schrader, *We Call it Home: A History of State Housing in New Zealand* (Auckland: Reed Publishing, 2005), 41.
710 Firth, *State Housing*, 6.
711 Schrader, *We Call it Home*, 83; R. T. Metge, "The House that Jack Built: The Origins of Labour State Housing 1935–8 With Particular Reference to the Role of J. A. Lee," MA thesis (Auckland: University of Auckland, 1972), 41.
712 Anon. to W. Nash, 28 March 1938, in R. T. Metge, "The House that Jack Built," 41.
713 B. Schrader, "Labour at Home," in *At Home in New Zealand: History, Houses, People*, B. Brookes, ed. (Wellington: Bridget Williams Books, 2000), 136.
714 *NZH*, 4 May 1937, 8.
715 Records of the Young Women's Christian Association (Auckland, N.Z.) (1885–1985), AWMML, ref. MS1131, 7.
716 *NZH*, 11 December 1937, 16.
717 *NZH*, 7 December 1937, 10.
718 J. Mulgan, *Report on Experience* (London: 1947; Barnsley: Frontline Books, 2010), 46.
719 *NZH*, 6 December 1939, 15.
720 J. Gatley, "Going Up Rather than Out," in Brookes, ed., *At Home in New Zealand*, 140.
721 *NZH*, 10 April 1941, 8.
722 *NZH*, 13 October 1938, 12.
723 M. Bassett and M. King, *Tomorrow Comes the Song. A Life of Peter Fraser* (Auckland: Penguin Publishing, 2000), 144; M. Nolan, "The reality and myth of New Zealand egalitarianism: Explaining the pattern of a labour historiography at the edge of empires," *Labour History Review* 72 (2007): 113–134.

6 The 1940s

724 Quoted in B. Gustafson, *From the Cradle to the Grave: A Biography of Michael Joseph Savage* (Auckland: Reed Methuen, 1986), 269.
725 Michael Joseph Savage. Original photograph, ATL, Box 1, Ref: PAColl-5471-055; I. Cross, *Such Absolute Beginners: A Memoir* (Auckland: David Ling, 2007), 103; B. Stagoll, "Coming across: family therapy in Australia and New Zealand," *Australian and New Zealand Journal of Family Therapy* 17, no. 1 (1996): 2.
726 R. Foster, "NZHPT Authority 2009/171. Michael Joseph Savage Memorial Garden, Bastion Point, Auckland Monitoring Report," (Auckland: Russell Foster and Associates, 2009), 2.

727 *NZH*, 29 March 1940, 9.
728 Annual Report of the Department of Internal Affairs, in *AJHR*, Session I, H-22 (1940), 2.
729 *NZH*, 1 April 1940, 12.
730 *NZH*, 1 April 1940, 11.
731 *Northern Advocate*, 31 July 1941, 2.
732 F. McGehan, Photo of Savage Memorial, Bastion Point, AL, Record ID 255A-35037.
733 M. J. Savage, in M. Logan, *Nordy: Arnold Nordmeyer, A Political Biography* (Wellington: Steele Roberts, 2008), 125.
734 *AS*, 3 January 1940, 8.
735 N. M. Taylor, *The Home Front* 2 (Wellington: Historical Publications Branch, 1986), 91.
736 Ibid., 79; *AS*, 6 February 1940, 3, 9 January 1940, 3.
737 *NZH*, 18 December 1940, 11.
738 *NZH*, 14 March 1941, 8.
739 *NZH*, 13 November 1940, 6.
740 R. Semple, in J. E. Cookson: "Illiberal New Zealand: The Formation of Government Policy on Conscientious Objection, 1940–1," *NZJH* 17, no. 2 (1983): 123.
741 *Nelson Evening Mail*, 12 February 1940, 3.
742 P. Fraser, in F. L. W. Wood, *Political and External Affairs* (Wellington: Historical Publications Branch, 1958), 124.
743 S. Robinson, *False Flags: Disguised German Raiders of World War II* (Wollombi: Exisle Publishing, 2016), 194.
744 S. D. Waters, *German Raiders in the Pacific* (Bennington: Merriam Press, 2005), 12; M. Turner, "RAN Sweeping of German Mines in Two World Wars," *Journal of Australian Naval History* 7, no. 2 (2010): 7–40.
745 *AS*, 19 June 1940, 8; 20 June 1940, 8.
746 J. Tonkin-Covell, "The collectors: Naval, Army and Air Intelligence in the New Zealand Armed Forces during the Second World War," PhD thesis (Hamilton: University of Waikato, 2000), 54.
747 *NZH*, 29 June 1940, 5.
748 W. Ngoei, "The Domino Logic of the Darkest Moment: The Fall of Singapore, the Atlantic Echo Chamber, and 'Chinese Penetration' in US Cold War Policy toward Southeast Asia," *Journal of American-East Asian Relations* 21, no. 3 (2014): 216–19; Ian Hamill, *The Strategic Illusion: The Singapore Strategy and the Defence of Australia and New Zealand, 1919–1942* (Singapore: Singapore University Press, 1981), 315–18.
749 *AS*, 24 December 1940, 6.
750 Report for the Social Security Department, in *AJHR*, Session I, H-09 (1941), 5; W. Nash, "New Zealand's Total War Effort," *Far Eastern Survey* 11, no. 12 (1942): 137.
751 Emergency Reserve Corps Regulations 1940, in *New Zealand Police Gazette* LXV, no. 35 (28 August 1940): 694.
752 M. Aldred, in M. King, *New Zealanders at War* (Auckland: Penguin Books, 2003), 220.
753 King, *New Zealanders at War*, 228–29.
754 D. Hume, in A. Parr, *Home: Civilian New Zealanders Remember the Second World War* (Auckland, Penguin Books, 2010), 94.
755 Ibid., 101.
756 M. Emery, J. Hooks and R. Stewart, "Born at the wrong time? An oral history of women professional accountants in New Zealand," *Accounting History* 7, no. 2 (2002): 17.
757 D. Montgomerie, *The Women's War: New Zealand Women 1939–45* (Auckland: Auckland University Press, 2001), 124.
758 Taylor, *The Home Front* 2, 1077.
759 Ibid., 1082–83.
760 J. Aitken, "Wives and Mothers First: The New Zealand Teachers' Marriage Bar and the Ideology of Domesticity, 1920–1947," *Women's Studies Journal* 12, no. 1 (1996): 83–87.
761 M. Nolan, "Unstitching the New Zealand state: Its role in domesticity and its decline," *International Review of Social History* 45, no. 2 (2000): 258.
762 Helen, "Uniform by Day," in *New Zealand Railways Magazine* 15, no. 2 (1 May 1940), 57.
763 Cited in Taylor, *The Home Front* 2, 1098–99.
764 *NZH*, 17 June 1944, 10; 1 November 1944, 8.
765 Taylor, *The Home Front* 2, 1059; *New Zealand Truth*, 11 March 1942, 25.
766 *AS*, 7 July 1940, 5.
767 *AS*, 4 December, 1943, 8.
768 A. Wanhalla and K. Stevens, "'I Don't Like Maori Girls Going Out with Yanks': Māori–American Encounters in New Zealand," in *Mothers' Darlings of the South Pacific: The Children of Indigenous Women and U.S. Servicemen, World War II*, J. A. Bennett and A. Wanhalla, eds (Honolulu: University of Hawai'i Press, 2016), 202.

769 *AS*, 1 September 1942, 2.
770 J. C. Beaglehole, *Meet New Zealand* (Wellington: Department of Internal Affairs, 1942), 1–10.
771 Cited in King, *New Zealanders at War*, 221.
772 J. Fleming, in A. Parr, *Home*, 219.
773 G. A. Carmichael, "Non-marital Pregnancies in New Zealand Since the Second World War," *Journal of Biosocial Science* 17, no. 2 (1985): 169.
774 *AS*, 21 November 1942, 7.
775 *White Ribbon*, 18 August 1943, 6.
776 Child Welfare, State Care of Children, Special Schools, and Infant-Life Protection, in *AJHR*, Session I, E-04 (1945), 2.
777 *AS*, 11 November 1941, 2.
778 *Alexandra Herald and Central Otago Gazette*, 4 February 1942, 3; *Patea Mail*, 28 August 1940, 4.
779 T. Stringer, *The Art of A. Lois White* (Auckland: The Wallace Arts Trust, 2017), n.p.
780 N. Green, *By the Waters of Babylon: The Art of A. Lois White* (Auckland: David Bateman, 1993), 53–80.
781 A. L. White, *Victims of Invasion*, in Green, *By the Waters of Babylon*, 47.
782 A. L. White, *Collapse*, in ibid., 71.
783 A. L. White, *Jubilation*, 1948, Auckland Art Gallery, Accession no. 1990/29.
784 *Wanganui Herald*, 8 May 1945, 7.
785 *AS*, 9 May 1945, 6.
786 *NZH*, 13 August 1945, 6.
787 Taylor, *The Home Front* 2, 1257–58.
788 *NZH*, 17 August 1945, 4.
789 *Franklin Times*, 26 September 1945, 3; *AS*, 5 September 1945, 4; Railways Statement, in *AJHR*, Session I, D-02 (1946), 4.
790 J. Mulgan, *Report on Experience* (London: 1947; Barnsley: Frontline Books, 2010), 50.
791 R. Winkelmann, "Immigration: The New Zealand Experience," *IZA Discussion Papers*, no. 61 (Bonn: Institute for the Study of Labor, 1999): 4–5.
792 M. Hutching, *Long Journey for Sevenpence: An Oral History of Assisted Immigration to New Zealand from the United Kingdom, 1947–1975* (Wellington: Victoria University Press, 1999), 9–10.
793 P. Ongley and D. Pearson, "Post-1945 International Migration: New Zealand, Australia and Canada Compared," *International Migration Review* 29, no. 3 (1995): 767.
794 B. Thomas, "Does our Migration Policy Make Sense?," *The Political Quarterly* 18, no. 3 (1947): 191.
795 Cited in Hutching, *Long Journey for Sevenpence*, 119.
796 *Ashburton Guardian*, 20 November 1948, 4.
797 Report of the Department of Labour and Employment, in *AJHR*, Session I, H-11 (1949), 9.
798 Cited in Hutching, *Long Journey for Sevenpence*, 76–77.
799 Pan American World Airways DC-4 Clipper "Kathay" at Whenuapai, Museum of Transport and Technology, Accession No. 16-0776.
800 P. Lewis, in "The Wings over New Zealand Aviation Forum," (8 November 2006), n.p.
801 Report on the Air Department, in *AJHR*, Session I, H-37 (1950), 40–43.
802 Interview with G. V. (March 2016).
803 I. Pool, "The baby boom in New Zealand and Other Western Developed Countries," *Journal of Population Research* 24, no. 2 (2007): 144.
804 Primary and Post-Primary Education, in *AJHR*, Session I, E-02 (1947), 1–2.
805 Report of the Minister of Education, in *AJHR*, Session I, E-01 (1944), 2.
806 W. Friesen, "The demographic transformation of inner city Auckland," *New Zealand Population Review* 35, no. 1 (2009): 58–61.
807 G. Bowron, "Tamaki State Housing Scheme," in *Long Live the Modern: New Zealand's New Architecture, 1904–1984*, J. Gatley, ed. (Auckland: Auckland University Press, 2008), 44; J. Arps, "Rise, Ruin & Regeneration: An Examination of the Regeneration of Post-War Suburban State Housing in New Zealand," MArch thesis (Wellington: Victoria University, 2012), 40.
808 F. Porter, "Digging in the Compost Heap," *Turnbull Library Record* 38, no 1 (January 2005): 43.
809 D. Brand, "Ernst Plischke and the Design of Urban New Zealand, 1939–47," *Journal of Urban Design* 19, no. 5 (2014): 682.
810 B. Schrader, *We Call It Home: A History of State Housing in New Zealand* (Auckland: Reed Publishing, 2005), 112, in Arps, 40.

811 Auckland Regional Council, *A Brief History of Auckland's Urban Form*, 13.
812 Greater London Authority, *Population Growth in London, 1939-2015* (London: Greater London Authority, 2015), 2-3.
813 E. Donovan, "State Housing Revival: Sustainable Regeneration Strategies for Post-war Suburban State Housing in New Zealand," *Housing and Welfare Conference: Boundaries, Encounters, Connections. Workshop 1: Polarization, Inequality and Affordable Housing* (Copenhagen, 2014), 3-4.
814 *Rehabilitation Act 1941*; *Servicemen's Settlement and Land Sales Act 1943*; *War Pensions Act 1943*.
815 V. Hopner, "Home from War," PhD thesis (Auckland: Massey University, 2014), 72.
816 *AS*, 21 February 1945, 8.
817 J. Frame, *The Carpathians* (London: Pandora, 1989), 69, in C. Mazlin, "Returned Soldiers in *Owls Do Cry*, *A State of Siege*, and *The Carpathians*: Janet Frame's Subversive Representations," *Antipodes* 28, no. 2 (2014): 336.
818 N. Hunt and I. Robbins, "The long-term consequences of war: the experience of World War II," *Aging & Mental Health* 5, no. 2 (2001): 183.
819 R. J. Bonwick and P. Morris, "Post-traumatic stress disorder in elderly war veterans," *International Journal of Geriatric Psychiatry* 11, no. 12 (1996): 1072; T. Jenks and A. Wanhalla, "Psychological Casualties: War Neurosis, Rehabilitation, and the Family in Post-World War II New Zealand," *Health and History* 22, no. 2 (2020): 1-25.
820 H. Robinson, "Lest We Forget? The Fading of New Zealand War Commemorations, 1946-1966," *NZJH* 44, no. 1 (2010): 76-77.
821 N. M. Taylor, *The Home Front* 2, 1284.
822 C. Brickell, "The politics of post-war consumer culture," *NZJH* 40, no. 2 (2006): 136-137.
823 s. 8, *Physical Welfare and Recreation Act 1937*; C. Daley, *Leisure & Pleasure: Reshaping & Revealing the New Zealand Body 1900-1960* (Auckland: Auckland University Press, 2003), 237-38.
824 A. Else, ed., *Women Together: A History of Women's Organisations in New Zealand: Ngā rōpū wāhine o te motu* (Wellington: Historical Branch, Department of Internal Affairs, 1993), 574; *Evening Star*, 7 March 1946, 3.
825 C. Macdonald, *Strong, Beautiful and Modern: National Fitness in Britain, New Zealand, Australia and Canada, 1935-1960* (Vancouver: University of British Columbia, 2013), 86-88; R. E. Wells, "A group of marching girls performing in front of a crowd in Dargaville, 1946," ATL, ref. 1/4-091100-F.
826 Else, ed., *Women Together*, 438.
827 *Franklin Times*, 21 February 1945, 3.
828 *AS*, 23 March 1945, 6.
829 *AS*, 24 March 1945, 14.
830 A. E. Birch, *The Story of the Boys' Brigade* (London: Frederick Muller, 1965), 29-30.
831 *Franklin Times*, 20 September 1944, 4.
832 *AS*, 8 April 1943, 6.
833 *NZH*, 3 January 1944, 5.
834 Interview with D. G. (Auckland, October 1990).
835 C. Ferrall and R. Ellis, *The Trials of Eric Mareo* (Wellington: Victoria University Press, 2002), 9-10.
836 D. Haworth and D. Miller, *Freda Stark: Her Extraordinary Life* (Auckland: HarperCollins, 2000), 83-87.
837 F. Matheson, in "Fever of the Fleet," documentary, Shani Bennett, Auckland University of Technology, (2010).
838 R. Salys, "Art Deco Aesthetics in Grigorii Aleksandrov's 'The Circus'," *The Russian Review* 66, no. 1 (2007): 25.
839 H. Robinson, in "Fever of the Fleet."
840 F. Sargeson, in G. Lay and J. Ross, *Golden Weather: North Shore Writers Past and Present* (Auckland: Cape Catley, 2004), 86.
841 *NZH*, 22 August 1936, 4.
842 L. Wallace, "Queer Chattels and Fixtures: Photography and Materiality in the Homes of Frank Sargeson and Patrick White," In *Domestic Imaginaries: Home in Global Literary and Visual Cultures*, B. Harper and H. Price, eds (Cham: Palgrave Macmillan, 2017), 191-209.
843 F. Sargeson, in L. Jones, "Frank Sargeson [Norris Frank Davey], 1903-1982," *Kōtare: New Zealand Notes & Queries* 7, no. 2 (2008): 158.
844 J. Sturm, "Anna Kavan Meets a New Zealand Writer on His Special Day," *Kōtare: New Zealand Notes & Queries* 5, no. 1 (2004): 36-37.
845 A. Kavan, "New Zealand: Answer to an Inquiry," *Horizon: A Review of Literature and Art* 8 (1943), 156, in M. Schwass, "Invention and reinvention: Greville Texidor meets Frank Sargeson," *Journal of New Zealand Literature* 34, no. 1 (2016): 8.

7 The 1950s

846 *White Ribbon*, 1 January 1954, 1.
847 Ibid.
848 J. Belich, *Paradise Reforged: A History of the New Zealanders from the 1880s to the Year 2000* (Auckland: Allen Lane/The Penguin Press, 2001), 83.
849 J. Phillips and T. Hearn, *Settlers: New Zealand Immigrants from England, Ireland and Scotland 1800-1945* (Auckland: Auckland University Press, 2008), 160, 161, 181; M. Watson, "'Of course you had to keep the cake tins full': Pakeha women and afternoon tea from 1930-50," PhD thesis (Wellington: Massey University, 2011), 78.
850 Watson, "'Of course you had to keep the cake tins full'," 78; D. Burton, *Two Hundred Years of New Zealand Food and Cookery* (Wellington: Reed, 1982), 32.
851 R. cited in Watson, "'Of course you had to keep the cake tins full'," 36, 57.
852 Interview with A. M. (May 2011).
853 *Otago Daily Times*, 9 February 1950, 4.
854 *Gisborne Herald*, 27 March 1950, 2.
855 Interview with D. W. (Auckland, 2019).
856 J. Clark and P. Walker, *Looking for the Local: Architecture and the New Zealand Modern* (Wellington: Victoria University Press, 2000), 29; G. Hochstein and J. Gatley, "A Golden Pedigree: Finding Mies in New Zealand Modernism through the Work of Edward Erickson," in *Proceedings of the Society of Architectural Historians, Australia and New Zealand*: 33, A. Brennan and P. Goad, eds (Melbourne: SAHANZ, 2016), 284.
857 A. Swenson and P. Chang, *Architectural Education at I.I.T., 1938-1978* (Illinois: Godwit, 1980), 21, cited in Hochstein and Gatley, 280.
858 M. Austin, "Round Table Connections: The House in the Auckland Scene," *Interstices: Journal of Architecture and Related Arts* 5 (2000): 133.
859 *Home and Building* 18, no. 1 (June 1955): 26-29.
860 Hochstein and Gatley, 281.
861 L. Tyler, "Imric Porsolt: The 'Messenger of Modernism' in Exile," *Interstices: Journal of Architecture and Related Arts* (2018): 64.
862 C. Buckenberger, "Meanings of housing qualities in suburbia: empirical evidence from Auckland, New Zealand," *Journal of Housing and the Built Environment* 27, no. 1 (2012): 74-75, 80-81.
863 Interview with K. P. (October 2020).
864 Odo Strewe, "Living in hand with nature," *New Zealand Modern Homes and Gardens* (Winter 1960), 63.
865 J. Beattie, J. M. Heinzen and J. P. Adam, "Japanese gardens and plants in New Zealand, 1850-1950: Transculturation and transmission," *Studies in the History of Gardens & Designed Landscapes* 28, no. 2 (2008): 231.
866 O. Strewe, in K. Francis, "Learning about Landscape: Odo Strewe and the Group," (Auckland: Unitec, 2010), 191.
867 R. Leydon, "Utopias of the Tropics: The Exotic Music of Les Baxter and Yma Sumac," in *Widening the Horizon: Exoticism in Post-War Popular Music*, P. Hayward, ed. (New Barnet: John Libbey Publishing, 1999), 45-47.
868 S. Sampson, "South Sea Island Magic: Bill Sevesi and the Auckland Music Scene," *Perfect Beat* 4, no. 1 (2015): 19-46.
869 Cited in D. L. Jenkins, *At Home: A Century of New Zealand Design* (Auckland: Godwit, 2006), 121.
870 *Home and Building* 12, no. 6 (June-July 1950): 17.
871 P. S. Morrison, *On the Falling Rate of Home Ownership in New Zealand* (Wellington: Centre for Housing Research Aotearoa New Zealand, 2007), 14.
872 J. Metge, *A New Maori Migration: Rural and Urban Relations in Northern New Zealand* (Melbourne: Melbourne University Press, 1964), 4.
873 M. Barcham, "The challenge of urban Maori: reconciling conceptions of indigeneity and social change," *Asia Pacific Viewpoint* 39, no. 3 (1998): 304-5.
874 Metge, 2.
875 M. Winiata, in *AS*, 6 September 1951, 3.
876 Metge, 2.
877 M. Bennett, in *Te Ao Hou* 18 (May 1957): 51.
878 D. T. Rowland, "Maori migration to Auckland," *New Zealand Geographer* 27, no. 1 (1971): 22.

879 M. Winiata, in *Te Ao Hou* 27 (June 1959): 21.
880 J. Carlyon and D. Morrow, *Urban Village: The Story of Ponsonby, Freemans Bay and St Mary's Bay* (Auckland: Random House, 2008), 249.
881 J. Taua, in *Te Ao Hou* 27 (June 1959): 57, 71; N. Jones, "Auckland's Māori Community Centre: 1947–1970," *Auckland History Initiative* (7 January 2020), n.p.
882 P. Tapsell, "Marae and tribal identity in urban Aotearoa/New Zealand," *Pacific Studies* 25, no. 1 (2002): 143.
883 T. Te Ua, in *Te Ao Hou* 1 (Winter 1952): 27.
884 E. Corbett, in *Te Ao Hou* 1 (Winter 1952): 55.
885 *Te Ao Hou* 1 (Winter 1952): 55–58.
886 B. Neho, in M. M. Williams, *Panguru and the City: Kāinga Tahi, Kāinga Rua — An Urban Migration History* (Wellington: Bridget Williams Books, 2015), 105.
887 M. Krivan, "The Department of Maori Affairs housing programme, 1935–1967," MA thesis (Palmerston North: Massey University, 1990), 3.
888 *Te Ao Hou* 27 (June 1959): 51.
889 H. A. Kersey, "Opening a Discourse on Race Relations in New Zealand: The Fern and the Tiki Revisited," *JNZS* 1 (2002): 12.
890 D. P. Ausubel, "Race relations in New Zealand: Maori and Pakeha: an American view," *Landfall* 12 (1958): 233–246; L. Johnson, "Maori activism across borders, 1950–1980s," PhD thesis (Palmerston North: Massey University, 2015), 81.
891 *Te Ao Hou* 15 (July 1956): 1.
892 Auckland Regional Council, *A Brief History of Auckland's Urban Form*, 40–41.
893 J. Broadbent, in Waitangi Tribunal, *Report of The Waitangi Tribunal on The Orakei Claim, Wai-9* (Wellington: Department of Justice, 1987), 125.
894 A. Tronson, *The Story of the British Empire Games* (Auckland: Organising Committee for the 1950 British Empire Games, 1950), 13.
895 The Police Force of the Dominion, in *AJHR*, Session I, H-16 (1949), 4; Session I, H-16 (1950), 3.
896 s. 5, *Finance Act no. 2, 1949*.
897 Newmarket Borough Council photographs. Auckland Council Archives Reference: NMB 020 Item 50; Architects Division, City Engineer's Department plans. Auckland Council Archives Reference: ACC 015-9631-2; Oblique aerial photograph of Mt Eden Borough, Whites Aviation photograph. Auckland Council Archives Reference: MEB 029 1j.
898 Ministry of Works Statement, in *AJHR*, Session I, D-01 (1950), 34.
899 C. Dheensaw, *The Commonwealth Games: The First 60 Years 1930–1990* (Victoria: Orca Book Publishers,1994), 35–41.
900 Tronson, 19.
901 *Hamilton Spectator*, 25 August 1930, 17, in K. Moore, "'The warmth of comradeship': the First British Empire Games and Imperial Solidarity," *The International Journal of the History of Sport* 6, no. 2 (1989): 242.
902 Tronson, 21.
903 J. Allum, in *Evening Post*, 1 February 1950, 9.
904 *Auckland Weekly News*, 15 February 1950, 7.
905 G. Ryan, "The Turning Point: The 1950 British Empire Games as an Imperial Spectacle," *Sport in History* 34, no. 3 (2014): 420–21.
906 *AS*, 4 February 1950, 1.
907 *The New Zealand Sportsman* 4, no. 8 (March 1950): 6.
908 British Empire Games, Auckland, New Zealand, 1950: Closing ceremony [and] Vice-Patrons of the New Zealand Olympic and British Empire Games Association. Official programme. NLNZ, Ref: Eph-A-SPORT-1950-03-20/21; *Ashburton Guardian*, 13 February 1950, 3.
909 *Sunday Mail*, 19 February 1950, 15.
910 D. J. Turkington, "The Trend of Strikes in New Zealand 1946–70: Part II," *Journal of Industrial Relations* 15, no. 2 (1973): 144, 150.
911 R. J. Towers, "The Mountain, the River, and the Big Blue: The 1951 Waterfront Dispute as it Occurred in the Taranaki and Wanganui Region," BA essay (Palmerston North: Massey University, 2001), 10.
912 S. Holland, 21 February 1951, in Radio New Zealand Sound Archives Ngā Taonga Kōrero, "Dispute: An Account of the 1951 Waterfront Conflict," 1968, ref no T81.
913 J. Scott, *151 Days: History of the Great Waterfront Lockout and Supporting Strikes* (Auckland: New Zealand Waterside Workers' Union, 1952), 39.
914 W. Goosman, in *NZPD* 294 (28 June 1951), 241.
915 *AS*, 1 May 1951, 1.
916 W. Nash, in K. Sinclair, *Walter Nash* (Auckland: Auckland University Press, 1976), 285.
917 J. Barnes, *Never a White Flag: The Memoirs of Jock Barnes*, T. Bramble, ed. (Wellington: Victoria University Press, 1998), 210.
918 Ibid., 211.
919 G. Millar, "'We never recovered': The social cost of the 1951 New Zealand waterfront dispute," *Labour History* 108 (2015): 96–99.
920 G. J. R. Linge, "The diffusion of manufacturing in Auckland, New Zealand," *Economic Geography* 39, no. 1 (1963): 25, 27.
921 *AS*, 7 January 1942, 1.
922 Business History Project, University of Auckland, "Fisher and Paykel," (Auckland: University of Auckland 2021), n.p.
923 A. LaRoche, "From Mt Wellington, 1950," Howick Historical Village, object no. 2017.296.02; Whites Aviation, Mt Wellington and Panmure, Aerial photograph, NLNZ, Ref: WA-45435.
924 J. Arbury, "From urban sprawl to compact city: an analysis of urban growth management in Auckland," MA thesis (Auckland: University of Auckland, 2005), 20.
925 Interviews with L. T. (June 2021), S. L. (July 2021); N. W. Derbyshire, "An anatomy of antipodean Anglicanism: the Anglican Church in New Zealand 1945 to 2012," PhD thesis (Auckland: Massey University, 2013), 122, 125.
926 S. M. Lange, *A Rising Tide: Evangelical Christianity in New Zealand, 1939–1965* (Dunedin: Otago University Press, 2013), 176–84.
927 K. Ward, "Towards 2015: the future of mainline Protestantism in New Zealand," *Journal of Beliefs and Values: Studies in Religion and Education* 27, no. 1 (2006): 13–23.
928 O. C. Mazengarb et al., *Report of the Special Committee on Moral Delinquency in Children and Adolescents* (Wellington: Government Printer, 1954).
929 Ibid., 13.
930 Ibid., 18.
931 Ibid., 19.
932 Ibid., 49.
933 A. Krzanich, "Murder, Mazengarb and a Moral Panic: The Intersection of Juvenile Delinquency and the Media in 1950s New Zealand," *Auckland University Law Review* 16 (2010): 170.
934 F. Belmer, in *NZH*, 13 July 1954, 8.
935 L. Guy, "'Moral Panic' or Pejorative Labelling? Rethinking the Mazengarb Inquiry into Underage Sex in the Hutt Valley in 1954," *Journal of Religious History* 33, no. 4 (2009): 435–451.
936 G. F. Whitcher, "'More than America': some New Zealand responses to American culture in the mid-twentieth century," PhD thesis (Christchurch: University of Canterbury, 2011), 184.
937 *Ashburton Guardian*, 29 December 1950, 3.
938 M. Hamilton, "Sexual politics and African-American music; or, placing Little Richard in history," *History Workshop Journal* 46, no. 1 (1998): 161–163.
939 H. Capper, in R. Yska, *All Shook Up: The Flash Bodgie and the Rise of the New Zealand Teenager in the Fifties* (Auckland: Penguin Books, 1993), 145.
940 Yksa, 154–58; P. Booth, *Deadline: My Story* (Auckland: Viking Adult, 1997), 103.
941 *NZH*, 15 January 2018, 9.
942 Yksa, 177–78.
943 A. E. Manning, *The Bodgie: A Study in Psychological Abnormality* (Wellington: Reed, 1958).
944 Ibid., 47–66.
945 Ibid., 93.
946 Ibid., 88.
947 B. J. Miller, "From 'jungles of terror' to 'God will begin a healing in this city': Billy Graham and evangelicals on cities and suburbs," *Journal of Urban History* (2020): 1–2.
948 J. Smart, "The Evangelist as Star: The Billy Graham Crusade in Australia, 1959," *The Journal of Popular Culture* 33, no. 1 (1999): 165–175.
949 B. D. Gilling, "'Back to the Simplicities of Religion': The 1959 Billy Graham Crusade in New Zealand and its Precursors," *Journal of Religious History* 17, no. 2 (1992): 223.
950 I. Harris, in *Otago Daily Times*, 9 March 2018; Smart, 168.
951 Gilling, 234.
952 G. S. Aldrete, *Daily Life in the Roman City: Rome, Pompeii and Ostia* (Westport: Greenwood Publishing Group, 2004), 35; M. E. Smith, "The archaeological study of neighborhoods and districts in ancient cities," *Journal of Anthropological Archaeology* 29, no. 2 (2010): 137–154.

953 Auckland's Last Tram, AM, ref. PH-CNEG-S1177.
954 Auckland Regional Planning Authority, "Master Transportation Plan for Metropolitan Auckland," (Auckland: Auckland Regional Planning Authority, 1955), 87, in M. Gunder, "Auckland's Motorway System: A New Zealand Genealogy of Imposed Automotive Progress 1946–66," *Urban Policy and Research* 20, no. 2 (2002): 134.
955 I. Muhammad, L. Matthews and J. Pearce, "Political path dependence in public transport in Auckland: an historical analysis," Australasian Urban History Planning History Group, Victoria University of Wellington, 12th Australasian Urban History Planning History Conference (2–5 February 2014, Wellington, New Zealand, 2014), 538.
956 H. B. Laurenson, "Myths and the City: A Social and Cultural History of Auckland, 1890–1990," PhD thesis (Auckland: University of Auckland, 2010), 186.
957 Ibid., 546; B. Labrum, *Real Modern: Everyday New Zealand in the 1950s and 1960s* (Wellington: Te Papa Press, 2015), 233; Laurenson, "Myths and the City," 186.
958 Gunder, 133.
959 S. L. McColley, "Historical GIS for Auckland suburbanisation: 1951–1981," MSc thesis (Auckland: University of Auckland, 2017), 2; W. Friessen, "The demographic transformation of inner-city Auckland," *New Zealand Population Review*, 35, no. 1 (2009): 55–74.
960 P. Mees and J. Dodson, "Backtracking Auckland?: Technical and Communicative Reason in Metropolitan Transport Planning," *International Planning Studies* 12, no.1 (2007): 35–53.
961 L. Kattan, S. Acharjee and R. Tay, "Pedestrian Scramble Operations: Pilot Study in Calgary, Alberta, Canada," *Transportation Research Record* 2140, no. 1 (2009): 79.
962 G. Riethmaier, photograph of Queen Street, ANZ, Ref. AAQT 6539 W3537 141/B4813.
963 Map of state and main highways showing load classification under the Heavy Motor Vehicles Regulations 1950, as at 1/4/1959, Auckland, New Zealand. Department of Lands and Survey, NLNZ, NZMS 19A; sheet 2.
964 A. W. Cliffe, "Auckland Harbour Bridge," *New Zealand Engineering* 13, no. 5 (1958): 202.
965 Royal Commission to Inquire into and Report Upon Transharbour Facilities in the Auckland Metropolitan Area and the Approaches Thereto, in *AJHR*, Session I, D-06 (1946), 7, 10, 13.
966 Ibid., 19.
967 C. E. Harris, "Slow train coming: the New Zealand state changes its mind about Auckland transit, 1949–56," *Urban Policy and Research* 23, no. 1 (2005): 47.
968 G. Roberts and O. A. Kerensky, "Auckland Harbour Bridge: Design (Including Plate)," *Proceedings of the Institution of Civil Engineers* 18, no. 4 (1961): 423.
969 NZPD 434 (15 October 1980), 4188.
970 I. Sharp, "The Big Meccano Set," *New Zealand Geographic* 7 (July–September 1990): 20–39.
971 *AS*, 30 May 1959, 4; Laurenson, "Myths and the City," 166.
972 C. McCahon, in *Home and Building* 18, no. 1 (June 1955): 44.
973 A. Snowball, "Delineating Nihilism: Colin McCahon's Last Paintings," BFA thesis (Brisbane: Griffith University, 2011), 12.
974 J. Luxford, in M. Stocker, "'The best thing ever seen in New Zealand': The Henry Moore Exhibition of 1956–57," *The Sculpture Journal* 16, no. 1 (2007): 74.
975 R. Hughes, *The Spectacle of Skill* (New York: Alfred Knopf, 2015), 3.

8 The 1960s

976 I. Hunter and M. Wilson, "Origins and opportunity: 150 years of New Zealand entrepreneurship," *Journal of Management & Organization* 13, no. 4 (2007): 303; *NZH*, 29 October 1963, 3.
977 D. L. Press, "Planned shopping centres: Impacts on retailers," *New Zealand Geographer* 50, no. 2 (1994): 15; P. J. Rimmer, "Planned Shopping Centres in New Zealand," *New Zealand Geographer* 23, no. 1 (1967): 76.
978 S. Feinberg, *What Makes Shopping Centers Tick* (New York: Fairchild Publications, 1960), 1.
979 C. Mawer and R. Kiddle, "Suburban shopping malls as spaces for community health and human flourishing: an Aotearoa New Zealand case study," *Journal of Urban Design* 25, no. 2 (2020): 237.
980 J. T. Diamond, View across plaza area at the newly opened shopping centre in New Lynn, photograph, AL, record I. D. JTD-11A-02070-2.

981 L. J. Truttman, *Heart of the Whau: The Story of the Centre of Avondale* (Auckland: Avondale-Waterview Historical Society, 2003), 117.
982 M. Smythe, *New Zealand by Design: A History of New Zealand Product Design* (Auckland: Godwit, 2011), 122.
983 K. Fallan, "One Must Offer 'Something for Everyone': Designing Crockery for Consumer Consent in 1950s' Norway," *Journal of Design History* 22, no. 2 (2009): 133–149.
984 J. Hawkins, "A Personal Recollection Of Four Years Work In The Crown Lynn Design Studio From 1978 To 1982," *Back Story: Journal of New Zealand Art, Media & Design History* 4 (2018): 96.
985 C. Bell, "'Not really beautiful, but iconic': New Zealand's Crown Lynn Ceramics," *Journal of Design History* 25, no. 4 (2012): 417.
986 F. Macdonald and R. Kerr, eds, *West: The History of Waitakere* (Auckland: Random House, 2009), 127.
987 C. Thompson, "Confronting design: case studies in the design of ceramics in New Zealand," PhD thesis (Auckland: Auckland University of Technology, 2003), 178.
988 F. McCahon-Jones, in F. Ralph, "Preserving the Legacy of Crown Lynn: The dedicated excavation efforts of one man have led to a museum that will preserve Crown Lynn's legacy," *Viva* (26 August 2015), n.p.
989 Factory worker, Crown Lynn, Te Papa MNZ, 1964, ref. F.013469; Crown Lynn workers, AWMM, ref. 72204N.
990 P. Andrews, interview, 13 April 2004, ATL, ref. OHInt-0899-14.
991 S. R. H. Jones, "Government policy and industry structure in New Zealand, 1900–1970," *Australian Economic History Review* 39, no. 3 (1999): 205; G. C. Billing, "The Industrial Pattern and New Zealand's Future," *The Economic Journal* 67, no. 265 (1957): 73.
992 T. Niall, *The Trekka Dynasty* (Auckland: Iconic Publishing, 2004), 107.
993 M. T. Maung, "Beneficiation of ironsands from Raglan, New Zealand," PhD thesis (Dunedin: University of Otago, 1962), 1.
994 S. 3, *Iron and Steel Industry Act 1959*.
995 E. Currie, "Old port town Waiuku," *Heritage Matters: The Magazine for New Zealanders Restoring, Preserving and Enjoying Our Heritage* 29 (2011): 26–28.
996 P. Joseph, "Maori and the Market: the Waitangi Tribunal," *Race and Class* 41, no. 4 (2000): 67; W. H. Oliver, *Claims to the Waitangi Tribunal* (Wellington: Department of Justice, 1991), 26.
997 Report of the Auckland Drainage Commission, in *AJHR*, Session I, H-03 (1947), 1–67.
998 S. Clark and S. Cameron, *Oxidation Pond Guidelines 2005* (Wellington: Ministry for the Environment, 2005), 5.
999 Auckland Regional Council, *A Brief History of Auckland's Urban Form*, 13, 15.
1000 Watercare, "The history of wastewater treatment in Auckland, 1878 to 2005," WWIS1-0918 (Auckland: Auckland City Council, 2010), 2–3.
1001 Mackintosh, "Shifting grounds: history, memory and materiality in Auckland landscapes c. 1350–2018," PhD thesis (Auckland: University of Auckland, 2019), 5.
1002 A. Taylor, "Maori Village is Rapidly Modernised," *Te Ao Hou* 9, no. 5 (September 1961): 37.
1003 I. Lawlor, *An assessment of heritage resources located within the proposed Otuataua Stonefields Historic Reserve Visitor Centre development 'footprint', and measures to avoid, remedy and mitigate effects* (Auckland: 2009), 103.
1004 Matthews and Matthews Architects Ltd, *Mangere Town Centre: Historic Heritage Survey*, Appendix 1 (Auckland: Matthews and Matthews Architects Ltd, 2013), 10.
1005 D. K. Lyon, "The Development and Performance of Airports in New Zealand as Commercial Entities," PhD thesis (Palmerston North: Massey University, 2011), 57, 151; G. T. Bloomfield, "Geographic Notebook: The Auckland International Airport," *New Zealand Geographer* 22, no. 1 (1966): 88.
1006 M. Thompson and A. Clements, *Where New Zealand Touches the World — From Farm Paddock to South Pacific Hub: A History of Auckland International Airport* (Auckland: Auckland International Airport, 2003), 137–38, 161.
1007 Bloomfield, 90.
1008 R. Bedford, "Pacific Islanders in New Zealand," *Espace Populations Sociétés* 12, no. 2 (1994): 187.
1009 T. Efi, in Isola Productions, *Dawn Raids*, documentary, R. Jean, producer (Auckland, 2005).

1010 S. U. Faemani, "The Impact of Remittances on Rural Development in Tongan Villages," *Asian and Pacific Migration Journal* 4, no. 1 (1995): 139-155.
1011 T. Brown Pulu, "Kakai Tonga 'i 'Okalani Nu'u Sila: Tongan Generations in Auckland New Zealand," PhD thesis (Hamilton: University of Waikato, 2007), 27, 121.
1012 S. D. Webb, *New Zealand Society: Contemporary Perspectives* (Sydney: John Wiley & Sons Australasia Pty, 1973), 322.
1013 J. R. McCreary, *Housing and Welfare Needs of Islanders in Auckland: A Report to the Minister of Island Territories* (Wellington: Victoria University, 1965), 25, 41-43.
1014 A. D. Trlin, "Attitudes Towards West Samoan Immigrants in Auckland, New Zealand," *The Australian Quarterly* 44, no. 3 (1972): 55.
1015 R. Loto, D. Hodgetts, K. Chamberlain, L. W. Nikora, R. Karapu and A. Barnett, "Pasifika in the news: The portrayal of Pacific peoples in the New Zealand press," *Journal of Community and Applied Social Psychology* 16, no. 2 (2006): 100.
1016 F. J. Taule'ale'ausumai, "The Samoan diaspora church in New Zealand: Patterns of movement and dynamics amongst three generations of Samoan families," PhD thesis (Auckland: Auckland University of Technology, 2019), 40.
1017 D. Ioka, "Origin and beginning of the Congregational Christian Church of Samoa (CCCS) in Aotearoa New Zealand," PhD thesis (Dunedin: University of Otago, 1998), 175.
1018 Cited in C. and L. Macpherson, "Evangelical Religion among Pacific Island Migrants: New Faiths or Brief Diversions?," *Journal of Ritual Studies* 15, no. 2 (2001): 33.
1019 Taule'ale'ausumai, 77-78.
1020 Ibid., 57.
1021 M. Anae, "From Kava to Coffee: The Browning of Auckland," in *Almighty Auckland*, I. Carter, D. Craig and S. Matthewman, eds (Palmerston North: Dunmore Press, 2004), 90 (emphasis in original).
1022 S. Jelicich and A. Trlin, "Croatian," in *Book & Print in New Zealand: A Guide to Print Culture in Aotearoa*, P. Griffith, K. Maslin and R. Harvey, eds (Wellington: Victoria University Press, 1997), 276.
1023 Interview with N. P. (July 2021).
1024 B. McEwan, M. Campbell and D. Swain, "New Zealand culture of intoxication: Local and global influences," *New Zealand Sociology* 25, no. 2 (2010): 16.
1025 N. J. Pollock, "Rugby, Racing and Beer in New Zealand: Colonising a Consumer Culture," in *Liquid Bread: Beer and Brewing in Cross-Cultural Perspective*, W. Schiefenhövel and H. Macbeth, eds (Oxford, Berghahn Books, 2011), 126.
1026 D. Kennedy, "Gourmet Restaurant (Auckland): The Gourmet. A la carte menu. Operated by Otto Groen (Amsterdam) and Jim Jennings (New York City) [ca 1960-1961?]," photo, NLNZ, Ref: Eph-C-DINING-1960-02.
1027 Heritage "Consultancy Services, North Shore Heritage — Thematic Review Report," Auckland Council Document TR 2011/010 (Auckland: Auckland Council, 2011), 66; G. Goodall. Colour postcard of the entrance of the new Mon Desir hotel, Takapuna, 1965. ALHC, ref. T0271; Gregory Riethmaier, "Takapuna Beer Garden," ANZ, ref. AAQT 6539, A84942.
1028 L. Neill, C. Bell and N. Hemmington, "A Pie Cart Story: The longevity of a Vernacular Fast Food Eatery," *Locale: The Australasian-Pacific Journal of Regional Food Studies* 2 (2012): 107.
1029 A. Gopnik, "Foreword," in R. L. Spang, *The Invention of the Restaurant: Paris and Modern Gastronomic Culture* (Cambridge, MA: Harvard University Press, 2000), 1-4.
1030 J. Mitchell, "Has 'foreign' food internationalized New Zealand's cuisine?," in *Culinary Arts and Sciences VII: Global, National and Local Perspectives*, H. H. Hartwell, P. Lugosi and J. S. A. Edwards, eds (Bournemouth: International Centre for Tourism and Hospitality Research, 2011): 238.
1031 "Tui Flower in full bloom," *New Zealand Woman's Weekly* (30 May 2010): n.p.
1032 Advertisement for 246, 1967, in K. Dix, "24 Shopping Centre," *New Zealand Fashion Museum* (September 2017), n.p.
1033 Dix, n.p.
1034 Interview with M. D. (June 2017).
1035 H. Keith, *New Zealand Yesterdays: A Look at Our Recent Past* (Sydney: Readers Digest Services, 1984), 190.
1036 Old Time Transport Preservation League, Minutes, correspondence, accounts etc., AML, ref. 88/28, MS-1651.
1037 A. Hare and E. Currie, "MOTAT Gems," *Heritage Matters: The Magazine for New Zealanders Restoring, Preserving and Enjoying our Heritage* 21 (2009): 24-26.

1038 MOTAT, *MOTAT: Moving History* (Auckland: MOTAT, 2006), 4-5.
1039 J. Cresswell, *MOTAT: Museum of Transport and Technology of New Zealand* (Auckland: Paul Hamlyn, 1976), 6.
1040 A. La Roche, *An Introduction to the Howick Historical Village* (Auckland: Howick and Districts Historical Society, 1997), 5.
1041 J. Walling, "Is Authenticity Necessary for Heritage? Official and Non-Official Views Through the Lens of the Open-Air Museum Howick Historical Village," PhD thesis (Auckland: University of Auckland: 2016), 49-51.
1042 H. Laurenson, *Going Up, Going Down: The Rise and Fall of the Department Store* (Auckland: Auckland University Press, 2005), 200; "Opening of the Centennial Street (Auckland 1866) exhibition at the Auckland War Memorial Museum," AM, ref. PH-RES-1699.
1043 *Reserves and Other Lands Disposal Act 1963*.
1044 A. Trapenznik and A. Gee, "'Each in his narrow cell for ever laid': Dunedin's Southern Cemetery and its New Zealand Counterparts," *Public History Review* 20 (2013): 45, 49, 59; S. Best and L. Furey, "Westney Road Denominational Graveyard. Report to the New Zealand Historic Places Trust," (Auckland: GFC Heritage Ltd, 2007), 19.
1045 United Nations Department of Economic and Social Affairs, "2019 Revision of World Population Prospects," (United Nations, 2019); D. C. Maré, A. Coleman and R. Pinkerton, *Patterns of population location in Auckland. Motu Working Paper 11-06* (Wellington: Motu Economic and Public Policy Research, 2011), 70.
1046 Auckland Regional Council, *A Brief History of Auckland's Urban Form*, 17.
1047 J. S. Whitelaw and G. T. Bloomfield, "Auckland, New Zealand's Largest Urban Area," *Geography* 54, no. 3 (1969): 306-7.
1048 Ibid.
1049 Auckland's Civic Administration Building, 5 October 1970. Sir George Grey Special Collections, AL, Ref: 580-20350; Auckland Council, "Fact Sheet: Civic Administration Building," (Auckland, 2017), 1.
1050 "Auckland City Council Administration Building," *Home and Building* 29, no. 6 (November 1966): 60-63.
1051 J. Gatley, "The Question of Auckland's Civic Building," *Docomomo Journal* 1 (2015): 83.
1052 J. Gottmann, "Why the Skyscraper?," *Geographical Review* 56, no. 2 (April 1966): 198, 200, 202, 211.
1053 "Auckland Synagogue and Community Centre," *New Zealand Institute of Architects Journal* 37, no. 5 (20 May 1970): 142, in A. Cusins-Lewer and J. Gatley, "The 'Myers Park Experiment' (1913-1916) and its Legacy in Auckland," *Fabrications* 12, no. 1 (2002): 71; Auckland Hebrew Congregation, "Submission on the proposed amendments to the Auckland Unitary Plan, (Operative in Part) Historic Heritage Overlay Schedule 14.1 as they relate to 108-116 Greys Avenue, Auckland (ID01965)," Appendix 2 (Auckland, 7 March 2018), 16, 21-25.
1054 T. Baldwin, "History of electricity security in New Zealand," (May 2005), 3.
1055 M. Abbott, "The long-term development of New Zealand's electricity supply industry," New Zealand Economic Papers 44, no. 1 (2010): 81.
1056 *Electricity Advisory Council Act 1962*.
1057 R. Murray, *Nuclear Energy: An Introduction to the Concepts, Systems, and Applications of Nuclear Processes* (Burlington, MA: Elsevier, 2009), 223.
1058 M. Templeton, *Standing Upright Here: New Zealand in the Nuclear Age, 1945-1990* (Wellington: New Zealand Institute of International Affairs/Victoria University Press, 2006), 51-53.
1059 World Nuclear Association, *Nuclear Energy Prospects in New Zealand* (London: World Nuclear Association, 2009), 2.
1060 J. A. Coll and R. Radicella, "Nuclear Activities in Argentina. A Short Review. Part 2," *Ciencia e Investigacion* 54, no. 1 (2002): 3-8.
1061 T. P. McCarthy, *Nuclear Power Generation in New Zealand: Report of the Royal Commission of Inquiry* (Wellington: Government Printer, 1978), 279.
1062 K. Clements, *Back from the Brink: The Creation of a Nuclear-Free New Zealand* (Wellington: Port Nicholson Press, 1988), 136.
1063 P. Williams, *A Passion for Justice* (Christchurch: Shoal Bay Press, 1997), 92.
1064 J. Banks, in S. Bainbridge, *The Bassett Road Machine-Gun Murders: New Zealand's Gangster Killings* (Auckland: Allen & Unwin, 2013), 26.

1065 P. Faulkner, in K. Ryan, *Justice Without Fear or Favour* (Auckland: Hodder, Moa, Beckett, 1997), 30.
1066 Ryan, 42ff.
1067 New Zealand Police, "Historic NZ Murder Rate Report 1926-2017," (Wellington, 2017), 1.
1068 P. B. Allen, in *NZPD* 338 (19 June 1964), 180.
1069 Bainbridge, 253–54.
1070 S. Del Visco, "Yellow peril, red scare: race and communism in National Review," *Ethnic and Racial Studies* 42, no. 4 (2019): 627.
1071 R. G. Rabel, "The Vietnam Antiwar Movement in New Zealand," *Peace and Change* 17, no. 1 (1992): 4.
1072 *White Ribbon*, 1 July 1960, 2.
1073 Interview with A. E. (June 2020).
1074 Interview with T. P. (May 2019).
1075 B. Lee, "Struggling to make the world a better place: Exploring some experiences of activists in the Auckland Progressive Youth Movement (1965-1977)," PhD thesis (Auckland: Auckland University of Technology, 2019), 56.
1076 Rabel, 7–8.
1077 Ibid., 11.
1078 'Jack', in Lee, 87.
1079 Anonymous, in S. M. Katavich, "Responses in New Zealand to the Vietnam War: a case study of the Palmerston North community," MA thesis (Palmerston North: Massey University, 2020), 68–69.
1080 B. Coutts and N. Fitness, *Protest in New Zealand* (Auckland: Pearson, 2013), 144.
1081 *New York Times*, 21 May 1967, 6.
1082 *NZH*, 30 October 1967, 1.
1083 Rabel, 21.
1084 'Daron', in M. Dorsey, "The Post-War Reconciliation Process of New Zealand Vietnam War Veterans," PhD thesis (Dunedin: University of Otago, 2014), 111.
1085 M. J. Heale, "The Sixties as History: A Review of the Political Historiography," *Reviews in American History* 33, no. 1 (2005): 133–152; T. Tsimpouki, "The Sixties Are Dead: Long Live Their Legacy: The Politics and Poetics of Counterculture," *Gramma: Journal of Theory and Criticism* 16 (2008): 45–66.
1086 A. J. Sepie, "Counterculture within a Counter-Culture: New Zealand, Psychedelic Rock, and the Moral Guardians of the 60s and 70s," *Rock Music Studies* 5, no. 3 (2018): 222.
1087 N. Whiteley, "Interior Design in the 1960s: Arenas for Performance," *Art History* 10, no. 1 (1987): 79–90.
1088 A. Blackburn, *Radio Pirates: How Hauraki Rocked the Boat* (Auckland: Shoestring Press, 2014), 121.
1089 Sepie, 223–24.
1090 H. Watt, in *NZPD* 369 (9 October 1970), 3901.

9 The 1970s

1091 J. Adam, V. Burgess and D. Ellis, *Rugged Determination: Historical Window on Swanson, 1854–2004* (Auckland: Swanson Residents and Ratepayers Association Incorporated, 2004), 101.
1092 K. I. Campbell, "The Beatles at Woodstock," *Popular Music and Society* 43, no. 2 (2020): 193.
1093 Redwood 70 Festival Poster (Auckland, 1970).
1094 A. Schmidt, "Redwood 70 National Music Convention — West Auckland January 31 to February 1, 1970," in *Audioculture: Iwi Waiata* (12 December 2013), n.p.
1095 P. Sinclair, in "Redwood 70," (New Zealand Broadcasting Corporation, 1970).
1096 Schmidt.
1097 Sinclair.
1098 Auckland Regional Council, *A Brief History of Auckland's Urban Form*, 19.
1099 Y. Liu, "Visualizing the urban development of Sydney (1971-1996) in GIS," in *Proceedings of the 10th Annual Colloquium of the Spatial Information Research Centre. Dunedin: The University of Otago* (Dunedin, 1998), 189–98; E. S. Mills and J. P. Tan. "A comparison of urban population density functions in developed and developing countries," *Urban Studies* 17, no. 3 (1980): 313–321.
1100 J. Polkinghorne, "New Zealand and the 1970s oil shocks — more than just 'carless days'," (Auckland, 2014), n.p.; D. Peterson, "Petrol Prices and Taxes," (Wellington: Parliamentary Library, 2001), 1; F. Delbruck, "Oil prices and the New Zealand economy," *Reserve Bank of New Zealand Bulletin* 68, no. 4 (2005): 5.
1101 Interview with M. J. (August 2021).
1102 *Municipal Corporations Act 1954*.
1103 Interview with E. M. (December 1999).
1104 I. Johnstone, "Johnstone's Journey — Settling for Suburbia," (New Zealand National Film Unit, 1978).
1105 Unnamed, in ibid.
1106 Johnstone.
1107 Interview with O. P. (July 2021).
1108 L. Shaw, "A Woman's Place," in *At Home in New Zealand: History, Houses, People*, B. Brookes, ed. (Wellington: Bridget Williams Books, 2000), 168.
1109 N. Isaacs, "House assembly — prefabrication and factory manufacture," *Build Magazine* 108 (2008): 95.
1110 O. Petersen, "Original P. C. L. Massey building fire," AM, ref. H-1988-9-F1-2.
1111 Interview with R. W. (February 2020).
1112 K. Gibson, M. Morgan, C. Woolley and T. Powis, "A different kind of family: Retrospective accounts of growing up at Centrepoint and implications for adulthood," (Palmerston North: Massey University, 2010).
1113 B. D. Zablocki, "Communes, Encounter Groups and the Search for Community," in *In Search for Community: Encounter Groups and Social Change*, K. W. Back, ed. (New York: Routledge, 2019), 97–144.
1114 F. Höllinger, "Does the counter-cultural character of New Age persist? Investigating social and political attitudes of New Age followers," *Journal of Contemporary Religion* 19, no. 3 (2004): 289–309.
1115 Cited in L. Oakes, *Inside Centrepoint: The Story of a New Zealand Community* (Auckland: Benton Ross, 1986), 114.
1116 Gibson, Morgan, Woolley and Powis, 4.
1117 Cited in ibid., 33.
1118 Ibid., 35.
1119 Ibid., 69.
1120 Ibid., 77.
1121 A. Richter, "Centrepoint: Neither Free nor Loving," Radio New Zealand broadcast, 7:45 pm (31 May 2021).
1122 J. Lawrence and R. Kearns, "Exploring the 'fit' between people and providers: refugee health needs and health care services in Mt Roskill, Auckland, New Zealand," *Health and Social Care in the Community* 13, no. 5 (2005): 454.
1123 J. Reidy, *Not Just Passing Through: The Making of Mt Roskill* (Auckland: Auckland City Council, 2007), 93.
1124 L. J. Francis, D. W. Lankshear and S. H. Jones, "The influence of the charismatic movement on local church life: A comparative study among Anglican rural, urban and suburban churches," *Journal of Contemporary Religion* 15, no. 1 (2000): 121–130.
1125 P. Lineham, "The place of small denominations in the religious landscape of New Zealand," *Stimulus: The New Zealand Journal of Christian Thought and Practice* 21, no. 2 (2014): 20.
1126 E. Van Ingen and N. Moor, "Explanations of changes in church attendance between 1970 and 2009," *Social Science Research* 52 (2015): 558–569.
1127 Interview with P. T. and A. T. (April 2018).
1128 K. Ward, "Towards 2015: the future of mainline Protestantism in New Zealand," *Journal of Beliefs and Values* 27, no. 1 (2006): 14.
1129 G. Davies, *Religion in Postwar Britain* (Oxford: Blackwell, 1994), 19.
1130 K. Ward, "Rugby and Church: Worlds in Conflict," *Reality* 53 (2002): 26–27.
1131 R. D. Putnam, "Bowling Alone: America's Declining Social Capital," *Journal of Democracy* 6, no. 1 (January 1995): 65–78.
1132 A. Drury, *Islam in New Zealand: The First Mosque* (Auckland: Abdullah Drury, 2006), 22.
1133 Ibid., 31.
1134 K. Ketola, "The Hare Krishna and the counterculture in the light of the theory of divergent modes of religiosity," *Method and Theory in the Study of Religion* 16, no. 3 (2004): 301.
1135 E. B. Rochford, "Recruitment strategies, ideology, and organization in the Hare Krishna movement," *Social Problems* 29, no. 4 (1982): 399–410.
1136 W. Dart, "Film," in *Rip It Up* 51 (October 1981), 22.
1137 D. Pepper, "Communes and the green vision: counterculture, lifestyle and the New Age," *Utopian Studies* 4, no. 1 (1993): 237–238.
1138 *The New Zealand Official Year-Book, 1986–7* (Wellington: Government Printer, 1987), 109.
1139 *AS*, 19 August 1971, 21.

1140 I. Brailsford, "'If there's not one near you now, there soon will be': American Fast-Food Chains Come to New Zealand," *NZJH* 39, no. 1 (2005): 59.
1141 I. Brailsford, "'US Image but NZ Venture': Americana and Fast-Food Advertising in New Zealand, 1971–1990," *Australasian Journal of American Studies* 22, no. 2 (2003): 10–11.
1142 R. Kumar, "A Comparative Study Between on Pizza Hut and Domino's Pizza," *International Journal of Marketing and Technology* 5, no. 9 (2015): 89.
1143 *Western Leader*, 10 September 1974, 18.
1144 Brailsford, "'US Image but NZ Venture'," 12.
1145 Jenna, in C. A. Russell, A. Cristel, H. J. Schau and P. Bliese, "Brand afterlife: Transference to alternate brands following corporate failure," *Journal of Business Research* 97 (2019): 257.
1146 Homestead Chicken, 1973, Dominion Post Collection, ATL (PAColl-7327), Ref: EP/1973/3746/26a.
1147 Brailsford, "'US Image but NZ Venture'," 12–14.
1148 S. Everingham, *Wild Ride: The Rise & Fall of Cobb & Co.* (Camberwell: Penguin, 2007), 1–12.
1149 P. Little, "A Brief History of Cobb & Co," *North & South* (29 May 2018), n.p.
1150 N. Bonney, in *NZH*, 7 October 2016, n.p.
1151 Interview with S. R. (August 2021).
1152 Kerry, "1970s Food," in H. Jackson, "Foodlovers," (Auckland, October 2007).
1153 A. F. Smith, *Eating History: 30 Turning Points in the Making of American Cuisine* (New York: Columbia University Press, 2009), 172.
1154 D. Harper, *Food Medicine* 1 (Bloomington: Balboa Press, 2020), chapter 3.
1155 Land March Itinerary, ANZ, ref: AAMK 869 W3074 Box 684/d 19/1/774 Part 1.
1156 R. Walker, *Ka Whawhai Tonu Matou: Struggle Without End* (Auckland: Penguin Books, 1990), 212.
1157 A. Harris, *Hīkoi: Forty Years of Māori Protest* (Wellington: Huia Publishers, 2004), 71–72.
1158 R. S. Hill, "Maori urban migration and the assertion of indigeneity in Aotearoa/New Zealand, 1945–1975," *Interventions* 14, no. 2 (2012): 270.
1159 Harris, 74.
1160 Te Roopu o te Matakite, "Why We March," (Auckland, 1975), 1.
1161 H. Smith, *E Tū Ake: Māori Standing Strong* (Wellington: Te Papa Press, 2011), 121.
1162 G. Lindsay, *Thousand-Eyed Eel* (Christchurch: Hawk Press, 1976), 3.
1163 W. Cooper, "Māori Land March. Whina Cooper," Radio New Zealand, Sound Archives T7113.
1164 Ibid.
1165 Cited in G. Stevens (director), *Te Matakite o Aotearoa — The Maori Land March*, television documentary, (Auckland: Television Two, 1975).
1166 H. Harawira, in *Takaparawhau: The People's Story. 1998 Bastion Point 20-Year Commemoration Book*, S. Hawke, ed. (Auckland: Moko Productions, 1998), 22.
1167 M. Johnson, "'The Land of the Wrong White Crowd': Anti-racist Organizations and Pakeha Identity Politics in the 1970s," *NZJH* 39, no. 2 (2005): 140.
1168 Waitangi Tribunal, *Report of The Waitangi Tribunal on The Orakei Claim, Wai-9* (Wellington: Department of Justice, 1987), 150.
1169 T. Dibble, in ibid., 153.
1170 M. Maihi, in *Takaparawhau*, 16.
1171 A. Robb, "Bastion Point: A desperate struggle and a dream fulfilled," in *E-Tangata* (3 June 2018), n.p.
1172 *NZH*, 29 September 1977, 1.
1173 J. Hawke, in *NZH*, 1 April 2010, 3.
1174 *Eastern Courier*, 30 May 1978, 1.
1175 Robb.
1176 Bastion Point Eviction, 25 May 1978, Television New Zealand Archive, Ref: P182678.
1177 R. Fowler, in *Takaparawhau*, 31.
1178 S. Hawke, in ibid., 19.
1179 R. Hawke, in ibid., 77.
1180 M. Wall, "National Party election advertisement," (Wellington, November 1975).
1181 Cited in Isola Productions, *Dawn Raids*, documentary, D. Fepuila'e, dir. (Auckland, 2005).
1182 T. Ross, "New Zealand's Overstaying Islander: A Construct of the Ideology of Race and Immigration," MA thesis (Wellington: Victoria University, 1994), 62.
1183 *AS*, 19 February 1976, 13.
1184 Cited in Isola Productions.
1185 D. V. Williams, "New Zealand Immigration Policies and the Law — A Perspective," *Otago Law Review* 4, no. 1 (1977): 185.
1186 S. Thomsen, J. Tavita and Z. Levi-Teu, *A Pacific Perspective on the Living Standards Framework and Wellbeing*, New Zealand Treasury Discussion Paper (Wellington: New Zealand Treasury, 2018), 5.
1187 H. Burnley, in *AS*, 26 October 1976, 3.
1188 J. Mitchell, "Immigration and national identity in 1970s New Zealand," PhD thesis (Dunedin: University of Otago, 2003), 254.
1189 T. Maloney, "Welfare reform and unemployment in New Zealand," *Economica* 69, no. 274 (2002): 273.
1190 T. Boraman, "A middle-class diversion from working-class struggle? The New Zealand new left from the mid-1950s to the mid-1970s," *Labour History* 103 (2012): 214.
1191 D. E. Wilton, "A note on the impact of government intervention in the petrol market, 1979–1980," *New Zealand Economic Papers* 17, no. 1 (1983): 123.
1192 D. Walker and R. Manning, "Rationing and Deterrence: General Theory and the Example of New Zealand's 'Carless Days' Scheme," Centre for the Economic Analysis of Property Rights. Economics and Law Workshop Papers, 83-09. London, ON: Department of Economics, University of Western Ontario (1983): 1–10.
1193 Interview with O. F. (July 2021).
1194 B. Roth, "Chronicle: April–June 1979," *New Zealand Journal of Industrial Relations* 4, no. 2 (1979), 1–2; B. Roth, "Chronicle: July–September 1979," *New Zealand Journal of Industrial Relations* 4, no. 3 (1979): 1–4.
1195 K. Nicholls, "Why was there no general strike in 1991? Corporatism, pluralism and neoliberal labour relations in New Zealand," *Commonwealth & Comparative Politics* 40, no. 1 (2002): 7; *NZH*, 21 September 1979, 16.
1196 H. Alleyne, "Traversing Memory: the last days of the old Mangere bridge," MA&D thesis (Auckland: Auckland University of Technology, 2014), 17.
1197 A. Reeves and J. McNeil, "The Design of the New Old Mangere Bridge," *Austroads Bridge Conference, 10th, 2017, Melbourne, Victoria, Australia* (2017), 1.
1198 Interview with J. O. (April 2021).
1199 Z. Wallace, in *Salient* 42, no. 5 (1979): 6.
1200 Interview with S. R. (April 2021).
1201 R. Willis, "Ten years of change in New Zealand manufacturing employment," *Labour, Employment and Work in New Zealand* (1994): 346.
1202 L. Murphy, "To the market and back: Housing policy and state housing in New Zealand," *GeoJournal* 59, no. 2 (2004): 119.
1203 Cited in D. I. Haigh, "Community development and New Zealand local authorities in the 1970s and 1980s," *New Zealand Sociology* 29, no. 1 (2014): 79–97.
1204 L. F. Tunufa'i, "The price of spiritual and social survival: investigating the reasons for the departure of young New Zealand-born Samoans from a South Auckland Samoan Seventh-day Adventist Church," PhD thesis (Auckland: Auckland University of Technology, 2005), 30.
1205 B. Ringer, "A History of Manukau City Centre," AL, Ref: LHE-004.
1206 A. Barrie, "Auckland City in the 1970s," *Itinerary No. 39, Block: The Broadsheet of the Auckland Branch of the New Zealand Institute of Architects* 10 (2011), 3.
1207 Manukau City Centre shopping mall, Auckland, 20 Oct 1976, NLNZ, Ref: WA-73691-G; Invitation to the official opening of the Manukau City Centre mall, outer and inner fold. (Ephemera, Commerce, 20/10/76) Auckland Libraries Heritage Collections MJ_4935.
1208 T. Parsons, *Essays in Sociological Theory* (New York: The Free Press, 1954), 423–29.
1209 Auckland Regional Council, *A Brief History of Auckland's Urban Form*, 19.
1210 *Sunday News*, 1 August 2021, 6; R. Beaglehole and R. Jackson, "Coronary heart disease mortality, morbidity, and risk factor trends in New Zealand," *Cardiology* 72, no. 1–2 (1985): 32.
1211 *NZH*, 7 December 1894, 3.
1212 Programmes for the annual Auckland Regatta, 1970, 1971, 1973, NLNZ, Ref: Eph-A-BOAT-AR-1970/1973.
1213 K. F. O'Connor and D. G. Simmons, "The use of islands for recreation and tourism: Changing significance for nature conservation," in *Ecological Restoration of New Zealand Islands*, D. R. Towns, C. H. Daugherty and I. A. E. Atkinson, eds, Conservation Sciences Publication No. 2 (Wellington: Department of Conservation, 1990): 187–188.

1214 University of Bradford, "The J. B. Priestley Archive: Interim Catalogue," Archive reference code: (GB 0532) PRI, Special Collections, J. B. Priestley Library (Bradford: University of Bradford, April 2013), 86.
1215 J. B. Priestley, *A Visit to New Zealand* (London: Heinemann, 1974), 124–25, 141–42 (emphases in original).

10 The 1980s

1216 s. 4, *Shop Trading Hours Amendment Act 1980*.
1217 s. 2, *Shops and Offices Amendment Act 1945*; J. E. Martin, "'Waging War on the Labour Market': The State and Wage Labour in Late Nineteenth-Century New Zealand," *The Turnbull Library Record* 26 (1993): 43.
1218 A. Kennedy, "The history of New Zealand shop trading hours," *International Journal of Retail & Distribution Management* 38, no. 8 (2010): 628.
1219 *AS*, 12 December 1979, 1.
1220 *National Business Review*, 24 January 1980, 4.
1221 *Metro*, 2 July 1981, 11.
1222 Ibid., 11–12.
1223 D. Lindsey, "A brief history of conscience voting in New Zealand," *Australian Parliamentary Review* 23, no. 1 (2008): 149.
1224 Cited in A. Kennedy, "Keep Sunday Free: Social Engineering Through Shop Trading Hours in New Zealand," PhD thesis (Auckland: Auckland University of Technology, 2009), 128.
1225 *Shop Trading Hours Act 1990*.
1226 C. Saunders, "The response of grassroots Christians to the introduction of Sunday trading to New Zealand in 1989: by what authority are you doing these things and who gave you this authority?," PhD thesis (Dunedin: University of Otago, 2011), 68–74.
1227 *Labour Relations Act 1987*.
1228 Cited in Kennedy, "Keep Sunday Free," 140.
1229 *AS*, 25 March 1988, 6.
1230 Kennedy, "Keep Sunday Free," 138.
1231 R. J. Osborne, "Toward Prosperity? Some Aspects of Recent Economic Deregulation in New Zealand," *UCLA Pacific Basin Law Journal* 7 (1990): 169.
1232 H. Clark, in *NZPD* 503 (5 December 1989), 13936.
1233 K. Witten et al., "New Zealand parents' understandings of the intergenerational decline in children's independent outdoor play and active travel," *Children's Geographies* 11, no. 2 (2013): 216–217; J. Vowles, "Civic engagement in New Zealand: Decline or demise?," Inaugural Professorial Address (Auckland: University of Auckland, 2004), 1–2.
1234 Welcome to Leisure Land. Theme Park. Te Atatu, Auckland. n.d., AM, ref. GV155 Box 2.
1235 Statement by Leisureland staff member, June 2019.
1236 Safari Land to move from Massey site to join Footrot Flats Fun Park, in Te Atatu North, AL, Ref: NZCI000128157.
1237 Institution of Professional Engineers New Zealand, *Engineering to 1990* (Wellington: Engineering Publications Ltd, 1990), 8.
1238 D. Grzelewski, "Kelly Tarlton," *New Zealand Geographic* 84 (March–April 2007); K. Wrigglesworth, "In retrospect: World-first fish world," *Engineering Insight* 13, no. 2 (2012): 24–26.
1239 P. K. Hamlin, "The 1981 Springbok Tour of New Zealand," *Auckland University Law Review* 4 (1980): 314–316.
1240 G. Chapple, *When the Tour Came to Auckland* (Wellington: Bridget Williams Books, 2014), 1.
1241 T. Richards, *Dancing on Our Bones: New Zealand, South Africa, Rugby and Racism* (Wellington: Bridget Williams Books, 1999), 3–44.
1242 E. Rankin, "Banners, batons and barbed wire: Anti-apartheid images of the Springbok rugby tour protests in New Zealand," *De Arte* 42, no. 76 (2007): 22.
1243 H. McDougall, "'The whole world's watching': New Zealand, international opinion, and the 1981 Springbok Rugby Tour," *Journal of Sport History* 45, no. 2 (2018): 202–223.
1244 S. Potgieter, "'Barbed-Wire Boks': The Long Shadow of the 1981 Springbok Tour of New Zealand and the United States of America," PhD thesis (Stellenbosch: Stellenbosch University, 2017), 85.
1245 Richards, *Dancing on Our Bones*, 224.
1246 R. Meurant, in *Sunday Star-Times*, 11 July 2021, 5.
1247 Television New Zealand commentary (12 September 1981).
1248 M. Jones, in *NZH*, 9 July 2006, 8.
1249 B. R. Davies, "Operation Rugby," *The Police Journal* 55, no. 1 (1982): 52.
1250 M. MacLean, "'Almost the same, but not quite … Almost the same, but not white': Maori and Aotearoa/New Zealand's 1981 Springbok Tour," *Kunapipi: Journal of Postcolonial Writing* 23, no. 1 (2001): 69–82.
1251 W. F. Keane, "'Ex-pats' and 'Poofters': The New Zealand All Whites," *Sport in Society* 4, no. 3 (2001): 49.
1252 M. A. Morrison, "The Grassroots of the 1981 Springbok Tour: An examination of the actions and perspectives of everyday New Zealanders during the 1981 Springbok Rugby Tour of New Zealand," MA thesis (Christchurch: University of Canterbury, 2017), 191.
1253 C. Little, "The forgotten game? A reassessment of the place of soccer within New Zealand society, sport and historiography," *Soccer & Society* 3, no. 2 (2002): 39.
1254 C. Dempsey, in Keane, 55.
1255 Papatoetoe A. F. C. Results, 10 & 11 May 1980, unpublished document.
1256 *New Zealand Listener*, 3 October 1981, 32; Keane, 59.
1257 *New Zealand Listener*, 26 September 1981, 20–21.
1258 Interview with S. C. (May 2021).
1259 K. Quinn, interview about 1987 Rugby World Cup, Television New Zealand (11 September 2007).
1260 J. Harris, "Definitely maybe: continuity and change in the Rugby World Cup," *Sport in Society* 16, no. 7 (2013): 854.
1261 S. Fitzpatrick, in Talksport Radio (19 November 2010).
1262 J. Vowles, "Social Structure. Political Attitudes and Trade Unionism: An Analysis of Aspects of the Fourth Labour Government's Election Coalition," New Zealand Political Science Association Conference Paper, (Auckland: University of Auckland, 1985), n.p.
1263 Interview with D. O. (September 2020).
1264 K. P. Clements, "New Zealand's Role in Promoting a Nuclear-Free Pacific," *Journal of Peace Research* 25, no. 4 (1988): 396.
1265 M. Templeton, *Standing Upright Here: New Zealand in the Nuclear Age, 1945–1990* (Wellington: New Zealand Institute of International Affairs/Victoria University Press, 2006), 382.
1266 Oppose Nuclear Visits, poster, 1983, AML, ref. EPH-2008-1-14.
1267 F. Barber, *The Christian Science Monitor* (5 December 1983), n.p.; E. Heath "David and Goliath cartoon," ATL, ref. B-144-034.
1268 United Press International, "About 50 protest boats tried to prevent the USS *Phoenix*," (9 November 1983), n.p.
1269 Vowles, n.p.
1270 P. Reynolds, "Popular responses to the New Zealand Government's Nuclear Weapons Policy: 1984–1986," *Politics* 22, no. 1 (1987): 63–64.
1271 D. Lange, "New Zealand's Security Policy," *Foreign Affairs* 63 (1984): 1011.
1272 R. Thakur, "Creation of the Nuclear-Free New Zealand Myth: Brinkmanship Without a Brink," *Asian Survey* 29, no. 10 (1989): 933.
1273 W. Woityra, K. Boda and M. Davanzo, "Lift the Ban on New Zealand Port Visits," *US Naval Institute Proceedings* 145, no. 7 (July 2019), 1397.
1274 J. Wexler, "The Rainbow Warrior Affair: State and Agent Responsibility for Authorized Violations of International Law," *Boston University International Law Journal* 5 (1987): 389.
1275 D. Robie, "The Rainbow Warrior bombers, the media and the judiciary," *Australian Journalism Review* 29, no. 2 (2007): 50.
1276 Radio New Zealand interview, Rainbow Warrior sinking, Radio New Zealand Sound Archives Ngā Taonga Kōrero, ref no COMP 3, 1985, tk6.
1277 H. Haazen, in *New Zealand Boating* (1 July 2015), 4.
1278 D. Lange, *My Life* (Auckland: Penguin Books, 2005), 214.
1279 *The Guardian*, 28 November 2005, n.p.
1280 A. Mafart, in Robie, 57.
1281 Haazen, 4.
1282 G. Hanly, "Crowd below rear of Museum awaiting Pope John Paul II, Auckland Domain," AM, ref. PH-2015-2-GH1596-33.
1283 Libreria Editrice Vaticana, "Homily of John Paul II, Auckland (New Zealand), 22 November 1986," (Vatican: 1986), n.p.
1284 J. P. Hanigan, "The centrality of marriage: Homosexuality and the Roman Catholic argument," *The Ecumenical Review* 50, no. 1 (1998): 54–63.
1285 ss 141, 142, 146, 153, 154, *Crimes Act 1961*.
1286 R. Bowman, "Public attitudes toward homosexuality in New Zealand," *International Review of Modern Sociology* 9, no. 2 (1979): 233–234.

1287 T. McCreanor, "'Why Strengthen the City Wall When the Enemy Has Poisoned the Well?' An Assay of Anti-Homosexual Discourse in New Zealand," *Journal of Homosexuality* 31, no. 4 (1996): 83–88.
1288 Auckland Co-ordinator of Petition to Oppose the Homosexual Law Reform Bill, submission to Select Committee, ANZ, ref. R314656.
1289 East Coast Bays Methodist Parish, 29 September 1985, submission to Select Committee, ANZ, ref. R314656.
1290 Waiheke County Council, submission to Select Committee, ANZ, ref. R314656.
1291 *AS*, 15 May 1985, 7.
1292 N. Jones addressing a public meeting in 1985, in LAGANZ 0080-B, Peter Nowland Collection.
1293 J. Peters, in *Sunday Star-Times*, 30 June 2016, 5.
1294 Stop the Killer Disease Aids, ANZ, ref. R314656.
1295 *NZPD* 467 (5 November 1985), 7733.
1296 M. N. R. Brown, "Packing down the scrum: an historical analysis of the 1981 Springbok tour and the homosexuality issue in the Presbyterian Church of Aotearoa New Zealand," PhD thesis (Dunedin: University of Otago, 1995), 55.
1297 *Homosexual Law Reform Act 1986.*
1298 L. Guy, "Between a Hard Rock and Shifting Sands: Churches and the Issue of Homosexuality in New Zealand, 1960–86," *Journal of Religious History* 30, no. 1 (2006): 76.
1299 K. Hay, in ibid., 76.
1300 Interview with former Mt Roskill minister (January 2018).
1301 M. T. Jones, "Adam Smith and the ethics of contemporary democratic capitalism in New Zealand," *International Journal of Social Economics* 20, no. 12 (1993): 4.
1302 T. B. Macaulay, in A. Hook, "Macaulay and America," *Journal of American Studies* 9, no. 3 (1975): 346.
1303 J. Keir, dir., *Close Up*, "Big Dealers," TVNZ (1987).
1304 J. Savells, "Who are the 'Yuppies'? A Popular View," *International Journal of Comparative Sociology* 27 (1986): 235.
1305 R. W. Smith, *Where's The Gold? My Story* (Auckland: R. M. & J. A. Jensen Ltd, 1994), 6.
1306 *NZH*, 16 June 2004, 11.
1307 J. Finn, in P. Ward, "Gloss: A Perspective," *NZ On Screen* (22 September 2008).
1308 P. Elliott, in G. Gracewood, "Gloss: the TV programme about Auckland city wankers," *Metro*, October 2017.
1309 Interview with D. M. (September 2021).
1310 B. Wheeler and M. Nash, *An Examination of the Sharemarket Crash and its Aftermath in New Zealand* (Wellington: Economic Development Commission, 1989), 1.
1311 I. Rodgers, in Gracewood.
1312 T. Gibbs, in N. Higgins, "Black Monday," Radio New Zealand broadcast, 3:30 pm (7 September 2017).
1313 L. Hoffman, *A Brief History of Auckland's Urban Form* (Auckland: Auckland Council Research and Evaluation Unit, 2019), 21.
1314 C. Lamers and B. Hall, "Auckland," *Cities* 6, no. 2 (1989): 85.
1315 L. Murphy, "Third-wave gentrification in New Zealand: The case of Auckland," *Urban Studies* 45, no. 12 (2008): 2521–2540.
1316 S. Tannock, "Nostalgia Critique," *Cultural Studies* 9, no. 3 (1995): 454.
1317 B. James, M. Rehm and K. Saville-Smith, "Impacts of leaky homes and leaky building stigma on older homeowners," *Pacific Rim Property Research Journal* 23, no. 1 (2017): 16.

11 The 1990s

1318 W. McIntyre, *The Significance of the Commonwealth, 1965–90* (London: Springer, 1991), 238.
1319 J. Culliford, "The Commonwealth Games Village — New Solutions to an Accommodation Problem," *New Zealand Engineering* 45, no. 2 (1990): 31.
1320 J. A. Hoek, P. J. Gendall and R. D. West, "The role of sponsorship in selected New Zealand companies," *New Zealand Journal of Business* 12 (1990): 87.
1321 Manukau Sports Bowl, Track marking layout. Archives Reference: MCC Barcode C9424; Brochure about the development of the West Auckland Swimming and Recreation Centre, pages 1–2. Commonwealth Games, Mount Albert City Council subject files. Archives Reference: MAC 108 Record C-1-11.
1322 Overall layout, XIV Commonwealth Games Village Development Company Ltd, 9 December 1988. Plans drawn by KRTA Ltd. Archives Reference: ACC 493 Item 44b.
1323 *Sunday Star-Times*, 1 April 2018, 9; *XIVth Commonwealth Games 1990 — Headquarters Operation Manual* (Auckland, 1989), Annex K.
1324 L. Baker, *The Way of the Jafa: A Guide to Surviving Auckland and Aucklanders* (Auckland: Penguin Publishing, 1998).
1325 W. Roger, in *North & South*, June 1999, 43.
1326 *Press*, 9 October 1897, 7; 11 March 1898, 2.
1327 *New Zealand Listener*, 10 November 1973, 12.
1328 H. B. Laurenson, "Myths and the City: A Social and Cultural History of Auckland, 1890–1990," PhD thesis (Auckland: University of Auckland, 2010), 283.
1329 S. Gee et al., "Producing and Consuming Masculinity: New Zealand's (Speight's) 'Southern Man'," in *Sport, Beer, and Gender: Promotional Culture and Contemporary Social Life*, L. A. Wenner and S. J. Jackson, eds (New York: Peter Lang, 2009), 189–90.
1330 P. L. Sunderland and R. M. Denny, "Finding Ourselves in Images: A Semiotic Excursion," *Journal of Research for Consumers* 8 (2005): 6.
1331 Auckland Tourism, Events, and Economic Development, *Auckland Growth Monitor* (Auckland: ATEED, 2017), 8.
1332 M. Jefferson, "Why geography? The law of the primate city," *Geographical Review* 79, no. 2 (1989): 228.
1333 Ibid., 226.
1334 Ibid., 229.
1335 K. B. Cumberland, *Auckland in Ferment: The Present and Future Brew* (Auckland: New Zealand Geographical Society, 1971), 3, in Laurenson, "Myths and the City," 300.
1336 W. Friesen, "New Asian migrants in Auckland: issues of employment and status," *Labour, Employment and Work in New Zealand* (1992): 149, 153.
1337 J. Livesey v The Dominion, New Zealand Media Council, CN 613 (May 1996), n.p.
1338 H. Ishizawa and D. Arunachalam, "Ethnic neighbourhoods in Auckland, New Zealand," *Urban Policy and Research* 32, no. 4 (2014): 419, 428–429.
1339 R. Johnston, M. Poulsen and J. Forrest, "Asians, Pacific Islanders, and ethnoburbs in Auckland, New Zealand," *Geographical Review* 98, no. 2 (2008): 217–220.
1340 H. Yoon, "Recent East Asian immigrants and their contribution to multi-culturalism in Auckland, New Zealand," *Japanese Journal of Human Geography* 55, no. 3 (2003): 95.
1341 Interview with R. J. (August 2021).
1342 Interview with C. S. (October 2014).
1343 J. Mackley-Crump, "A 'Pacific renaissance'?: exploring the Pacific diaspora in Aotearoa New Zealand through the evolution of festivals and popular music," *Journal of New Zealand & Pacific Studies* 3, no. 2 (2015): 149–166.
1344 J. Mackley-Crump, *The Pacific Festivals of Aotearoa New Zealand: Negotiating Place and Identity in a New Homeland* (Honolulu: University of Hawai'i Press, 2015), 195.
1345 R. Vaughan, in Mackley-Crump, "A 'Pacific renaissance'?," 155.
1346 Ibid.
1347 Cited in T. Buch, S. Milne and G. Dickson, "Multiple stakeholder perspectives on cultural events: Auckland's Pasifika Festival," *Journal of Hospitality Marketing & Management* 20, nos. 3–4 (2011): 322.
1348 P. Leiser, in Mackley-Crump, *The Pacific Festivals of Aotearoa New Zealand*, 79.
1349 D. Ozich, "History of the Croatian Cultural Society," (Auckland: Croatian Cultural Society, 2012), n.p.
1350 M. Krtalić and I. H. Grgić, "Cultural societies and information needs: Croats in New Zealand," *Global Knowledge, Memory and Communication* 68, nos. 8/9 (2019): 652–673.
1351 D. Simon, "Dancing the Kolo Under the Long White Cloud," in *Moving Oceans: Celebrating Dance in the South Pacific*, R. Buck and N. Rowe, eds (London: Routledge, 2017), 112.
1352 A. P. Butcher, "Educate, consolidate, immigrate: educational immigration in Auckland, New Zealand," *Asia Pacific Viewpoint* 45, no. 2 (2004): 259, 261.
1353 P. Spoonley and C. Meares, "Laissez-faire multiculturalism and relational embeddedness: Ethnic precincts in Auckland," *Cosmopolitan Civil Societies: An Interdisciplinary Journal* 3, no. 1 (2011): 44, 48.
1354 H. Bradstock, "'Let's Talk about Something Else': Religion and Governmentality in New Zealand's State Primary Schools," PhD thesis (Dunedin: University of Otago, 2016), 231.

1355 Journey NZ, "Coca-Cola Christmas in the Park: 25 years of Memories, History and Fun," (Auckland, 31 August 2018), n.p.
1356 W. Ihimaera, *Out There: Portraits of the Hero Parade* (Auckland: Savidan Productions Ltd, 2000), n.p.
1357 Anon., (22 September 1995), in L. Johnston, "Borderline Bodies," in *Subjectivities, Knowledges and Feminist Geographies: The Subjects and Ethics of Social Research*, L. Bondi, H. Avis, R. Bankey, V. Einagel, A. Bingley and J. Davidson, eds (Lanham: Rowman & Littlefield, 2002), 78.
1358 Ibid., (1997), 81 (emphasis in original).
1359 L. Smith, in N. Gearing, *Emerging Tribe: Gay Culture in New Zealand in the 1990s* (Auckland: Penguin, 1997), 89.
1360 Cited in Gearing, 91.
1361 L. Mills, in C. Brickell, "Heroes and invaders: Gay and lesbian pride parades and the public/private distinction in New Zealand media accounts," *Gender, Place and Culture: A Journal of Feminist Geography* 7, no. 2 (2000): 167.
1362 D. Hay, in Auckland Library, "The Hero Parade's Seven Fabulous Outings," (19 February 2019), n.p.
1363 N. Stephenson, in ibid.
1364 A. Hughes and P. Saxton, "Geographic micro-clustering of homosexual men: implications for research and social policy," *Social Policy Journal of New Zealand* 28 (2006): 170.
1365 Brickell, "Heroes and invaders," 163-170.
1366 M. Smith, in "The chainsaw used on One Tree Hill and heard across Aotearoa," in *The Spinoff, The Single Object*, video (13 April 2021).
1367 M. Smith, in *NZH*, 28 October 2004, 5.
1368 H. Joyce, "Out from nowhere: *Pakeha* anxieties in *Ngati* (Barclay, 1987), *Once Were Warriors* (Tamahori, 1994) and *Whale Rider* (Caro, 2002)," *Studies in Australasian Cinema* 3, no. 3 (2009): 245.
1369 L. Tamahori, in K. M. Thompson, "Once Were Warriors: New Zealand's First Indigenous Blockbuster," in *Movie Blockbusters*, J. Stringer, ed. (London: Routledge, 2013), 237.
1370 J. Pule, *The Shark that Ate the Sun* (Auckland: Penguin, 1992), 194, in P. Fresno-Calleja, "Trans/locating Pacific Identities," in *Postcolonial Translocations: Cultural Representation and Critical Spatial Thinking*, M. Munkelt et al., eds (Amsterdam: Ropoti, 2013): 209.
1371 A. de Bruin, "From cultural to economic capital: Community employment creation in Otara," in *Labour, Employment and Work in New Zealand* (1996): 90.
1372 J. Lunday, Enterprise Otara, 1993, in de Bruin, 91.
1373 A. de Bruin and A. Dupuis, "The dynamics of New Zealand's largest street market; the Otara flea market," *International Journal of Sociology and Social Policy* 20, nos. 1/2 (2000): 55.
1374 G. Pacheco and T. Maloney, "Are the Determinants of Intergenerational Welfare Dependency Gender-Specific?," *Australian Journal of Labour Economics* 6, no. 3 (2003): 371–382; M. Olssen, "In defence of the welfare state and publicly provided education: A New Zealand perspective," *Journal of Education Policy* 11, no. 3 (1996): 337-362.
1375 J. Campion, in M. Bilborough, "The Making of the Piano," in *The Piano*, J. Campion and J. Chapman, eds (New York: Hyperion, 1993), 139.
1376 Interview with W. G. (July 2004).
1377 *Press*, 28 December 1961, 8.
1378 J. Boon, "The interplay of market forces and government action in the achievement of urban intensification: the case of Auckland, New Zealand," *Journal of Urbanism* 3, no. 3 (2010): 298-299.
1379 Interview with E. C. (December 2020).
1380 Auckland Regional Council, *A Brief History of Auckland's Urban Form*, 23.
1381 J. Boon, "Urban Regeneration in Moderate Size Cities — The Case for Minimal Government Intervention," Asian Planning Schools Association Congress (Bandung, 1997), 4.
1382 Statistics New Zealand, "Apartments Hit Record High," (Wellington: Statistics New Zealand, 31 August 1999), n.p.
1383 J. Ge and F. P. Lai, "A study into the demand for apartments in central Auckland," Asian Real Estate Society Annual Meeting and International Conference (Shanghai: Shanghai University of Finance and Economics, 2008).
1384 Boon, "Urban Regeneration," 4–7.
1385 M. Horton, "The Art of Poetry: The (Frank Lloyd) Wright Stuff," *Carolina English Teacher* 31, no. 4 (2005): 13.
1386 A. Krukziener, in *NZH*, 5 June 2010, 9.
1387 A. Krukziener, in *NZH*, 18 March 2002, 2.
1388 *NZH*, 30 June 2000, 7.
1389 A. Barrie, "Auckland City in the 1990s," *Itinerary No. 37, Block: The Broadsheet of the Auckland Branch of the New Zealand Institute of Architects* 3 (2011): 1–3.
1390 F. Monsalve, "ASB Theatre," *Architecture Now* 10 (December 2013), n.p.
1391 Barrie, 2.
1392 G. M. Griffiths, N. Talbot, K. N. Dirks, G. Betti and J. A. Salmond, "Forecasting brown haze in Auckland," *Weather and Climate* 39, no. 1 (2019): 2–13.
1393 P. Wilson-Jackson, "Vertigo as Entertainment: Sky Tower Data," *New Zealand Engineering* 52, no. 7 (1997): 20–23.
1394 E. Burke, *Burke's Philosophical Inquiry into the Origin of Our Ideas of the Sublime and Beautiful* (London: J. F. Dove, 1827), 34.
1395 E. Durkheim, in P. Thijssen, "From Mechanical to Organic Solidarity, and back: With Honneth beyond Durkheim," in *European Journal of Social Theory* 15, no. 4 (2012): 455–456.
1396 B. Leyland, "Auckland central business district power failure," *Power Engineering Journal* 12, no. 3 (1998): 109–114.
1397 Ibid., 109.
1398 H. Rennie, *Auckland power supply failure 1998: the report of the Ministerial Inquiry into the Auckland Power Supply Failure* (Wellington: Ministry of Commerce, 1998), 50–88.
1399 Mercury Energy Statement (20 February 1998), in J. Walker, "Auckland lights out from failure to recovery [power system disturbance]," in *21st International Telecommunications Energy Conference. INTELEC' 99*, Cat. No. 99CH37007 (Chester, 1999), 1.
1400 P. Gutman, "Auckland's Power Outage, or, Auckland — Your Y2K Beta Test Site," (Auckland, 24 May 1998), n.p.
1401 Radio New Zealand broadcast, "The night the lights went out in Auckland," 3:30 pm (22 March 2018).
1402 Leyland, 109.
1403 Rennie, 50–88.
1404 OECD, *Mobile Phones: Pricing Structures and Trends* (Paris: OECD, 2000), 92, 98.
1405 OECD, *Communications Outlook 1999* (Paris, OECD, 1999), 178.
1406 OECD, *Mobile Phones*, 80.
1407 Interview with S. M. (October 2021).
1408 Ministry of Commerce, *Statistics on Information Technology in New Zealand* (Wellington: Ministry of Commerce, 2006), s. 7.1.
1409 Interview with M. D. (April 2016).
1410 Interview with S. R. (September 2021).
1411 *Local Government (Millennium Events) Amendment Act 1999*.
1412 P. N. Edwards, "Y2K: Millennial reflections on computers as infrastructure," *History and Technology, an International Journal* 15, no. 1-2 (1998): 8.
1413 D. Tewksbury, P. Moy and D. S. Weis, "Preparations for Y2K: Revisiting the behavioral component of the third-person effect," *Journal of Communication* 54, no. 1 (2004): 141.
1414 Interview with P. O. (August 2020).
1415 M. Williamson, in Radio New Zealand broadcast, "Are You Y2K OK?," 7:00 am (13 December 2018).
1416 G. Ellis, in *NZH*, 13 December 2009, 8.
1417 Ibid.
1418 Auckland City Council, "Listen to Ken! Y2K," media release (Auckland, 23 August 1999), 1.
1419 J. Elder, in Department of Internal Affairs, "Auckland Millennium Celebrations Get Lottery Funding," (Wellington, 16 July 1999), 1.
1420 Ibid.

Epilogue

1421 B. Mason, *The End of the Golden Weather: A Voyage into a New Zealand Childhood* (Wellington: Victoria University Press, 1998), 39.

Index

246 Queen Street 217–18

A

Advances to Workers Act 43
Akarana Maori Association 117
Albany 199, 237–38, 287, 303–304
Albert Park 31
Aotea Centre 308
Apartments 305–307
Arch Hill 166
Auckland Airport 210–11
Auckland and Manukau Canal Act 53
Auckland Art Gallery 30, 47, 68, 72, 87, 202
Auckland Automobile Association 52
Auckland Beautifying Society 111
Auckland Centennial Memorial Park Act 139
Auckland City Mission 100, 127
Auckland Cyclists' Road League 52
Auckland Domain 27, 30, 33–34, 75–76, 78, 88, 112, 152, 190–91, 279–80, 297, 315–16, 318
Auckland Exhibition 75–76, 112
Auckland Harbour Bridge 13, 200–201, 221, 248, 316
Auckland Museum 36
Auckland Peace Association 60–61
Auckland Public Library 28, 30, 72, 308
Auckland Scenery Conservation Society 29–30
Auckland Society of Arts 67–69, 201–202
Auckland Town Hall 57, 70–71, 74, 87, 97–99, 106, 111, 130–32, 141, 162, 187, 226, 298, 308
Auckland University College 27–28
Auckland War Memorial Museum 112–13, 219
Avondale 51, 91, 108, 135–36, 200, 231, 264

B

Bastion Point 26, 149–51, 249–52, 256
Bayswater 71
Birkenhead 63–64, 71, 255, 260, 286
Boer War 41, 56–58, 60, 86
British immigration 163–66
Bungalows 104–107, 176, 262, 287, 305

C

Cabaret 103–104
Carless days 256–57
Centrepoint 237–39
Chatswood 287
Chief Post Office (Central Post Office) 71, 198, 308
Chinese immigration 28, 49–50, 115–19, 292–93, 296
Christchurch 27, 262, 291
Christianity 33–34, 37–38, 57, 62, 89, 94–103, 137, 152, 183, 192, 197, 213–14, 239–42, 259–60, 279–83, 296
Christmas in the Park 297, 318
Civic Administration Building 221–22
Civic Theatre 114, 171–72
Clark, Helen 265–67
Coatesville 199, 241
Cobb & Co 245
Commonwealth Games 289–90
Commercial Bay 22
Communism 225–28
Cooper, Whina 247–49
Cornwall Park 48, 300
Coromandel 15, 229
Craig's Museum 36–37
Crime 79–80, 192–96, 223–25, 239
Croatian/Yugoslavia immigration 53, 141–42, 215, 295
Crown Lynn 205–206
Cyclists 52

D

Dairy Flat 200
Dawn raids 253–55
Devonport 34, 57, 63–64, 71, 108, 120, 135, 260, 276
Dominion Day 59
Dominion Road 50, 107
Drury 26
Duke and Duchess of Cornwall and York 44, 46–47
Dunedin 27, 76, 262

E

East Tamaki Heights 14
Eden, George 21
Eden Park 56, 187–88, 270–71, 273–74
Eden Terrace 136, 142, 166
Ellerslie 34, 91, 148, 191, 198, 260, 286
Empire Games 187–89
Epsom 106, 170, 196, 238, 305

F

Fairburn, William 19–20
Farmers' Trading Company 134–36, 205
Ferry Building 71
First World War 84–90, 96, 99, 111–13, 143–44, 151–53, 160
Foodtown 204
Freemans Bay 21, 61, 166, 184

G

Georgie Pie 244
Glenbrook Steel Mill 208–209
Glen Eden 178
Glen Innes 166, 290, 301
Gloss 285–286
Goldie, Charles 66–67
Grafton Bridge 69–70, 88, 220
Graham, Billy 197
Grand Hotel 44–46
Great Barrier Island 55, 154, 229, 260
Great Depression 119, 126–33, 137, 145, 149
Great White Fleet 58–59
Greenhithe 21
Greenlane 108
Grey, George 25, 30, 99
Grey Lynn 62, 91, 135, 148, 166, 214, 260, 287
Group housing 235–37

H

Hare Krishna movement 241
Henderson 51, 54, 214, 260, 264, 286, 290, 303
Helensville 96, 260
Herne Bay 63, 166
Hero Parade 297–99
Highbury 255, 287
Hika, Hongi 17–18
Hillsborough 209, 292
Hobson, William 21
Hobsonville 54, 152, 205
Homosexual Law Reform Bill 280–83, 298–99
Howick 24, 120, 219–20, 223, 260, 292

Howick Historical Village 219–20
Hyde, Robin 123, 130, 140

I

Immigration Restriction Amendment Act 116
Indian immigration 115–19

J

Jazz 102–103, 140
Jewish community 37, 96–97, 144, 222

K

Karangahape Road 50, 135–36, 198, 255
Karekare 203
Kauri 12, 27, 42, 55, 172
Kawau Island 34
Kelly Tarlton's 268
Kentucky Fried Chicken 243, 246
Khyber Pass 37, 41, 95
Kinetoscope 38–39
Kingseat 142–43
Kingsland 50, 56, 136
Knox Presbyterian Church 33, 38, 94, 101
Kohimarama 16, 25, 71
Kumeu 119

L

Land March 247–49
Lange, David 274–76
Leaky homes 288
Leisureland 267
Liston, Bishop James 98–99
Logan Campbell, John 20, 29, 46–47, 68, 91, 148
LynnMall 204–205
Lyric Theatre 72–73

M

Māngere 16, 53, 63, 117, 139, 208–211, 247, 257–58, 272, 274–75, 301–302
Māngere Bridge 257–58
Manukau 11, 208–210, 259–60, 266–67, 290
Manukau Harbour 13–16, 28, 53, 62–63, 138, 208–209, 211, 257
Manurewa 99, 160, 275, 302
Māori urbanisation 181–86
Massey 234–37
Mathew, Felton 21–22
Mazengarb Report 192–95
McCahon, Colin 201–202
McDonald's 243–45, 318

Meadowbank 287, 292
Melville, Ellen 80, 134
Metropolis 306–307
Milford 103–104, 108
Mitchell, Thomas 19–20
Modernist housing 176–78, 181, 287–88
Mon Desir Hotel 64, 216
Motuihe Island 144
Motutapu Island 34
Mt Albert 62, 96, 106, 121, 135–36, 148, 160, 241, 260, 265, 304
Mt Eden 41, 50, 62, 88–89, 106, 135, 139, 171, 175, 227, 241, 260, 286–87, 305, 309
Mt Roskill 42, 50, 62, 106, 108, 135, 239–40, 242, 260, 264, 281, 283
Mt Smart Stadium 289–90
Mt Wellington, 191–92, 198, 260
Muldoon, Robert 225, 252, 274–75
Mulgan, John 129, 163
Museum of Transport and Technology (MOTAT) 219–20
Muslims 241, 296

N

New Lynn 53–54, 96, 108, 119, 135–36, 191, 204–206, 243, 260
Newmarket 61–62, 104, 166, 187, 260
Newton 104, 166, 179, 214
New Year's celebrations 33–35, 170, 289, 315–16
Ngāpuhi 17–19, 300
Ngāti Pāoa 16–19
Ngāti Whātua 13, 16–17, 20, 22, 26, 122, 124, 126, 186, 248–49, 252, 318
Northcote 71, 96, 108, 136, 260

O

Old Colonists' Museum 72
Once Were Warriors 300–301
Onehunga 24, 26, 62–63, 108, 135, 139, 148, 191, 253, 257, 260, 301
One Tree Hill/Maungakiekie 15–16, 20, 48–49, 68, 148, 260, 300, 309
Ōrākei 13, 16, 25, 71, 104, 122–126, 147–48, 150, 186, 249–52
Orange Hall 104, 179
Ōrewa 304
Ōtāhuhu 26, 53, 63, 108, 147, 150, 155, 204, 206–207, 260, 302
Ōtara 260, 272, 301–302
Ōtuataua Stonefields 209–210
Ōwairaka 184–85

P

Pacific immigration 211–14
Pākiri 96
Panmure 18, 24, 111, 117, 166, 191, 198, 243
Papakura 91, 135, 142, 151, 162, 170, 260, 272
Parnell 38, 47, 61, 91, 94, 101, 104, 135, 166, 177, 191, 202, 262, 284, 308
Parnell Baths 202–203
Pasifika Festival 293–96
Penrose 53, 191, 310
Piha 91
Ponsonby 45, 50, 61, 109, 135, 160, 166, 184, 214, 241, 256, 286–87, 299
Pōnui Island 7, 15
Pope John Paul II 279–80
Port Albert 96, 120
Power cut 310–12
Prostitution 82–84, 192–93
Pt Chevalier 106, 135, 148, 226
Pt England 166
Public Works Act 25
Pūhoi 64
Pukekohe 91, 99, 111, 116–18, 135, 147, 170–71, 185, 260–61

Q

Queen Elizabeth II 174–75, 290
Queen Street 22, 31, 33, 35, 39, 52, 61, 71, 85, 88, 97, 103, 114, 129, 131–32, 134–36, 157, 161–62, 190, 195–96, 199, 215, 217–18, 227, 241, 248, 263, 285, 297, 299, 307–308, 311, 316
Queens Wharf 33, 85

R

Radio Hauraki 229
Railways 26, 32, 35, 51, 53–54, 62, 109, 120, 136, 150, 190, 201, 219, 257, 308
Rainbow's End 267–68
Rainbow Warrior 276–79
Rangitoto 11, 13, 58, 144, 201, 300, 316, 319
Redwood 70 231–33
Remuera 23–24, 50, 62, 224, 286
Riverhead 34, 199
Rock and roll 195–96, 229
Rodney 65, 260
Rosebank, 287
Round the Bays 261
Rugby World Cup 273–74

S

Sandringham 40, 135, 293
Sargeson, Frank 172–73
Savage, Michael 128, 149–51, 153
Second World War 151–63, 169–71, 181, 222, 228, 274
Seddon, Richard 56
Sewage 22, 121–23, 208–209, 210, 268, 311
Shop Trading Hours Amendment Act 263–67
Six o'clock swill 215–16
Sky Tower 201, 308–309, 316–17
Smith & Caughey's 134–35
Soccer 272–73
Spanish influenza 90–93
Springbok rugby tour 268–72
Stanley Bay 71
Stark, Freda 171–73
State Advances Amendment Act 109–110
State housing 147–48
St Heliers 71, 95
St Johns 287
Strikes 76–79, 189–91, 257
Sunday school 33–34, 99, 171
Swanson 34, 139, 231–33

T

Takapuna 64, 148, 170, 172, 216, 243, 260, 284, 319
Taupaki 199
Te Waiohua 15–17
The End of the Golden Weather 319
The Piano 203
Three Kings 62
Titirangi 55, 74, 136–39, 177, 202
Titirangi Hotel (Lopdell House) 138–39
Trams 35, 50–51, 53, 63, 65, 74, 77, 88, 107, 135, 148, 156, 198, 219, 230
Trekka 207
Tūākau 122

V

Vietnam War 225–28
Villas 39–42, 64, 105–106, 148, 176, 181, 287, 305

W

Waiheke Island 13, 20, 34, 144, 260, 281
Waimauku 96
Waitākere Dam 73–74
Waitākere Ranges 12, 55, 137, 139
Waitematā Harbour 13, 15, 18–19, 21, 25, 28, 34, 47, 53, 58, 62–63, 71, 76, 88, 154, 165, 201, 261, 275–77
Waiuku 208, 260–61, 272
Waiwera 34, 64
Warkworth 64–65, 120
Waterview 121
Wellington 21, 26–27, 62, 76, 149, 247, 262, 291–92, 318
Wellsford 177, 261
Western Springs 27, 139, 187–89, 219, 293
Westgate 303–304
Westmere 135
Whangaparāoa 304
Whenuapai 21, 165–66, 199–200, 210, 303
White New Zealand League 117
Wintergardens 113–14
Women's Christian Temperance Union 57–58, 79–80, 83, 102, 159

Y

Y2K 314–15, 317
Yugoslavian/Croatian immigration 53, 141–42, 215, 295
Yuppies 283–86